Paris Exposition, 1900;
Sirot Collection.

THE PROUD TOWER

BY BARBARA W. TUCHMAN

Bible and Sword (1956)
The Zimmermann Telegram (1958)
The Guns of August (1962)
The Proud Tower (1966)

Barbara W. Tuchman

THE
PROUD
TOWER

A Portrait of the World
Before the War

1890–1914

MACMILLAN PUBLISHING CO., INC.

NEW YORK

Chapter 2 appeared, in part, in *The Atlantic Monthly* for
May 1963. Parts of Chapter 3 were published in *American
Heritage* for December 1962 and in *The Nation* 100th Anniversary issue, September 1965. Parts of Chapter 1 were
published in *Vogue* in 1965.

Permission to quote copyrighted material is gratefully
acknowledged to publishers and authors as follows:
   Holt, Rinehart and Winston, Inc. for stanzas from "On
the idle hill of summer" from "A Shropshire Lad"—Author-
ized Edition—from *The Collected Poems of A. E. Hous-
man,* copyright 1939, 1940, © 1959 by Holt, Rinehart and
Winston, Inc.
   Macmillan Publishing Co., Inc. for four lines from "The
Valley of the Black Pig" by William Butler Yeats, reprinted
by permission of Macmillan Publishing Co., Inc., from
Collected Poems by W. B. Yeats, copyright 1906 by Mac-
millan Publishing Co., Inc., renewed 1934 by W. B. Yeats.
   Houghton Mifflin Company for four lines from William
Vaughan Moody's "Ode in a Time of Hesitation."
   Doubleday & Company, Inc. for lines from "The Truce
of the Bear" and "The White Man's Burden" by Rudyard
Kipling, from *Rudyard Kipling's Verse: Definitive Edition.*

While from a proud tower in the town
Death looks gigantically down.

From "The City in the Sea"
EDGAR ALLAN POE

Acknowledgments

To Mr. Cecil Scott of Macmillan Publishing Co., Inc., a participant in this book from the first outline to the end, I owe a writer's most important debt: for the steady companionship of an interested reader and for constructive criticism throughout mixed with encouragement in times of need.

For advice, suggestions and answers to queries I am grateful to Mr. Roger Butterfield, author of *The American Past;* Professor Fritz Epstein of Indiana University; Mr. Louis Fischer, author of *The Life of Lenin;* Professor Edward Fox of Cornell University; Mr. K. A. Golding of the International Transport Workers' Federation, London; Mr. Jay Harrison of Columbia Records; Mr. John Gutman of the Metropolitan Opera; Mr. George Lichtheim of the Institute on Communist Affairs, Columbia University; Mr. William Manchester, author of *The House of Krupp;* Professor Arthur Marder, editor of the letters of Sir John Fisher; Mr. George Painter, the biographer of Proust; Mr. A. L. Rowse, author of an introduction to the work of Graham Wallas; Miss Helen Ruskell and the staff of the New York Society Library; Mr. Thomas K. Scherman, director of the Little Orchestra Society; Mrs. Janice Shea for information about the circus in Germany; Professor Reba Soffer of San Fernando Valley State College for information on Wilfred Trotter; Mr. Joseph C. Swidler, chairman of the Federal Power Commission; and Mr. Louis Untermeyer, editor, among much else, of *Modern British Poetry.* Equal gratitude extends to the many others who gave me verbal aid of which I kept no record.

For help in finding certain of the illustrations I am indebted to Mr. A. J. Ubels of the Royal Archives at The Hague; to the staffs of the Art and Print Rooms of the New York Public Library; and to Mr. and Mrs. Harry Collins of Brown Brothers.

I would like to express particular thanks to two indefatigable readers of the proofs, Miss Jessica Tuchman and Mr. Timothy Dickinson, for improvements and corrections, respectively; and to Mrs. Esther Bookman, who impeccably typed the manuscript of both this and my previous book, *The Guns of August.*

BARBARA W. TUCHMAN

Contents

Illustrations

British delegation to The Hague, 1899
Paris Exposition, 1900: Porte Monumentale and the Palace of Electricity
Alfred Nobel
Bertha von Suttner
The Krupp works at Essen, 1912

Richard Strauss
Friedrich Nietzsche watching the setting sun, Weimar, 1900
A beer garden in Berlin
Nijinsky as the Faun: design by Léon Bakst

Arthur James Balfour
Coal strike, 1910: mine owners arriving at 10 Downing Street
Seaman's strike, 1911
David Lloyd George

August Bebel
Keir Hardie
"Strike," painting by Steinlen
Jean Jaurès

Foreword

The epoch whose final years are the subject of this book did not die of old age or accident but exploded in a terminal crisis which is one of the great facts of history. No mention of that crisis appears in the following pages for the reason that, as it had not yet happened, it was not a part of the experience of the people of this book. I have tried to stay within the terms of what was known at the time.

The Great War of 1914–18 lies like a band of scorched earth dividing that time from ours. In wiping out so many lives which would have been operative on the years that followed, in destroying beliefs, changing ideas, and leaving incurable wounds of disillusion, it created a physical as well as psychological gulf between two epochs. This book is an attempt to discover the quality of the world from which the Great War came.

It is not the book I intended to write when I began. Preconceptions dropped off one by one as I investigated. The period was not a Golden Age or *Belle Epoque* except to a thin crust of the privileged class. It was not a time exclusively of confidence, innocence, comfort, stability, security and peace. All these qualities were certainly present. People *were* more confident of values and standards, more innocent in the sense of retaining more hope of mankind, than they are today, although they were not more peaceful nor, except for the upper few, more comfortable. Our misconception lies in assuming that doubt and fear, ferment, protest, violence and hate were not equally present. We have been misled by the people of the time themselves who, in looking back across the gulf of the War, see that earlier half of their lives misted over by a lovely sunset haze of peace and security. It did not seem so golden when they were in the midst of it. Their memories and their nostalgia have conditioned our view of the pre-war era but I can offer the reader a rule based on adequate research: all statements of how lovely it was in that era made by persons contemporary with it will be found to have been made after 1914.

A phenomenon of such extended malignance as the Great War does not come out of a Golden Age. Perhaps this should have been obvious to me when I began but it was not. I did feel, however, that the genesis of the war did not lie in the *Grosse Politik* of what Isvolsky said to Aehrenthal and Sir Edward Grey to Poincaré; in that tortuous train of Reinsurance treaties, Dual and Triple Alliances, Moroccan crises and Balkan imbroglios which historians have painstakingly followed in their search for origins. It was necessary that these events and exchanges be examined and we who come after are in debt to the examiners; but their work has been done. I am with Sergei Sazonov, Russian Foreign Minister at the time of the outbreak of the War, who after a series of investigations exclaimed at last, "Enough of this chronology!" The *Grosse Politik* approach has been used up. Besides, it is misleading because it allows us to rest on the easy illusion that it is "they," the naughty statesmen, who are always responsible for war while "we," the innocent people, are merely led. That impression is a mistake.

The diplomatic origins, so-called, of the Great War are only the fever chart of the patient; they do not tell us what caused the fever. To probe for underlying causes and deeper forces one must operate within the framework of a whole society and try to discover what moved the people in it. I have tried to concentrate on society rather than the state. Power politics and economic rivalries, however important, are not my subject.

The period of this book was above all the culmination of a century of the most accelerated rate of change in man's record. Since the last explosion of a generalized belligerent will in the Napoleonic wars, the industrial and scientific revolutions had transformed the world. Man had entered the Nineteenth Century using only his own and animal power, supplemented by that of wind and water, much as he had entered the Thirteenth, or, for that matter, the First. He entered the Twentieth with his capacities in transportation, communication, production, manufacture and weaponry multiplied a thousandfold by the energy of machines. Industrial society gave man new powers and new scope while at the same time building up new pressures in prosperity and poverty, in growth of population and crowding in cities, in antagonisms of classes and groups, in separation from nature and from satisfaction in individual work. Science gave man new welfare and new horizons while it took away belief in God and certainty in a scheme of things he knew. By the time he left the

Nineteenth Century he had as much new unease as ease. Although *fin de siècle* usually connotes decadence, in fact society at the turn of the century was not so much decaying as bursting with new tensions and accumulated energies. Stefan Zweig who was thirty-three in 1914 believed that the outbreak of war "had nothing to do with ideas and hardly even with frontiers. I cannot explain it otherwise than by this surplus force, a tragic consequence of the internal dynamism that had accumulated in forty years of peace and now sought violent release."

In attempting to portray what the world before the war was like my process has been admittedly highly selective. I am conscious on finishing this book that it could be written all over again under the same title with entirely other subject matter; and then a third time, still without repeating. There could be chapters on the literature of the period, on its wars—the Sino-Japanese, Spanish-American, Boer, Russo-Japanese, Balkan—on imperialism, on science and technology, on business and trade, on women, on royalty, on medicine, on painting, on as many different subjects as might appeal to the individual historian. There could have been chapters on Leopold II, King of the Belgians, Chekhov, Sargent, The Horse, or U.S. Steel, all of which figured in my original plan. There should have been a chapter on some ordinary everyday shopkeeper or clerk representing the mute inglorious anonymous middle class but I never found him.

I think I owe the reader a word about my process of selection. In the first place I confined myself to the Anglo-American and West European world from which our experience and culture most directly derive, leaving aside the East European which, however important, is a separate tradition. In choice of subjects the criterion I used was that they must be truly representative of the period in question and have exerted their major influence on civilization before 1914, not after. This consideration ruled out the automobile and airplane, Freud and Einstein and the movements they represented. I also ruled out eccentrics, however captivating.

I realize that what follows offers no over-all conclusion but to draw some tidy generalization from the heterogenity of the age would be invalid. I also know that what follows is far from the whole picture. It is not false modesty which prompts me to say so but simply an acute awareness of what I have not included. The faces and voices of all that I have left out crowd around me as I reach the end.

BARBARA W. TUCHMAN

I

The Patricians

ENGLAND: 1895–1902

I

The Patricians

THE LAST government in the Western world to possess all the attributes of aristocracy in working condition took office in England in June of 1895. Great Britain was at the zenith of empire when the Conservatives won the General Election of that year, and the Cabinet they formed was her superb and resplendent image. Its members represented the greater landowners of the country who had been accustomed to govern for generations. As its superior citizens they felt they owed a duty to the State to guard its interests and manage its affairs. They governed from duty, heritage and habit—and, as they saw it, from right.

The Prime Minister was a Marquess and lineal descendant of the father and son who had been chief ministers to Queen Elizabeth and James I. The Secretary for War was another Marquess who traced his inferior title of Baron back to the year 1181, whose great-grandfather had been Prime Minister under George III and whose grandfather had served in six cabinets under three reigns. The Lord President of the Council was a Duke who owned 186,000 acres in eleven counties, whose ancestors had served in government since the Fourteenth Century, who had himself served thirty-four years in the House of Commons and three times refused to be Prime Minister. The Secretary for India was the son of another Duke whose family seat was received in 1315 by grant from Robert the Bruce and who had four sons serving in Parliament at the same time. The President of the Local Government Board was a pre-eminent country squire who had a Duke for brother-in-law, a Marquess for son-in-law, an ancestor who had been Lord Mayor of London in the reign of Charles II, and who had himself been a Member of Parliament for twenty-seven years. The Lord Chancellor bore a family name brought to England by a Norman follower of William the Conqueror and maintained thereafter over eight centuries without a title. The Lord Lieutenant for Ireland was an Earl, a grandnephew of the Duke of Wellington and a hereditary trustee of the British Museum. The Cabinet also included a Viscount, three Barons and two Baronets. Of its six commoners, one was a director of the Bank of England, one was a squire whose family had represented the same county in Parliament since the Sixteenth Century, one—who acted as Leader of the House of Commons—was the Prime Minister's nephew and inheritor of a Scottish fortune of £4,000,000, and one, a notable and disturbing cuckoo in the nest, was a Birmingham manufacturer widely regarded as the most successful man in England.

Besides riches, rank, broad acres and ancient lineage, the new Government also possessed, to the regret of the Liberal Opposition and in the words of one of them, "an almost embarrassing wealth of talent and capacity." Secure in authority, resting comfortably on their electoral majority in the House of Commons and on a permanent majority in the House of Lords, of whom four-fifths were Conservatives, they were in a position, admitted the same opponent, "of unassailable strength."

Enriching their ranks were the Whig aristocrats who had seceded from the Liberal party in 1886 rather than accept Mr. Gladstone's insistence on Home Rule for Ireland. They were for the most part great landowners who, like their natural brothers the Tories, regarded union with Ireland as sacrosanct. Led by the Duke of Devonshire, the Marquess of Lansdowne and Mr. Joseph Chamberlain, they had remained independent until 1895, when they joined with the Conservative party, and the two groups emerged as the Unionist party, in recognition of the policy that had brought them together. With the exception of Mr. Chamberlain, this coalition represented that class in whose blood, training and practice over the centuries, landowning and governing had been inseparable. Ever since Saxon chieftains met to advise the King in the first national assembly, the landowners of England had been sending members to Parliament and performing the duties of High Sheriff, Justice of the Peace and Lord Lieutenant of the Militia in their own counties. They had learned the practice of government from the possession of great estates, and they undertook to manage the affairs of the nation as inevitably and unquestionably as beavers build a dam. It was their ordained role and natural task.

But it was threatened. By a rising rumble of protest from below, by the Radicals of the Opposition who talked about taxing unearned increment on land, by Home Rulers who wanted to detach the Irish island from which so much English income came, by Trade Unionists who talked of Labour representation in Parliament and demanded the legal right to strike and otherwise interfere with the free play of economic forces, by Socialists who wanted to nationalize property and Anarchists who wanted to abolish it, by upstart nations and strange challenges from abroad. The rumble was distant, but it spoke with one voice that said Change, and those whose business was government could not help but hear.

Planted firmly across the path of change, operating warily, shrewdly yet with passionate conviction in defence of the existing order, was a peer who was Chancellor of Oxford University for life, had twice held the India Office, twice the Foreign Office and was now Prime Minister for the third time. He was Robert Arthur Talbot Gascoyne-Cecil, Lord Salisbury, ninth Earl and third Marquess of his line.

Lord Salisbury was both the epitome of his class and uncharacteristic of it—except insofar as the freedom to be different was a class characteristic. He was six feet four inches tall, and as a young man had been thin, ungainly, stooping and shortsighted, with hair unusually black for an Englishman. Now sixty-five, his youthful lankiness had turned to bulk, his shoulders had grown massive and more stooped than ever, and his heavy bald head with full curly gray beard rested on them as if weighted down. Melancholy, intensely intellectual, subject to sleepwalking and fits of depression which he called "nerve storms," caustic, tactless, absent-minded, bored by society and fond of solitude, with a penetrating, skeptical, questioning mind, he had been called the Hamlet of English politics. He was above the conventions and refused to live in Downing Street. His devotion was to religion, his interest in science. In his own home he attended private chapel every morning before breakfast, and had fitted up a chemical laboratory where he conducted solitary experiments. He harnessed the river at Hatfield for an electric power plant on his estate and strung up along the old beams of his home one of England's first electric light systems, at which his family threw cushions when the wires sparked and sputtered while they went on talking and arguing, a customary occupation of the Cecils.

Lord Salisbury cared nothing for sport and little for people. His aloofness was enhanced by shortsightedness so intense that he once failed to recognize a member of his own Cabinet, and once, his own butler. At the close of the Boer War he picked up a signed photograph of King Edward and, gazing at it pensively, remarked, "Poor Buller [referring to the Commander-in-Chief at the start of the war], what a mess he made of it." On another occasion he was seen in prolonged military conversation with a minor peer under the impression that he was talking to Field Marshal Lord Roberts.

For the upper-class Englishman's alter ego, most intimate companion and constant preoccupation, his horse, Lord Salisbury had no more regard. Riding was to him purely a means of locomotion to which the horse was "a necessary but extremely inconvenient adjunct." Nor was he addicted to shooting. When Parliament rose he did not go north to slaughter grouse upon the moors or stalk deer in Scottish forests, and when protocol required his attendance upon royalty at Balmoral, he would not go for walks and "positively refused," wrote Queen Victoria's Private Secretary, Sir Henry Ponsonby, "to admire the prospect or the deer." Ponsonby was told to have his room in the dismal castle kept "warm"—a minimum temperature of sixty degrees. Otherwise he retired for his holidays to France, where he owned a villa at Beaulieu on the Riviera and where he could exercise his fluent French and lose himself in *The Count of Monte Cristo,* the only book, he once told Dumas *fils,* which allowed him to forget politics.

His acquaintance with games was confined to tennis, but when elderly he invented his own form of exercise, which consisted in riding a tricycle through St. James's Park in the early mornings or along paths cemented for the purpose in the park of his estate at Hatfield. Wearing for the occasion a kind of sombrero hat and a short sleeveless cloak with a hole in the middle in which he resembled a monk, he would be accompanied by a young coachman to push him up the hills. At the downhill slopes, the young man would be told to "jump on behind," and the Prime Minister, with the coachman's hands on his shoulders, would roll away, cloak flying and pedals whirring.

Hatfield, twenty miles north of London in Hertfordshire, had been the home of the Cecils for nearly three hundred years since James I had given it, in 1607, to his Prime Minister, Robert Cecil, first Earl of Salisbury, in exchange for a house of Cecil's to which the King had taken a fancy. It was the royal residence where Queen Elizabeth had spent her childhood and where, on receiving news of her accession, she held her first council, to swear in William Cecil, Lord Burghley, as her chief Secretary of State. Its Long Gallery, with intricately carved paneled walls and gold-leaf ceiling, was 180 feet in length. The Marble Hall, named for the black and white marble floor, glowed like a jewel case with painted and gilded ceiling and Brussels tapestries. The red King James Drawing Room was hung with full-length family portraits by Romney and Reynolds and Lawrence. The library was lined from floor to gallery and ceiling with 10,000 volumes bound in leather and vellum. In other rooms were kept the Casket Letters of Mary Queen of Scots, suits of armor taken from men of the Spanish Armada, the cradle of the beheaded King, Charles I, and presentation portraits of James I and George III. Outside were yew hedges clipped in the form of crenelated battlements, and the gardens, of which Pepys wrote that he never saw "so good flowers, nor so great gooseberries as big as nutmegs." Over the entrance hall hung flags captured at Waterloo and presented to Hatfield by the Duke of Wellington, who was a constant visitor and devoted admirer of the Prime Minister's mother, the second Marchioness. In her honor Wellington wore the hunt coat of the Hatfield Hounds when he was on campaign. The first Marchioness was painted by Sir Joshua Reynolds and hunted till the day she died at eighty-five, when, half-blind and strapped to the saddle, she was accompanied by a groom who would shout, when her horse approached a fence, "Jump, dammit, my Lady, jump!"

It was this exceptional person who reinvigorated the Cecil blood, which, after Burghley and his son, had produced no further examples of superior mentality. Rather, the general mediocrity of succeeding generations had been varied only, according to a later Cecil, by instances of "quite exceptional stupidity." But the second Marquess proved a vigorous and able man with a strong sense of public duty who served in several mid-century Tory cabinets. His second son, another Robert Cecil, was the Prime Minister of 1895. He in turn produced five sons who were to distinguish themselves. One became a general, one a bishop, one a minister of state, one M.P. for Oxford, and one, through service to the government, won a peerage in his own right. "In human beings as in horses," Lord Birkenhead was moved to comment on the Cecil record, "there is something to be said for the hereditary principle."

At Oxford in 1850 the contemporaries of young Robert Cecil agreed that he would end as Prime Minister either because or in spite of his remorselessly uncompromising opinions. Throughout life he never bothered to restrain them. His youthful speeches were remarkable for their virulence and insolence; he was not, said Disraeli, "a man who measures his phrases." A "salisbury" became a synonym for a political imprudence. He once compared the Irish in their incapacity for self-government to Hottentots and spoke of an Indian candidate for Parliament as "that black man." In the opinion of Lord Morley his speeches were always a pleasure to read because "they were sure to contain one blazing indiscretion which it is a delight to remember." Whether these were altogether accidental is open to question, for though Lord Salisbury delivered his speeches without notes, they were worked out in his head beforehand and emerged clear and perfect in sentence structure. In that time the art of oratory was considered part of the equipment of a statesman and anyone reading from a written speech would have been regarded as pitiable. When Lord Salisbury spoke, "every sentence," said a fellow member, "seemed as essential, as articulate, as vital to the argument as the members of his body to an athlete."

Appearing in public before an audience about whom he cared nothing, Salisbury was awkward; but in the Upper House, where he addressed his equals, he was perfectly and strikingly at home. He spoke sonorously, with an occasional change of tone to icy mockery or withering sarcasm. When a recently ennobled Whig took the floor to lecture the House of Lords in high-flown and solemn Whig sentiments, Salisbury asked a neighbor who the speaker was and on hearing the whispered identification, replied perfectly audibly, "I thought he was dead." When he listened to others he could become easily bored, revealed by a telltale wagging of his leg which seemed to one observer to be saying, "When will all this be over?" Or sometimes, raising his heels off the floor, he would set up a sustained quivering of his knees and legs which could last for half an hour at a time. At home, when made restless by visitors, it shook the floor and made the furniture rattle, and in the House his colleagues on the front bench complained it made them seasick. If his legs were at rest his long fingers would be in motion, incessantly twisting and turning a paper knife or beating a tattoo on his knee or on the arm of his chair.

He never dined out and rarely entertained beyond one or two political receptions at his town house in Arlington Street and an occasional garden party at Hatfield. He avoided the Carlton, official club of the Conservatives, in favor of the Junior Carlton, where a special luncheon table was set aside for him alone and the library was hung with huge placards inscribed SILENCE. He worked from breakfast to one in the morning, returning to his desk after dinner as if he were beginning a new day. His clothes were drab and often untidy. He wore trousers and waistcoat of a dismal gray under a broadcloth frock coat grown shiny. But though careless in dress, he was particular about the trimming of his beard and carefully directed operations in the barber's chair, indicating "just a little more off here" while "artist and subject gazed fixedly in the mirror to judge the result."

Despite his rough tongue and sarcasms, Salisbury exerted a personal charm upon close colleagues and equals which, as one of them said, "was no small asset in the conduct of affairs." He gave detailed attention to party affairs and even sacrificed his exclusiveness for their sake. Once he astonished everyone by accepting an invitation to the traditional dinner for party supporters given by the Leader of the House of Commons. He asked to be given in advance biographical details about each guest. At the dinner the Prime Minister charmed his neighbor at table, a well-known agriculturist, with his expert knowledge of crop rotation and stock-breeding, chatted amiably afterward with every guest in turn, and before leaving, beckoned to his Private Secretary, saying, "I think I have done them all, but there was someone I have not identified who, you said, made mustard."

Mr. Gladstone, though in political philosophy his bitterest antagonist, acknowledged him "a great gentleman in private society." In private life he was delightful and sympathetic and a complete contrast to his public self. In public acclaim, Salisbury was uninterested, for—since the populace was uninstructed—its opinions, as far as he was concerned, were worthless. He ignored the public and neither possessed nor tried to cultivate the personal touch that makes a political leader a recognizable personality to the man in the street and earns him a nickname like "Pam" or "Dizzy" or the "Grand Old Man." Not in the press, not even in *Punch,* was Lord Salisbury ever called anything but Lord Salisbury. He made no attempt to conceal his dislike for mobs of all kinds, "not excluding the House of Commons." After moving to the Lords, he never returned to the Commons to listen to its debates from the Peers' Gallery or chat with members in the Lobby, and if compelled to allude to them in his own House, would use a tone of airy contempt, to the amusement of visitors from the Commons who came to hear him. But this was merely an outward pose designed to underline his deep inner sense of the patrician. He was not rank-conscious; he was indifferent to honors or any other form of recognition. It was simply that as a Cecil, and a superior one, he was born with a consciousness in his bones and brain cells of ability to rule and saw no reason to make any concessions of this prescriptive right to anyone whatever.

Having entered the House of Commons in the customary manner for peers' sons, from a family-controlled borough in an uncontested election at the age of twenty-three, and, during his fifteen years in the House of Commons, having been returned unopposed five times from the same borough, and having for the last twenty-seven years sat in the House of Lords, he had little personal experience of vote-getting. He regarded himself not as responsible *to* the people but as responsible *for* them. They were in his care. What reverence he felt for anyone was directed not down but up—to the monarchy. He revered Queen Victoria, who was some ten years his senior, both as her subject and, with chivalry toward her womanhood, as a man. For her he softened his brusqueness even if at Balmoral he could not conceal his boredom.

She in turn visited him at Hatfield and had the greatest confidence in him, giving him, as she told Bishop Carpenter, "if not the highest, an equal place with the highest among her ministers," not excepting Disraeli. Salisbury, who was "bad on his legs at any time," was the only man she ever asked to sit down. Unalike in every quality of mind except in their strong sense of rulership, the tiny old Queen and the tall, heavy, aging Prime Minister felt for each other mutual respect and regard.

In unimportant matters of state as in dress, Salisbury was inclined to be casual. Once when two clergymen with similar names were candidates for a vacant bishopric, he appointed the one not recommended by the Archbishop of Canterbury, and this being sorrowfully drawn to his attention, he said, "Oh, I daresay he will do just as well." He reserved high seriousness for serious matters only, and the most serious to him was the maintenance of aristocratic influence and executive power, not for its own sake, but because he believed it to be the only element capable of holding the nation united against the rising forces of democracy which he saw "splitting it into a bundle of unfriendly and distrustful fragments."

Class war and irreligion were to him the greatest evils and for this reason he detested Socialism, less for its menace to property than for its preaching of class war and its basis in materialism, which meant to him a denial of spiritual values. He did not deny the need of social reforms, but believed they could be achieved through the interplay and mutual pressures of existing parties. The Workmen's Compensation Act, for one, making employers liable for work-sustained injuries, though denounced by some of his party as interference with private enterprise, was introduced and passed with his support in 1897.

He fought all proposals designed to increase the political power of the masses. When still a younger son, and not expecting to succeed to the title, he had formulated his political philosophy in a series of some thirty articles which were published in the *Quarterly Review* in the early 1860's, when he was in his thirties. Against the growing demand at that time for a new Reform law to extend the suffrage, Lord Robert Cecil, as he then was, had declared it to be the business of the Conservative party to preserve the rights and privileges of the propertied class as the "single bulwark" against the weight of numbers. To extend the suffrage would be, as he saw it, to give the working classes not merely a voice in Parliament but a preponderating one that would give to "mere numbers a power they ought not to have." He deplored the Liberals' adulation of the working class "as if they were different from other Englishmen" when in fact the only difference was that they had less education and property and "in proportion as the property is small the danger of misusing the franchise is great." He believed the workings of democracy to be dangerous to liberty, for under democracy "passion is not the exception but the rule" and it was "perfectly impossible" to commend a farsighted passionless policy to "men whose minds are unused to thought and undisciplined to study." To widen the suffrage among the poor while increasing taxes upon the rich would end, he wrote, in a complete divorce of power from responsibility; "the rich would pay all the taxes and the poor make all the laws."

He did not believe in political equality. There was the multitude, he said, and there were "natural" leaders. "Always wealth, in some countries birth, in all countries intellectual power and culture mark out the man to whom, in a healthy state of feeling, a community looks to undertake its government." These men had the leisure for it and the fortune, "so that the struggles for ambition are not defiled by the taint of sordid greed. . . . They are the aristocracy of a country in the original and best sense of the word. . . . The important point is, that the rulers of a country should be taken from among them," and as a class they should retain that "political preponderance to which they have every right that superior fitness can confer."

So sincere and certain was his conviction of that "superior fitness" that in 1867 when the Tory Government espoused the Second Reform Bill, which doubled the electorate and enfranchised workingmen in the towns, Salisbury at thirty-seven flung away Cabinet office within a year of first achieving it rather than be party to what he considered a betrayal and surrender of Conservative principles. His party's reversal, engineered by Disraeli in a neat enterprise both to "dish the Whigs" and to meet political realities, was regarded with abhorrence by Lord Cranborne (as Lord Robert Cecil had then become, his elder brother having died in 1865). Though it might ruin his career he resigned as Secretary for India and in a bitter and serious speech spoke out in the House against the policy of the party's leaders, Lord Derby and Mr. Disraeli. He begged the members not to do for political advantage what would ultimately destroy them as a class. "The wealth, the intelligence, the energy of the community, all that has given you that power which makes you so proud of your nation and which makes the deliberations of this House so important, will be numerically absolutely overmatched." Issues would arise in which the interests of employers and employed would clash and could only be decided by political force, "and in that conflict of political force you are pitting an overwhelming number of employed against a hopeless minority of employers." The outcome would "reduce to political insignificance and extinction the classes which have hitherto contributed so much to the greatness and prosperity of their country."

A year later, on his father's death, he entered the House of Lords as third Marquess of Salisbury. In 1895, after the passage of nearly thirty years, his principles had not shifted an inch. With no belief in change as improvement, nor faith in the future over the present, he dedicated himself with "grim acidity" to preserving the existing order. Believing that "rank, without the power of which it was originally the symbol, was a sham," he was determined, while he lived and governed England, to resist further attack on the power of that class of which rank was still the visible symbol. Watchful of approaching enemies, he stood against the coming age. The pressures of democracy encircled, but had not yet closed in around, the figure whom Lord Curzon described as "that strange, powerful, inscrutable, brilliant, obstructive deadweight at the top."

The average member of the ruling class, undisturbed by Lord Salisbury's too-thoughtful, too-prescient mind, did not worry deeply about the future; the present was so delightful. The Age of Privilege, though assailed at many points and already cracking at some, still seemed, in the closing years of the Nineteenth Century and of Victoria's reign, a permanent condition. To the privileged, life appeared "secure and comfortable. . . . Peace brooded over the land." Undoubtedly Sir William Harcourt's budget of 1894, enacted by the Liberals during the premiership of Lord Rosebery, Mr. Gladstone's rather inappropriate successor, sent a tremor through many. It introduced death duties—and what was worse, introduced them on a graduated principle from 1 per cent on estates of £500 to 8 per cent on estates of over a million pounds. And it increased the income tax by a penny to eightpence in the pound. Although to soften the blow and equalize the burden it imposed a tax on beer and spirits so that the working class, who paid no income tax, would contribute to the revenue, this failed to muffle the drumbeat of the death duties. The eighth Duke of Devonshire was moved to predict a time which he "did not think can be deferred beyond the period of my own life" when great estates such as his of Chatsworth would be shut up solely because of "the inexorable necessities of democratic finance."

But a greater, and from the Conservative point of view a happier, event of 1894 compensated for the budget. Mr. Gladstone retired from Parliament and from politics. His last octogenarian effort to force through Home Rule had been defeated in the House of Lords by a wrathful assembly of peers gathered for the purpose in numbers hardly before seen in their lifetime. He had split his party beyond recall, he was eighty-five, the end of a career had come. With the Conservative victory in the following year there was a general feeling, reflected by *The Times*, that Home Rule, that "germ planted by Mr. Gladstone in our political life which has threatened to poison the whole organism," being now disposed of, at least for the present,

England could settle down sensibly to peace and business. The "dominant influences" were safely in the saddle.

"Dominant influences" was a phrase, not of the Conservative-minded *Times,* but strangely enough of Mr. Gladstone himself, who was a member of the landed gentry and never forgot it nor ever abandoned the inborn sense that property is responsibility. He owned an estate of 7,000 acres at Hawarden with 2,500 tenants producing an annual rent roll between £10,000 and £12,000. In a letter to his grandson who would inherit it, the Great Radical urged him to regain lands lost through debt by earlier generations and restore Hawarden to its former rank as a "leading influence" in the county, because, as he said, "society cannot afford to dispense with its dominant influences." No duke could have put it better. This was exactly the sentiment of the Conservative landowners, who were his bitterest opponents but with whom, at bottom, he shared a belief both in the "superior fitness" conferred by inherited ownership of land and in the country's need of it. Their credo was the exact opposite of the idea prevailing in the more newly minted United States, that there was a peculiar extra virtue in being lowly born, that only the self-made carried the badge of ability and that men of easy circumstances were more likely than not to be stupid or wicked, if not both. The English, on the contrary, having evolved slowly through generations of government by the possessing class, assumed that prolonged retention by one family of education, comfort and social responsibility was natural nourishment of "superior fitness."

It qualified them for government, considered in England as nowhere else the proper and highest profession of a gentleman. A private secretaryship to a ministerial uncle or other relative could be either a serious apprenticeship for Cabinet office or merely a genial occupation for a gentleman like Sir Schomberg McDonnell, Lord Salisbury's Private Secretary, a brother of the Earl of Antrim. Diplomacy, too, offered a desirable career, often to persons of talent. The Marquess of Dufferin and Ava, when British Ambassador in Paris in 1895, taught himself Persian and noted in his diary for that year that besides reading eleven plays of Aristophanes in Greek, he had learned by heart 24,000 words from a Persian dictionary, "8,000 perfectly, 12,000 pretty well, and 4,000 imperfectly." Military service in one of the elite regiments of Guards or Hussars or Lancers was an equally accepted role for men of wealth and rank, although it tended to attract the weaker minds. The less wealthy went into the Church and the Navy; the bar and journalism provided careers when earning power was a necessity. But Parliament above all was the natural and desirable sphere for the exercise of "superior fitness." A seat in Parliament was the only way to a seat in the Cabinet, where power and influence and a membership in the Privy Council, and on retirement a peerage, were to be won. The Privy Council, made up of 235 leaders in all fields, though formal and ceremonial in function, was the badge of importance in the nation. A peerage was still the magic mantle that set a man apart from his fellows. Cabinet office was highly coveted and the object of intense maneuvering behind the scenes. When governments changed, nothing so absorbed the attention of British society as the complicated minuet of Cabinet-making. Clubs and drawing rooms buzzed, cliques and alliances formed and re-formed, and the winners emerged proudly wearing fortune's crown of laurel. The prize required hard work and long hours, though rarely knowl-edge of the department. A minister's function was not to do the work but to see that it got done, much as he managed his estate. Details such as decimal points, which Lord Randolph Churchill when Chancellor of the Exchequer shrugged aside as "those damned dots," were not his concern.

The members of Lord Salisbury's Government, of whom the majority, though not all, enjoyed inherited land, wealth or titles, had not entered government for material advantages. Indeed, from their point of view, it was right and necessary that public affairs should be administered, as Lord Salisbury said, by men unaffected "by the taint of sordid greed." A par-liamentary career—which was of course unsalaried—conferred, not gain, but distinction. The House of Commons was the center of the capital, of the Empire, of Society; its company was the best in the kingdom. Ambition led men there as well as duty; besides, it was the expected thing to do. Fathers in Parliament were followed by sons, both often serving at the same time. James Lowther, Deputy Speaker of the House from 1895 to 1905 and afterward Speaker, came from a family which had represented Westmorland constituencies more or less continuously over six centuries. His great-grandfather and grandfather each had sat for half a century and his father for twenty-five years. The representative of a county division in Parliament was usually someone whose home was known for seventy miles around as "The House," whose family had been known in the district for several hundred years and the candidate himself since his birth. Since the cost of candidacy and election and of nursing a constituency afterward was borne by the member himself, the privilege of representing the people in Parliament was a luxury largely confined to the class that could afford it. Of the 670 members in the House of Commons in 1895, 420 were gentlemen of leisure, country squires, officers and barristers. Among them were twenty-three eldest sons of peers, besides their innumerable younger sons, brothers, cousins, nephews and uncles, including Lord Stanley, heir of the sixteenth Earl of Derby, who, after the Dukes, was the richest peer in England. As a junior Government Whip, Stanley was obliged to stand at the door of the Lobby and bully or cajole members to be on hand for a division, though himself not allowed inside the chamber while performing this duty. It was as if he were, wrote an observer, "an Upper Class Servant." To see "this heir to a great and historic name and a vast fortune doing work almost menial" was testimony both to a sense of political duty and the allure of a political career.

The ruling class did not grow rulers only. It produced the same proportion as any other class of the unfit and misfit, the bad or merely stupid. Besides prime ministers and empire-builders it had its bounders and club bores, its effete Reggies and Algies caricatured in *Punch* discussing their waistcoats and neckwear, its long-legged Guardsmen whose conversation was confined to "haw, haw," its wastrels who ruined themselves through drink, racing and cards, as well as its normal quota of the mediocre who never did anything noticeable, either good or bad. Even Eton had its "scugs," boys who, in the words of an Etonian, were "simply not good form . . . and if not naturally vicious, certainly imbecile, probably degenerate." Though a scug at Eton—not to be confused with "swat," or grind—could as often as not turn out to be a Privy Councillor thirty years later, some were scugs for life. One of Lord Salisbury's nephews, Cecil Balfour, disappeared to Australia, over an affair of a forged check, and died there, it was said, of drink.

Despite such accidents, the ruling families had no doubts of their inborn right to govern and, on the whole, neither did the rest of the country. To be a lord, wrote a particularly picturesque exemplar, Lord Ribblesdale, in 1895, "is still a popular thing." Known as the "Ancestor" because of his Regency appearance, Ribblesdale was so handsome a personification of the patrician that John Singer Sargent, glorifier of the class and type, asked to paint him. Standing at full length in the portrait, dressed as Master of the Queen's Buckhounds in long riding coat, top hat, glistening boots and holding a coiled hunting whip, Sargent's Ribblesdale stared out upon the world in an attitude of such natural arrogance, elegance and self-confidence as no man of a later day would ever achieve. When the picture was exhibited at the Salon in Paris and Ribblesdale went to see it, he was followed from room to room by admiring French crowds who, recognizing the subject of the portrait, pointed out to each other in whispers *"ce grand diable de milord anglais."*

At the opening of Ascot Race Week when Lord Ribblesdale led the Royal Procession down the green turf, mounted on a bright chestnut against a blue June sky, wearing a dark-green coat with golden hound-couplings hanging from a gold belt, he made a sight that no one who saw it could ever forget. As Liberal Whip in the House of Lords, an active member of the London County Council and chief trustee of the National Gallery, he too took his share of government. Like most of his kind he had a sense of easy communion with the land-based working class who served the sports and estates of the gentry. When the Queen presented J. Miles, a groom of the Buckhounds, with a medal in honor of fifty years' service, Ribblesdale rode over from Windsor to congratulate him and stayed "for tea and a talk" with Mrs. Miles. As he himself wrote of the average noble-man, "the ease of his circumstances from his youth up tends to produce a good-humored attitude. . . . To be pleased with yourself may be selfish or it may be stupid, but it is seldom actively disagreeable and usually it is very much the reverse." Despite a tendency of the Liberal press to portray the peerage as characterized "to a melancholy degree by knock-knees and receding foreheads," the peer still retained, Ribblesdale thought, the respect of his county. Identifying himself with its interests and affairs, maintaining mutually kindly relations toward his tenants, cottagers and the tradesmen of his market town, he would have to seriously misconduct himself before he would "outrun the prestige of an old name and tried associations." Yet for all this comfortable picture, Ribblesdale too heard the distant rumble and thirty years later chose for the motto of his memoirs the claim of Chateaubriand: "I have guarded that strong love of liberty peculiar to an aristocracy whose last hour has sounded."

Midsummer was the time when the London season was at its height and Society disported and displayed itself in full glory. To a titled visitor from Paris it seemed as if "a race of gods and goddesses descended from Olympus upon England in June and July." They appeared "to live upon a golden cloud, spending their riches as indolently and naturally as the leaves grow green." In the wake of the Prince of Wales followed a "flo-tilla of white swans, their long necks supporting delicate jewelled heads," who went by the names of Lady Glenconner, the Duchess of Leinster and Lady Warwick. The Duchess, who died young in the eighties, was, in the words of Lord Ernest Hamilton, "divinely tall, . . . of a beauty so dazzling as to be almost unbelievable." Her successor, the Countess of Warwick, "the prettiest married woman in London," was an inamorata of the Prince of Wales and the cause of a famous fracas in which Lord Charles Beresford almost struck his future sovereign. She shimmered before the eyes of a Society journal as "a goddess with a rounded figure, diaphanously draped, and a brilliant haughty beautiful countenance whose fame had penetrated to the dim recesses of the placid country." She was a Beauty, a magic title of the time that conferred upon its bearer a public character. "Get up, Daisy," cried her mother when their ship docked after a particularly sea-sick crossing of the Irish Channel which had left her prostrate, "the crowd is waiting to have a look at you."

In and out of Adam doorways in Berkeley and Belgrave Squares the constant procession flowed. No one unless dying ever stayed home. The day began at ten with a gallop in the Park and ended at a ball at three in the morning. At a select spot between the Albert and Grosvenor Gates in Hyde Park, a small circle of all the Society that counted was sure of meeting its members on a morning ride or a late afternoon drive between tea and dinner. London had not lost her Georgian air. Window boxes were bright with flowers in houses and squares lived in by the families whose names they bore: Devonshire House and Lansdowne House, Grosvenor Square and Cadogan Place. Splendid equipages filled the streets. Ladies driving in victorias drawn by smart, high-stepping cobs with a "tiger" sitting very straight with folded arms beside the coachman on the box, excited approving masculine gaze as they passed under club windows. Gentlemen sighed and told each other "what a pretty thing it was to see a lovely woman drive in London behind a well-matched pair." Down another street came trotting the Royal Horse Guards in blue tunics and white breeches on black horses with bridles and halter-chains shining and jingling. Tall silhouettes of hansom cabs carried the well-known profiles of statesmen and clubmen on their round of visits to the great houses and to the clubs in Pall Mall and Piccadilly, the Carlton for Conservatives, the Reform for Liberals, the Athenæum for distinction, the Turf for sportsmen, the Travellers' or White's, Brooks's or Boodle's for social converse with like-minded gentlemen. The business of government and empire went on in "the best club in London," the House of Commons, which sat through the season. Its library, smoking room and dining room, its servants, waiters and wine cellars were of a quality befitting the profession of a gentleman. Ladies in wide hats and trailing skirts took tea with members and ministers on the terrace overhanging the Thames where they could look out on the episcopal dignity of Lambeth Palace across the river and gossip about political preferment.

At private dinner tables draped in smilax, with a footman behind each chair, gentlemen in white tie and tails conversed with ladies in clouds of tulle over bare shoulders, wearing stars or coronets in their elaborately piled hair. Conversation was not casual but an art "in which competence conferred prestige." At the opera, made fashionable by its most energetic patroness, Lady de Grey, Nellie Melba sang love duets in her pure angelic soprano with the handsome idol Jean de Reszke. In the Royal Box glowed a vision in low-cut velvet, Lady Warwick, with "only a few diamonds on her Mephistophelian scarlet dress" and a scarlet aigrette in her hair. A battle array of lorgnettes was raised to see what Lady de Grey, her rival as London's best-dressed woman, was wearing. Afterwards at Lady de Grey's parties, called "Bohemia in tiaras," the guests might include Mme Melba herself and the Prince of Wales and—before his fatal year of 1895 —Oscar Wilde. Every night there were political receptions lasting till midnight or dances continuing until dawn. At the top of a sweeping curve of staircase the Duchess of Devonshire or Lady Londonderry, the two arbiters of Society, glittering in diamonds, received a brilliant stream of guests while a major-domo in a stentorian orgy of titles announced, "His Grace . . . Her Highness . . . The Right Honorable . . . Lord and Lady . . . His Excellency the Ambassador of . . ." and down in the lamplit square a footman bellowed for some departing Lordship's carriage.

Society was divided into several sets whose edges overlapped and members mingled. At the head of the "fast," or sporting, Marlborough House set was the cigar and paunch, the protruding Hanoverian countenance finished off by a short gray beard, the portly yet regal figure of the Prince of Wales. Eclectic, sociable, utterly bored (as was everyone who suffered under it) by the dull monotony of the royal regimen prescribed by his widowed mother, the Prince opened his circle of the nobility to a variety of disturbing outsiders, provided they were either beautiful, rich or amusing: Americans, Jews, bankers and stockbrokers, even an occasional manufacturer, explorer or other temporary celebrity. Professionally the Prince met everybody: among his personal friends he included some of the country's ablest men, such as Admiral Sir John Fisher, and it was an unkind canard to say he never read a book. True, he preferred Marie Corelli to any living author, yet he read Lieutenant Winston Churchill's first book, *The Malakand Field Force,* with "the greatest possible interest" and kindly wrote the author an appreciative note saying he thought "the descriptions and language generally excellent." But on the whole, in his circle, intellectuals and literary people were not welcome and brains not appreciated, because, according to Lady Warwick, Society, or this section of it, "did not want to be made to think." It was pleasure-loving, reckless, thoughtless and wildly extravagant. The newcomers, especially the Jews, were in most cases resented, "not because we disliked them individually, for some of them were charming and even brilliant, but because they had brains and understood finance." This was doubly disturbing because society most particularly did not want to think about making money, only about spending it.

On the right of the sporting set were the "Incorruptibles," the strict, reactionary, intensely class-conscious long-established families who regarded the Prince's circle as "vulgar" and themselves as upholding the tone of Society. Each family was encircled by a tribe of poorer country cousins who appeared in London once or twice a generation to bring out a daughter, but otherwise had hardly emerged from the Eighteenth Century. On the left were the "Intellectuals," or "Souls," who gathered in worship around their sun and center, Arthur Balfour, nephew of Lord Salisbury and the most brilliant and popular man in London. As a group they were particularly literate, self-consciously clever and endlessly self-admiring. They enjoyed each other's company in the same way that an unusually handsome man or woman enjoys preening before a mirror. "You all sit around and talk about each other's souls," remarked Lord Charles Beresford at a dinner in 1888. "I shall call you the 'Souls,'" and so they were named. An admiral of the Navy and vivid ornament of the Prince of Wales's set, Lord Charles was not himself one of the Souls, although he had married an unusual wife who wore a tiara with her tea gowns and was painted by Sargent with two sets of eyebrows because, as the painter briefly explained, she *had* two sets, a penciled one above the real.

The men of the Souls all followed political careers and nearly all were junior ministers in Lord Salisbury's Government. A leading member was George Wyndham, who had written a book on French poets and an introduction to North's *Plutarch* and after serving as Mr. Balfour's Parliamentary Private Secretary was named Under-Secretary of War in 1898, despite Lord Salisbury's reluctant remark, "I don't like poets." George Curzon, Under-Secretary for Foreign Affairs and soon to be appointed Viceroy of India, was another Soul, as was St. John Brodrick, a later Secretary for War. Both were heirs to peerages who staged a vain protest against their anticipated fate of enforced removal to the House of Lords. Others were the Tennant connection: Alfred Lyttelton, a champion cricketer who was to become Colonial Secretary and who had been married, before she died, to Laura Tennant; Lord Ribblesdale, who was married to Charlotte Tennant; and the uninhibited third sister, Margot, whose marriage to the outgoing Liberal Home Secretary, Mr. Asquith, was attended by two past prime ministers, Mr. Gladstone and Lord Rosebery, and two future ones, Mr. Balfour and the groom. A particularly admired member was Harry Cust, heir of the Brownlow barony, a scholar and athlete with a blazing wit who on sheer reputation alone, with no previous experience, was asked across the dinner table to be editor of the *Pall Mall Gazette*; he accepted on the spot and served for four years. Flawed by a "fatal self-indulgence" with regard to women—to whom he was "irresistibly fascinating"—his public career suffered and never fulfilled its early promise.

Society was small and homogeneous and its *sine qua non* was land. For an outsider to break in, it was essential first to buy an estate and live on it, although even this did not always work. When John Morley, at that time a Cabinet minister, was visiting Skibo, where Mr. Andrew Carnegie had constructed a swimming pool, he took his accompanying detective to see it and asked his opinion. "Well, sir," the detective replied judiciously, "it seems to me to savour of the parvenoo."

In the "brilliant and powerful body," as Winston Churchill called it, of the two hundred great families who had been governing England for generations, everyone knew or was related to everyone else. Since superiority and comfortable circumstances imposed on the nobility and gentry a duty to reproduce themselves, they were given to large families, five or six children being usual, seven or eight not uncommon, and nine or more not unknown. The Duke of Abercorn, father of Lord George Hamilton in Salisbury's Government, had six sons and seven daughters; the fourth Baron Lyttelton, Gladstone's brother-in-law and father of Alfred Lyttelton, had eight sons and four daughters; the Duke of Argyll, Secretary for India under Gladstone, had twelve children. As a result of the marriages of so many siblings, and of the numerous second marriages, everyone was related to a dozen other families. People who met each other every day, at each other's homes, at race meetings and hunts, at Cowes, for the Regatta, at the Royal Academy, at court and in Parliament, were more often than not meeting their second cousins or brother-in-law's uncle or stepfather's sister or aunt's nephew on the other side. When a prime minister formed a government it was not nepotism but almost unavoidable that some of his Cabinet should be related to him or to each other. In the Cabinet of 1895 Lord Lansdowne, the Secretary for War, was married to a sister of Lord George Hamilton, the Secretary for India, and Lansdowne's daughter was married to the nephew and heir of the Duke of Devonshire, who was Lord President of the Council.

The country's rulers, said one, "knew each other intimately quite apart from Westminster." They had been at school together and at one of the two favored colleges, Christ Church at Oxford or Trinity College at Cambridge. Here prime ministers—including Lords Rosebery and Salisbury, at Christ Church, and their immediate successors, Mr. Balfour and Sir Henry Campbell-Bannerman, at Trinity—were grown naturally. The forcing house of statesmanship, however, was Balliol, whose mighty Master, Benjamin Jowett, frankly spent his teaching talents on intelligent undergraduates "whose social position might enable them to obtain high offices in the public service." Christ Church, known simply as the "House," was the particular habitat of the wealthy and landed aristocracy. During the youth of the men who governed in the nineties, it was presided over by Dean Liddell, a singularly handsome man of great social elegance and formidable manner who had a daughter, Alice, much admired by an obscure lecturer in mathematics named Charles Dodgson. Activities at the "House" were chiefly fox-hunting, racing, a not too serious form of cricket and "no end of good dinners in the company of the best fellows in the world, as they knew it."

When such fellows in after life wrote their memoirs, the early pages were thick with footnotes identifying the Charles, Arthur, William and Francis of the author's school days as "afterwards Chief of Imperial General Staff" or "afterwards Bishop of Southhampton" or Speaker of the House or Minister at Athens as the case might be. Through years of familiarity they knew each other's characters and could ask each other favors. When Winston Churchill, at twenty-three, wanted to join the Sudan expedition in 1898 over the firm objections of its Commander-in-Chief, Sir Herbert Kitchener, the matter was not beyond accomplishment. Winston's grandfather, the seventh Duke of Marlborough, had been Lord Salisbury's colleague under Disraeli, and Lord Salisbury as Prime Minister listened amiably to the young man and promised his help. When it turned out to be needed on short notice, Winston had recourse to the Private Secretary, Sir Schomberg McDonnell, "whom I had seen and met in social circles since I was a child." Winston found him dressing for dinner and on the errand being explained, " 'I'll do it at once,' said this gallant man, and off he went, discarding his dinner party." In this way affairs were managed.

The mold in which they were all educated was the same, and its object was not necessarily the scientific spirit or the exact mind, but a "graceful dignity" which entitled the bearer to the status of English gentleman, and an unshatterable belief in that status as the highest good of man on earth. As such, it obligated the bearer to live up to it. In every boy's room at Eton hung the famous picture by Lady Butler of the disaster at Majuba Hill showing an officer with uplifted sword charging deathward to the cry of *"Floreat Etona!"* The spirit instilled may have accounted for, as has been suggested, the preponderance of bravery over strategy in British officers. Yet to be an Etonian was "to imbibe a sense of effortless superiority and be lulled in a consciousness of unassailable primacy." Clothed in

this armor, its wearers were serenely sure of their world and sorry for anyone who was not of it. When Sir Charles Tennant and a partner at golf
were preparing to drive and were rudely interrupted by a stranger who
pushed in ahead and placed his own ball on the tee, the enraged partner
was about to explode. "Don't be angry with him," Sir Charles soothed.
"Perhaps he isn't quite a gentleman, poor fellow, poor fellow."

This magic condition was envied and earnestly imitated abroad by all
the continental aristocracy (except perhaps the Russians, who spoke
French and imitated nobody). German noblemen relentlessly married
English wives and put on tweeds and raglan coats, while in France the life
of the *haut monde* centered upon the Jockey Club, whose members played
polo, drank whiskey and had their portraits painted in hunting pink by
Helleu, the French equivalent of Sargent.

It was no accident that their admired model was thought of in equestrian terms. The English gentleman was unthinkable without his horse.
Ever since the first mounted man acquired extra stature and speed (and,
with the invention of the stirrup, extra fighting thrust), the horse had distinguished the ruler from the ruled. The man on horseback was the symbol
of dominance, and of no other class anywhere in the world was the horse
so intrinsic a part as of the English aristocracy. He was the attribute of
their power. When a contemporary writer wished to describe the point of
view of the county oligarchy it was equestrian terms that he used: they
saw society, he wrote, made up of "a small select aristocracy born booted
and spurred to ride and a large dim mass born saddled and bridled to be
ridden."

In 1895 the horse was still as inseparable from, and ubiquitous in,
upper-class life as the servant, though considerably more cherished. He
provided locomotion, occupation and conversation; inspired love, bravery,
poetry and physical prowess. He was the essential element in racing,
the sport of kings, as in cavalry, the elite of war. When an English patrician
thought nostalgically of youth, it was as a time "when I looked at life from
the saddle and was as near heaven as it was possible to be."

The gallery at Tattersall's on Sunday nights when Society gathered to
look over the horses for the Monday sales was as fashionable as the opera.
People did not simply go to the races at Newmarket; they owned or took
houses in the neighborhood and lived there during the meeting. Racing was
ruled by the three Stewards of the Jockey Club from whose decision there
was no appeal. Three Cabinet ministers in Lord Salisbury's Government,
Mr. Henry Chaplin, the Earl of Cadogan and the Duke of Devonshire,
were at one time or another Stewards of the Jockey Club. Owning a stud

and breeding racehorses required an ample fortune. When Lord Rosebery, having married a Rothschild, won the Derby while Prime Minister in 1894, he received a telegram from Chauncey Depew in America, "Only heaven left." Depew's telegram proved an underestimate, for Rosebery won the Derby twice more, in 1895 and 1905. The Prince of Wales won it in 1896 with his great lengthy bay Persimmon, bred at his own stud, again in 1900 with Persimmon's brother Diamond Jubilee, and a third time, as King, in 1909 with Minoru. As the first such victory by a reigning monarch, it was Epsom's greatest day. When the purple, scarlet and gold of the royal colors came to the front at Tattenham Corner the crowd roared; when Minoru neck and neck with his rival battled it out at a furious pace along the rails they went mad with excitement and wept with delight when he won by a head. They broke through the ropes, patted the King on the back, wrung his hand, and "even policemen were waving their helmets and cheering themselves hoarse."

Distinction might also be won by a famous "whip" like Lord Londesborough, president of the Four-in-Hand Club, who was known as a "swell," the term for a person of extreme elegance and splendor, and was renowned for the smartness of his turnouts and the "gloss, speed and style" of his carriage horses. The carriage horse was more than ornamental; he was essential for transportation and through this role his tyranny was exercised. When a niece of Charles Darwin was taken in 1900 to see Lord Roberts embark for South Africa, she saw the ship but not Lord Roberts "because the carriage had to go home or the horses might have been tired." When her Aunt Sara, Mrs. William Darwin, went shopping in Cambridge she always walked up the smallest hill behind her own carriage, and if her errands took her more than ten miles the carriage and horses were sent home and she finished her visits in a horsecab.

But the true passion of the horseman was expressed in the rider to hounds. To gallop over the downs with hounds and horsemen, wrote Wilfrid Scawen Blunt in a sonnet, was to feel "my horse a thing of wings, myself a God." The fox-hunting man never had enough of the thrills, the danger, and the beauty of the hunt; of the wail of the huntsman's horn, the excited yelping of the hounds, the streaming rush of red-coated riders and black-clad ladies on sidesaddles, the flying leaps over banks, fences, stone walls and ditches, even the crashes, broken bones and the cold aching ride home in winter. If it was bliss in that time to be alive and of the leisured class, to hunt was rapture. The devotee of the sport—man or woman—rode to hounds five and sometimes six days a week. It was said of Mr. Knox, private chaplain to the Duke of Rutland, that he wore boots and spurs

under his cassock and surplice and "thought of horses even in the pulpit."
The Duke's family could always tell by the speed of morning prayers if
Mr. Knox were hunting that day or not.

Mr. Henry Chaplin, the popular "Squire" in Lord Salisbury's Cabinet,
who was considered the archetype of the English country gentleman and
took himself very seriously as representative in Parliament of the agricultural interest, took himself equally seriously as Master of the Blankney
Hounds and could not decide which duty came first. During a debate or a
Cabinet he would draw little sketches of horses on official papers. When
his presence as a minister was required at question time he would have a
special train waiting to take him wherever the hunt was to meet next
morning. Somewhere between stations it would stop, Mr. Chaplin would
emerge, in white breeches and scarlet coat, climb the embankment, and
find his groom and horses waiting. Weighing 250 pounds, he was constantly in search of horses big and strong enough to carry him and frequently "got to the bottom of several in one day." "To see him thundering
down at a fence on one of his great horses was a fine sight." On one
occasion the only opening out of a field was a break in a high hedge where
a young sapling had been planted surrounded by an iron cage 4 feet 6
inches high. "There were shouts for a chopper or a knife when down
came the Squire, forty miles an hour, with his eyeglass in his eye seeing
nothing but the opening in the hedge. There was no stopping him; neither
did the young tree do so, for his weight and that of his horse broke it off
as clean as you would break a thin stick and away he went without an
idea that the tree had ever been there."

The cost of being a Master who, besides maintaining his own stable,
was responsible for the breeding and upkeep of the pack was no small
matter. So extravagant was Mr. Chaplin's passion that he at one time
kept two packs, rode with two hunts and, what with keeping a racing stud,
a deer forest in Scotland and entertaining that expensive friend, the Prince
of Wales, he ultimately ruined himself and lost the family estates. On
one of his last hunts in 1911, when he was over seventy, he was thrown
and suffered two broken ribs and a pierced lung, but before being carried
home, insisted on stopping at the nearest village to telegraph the Conservative Whip in the House of Commons that he would not be present to vote
that evening.

George Wyndham, who was to acquire Cabinet rank as Chief Secretary for Ireland in 1902, was torn like Mr. Chaplin between passion for
the hunt and duty to politics. In Wyndham's case, the duty was not un-
tinged by ambition, since he had every intention of becoming Prime

Minister. As he likewise wrote poetry and had leanings toward art and literature, life was for him full of difficult choices. A sporting friend advised him against "sacrificing my life to politics and gave Harry Chaplin as a shocking example of whom better things were expected in his youth." It was hard not to agree and prefer the carefree life when gentlemen came down to breakfast in their pink coats with an apron tied on to protect the chalked white of their breeches, or when on a Christmas night, as Wyndham described it, "we sat down thirty-nine to dinner" and thirty hunted next day. "Today we are all out again. . . . Three of us sailed away [fifty lengths in front of the nearest followers]. The rest were nowhere. We spreadeagled the field. The pace was too hot to choose your place by a yard. We just took everything as it came with hounds screaming by our side. Nobody could gain an inch. These are the moments . . . that are the joy of hunting. There is nothing like it."

Older than fox-hunting, the oldest role of the horseman was in war. Cavalry officers considered themselves the cream of the Army and were indeed more notable for social prestige than for thought or imagination. They were "sure of themselves," wrote a cavalry officer from a later vantage point, "with the superb assurance that belonged to those who were young at this time and came of their class and country." In their first years with the regiment they managed, by a daily routine of port and a weekly fall on the head from horseback, to remain in "that state of chronic numb confusion which was the aim of every cavalry officer." Polo, learned on its native ground by the regiments in India, was their passion and the cavalry charge the sum and acme of their strategy. It was from the cavalry that the nation's military leaders were drawn. They believed in the cavalry charge as they believed in the Church of England. The classical cavalry officer was that magnificent and genial figure, a close friend of the Prince of Wales, "distinguished at Court, in the Clubs, on the racecourse, in the hunting field . . . one of the brightest military stars in London Society," Colonel Brabazon of the 10th Hussars. Six feet tall, with clean and symmetrical features, bright gray eyes and strong jaw, he had a moustache the Kaiser would have envied, and ideas to match. Testifying before the Committee of Imperial Defence in 1902 on the lessons of the Boer War, in which he had commanded the Imperial Yeomanry, General Brabazon (as he now was) "electrified the Commission by a recital of his personal experiences in hand to hand fighting and his theories of the use of the Cavalry Arm in war." These included, as reported by Lord Esher to the King, "life-long mistrust of the weapons supplied to the Cavalry and his preference for shock tactics by men armed

with a Tomahawk." Giving his evidence "in a manner highly characteristic
of that gallant officer . . . he drew graphic pictures of a Cavalry charge
under these conditions which proved paralyzing to the imagination of the
Commissioners." They next heard Colonel Douglas Haig, lately chief Staff
officer of the cavalry division in the South African War, deplore the
proposed abolition of the lance and affirm his belief in the *arme blanche*,
that is, the cavalry saber, as an effective weapon.

At home in the country, among his tenants and cottagers, crops and
animals, on the estate that dominated the life of the district of which "The
House" was the large unit and the village the small, on the land that his
family had owned and cultivated and rented out and drawn income from
for generations, the English patrician bloomed in his natural climate.
Here from childhood on he lived closely with nature, with the sky and
trees, the fields and birds and deer in the woods. "We were richly endowed
in the surpassing beauty of the homes in which we were reared," wrote
Lady Frances Balfour. The stately houses—Blenheim of the Dukes of
Marlborough, Chatsworth of the Dukes of Devonshire, Wilton of the
Earls of Pembroke, Warwick Castle of the Earls of Warwick, Knole of
the Sackvilles, Hatfield of the Salisburys—had three or four hundred
rooms, a hundred chimneys, and roofs measured in acres. Others less
grand often had been lived in longer, like Renishaw, inhabited by the
Sitwells for at least seven hundred years. Owners great and small never
finished adding on to or altering the house and improving the landscape.
They removed or created hills, conjured up lakes, diverted streams, and
cut vistas through their woods finished off by a marble pavilion to fix
the eye.

Their homes proliferated. A town house, a family estate, a second
country home, a shooting box in a northern county, another in Scotland,
possibly a castle in Ireland were not out of the ordinary. Besides Hatfield
and his London house on Arlington Street, Lord Salisbury owned
the Manor House at Cranborne in Dorsetshire, his villa in France,
and if he had been a sporting man, would have had a place in
Scotland or a racing stud near Epsom or Newmarket. There were 115
persons in Great Britain who owned over 50,000 acres each, and forty-
five of these owned over 100,000 acres each, although much of this was
uncultivatable land in Scotland whose income yield was low. There were
some sixty to sixty-five persons, all peers, who possessed both land over
50,000 acres and income over £50,000, and fifteen of these—seven
dukes, three marquesses, three earls, one baron and one baronet—had

landed incomes of over £100,000. In all of Great Britain, out of a population of 44,500,000, there were 2,500 landowners who owned more than 3,000 acres apiece and had landed incomes of over £3,000.

Income taxes were not payable on incomes under £160 and in this category there were approximately eighteen to twenty million people. Of these, about three million were in white-collar or service trades—clerks, shopmen, tradesmen, innkeepers, farmers, teachers—who earned an average of £75 a year. Fifteen and a half million were manual workers, including soldiers, sailors, postmen and policemen and those in agricultural and domestic service who earned less than £50 a year. The "poverty line" had been worked out at £55 a year, or 21s. 8d. a week, for a family of five. Indoor servants slept in attics or windowless basements. Agricultural laborers lived in houses for which they paid a shilling a week, and worked with scythe, plow and sickle in the fields from the time when the great horn boomed at five o'clock in the morning until nightfall. When their houses leaked or rotted they were dependent on the landlord for repairs, and unless the landlord took care of them when their earning power came to an end, they went to the workhouse to finish out their days. Estate servants—grooms, gardeners, carpenters, blacksmiths, dairymen and field hands—whose families had lived on the land as long as its owners, gave service that was "wholehearted and passionate. . . . Their pride was bound up in it."

With the opening of the grouse season in August, and until the reopening of Parliament in January, the great landowners engaged in continuous entertainment of each other in week-long house parties of twenty to fifty guests. With each guest bringing his own servant, the host fed as many as a hundred, and on one occasion at Chatsworth, four hundred extra mouths while his house party lasted. Shooting was the favored pastime and consisted in displaying sufficient stamina and marksmanship, assisted by a loader and three or four guns, to bring down an unlimited bag of small game flushed out of its coverts by an army of beaters. From county to county and back and forth into Scotland, their trail marked by thousands upon thousands of dead birds and hares, the gentry were constantly on the move: for shooting with the Prince at Sandringham, for hunting (in blue and buff instead of scarlet coats) with the Duke of Beaufort's hounds in Wiltshire, for deer stalking amid Scottish lochs and crags and trackless forests ("Keep doon, Squire, keep doon"—his ghillie whispered to Mr. Chaplin, forced to crawl into the open to come within shooting distance of his stag—"ye're so splendidly built about the haunches I'm afeert the deer will be seeing ye"), for Christmas parties and coming-of-

age parties and occasional time out at Homburg and Marienbad to purge
satiated stomachs and allow the round to begin again.

Morning was the gentlemen's time on the moors; ladies came down
to breakfast in hats and at afternoon tea reigned in elaborate and languor-
ous tea gowns of, it might be, "*eau de Nil* satin draped with gold-spangled
mousseline de soie and bands of sable at hem and neck." Formal dinners
followed in full evening dress. All day, herds of servants glided silently
about, bringing early morning tea and *The Times*, carrying up bath water
and coal for the fireplaces, replenishing vases daily with fresh flowers,
murmuring "His Grace is in the Long Library," sounding gongs at meal
times and waiting up to uncorset Her Ladyship for bed.

Each guest at the house parties had his name on a card fitted into a
brass frame on his bedroom door and a corresponding card beside the
bell indicator in the butler's pantry. In assigning rooms the recognized, if
unacknowledged, liaisons had to be considered. As long as the partners
in these intramural infidelities did nothing to provoke a public scandal
by outraged wife or cuckolded husband, they could do as they pleased.
The overriding consideration was to prevent any exposure of misconduct
to the lower classes. In that respect the code was rigid. Within the closed
circle of the ruling class the unforgivable sin was to give away any
member of the group; there must be no appeal to the Divorce Court, no
publicity that would bring the members as a class into disrepute. If,
regrettably, a husband refused absolutely to be complaisant and threatened
action, all the arbiters of Society, including, if necessary, the Prince of
Wales (despite his own hardly faultless record), rallied to stop him. He
must not, they reminded him, sacrifice his class to such exposure. It was
his duty to preserve appearances and an unsullied front before the gaze
of the vulgar. Subdued, he would obey, even at the cost, in the case of one
couple, of not speaking to his wife except in public for twenty years.

In their luxurious and lavish world, self-indulgence was the natural
law. Notable eccentrics like the nocturnal Duke of Portland and bad-
tempered autocrats like Sir George Sitwell and Sir William Eden were
merely representatives of their class in whom the habit of having their
own way had gone to extremes. But for the majority it was easy to be
agreeable when everything was done to keep them in comfort and ease
and to make life for the great and wealthy as uninterruptedly pleasant as
possible.

The lordly manner was the result. When Colonel Brabazon, who
affected a fashionable difficulty with his *r*'s, arrived late at the railroad
station to be informed that the train for London had just left, he instructed

the station master, "Then bwing me another." Gentlemen who did not relish a cold wait at a country station or a slow journey on a local made a habit of special trains which cost £25 for an average journey. There were not a few among them who, like Queen Victoria, had never seen a railway ticket. Ladies had one-of-a-kind dresses designed exclusively for them by Worth or Doucet, who devoted as much care to each client as if he were painting her portrait. "So as to be different from other people," the English-born beauty, Daisy, Princess of Pless, had "a fringe of real violets" sewn down the train of her court dress, which was of transparent lace lined with blue chiffon and sprinkled with gold sequins.

Fed upon privilege, the patricians flourished. Five at least of the leading ministers in Lord Salisbury's Government were over six feet tall, far above the normal stature of the time. Of the nineteen members of the Cabinet, all but two lived to be over seventy, seven exceeded eighty, and two exceeded ninety at a time when the average life expectancy of a male at birth was forty-four and of a man who had reached twenty-one was sixty-two. On their diet of privilege they acquired a certain quality which Lady Warwick could define only in the words, "They have an air!"

Now and then the sound of the distant rumble in the atmosphere caused them vague apprehensions of changes coming to spoil the fun. With port after dinner the gentlemen talked about the growth of democracy and the threat of Socialism. Cartoons in newspapers pictured John Bull looking over a fence at a bull called Labour. Most people were aware of problems without seriously imagining any major change in the present order of things, but a few were deeply disturbed. Young Arthur Ponsonby saw every night along the embankment from Westminster to Waterloo Bridge the "squalid throng of homeless, wretched outcasts sleeping on the benches," and broke with the courtier tradition of his father and brother to become a Socialist. Lady Warwick tried to smother nagging doubts about a life devoted to the pursuit of pleasure in "recurrent fits of philanthropy" which she indulged in from "an impelling desire to help put things right and a deep conviction that things as they were, were not right." In 1895, on reading an attack by the Socialist editor Robert Blatchford in his paper the *Clarion* on a great ball given at Warwick Castle to celebrate her husband's accession to the title, she rushed in anger to London, leaving a house full of guests, to confront the enemy. She explained to him how during a hard winter when many were out of work the Warwick celebrations provided employment. Mr. Blatchford explained to his beautiful caller the nature of productive labour and the principles of Socialist theory. She returned to Warwick in a daze of new ideas and thereafter devoted her energy, money and influence to propagating them, to the acute discomfort of her circle.

Lady Warwick was a straw, not a trend. As a nation, Britain in 1895 had an air of careless supremacy which galled her neighbors. The attitude, called "splendid isolation," was both a state of mind and a fact. Britain did not worry seriously about potential enemies, felt no need of allies and had no friends. In a world in which other national energies were bursting old limits, this happy condition gave no great promise of permanence. On July 20, when Salisbury's Government was less than a month old, it was suddenly and surprisingly challenged from an unexpected quarter, the United States. The affair concerned a long-disputed frontier between British Guiana and Venezuela. Claiming that the British were expanding territorially at their expense in violation of the Monroe Doctrine, the Venezuelans had been goading the United States to open that famous umbrella and insist on arbitration. Although the American President, Grover Cleveland, was a man of ordinarily sound judgment and common sense, his countrymen were in a mood of swelling self-assertion and, as Rudyard Kipling pointed out, for purposes of venting chauvinist sentiments, France had Germany, Britain had Russia, and America had Britain, the only feasible country "for the American public speaker to trample upon." On July 20, Cleveland's Secretary of State, Richard Olney, delivered a Note to Great Britain stating that disregard of the Monroe Doctrine would be "deemed an act of unfriendliness toward the United States," whom he described in terms of not very veiled belligerence as "master of the situation and practically invulnerable against any and all comers."

This was truly astonishing language for diplomatic usage; but it was deliberately provocative on Olney's part, because, as he said, "in English eyes the United States was then so completely a negligible quantity" that he felt "only words the equivalent of blows would be effective." Upon Lord Salisbury who was acting as his own Foreign Secretary they failed of effect. He was no more disposed to respond to this kind of prodding than he would have been if his tailor had suddenly challenged him to a duel. Foreign policy had been his métier for twenty years. He had been at the Congress of Berlin with Disraeli in 1878 and had maneuvered through all the twists and turns of that perennial entanglement, the Eastern Question. His method was not that of Lord Palmerston, whom the Prince of Wales admired because he "knew his own mind and put down his foot." Issues in foreign affairs were no longer as forthright as in the days of

Lord Palmerston's flourishing, and Lord Salisbury sought no dramatic successes in their conduct. The victories of diplomacy, he said, were won by "a series of microscopic advantages; a judicious suggestion here, an opportune civility there, a wise concession at one moment and a farsighted persistence at another; of sleepless tact, immovable calmness and patience that no folly, no provocation, no blunder can shake." But he regarded these refinements as wasted on a democracy like the United States, just as he regarded the vote as too good for the working class. He simply let Olney's note go unanswered for four months.

When he finally replied on November 26 it was to remark coldly that "the disputed frontier of Venezuela has nothing to do with any of the questions dealt with by President Monroe" and to refuse flatly to arbitrate "the frontier of a British possession which belonged to the Throne of England before the Republic of Venezuela came into existence." He did not even bother to obey diplomacy's primary rule: leave room for negotiation. The rebuff was too much even for Cleveland. In a Message to Congress on December 17 he announced that after an American Committee of Inquiry had investigated and established a boundary line, any British extension over the line would be regarded as "wilful aggression" upon the rights and interests of the United States. Cleveland became a hero; a tornado of jingoism swept the country; "WAR IF NECESSARY," proclaimed the New York *Sun*. The word "war" was soon being used as recklessly as if it concerned an expedition against the Iroquois or the Barbary pirates.

Britain was amazed, with opinion dividing according to party. The Liberals were mortified by Lord Salisbury's haughty tone, the Tories angered at American presumption. "No Englishman with imperial instincts," wrote the Tory journalist and novelist Morley Roberts in the inevitable letter to *The Times*, "can look with anything but contempt on the Monroe Doctrine. The English and not the inhabitants of the United States are the greatest power in the two Americas; and no dog of a Republic can open its mouth to bark without our good leave." If the tone was overdone, the outrage was real. Although the absurdity of the issue was recognized on both sides of the Atlantic, belligerence surged and blood boiled. Aggressiveness born of power and prosperity was near the surface. The quarrel was becoming increasingly difficult to terminate when happily a third force caused a distraction.

No one was more useful as a magnet of other nations' animosities than that catalyst of his epoch, Kaiser Wilhelm II of Germany. Forever spoiling to emphasize his own and his country's importance, to play a role, to strike a pose, to twist the course of history, he never overlooked an opportunity. He hankered to be influential and usually was.

On December 29, 1895, the long-standing conflict between the Boer Republic of the Transvaal and the British of the Cape Colony was broken open by the Jameson Raid. Nominally under British suzerainty but virtually independent, the Boer Republic was a block in the march of British red down the length of Africa and an oppressor of the Uitlanders within its borders. These were British and other foreigners who, drawn by gold, had flocked to, and settled in, the Transvaal until they now outnumbered the Boers, but were kept by them without suffrage and other civil rights, and were seething with grievances. Inspired by imperialism's impatient genius, Cecil Rhodes, Dr. Jameson led six hundred horsemen over the border with intent to bring about an uprising of the Uitlanders, overthrow the Boer government and bring the South African Republic under British control. His troop was surrounded and captured within three days, but his mission released a train of events that was to take full effect four years later.

For the moment it provided the ever alert Kaiser with an opening. He telegraphed congratulations to President Kruger of the Boer Republic on his success in repelling the invaders "without appealing to the help of friendly powers." The implication that such help would be available on future request was clear. Instantly, every British gaze, like spectators' heads at a tennis match, turned from America to Germany, and British wrath was diverted from President Cleveland, always unlikely in the role of menace, to the Kaiser, who played it so much more suitably. In helping to bring on the ultimate encirclement that he most dreaded, the Kruger telegram was one of the Kaiser's most effective efforts. It revealed a hostility that startled the British. From that moment the possibility that isolation might prove more hazardous than splendid began to trouble the minds of their policy-makers.

The year 1895 was prolific of shocks, and one that shook society unpleasantly occurred two months before the Conservatives took office. The trial and conviction of Oscar Wilde under Section 11 of the Criminal Law Amendment Act, for acts of gross indecency between males, destroyed both a brilliant man of letters and the mood of decadence he symbolized.

The presumption of decay had been heavily reinforced two years earlier by Max Nordau in a widely discussed book called *Degeneration*.

Through six hundred pages of mounting hysteria he traced the decay lurking impartially in the realism of Zola, the symbolism of Mallarmé, the mysticism of Maeterlinck, in Wagner's music, Ibsen's dramas, Manet's pictures, Tolstoy's novels, Nietzsche's philosophy, Dr. Jaeger's woollen clothing, in Anarchism, Socialism, women's dress, madness, suicide, nervous diseases, drug addiction, dancing, sexual license, all of which were combining to produce a society without self-control, discipline or shame which was "marching to its certain ruin because it is too worn out and flaccid to perform great tasks."

Wilde, conforming to the duty of a decadent, was already engaged in destroying himself. In his role of aesthete, voluptuary and wit, he had hitherto been protected by the enamel of success. His incomparable talk enraptured friends as his plays did the public. But his arrogance as artist became overweening and his appetites uncontrolled, so that he grew fat and loose and heavy-jowled and, as a friend remarked, "all his bad qualities began to show in his face." Nor did success satisfy him, for satiety required that he must taste the ultimate sensation of ruin. "I was a problem," he said in sad self-knowledge, "for which there was no solution." He precipitated his own arrest by taking action for libel against the Marquess of Queensberry. The ensuing trials tore away Society's screen of discretion and gave everyone a shuddering look at the livid gleam of vice: panders, male prostitutes, hotel-room assignations with a valet, a groom, a boat-attendant picked up on a beach, and blackmail. No charges were brought against Lord Alfred Douglas, son of the Marquess of Queensberry, the flowery and seductive young man who shared these practices as well as Wilde's company and affections. Nor had there been any charges when Lord Arthur Somerset, a son of the Duke of Beaufort and a friend of the Prince of Wales, had been found in a homosexual brothel raided by the police in 1889. He had been allowed to take himself off and live comfortably after his fashion on the Continent while the Prince had asked Lord Salisbury that he might occasionally be permitted to visit his parents quietly in the country "without fear of being apprehended on this awful charge."

Frank Harris, then editor of the *Fortnightly Review*, thought that the solidarity of the governing class would close protectively around his friend Oscar in the same way. He supposed that aristocratic prejudice was a matter of favoring the exceptional over the common and would operate equally for the lord, the millionaire and the "man of genius." He was mistaken. Wilde had done the unforgivable in forcing public notice of his sin. And as artist-intellectual caught in scarlet depravity he evoked the howl of the philistines and plunged the British public into one of the most virulent of its periodic fits of morality. The judge was malevolent, the public vituperative, the society which he had amused turned its back, cabbies and newsboys exchanged vulgar jokes about "Oscar," the press reviled him, his books were withdrawn from sale and his name pasted out on the playbills advertising *The Importance of Being Earnest*, his brightest diamond, then playing to enchanted audiences. His downfall, said the gentleman-Socialist H. M. Hyndman, "was the most grievous thing I have ever known in the literary world." With it was dissipated, in England, if not on the Continent, the yellow haze of *fin de siècle* decadence.

Lord Salisbury's appointment of a Poet Laureate at the end of the year could not have provided a greater contrast in men of letters or done more to re-enthrone Respectability. Since the death of Tennyson in 1892, the post had remained vacant because neither Mr. Gladstone nor Lord Rosebery, who took their responsibility to literature seriously, could find a worthy successor. Swinburne, owing to his distressing habits and opinions, was, regrettably, "absolutely impossible" (although Mr. Gladstone "admired his genius"), William Morris was a Socialist, Hardy was known so far only by his novels and the younger poetic talents tended to wear the colors of the Yellow Book and the Mauve Decade. The young Anglo-Indian, Rudyard Kipling, in his *Barrack Room Ballads* of 1892, had certainly sounded a virile and imperial note but in a rather rough idiom, and neither he nor W. E. Henley nor Robert Bridges was considered. All other candidates were mediocrities, one of whom, Sir Lewis Morris, offered an opening to what a contemporary called "the most spontaneously witty thing ever uttered in England." Morris, author of an effusion entitled *The Epic of Hades*, who wanted the Laureateship badly, complained to Oscar Wilde in the days before his ruin, "There is a conspiracy of silence against me, a conspiracy of silence. What ought I to do, Oscar?" "Join it," replied Wilde.

On the principle that, like bishops, one Laureate would do as well as another, Lord Salisbury, when he became Prime Minister, appointed Alfred Austin. A journalist of deep Conservative dye, founder and editor of the *National Review*, Austin was also the producer of fervent topical verse on such occasions as the death of Disraeli. When a friend pointed out grammatical errors in his poems, Austin said, "I dare not alter these things. They come to me from above." He was a tiny man—five feet high —with a round face and neat white moustache who, as a contributor of articles expounding Conservative foreign policy which he signed "Diplomaticus," was personally acquainted with the Prime Minister and a fre-

quent visitor to Hatfield. He had begun his career as a correspondent in
the war of 1870 by gaining an interview with Bismarck at Versailles, and
thirty years later was forced to the painful conclusion that Germany, in
her wars of 1859–70, had "unquestionably resorted to means which one
could not conceive Alfred the Great or any modern British minister employing." His most popular work so far had been a prose book on English
gardens, but within two weeks of his appointment as Laureate, he exceeded
expectations with a poem in *The Times* celebrating Dr. Jameson's exploit:

> There are girls in the gold-reef city,
> There are mothers and children too!
> And they cry, Hurry up! for pity!
> So what could a brave man do? . . .
>
> So we forded and galloped forward,
> As hard as our beasts could pelt,
> First eastward, then trending northward,
> Right over the rolling veldt. . . .

Some echo of the hilarity this provoked reaching the Queen, she queried
Salisbury, who had to admit that her new Laureate's first effusion was "un-
luckily to the taste of the galleries in the lower class of theatres who sing
it with vehemence." Salisbury never bothered to explain his choice of
Austin beyond an off-hand remark once that "he wanted it"; but if the
choice did not honor British poetry, it was a shrewd match of the British
mood.

The Englishman, as an American observer noticed, felt himself the
best-governed citizen in the world even when in Opposition he believed
the incumbents were ruining the country. The English form of government
"is the thing above all others that he is proud of . . . and he has an un-
shakeable confidence in the personal integrity of statesmen." Austin reflected that comfortable pride. In the radiant summer of Jubilee Year,
1897, a visitor found him in linen suit and panama hat, sitting in a
high-backed wicker chair, on the lawn of his country home enjoying
conversation with Lady Paget and Lady Windsor. They agreed that each
person should tell what was his idea of heaven. Austin's wish was noble.
He desired to sit in a garden and receive a flow of telegrams announcing
alternately a British victory by sea and a British victory by land.

It was easy to make fun of Alfred Austin, with his small size, large
pomposity and banal verse, and many did. Yet in his Jubilee wish there
was something simple and devoted, an assurance, a complete and happy

love and admiration for his country, a noncognizance of wrong, which expressed a mood and a condition which, like Lord Ribblesdale's appearance, were to become beyond recapture.

The House of Lords, now that the Conservatives had replaced the Liberals, could lean back comfortably and follow its natural bent, which was to do as little work as possible. In the last years of the Liberals it had roused itself to "stop the rot" induced by Radical legislation and had thrown out an Employers' Liability Bill, a Parish Councils Bill designed to make local government councils more democratic, and finally the Home Rule Bill. In the last speech of his career on March 1, 1894, Gladstone had solemnly warned that differences of "fundamental tendency" between the two Houses had reached a point in the past year which required that some solution would have to be found for "this tremendous contrariety and incessant conflict upon matters of high principle and profound importance." Proposals for reform of the Upper House to redress the imbalance when a Liberal Government was in power and thus remove the grounds of criticism had been many. But now that a state of happy harmony had succeeded conflict, the urgency relaxed, Gladstone's warning was forgotten and the Lords could resume their customary quiescence.

Out of 560 members, many "backwoods" peers, as they were called, never took their seats at all. Others appeared only at times of crisis and hardly more than fifty regularly attended the sessions. It was, said Lord Newton, "the most good-natured assembly that exists," hearing out speakers who would not be listened to for five minutes in the Commons. Its debates were "always polite" and conducted with a restraint which seemed to show "detachment almost amounting to indifference." Party animosity was concealed "under a veil of studied courtesy." It was not a stimulating audience, especially to Liberals, whose leader, Lord Rosebery, complained that "every auditor gives the impression of profound weariness and boredom."

While Lord Salisbury was Prime Minister the House of Lords was entirely under his dominance, although its official ruler was the Lord Chancellor, who acted as Speaker. This office was now held by Lord Halsbury, born a commoner, by name Hardinge Giffard, a member of one of the oldest families in England. Its founder had fought at Hastings and was later created Earl of Buckingham by William Rufus. Although the title died out in the next generation, the family persisted with vigor if not riches and the sprightly Lord Chancellor, seventy-two at this time, lived to be ninety-eight. A stubby Pickwickian figure with short legs, red cheeks, white tufts of hair over his ears and a humorous expression, Lord Halsbury, despite his genial manner, was a hard opponent, implacable at the bar, with a relentless memory. He wore a frock coat, a square-topped derby hat, a "true blue" Tory tie and, according to a younger member of the Upper House, "invariably objected on principle to all change." Owing to meagre family finances, he had been educated at home by his father, a barrister and editor of a high Tory daily paper, the *Standard*, who gave him lessons in Greek, Latin and Hebrew until 4 A.M. and was so upright that he refused an offer from the Duke of Newcastle, an admirer of his paper, to put his three sons through Oxford. The youngest son went through Merton College nevertheless, rose rapidly to the top of the legal profession, acquiring wealth and friends on the way as well as the accusation from some quarters that he "filled his great office with jolly cynicism" and made unscrupulous use of the Bench for political patronage. However, when from among many rival claimants he was named Lord Chancellor, making him the highest-ranking personage after the royal family and the Archbishop of Canterbury, the "Carlton Club supported him to a man," and Lord Coleridge, the Lord Chief Justice and a Liberal, wrote, "Your politics are of course unintelligible to me but in everything else, as a scholar, a gentleman and a lawyer, there is no one fitter to be our head."

Two high-ranking peers in Lord Salisbury's Cabinet, the fifth Marquess of Lansdowne and the eighth Duke of Devonshire, were both Whigs of pedigree and converts to the Conservatives. Lord Lansdowne, the Secretary for War, was an aristocrat who looked it every inch. Smooth and cold as polished stone, elegant, correct and courteous, he was an obvious choice for the great ceremonial posts and had been Governor-General of Canada at thirty-eight and Viceroy of India at forty-three. His family name was Fitzmaurice. In the Twelfth Century the first of his line had settled in Ireland in county Kerry and the current Marquess was twenty-eighth Lord of Kerry in the direct male line. He was one of those Anglo-Irishmen, said the *Spectator* in commenting on the quality of Lord Salisbury's Government, "who can rule by a sort of instinct." The instinct had flourished in his great-grandfather, the first Marquess, who as Earl of Shelburne had been a secretary of state under George III, and had served briefly as Prime Minister in the last year of the war with the American Colonies. The same instinct carried his grandfather, the third Marquess, to the Home Office and other posts in six governments between 1827 and 1857, after which he had declined to be Prime Minister and had refused a dukedom. The present Marquess seemed to his brother-in-law, Lord

Ernest Hamilton, to be "the greatest gentleman of his day," who in any international competition for gentlemen must surely be nominated the British representative.

Senior to, and even grander than, Lansdowne—but wearing the patrician air without self-consciousness—was Spencer Compton Cavendish, eighth Duke of Devonshire, probably the only man in England both secure enough and careless enough to forget an engagement with his sovereign. Edward VII, having informed the Duke that he proposed to dine quietly with him at Devonshire House on a certain day, duly arrived, to the consternation of the household, for the Duke was not at home and had to be hurriedly retrieved from the Turf Club.

He was sixty-two in 1895, tall and bearded, with heavy-lidded eyes in a long Hapsburg face and a straight, lordly, high-ridged nose. Formerly Lord Hartington during his thirty-four years in the House of Commons, he was now Lord President of the Council in Salisbury's Cabinet. He owned 186,000 acres and had an income of £180,000 from land alone, not counting investments. Though famous for his lassitude, he had managed to serve in more Cabinet offices under more governments than any man living: as First Lord of the Admiralty under Lord Palmerston, Secretary for War under Lord John Russell, Postmaster-General, Secretary for Ireland, for India and again for War in successive Gladstone governments. A familiar sight coming down Whitehall was Lord Hartington driving himself to the House in a light phaeton with a careless hold on the reins, a large cigar in his mouth and a collie sitting next to him.

He had played a leading role in growing opposition to Mr. Gladstone in the two crises of the eighties that broke apart the Liberal party: the imperialist issue over General Gordon's expedition to the Sudan and the Irish issue over Home Rule. Though he was not one of the polished and impassioned orators, his speech in 1886 announcing his break with Gladstone made a profound impression. By stating plainly that men could not remain in the false position of continuing to support a government, even of their own party, whose principles they disapproved, he gave, said a member, "a new sense of duty and a new power of action to hundreds of men throughout the country." Henry Chaplin thought the speech ought "to make you Prime Minister for certain." Some years earlier the Queen, in her stubborn effort to avoid the inevitability of Mr. Gladstone, had already asked Lord Hartington to form a government; but he had refused, bowing to Gladstone, who, he knew, would not serve except in first place.

In the opinion of Mr. Balfour, an expert, Lord Hartington was "of all the statesmen I have known . . . the most persuasive speaker," less for his words than for the character behind them. He made every listener feel that here was a man "who has done his best to master every aspect of this question, who has been driven by logic to arrive at certain conclusions, and who is disguising from us no argument on either side. . . . How can we hope to have a more honest guide?" It was this quality, said Balfour, which Hartington possessed "in far greater measure than any man I have ever known," which gave him his great influence with the public, made him indispensable to governments and, whether in the Cabinet, in Parliament, or on the public platform, "gave him a dominant position in any assembly."

The Duke would have preferred to be anywhere else, for he undertook the hard work and confining hours of government office more from duty than desire. But he was requited by the feeling of sovereign and country that he was one of the pillars on which the state reposed. "The Queen cannot conclude this letter," Victoria wrote to him in 1892, "without expressing to the Duke . . . how much she relies on him to assist in maintaining the safety and honor of her vast Empire. All must join"—she finished in simple summary of her faith—"in this great and necessary work."

The Duke joined with no visible zest. "Never angry though often bored," according to one friend, "he takes things very easy indeed," according to another. Some said his lethargy was laziness, others that it was a well-considered reluctance to hurry; in either event it was underlined by a habit of going to sleep in the midst of things. Even his own speeches bored him and once when speaking on the Indian budget he paused, leaned over to the colleague nearest him on the bench, and suppressing a yawn, whispered, "This is damned dull."

His only passion was for his racing stud, although he also maintained, whether from passion, habit or indolence, a thirty-year liaison with "one of the handsomest women in Europe," as she was when the affair began, the domineering, ambitious, German-born Louise, Duchess of Manchester. Her first Duke disappointed her by impoverishing himself, but obedient to his caste, refrained or was persuaded to refrain from bringing any unpleasant public action, leaving his wife and Lord Hartington to enjoy both each other and an unassailable moral and social position. When Manchester died, his widow married the Duke of Devonshire in 1892 just after he had succeeded to his title. Thereafter known as the "Double Duchess," she continued to exercise her formidable talents toward her major goal, that of making her husband Prime Minister.

The Duke did not give her the necessary help. He was not the kind in whom a burning ambition for the highest post erases every other consideration. When, after he had led the Liberal Unionists out of the party, Lord Salisbury twice offered to serve under him, he again refused, not yet prepared for coalition. By 1895, however, the split between moderate and radical Whigs having widened and the habit of voting in concert with the Tories having made a bridge, the Duke with four other Liberal Unionists crossed over it to serve under Lord Salisbury.

This was the Conservative—now Unionist—Government which took office in June, 1895. A delicate situation was expected at Windsor when the Duke and the other former Liberals, arriving as members of Lord Salisbury's Ministry to receive their seals of office, would pass their former colleagues on the way out. To avoid embarrassment, the Queen's Private Secretary tactfully arranged that the outgoing Liberals should deliver up their seals at 11 A.M. while the new ministers waited in another drawing room until their predecessors had left. All would have gone off smoothly but for the Duke, who, arriving late as usual, missed the designated waiting room and met his old associates coming out, who peppered him with taunts about his new friends. "No face was more suited to a difficult situation," wrote a witness, for the Duke, quite unperturbed, "passed through them with his mouth wide open and his eyes half closed."

The Cavendishes stemmed from an ancestor who had been Chief Justice of the Court of King's Bench during the Peasants' Revolt of 1381. His son John was the man who killed Wat Tyler, for which he was knighted on the spot by Richard II, while the father was seized elsewhere by the mob and beheaded in revenge. Dutifully, if none too enthusiastically, the Cavendishes down through the centuries helped to govern the country. The fourth Duke served briefly as Prime Minister in 1756–57, while Pitt and Newcastle were feuding, but resigned as soon as he could be replaced. His brother, Lord John Cavendish, was twice Chancellor of the Exchequer, in which capacity Edmund Burke praised him for his "great integrity . . . and perfect disinterestedness" but wished that Lord John could be "induced to show a certain degree of regular attendance on business" and be allowed only "a certain reasonable proportion of fox-hunting" and no more. The fifth Duke excelled by marrying the ravishing Georgiana, Duchess of Devonshire, whom Gainsborough painted in a pale shining glow against storm clouds, and Reynolds painted laughing with a full-skirted baby on her knee. Her beauty and irresistible charm came in the same excess as her gambling debts, which cost her husband £1,000,000. Fortunately, the Cavendishes were one of the two or three richest families in the kingdom. When his steward regretted to inform the fifth Duke that his heir, the Lord Hartington of that day, was "disposed to spend a great deal of money," the Duke replied, "So much the better; Lord Hartington will have a great deal of money to spend."

In the Duke of 1895, neither fortune, nor position as eldest son, nor disinclination to exert himself, nor desire to follow his heart upon the turf were enough to outweigh in him "certain hereditary government instincts." He felt that "he owed a debt to the State that must be paid." This sense of obligation, remarked on by all who knew him, originated not only in family estate but also in a consciousness of superior ability. His father, a student of mathematics and the classics, known as the "Scholar" Duke, had educated him at home. Later at Trinity College, Cambridge, despite an idle, sporting, sociable life among the "tufts," Lord Hartington was the only one of his set to take an Honours degree, a second class in the mathematical tripos. He entered Parliament at twenty-four and achieved his first Cabinet office at thirty. His brother, Lord Frederick Cavendish, also undertook a political career, and in 1882, on his first day as Chief Secretary for Ireland, was assassinated in Phoenix Park in Dublin. The killing of an English minister of the Crown by Irish malcontents created a sensation as great as the death of General Gordon at Khartoum. Whether because of his brother's murder or some other less obvious reason, the Duke made a habit of always carrying a loaded revolver about with him, and this was a constant source of worry to his family. "He was always losing them and buying new ones," wrote his nephew, "and there were no less than twenty of them knocking about Devonshire House when he died."

With the advent of the Duchess, an indefatigable hostess, Devonshire entertainments became the stateliest in Society. Every year on the opening of Parliament, the Duke and Duchess gave a great reception. Every year on Derby Day, Devonshire House, filled with roses and June flowers from the Duke's gardens, was the scene of a sparkling ball. Before the ball, the King gave a dinner to members of the Jockey Club at Buckingham Palace while the Queen came to dine with the Duchess. In Jubilee Year of 1897 the Devonshire fancy-dress ball was the most famous and lavish party of the era. At Chatsworth in Derbyshire, home of the Cavendishes for four hundred years, house parties reached their peak with the annual visit of the Prince and Princess of Wales, which continued when they were King and Queen. Every royal comfort was anticipated and satisfied, including the presence of the King's mistress, Mrs. Keppel, brilliant in diamonds, with whom, according to Princess Daisy of Pless, "the King has his bridge in a separate room while in other rooms people are massed together also of course playing bridge."

Built of the golden stone of the district, Chatsworth was surrounded by an Eighteenth Century park designed by Capability Brown. Luxury was everywhere. Cascades rippled over a series of stone steps six hundred feet long copied after the Renaissance water-landscaping of Italy. A copper willow tree, by an ingenious mechanism, could weep water from every leaf. Elaborate and exquisite garlands of flowers and fruit carved in wood festooned the walls. The library and collection of pictures and sculpture were on a princely scale like the Medicis' and administered almost as a public trust. Curators in the Duke's employ kept them open to scholars and connoisseurs, made new purchases and liberally loaned the treasures to exhibitions. The Chatsworth Memling went to Bruges, its Van Dycks to Antwerp, and all year the house was open to the public, who tramped through the halls in thousands. The Duke liked to watch them, and thinking his face as unknown to them as theirs to him, would stand, unconscious of being recognized, "wondering why the housemaid who acted as guide and the whole party had suddenly stood still and were staring at him." Though racehorses were more to him than books, he once astonished his librarian who was showing him his own first edition of *Paradise Lost* by sitting down and reading it aloud from the first line with simple pleasure, until the Duchess came in and, poking the Duke with her parasol, remarked, "If he reads poetry he will never go for his walk."

He was bored by pomp and hated pomposity. When the King decided to make him a Grand Commander of the new Victorian Order, the Duke, "in his sleepy way," asked the King's Private Secretary, Sir Frederick Ponsonby, what he was supposed to do with "the thing." "Anyone less anxious to receive an order I have never seen. He seemed to think it would only complicate his dressing." At the rehearsal for King Edward's coronation in 1902, at which the appearance of the peers wearing coronets with morning dress produced a comical effect, the Duke arrived late as usual and, with his right hand in his trouser pocket and an inexpressibly bored look on his face, strolled about the stage at the bidding of the Earl Marshal. He liked old baggy, casual clothes, never took the slightest trouble with his guests, deliberately ignored those who might prove tiresome, and once, when a speaker in the House of Lords was declaiming on "the greatest moments in life," the Duke opened his eyes long enough to remark to his neighbor, "My greatest moment was when my pig won first prize at Skipton Fair." His favorite club, after the Turf, was the Travellers', known for exclusiveness and an atmosphere of "solemn tranquillity" in which reading, dozing and meditation took precedence over conversation. For the disagreeable task of speaking at public meetings he trained himself by a method he once revealed to the young Winston Churchill when they were appearing together at a Free Trade meeting in Manchester. "Do you feel nervous, Winston?" asked the Duke, and on receiving an affirmative reply, told him, "I used to, but now, whenever I get up on a public platform, I take a good look around and as I sit down I say, 'I never saw such a lot of damned fools in my life' and then I feel a lot better."

When he chose he could be "the best of company, . . . delightful to talk to," that is, if conditions were right. At a dinner party in 1885 he arrived tired and hungry after a long day in Committee and sulked in silence when the first courses proved to be fancy but insubstantial French dishes instead of the solid fare that he liked. When a roast beef was brought in, he exclaimed in deep tones, "Hurrah! something to eat at last" and thereafter joined in the conversation. A fellow guest, the writer Wilfred Ward, noticed that in every case where he differed from Mr. Gladstone, who was of the company, Lord Hartington "put his finger on the weak point in the logic which Mr. Gladstone's rhetoric tended to obscure." Eighteen years later Ward met the Duke again at the British Embassy in Rome and confronted by a blank face reminded him of the place of their previous meeting. Thereupon the Duke exclaimed with feeling, "Of course I remember. We had nothing to eat." The inadequate French dishes, as Ward told the story, "had dwelt in his mind for nearly twenty years."

After succeeding to the title in 1891, he still returned, unlike Salisbury, to visit the House of Commons and "could generally be seen yawning in the front row of the Peers' Gallery" on the nights of big debates. As Duke he had more work to do than ever. He owned estates in Derbyshire, Yorkshire, Lancashire, Lincolnshire, Cumberland, Sussex, Middlesex and Ireland and personally went over all accounts of his properties and all important questions with his estate agents. He was Lord Lieutenant of Derbyshire, Chancellor of Cambridge University, President of the British Empire League and patron of various clerical livings to which he had to make appointments. He was director or chairman of various companies in which he had investments, including two railway lines, a steel company, a waterworks and a naval construction company. Though he distrusted his knowledge of business, "once he got a grip of a subject," according to one of his staff, "then no one was better able to confute a false argument or to see what the real point was." His mind worked slowly, and if he did not understand a matter at once, he would insist on its being thrashed out all over again until it was clear to him. He performed all his functions while continuing to maintain that he was happiest with his racing stud at Newmarket. Once at Aix-les-Bains he met W. H. Smith, then Conservative Leader of the House of Commons, and promptly sat down to talk politics for half an hour, saying, "it was pleasant in a place like this to have some work to do." It is possible he would have been more bored out of office than in.

To the Conservative Government of 1895 he brought, besides long experience and the prestige of his name and rank, an immense fund of public confidence banked over the four decades of his career. His disinterestedness was beyond question. So obviously was he above private ambition, wrote the editor of the *Spectator*, "that no one ever attributed to him unworthy motives or insinuated that he was playing for his own hand. If anyone had ventured to do so, the country would simply have regarded the accuser as mad." When the Duke took a position, people felt they had been given a lead. He never became Prime Minister or won the Derby but "no one," said *The Times,* "had a greater authority in moulding the political convictions of his countrymen." He remained vaguely puzzled by the extent of his own influence. "I don't see why I should tell the people what I should do if I had the vote," he protested. "They will do what they think right and I shall do what I think right. They don't want me to interfere." And when the Prince, who, no less than his subjects, relied on the Duke's judgment of men and issues, consulted him as arbiter of delicate social matters, he complained, "I don't know why it is but whenever a man is caught cheating at cards the case is referred to me." He had become, through a combination of heritage and character, a keeper of the national conscience. When a Presence was required for a solemn or ceremonial occasion, the solid, rather melancholy dignity of the Duke fulfilled the need. He was, Lord Rosebery said, "one of the great reserve forces of this country."

Among Lord Salisbury's ministers who took their seats in 1895 on the Government Front Bench in the House of Commons were two baronets, the ninth and sixth of their lines, Sir Michael Hicks-Beach, Chancellor of the Exchequer, and Sir Matthew White Ridley, Home Secretary. The former, tall, thin and austere, was an arch Conservative, a champion of the Church of England and of the landowning class, known as "Black Michael." Tart and sharp-tongued, he once, after reading over a Liberal member's remarks on his budget, said to his secretary succinctly, "Go and tell him he is a pig." Beside them sat the two squires, Mr. Henry Chaplin and Mr. Walter Long, representatives of the landed gentry, the old untitled aristocracy who "scorned a peerage but made it a point of honor to stand for their county at the first general election after they came of age." Mr. Long, President of the Board of Agriculture and youngest member of the Government at forty-one, "never said anything in his life that anybody remembered." He "gently dozes," as an observer saw him, "his arms folded, his head sunk back upon a cushion, his ruddy October face giving a touch of color to the scene," while the older Mr. Chaplin "vigorously, wakefully, alertly guards the Empire against the knavish tricks of the Opposition."

Mr. Chaplin at fifty-four, with his magnificent stature, big handsome head, long nose, prominent chin, sideburns and monocle, was a marked personality, one of the most popular men of his generation, "easily recognizable, familiar to the public. Everyone knew him by sight." He was the visible symbol of the English country gentleman. His post was the Local Government Board, which dealt with the poor law, housing, town planning, public health and municipal government. Its functions were best described by Winston Churchill, who, on being offered the post in 1908, said, "I refuse to be shut up in a soup kitchen with Mrs. Sidney Webb." Chaplin performed its duties and those of M.P. with tremendous gravity. He regarded himself, as did his constituents, as the bulwark of the essential Britain, and used to practice his speeches behind hedges the better to do credit to his role. His jovian thunders, the noble sweep of his arm as he spoke from the Front Bench, said a witness, expressed, not vanity, but "the calm, ineradicable conviction of the ruling class." Undaunted by the most abstruse problems of government, he would tackle the tariff or the Education Bill in the same spirit as a difficult ditch in the hunting field and even undertook the fervent advocacy of bimetalism as a cure for economic ills. Once after a two-hour discourse on this recondite subject, he mopped his brow and leaning over to Mr. Balfour, asked, "How did I do, Arthur?"

"Splendidly, Harry, splendidly."

"Did you understand me, Arthur?"

"Not a word, Harry, not a word."

Arthur Balfour, prince of the Cecil line, nephew of the Prime Minister and his political heir apparent, artist of debate and idol of Society, was the paragon of his party and its official Leader in the House of Commons. He was forty-seven in 1895 and, when his uncle retired in 1902, was to succeed him as Prime Minister. Over six feet tall, he had blue eyes, waving brown hair and moustache, and a soft, bland face that might have seemed vulnerable if it had not been smoothed to an external serenity. His expression was gentle, his figure willowy, his manner nonchalant, but there remained a mystery in his face. No one could tell what banked fires burned behind it or whether they burned or even if they existed.

Rarely seen to sit upright, he reclined in indolent attitudes as close to the horizontal as possible, "as if to discover," wrote *Punch*'s parliamentary correspondent, "how nearly he could sit on his shoulder blades." In him all the gifts of privilege had combined. He had wealth, blue blood, good looks, great charm and "the finest brain that has been applied to politics in our time." He was a philosopher on a serious level whose second major work, *The Foundations of Belief,* published in 1895, was read by the American philosopher William James with "immense gusto. There is more real philosophy in such a book," he wrote to his brother Henry, "than in fifty German ones heaped with subtleties and technicalities."

Although ultimately aloof and detached, Balfour had a winning manner that encircled him with admiration. His charm was of the kind that left everyone feeling happy who talked with him. "Although he was the best talker I have ever known," said John Buchan, "he was not a monopolist of the conversation but one who quickened and elevated the whole discussion and brought out the best of other people." After an evening in his company, wrote Austen Chamberlain, "one left with the feeling that one had been at the top of one's form and really had talked rather well." Political opponents were affected no less than allies. He was the only Conservative to whom Gladstone in debate accorded the term usually reserved for members of his own party, "my honourable friend." Women succumbed equally. "Oh dear," sighed Constance Lady Battersea after a visit to his home in 1895, "what a gulf between him and most men!" Margot Asquith found his "exquisite attention" and "lovely bend of the head," when he talked to her, "irresistible"; so much so that earlier, when she was Margot Tennant, and herself a social star of high voltage, she had "moved heaven and earth," according to Lady Jebb, to marry him. Queried on the rumor of this marriage, Balfour replied, "No, that is not so. I rather think of having a career of my own."

As the eldest son of Lord Salisbury's sister, Lady Blanche Balfour, he was named Arthur for the Duke of Wellington, who acted as his godfather. On the paternal side the Balfours were of ancient Scottish lineage, their fortune having been made in the late Eighteenth Century by Arthur's grandfather, James Balfour, a nabob of the East India Company. James acquired in Scotland an estate of 10,000 acres, at Whittinghame overlooking the Firth of Forth, which became the family home, as well as a deer forest, a salmon river, a shooting lodge, a seat in Parliament and a daughter of the eighth Earl of Lauderdale as wife. A daughter of this marriage, Balfour's aunt, married the Duke of Grafton, so that along with the Salisbury connection, Balfour, as a friend said, "can call cousins with half the nobility of England." His younger brother Eustace subsequently married Lady Frances Campbell, daughter of the Duke of Argyll, granddaughter of the Duke of Sutherland, niece of the Duke of Westminster and sister-in-law of Princess Louise, daughter of Queen Victoria.

Balfour's father, also an M.P., died at thirty-five, when Arthur was seven, leaving Lady Blanche, in whom the Cecil streak of religious feeling was particularly marked, to govern her family of five sons and three daughters. Besides teaching Arthur to admire Jane Austen and her brother's favorite, *The Count of Monte Cristo*, she also communicated the Cecil sense of duty. When her son at Cambridge became enamored of philosophy and wished to make over his inheritance to a brother in favor of the studious life, she scolded him severely for poor spirit in wanting to shirk the responsibilities of his position.

At Trinity College, where Balfour read Moral Science, his failure to take a First did not depress his imperturbable good nature or good spirits. He was, wrote Lady Jebb, the doyenne of Cambridge society, "a young prince in his way and almost as much spoiled." Of his four brothers, Frank was a professor of embryology who according to Darwin would have become "the first of English biologists" if he had not been killed climbing in the Swiss Alps at the age of thirty-one; Gerald, superbly handsome, was, according to Lady Jebb, "the most superior man I ever met," although her niece thought him "the most conceited"; Eustace was merely average and Cecil was the bad apple in the barrel, who died disgraced in Australia. But Arthur, decided Lady Jebb, was "the best in a family all of whom are best, . . . a man that almost everyone loves." She thought his nature, however, was "emotionally cold" and that his one essay in love, with May Lyttelton, sister of a Cambridge friend and Gladstone's niece, who died when she was twenty-five and Balfour twenty-seven, had "exhausted his powers in that direction." This was the accepted supposition in later years to explain Balfour's bachelorhood. In fact, it was not so much that he was emotionally cold as that he was warmly attached to his complete freedom to do as he pleased.

Among his friends were two of Trinity's outstanding scholars: his tutor Henry Sidgwick, later Professor of Moral Philosophy, and the physicist John Strutt, later third Baron Rayleigh, a future Nobel prize winner and Chancellor of the University, each of whom married a sister of Balfour. At that time, when to be an intellectual was to be agnostic, Balfour's inherited religious sense caused his Cambridge friends to regard him as "a curious relic of an older generation." His Society friends, on the other hand, when he published his first book, *A Defence of Philosophic Doubt*, in 1879, assumed from the title that Arthur was championing agnosticism, and when his name was mentioned, "they went about looking very solemn." In fact, by expressing doubt of material reality, the book was paradoxically asserting the right to spiritual faith, a position more explicitly stated in his later book, *The Foundations of Belief*. At Whittinghame, which was run for him by his maiden sister, Alice, and shared by his married brothers and their numerous children, he read family prayers every Sunday evening. Steeped in the Hebraism of the Old Testament, he felt a particular interest in the "people of the Book" and was concerned about the problem of the Jew in the modern world. His niece and biographer in her childhood imbibed from him "the idea that Christian religion and civilization owes to Judaism an immeasurable debt, shamefully ill repaid."

He was the most dined-out man in London. Blandly ignoring the implacable rule that required the Leader of the House to be in his place throughout a sitting, he would often disappear during the dinner hour, reappearing shamelessly some hours later in evening dress. Every diary of the time finds him at house parties and dinner parties: "at the Rothschilds," wrote John Morley, "only Balfour there, *partie carrée,* always most pleasurable." He was one of twenty men at dinner at Harry Cust's, where the talk was so absorbing that when the house caught fire upstairs the dinner continued while the footmen passed bath towels with the port for protection against water from the firemen's hoses; he was at Blenheim Palace with the Marlboroughs in a party including the Prince and Princess of Wales, the Curzons, the Londonderrys, the Grenfells and Harry Chaplin; he was at Chatsworth with the Devonshires in a party including the Duke and Duchess of Connaught, Count Mensdorff, the Austrian Ambassador, the ugly, fascinating and ribald Marquis de Soveral, Ambassador of Portugal, the de Greys, Ribblesdales and Grenfells; he was at Hatfield with the Salisburys in a party including the Duke of Argyll, Mr. Speaker Peel and his daughter, Mr. Buckle of *The Times*, George Curzon and General Lord Methuen; he was at Cassiobury, home of Lord Essex, one Sunday at the end of a brilliant London season, when Edith Wharton, arriving for tea, "found scattered on the lawn under the great cedars the very flower and pinnacle of the London world: Mr. Balfour, Lady Desborough, Lady Elcho, John Sargent, Henry James and many others of that shining galaxy, so exhausted by their social labors of the past weeks . . . that beyond benevolent smiles they had little to give."

Most often Balfour was to be found at Clouds, home of the baronet Sir Percy Wyndham and favored country house of the Souls. Among their congenial company the particular attraction for Balfour was Lady Elcho, one of the three beautiful Wyndham sisters, with whom, though she was the wife of a friend, Balfour pursued a discreet affair over a period of some twelve years, of which the letters survive. Sargent, when he painted the sisters in 1899, was hampered by no such compelling realism as affected him in the matter of Lady Charles Beresford's eyebrows. The group portrait of Lady Elcho, Mrs. Tennant and Mrs. Adeane, gowned in porcelain whiteness and draped in poses of careless but haughty elegance upon a sofa, is a dazzling dream of feminine aristocracy.

The ladies of the Souls, in conscious reaction to the Victorian feminine ideal, determined to be intellectual, to be slim and likewise to allow themselves a new freedom of private morality. Their only American member, the beautiful Daisy White, wife of Henry White, First Secretary of the American Embassy, was once congratulated by a friend on not allowing herself to be changed by "all those people who have lovers." In this activity the Souls were no different from the more philistine members of the Prince of Wales's set. All were engaged in the same open conspiracy in which Society managed to depart from Victorian morality without deserting propriety. Balfour's liaison with Lady Elcho was for a while serious enough to cause their friends some anxiety. The feelings of the husband, Hugo, Lord Elcho, heir of the Earl of Wemyss and a member, though a silent one, of the same circle, are unknown. The affair, like the Duke of Devonshire's, was the permitted excursion of a person of character and position sufficiently lofty to be above reproach.

When Balfour first entered Parliament at twenty-six from a family-controlled borough, it had been less from personal desire than from ordained fate as an eldest son and a Cecil. By the time he moved into Downing Street in 1895 as First Lord of the Treasury and Leader of the House, in lieu of his uncle, who preferred to live at home, the passion for politics latent in his blood had grown with growing skill and power. Yet it did not disturb his temperamental detachment. When meeting criticism he would regard it, not as something to resent, but as a thing to be examined like an interesting beetle. "Quite a good fellow," he would

say of an opponent, "has a curious view, not uninteresting." He was at
heart both a conservative who wanted to retain the best of the world
he knew and a liberal with, as his sister-in-law remarked, "a sympathetic
outlook for all progress." People felt in him "a natural spring of youth,"
in the words of one friend, and a "freshness, serenity and buoyancy" in the
words of another. Later, as Prime Minister, he was the first in that office to
go to Buckingham Palace in a motorcar and the first to go to the House of
Commons in a Homburg hat.

He thought of himself as belonging to the younger generation of Tories
who recognized the necessity of responding to the rising challenge of the
working class. Yet bred as they were in privilege they could not, when
issues came to a test, range themselves on the side of the invaders. In his
first years in Parliament, Balfour had joined the four "Radical" Tories of
the Fourth Party led by Lord Randolph Churchill. They occupied the
Front Bench below the gangway and Balfour sat with them, because, he
said, he had room there for his legs, but the choice indicated a point of
view. The Fourth Party were gadflies in the cause of what was called "Tory
Democracy," the belief that the rising political power of Labour could be
harnessed in partnership with the Tories. If Labour, stated Lord Randolph
in 1892, found that it could "obtain its objects and secure its own
advantage" under the existing constitution—which it was the Tories' business to preserve—then all would be well; but if the Conservatives stubbornly resisted these demands in "unreasoning and shortsighted support
of all the present rights of property," then Labour would be ranged against
them. Since the Tories were a minority in the country, it was incumbent
on them to enlist in their support "a majority of the votes of the masses
of Labour."

Balfour was never thoroughly persuaded of this convincingly worded
argument, any more than, when it came to a practical test, was Lord
Randolph himself. In the abstract, Balfour believed in democracy and
extension of the suffrage and in improvement of working conditions and
of the rights of Labour but not at the cost of breaking down the walls of
privilege that protected the ruling class. Here was the fundamental difficulty
of Tory Democracy. Its advocates thought it possible to meet the demands
of the workers while at the same time preserving intact the citadel of
privilege, but Balfour suspected the bitter truth of history: that progress
and gain by one group is never accomplished without loss of some permanent value of another. He continued to express his belief that Socialism
would never get possession of the working classes "if those who wield the
collective forces of the community show themselves desirous . . . to

ameliorate every legitimate grievance." But when it came to specific acts of amelioration he was not enthusiastic or deeply concerned. "What exactly *is* a 'Trade Union'?" he once asked a Liberal friend. Margot Asquith said to him that he was like his uncle in having a wonderful sense of humor, literary style and a deep concern with science and religion. Was there any difference between them? "There is a difference," Balfour replied. "My uncle is a Tory—and I am a liberal." Yet the fact that his uncle remained undisturbed by Balfour's early association with the Tory "Radicals" and that the perfect confidence between them remained unclouded suggests that there was a basic identity of belief stronger than the difference.

Balfour seemed an enigma to his contemporaries because his nature was paradoxical, his opinions often irreconcilable, and because he did not see life or politics in terms of absolutes. As a result, he was often charged with being cynical, and people who looked at the world from a liberal point of view thought him perverse. H. G. Wells portrayed him as Evesham in *The New Machiavelli*. "In playing for points in the game of party advantage Evesham displayed at times a quite wicked unscrupulousness in the use of his subtle mind. . . . Did he really care? Did anything matter to him?" Winston Churchill, too, once used the word "wicked" in speaking of him to Mrs. Asquith. She thought the secret of Balfour's imperturbability in a crisis was that he did not "really care for the things at stake or believe that the happiness of mankind depends on events going this way or that." Balfour did, in fact, hold certain basic convictions, but he could see arguments on both sides of a matter, which is the penalty of the thoughtful man. On one occasion, arriving for an evening party at a great house whose staircase split in twin curves, he stood at the bottom for twenty minutes trying to work out, as he explained to a puzzled observer, a logical reason for taking one side rather than the other.

In 1887 Salisbury's surprising appointment of his nephew to the difficult and dangerous post of Chief Secretary for Ireland was expected to prove a fiasco. Balfour was then regarded as a languid intellectual whom the press delighted to call "Prince Charming," or even "Miss Balfour." Ireland was seething in its chronic war between landlord and tenant made fiercer by agitators for Home Rule. Police daily evicted tenants unable to pay their rent and were in turn bombarded with stones, vitriol and boiling water by the mob. The memory of Lord Frederick Cavendish's fate five years earlier had been kept fresh by continued assaults and "everybody right up to the top was trembling." Balfour, ignoring threats to his life, astonished both islands. He said he intended to be "as relentless as

Cromwell" in enforcing the law and as "radical as any reformer" in redressing grievances with regard to the land. His resolute rule "took his foes by surprise," wrote John Morley, "and roused in his friends a delight hardly surpassed in the politics of our day." It made him a popular celebrity and brought him in one bound to recognition as "Bloody" Balfour in Ireland and as the coming natural leader of his party in England.

In 1891, on the resignation of W. H. Smith as Leader of the House, he succeeded by unanimous choice. As Irish Secretary, his absolute disregard for personal danger had revealed a courage—or absence of fear—that his contemporaries had not suspected. George Wyndham, then serving as Balfour's Private Secretary, wrote from Dublin that the Irish loyalists' admiration for him was "almost comic" and ascribed it to the fact that "great courage being so rare a gift and so large a part of human misery being due to Fear, all men are prepared to fall down before anyone wholly free from fear." Winston Churchill ascribed Balfour's lack of nerves to a "cold nature" but acknowledged him "the most courageous man alive. I believe if you held a pistol to his face it would not frighten him."

The same quality gave him mastery in debate. Sure of his own powers, he feared no opponent or embarrassment. According to Morley, he operated on Dr. Johnson's principle that "to treat your adversary with respect is to give him an advantage to which he is not entitled." He debated with "dauntless ingenuity and polished raillery." Although in public he rarely indulged in hurtful sarcasm, his private epigrams could be sharp. He once said of a colleague, "If he had a little more brains he would be a half-wit." In the House he maintained toward opponents an almost deferential courtesy, and when under bitter attack by the Irish members, would sit quietly with a placid smile, and when he rose to reply, demolish them with words which had the effect "of a bullet on a bubble." Yet it was not done without strain. He confessed to a friend that he never slept well after a rough night in the House. "I never lose my temper but one's nerves get on edge and it takes time to cool." He admired Macaulay, finding his narrative irresistible and his style a delight. His own speeches, delivered without notes, were unstudied yet perfectly finished. Lord Willoughby de Broke, an active young member of the other House, who liked to come over to listen to Balfour, said the pleasure lay in hearing "ideas and arguments being produced in exactly the right sequence without any appearance of premeditation, the whole masterly process of thought, argument and phrasing being carried out with such consummate skill and such perfect ease, that to witness the exercise of the art was sheer delight."

Balfour was careless of facts, unsafe with figures, and memory was not his strong point, but he surmounted this weakness by a technique that never failed to amuse the House. When dealing with a complicated bill he would take care to be flanked by a knowledgeable minister such as the Home Secretary or Attorney-General, and if he floundered over details his colleague could whisper a correction. As described by Sir Henry Lucy, parliamentary correspondent of *Punch*, Mr. Balfour would pause, regard the colleague with a friendly glance tinged with gentle admonition, and say, "Exactly." At the next mistake and whispered correction, he would repeat the performance with a sterner note in his "Exactly," conveying the impression that there was a limit to toleration in these matters and the colleague could be forgiven once but he really must not go on blundering.

Promptness was not one of his virtues and often he would come lounging gracefully in when Questions were almost over. He effected a revolution by changing the Wednesday short sitting of the House to Fridays for the sake of the weekend, an institution which he, in fact, invented to allow time for his golf. "This damned Scotch croquet," as a disgusted sportsman called it, owed its popularity to Balfour's influence. With perfect insouciance and contrary to all custom, he played it even on Sundays except in Scotland and such was his magnetism that Society followed where he went, and so the custom of the country-house weekend was born. He neither shot nor hunted but in addition to golf played vigorous tennis, bicycled whenever possible, on occasion twenty miles at a stretch, and indulged a guilty passion for the thrilling new experience of the motorcar. His idea of distraction was not everyone's. When visiting his sister, Lady Rayleigh, and asked by her what he would like in the way of entertainment, he replied, "Oh something amusing; get some people from Cambridge to talk science." Music was another enthusiasm. He wrote an essay on Handel for the *Edinburgh Review*, and went on a musical tour of Germany during which he charmed that difficult relict Frau Wagner.

His nonchalance and languid air covered an immense capacity for work. Besides leading the Government in the House of Commons he frequently doubled for his uncle at the Foreign Office. When in 1902 Salisbury retired, Lord Esher felt that his absence would be made up by "the supreme energy of Arthur." To conserve energy Balfour transacted as much business as possible in bed and rarely rose before noon.

He read incessantly: a book on science was propped open on the mantelpiece while he dressed, a detective story lay on his bedside table, the shelves of his private sitting room were stacked with volumes of philosophy and theology, the overflow was piled on the sofa, periodicals littered table and chairs and his sponge was used to support the reading of French novels in his bathtub. He never read the newspapers. Overnight guests found he did not even subscribe to them, a negligence for which he was scolded by Mr. Buckle, editor of *The Times*. Once the journalist, W. T. Stead, in conversation with the Prince of Wales, remarked that Balfour was a good man to have at one's back in a fight but he was a little too indifferent. "Ah," replied the Prince, nodding, "he never reads the papers, you know."

The Prince never cared for Balfour, who, he felt, condescended to him. Queen Victoria on the other hand admired him. On a visit to Balmoral, reported Sir Henry Ponsonby, Balfour discussed matters with the Queen, "showing where he differs from her in a way which makes her think it over. . . . I think the Queen likes him but is a little afraid of him." The younger Ponsonby considered him a great success with the Queen, "although he never seemed to treat her seriously." The Queen set down her own opinion in 1896 after a talk with Balfour on Crete, Turkish horrors, the Sudan and the Education Bill. She was "much struck by Mr. Balfour's extreme fairness, impartiality and large-mindedness. He sees all sides of a question, is wonderfully generous in his feelings toward others and very gentle and sweet-tempered."

The supremacy and security of that time had not long to endure, and Balfour had weaknesses which, as the century turned over into less indulgent years, were to become apparent. Including the weaknesses, he was in character and attributes the final flower of the patrician and of him might have been said what Proust's housekeeper, Celeste, said on the death of her employer, "When one has known M. Proust everyone else seems vulgar."

Not since Rome had imperial dominion been flung as wide as Britain's now. It extended over a quarter of the land surface of the world, and on June 22, 1897, the Queen's Diamond Jubilee, its living evidence marched in splendid ranks to the Thanksgiving service at St. Paul's. The occasion being designed to celebrate the imperial family under the British Crown, none of the foreign kings who had assisted at the Golden Jubilee in 1887 were this time invited. In their place, carriages of state carried the eleven colonial premiers of Canada, New Zealand, the Cape Colony, Natal, Newfoundland and the six states of Australia. In the parade rode cavalry from every quarter of the globe: the Cape Mounted Rifles, the Canadian Hussars, the New South Wales Lancers, the Trinidad Light Horse, the magnificent turbaned and bearded Lancers of Khapurthala, Badnagar and other Indian states, the Zaptichs of Cyprus in tasseled fezzes on black-maned ponies. Dark-skinned infantry regiments, "terrible and beautiful to behold," in the words of a rhapsodic press, swung down the streets in a fantasy of variegated uniforms: the Borneo Dyak Police, the Jamaica Artillery, the Royal Nigerian Constabulary, giant Sikhs from India, Houssas from the Gold Coast, Chinese from Hong Kong, Malays from Singapore, Negroes from the West Indies, British Guiana and Sierra Leone; company after company passed before a dazzled people, awestruck at the testimony of their own might. At the end of the procession in an open state landau drawn by eight cream horses came the day's central figure, a tiny person in black with cream-colored feathers nodding from her bonnet. The sun shone, bright banners rippled in the breeze, lampposts were decked in flowers and along six miles of streets millions of happy people cheered and waved in an ecstasy of love and pride. "No one ever, I believe, has met with such an ovation as was given me," wrote the Queen in her Journal. "Every face seemed to be filled with real joy. I was much moved and gratified."

Already for some months there had been an aura of self-congratulation in the air, "a certain optimism," said Rudyard Kipling, "that scared me." It moved him to write, and on the morning after the parade the stern warning of "Recessional" appeared in *The Times*. Its impact was immense— "The greatest poem that has been written by any living man," pronounced the distinguished jurist, Sir Edward Clarke. Yet however solemnly people took its admonition, how could they believe, as the ceremonies and salutes continued and top-hatted personages came and went to the Imperial Conference in Whitehall, that all this visible greatness was really "one with Nineveh and Tyre"?

On October 11, 1899, a distant challenge, which had been growing stronger ever since the Jameson Raid, became explicit and the Boer War began. "Joe's War," Lord Salisbury called it in tribute to the aggressive role of the cuckoo in his nest, Mr. Joseph Chamberlain, the Colonial Secretary. Although he had started life as a Radical Liberal among men opposed on principle to imperialism, Mr. Chamberlain had since learned to "think imperially," as he put it. It was a change of mind easily understood in a man with his keen sense of opportunity, for in the last twelve years alone, territories equal to twenty-four times the area of Great Britain had been added to the Empire. On joining the Government of 1895, Chamberlain had chosen the Colonial Office in the conviction that here was the key to empire and "manifest destiny," a categorical imperative that was just then directing American eyes toward Cuba and Hawaii and stimulating Germans, Belgians, French, and even Italians, to join in the scramble for choice cuts of Africa.

Chamberlain was a man of surpassing force, ability, and a consuming ambition which had never been satisfied. Not born to the landowning class, he had perfected an appearance of authority and poise that was distinctly his own. He had sharp, rather elegant features, eyes that revealed nothing and jet-black hair smoothly brushed. His face was a mask adorned by a monocle on a black ribbon; his tailoring was faultless, adorned by a daily orchid in his buttonhole. Having made sufficient fortune as a manufacturer of screws in Birmingham to retire from business at thirty-eight, he had become Mayor of his city, where his accomplishments in education and other social reforms had won national attention. Wasting no time, he had entered Parliament at forty as member for Birmingham, became a vehement spokesman of the Radicals, denouncing aristocrats and plutocrats as ardently as any Socialist, and quickly achieved Cabinet office as President of the Board of Trade in Gladstone's Ministry of 1880. A hard-hitting, cool and masterful character whose popularity in the Midlands swung many votes, he was a political factor to be reckoned with and saw himself as Gladstone's successor. But the Grand Old Man was in no hurry to have one, and Chamberlain, too impatient to wait, found reason in the Home Rule issue to leave the party with a considerable following. In preparing for the election of 1895 the Conservatives were glad, if nervous, to attach him. He did not share the patrician's indifference to public opinion, but in mannerisms and dress, played up to it, making himself a memorable personality. To the public he was "Pushful Joe" the "Minister for Empire" and the best-known figure in the new Government.

Only Lord Salisbury remained unimpressed. "He has not persuaded himself that he has any convictions," he had written to Balfour in 1886, "and therein lies Gladstone's infinite superiority." Balfour, characteristically, was kinder but plain. "Joe, though we all love him dearly," he wrote to Lady Elcho, "somehow does not absolutely or completely mix, does not form a chemical combination with us." This was not surprising. Chamberlain had not been to public school or the University (that is, Oxford or Cambridge), where, as Lord Esher remarked, "everyone with his capacity learns self-restraint," and was not even a member of the Church of England. He nevertheless moved suavely among his new associates and was seen entertaining to tea on the terrace of the House of Commons a large party that included three duchesses. He could certainly never be accused like Balfour of being too indifferent. Chamberlain was always in the grip of one passionate conviction or another which he would pursue, while he held it, with ruthless intensity. But he lacked a permanent, rooted point of view. Though only five years younger than Salisbury and twelve years older than Balfour, he represented the forces and methods of a new time to which Salisbury's Government was essentially opposed. "The difference between Joe and me," said Balfour, "is the difference between youth and age: I am age." Balfour had behind him the long stability of belonging on top; Joe was the new tycoon in a hurry. The ways in which they did not "mix" were fundamental.

For the present the collaboration between Chamberlain and his new colleagues was mutually loyal. When his hand was suspected behind the Jameson Raid and the Liberals made furious accusations, the Government closed ranks around him and a parliamentary committee of investigation found itself unable to trace anything definite back to the Colonial Office. Joe emerged with power undiminished and aggressiveness undimmed. "I don't know which of our many enemies we ought to defy," he wrote to Salisbury after the Kruger telegram, "but let us defy someone." As the minister in charge of the increasingly inimical negotiations with the Boer Republic, his favorite method, reported Balfour to Salisbury, "is the free application of irritants." While these were taking effect an old defeat was avenged: in 1898 Kitchener retook Khartoum and raised the British flag over the grave of General Gordon. Farther up the Nile, at Fashoda, a French military expedition penetrating the Sudan was confronted eye to eye by the British and, after a period of suspense during which the French recognized realities, withdrew without the firing of a shot. Britain's unpopularity rose with her prestige.

Then came the Boer War. The British Army, on which years of splendid isolation had conferred a certain rigidity, was revealed fully prepared for the Crimean War and it met a series of defeats. The Boers, it turned out, possessed cannon from Krupp's and Creusot and their gunners were often German or French. President Kruger had used the reparations awarded for the Jameson Raid to buy artillery, Maxim guns and large stores of rifles and ammunition in preparation for the ultimate clash of arms. In one "Black Week" of December, 1899, Lord Methuen was defeated at Magersfontein, General Gatacre at Stormberg, and Sir Redvers Buller, the Commander-in-Chief, at Colenso with the loss of eleven guns, leaving Kimberley and Ladysmith invested. At home, people were stunned with unbelief. The Duke of Argyll, who was in his last illness, never rallied from the shock and died murmuring Tennyson's line on the Duke of Wellington, "Who never lost an English gun."

With Black Week went the last time Britons felt themselves unquestionably masters of the earth. And the point was brought home when the Kaiser, a few months later, was able to insist successfully on a German commander for the expedition embarking to punish the Boxers at Peking. True, it was a largely German effort, the main British force being already on the spot, but Salisbury objected on principle. It was a British characteristic, even if unreasonable, he told the German Ambassador, "not to endure the command of a foreigner." But he could not afford at that moment to court a conflict which might result in help for the Boers and was forced to acquiesce.

In the new year, with new vigor, reinforcements and a new commander-in-chief to replace the disastrous Buller, the war gradually came under control. Mafeking was relieved in May, 1900—to the accompaniment of hysterics at home—Lord Roberts entered Pretoria in June and the annexation of the Transvaal was proclaimed on September 1 in the belief that only mopping-up was left. On a wave of renewed self-confidence and good spirits, the Conservatives called for a renewed mandate in what was known as the "Khaki" election in October. Using the slogan, "Every seat won by the Liberals is a seat won by the Boers," they were comfortably returned to office. But though patriotic fervor was dominant, there was a current of antipathy to the war which came not only from "Little Englanders" of the orthodox Gladstone tradition but more particularly, this time, from an uneasy sense of ignoble motive, a glitter of the gold mines of the Rand, an aura of predatory capitalism, commercialism and profit. Opposition to the war provided a cause in which a young M.P., David Lloyd George, made himself known, although he did not go so far as to oppose annexation but only to propose negotiation to stop the war.

There were many inside and outside the Government who awaited the approaching Twentieth Century with certain illusions lost which were never to be restored. Lady Salisbury, shortly before she died in November, 1899, said to a young relative, "The young generation may criticize us as they like; will they ever provide anything as good as what we have known?"

The year 1900, rather than 1899, the Astronomer Royal had decided, after much weighing of the pros and cons, was the hundredth and last year of the Nineteenth Century. The moment of its passing was at hand; the end of the most hope-filled, change-filled, progressive, busiest and richest century the world had even known. Three weeks after it closed, on January 24, 1901, Queen Victoria died, redoubling the general sense of an era's end. Lord Salisbury, tired of office, wanted to go too, but felt he could not until victory, still elusive in South Africa, was won. It came finally in June, 1902, and on July 14 Lord Salisbury stepped down. Again was felt the somber consciousness of something coming to an end: an Authority, a type, a tradition had departed. A French paper, *Le Temps* of Paris, still smarting from the humiliation of Fashoda, said, "What closes today with Lord Salisbury's departure is a whole historic era. It is ironic that what he hands on is a democratized, imperialized, colonialized and vulgarized England—everything that is antithetic to the Toryism, the aristocratic tradition and the High Church that he stood for. It is the England of Mr. Chamberlain, not, despite his nominal leadership, of Mr. Balfour."

Queen Victoria, Lord Salisbury and the Nineteenth Century were gone. A year before she died, the Queen, returning on her yacht from a visit to Ireland, was disturbed by rough seas. After a particularly strong wave buffeted the ship, she summoned her doctor, who was in attendance, and said, in unconscious echo of a distant predecessor, "Go up at once, Sir James, and give the Admiral my compliments and tell him the thing must not occur again."

But the waves would not stand still.

2

The Idea and the Deed

THE ANARCHISTS:

1890–1914

2

The Idea and the Deed

S O ENCHANTING was the vision of a stateless society, without government, without law, without ownership of property, in which, corrupt
institutions having been swept away, man would be free to be
good as God intended him, that six heads of state were assassinated for
its sake in the twenty years before 1914. They were President Carnot of
France in 1894, Premier Canovas of Spain in 1897, Empress Elizabeth
of Austria in 1898, King Humbert of Italy in 1900, President McKinley of
the United States in 1901, and another Premier of Spain, Canalejas, in
1912. Not one could qualify as a tyrant. Their deaths were the gestures
of desperate or deluded men to call attention to the Anarchist idea.

No single individual was the hero of the movement that swallowed up
these lives. The Idea was its hero. It was, as a historian of revolt has
called it, "a daydream of desperate romantics." It had its theorists and
thinkers, men of intellect, sincere and earnest, who loved humanity. It
also had its tools, the little men whom misfortune or despair or the anger,
degradation and hopelessness of poverty made susceptible to the Idea until
they became possessed by it and were driven to act. These became the
assassins. Between the two groups there was no contact. The thinkers
in press and pamphlet constructed marvelous paper models of the Anarchist millennium; poured out tirades of hate and invective upon the ruling
class and its despised ally, the bourgeoisie; issued trumpet calls for action,
for a "propaganda of the deed" to accomplish the enemy's overthrow.
Whom were they calling? What deed were they asking for? They did not
say precisely. Unknown to them, down in the lower depths of society lonely
men were listening. They heard echoes of the tirades and the trumpets and
caught a glimpse of the shining millennium that promised a life without

hunger and without a boss. Suddenly one of them, with a sense of injury or a sense of mission, would rise up, go out and kill—and sacrifice his own life on the altar of the Idea.

They came from the warrens of the poor, where hunger and dirt were king, where consumptives coughed and the air was thick with the smell of latrines, boiling cabbage and stale beer, where babies wailed and couples screamed in sudden quarrels, where roofs leaked and unmended windows let in the cold blasts of winter, where privacy was unimaginable, where men, women, grandparents and children lived together, eating, sleeping, fornicating, defecating, sickening and dying in one room, where a teakettle served as a wash boiler between meals, old boxes served as chairs, heaps of foul straw as beds, and boards propped across two crates as tables, where sometimes not all the children in a family could go out at one time because there were not enough clothes to go round, where decent families lived among drunkards, wife-beaters, thieves and prostitutes, where life was a seesaw of unemployment and endless toil, where a cigar-maker and his wife earning 13 cents an hour worked seventeen hours a day seven days a week to support themselves and three children, where death was the only exit and the only extravagance and the scraped savings of a lifetime would be squandered on a funeral coach with flowers and a parade of mourners to ensure against the anonymity and last ignominy of Potter's Field.

The Anarchists believed that with Property, the monarch of all evil, eliminated, no man could again live off the labour of another and human nature would be released to seek its natural level of justice among men. The role of the State would be replaced by voluntary cooperation among individuals and the role of the law by the supreme law of the general welfare. To this end no reform of existing social evils through vote or persuasion was of any use, for the ruling class would never give up its property or the powers and laws which protected ownership of property. Therefore, the necessity of violence. Only revolutionary overturn of the entire malignant existing system would accomplish the desired result. Once the old structure was in rubble, a new social order of utter equality and no authority, with enough of everything for everybody, would settle smilingly upon the earth. So reasonable seemed the proposition that once apprised of it the oppressed classes could not fail to respond. The Anarchist task was to awaken them to the Idea by propaganda of the word and of the Deed, and one day, one such deed would flash the signal for revolt.

During the first and formulative period of Anarchism, beginning around the time of the revolutionary year 1848, its two major prophets were Pierre Proudhon of France and his disciple, Michael Bakunin, a Russian exile who became the active leader of the movement.

"Whoever lays his hand on me to govern me," Proudhon proclaimed, "is a usurper and a tyrant; I declare him to be my enemy. . . . Government of man by man is slavery" and its laws are "cobwebs for the rich and chains of steel for the poor." The "highest perfection" for free society is no government, to which Proudhon was the first to give the name "An-archy." He excoriated government in a passion of contempt. "To be governed is to be watched, inspected, spied on, regulated, indoctrinated, preached at, controlled, ruled, censored, by persons who have neither wisdom nor virtue. It is every action and transaction to be registered, stamped, taxed, patented, licensed, assessed, measured, reprimanded, corrected, frustrated. Under pretext of the public good it is to be exploited, monopolized, embezzled, robbed and then, at the least protest or word of complaint, to be fined, harassed, vilified, beaten up, bludgeoned, disarmed, judged, condemned, imprisoned, shot, garroted, deported, sold, betrayed, swindled, deceived, outraged, dishonored. That's government, that's its justice, that's its morality! And imagine that among us there are democrats who believe government to be good, socialists who in the name of liberty, equality and fraternity support this ignominy, proletarians who offer themselves candidates for President of the Republic! What hypocrisy!"

Proudhon believed that the "abstract idea of right" would obviate the need of revolution and man would be persuaded to adopt the stateless society through reason. What Bakunin added, learning from Russia under Nicholas I, was the necessity of violent revolution. As opposed to his rival, Karl Marx, who maintained that revolution would come only from an industrial proletariat, organized and trained for the task, Bakunin believed that immediate revolution could explode in one of the more economically backward countries—Italy, Spain or Russia—where the workers, though untrained, unorganized and illiterate, with no understanding of their own wants, would be ready to rise because they had nothing to lose. The task of the conscientious revolutionist was to popularize the Idea among the masses, hitherto bound in ignorance and prejudice by the ruling class. It was necessary to make them conscious of their own wants and "evoke" from them thoughts to match their impulses, thoughts of revolt. When this happened the workers would know their own will and then "their power will be irresistible." Bakunin, however, lost control of the First International to Marx, who believed in organization.

There was an inherent paradox within the body of Anarchism that frustrated progress. Anarchism rejected the political party, which Proudhon had called a mere "variety of absolutism"; yet to bring about a revolution it was necessary to submit to authority, organization and discipline. Whenever Anarchists met to prepare a program, this terrible necessity rose up to face them. Loyal to their Idea, they rejected it. Revolution would burst from the masses spontaneously. All that was needed was the Idea—and a spark.

Each strike or bread riot or local uprising the Anarchist hoped—and the capitalist feared—might be the spark. Mme Hennebau, the manager's wife in Zola's *Germinal,* watching the march of the striking miners under the bloody gleam of the setting sun, saw "the red vision of revolution that on some sombre evening at the end of the century would carry everything away. Yes, on that evening the people, unbridled at last, would make the blood of the middle class flow, . . . in a thunder of boots the same terrible troop, with their dirty skins and tainted breath, would sweep away the old world. . . . Fires would flame, there would be nothing left, not a *sou* of the great fortunes, not a title deed of acquired properties."

Yet each time, as when Zola's miners faced the guns of the gendarmerie, the spark was stamped out. The magic moment when the masses would awaken to their wants and their power did not come. The Paris Commune flared and died in 1871 and failed to signal a general insurrection. "We reckoned without the masses who did not want to be roused to passion for their own freedom," wrote Bakunin, disillusioned, to his wife. "This passion being absent what good did it do us to have been right theoretically? We were powerless." He despaired of saving the world and died, disillusioned, in 1876, a Columbus, as Alexander Herzen said, without America.

Meanwhile in his native land his ideas took root in the Narodniki, or Populists, otherwise the Party of the People's Will, founded in 1879. Because of communal use of land peculiar to the Russian peasant, reformers worshipped the peasant as a natural Socialist who needed only the appearance of a Messiah to be awakened from his lethargy and impelled upon the march to revolution. The bomb was to be the Messiah. "Terrorist activity," stated the Narodniki program, "consisting in destroying the most harmful person in government, aims to undermine the prestige of the government and arouse in this manner the revolutionary spirit of the people and their confidence in the success of the cause."

In 1881 the Narodniki struck a blow that startled the world: they assassinated the Czar, Alexander II. It was a triumphant coup, equal, they imagined, to the battering down of the Bastille. It would shout aloud their protest, summon the oppressed and terrorize the oppressors. Instead it ushered in reaction. The dead Czar, whose crown may have been the symbol of autocracy but who in person was the "Liberator" of the serfs, was mourned by the peasants, who believed "the gentry had murdered the Czar to get back the land." His ministers opened a campaign of savage repression, the public, abandoning all thoughts of reform, acquiesced, and the revolutionary movement, "broken and demoralized, withdrew into the conspirators' cellar." There Anarchism's first period came to an end.

Before the movement burst into renewed bloom in the nineties, a single terrible event which enlarged the stature of Anarchism took place, not in Europe, but in America, in the city of Chicago. There in August, 1886, eight Anarchists were sentenced by Judge Joseph Gary to be hanged for the murder of seven police killed on the previous May 4 by a bomb hurled into the midst of an armed police force who were about to break up a strikers' meeting in Haymarket Square.

The occasion was the climax of a campaign for the eight-hour day, which in itself was the climax of a decade of industrial war centering on Chicago. In every clash the employers fought with the forces of law—police, militia and courts—as their allies. The workers' demands were met with live ammunition and lockouts and with strikebreakers protected by Pinkertons who were armed and sworn in as deputy sheriffs. In the war between the classes, the State was not neutral. Driven by misery and injustice, the workers' anger grew and with it the employers' fear, their sense of a rising menace and their determination to stamp it out. Even a man as remote as Henry James sensed a "sinister anarchic underworld heaving in its pain, its power and its hate."

Anarchism was not a labour movement and was no more than one element in the general upheaval of the lower class. But Anarchists saw in the struggles of labour the hot coals of revolution and hoped to blow them into flame. "A pound of dynamite is worth a bushel of bullets," cried August Spies, editor of Chicago's German-language Anarchist daily, *Die Arbeiter-Zeitung.* "Police and militia, the bloodhounds of capitalism, are ready to murder!" In this he was right, for in the course of a clash between workers and strikebreakers, the police fired, killing two. "Revenge! Revenge! Workingmen to arms!" shrieked handbills printed and distributed by Spies that night. He called for a protest meeting the next day. It took place in Haymarket Square, the police marched to break it up, the bomb was thrown. Who threw it has never been discovered.

The defendants' speeches to the court after sentence, firm in Anarchist principle and throbbing with consciousness of martyrdom, resounded throughout Europe and America and provided the best propaganda Anarchism ever had. In the absence of direct evidence establishing their guilt, they knew and loudly stated that they were being tried and sentenced for the crime, not of murder, but of Anarchism. "Let the world know," cried August Spies, "that in 1886 in the state of Illinois eight men were sentenced to death because they believed in a better future!" Their belief had included the use of dynamite, and society's revenge matched its fright. In the end the sentences of three of the condemned were commuted to prison terms. One, Louis Lingg, the youngest, handsomest and most fervent, who was shown by evidence at the trial to have made bombs, blew himself up with a capsule of fulminate of mercury on the night before the execution and wrote in his blood before he died, "Long live anarchy!" His suicide was regarded by many as a confession of guilt. The remaining four, including Spies, were hanged on November 11, 1887.

For years afterward the silhouette of the gallows and its four hanging bodies decorated Anarchist literature, and the anniversary of November 11 was celebrated by Anarchists in Europe and America as a revolutionary memorial. The public conscience, too, was made aware by the gallow's fruit of the misery, protest and upheaval in the working class.

Men who were Anarchists without knowing it stood on every street corner. Jacob Riis, the New York police reporter who described in 1890 *How the Other Half Lives,* saw one on the corner of Fifth Avenue and Fourteenth Street. The man suddenly leaped at a carriage carrying two fashionable ladies on an afternoon's shopping and slashed at the sleek and shining horses with a knife. When arrested and locked up, he said, "They don't have to think of tomorrow. They spend in an hour what would keep me and my little ones for a year." He was the kind from which Anarchists of the Deed were made.

Most of them were voiceless or could speak their protest only in the wail of a dispossessed Irish peasant spading his field for the last time, who was asked by a visitor what he wanted. "What is it I am wantin'?" cried the old man, shaking his fist at the sky. "I want the Day av Judgment!"

The poor lived in a society in which power, wealth and magnificent spending were never more opulent, in which the rich dined on fish, fowl and red meat at one meal, lived in houses of marble floors and damask walls and of thirty or forty or fifty rooms, wrapped themselves in furs in winter and were cared for by a retinue of servants who blacked their boots, arranged their hair, drew their baths and lit their fires. In this world, at a luncheon for Mme Nellie Melba at the Savoy, when perfect peaches, a delicacy of the season, were served up "fragrant and delicious in their cotton wool," the surfeited guests made a game of throwing them at passers-by beneath the windows.

These were the rulers and men of property whose immense possessions could, it seemed, only be explained as having been accumulated out of the pockets of the exploited masses. "What is Property?" asked Proudhon in a famous question and answered, "Property is theft." "Do you not know," cried Enrico Malatesta in his *Talk Between Two Workers,* an Anarchist classic of the nineties, "that every bit of bread they eat is taken from your children, every fine present they give to their wives means the poverty, hunger, cold, even perhaps prostitution of yours?"

If in their economics the Anarchists were hazy, their hatred of the ruling class was strong and vibrant. They hated "all mankind's tormentors," as Bakunin called them, "priests, monarchs, statesmen, soldiers, officials, financiers, capitalists, moneylenders, lawyers." To the workers themselves it was not the faraway rich but their visible representatives, the landlord, the factory owner, the boss, the policeman, who were the Enemy.

They could hate but only a few were rebels. Most existed in apathy, stupefied by poverty. Some gave up. A woman with four children who made match boxes at 4½ cents a gross, and by working fourteen hours could make seven gross a day for a total of 31½ cents, threw herself out of the window one day and was carried from the street dead. She was "discouraged," a neighbor said. A young man who had a sick mother and had lost his job was charged in magistrate's court with attempted suicide. The lockkeeper's wife who pulled him out of the river testified how "as fast as I pulled to get him out, he crawled back" until some workmen came to assist her. When the magistrate congratulated the woman on her muscular powers, the courtroom laughed, but an observer named Jack London wrote, "All I could see was a boy on the threshold of life passionately crawling to a muddy death."

The failure of practical attempts at Anarchism in Bakunin's period caused Anarchist theory and practice to veer off in a direction not toward the earth but toward the clouds. In the new period beginning in the nineties, its aims, always idyllic, became even more utopian and its deeds less than ever connected with reality. It became impatient. It despised the puny efforts of Socialists and trade unionists to achieve the eight-hour day. "Eight hours of work for the boss is eight hours too much," proclaimed the Anarchist paper, *La Révolte.* "We know that what is wrong with our society is not that the worker works ten, twelve or fourteen hours, but that the boss exists."

The most prominent among the new Anarchist leaders was Prince Peter Kropotkin, by birth an aristocrat, by profession a geographer, and by conviction a revolutionist. His sensational escape after two years' imprisonment from the grim fortress of Peter and Paul in 1876 had endowed him with a heroic aura, kept bright afterwards during his years of exile in Switzerland, France and England by unrepentant and unremitting preaching in the cause of revolt.

Kropotkin's faith in mankind, despite a life of hard experience, was inexhaustible and unshatterable. He gave the impression, said the English journalist Henry Nevinson, who knew him well, of "longing to take all mankind to his bosom and keep it warm." Kindliness shone from his bald and noble dome ringed with a low halo of bushy brown hair. An ample beard spread comfortably beneath his chin. He was very short, "with hardly enough body to hold up the massive head." Descended from princes of Smolensk who, according to family tradition, belonged to the Rurik Dynasty, which had ruled Russia before the Romanovs, Kropotkin took his place in that long line of "conscience-stricken" Russian nobility who felt guilty for belonging to a class which had oppressed the people for centuries.

He was born in 1842. After service as an officer of Cossacks in Siberia, where he studied the geography of the region, he became Secretary of the Geographical Society, for whom he explored the glaciers of Finland and Sweden in 1871. Meanwhile he had become a member of a secret revolutionary committee, and on this being discovered, his arrest and imprisonment followed. After his escape in 1876—the year Bakunin died—he went to Switzerland, where he worked with Elisée Reclus, the French geographer and a fellow Anarchist, on Reclus' monumental geography of the world. Kropotkin wrote the volume on Siberia and, with Reclus, founded and for three years edited *Le Révolté*, which, after suppression and a rebirth in Paris as *La Révolte*, was to become the best-known and longest-lived Anarchist journal. His stream of convincing and passionate polemics, the prestige of his escape from the most dreaded Russian prison, his active work with the Swiss Anarchists of the Jura—which caused his expulsion from Switzerland—all topped by his title of Prince, made him Bakunin's recognized successor.

In France, where he came next in 1882, the traditions of the Commune had nourished a militant Anarchist movement of which there was a flourishing group in Lyons. A police raid and a retaliatory bomb causing one death had been followed by the arrest and trial of fifty-two Anarchists, including Kropotkin, on charges of belonging to an international league dedicated to the abolition of property, family, country and religion. Sentenced to prison for five years, Kropotkin had served three, had then been pardoned by President Grévy and, with his wife and daughter, had settled in England, the inevitable refuge of political exiles at the time.

In a small house in Hammersmith, a drearily respectable dormitory of outer London, he continued to write fiery paeans to violence for *La Révolte*, scholarly articles for geographical journals and for the *Nineteenth Century,* to entertain visiting radicals in five languages, to lecture Anarchist club meetings in a cellar off Tottenham Court Road, to thump the piano, and paint, and to charm with his sweet temper and genial manners everyone who met him. "He was amiable to the point of saintliness," wrote George Bernard Shaw, "and with his full beard and lovable expression might have been a shepherd from the Delectable Mountains. His only weakness was the habit of prophesying war within the next fortnight. And he was right in the end." This weakness was in fact an expression of Kropotkin's optimism, for war to him was the expected catastrophe that was to destroy the old world and clear the way for the triumph of Anarchy. The "galloping decay" of states was hastening the triumph. "It cannot be far off," he wrote. "Everything brings it nearer."

This agreeable person, conventionally dressed in the black frock coat of a Victorian gentleman, was an uncompromising apostle of the necessity of violence. Man's progress toward perfection was being held back, he wrote, by the "inertia of those who have a vested interest in existing conditions." Progress needed a violent event "to hurl mankind out of its ruts into new roads. . . . Revolution becomes a peremptory necessity." The spirit of revolt must be awakened in the masses by repeated "propaganda of the deed." This phrase, which became the banner of Anarchist violence, was first used by a French Socialist, Paul Brousse, in 1878, a year which saw four attempts on crowned heads: two on Wilhelm I of Germany and one each on the Kings of Spain and Italy. "The Idea is on the march," Brousse wrote, "and we must seek to inaugurate the propaganda of the deed. Through a royal breast is the way to open the road to revolution!"

The next year at an Anarchist Congress in the Swiss Jura, Kropotkin specifically advocated propaganda of the Deed, if somewhat less explicit as to method. Though never recommending assassination in so many words, he continued during the eighties to urge a propaganda by "speech and written word, by dagger, gun and dynamite." He sounded an inspiring summons in the pages of *La Révolte* to "men of courage willing not only to speak but to act, pure characters who prefer prison, exile and death to a life that contradicts their principles, bold natures who know that in order to win one must dare." Men such as these must form an advance guard of revolution long before the masses were ready, and in the midst of "talking, complaining, discussing," must do the "deed of mutiny."

"A single deed," Kropotkin wrote at another time, "is better propaganda than a thousand pamphlets." Words are "lost in the air like the sound of church bells." Acts are needed "to excite hate for the exploiters, to ridicule the Rulers, to show up their weakness and above all and always to awaken the spirit of revolt." The acts he loftily called for on paper were performed, but not by him.

In the nineties, when he was in his fifties, Kropotkin, though never altering his demand for revolt, subdued a little his enthusiasm for the individual Deed. Although "the revolutionary spirit gains immensely through such deeds of individual heroism," he wrote in *La Révolte* of March, 1891, "nevertheless it is not these heroic acts that make revolutions. Revolution is above all a mass movement. . . . Institutions rooted in centuries of history are not destroyed by a few pounds of explosives. The time for such action has passed and the time for the anarchist and communist idea to penetrate the masses has come." Disclaimers, however, rarely have the same force as the original proposition.

In London, in a restaurant in Holborn during the coal strike of 1893, Kropotkin was arguing with Ben Tillett and Tom Mann, two tough-minded trade unionists. "We must destroy! We must pull down! We must be rid of the tyrants!" shouted Mann.

"No," said Kropotkin in his foreign accent, with the eyes of a scientist gleaming behind his spectacles, "we must build. We must build in the hearts of men. We must establish a kingdom of God."

He had the plans for the kingdom already drawn. After the revolution— which he calculated would take three to five years to accomplish the overthrow of governments, the destruction of prisons, forts and slums and the expropriation of land, industries and all forms of property—volunteers would take inventory of all food stocks, dwellings, and means of production. Printed lists would be distributed by the million. Everyone would take what he needed of the things which existed in plenty and there would be rationing of the things of which there was shortage. All property would be community property. Everyone would draw upon the community warehouse for food and goods according to his needs and would have the right "to decide for himself what he needs for a comfortable life." As there would be no more inheritance, there would be no more greed. All able-bodied males would enter into "contracts" with society through their groups and communes by which they would engage to do five hours' daily work from the age of twenty-one to about forty-five or fifty, each in a labour of his choice. In return, society would guarantee them the enjoyment of "houses, stores, streets, conveyances, schools, museums, etc." There would be no need for enforcement or judges or penalties because people would fulfill their contracts out of their own need of "cooperation, support and sympathy" from their neighbors. The process would work because of its very reasonableness, although even Kropotkin might have noticed that the reasonableness of something is rarely a motive in human affairs.

Shaw, with his unrelenting common sense, picked out the trouble in a Fabian Tract called *The Impossibilities of Anarchism*, published in 1893 and reprinted several times during the next ten years. If man is good and institutions bad, he asked, if man will be good again as soon as the corrupt system ceases to oppress him, "how did the corruption and oppression under which he groans ever arise?" Yet the fact that Shaw felt required to write the Tract was his tribute to the force of the Idea.

The most vexing problem of the Anarchist plan was the question of an accounting of the value of goods and services. According to the theories of Proudhon and Bakunin, everyone would be paid in goods in proportion to what he produced. But this required a body to establish values and do the accounting, an Authority, which was anathema to "pure" Anarchy. As resolved by Kropotkin and Malatesta, the solution was to assume that everyone would *want* to work for the good of the whole, and since all work would be agreeable and dignified, everyone would contribute freely and take from the community storehouse freely without the necessity of accounting.

In proof Kropotkin evolved his theory of "mutual aid" to show that Anarchism had a scientific basis in the laws of nature. Darwin's thesis, he argued, had been perverted by capitalist thinkers. Nature was not, in fact, red in tooth and claw nor animated by the instinct of each living thing to survive at the cost of its fellow but, on the contrary, by the instinct of each to *preserve* the species through "mutual assistance." He drew examples from the ants and the bees and from wild horses and cattle—who form a ring when attacked by wolves—and from the communal field and village life of men in the Middle Ages. He greatly admired the rabbit, which, though defenceless and adapted to nothing in particular, yet survived and multiplied. The rabbit symbolized for him the durability of the meek who, an earlier Preacher had claimed, would inherit the earth.

Although Kropotkin never slackened his lust for the total destruction of the bourgeois world, that world could not forbear to honor him. He was such a distinguished scholar—and besides, a Prince. When he refused membership in the Royal Geographic Society because it was under royal patronage, he was invited anyway to the Society's dinner, and when he refused to rise upon the chairman's toast to "The King!" the chairman promptly rose again to propose "Long live Prince Kropotkin!" and the whole company stood up to join in the toast. When he visited the United States in 1901 and lectured to the Lowell Institute in Boston, he was entertained by its intellectual elite and, not to be outdone, by Mrs. Potter Palmer in Chicago. His memoirs were commissioned by the *Atlantic Monthly*; his books bore the imprint of the most respectable publishers. When *Mutual Aid* appeared, the *Review of Reviews* called it "a good healthy cheerful, delightful book which does one good to read."

Aside from Kropotkin, Anarchist thought was most highly developed in France. Among a wide assortment, some serious and some frivolous, the leaders were Elisée Reclus and Jean Grave. Reclus, with a dark-bearded melancholy face of somber beauty like that of a Byzantine Christ, was the soothsayer of the movement. He had fought on the barricades of the Commune and marched to prison down the dusty blood-stained road to Versailles. He came from a distinguished family of scholars and, besides his work as a geographer, had devoted years to explaining and preaching the Anarchist system through his books and through the journals he edited at one time or another with Kropotkin and Grave. In his lectures at the Université Nouvelle of Brussels, where he held for a time the chair of Geography, he exerted on listeners, wrote one of them, an "irresistible magnetism." He moved from the formation of the earth to the future of man and "affirmed, like Rousseau, his unalterable faith in human goodness once it was released from the blemishes of a society founded on force."

In contrast, Grave came from a working-class family. Once a shoemaker and then, like Proudhon, a typesetter and printer, he had, in the eighties, practiced making fulminate of mercury to blow up the Prefecture of Police or the Palais Bourbon, seat of the French parliament. His book, *The Dying Society and Anarchism*, so persuasively argued the overthrow of the State and offered so many insidious suggestions that it cost him two years in prison. While there he wrote another book, *Society After the Revolution*, which he promptly printed himself and published upon his release. Being utopian, it was not considered dangerously subversive by the authorities. In a fifth-floor garret in a working-class street, the Rue Mouffetard, he now edited, largely wrote, and printed on a hand press *La Révolte*, at the same time working on his great history, *Le Mouvement libertaire sous la troisième république.* In a room furnished with a table and two chairs, he lived and worked, dressed invariably in a French workman's long black blouse, surrounded by pamphlets and newspapers, "simple, silent, indefatigable," and so absorbed in his thought and task that "he seemed like a hermit from the Middle Ages who forgot to die eight hundred years ago."

The followers who were the body of the movement never formed a party but associated only in small, localized clubs and groups. A few comrades would pass out notices informing friends that, for instance, "the Anarchists of Marseilles are establishing a group to be called The Avengers and Famished which will meet every Sunday at ————. Comrades are invited to come and bring reliable friends to hear and take part in the discussions." Such groups existed not only in Paris but in most of the large cities and many small towns. Among them were the "Indomitables" of Armentières, the "Forced Labour" of Lille, the "Ever-Ready" of Blois, "Land and Independence" of Nantes, "Dynamite" of Lyons, the "Anti-Patriots" of Charleville. With similar groups from other countries, they occasionally held Congresses, such as the one in Chicago during the World's Fair in 1893, but they neither organized nor federated.

Enrico Malatesta, the firebrand of Anarchism, was an Italian, always carrying the flame to whatever corner of the world there was an Anarchist group. Ten years younger than Kropotkin, he looked like a romantic bandit who might have befriended the Count of Monte Cristo. In fact, he came from a well-off bourgeois family and as a young medical student had been expelled from the University of Naples for participating in a student riot at the time of the Paris Commune. Thereafter he learned the electrician's trade in order to make a living, joined the Italian section of the International, sided with Bakunin against Marx, led an abortive peasant revolt in Apulia, went to prison and then into exile. He tried to direct the Belgian general strike of 1891 away from its petty aim of manhood suffrage because the vote, in his Anarchist credo, was merely another booby trap of the bourgeois state. He was expelled for similar revolutionary efforts from one country after another and condemned to five years on the prison island of Lampedusa, from which he escaped in a rowboat during a storm. When confined to Italy he escaped in a packing case marked "sewing machines." It was loaded on a boat for Argentina, where he hoped to prospect for gold in Patagonia to provide funds for the cause, and where, in fact, he found it, only to have his claim confiscated by the Argentine government.

Not content merely with talking about the coming disappearance of the State, Malatesta was constantly embroiled in practical attempts designed to help it disappear. This caused him to be suspected of deviating from "pure" Anarchism and even of leaning toward Marxism. On one occasion he was shot by an Italian fellow-Anarchist of the extreme *anti-organizzatori* wing. Never discouraged, no matter how many of the insurrections he mid-wifed were stillborn, Malatesta was always just in or out of prison, fresh from some dramatic escape or desperate adventure, forever an exile without a home or with hardly a room to call his own, always turning up, as Kropotkin said, "just as we saw him last, ready to renew the struggle, with the same love of man, the same absence of hatred for adversaries or jailers."

Their optimism was the outstanding characteristic of these leaders. They were certain that Anarchism because of its rightness must triumph and the capitalist system because of its rottenness must fall, and they sensed a mysterious deadline in the approaching end of the century. "All are awaiting the birth of a new order of things," wrote Reclus. "The century which has witnessed so many grand discoveries in the world of science cannot pass away without giving us still greater conquests. After so much hatred we yearn to love each other and for this reason we are the enemies of private property and the despisers of law."

Kropotkin's benevolent eyes peering at the world around him found encouraging signs everywhere. The increasing number of free museums, free libraries and free parks, for instance, seemed to him to be progress toward the Anarchist day when all private property would eventually become common property. Were not turnpikes and toll bridges becoming free? Were not municipalities providing free water and free street lights? Proof of the Anarchists' contention that the society of the future would no longer be held together by government but by the "free association of men into groups" was, he thought, appearing in such developments as the International Red Cross, the trade unions and even the cartels of shipowners and railroads (elsewhere being denounced as "Trusts" by a rather different type of reformer in America).

As formulated by men like Kropotkin, Malatesta, Jean Grave and Reclus, Anarchism at the end of the century may have attained, in the words of one of its recorders, "a shining moral grandeur," but only at the cost of a noticeable removal from reality. These men had all suffered prison more than once for their beliefs. Kropotkin himself had lost his teeth as a result of prison scurvy. They were not men of the ivory tower except in so far as their heads were in ivory towers. They were able to draw blueprints of a state of universal harmony only by ignoring the evidence of human behavior and the testimony of history. Their insistence on revolution stemmed directly from their faith in humanity, which, they believed, needed only a shining example and a sharp blow to start it on its way to the golden age. They spoke their faith aloud. The consequences were frequently fatal.

Anarchism's new era of violence opened in France just after the hundredth anniversary of the French Revolution. A two-year reign of dynamite, dagger and gunshot erupted, killed ordinary men as well as great ones, destroyed property, banished safety, spread terror and then subsided. The signal was given in 1892 by a man whose name, Ravachol, seemed to "breathe revolt and hatred." His act, like nearly all that followed it, was a gesture of revenge for comrades who had suffered at the hands of the State.

On the previous May Day of 1891, at Clichy, a working-class suburb of Paris, a workers' demonstration led by *les anarchos* carrying red banners with revolutionary slogans was charged by mounted police. In the melee five police were slightly, and three Anarchist leaders severely, wounded. Dragged to the police station, the Anarchists were subjected, while still bleeding and untended, to a *passage à tabac* of uncontrolled savagery, being made to pass between two lines of policemen under kicks and blows and beatings with revolver butts. At their trial, Bulot, the prosecuting attorney, charged that one of them, on the day before the riot, had called on the workers to arm themselves, and told them, "If the police come, let no one fear to kill them like the dogs they are! Down with Government! *Vive la révolution!*" Bulot thereupon demanded the death penalty for all three, which, since no one had been killed, was an impossible demand that he might better not have made. It was to start a train of dynamite. For the moment, M. Benoist, the presiding judge, acquitted one defendant and sentenced the other two to five and three years' imprisonment respectively, the maximum allowable in the circumstances.

Six months after the trial, the home of M. Benoist on the Boulevard St-Germain was blown up by a bomb. Two weeks later, on March 27, another bomb blew up the home of Bulot, the prosecuting attorney, in the Rue de Clichy. Between the two explosions the police had circulated a description of the suspected criminal as a thin but muscular young man in his twenties with a bony, yellowish face, brown hair and beard, a look of ill health and a round scar between thumb and first finger of the left hand. On the day of the second explosion a man of this appearance took dinner at the Restaurant Véry in the Boulevard Magenta, where he talked volubly to a waiter named Lhérot about the explosion, which no one in the quarter yet knew had taken place. He also expressed anti-militarist and Anarchist opinions. Lhérot wondered about him but did nothing. Two days later the man returned and this time Lhérot, noticing the scar, called the police. When they arrived to arrest him the slight young man suddenly became a giant of maniacal strength and it required ten men and a terrific struggle to subdue and take him prisoner.

This was Ravachol. He had adopted his mother's name in preference to Koenigstein, the name of his father, who had abandoned his wife and four children, leaving Ravachol at eight years of age as chief breadwinner of the family. At eighteen, after reading Eugène Sue's *The Wandering Jew*, he had lost faith in religion, adopted Anarchist sentiments, attended their meetings, and as a result, was dismissed with a younger brother from his job as a dyer's assistant. Meanwhile, his younger sister died and his elder sister bore an illegitimate child. Although Ravachol found other jobs, they did not pay enough to keep the family from misery. Accordingly, he took to illegal supplements, but with a certain fierce pride of principle. Robbery of the rich was the right of the poor "to escape living like beasts," he said in prison. "To die of hunger is cowardly and degrading. I preferred to turn thief, counterfeiter, murderer." He had in fact been all these and grave robber as well.

At his trial on April 26, 1892, he stated that his motive had been to avenge the Anarchists of Clichy who had been beaten up by the police and "not even given water to wash their wounds," and upon whom Bulot and Benoist had imposed the maximum penalty although the jury had recommended the minimum. His manner was resolute and his eyes had the peculiarly piercing gaze expressive of inner conviction. "My object was to terrorize so as to force society to look attentively at those who suffer," he said, putting volumes into a sentence. While the press described him as a figure of sinister violence and cunning and a "colossus of strength," witnesses testified that he had given money to the wife of one of the imprisoned Clichy Anarchists and bought clothes for her children. At the end of the one-day trial he was sentenced to imprisonment at hard labour for life. But the Ravachol affair had just begun.

The waiter Lhérot, meanwhile, was winning heroic notoriety by regaling customers and journalists with his story of the Scar, the Recognition and the Arrest. As a result he attracted an unknown avenger who set off a bomb in the Restaurant Véry which killed, not Lhérot, but his brother-in-law, M. Véry, the proprietor. The act was hailed by *Le Père Peinard*, an Anarchist journal given to coarse street argot, with the ghoulish double pun, *"Vérification!"*

By now the police had uncovered a whole series of Ravachol's crimes,

Lord Salisbury

Lord Ribblesdale (portrait by Sargent, 1902)

The Wyndham sisters: Lady Elcho, Mrs. Tennant, and Mrs. Adeane
(portrait by Sargent, 1899)

Chatsworth

Prince Peter Kropotkin

Editorial office of *La Révolte*

"Slept in That Cellar Four Years" (photograph by Jacob A. Riis, about 1890)

"Lockout" (drawing by Théophile Steinlen; signed "Petit Pierre")

including a grave robbery for the jewelry on a corpse, the murder of a ninety-two-year-old miser and his housekeeper, the further murder of two old women who kept a hardware shop—which had netted him forty sous—and of another shopkeeper, which had netted him nothing. "See this hand?" Ravachol was quoted as saying; "it has killed as many bourgeois as it has fingers." At the same time he had been living peaceably in lodgings, teaching the little daughter of his landlord to read.

His trial for these murders opened on June 21 in an atmosphere of terror induced by the avenger's bomb in the Restaurant Véry. Everyone expected the Palais de Justice to be blown up; it was surrounded by troops, every entrance guarded, and jurors, judges and counsel heavily escorted by police. Upon being sentenced to death, Ravachol said that what he had done had been for the "Anarchist idea" and added the prophetic words, "I know I shall be avenged."

Faced with this extraordinary person, at once a monster of criminality and a protector and avenger of the unfortunate, the Anarchist press fell into discord. In *La Révolte* Kropotkin repudiated Ravachol as "not the true, the authentic" revolutionary but the "*opéra-bouffe* variety." These deeds, he wrote, "are not the steady, daily work of preparation, little seen but immense, which the revolution demands. This requires other men than Ravachols. Leave them to the *fin de siècle* bourgeois whose product they are." Malatesta likewise, in the literary Anarchist journal, *l'En Dehors*, rejected Ravachol's gesture.

The difficulty was that Ravachol belonged almost but not quite to that class of Ego Anarchists who had one serious theorist in the German Max Stirner and a hundred practitioners of the *culte de moi*. They professed an extreme contempt for every bourgeois sentiment and social restraint, recognizing only the individual's right to "live anarchistically," which included burglary and any other crime that served the need of the moment. They were interested in themselves, not in revolution. The unbridled operations of these "miniature Borgias," usually ending in gun battles with the police and flaunted under the banner of "Anarchism," added much to the fear and anger of the public, who did not distinguish between the aberrant and the true variety. Ravachol was both. There was in him a streak of genuine pity and fellow feeling for the oppressed of his class which led one Anarchist paper to compare him with Jesus.

On July 11, calm and unrepentant, he went to the guillotine, crying at the end, "*Vive l'anarchie!*" At once the issue was clear. Overnight he became an Anarchist martyr and among the underworld, a popular hero. *La Révolte* reversed itself. "He will be avenged!" it proclaimed, adding its bit to the unfolding cycle of revenge. *L'En Dehors* opened a subscription for the children of an accomplice tried along with Ravachol. Among the contributors were the painter Camille Pissarro, the playwright Tristan Bernard, the Belgian Socialist and poet Emile Verhaeren, and Bernard Lazare (soon to be an actor in the Dreyfus case). A verb, *ravacholiser*, meaning "to wipe out an enemy," became current, and a street song called "La Ravachole," sung to the tune of "La Carmagnole," carried the refrain:

> It will come, it will come,
> Every bourgeois will have his bomb.

Ravachol's significance was not in his bombs but in his execution. Meantime, violence erupted across the Atlantic.

Anarchism, which rejected government in sexual matters as in all others, had its love affairs, and one that was to have explosive effect upon the movement in America was at this time in progress in New York. It began in 1890 at a memorial meeting for the Haymarket martyrs at which the speaker was the German exile Johann Most, with the twisted face and deformed body, who edited the Anarchist weekly *Freiheit* in New York.

An untended childhood accident which caused his facial disfigurement, a scorned and lonely youth spent wandering from place to place, sometimes starving, sometimes finding odd jobs, was natural food for an animus against society. In Most it sprouted with the energy of a weed. In Germany he learned the bookbinder's trade, wrote wrathfully for the revolutionary press, and achieved one term as deputy in the Reichstag in the seventies. Exiled for his revolutionary incitement, he had taken refuge first in England, where he became an Anarchist, founded his journal of fiery sentiments and welcomed the regicide of Alexander II in 1881 with such enthusiasm that he received a prison term of eighteen months. When his comrades, while he was in gaol, applauded equally the assassination of Lord Frederick Cavendish by Irish rebels in Dublin, England's traditional tolerance was outraged at last; *Freiheit* was suppressed and Most, when he emerged, took his paper and his passion to the United States.

Freiheit's incitements and ferocity continued unabated and to one reader seemed like "lava shooting forth flames of ridicule, scorn and defiance . . . and breathing hatred." After working secretly for a time in an explosives factory in Jersey City, Most published a manual on the manufacture of bombs and expounded in uninhibited language in *Freiheit* on the uses of dynamite and nitroglycerine. His goal, like his hate, was generalized and directed toward destruction of the "existing class rule" by "relentless" revolutionary action. Most cared nothing for the eight-hour day, that "damned thing" as he called it, which even if gained would serve only to distract the masses from the real issue: the struggle against capitalism and for a new society.

In 1890 Most was forty-four, of medium height with gray, bushy hair crowning a large head, of which the lower part was twisted to the left by the dislocated jaw. A harsh, embittered man, he was yet so eloquent and impassioned when he spoke at the memorial meeting that his repellent appearance was forgotten. To one female member of the audience, his blue eyes were "sympathetic" and he seemed to "radiate hatred and love."

Emma Goldman, a recent Russian Jewish immigrant of twenty-one, with a rebellious soul and a highly excitable nature, was transported. Her companion of the evening was Alexander Berkman, like herself a Russian Jew, who had lived in the United States less than three years. Persecution in Russia and poverty in America had endowed both these young people with exalted revolutionary purpose. Anarchism became their creed. Emma's first job in the United States was sewing in a factory ten and a half hours a day for $2.50 a week. Her room cost $3.00 a month. Berkman came from a slightly better-class family which in Russia had been sufficiently well-off to employ servants and send him to the *gymnasium*. But economic disaster had overtaken them; a favorite uncle of revolutionary sentiments had been seized by the police and never seen again and Sasha (Alexander) had been expelled from school for writing a Nihilist and atheistic composition. Now twenty, he had "the neck and chest of a giant," a high studious forehead, intelligent eyes, and a severe expression. From the "tension and fearful excitement" of Most's speech about the martyrs, Emma sought "relief" in Sasha's arms and subsequently her enthusiasm led her to Most's arms as well. The tensions of this arrangement proved no different from those of any bourgeois triangle.

In June, 1892, in Homestead, Pennsylvania, the steelworkers' union struck in protest against a reduction of wages by the Carnegie Steel Company. The company had ordered the wage cut in a deliberate effort to crush the union, and in expectation of battle, set about erecting a military stockade topped with barbed wire behind which it planned to operate the mills with three hundred strikebreakers recruited by the Pinkerton Agency. Having become a philanthropist, Andrew Carnegie discreetly retreated for the summer to a salmon river in Scotland, leaving his manager, Henry Clay Frick, to do battle with organized labour. No one was more competent or more willing. A remarkably handsome man of forty-three, with a strong black moustache merging into a short black beard, a courteous controlled manner and eyes which could become suddenly "very steely," Frick came from a well-established Pennsylvania family. He dressed with quiet distinction in dark blue with a hairline stripe, never wore jewelry and when offended by a cartoon of himself in the Pittsburgh *Leader*, said to his secretary, "This won't do. This won't do at all. Find out who owns this paper and buy it."

On July 5 the strikebreakers recruited by Frick were to be brought in to operate the plant. When they were ferried in armored barges across the Monongahela and were about to land, the strikers attacked with homemade cannon, rifles, dynamite and burning oil. The day of furious battle ended with ten killed, seventy wounded, and the Pinkertons thrown back from the plant by the bleeding but triumphant workers. The Governor of Pennsylvania sent in eight thousand militia, the country was electrified, and Frick in the midst of smoke, death, and uproar, issued an ultimatum declaring his refusal to deal with the union and his intention to operate with non-union labour and to discharge and evict from their homes any workers who refused to return to their jobs.

"Homestead! I must go to Homestead!" shouted Berkman on the memorable evening when Emma rushed in waving the newspaper. It was, they felt, "the psychological moment for the deed. . . . The whole country was aroused against Frick and a blow aimed at him now would call the attention of the whole world to the cause." The workers were striking not only for themselves but "for all time, for a free life, for Anarchism"— although they did not know it. As yet they were only "blindly rebellious," but Berkman felt a mission to "illumine" the struggle and impart the "vision of Anarchism which alone could imbue discontent with conscious revolutionary purpose." The removal of a tyrant was not merely justifiable; it was "an act of liberation, the giving of life and opportunity to an oppressed people" and it was the "highest duty" and the "test of every true revolutionist" to die in its cause.

Berkman boarded the train for Pittsburgh bent on killing Frick but surviving long enough himself "to justify my case in court." Then in prison he would "die by my own hand like Lingg."

On July 23 he made his way to Frick's office, where he was admitted when he presented a card on which he had written, "Agent of a New York employment firm." Frick was conferring with his vice-chairman, John Leishman, when Berkman entered, pulled out a revolver and fired. His bullet wounded Frick on the left side of his neck; he fired again wounding him on the right side, and as he fired the third time, his arm was knocked up by Leishman so that he missed altogether. Frick, bleeding, had risen and lunged at Berkman, who, attacked also by Leishman, fell to the floor dragging the other two men with him. Freeing one hand, he managed to extract a dagger from his pocket, and stabbed Frick in the side and legs seven times before he was finally pulled off by a deputy sheriff and others who rushed into the room.

"Let me see his face," whispered Frick, his own face ashen, his beard and clothes streaked with blood. The sheriff jerked Berkman's head back by his hair, and the eyes of Frick and his assailant met. At the police station two caps of fulminate of mercury of the same kind Lingg had used to blow himself up were found on Berkman's person (some say, in his mouth). Frick lived, the strike was broken by the militia, and Berkman went to prison for sixteen years.

All this left the country gasping, but the public shock was as nothing compared to that which rocked Anarchist circles when in *Freiheit* of August, 27, Johann Most, the priest of violence, turned apostate to his past and denounced Berkman's attempt at tyrannicide. He said the importance of the terrorist deed had been overestimated and that it could not mobilize revolt in a country where there was no proletarian class-consciousness, and he dealt with Berkman, now a hero in Anarchist eyes, in terms of contempt. When he repeated these views verbally at a meeting, a female fury rose up out of the audience. It was Emma Goldman, armed with a horsewhip, who sprang upon the platform and flayed her former lover across his face and body. The scandal was tremendous.

That personal emotions played a part both in Most's act and hers can hardly be doubted. Most may have taken his cue from Kropotkin and Malatesta, who already in Ravachol's case had begun to question the value of gestures of violence. But the dedicated Berkman was no Ravachol and it was clearly jealousy of him as a younger rival both in love and in the revolutionary movement that galled Most. His splenetic attack on a fellow Anarchist who had been ready to die for the Deed was a stunning betrayal from which the movement in America never fully recovered.

It had no effect on the public at large, who were aware only of the Anarchists' blows, or *attentats*, as the French called them. Society's fear of the disruptive force within its bowels grew with each attack. In the year after Homestead the fear burst out when Governor John P. Altgeld of Illinois pardoned the three remaining Haymarket prisoners. A strange, hard, passionate man who had been born in Germany and brought to the United States at the age of three months, Altgeld had come from a boyhood of hardship and manual labour. He had fought in the Civil War at sixteen, had studied law, become State's Attorney, judge and finally Governor and had made a fortune in real estate, and was an almost demonic liberal. He had pledged himself to right the injustice done by the drumhead trial as soon as he had the power and he was also not unmotivated by a personal grudge against Judge Gary. As soon as he was elected Governor he set in motion a study of the trial records and on June 26, 1893, issued his pardon along with an 18,000-word document affirming the illegality of the original verdict and sentence. He showed the jury to have been packed and "selected to convict," the judge prejudiced against the defendants and unwilling to conduct a fair trial, and the State's Attorney to have admitted that there was no case against at least one of the defendants. These facts had not been unknown, and in the year between the verdict and the hanging, many prominent Chicagoans, uneasy over the death sentence, had worked privately for pardon and had in fact been responsible for the commutation of the sentence of the three defendants now still alive. But when Altgeld displayed publicly the cloven hoof of the Law, he shook public faith in a fundamental institution of society. Had he pardoned the Anarchists as a pure act of forgiveness, there would have been little excitement. As it was, he was excoriated by the press, by ministers in their pulpits, by important persons of all varieties. The Toledo *Blade* said he had encouraged "the overthrow of civilization." So outraged was the New York *Sun* that it resorted to verse:

> Oh wild Chicago . . .
> Lift up your weak and guilty hands
> From out the wreck of states
> And as the crumbling towers fall down,
> Write ALTGELD on your gates!

Altgeld was defeated for office at the next election. Although there were other reasons besides the pardon, he never held office again before he died at fifty-five in 1902.

Simultaneously with these events the era of dynamite exploded in Spain. There it opened with more ferocity, continued in more savagery and excess and lasted longer than in any other country. Spain is the desperado of countries, with a tragic sense of life. Its mountains are naked, its cathedrals steeped in gloom, its rivers dry up in summer, one of its greatest kings built his own mausoleum to inhabit while he lived. Its national sport is not a game but a ritual of danger and blood-letting. Its special quality was expressed by the deposed Queen, Isabella II, who, on a visit to the capital in 1890, wrote to her daughter, "Madrid is sad and everything is more unusual than ever."

In Spain it was natural that the titans' struggle between Marx and Bakunin for control of the working-class movement should have ended in victory for the Anarchist tendency. In Spain, however, where everything is more serious, the Anarchists organized, with the result that they took root and their power lasted long into the modern period. Like Russia, Spain was a cauldron in which the revolutionary element boiled against a tight lid of oppression. The Church, the landowners, the *Guardia Civil,* all the guardians of the State held the lid down. Although Spain had a Cortes and a façade of the democratic process, in reality the working class did not have open to it the legal means for reform and change which existed in France and England. Consequently, the appeal of Anarchism and its explosive methods was stronger. But unlike "pure" Anarchism, the Spanish form was collectivist because it had to be. Oppression was too heavy to allow hopes of individual action.

In January, 1892, occurred an outburst which, like the May Day affair at Clichy, was to inaugurate a terrible cycle of deed, retaliation and revenge. Agrarian revolt was endemic in the south where the immense *latifundia* of absentee landlords were farmed by peasants who worked all day for the price of a loaf of bread. Four hundred of them now rose in revolt, and armed with pitchforks, scythes and what firearms they could lay hold of, marched on the village of Jerez de la Frontera in Andalusia. Their object was the rescue of five comrades sentenced to life imprisonment in chains for complicity in a labour affair ten years earlier. The rising was promptly suppressed by the military and four of the leaders garroted, a Spanish form of execution in which the victim is tied with his back to a post and strangled with a scarf which the executioner twists from behind by means of a wooden handle. Zarzuela, one of the condemned, died calling upon the people to "avenge us."

A bulwark of the Spanish government was General Martínez de Campos, whose strong arm had restored the monarchy in 1874. After this he had defeated the Carlists, suppressed an early Cuban insurrection, and served as Premier and Minister of War. On September 24, 1893, he was reviewing a parade of troops in Barcelona. From the front row of the crowds an Anarchist named Pallas, who had been with Malatesta in the Argentine, threw first one bomb and then a second, killing the General's horse, one soldier and five bystanders, but erratically leaving its intended victim, who was thrown under the body of his horse, only bruised. Pallas, as he confessed with pride, had planned to kill the General and "his whole staff." When condemned to death by court-martial he cried, "Agreed! There are thousands to continue the work." He was allowed to take farewell of his children but, for some barbaric reason, not of his wife and mother. Sentenced to be shot with his back to a firing squad, another Spanish variant of usual custom, he repeated the cry of Andalusia, "Vengeance will be terrible!"

It came within weeks, again in the Catalan capital, and in the number of its dead was the most lethal of all the Anarchist assaults. November 8, 1893, almost coinciding with the Haymarket anniversary, was opening night of the opera season at the Teatro Lyceo and the audience in glittering evening dress was listening to *William Tell*. In the midst of this drama of defiance to tyrants, two bombs were thrown down from the balcony. One exploded, killing fifteen persons outright, and the other lay unexploded, threatening to burst at any moment. It caused a pandemonium of "terror and dismay," shrieks and curses and a wild rush for the exits in which people "fought like wild beasts to escape, respecting neither age nor sex." Afterwards, as the wounded were carried out, their splendid dresses torn, blood streaming over their starched white shirt fronts, crowds gathered outside "cursing both Anarchists and police," according to a reporter. Seven more died of their wounds, giving a total of twenty-two dead and fifty wounded.

The answer of the government was as fierce. Police raided every known club or home or meeting place of social discontent. Hundreds, even thousands, were arrested and thrown into the dungeons of Montjuich, the prison fortress seven hundred feet above the sea, whose guns dominate the harbor and city of Barcelona and foredoom any revolt by that chronically rebellious city. So full were the cells that new prisoners had to be kept shackled in warships anchored below. There being in this case no one to admit to the guilt of so many deaths, torture was applied mercilessly to extract a confession. Prisoners were burned with irons or forced with whips to keep walking thirty, forty, or fifty hours at a time and subjected to other procedures indigenous to the country of the Inquisition. By these means information was extorted that led to the arrest in January, 1894, of an Anarchist named Santiago Salvador who admitted to the crime in the Opera House as an act of revenge for Pallas. His arrest was immediately answered by his fellow Anarchists of Barcelona with another bombing, which killed two innocent persons. The government replied with six death sentences carried out in April upon prisoners from whom some form of confession had been extracted by torture. Salvador, who had attempted ineffectively to kill himself by revolver and poison, was tried separately in July and executed in November.

The ghastly tale of the Opera House explosion in Spain excited the nerves of authorities everywhere and caused even the English to question whether allowing Anarchists to preach their doctrines openly was advisable. When, three days later, the Anarchists held their traditional memorial meeting for the Haymarket martyrs, questions were put in Parliament about the conduct of the Liberal Home Secretary, Mr. Asquith, in permitting it, since such meetings required specific approval by the Home Office in advance. Mr. Asquith endeavored to shrug the matter aside as insignificant but was "crushed," according to a reporter, by the Leader of the Opposition, Mr. Balfour, who in his languid way suggested that the right to throw bombs was not an open question for public meetings nor defensible on the ground that society was badly organized. Whether convinced by Balfour or by second thoughts about the Spanish deaths, Asquith in any event reversed himself and announced a few days later that, as "the propagation of Anarchist doctrine was dangerous to the social order," no further open meetings of Anarchists would be permitted.

London's Anarchists at this time were mostly Russians, Poles, Italians and other exiles who centered around the "Autonomie," an Anarchist club, and a second group among Jewish immigrants who lived and worked in desperate poverty in the East End, published a Yiddish-language paper, *Der Arbeiter-Fraint*, and gathered at a club called the "International," in Whitechapel. The English working class, to whom acts of individual violence came less naturally than to Slavs and Latins, was on the whole not interested. An occasional intellectual like William Morris was a torchbearer; but he was mainly interested in his personal version of a utopian state, and his influence having waned by the end of the eighties, he lost control of *Commonweal*, the journal he had founded and edited, to more militant, plebeian and orthodox Anarchists. Another journal, *Freedom*, was the organ of an active group whose mentor was Kropotkin, and a third, called *The Torch*—edited by the two daughters of William Rossetti—published the voices of Malatesta, Faure and other French and Italian Anarchists.

In 1891 with the appearance of *The Soul of Man Under Socialism* a strange recruit alighted briefly on the movement like a gorgeous butterfly and then flew off. The author of the essay was Oscar Wilde. He had been much moved by the personality of Kropotkin and saw true freedom for the Artist in a society in which, "of course, authority and compulsion are out of the question." Despite his title he objected to Socialism on the same ground as the orthodox Anarchist, namely, that it was "authoritarian." If governments are to be armed with economic power, "if in a word, we are to have Industrial Tyrannies, then the last state of man will be worse than the first." Wilde's vision was of Socialism founded upon Individualism, and when this had set free the true personality of man, the Artist would at last come into his own.

In France meanwhile there had been no pause in the assaults. On November 8, 1892, at the time of a miner's strike against the Société des Mines de Carmaux, a bomb was deposited in the Paris office of the company on the Avenue de l'Opéra. Discovered by the concierge, it was taken out to the sidewalk and carefully carried off by a policeman to the nearest precinct station, in the Rue des Bons Enfants. As the policeman was bringing it in, it burst with a devastating explosion, killing five other policemen who were in the room. They were blown to fragments, blood and bits of flesh were splashed over shattered walls and windows, pieces of arms and legs lay about. Police suspicion centered on Emile Henry, younger brother of a well-known radical orator and son of Fortuné Henry who had escaped to Spain after being condemned to death in the Commune. When Emile Henry's movements during the day were traced, it appeared impossible that he could have been in the Avenue de l'Opéra at the right moment, and for the time being, no arrests were made.

The bomb in the police station threw Paris into a panic; no one knew where the next bomb would hit. Anyone connected with the law or police was regarded by his neighbors—since Parisians live largely in apartments—as if he had the plague and was often given notice to leave by his landlord. The city, wrote an English visitor, was "absolutely paralyzed" with fear. The upper classes "lived again as if in the days of the Commune. They dared not go to the theatres, to restaurants, to the fashionable shops in the Rue de la Paix or to ride in the Bois where Anarchists were suspected behind every tree." People exchanged terrible rumors: the Anarchists had mined the churches, poured prussic acid in the city's reservoirs, were hiding beneath the seats of horsecabs ready to spring out upon passengers and rob them. Troops were assembled in the suburbs ready to march, tourists took flight, the hotels were empty, busses ran without passengers, theatres and museums were barricaded.

The time was in any case one of public rancor and disgust. Hardly had the Republic warded off the Boulanger coup d'état than it was put to shame by the nexus of corruption revealed in the Panama scandal and in the official traffic in decorations. Day after day in Parliament during

1890–92 the chain of Panama financing through loans, bribes, slush funds and sales of influence was uncovered, until, it was said, 104 deputies were involved. Even Georges Clemenceau was smeared by association and lost his seat in the next election.

In proportion as the prestige of the State sank, Anarchism flourished. Intellectuals flirted with it. The buried dislike of government and law that exists in most men is nearer to the surface in some. Like the fat man who has a thin man inside crying to get out, even the respectable have a small Anarchist hidden inside, and among the artists and intellectuals of the nineties his faint cry was frequently heard. The novelist Maurice Barrès, who at one time or another tried every position in the political spectrum as a tribune for his talents, glorified Anarchist philosophy in his *l'Ennemi des Lois* and *Un Homme Libre*. The poet Laurent Tailhade hailed the future Anarchist society as a "blessed time" when aristocracy would be one of intellect and "the common man will kiss the footprints of the poets." Literary anarchism enjoyed a vogue among the Symbolists, like Mallarmé and Paul Valéry. The writer Octave Mirbeau was attracted to Anarchism because he had a horror of authority. He detested anyone in uniform: policemen, ticket-punchers, messengers, concierges, servants. In his eyes, said his friend Léon Daudet, a landlord was a pervert, a Minister a thief, lawyers and financiers made him sick and he had tolerance only for children, beggars, dogs, certain painters and sculptors and very young women. "That there need be no misery in the world was his fixed belief," said a friend; "that there nevertheless was, was the occasion of his wrath." Among painters, Pissarro contributed drawings to *Le Père Peinard* and several brilliant and savage Parisian illustrators, including Théophile Steinlen, expressed in the Anarchist journals their disgust at social injustice; sometimes, as when the President of France was caricatured in soiled pajamas, in terms unprintable in a later day.

Scores of these ephemeral journals and bulletins appeared, with names like *Antichrist*, *New Dawn*, *Black Flag*, *Enemy of the People*, the *People's Cry*, *The Torch*, *The Whip*, *New Humanity*, *Incorruptible*, *Sans-Culotte*, *Land and Liberty*, *Vengeance*. Groups and clubs calling themselves "Antipatriots' League" or "Libertarians" held meetings in dimly lit halls furnished with benches where members vented their contempt for the State, discussed revolution, but never organized, never affiliated, accepted no leaders, made no plans, took no orders. To them the State, in its panic over the Ravachol affair, in its rottenness revealed by the Panama affair, appeared to be already crumbling.

In March of 1893 a man of thirty-two named August Vaillant returned to Paris from Argentina, where he had gone in the hope of starting a new life in the New World but had failed to establish himself. Born illegitimate, he was ten months old when his mother married a man not his father, who refused to support the child. He was given to foster parents. At twelve, the boy was on his own in Paris, living by odd jobs, petty theft and begging. Somehow he went to school and found white-collar jobs. At one time he edited a short-lived weekly called *l'Union Socialiste* but soon, like others among the disinherited, gravitated to Anarchist circles. As secretary of a *Fédération des groupes indépendants,* he had some contact with Anarchist spokesmen, among them Sebastien Faure, whose "harmonious and caressing voice," beautiful phrases and elegant manners could make anyone believe in the millennium as long as they were listening to him. Vaillant married, parted from his wife, but kept with him their daughter, Sidonie, and acquired a mistress. Not the footloose or libertarian type, he held together his tiny family until the end. After his failure in Argentina he tried again to make a living in Paris, and like his contemporary Knut Hamsun, then hungrily wandering the streets of Christiania, experienced the humiliation of "the frequent repulses, half-promises, the curt noes, the cherished deluded hopes and fresh endeavors that always resulted in nothing," until the last frustration when he no longer had any respectable clothes to wear when applying for a job. Unable to afford a new pair of shoes, Vaillant wore a pair of discarded galoshes he had picked up in the street. Finally he found work in a sugar refinery paying 3 francs a day, too little to support three people.

Ashamed and bitter to see his daughter and mistress go hungry, disillusioned with a world he never made, he decided to end his life. He would not go silently but with a cry of protest, "a cry of that whole class," as he wrote the night before he acted, "which demands its rights and some day soon will join acts to words. At least I shall die with the satisfaction of knowing that I have done what I could to hasten the advent of a new era."

Not a man to kill, Vaillant planned a gesture that had some logic. He saw the disease of society exemplified by the scandal-ridden Parliament. He manufactured a bomb out of a saucepan filled with nails and with a non-lethal charge of explosive. On the afternoon of December 9, 1893, he took it with him to a seat in a public gallery of the Chambre des Députés. An observer saw a tall gaunt figure with a pale face rise to his feet and hurl something down into the midst of the debate. Vaillant's bomb detonated with the roar of a cannon, spraying the deputies with metal fragments, wounding several but killing none.

The sensation, as soon as the news was known, was enormous, and was made memorable by an enterprising journalist. He asked for comment that night at a dinner given by the journal *La Plume* to a number of celebrities, including Zola, Verlaine, Mallarmé, Rodin and Laurent Tailhade. The last-named replied grandly and in exquisite rhythm, *"Qu'importe les victimes si le geste est beau?"* (What do the victims matter if it's a fine gesture?) Published in *Le Journal* next morning, the remark was soon to be recalled in gruesome circumstances. That same morning Vaillant gave himself up.

All France understood and some, other than Anarchists, even sympathized with his gesture. Ironically, these sympathizers came from the extreme right, whose anti-Republican forces—Royalists, Jesuits, floating aristocracy and anti-Semites—despised the bourgeois state for their own reasons. Edouard Drumont, author of *La France Juive* and editor of *La Libre Parole*, who was busy raging at the Jews involved in the Panama scandal, produced a piece richly entitled "On Mud, Blood and Gold—From Panama to Anarchism." "The men of blood," he said, "were born out of the mud of Panama." The Duchesse d'Uzès, married into one of the three premier ducal families, offered to give a home and education to Vaillant's daughter (whom Vaillant, however, preferred to leave to the guardianship of Sebastien Faure).

In an angry mood, and determined to finish off the Anarchists once and for all, the government acted to stifle their propaganda. Two days after Vaillant's bomb, the Chamber unanimously passed two laws making it a crime to print any direct or "indirect" provocation of terrorist acts or to associate with intent to commit such acts. Although known as *les lois scélérates* (the scoundrelly laws), they were hardly an unreasonable measure, since the preaching of the Deed was in fact the principal incitement. Police raided Anarchist cafés and meeting places, two thousand warrants were issued, clubs and discussion groups scattered, *La Révolte* and *Le Père Peinard* closed down, and leading Anarchists left the country.

On January 10, Vaillant came to trial before five judges in red robes and black gold-braided caps. Charged with intent to kill, he insisted that he had intended only to wound. "If I had wanted to kill I could have used a heavier charge and filled the container with bullets; instead, I used only nails." His counsel, Maître Labori, who was destined for drama and violence in a far more famous case, defended him with spirit as *un exaspéré de la misère*. It was parliament, Labori said, which was guilty, for failing to remedy "the misery of poverty that oppresses one third of a nation." Despite Labori's efforts, Vaillant received the death penalty, the first time in the Nineteenth Century it had been imposed on a person who had not killed. Trial, verdict and sentence were rushed through in a single day. Almost immediately petitions for pardon began to assail President Sadi Carnot, including one from a group of sixty deputies led by Abbé Lemire, who had been one of those wounded by the bomb. A fiery Socialist, Jules Breton, predicted that if Carnot "pronounced coldly for death, not a single man in France would grieve for him if he were one day himself to be victim of a bomb." As incitement to murder, this cost Breton two years in prison and proved to be the second comment on the Vaillant affair, which was to end in strange and sinister coincidence.

The government could not pardon an Anarchist attack upon the State. Carnot refused to remit the sentence and Vaillant was duly executed on February 5, 1894, crying, "Death to bourgeois society! Long live Anarchy!"

The train of death gathered speed. Only seven days after Vaillant went to the guillotine, he was avenged by a blow of such seemingly vicious unreason that the public felt itself in the midst of nightmare. This time the bomb was aimed not against any representative of law, property or State, but against the man in the street. It exploded in the Café Terminus of the Gare St-Lazare in the midst, as *Le Journal* wrote, "of peaceful, anonymous citizens gathered in a café to have a beer before going to bed." One was killed and twenty wounded. As later became clear, the perpetrator acted upon a mad logic of his own. Even before he came to trial, the streets of Paris rocked with more explosions. One in the Rue St-Jacques killed a passer-by, one in the Faubourg St-Germain did no damage and a third exploded in the pocket of Jean Pauwels, a Belgian Anarchist, as he was entering the Church of the Madeleine. He was killed and proved to have set off the other two. On April 4, 1894, a fourth exploded in the fashionable Restaurant Foyot, where, though it killed no one, it put out the eye of Laurent Tailhade, who happened to be dining there and who only four months earlier had shrugged aside the victims of a "fine gesture."

Public hysteria mounted. When, at a theatrical performance, some scenery back stage fell with a clatter, half the audience rushed for the exits screaming, "*Les Anarchistes! Une bombe!*" Newspapers took to printing a daily bulletin under the heading, "La Dynamite." When the trial of the bomber of the Café Terminus opened on April 27, the terrible capacity of the Anarchist idea to be transformed from love of mankind to hatred of men was revealed.

The accused turned out to be the same Emile Henry who had been suspected of setting the earlier bomb in the office of the Mines de Carmaux which had ultimately killed the five policemen. Already charged for murder in the Café Terminus, he now claimed credit for the other deaths as well, although no proof could be found. He stated that he had bombed the Café Terminus to avenge Vaillant and with full intention to kill "as many as possible. I counted on fifteen dead and twenty wounded." In fact, police had found in his room enough equipment to make twelve or fifteen bombs. In his cold passion, intellectual pride and contempt for the common man, Henry seemed the "St. Just of Anarchism." A brilliant student who had been admitted to the arcane Ecole Polytechnique and had been expelled for insulting a professor, he had been left to occupy his mind as a draper's clerk at 120 francs a month. At twenty-two he was, along with Berkman, the best educated and best acquainted with Anarchist theory of all the assassins, and of them all, the most explicit.

In prison he wrote a long, closely reasoned account of his experience of the cynicism and injustice of bourgeois society, of his "too great respect for individual initiative" to permit him to join the herd-like Socialists, and of his approach to Anarchism. He showed himself thoroughly familiar with its doctrines and with the writings of Kropotkin, Reclus, Grave, Faure and others, although he affirmed that Anarchists were not "blind believers" who swallowed whole any or all the ideas of the theorists.

But it was when he explained his choice of the Café Terminus that he suddenly set himself apart. There, he said, come "all those who are satisfied with the established order, all the accomplices and employees of Property and the State, . . . all that mass of good little bourgeois who make 300 to 500 francs a month, who are more reactionary than their masters, who hate the poor and range themselves on the side of the strong. These are the clientele of the Terminus and the big cafés of its kind. Now you know why I struck where I did."

In court, when reproached by the judge for endangering innocent lives, he replied with icy hauteur, in words that should have been blazoned on some Anarchist banner, "There are no innocent bourgeois."

As for the Anarchist leaders, he said, who "dissociate themselves from the propaganda of the deed," like Kropotkin and Malatesta in the case of Ravachol, and "who try to make a subtle distinction between theorists and terrorists, they are cowards. . . . We who hand out death know how to take it. . . . Mine is not the last head you will cut off. You have hung in Chicago, beheaded in Germany, garroted at Jerez, shot in Barcelona, guillotined in Paris, but there is one thing you cannot destroy: Anarchism. . . . It is in violent revolt against the established order. It will finish by killing you."

Henry himself took death staunchly. Even the caustic Clemenceau, who witnessed the execution on May 21, 1894, was moved and disturbed. He saw Henry "with the face of a tormented Christ, terribly pale, implacable in expression, trying to impose his intellectual pride upon his child's body." The condemned man walked quickly, despite his shackles, up the steps of the scaffold, glanced around and called out in a raucous strangled cry, *"Courage, Camarades! Vive l'anarchie!"* Society's answer to Henry seemed to Clemenceau at that moment "an act of savagery."

Almost without pause fell the next blow, the last in the French series and the most important in its victim, although the least in its assassin. In Lyons on June 24, 1894, during a visit to the Exposition in that city, President Sadi Carnot was stabbed to death by a young Italian workman with the cry, *"Vive la révolution! Vive l'anarchie!"* The President was driving in an open carriage through crowds that lined the streets, and had given orders to his escort to let people approach if they wanted to. When a young man holding a rolled-up newspaper thrust himself forward from the front row, the guards did not stop him, thinking the newspaper contained a bouquet of flowers for the President. Instead it contained a dagger and, with a terrible blow, the young man plunged it six inches into the President's abdomen. Carnot died within three hours. His wife next day received a letter mailed before the attack and addressed to the "Widow Carnot" which enclosed a photograph of Ravachol inscribed, "He is avenged."

The assassin was a baker's apprentice, not yet twenty-one, named Santo Caserio. Born in Italy, he had become acquainted with Anarchist groups in Milan, the home of political turbulence. At eighteen he was sentenced for distributing Anarchist tracts to soldiers. Following the drift of other restless and troublesome characters, he went to Switzerland and then to Cette in the south of France, where he found work and a local group of Anarchists which went by the name "Les Coeurs de Chêne" ("Hearts of Oak"). He was brooding over Vaillant's case and the refusal of the President to give a reprieve when he read in the newspapers of the President's forthcoming visit to Lyons. Caserio decided at once to do a "great deed." He asked for a holiday from his job and for twenty francs that were due him, and with the money, bought a dagger and took the train for Lyons. There he followed the crowds until he met his opportunity.

Afterwards, in the hands of his captors and in court he was docile, smiling and calm. His wan and rather common but gentle face looked to one journalist like "the white mask of a floured Pierrot illuminated by two bright little blue eyes, obstinately fixed. His lip was ornamented by a poor little shadow of a moustache which seemed to have sprouted almost apologetically." During his interrogation and trial he remained altogether placid and talked quite rationally about Anarchist principles, by which he appeared obsessed. He described his act as a deliberate "propaganda of the deed." His only show of emotion was at mention of his mother, to whom he was greatly attached and to whom he had been writing letters regularly when away from home. When the gaoler came to wake him on August 15, the day of execution, he wept for a moment and then made no further sound on the way to the guillotine. Just as his neck was placed on the block he murmured a few words which were interpreted by some as the traditional *"Vive l'anarchie!"* and by others as *"A voeni nen,"* meaning, in the Lombard dialect, "I don't want to."

When Anarchism slew the very chief of State, it reached a climax in France after which, suddenly, face to face with political realities and the facts of life in the labour movement, it retreated. At first, however, it looked as if the Anarchists would be handed a magnificent opportunity for either propaganda or martyrdom. Charging to the offensive, the Government on August 6 staged a mass trial of thirty of the best known Anarchists in an effort to prove conspiracy between theorists and terrorists. As the known terrorists had already been executed, the only examples the Government could produce were three minor characters of the "burglar" type, none of them Ravachols. Of the leaders, Elisée Reclus had left the country, but his nephew Paul Reclus, Jean Grave, Sebastien Faure and others were in the dock. In the absence of a party or corporate body as defendant, the prosecution was in a difficulty similar to having no *corpus delicti*. Nevertheless it accused what it called the "sect" of aiming at the destruction of the State through propaganda that encouraged theft, pillage, arson and murder "in which each member of the sect cooperates according to his temperament and facilities." In dread perhaps of the irresistible oratory of Faure, the prosecution did all the talking, hardly allowing the defendants to open their mouths and regretting it when they did. Addressing Felix Fenéon, the art critic and first champion of the Impressionists, who was one of the defendants, the presiding judge said, "You were seen talking with an Anarchist behind a lamppost."

"Can you tell me, Your Honor," replied Fenéon, "where is 'behind a lamppost'?"

In the absence of evidence connecting the accused with the deeds, the jury was not impressed and acquitted everyone except the three burglars, who were given prison terms. Once again French common sense had reasserted itself.

The jury's sensible verdict deprived Anarchism of a *cause célèbre*, but a greater reason for the decline that followed was that the French working class was too realistic to be drawn into a movement suffering from self-inflicted impotence. The sterility of deeds of terror was already beginning to be recognized by leaders like Kropotkin, Malatesta, Reclus and even Johann Most. Searching for other means of bringing down the State, they were always tripped up by the inherent paradox: Revolution demands organization, discipline and Authority; Anarchism disallows them. The futility of their position was beginning to make itself felt.

Banished from the meeting of the Socialist Second International in London in 1896, because of their refusal to subscribe to the necessity of political action, Anarchist groups called a Congress of their own in Paris in 1900. They made efforts to arrive at a formula of union which the comrades could accept, but every proposal foundered against the stubborn devotion to singleness of Jean Grave. A second attempt in a Congress at Amsterdam in 1907 produced a short-lived International Bureau which, for lack of support, soon withered and ceased to function.

Yet in the end there was a kind of tragic sense in the Anarchist rejection of Authority. For, as the Jesuit-educated Sebastien Faure said in a moment of cold realism, "Every revolution ends in the reappearance of a new ruling class."

Realists of another kind during these years began to come to terms with the labour movement. It was the eight-hour day that the French working class wanted, not bombs in parliament or murdered presidents. But it was the Anarchist propaganda of the Deed that woke them to recognition of what they wanted and the necessity of fighting for it. That was why Ravachol, whom they understood, became a popular hero and songs were sung about him in the streets. Ever since the massacres of the Commune, the French proletariat had been prostrate; it was the Anarchist assaults that brought them to their feet. They sensed that their strength lay in collective action, and in 1895, only a year after the last of the *attentats,* there was formed the Confédération Générale de Travail (CGT), France's federation of labour.

Upon the Anarchists, frustrated by their own inherent paradox, it exerted a strong pull. One by one they drifted into the trade unions, bringing with them as much of their doctrine as could be applied. This merger of Anarchist theory and trade-union practice took the form known as Syndicalism, derived from *syndicat,* the French word for trade union. In this altered form, though extremists of the "pure" kind like Jean Grave shunned it, French Anarchism developed during the years 1895–1914.

Its dogma was direct action through the general strike and its new prophet was Georges Sorel. Under his banner the general strike was to replace propaganda of the deed. The overthrow of capitalism, Sorel argued, could only be accomplished when the working class developed a will to power. The use of violence was to be the means of fostering and training the revolutionary will. The Syndicalists continued to abhor the State or anyone willing, like the Socialists, to cooperate with it, and they had no more use than their Anarchist predecessors for half-way reformist measures. The strike was all, the general strike and nothing but the strike. They retained the sinews of the old movement; but something of its soul, its mad marvelous independence, was gone.

In Spain the cycle had far from run its course. On June 7, 1896, during the festival of Corpus Christi in Barcelona, a bomb was thrown into the midst of a religious procession as it was entering the church door led by the Bishop and the Commanding General of Barcelona. The two representatives of the Church and the Army at whom the bombs were aimed escaped injury, but eleven others were killed and forty wounded amid scenes of blood and terror comparable to the slaughter in the Opera House three years before. The Anarchists succeeded in thoroughly frightening the country, if not its Premier, Antonio Canovas del Castillo, who was not a man to tremble.

Recalled in 1895 for his fifth term as Prime Minister, Canovas was a man of "humble origin," as the phrase then was, who had risen—through engineering, journalism, diplomacy and election to the Cortes—to the top post of the Conservative Party. He had been the political arm of the restoration of the crown in 1874. In addition to practicing politics, he wrote poetry, literary criticism, a life of Calderón, a ten-volume history of Spain, and was President of the Royal Academy of History. He collected paintings, rare china, old coins and walking sticks, lived in a sumptuous palace in Madrid, dressed always in black and, like Frick, never allowed jewels "to obtrude their vulgarity" upon his person. Whether considered a man of reaction by the republicans or the ablest statesman of his time by others, he was acknowledged to be the only man who could hold the Conservative Party together and hold Cuba for Spain. Although he had formulated a plan for Cuban autonomy, he had also sent out General Weyler to quell the *insurrectos*, and already a firm hand and stern measures, in contrast to that of his Liberal predecessors, were taking effect. Against the Anarchists Canovas had no compunctions about proceeding ruthlessly.

With his sanction the mass arrests began again. Over four hundred persons were imprisoned, the Government as usual seizing the pretext to proceed against any or all enemies of the regime, whether Anarchists, anti-Clericals, or Catalan Republicans. The cries of agony from Montjuich were heard again, followed by the fearsome report that the Attorney-General would ask the death penalty for no less than twenty-eight out of eighty-four accused persons who were to be tried by court-martial. This was under a law passed by the Cortes after the Opera House explosion, making all crimes committed with explosives subject to court-martial and providing the death penalty for the guilty. Life imprisonment was decreed for those guilty of advocating violence through speeches, articles or pictures. The trial took place behind the stone curtain of Montjuich with only military personnel permitted to be present. Only the sentences were announced: eight condemned to die, of whom four were reprieved and four executed. Seventy-six were sentenced to prison terms ranging from eight to nineteen years, of whom sixty-one were sent to the penal colony of Rio de Oro, the Spanish Devil's Island.

At the same time the outside world learned from a firsthand report of the tortures inflicted at Montjuich upon the prisoners of 1893. Tarrida del Marmol, member of a leading Catalan family and director of the Polytechnic Academy of Barcelona, had, because of his liberal opinions, been caught up in the arrests, and his account, published in Paris in 1897 under the title *Les Inquisiteurs de l'Espagne*, aroused horrified protests. It included a posthumous cry for help in the form of a letter from a fellow prisoner, written before his execution and addressed to "All good men on earth." It told how he had been taken at night from his cell to a cliff over the sea where the guards loaded their guns and threatened to shoot him unless he said everything the lieutenant told him to say. When he refused, his genital organs were twisted and later, back in prison, this torture was repeated while he was hung from the door of his cell for ten hours. He was also subjected to the enforced walking for a period of five days. "Finally I declared everything they wanted and in my weakness and cowardice signed my declaration."

Some time later, in August, 1897, Premier Canovas went for a summer holiday to Santa Agueda, a spa in the Basque mountains. During tranquil days there, he noticed a fair-haired well-mannered fellow guest at the hotel who spoke Spanish with an Italian accent and several times saluted him politely. Canovas was moved to ask his secretary if he knew who the strange young man was and found he was registered as correspondent from the Italian newspaper *Il Popolo*. One morning as the Premier was sitting with his wife on the terrace reading his newspaper, the young Italian suddenly appeared, pulled a revolver from his pocket, and at three yards' distance fired three shots into Canovas' body, killing him instantly, Mme Canovas, in a passion of rage and grief, flew at the man still holding the revolver and struck him in the face with her fan, crying, "Murderer! Assassin!"

"I am not an assassin," replied the Italian sternly. "I am the Avenger of my Anarchist comrades. I have nothing to do with you, Madame."

Upon arrest and examination, his real name proved to be Michel Angiollilo. When in the Italian Army, he had served three terms in the disciplinary battalion for insubordination. On release from the Army he became a printer, a trade with an affinity for Anarchism, either because the Anarchist seeks contact with the printed word or because contact with the printed word leads to Anarchism. In any case Angiollilo was shortly sentenced to eighteen months in prison for printing subversive literature. In 1895, following a futile attempt, along with some Italian Anarchist comrades, to set up a clandestine press in Marseilles, he went to Barcelona and left after the Corpus Christi explosion. He drifted to Belgium and then London, where he bought a revolver with the intention of killing the Spanish Premier for "ordering the mass torture and execution of Anarchists." He returned to Spain, stalked Canovas in Madrid but failed to find his opportunity, followed him to Santa Agueda and found it there. Tried by court-martial a week later, he attempted to expound his Anarchist principles, and when silenced by the Court, shouted, "I must justify myself!" but was not allowed to speak. At his execution by the garrote he refused religious rites and maintained an unbroken sangfroid.

The European press erupted in agitated demand for a concerted effort to suppress the "mad dogs" of Anarchism. There was a sense that the loss of a man of Canovas' stature could be grave for Spain if not, as the *Nation* of New York predicted, a "national disaster." In fact, his death proved to be one of those accidents that give a decisive jerk to the course of events. With Canovas gone, the Liberals succeeded in taking office and soon retreated before the wild howls of Hearst-engendered indignation against "Butcher" Weyler then reverberating from the United States. General Weyler was relieved just when he was close to restoring order and the Cuban insurrection flared up again, providing the imperialists in the United States with the excuse for the most deliberately manufactured war of the century. Had Canovas lived, the excuse might not have been available.

For his death there was a reason; for two of the three that followed within the next three years there was none whatever. They were the product partly of Anarchist propaganda, which supplied the suggestion, but even more of public excitement over Anarchist deeds, which gave assassins promise of heroic notoriety and acted as an intoxicant to unsound minds.

The first death took place by dagger on September 10, 1898, alongside the lake steamer at the Quai Mont Blanc in Geneva. Here met, in mortal junction, as meaningless as when a stroke of lightning kills a child, two persons so unconnected, so far apart in the real world, that their lives could never have touched except in a demented moment. One was the Empress Elizabeth of Austria, wife of the Emperor Franz Joseph, the other Luigi Lucheni, a vagrant Italian workman.

The most beautiful and the most melancholy royal personage in Europe, married and crowned at sixteen, Elizabeth was still, at sixty-one, forever moving restlessly from one place to another in endless escape from an unquiet soul. Renowned for her loveliness, her golden-brown hair a yard long, her slender elegance and floating walk, her sparkling moods when she was the "incarnation of charm," she suffered also from "court-ball headaches," and could not appear in public without holding a fan before her face. She was "a fairies' child," wrote Carmen Sylva, the Queen of Rumania, "with hidden wings, who flies away whenever she finds the world unbearable." She wrote sad romantic poetry and had seen her son's life end in the most melodramatic suicide of the century. Her first cousin, King Ludwig of Bavaria, had died insane by drowning; her husband's brother, Maximilian, by firing squad in Mexico; her sister by fire at a charity bazaar in Paris. "I feel the burden of life so heavily," she wrote her daughter, "that it is often like a physical pain and I would far rather be dead." She would rush off to England or Ireland to spend weeks in the hunting field riding recklessly over the most breakneck fences. In Vienna she took lessons in the most dangerous tricks of circus riding. At times she adopted frenetic diets, reducing her nourishment to an orange or a glass of milk a day, and when her health could no longer sustain hunting, she indulged in orgies of walking for six or eight hours at a time at a forced pace no companion could keep up with. What she was seeking was plain: "I long for death," she wrote her daughter four months before she reached Geneva.

On September 9 she visited the lakeside villa of the Baroness Adolfe de Rothschild, a remote, enchanted world where tame miniature porcupines from Java and exotic colored birds decorated a private park planted with cedars of Lebanon. As she left her hotel next morning to take the lake steamer, the Italian, Lucheni, was waiting outside on the street.

He had come from Lausanne, where he recently had been reported to the police as a suspicious character. The orderly of a hospital where he had been taken for an injury suffered during a building job had found among his belongings a notebook containing Anarchist songs and the drawing of a bludgeon labeled *"Anarchia"* and underneath, in Italian, "For Humbert I." Accustomed to misfits, radicals and exiles of all kinds, the Swiss police had not considered this sufficient cause for arrest or surveillance.

According to what he told the hospital orderly, Lucheni's mother, pregnant at eighteen with an illegitimate child, had made her way to Paris to give birth among the anonymous millions of a great city. Later she was able to return to Italy, where she left her child in the poorhouse in Parma and disappeared to America.

At nine the boy was a day laborer on an Italian railroad. Later when drafted into a cavalry regiment of the Italian Army, he made a good record and was promoted to corporal. Upon his discharge in 1897, having neither savings nor prospects, he became manservant to his former Captain, the Prince d'Aragona, but on being denied a raise, left in anger. Later he asked to come back, but the Prince, considering him too insubordinate for domestic service, refused. Resentful and jobless, Lucheni took to reading *L'Agitatore*, *Il Socialista*, *Avanti* and other revolutionary papers and pamphlets whose theme at the moment was the rottenness of bourgeois society as demonstrated by the Dreyfus case. A single Samson, they indicated, could bring down the State at a blow. Lucheni, now in Lausanne, sent clippings from these papers with his comments to comrades in his former cavalry regiment. Apropos of a workman killed in a quarrel, he remarked to a friend at this time, "Ah, how I'd like to kill somebody. But it must be someone important so it gets into the papers." He attended meetings of Italian Anarchists who fiercely discussed plans to shake the world by a great deed, of which the favored victim was to be King Humbert of Italy.

Meanwhile the Swiss papers reported the coming visit of the Empress Elizabeth to Geneva. Lucheni tried to buy a stiletto but lacked the necessary 12 francs. In its place he fashioned a homemade dagger out of an old file, carefully sharpened and fitted to a handle made from a piece of firewood. As the Empress and her lady-in-waiting, Countess Sztaray, walked toward the Quai Mont Blanc, Lucheni stood in their path. He rushed upon them with hand upraised, stopped and peered beneath her parasol to make sure of the Empress' identity, then stabbed her through the heart. She died four hours later. Lucheni, seized by two gendarmes, was caught in his great moment by an alert passer-by with a camera. The picture shows him walking jauntily between his captors with a satisfied smile, almost a smirk, on his face. At the police station he eagerly described all his proceedings and preparations and when later it was learned that the Empress had died, expressed himself as "delighted." He declared himself an Anarchist and insisted on its being understood that he had acted on his own initiative and not as a member of any group or party. Asked why he had killed the Empress, he replied, "As part of the war on the rich and the great. . . . It will be Humbert's turn next."

From prison he wrote letters to the President of Switzerland and to the newspapers proclaiming his creed and the coming downfall of the State, and signing himself, "Luigi Lucheni, Anarchist, and one of the most dangerous of them." To the Princess d'Aragona he wrote, "My case is comparable to the Dreyfus case." Yet behind the poor foolish megalomania, even in Lucheni, glowed the Idea, for he also wrote to the Princess that he had learned enough of the world during his twenty-five years in it to feel that "never in my life have I felt so contented as now. . . . I have made known to the world that the hour is not far distant when a new sun will shine upon all men alike."

There being no death penalty in Geneva, Lucheni was sentenced to life imprisonment. Twelve years later, after a quarrel with the warder which resulted in his being given a term of solitary confinement, he hanged himself by his belt.

In the month following the Empress' death, the Kaiser, Wilhelm II, in the course of a widely heralded royal progress to Jerusalem, was the most conspicuous ruler of the moment. Police rounded up all known Anarchists along the route and international excitement reached a peak when an Italian Anarchist was arrested in Alexandria in possession of two bombs, a ticket for Haifa and obviously murderous intent upon the Kaiser. That sovereign had little to fear, however, from the Anarchists of his own country, for the two who had attempted to kill his grandfather were the last and only activists. Otherwise, German Anarchists remained theorists, except for those who got away to America. Germans were not fit for Anarchism, as Bakunin had said with disdain, for with their passion for Authority, "they want to be at once both masters and slaves and Anarchism accepts neither."

The assassins of the President of France, the Premier of Spain, and the Empress of Austria, as well as the would-be assassins of the Kaiser, had all been Italians. Inside Italy itself, in 1897, an Anarchist blacksmith named Pietro Acciarito had attempted to kill King Humbert, leaping upon him in his carriage with a dagger in the identical manner of Caserio upon President Carnot. More alert than Carnot to these occupational hazards, the King jumped aside, escaped the blow, and remarking with a shrug to his escort, *"Sono gli incerti del mestiere"* ("These are the risks of the job"), ordered his coachman to drive on. Acciarito told the police that he would have preferred to have "stuck that old monkey" Pope Leo XIII, but that as he could not get inside the Vatican, he chose to attack the monarchy as the next evil after the papacy.

The hatred for constituted society that seethed in the lower classes and the helplessness of society to defend itself against these attacks was becoming more and more apparent. As usual, the police, in wishful hunt for a "plot," arrested half a dozen alleged accomplices of Acciarito, none of whom in the end could be proved to have had any connection with him. Plots by groups or parties could be dealt with; there were always informers. But how could the sudden spring of these solitary tigers be prevented?

So serious was the problem that the Italian Government convened an international conference of police and home ministry officials in Rome in November, 1898, to try to work out a solution. Secret sessions lasted for a month with no known result except the admirable if negative one that Belgium, Switzerland and Great Britain refused to give up the traditional right of asylum or agree to surrender suspected Anarchists upon demand of their native countries.

In the following year, 1899, there were bread riots in Italy, caused by taxes and an import duty on grain, which the Anarchists saw as another aspect of the war on the poor by the State. The riots spread north and south despite repressive measures and bloody collision between troops and people. In Milan, streetcars were overturned to make barricades, people hurled stones at police armed with guns, women threw themselves in front of trains to prevent the arrival of troops, a state of siege was declared, and all Tuscany put under martial law. The cry that at last the revolution had come brought thousands of Italian workmen back from Spain, Switzerland and the south of France to take part. Control was only regained by the dispatch of half an army corps to Milan. All Socialist and revolutionary papers were suppressed, parliament was prorogued, and although the Government succeeded in re-establishing order, it was only on the surface.

The inoffensive monarch who found himself presiding over this situation had a fierce white moustache, personal courage, a gallant soul and no more noticeable talent for kingship than any of the House of Savoy.

Humbert was passionately fond of horses and hunting, totally impervious to the arts, which he left to the patronage of his Queen, and very regular in his habits. He rose at six every morning, attended to the management of his private estates (whose revenues were large and deposited in the Bank of England), visited his stables and drove out in his carriage every afternoon at the same hour over the same route through the Borghese Gardens. Every evening at the same hour he visited a lady to whom he had remained devotedly faithful since before his marriage thirty years earlier. On July 29, 1900, he was distributing prizes from his carriage to athletic competitors in Monza, the royal summer residence near Milan, when he was shot four times by a man who stepped up to the carriage and fired at hardly two yards' distance. The King gazed at him reproachfully for a moment, then fell over against the shoulder of his aide-de-camp, murmured "*Avanti!*" to his coachman and expired.

The assassin, "holding his smoking weapon exultantly aloft," was immediately seized. He was identified as Gaetano Bresci, a thirty-year-old Anarchist and silk-weaver who had come from Paterson, New Jersey, to Italy with intent to assassinate the King. His act was the only instance of Anarchist propaganda of the deed for which there is some evidence, though unproven, of previous conspiracy.

Paterson was a center of Italians and of Anarchism. Certainly the Anarchists of Paterson held many meetings and heatedly discussed a Deed which would be the signal for overthrow of the oppressor. Certainly the King of Italy figured as their preferred target, but whether, as charged in reports after the event, lots were actually chosen to select the person to do the deed, or whether the discussions simply inspired Bresci to act of his own accord, is not certain. The picture of a cabal of Anarchists in a cellar drawing lots to select an assassin was a favorite journalistic imagery of the time.

One imaginative reporter pictured Bresci as having been "indoctrinated" by Malatesta, "the head and moving spirit of all the conspiracies which have recently startled the world by their awful success." He claimed that Malatesta had been glimpsed quietly drinking at an Italian bar in Paterson, but the police found no evidence that Bresci had ever met Malatesta. He had, however, either obtained or been given a revolver in Paterson with which he practiced shooting in the woods while his wife and three-year-old daughter picked flowers nearby. Also, he was given by his comrades, or somehow obtained, money to buy a steerage ticket on the French Line with enough left over to make his way from Le Havre to Italy.

"He was not insane enough to expect that the change of Government would follow his act," explained Pedro Esteve, editor of the Paterson Anarchist journal, to a reporter. "But how else could he let the people of Italy know that there was any such force in the world as Anarchy?" An amiable and scholarly person whose bookshelves held the works of Emerson next to those of Jean Grave, Esteve accepted as quite reasonable that one of his own readers should go out and express the protest of the masses in a magnificent gesture.

Bresci's comrades sent him a congratulatory telegram in prison and wore his picture on buttons in their coat lapels. They also insisted at a mass meeting in Paterson, attended by over a thousand persons, that there had been no plot. "We don't need to make plots or talk," said Esteve, who was the principal speaker. "If you are an Anarchist you know what to do and you do it individually and of your own accord."

Bresci himself suffered the same fate as other instruments of the Idea. As Italy had abolished the death penalty, he was sentenced to life imprisonment, the first seven years to be spent in solitary confinement. After the first few months he killed himself in prison.

In the United States the newspaper account of King Humbert's assassination was read over and over again by a Polish-American named Leon Czolgosz. The clipping became a precious possession which he took to bed with him every night. Twenty-eight at this time, he was small and slight, with a peculiar fixed gaze in his light-blue eyes. Born in the United States shortly after his parents came to America, he was one of six brothers and two sisters, and lived with his family on a small farm in Ohio. According to his father, he had "the appearance of thinking more than most children," and because of his fondness for reading, was considered the intellectual of the family. In 1893, when he was twenty years old, he had been laid off during a strike in the wire factory where he worked, and afterward, according to his brother, "he got quiet and not so happy." Prayer and the local priest having proved ineffective, he broke away from the Catholic Church, took to reading pamphlets issued by "Free Thinkers" and through these became interested in political radicalism. He joined a Polish workers' circle where Socialism and Anarchism were among the topics discussed, and also, as he said later, "we discussed Presidents and that they were no good."

In 1898 he suffered some undefined illness which left him moody and dull. He gave up work, stayed home, took his meals upstairs to his bedroom, kept to himself, read the Chicago Anarchist paper *Free Society* and Bellamy's utopia, *Looking Backward*, and brooded. He made trips to

Chicago and Cleveland, where he attended Anarchist meetings, heard speeches by Emma Goldman and had talks with an Anarchist named Emil Schilling to whom he expressed himself as troubled by the conduct of the American Army, which, after liberating the Philippines from Spain, was now engaged in war upon the Filipinos. "It does not harmonize with the teaching in our public schools about our flag," said Czolgosz worriedly.

As flags were a matter of no respect to Anarchists, Schilling became suspicious of him and published a warning in *Free Society* that the oddly behaved Polish visitor might be an *agent provocateur*. This was on September 1, 1901, and was wide of the mark. Five days later Czolgosz turned up in Buffalo, where, in a receiving line at the Pan-American Exposition, he shot President McKinley. The President died eight days later and was succeeded by Theodore Roosevelt. Thus Czolgosz, on the lowest level of understanding among Anarchist assassins, performed of them all the act with the greatest consequences.

"I killed President McKinley," Czolgosz wrote in his confession, "because I done my duty," and later added, "because he was an enemy of the good working people." He told reporters that he had heard Emma Goldman lecture and her doctrine "that all rulers should be exterminated . . . set me to thinking so that my head nearly split with pain." He said, "McKinley was going around the country shouting prosperity when there was no prosperity for the poor man." And further, "I don't believe we should have any rulers. It is right to kill them. . . . I know other men who believe what I do that it would be a good thing to kill the President and to have no rulers. . . . I don't believe in voting; it is against my principles. I am an Anarchist. I don't believe in marriage. I believe in free love."

The Idea of Anarchism, its vision of a better society, had not come within Czolgosz's ken. Like Caserio, the simple assassin of President Carnot, he was of the type of regicide who becomes obsessed by the delusion that it is his mission to kill the sovereign. This was brought out, shortly after Czolgosz's hurried trial and electrocution on October 29, by Dr. Walter Channing, Professor of Mental Diseases at Tufts, and son of the poet William Ellery Channing. Dissatisfied with the official alienists' report, Channing made his own study and concluded that Czolgosz had been "drifting in the direction of *dementia praecox*" and was a victim of a delusion already isolated and described by a French alienist, Dr. Emanuel Regis, in 1890. According to Dr. Regis, the regicide type is much given to cogitations and solitude and "whatever sane reason he may have possessed gives way to a sickly fixation that he is called on to deal a great blow, sacrifice his life to a just cause and kill a monarch or a dignitary in the name of God, Country, Liberty, Anarchy or some analogous principle." He is characterized by premeditation and obsession. He does not act suddenly or blindly, but on the contrary, prepares carefully and alone. He is a *solitaire*. Proud of his mission and his role, he acts always in daylight and in public, and never uses a secret weapon like poison but one that demands personal violence. Afterwards, he does not seek to escape but exhibits pride in his deed and desire for glory and for death, either by suicide or "indirect suicide" as an executed martyr.

The description fits, but for the delusions to become active there is required a certain climate of protest—and an example. This the Anarchist creed and deeds provided. There may be at any time a hundred Czolgoszes living mute, inactive lives; it took the series of acts from Ravachol to Bresci to inspire one to kill the President of the United States.

The public was by now thoroughly aroused, and the public was composed not only of the rich but of the imitators of the rich. The ordinary man, the petty bourgeois, the salaried employee, associated himself—as Emile Henry knew when he threw his bomb in the Café Terminus—with his employers. His living, as he thought, depended on their property. When this was threatened, he felt threatened. He felt a peculiar horror at the Anarchist's desire to destroy the foundations on which everyday life was based; the flag, the legal family, marriage, the church, the vote, the law. The Anarchist became everybody's enemy. His sinister figure became synonymous with everything wicked and subversive, synonymous, said a professor of political science in *Harper's Weekly,* with "the king of all Anarchists, the arch-rebel Satan." His doctrine, said the *Century Magazine* after the death of McKinley, "bodes more evil to the world than any previous conception of human relations."

The new President, an extraordinarily mixed man equally capable of subtle understanding, courageous action and extremes of banality, saw in the Anarchist simply a criminal, more "dangerous" and "depraved" than the ordinary kind. In his message to Congress on December 3, 1901, Theodore Roosevelt said, "Anarchism is a crime against the whole human race and all mankind should band against the Anarchist." He was not the product of social or political injustice and his protest of concern for the workingman was "outrageous." The institutions of the United States, the President insisted, offered open opportunity "to every honest and intelligent son of toil." He urged that Anarchist speeches, writings and meetings should henceforth be treated as seditious, that Anarchists should no longer be allowed at large, those already in the country should be deported, Congress should "exclude absolutely all persons who are known

to be believers in Anarchistic principles or members of Anarchistic societies," and their advocacy of killing should by treaty be made an offense
against international law, like piracy, so that the federal government would
have the power to deal with them.

After much discussion and not without strong objections to the denial
of the traditional right of ingress, Congress in 1903 amended the Immigration Act to exclude persons disbelieving in or "teaching disbelief in or
opposition to all organized government." The amendment provoked liberal
outcries and sorrowful references to the Statue of Liberty.

Of the dual nature of Anarchism, half hatred of society, half love of
humanity, the public was aware only of the first. It was the bombs and
explosions, the gunshots and the daggers, that impressed them. They knew
nothing of the other side of Anarchism which hoped to lead humanity
through the slough of violence to the Delectable Mountains. The press
showed them Malatesta, for instance, as the evil genius of Anarchism,
"silent, cold, plotting." It did not show him as the man whose philosophy
of altruism caused him to deed two houses he inherited from his parents
in Italy to the tenants inhabiting them. Since the public likewise knew nothing of the theory of propaganda by the deed, it could make no sense of
the Anarchist acts. They seemed purposeless, mad, a pure indulgence in
evil for its own sake. The press customarily referred to Anarchists as "wild
beasts," "crypto-lunatics," degenerates, criminals, cowards, felons, "odious
fanatics prompted by perverted intellect and morbid frenzy." "The mad dog
is the closest parallel in nature to the Anarchist," pronounced *Blackwood's*,
the dignified British monthly. How was it possible, asked Carl Schurz
after the murder of Canovas, to protect society against "a combination
of crazy people and criminals"?

That was the unanswerable question. All sorts of proposals were put
forward, including the establishment of an international penal colony for
Anarchists, or disposal of them in hospitals for the insane, or universal
deportation, although it was not explained what country would receive
them if every country was engaged in sending them away.

Yet the cry of protest in the throat of every Anarchist act was heard
by some, and understood. In the midst of the hysteria over McKinley,
Lyman Abbott, editor of the *Outlook* and a spokesman of the New
England tradition which had produced the Abolitionists, had the courage
to ask if the Anarchist's hatred of government and law did not derive
from the fact that government and law operated unjustly. So long, he said,
as legislators legislate for special classes, "encourage the spoliation of

the many for the benefit of the few, protect the rich and forget the poor," so long will Anarchism "demand the abolition of all law because it sees in law only an instrument of injustice." Speaking to the comfortable gentlemen of the Nineteenth Century Club, he suggested that "the place to attack Anarchism is where the offenses grow." He was echoing a concern that was already expressing itself in movements of reform, in Jane Addams and the social welfare work she inspired from Hull House, in the Muckrakers who within a year or two were to begin exposing the areas of injustice, rottenness and corruption in American life.

With McKinley the era of Anarchist assassinations came to an end in the western democracies. Even Alexander Berkman in his prison cell recognized, as he wrote to Emma Goldman, the futility of individual acts of violence in the absence of a revolutionary-minded proletariat. This second disavowal sent his correspondent, who still believed, into "uncontrollable sobbing," and left her "shaken to the roots," so that she took to her bed, ill. Although she retained an ardent following, especially among the press, who referred to her as the "Queen of the Anarchists," Anarchist passion on the whole passed, as it had in France, into the more realistic combat of the Syndicalist unions. In the United States it was absorbed into the Industrial Workers of the World, founded in 1905, although in every country there remained irreconcilables who stayed lonely and true to the original creed.

In the two countries on Europe's rim, Spain and Russia, each industrially backward and despotically governed, bombs and assassinations mounted as the world moved into the Twentieth Century. When in Spain a bomb was thrown at King Alfonso and his young English bride on their wedding day in 1906, killing twenty bystanders, it spread a fearful recognition of the deep reservoir of hatred which could have impelled such a deed. The reciprocal hatred of the ruling class was confirmed in 1909, when as a result of an abortive revolt in Barcelona known as "Red Week," the Government executed Francisco Ferrer, a radical and anticlerical educator, though not a true Anarchist. The case raised storms of protest in the rest of Europe, where, as usual, Spanish iniquities provided a vent for liberal consciences. In 1912 a Spanish Anarchist named Manuel Pardinas stalked the Premier, José Canalejas, through the streets of Madrid and shot him dead from behind as he was looking into the window of a bookstore in the Puerta del Sol. It was a poor choice, for Canalejas, carried into office in the wake of Ferrer's death, was attempting some reforms of the unbridled power of Church and landlords, but it was evidence that in their continuing combat against society, Spanish Anarchists were moved, as Shaw wrote, by "consciences outraged beyond endurance."

In Russia the tradition of revolution was old and deep and as full of despair as of hope. Each generation turned up new fighters in the long war between rebel and despot. In 1887, the year the Haymarket Anarchists were hanged, five students of the University of St. Petersburg were hanged for the attempted murder by bomb of Alexander III. Their leader, Alexander Ulyanov, justified the use of terror at his trial as the only method possible in a police state. He was one of three brothers and three sisters, all revolutionaries, of whom a younger brother, Vladimir Ilyich, swore revenge, changed his last name to Lenin, and went forth to work for revolution.

Increasing unrest during the nineties encouraged the revolutionists to believe that the time was ripening for insurrection. A new Czar who was that most dangerous of rulers, a weak autocrat, marked his accession as Nicholas II in 1895 by flatly dismissing all pleas for a constitution as "nonsensical dreams," thereby causing democrats to despair and extremists to exult. In the cities, strikes by newly industrialized workers followed one upon another. Over all, exerting a mysterious intangible pull, like the moon upon the tides, loomed the approaching moment of the end of the century. There was a sense of an end and a beginning, of "a time to break."

All the groups of discontent felt the need to prepare for a time of action, to gather their strength in parties and to state their program. But there was conflict between the followers of Marxism, with its hard-bitten insistence on organization and training, and the inheritors of the Narodniki tradition, who believed in spontaneous revolution brought on by some deed of terror. As a result, two parties took shape in the years 1897 and 1898, the Marxist Social-Democratic party on the one hand, and on the other, the Populist Socialist-Revolutionaries, whose various groups merged into a definitive party in 1901.

In so far as they accepted organization as a party, the Socialist-Revolutionaries were not Anarchists of the true breed, but they shared the Anarchists' belief that deeds of terror could precipitate revolution. Like them they saw revolution as a sunburst on the horizon under whose benevolent beams the future would take care of itself. The public's identification of Anarchists with Russians stemmed partly from their addiction to the bomb, which, ever since the killing of the Czar in 1881, seemed peculiarly a Russian weapon, and partly from the unconscious syllogism: Russians were revolutionists; Anarchists were revolutionists; ergo, Anarchists were Russians. Orthodox Anarchists, of whom there were small groups who published Russian-language journals in Geneva and Paris, and took their inspiration from Kropotkin, were not a significant force inside Russia.

In 1902 Maxim Gorky put into *The Lower Depths* all the woe, the wretchedness and the despair of Russia. "Man must live for something better!" cries the drunken cardsharp in the play, "something better," and searching for words, for meaning, for a philosophy, he can only repeat, "something better." Toward that end, in the years 1901–03 the Terror Brigade of the Socialist-Revolutionaries assassinated the Minister of Education, Bogolepov; the Minister of Interior, Sipiagin, who directed the Secret Police; and the Governor of Ufa, Bogdanovitch, who had put down a miners' strike in the Urals with particular brutality. On July 15, 1904, in the midst of the Russo-Japanese War, they disposed of a second Minister of Interior, Wenzel von Plehve, the most hated man in Russia. An ultra-reactionary, Plehve was if anything even firmer than the Czar in the belief that autocracy must be kept unimpaired by the slightest concession to democratic processes. His sole policy was to smash every possible source of antipathy to the regime. He arrested revolutionaries, suppressed the orthodox "old believers," restricted the *zemstvos*, or village governments, victimized the Jews, forcibly Russified the Poles, Finns and Armenians and, as a result, increased the enemies of Czarism, and convinced them of the need for a final change.

A method he favored for diverting popular discontent was expressed to a colleague in the words, "We must drown the revolution in Jewish blood." Stirred up by his agents, watched tolerantly by the police, Russian citizens of Kishinev during the Passover of 1903 burst into a frenzy of violence against the eternal scapegoat, killing and beating, burning and plundering homes and shops, desecrating synagogues, tearing the sacred Torah from the arms of a white-bearded rabbi whose horror at seeing it defiled by Gentiles was shortened by his death under their clubs and boots. The Kishinev pogrom not only resounded around the world but succeeded in penetrating under the skin of the leader of the Terror Brigade, Evno Azev, who was at the same time an agent of the Secret Police and also happened to be a Jew. Azev took care not to inform on the plan for the assassination of Plehve which duly took place. It made an enormous impression upon everyone in Russia as a terrible blow against the system of which Plehve was the incarnation. So ominous did it seem that the assassin was condemned to hard labour in Siberia for life instead of to death by Plehve's successor, Prince Svyatopolk-Mirsky, in the hope that a mild policy might accomplish something.

Six months later, in January, 1905, occurred the massacre in front of the Winter Palace known as "Bloody Sunday," when troops fired on a crowd of workingmen who had come to petition the Czar for a constitution. About one thousand were killed. The terrorists now made plans to assassinate the Czar and his uncles, the Grand Duke Vladimir, who was held responsible for the massacre, and the Grand Duke Sergei, who was said to be the person with the greatest influence on the Czar. As Governor-General of Moscow, Sergei was known for the merciless brutality of his rule, for a capricious and domineering character and extremes of autocratic temperament bordering on derangement. According to an English observer, he was "conspicuous for his cruelty and renowned, even among the Russian aristocracy, for the peculiarity of his vices." Although in the pay of the police, Azev had to allow the Brigade enough successes to satisfy them and to maintain his position as their chief, without which he would have been of far less value to the police. In February, 1905, Sergei was blown up with a bomb thrown by a young revolutionary named Kaliaev who was left standing alive in the midst of the debris, in his old blue coat with a red scarf, his face bleeding, but otherwise unhurt. All that was left of the Grand Duke and of his carriage and horses was "a formless mass of fragments about eight or ten inches high." That evening when the Czar heard the news he came down to dinner as usual and did not mention the murder, but, according to a guest who was present, "after dinner the Czar and his brother-in-law amused themselves by trying to edge one another off the long narrow sofa."

At his trial in April, 1905, Kaliaev, thin, haggard and with eyes sunken in their sockets, said to the judges, "We are two warring camps, . . . two worlds in furious collision. You, the representatives of capital and oppression; I, one of the avengers of the people." Russia was in the midst of war, outside against the Japanese, and inside against her own people, who were in open revolt. "What does all this mean? It is the judgment of history upon you." When sentence of death was pronounced, Kaliaev said he hoped his executioners would have the courage to carry it out openly and publicly. "Learn to look the advancing revolution straight in the eye," he told the Court. But he was hanged, dressed in black, after midnight in the prison yard and buried beneath the prison wall.

In October the Revolution came; propaganda of the deed, in the murders of von Plehve and the Grand Duke Sergei, had helped to excite the nerves of the masses toward the point of insurrection. Neither organized nor led by the Socialist-Revolutionaries, Social-Democrats or Anarchists, it was the spontaneous revolution Bakunin had believed in and did not live to see. In accordance with Syndicalist theory it erupted out of a general strike by the workers, and during the regime's first fright, succeeded in forcing the concession of a constitution and a Duma. Although these were subsequently withdrawn, and the Revolution, when the regime had recovered its nerve, ferociously suppressed, it heartened the Syndicalists' belief in "direct action" through the general strike, and re-enforced the movement of Anarchists into the industrial unions. In Russia the Terror Brigade accomplished several more deaths before it disintegrated under the shock of the exposure of Azev in 1908. By the time the Premier, Stolypin, was assassinated in 1911 the half-lunatic world of the Romanov twilight had so darkened that it was never clear whether the assassins were genuine revolutionaries or *agents provocateurs* of the police.

However self-limited its acts, however visionary its dream, Anarchism had terribly dramatized the war between the two divisions of society, between the world of privilege and the world of protest. In the one it shook awake a social conscience; in the other, as its energy passed into Syndicalism, it added its quality of violence and extremism to the struggle for power of organized labour. It was an idea which drew men to follow it but because of its built-in paradox could not draw them together into a group capable of concerted action. It was the last cry of individual man, the last movement among the masses on behalf of individual liberty, the last hope of living unregulated, the last fist shaken against the encroaching State, before the State, the party, the union, the organization closed in.

3

End of a Dream

THE UNITED STATES:
1890–1902

3

End of a Dream

IN THE United States on the opening of Congress in January, 1890, a
newly elected Speaker of the House of Representatives was in the
Chair. A physical giant, six feet three inches tall, weighing almost
three hundred pounds and dressed completely in black, "out of whose
collar rose an enormous clean-shaven baby face like a Casaba melon
flowering from a fat black stalk, he was a subject for a Frans Hals, with
long white fingers that would have enraptured a Memling." Speaking in a
slow drawl, he delighted to drop cool pearls of sarcasm into the most
heated rhetoric and to watch the resulting fizzle with the bland gravity of
a New England Buddha. When a wordy perennial, Representative
Springer of Illinois, was declaiming to the House his passionate preference
to be right rather than President, the Speaker interjected, "The gentleman
need not be disturbed; he will never be either." When another member, notorious for ill-digested opinions and a halting manner, began some remarks
with, "I was thinking, Mr. Speaker, I was thinking . . ." the Chair expressed
the hope that "no one will interrupt the gentleman's commendable innovation." Of two particularly inept speakers, he remarked, "They never open
their mouths without subtracting from the sum of human knowledge." It
was said that he would rather make an epigram than a friend. Yet among
the select who were his chosen friends he was known as "one of the most
genial souls that ever enlivened a company," whose conversation, "sparkling
with good nature, was better than the best champagne." He was Thomas
B. Reed, Republican of Maine, aged fifty. Already acknowledged after
fourteen years in Congress as "the ablest running debater the American
people ever saw," he would, before the end of the session, be called "the

greatest parliamentary leader of his time, . . . far and away the most brilliant figure in American politics."

Although his roots went back to the beginning of New England, Reed was not nurtured for a political career by inherited wealth, social position or landed estate. Politics in America made no use of these qualities, and men who possessed them were not in politics. Well-to-do, long-established families did not shoulder—but shunned—the responsibilities of government. Henry Adams' eldest brother, John, "regarded as the most brilliant of the family and the most certain of high distinction," who made a fortune in the Union Pacific Railroad, "drew himself back" from government, according to his brother. "He had all he wanted; wealth, children, society, consideration; and he laughed at the idea of sacrificing himself in order to adorn a Cleveland Cabinet or get cheers from an Irish mob." This attitude was not confined to the rather worn-out Adamses. When the young Theodore Roosevelt announced his intention of entering politics in New York in 1880, he was laughed at by the "men of cultivated and easy life" who told him politics were "low" and run by "saloon-keepers, horse-car conductors and the like," whom he would find "rough, brutal and unpleasant to deal with."

The abdication of the rich was born out of the success of the American Revolution and the defeat of Hamilton's design to organize the State in the interests of the governing class. Jefferson's principles and Jackson's democracy had won. The founding fathers and the signers of the Declaration had been in the majority men of property and position, but the very success of their accomplishment ended by discouraging men of their own kind from participating in government. With the establishment of universal manhood suffrage, men of property found themselves counting for no more at the polls than the common man; being far outnumbered they retired from the combat. No President after the first six came from a well-established family (unless the Harrisons could be considered to so qualify). Retreating to the comfort of their homes and the pursuits of their class, they left government increasingly to hard-driving newcomers pushing up from below. Such energies as they had they devoted to making money in banking and trade, rather than from the land which they gradually abandoned. The great estates of the Dutch-descended patroons of New York declined first; the Southern plantations went with the Civil War; Boston's old families remained active and prosperous but on the whole aloof from government. The proud "Hub" had produced no President after the first two Adamses. "The most valuable, most moderate, able and cultivated part of the population," wrote Emerson, in his essay on Politics, "is timid and merely defensive of property."

Forty years later the Englishman James Bryce was struck by the "apathy among the luxurious classes and fastidious minds," and devoted a whole chapter in *The American Commonwealth* to "Why the Best Men Do Not Go into Politics." They lacked a sense of noblesse oblige. The "indifference of the educated and wealthy classes" was due partly, he thought, to the lack of respect in which they were held by the masses. "Since the masses do not look to them for guidance, they do not come forward to give it."

Without land to hold on to, a hereditary governing class had failed to develop, and the absence of such a class bound by a traditional morality left America open to the unrestricted exploits of the "plungers" and plunderers, the builders and malefactors and profiteers—and through them to the corruption of politics. With the great release and surge of enterprise after the Civil War, America was in a period of unprecedented expansion. The population increased by 50 per cent from fifty million to seventy-five million in the years 1880–1900. With opportunity opening on every hand, government in America through the seventies and eighties functioned chiefly to make the country safe—and lucrative—for the capitalist. Government was a paid agent. Its scandals and deals, becoming blatant, had aroused anger and people were demanding reform. But meanwhile gentlemen did not "stoop to politics," as Edith Wharton said of New York "Society." Few of her friends of "the best class" made use of their abilities or rendered the public services they could have. America "wasted this class instead of using it."

With no role in government and no security from the land, the American rich panicked easily. When the financial crisis of 1893 threatened the loss of John Adams' fortune, "he went all to pieces," wrote Henry. "The entire nervous system of Boston seemed to give way and he broke down with a whole crowd of other leading men. I have certainly no reason to think that any of us are stronger than he. My own nerves went to pieces long ago." Although many of his class were stronger-fibered than Adams, they were a far cry from Lewis Morris, lord of the manor of Morrisania, who, when urged by his brother not to sign the Declaration of Independence because of the consequences to his property, replied, "Damn the consequences, give me the pen!"

Speaker Reed in character, intellect and a kind of brutal independence represented the best that America could put into politics in his time. He was sprung from a rib of that hard northern corner of New England with the uncompromising monosyllabic name. At the time of his birth in 1839 his ancestors had been living in Maine for two hundred years. Through his mother he was descended from a *Mayflower* passenger and through his father's mother from George Cleve, who came from England in 1632, built the first white man's house in Maine and was founder of the Portland Colony and its first Governor. The Reed who married Cleve's great-great-granddaughter came of a fishing and seafaring family. Never landed in a large sense, nor wealthy, these forbears and their neighbors had striven over the generations to maintain a settlement on the rock-ribbed soil, to survive Indian attack and isolation and snowbound winters. The habit of struggle against odds was bred into Thomas Reed's blood. His father, captain of a small coastal vessel, had mortgaged his home to send his son to Bowdoin. To maintain himself at college, Reed taught school, walking six miles to and from his lodgings each day. The sons of Portland families went to Bowdoin, not to satisfy social custom, but to gain a serious education. As most of them were situated in circumstances like Reed's, the semesters were arranged to allow for teaching school in winter. Reed intended himself for the ministry, but sitting up nights on the bed in his attic room reading aloud with a college friend Carlyle's *French Revolution*, Goethe's *Faust* and *Werther*, Macaulay's *Essays* and the novels of Thackeray and Charles Reade, he formed religious convictions that were too individual to submit to a formal creed. After graduating in 1861 he studied law while continuing to teach for $20 a month and "boarding round" in local families.

The Civil War did not engulf him until 1864 when he joined the Navy and saw service of a none too bellicose nature on a Mississippi gunboat. He was commissary officer and would freely admit in later life that he had never been under fire. The usual aura of glory and glitter of gallantry which gradually encrust most wartime memories were no part of Reed's. "What a charming life that was, that dear old life in the Navy," he would say when others took to recalling the war, "when I kept grocery on a gunboat. I knew all the regulations and the rest of them didn't. I had all my rights and most of theirs." He was to repeat the method and gain the same result in Congress.

When admitted to the bar in Maine in 1865, Reed was a tall, strong young man of twenty-five with a square handsome hard-boned face and thick blond hair. During the next ten years he served as City Counsel for Portland, was elected to the state Legislature and then to the state Senate, was appointed Attorney-General for Maine, married, and grew fat. He had two children, a son who died young and a daughter. His hair thinned until he was almost bald, his figure bellied out until, as he walked down the streets of Portland, he resembled "a human frigate among shallops." Silent, impassive, with an inward-turned eye, noticing no one, he moved along with the ponderous, gently swaying gait of an elephant. "How narrow he makes the street look!" a passer-by once exclaimed.

In 1876, Reed, now thirty-six, was elected to Congress in place of Blaine, who moved up to the Senate. As a member of the committee formed to investigate the Democrats' charges of electoral fraud in the Hayes-Tilden election, his cross-examination of witnesses drew spectators for its forensic artistry and made him nationally prominent. In subsequent Congresses he became a member of the all-important Rules Committee and chairman of the Judiciary Committee while session by session perfecting his knowledge of House procedure and parliamentary device.

A body of rules had grown up "calculated better than anything else," as a colleague said, "to obstruct legislation," a body as full of "intricacies and secrets" as the armamentarium of a medieval cabalist. Reed mastered it. "In my opinion there never has been a more perfectly equipped leader in any parliamentary body at any period," said a professional observer, Senator Henry Cabot Lodge, who had served with him for seven years in the House. Reed not only knew parliamentary practice and law but "understood as few men do the theory and philosophy of the system." Whether consciously or not, he was preparing for the time when as Speaker he would be able to impress upon the House a sense that no one on the floor could compete with the Chair in command of the rules.

Even with this he could not have imposed his authority if he had not also been "the finest, most effective debater," in Lodge's opinion, "that I have ever seen or heard." He never used an extra word, never stumbled in his syntax, was never at a loss, never forced to retreat or modify a position. He was instant in rejoinder, terse, forcible, lucid. He could state a case unanswerably, illuminate an issue, destroy an argument or expose a fallacy in fewer words than anyone else. His language was vivid and picturesque. "Hardly time to ripen a strawberry," he said to describe a lapse of two months. He had a way of phrasing things that was peculiarly apt and peculiarly his own. In an argument over which of two fellow members, Berry or Curtis, was the taller, he asked them to stand up and be measured. When Berry uncoiled slowly to his full height, Reed said, "My God, Berry, how much of yourself do you keep in your pockets?" His epigrams were famous. "All the wisdom in the world consists in shouting with the majority" was one. "A statesman is a politician who is dead" was another. He rarely made a gesture when speaking. "When he stood up," said Lodge, "waiting for an opponent to conclude, filling the narrow aisle, with his hands resting upon the desk, with every trace of expression banished from his face and looking as if he had not an idea and barely heard what was being said, then he was most dangerous." After one retort which left its victim limply speechless, Reed, looking about him sweetly, remarked, "Having embedded that fly in the liquid amber of my remarks, I will proceed."

His lucidity and logic were particularly effective under the "five-minute" rule. "Russell," he said to a Representative from Massachusetts, "you do not understand the theory of five-minute debate. The object is to convey to the House either information or misinformation. You have consumed several periods of five minutes this afternoon without doing either."

Reed made his point by narrating, not orating. Once when engaged in his favorite sport of baiting the adjoining chamber for which he felt a profound disrespect, he described a Presidential election fifty years in the future when by Constitutional amendment the President would be selected from among and by the Senators. "When the ballots had been collected and spread out, the Chief Justice who presided was observed to hesitate and those nearest could see by his pallor that something unexpected had happened. But with a strong effort he rose to his feet and through a megaphone, then recently invented by Edison, shouted to the vast multitude the astonishing result: seventy-six Senators had each received one vote."

Discussing economic privilege during a tariff debate he told how, when walking through the streets of New York and contrasting "the brownstone fronts of the rich merchants with the unrewarded virtue of the people on the sidewalk, my gorge rises, . . . I do not feel kindly to the people inside. But when I feel that way I know what the feeling is. It is good honest high-minded envy. When the gentlemen across the aisle have the same feeling they think it is political economy."

When word ran down the corridors that Reed was on his feet, about to speak, gossiping groups dissolved, members hurried to their seats, boredom and inattention vanished as the House listened expectantly for the sculptured prose, the prick of sarcasm and the flash of wit. Every member coveted the notoriety of debating with Reed, but he refused to be drawn by the "little fellows," reserving himself only for those he considered worthy opponents.

Reporters, in the hope of eliciting a witticism, were always asking him for comments on the news of the day. They were not always successful. Asked to comment on a Papal message, he replied, "The overpowering unimportance of this makes me speechless." Asked what was the greatest problem confronting the American people, he replied, "How to dodge a bicycle."

After his first term, his nomination as Representative of Maine's First District was never afterward contested. Elections were another matter and he almost lost the one of 1880 when he refused to compromise or equivocate on free silver despite strong "greenback" sentiment in Maine. He kept his seat on that occasion by only 109 votes. But as his fame grew he generally ran ahead of his ticket in the biennial elections. Even Democrats confessed to "voting for him on the sly." "He suited the taste of New England," said Senator Hoar of Massachusetts. "The people liked to hear him on public questions better than any other man not excepting Blaine or McKinley." The reason was perhaps the same as that given by an Englishman to explain the secret of Palmerston's popularity: "What the nation likes in Palmerston is his you-be-damnedness!"

Though Reed scorned fence-building and never encouraged familiarity with the public, among intellectual equals "no more agreeable companion ever lived." In the small world that was then Washington's elite he was a jovial and radiant personality, a poker-player, storyteller and sought-after dinner guest. At one dinner party when the conversation turned on gambling, another famous raconteur, Mr. Joseph H. Choate of New York, remarked somewhat unctuously that he had never made a bet on a horse or card or anything else in his life. "I wish I could say that," a fellow guest said earnestly. "Why caaan't you?" asked Reed with his peculiar twang. "Choate did."

His table talk was enriched by the resources of a cultivated mind. His favorite poets were Burns, Byron and Tennyson, his favorite novel Thackeray's *Vanity Fair*. He habitually read *Punch*, and Balzac in the original, of whom he said, "There is hardly a book of his which is not sad beyond words." He had learned French after he was forty and kept a diary in that language "for practise." The existence of a national library is owed to Reed, whose persistent and eloquent insistence finally wore out the natural parsimony of the House to secure adequate funds for the Library of Congress.

"No one was ever better to listen to or a better listener," said Lodge, "for his sympathies were wide, his interests unlimited and nothing human was alien to him." "We asked the Tom Reeds to dinner," wrote a young friend of Lodge from New York, "and he was delightful." Shortly afterward Reed, an advocate of civil service reform, obtained for the young man a post in Washington on the Civil Service Commission and thereafter, whenever the new Commissioner needed help on the Hill, Reed was ready to give it. Later when the young man from New York bestrode the national scene, Reed composed probably the most memorable tribute ever made to him: "Theodore, if there is one thing more than another for which I admire you, it is your original discovery of the Ten Commandments." With a little less prescience he had also said, "Theodore will never be President; he has no political background."

In 1889, however, Theodore Roosevelt proved politically useful to Reed in his intra-party contest against McKinley, Joe Cannon and two others for the Speakership. While ranching and hunting in the Northwest, Roosevelt campaigned vigorously, and with success, to ensure that the four new states which had just entered the Union—Washington, Montana and the two Dakotas—would send Republicans to the next Congress. On his return to Washington he opened personal headquarters in a back room of the old Wormley Hotel where he "rounded up" the new Congressmen's votes for Reed. Although, to the despair of his supporters, Reed refused to fish for votes with the bait of promised committee appointments, he won nevertheless.

He now occupied the highest electoral office in the gift of his party next to the Presidency. "Ambitious as Lucifer," in the opinion of Representative Champ Clark, who knew him well, he did not intend to stop there. He was determined, on taking up the gavel as Speaker, to put into effect a plan on which he had long deliberated, consulting no one, and on which he risked his political future. He knew that the fight would focus upon him the nation's attention and also that if he failed his Congressional career would be over. The stakes were high: he would either break "the tyranny of the minority" by which the House was paralyzed into a state of "helpless inanity," or he would resign.

The system Speaker Reed had decided to challenge was known as the silent—or disappearing—quorum. It was a practice whereby the minority party could prevent any legislation obnoxious to it by refusing a quorum, that is, by demanding a roll call and then remaining silent when their names were called. Since the rules prescribed that a member's presence was established only by a viva voce reply to the roll, and since it required a majority of the whole to constitute a quorum, the silent filibuster could effectively stop the House from doing business.

The recent election of 1888 had been a Republican victory in which for the first time in sixteen years one party controlled both Executive and Congress. But by barely a hair. The dour Benjamin Harrison was a minority President who had lost to Cleveland in popular vote and sat on that unstable throne so oddly carpentered by the electoral college system. The Republican majority in the House of 168–160 was wafer-thin, only three more than a quorum, which was set at 165. With this the Republicans faced the task of enacting two major pieces of party legislation, the Mills Bill for revising the tariff and the Force Bill directed against the poll tax and other Southern devices to keep the Negroes from voting. The Democrats were prepared to obstruct this legislation and also to prevent a vote on the seating of four Republicans, two of them Negroes, in contested elections from Southern districts.

To Reed the issue was survival of representative government. If the Democrats could prevent that legislation which the Republicans by virtue of their electoral victory could rightfully expect to enact, they would in effect be setting aside the verdict of the election. The rights of the minority, he believed, were preserved by freedom to debate and to vote but when the minority was able to frustrate action by the majority, "it becomes a tyranny." He believed that legislation, not merely deliberation, was the business of Congress. The duty of the Speaker to his party and country was to see that that business was accomplished, not merely to umpire debate.

The Speakership was a post of tremendous influence, still possessed of all the powers which in 1910, in the revolt against Joe Cannon, were to be transferred to the committees. Since the Speaker was ex officio Chairman of the Committee on Rules, whose two Republican and two Democratic members canceled each other out, and since he had the right to appoint all committees, the careers of members and the course of legislation depended upon his will. In Reed's hands was now the "power with responsibility," and notwithstanding a famous dictum, power has other effects than only to corrupt: it can also enlarge the understanding. It sometimes begets greatness. The Speaker's office, which the Washington *Post* called "no less consequential than the Presidency," could be the stepping stone to that ultimate peak. Reed was not the man either to miss his opportunity or to meet it feebly.

He reached his decision to attack the silent quorum, and planned his campaign, alone, partly because no one else would have thought there was a chance of success and partly because he was not sure that even his own party would support him. There were indications that they might not. Because of Reed's known views on the silent filibuster it was clear that quorum-counting would be an issue in the new Congress. REED WILL COUNT THEM, predicted a headline in the Washington *Post*, and the story beneath it said that even Mr. Cannon, Reed's closest lieutenant, was opposed to the attempt. The Democrats were manning their defences. Ex-Speaker Carlisle let it be known that any legislation enacted by a quorum which had not been established by a "recorded vote" would be taken to court as unconstitutional.

Reed, however, had satisfied himself that he would be upheld if it came to law, and on the attitude of his own party he was prepared to gamble. He shrewdly judged that the Democrats in their rage would provoke the Republicans to rally to his support. When the first of the contested elections appeared on the schedule for January 29 he was ready. As expected, the Democrats raised a cry of no quorum and demanded a roll call. It produced 163 yeas, all Republican, two less than a quorum. Reed's moment had come. Without a flicker of expression on the great white moon face, "the largest human face I ever saw," as a colleague described it, without any quickening of the drawling voice, he announced, "The Chair directs the Clerk to record the names of the following members present and refusing to vote," and began reading off the names himself. Instantly, according to a reporter, "pandemonium broke loose. The storm was furious . . . and it is to be doubted if ever there was such wild excitement, burning indignation, scathing denunciation and really dangerous conditions as existed in the House" during the next five days. Republicans were wildly applauding, all the Democrats were "yelling and shrieking and pounding their desks" while the voice of their future Speaker, Crisp of Georgia, boomed, "I appeal! I appeal from the decision of the Chair!" The explosion was "as violent as was ever witnessed in any parliament," a member recalled later. Unruffled, expressionless, the Speaker continued his counting, "Mr. Blanchard, Mr. Bland, Mr. Blount, Mr. Breckinridge of Arkansas, Mr. Breckinridge of Kentucky . . ."

Up jumped the Kentuckian, "famous for his silver hair and silver tongue." "I deny the power of the Speaker and denounce it as revolutionary!" he called.

The resonant twang from the Chair continued unregarding, "Mr. Bullock, Mr. Bynum, Mr. Carlisle, Mr. Chipman, Mr. Clement, Mr. Covert, Mr. Crisp, Mr. Cummings"—through hisses and catcalls and cries of "Appeal!" irresistibly rolling down the alphabet—"Mr. Lawler, Mr. Lee, Mr. McAdoo, Mr. McCreary . . ."

"I deny your right, Mr. Speaker, to count me as present!" bellowed McCreary.

For the first time the Speaker stopped, held the hall in silence for a pause as an actor holds an audience, then blandly spoke: "The Chair is making a statement of fact that the gentleman is present. Does he deny it?"

He went on with his count, unmoved by the protests, denials, cries of "Order!" that rose to bedlam, through the *S*'s and *T*'s to the end. Then suddenly, seeming to gather all the power of his huge body, projecting all the force of his commanding personality and raising the voice which could fill any hall when he wanted, he announced, "The Chair thereupon rules that there is a quorum present within the meaning of the Constitution."

Tumult even worse than before followed. Breckinridge of Kentucky demanded a point of order on the ground that the Chair had no right to make such a ruling. "The Chair overrules the point of order," declared Reed coolly.

"I appeal the decision of the Chair!" shouted Breckinridge.

"I move to lay the appeal on the table," quickly interposed an alert Republican, Payson of Illinois. As this motion, if carried, would have shut off debate, the Democrats foamed with rage. A hundred of them "were on their feet howling for recognition," wrote a reporter. "Fighting Joe" Wheeler, the diminutive former Confederate cavalry general, unable to reach the front because of the crowded aisles, came down from the rear "leaping from desk to desk as an ibex leaps from crag to crag." As the excitement grew wilder, the only Democrat not on his feet was a huge Representative from Texas who sat in his seat significantly whetting a bowie knife on his boot. When a Republican member said he believed "we should have debate" on such an important matter, Reed allowed it. The debate was to last four days with the Democrats fighting every inch of the way, insisting on readings of every word of the Journal, on appeals and points of order and roll calls, each of which were met by Reed imperturbably counting off the silent members as present and evoking each time further infuriated defiance. Once Representative McKinley, striving to please as usual, inadvertently yielded the floor, and had to be prompted by Reed, "The gentleman from Ohio declines to be interrupted."

"I decline to be interrupted," echoed McKinley valiantly closing the breach.

As implacably at each juncture Reed counted heads and repeated his formula, "A Constitutional quorum is present to do business," the fury and frustration of the Democrats mounted. A group breathing maledictions advanced down the aisle threatening to pull him from the Chair and for a moment it looked to a spectator "as if they intended to mob the Speaker." Reed remained unmoved. Infected by the passion on the floor, visitors and correspondents in the galleries leaned over the railings to shake their fists at the Speaker and join in the abuse and profanity. "Decorum," lamented a reporter, "was altogether forgotten. Members rushed madly about the floor, the scowl of battle upon their brows, . . . shouting in a mad torrent of eloquent invective." They called Reed tyrant, despot and dictator, hurling epithets like stones. Among all the variants on the word "tyrant," "czar" emerged as the favorite, embodying for its time the image of unrestrained autocracy, and as "Czar" Reed, the Speaker was known thereafter. The angrier the Democrats became, the cooler Reed remained, bulking hugely in the chair, "serene as a summer morning." Although his secretary saw him in his private room, during an interval, gripping the desk and shaking with suppressed rage, he never gave a sign in the hall to show that the vicious abuse touched him. He maintained an iron control, "cool and determined as a highwayman," said the New York *Times*.

The secret of his self-possession, as he told a friend long afterward, was that he had his mind absolutely made up as to what he would do if the House did not sustain him. "I would simply have left the Chair and resigned the Speakership and my seat in Congress." He had a place waiting for him for the private practice of law in Elihu Root's New York firm, and "I had made up my mind that if political life consisted in sitting helplessly in the Speaker's Chair and seeing the majority helpless to pass legislation, I had had enough of it and was ready to step down and out." Coming to such a decision, he said, "you have made yourself equal to the worst" and are ready for it. This has a very "soothing" effect on the spirit.

It did more than soothe: it gave him an embedded strength which men who fear the worst, or will yield principles to avoid the worst, can never possess. It endowed him with a moral superiority over the House which members without knowing why could sense in the atmosphere.

Now the Democrats, changing their strategy, decided to absent themselves in actuality, counting on the inability of the Republicans to round up a quorum of themselves alone. As one by one the Democrats slipped out, Reed, divining their intention, ordered the doors locked. At once there followed a mad scramble to get out before the next vote. Losing "all sense of personal or official dignity," Democrats hid under desks and behind screens. Representative Kilgore of Texas, kicking open a locked door to make his escape, made "Kilgore's Kick" the delight of cartoonists.

On the fifth day, the Democrats absented themselves altogether and when a vote was called the Republicans were still short of a quorum. Two of their number were brought in on cots from their sickbeds. There was still one too few. One member was known to be on his way to Washington. Suddenly a door opened, and, as a reporter told it, "there was a flash of red whiskers and a voice saying, 'One more, Mr. Speaker.'" Sweney of Iowa was counted in, the quorum was filled, and the vote recorded at

166–0. The battle was over. Democrats sullenly filed back to their seats. The Rules Committee reported out a new set of rules, composed, needless to say, and imposed by the Chairman. Known thereafter as "Reed's Rules" and adopted on February 14, they provided among other things that (1) all members must vote; (2) one hundred shall constitute a quorum; (3) all present shall be counted; and (4) no dilatory motion shall be entertained and the definition of what is dilatory to be left to the judgment of the Speaker.

Five years later Theodore Roosevelt wrote that in destroying the silent filibuster, Reed's reform was of "far greater permanent importance" than any piece of legislation it brought to enactment at the time. Reed knew this as soon as he had won. In his speech closing the Fifty-first Congress he said that "the verdict of history" was the only one worth recording and he was confident of its outcome "because we have taken here so long a stride in the direction of responsible government."

More immediate than a verdict by history, and, indeed, then widely considered its equivalent, was a portrait by Sargent. Commissioned as a tribute to the Speaker by his Republican colleagues, it was a memorable failure. "He is supposed to be in the act of counting a quorum," a critic observed, "but in fact has just been inveigled into biting a green persimmon."

The death of the silent quorum was discussed in parliamentary bodies all over the world. At home it made Reed a leading political figure and obvious candidate for the Presidential nomination in 1892. But his time had not yet come, as he correctly judged, for when asked if he thought his party would nominate him, he replied, "They might do worse and I think they will."

They did. Reed's "czardom" was still resented and his sarcasm had not made friends. Nor did his disgust for deals, his refusal to woo the public with smiles and handshakes, or politicians with promises, enlarge his circle of supporters. The party regulars preferred to nominate the incumbent Harrison, incorruptible but sour, known as the "White House Iceberg," whom Reed disliked with no concealment whatever. When Harrison appointed as Collector of Portland, Reed's home town, a man Reed despised, he thereafter refused to enter the White House or meet Harrison until the day he died.

When, in 1892, the Democrats won control of the House by so large a majority that they could always assemble a quorum among themselves, they triumphantly threw out Reed's reform. He waited for history, not without some faith, as he used to say, that "the House has more sense than anyone in it." History did not keep him waiting long. In the next Congress, with the Democratic majority reduced by half and split over the currency and other heated issues, Reed enjoyed a delicious revenge. Over and over he demanded roll calls and when Bland of Missouri stormed against this "downright filibuster," he countered instantly, "Downright? You mean upright." His control over his party, as minority leader no less than as Speaker, remained total. "Gentlemen on that side blindly follow him," Speaker Crisp said wistfully. "You will hear them privately saying, 'Reed ought not to do that,' or 'This is wrong,' but when Reed says 'Do it,' they all step up and do it." When at last the Democrats had to give way, and for the sake of their own program, re-adopt his quorum-counting rule, Reed refrained from crowing. "This scene here today is a more effective address than any I could make," he said. "I congratulate the Fifty-third Congress."

In 1890, when the last armed conflict between Indians and whites in the United States took place at Wounded Knee Creek and the Census Bureau declared there was no longer a land frontier, a further test was shaping for Reed. In that year Captain A. T. Mahan, president of the Naval War College, announced in the *Atlantic Monthly,* "Whether they will or no, Americans must now begin to look outward."

A quiet, tight-lipped naval officer with one of the most forceful minds of his time, Alfred Thayer Mahan had selected himself to fill the country's need of "a voice to speak constantly of our external interests." Few Americans were aware that the United States had external interests and a large number believed she ought not to have them. The immediate issue was annexation of Hawaii. A naval coaling base at Pearl Harbor had been acquired in 1887, but the main impulse for annexation of the Islands came from American property interests there which were dominated by Judge Dole and the sugar trust. With the support of the United States Marines they engineered a revolt against the native Hawaiian government in January, 1893; Judge Dole became President Dole and promptly negotiated a treaty of annexation with the American Minister which President Harrison hurriedly sent to the Senate in February. Having been defeated for re-election by former President Cleveland, who was due to be inaugurated on March 4, Harrison asked for immediate action by the Senate in the hope of obtaining ratification before the new President could take office. The procedure was too raw and the Senate balked.

Opposed to expansion in any form, Cleveland was a man of integrity, as well as shape, similar to Reed's. Once, when mistaken for Cleveland in an ill-lit room, Reed said, "Mercy! Don't tell Grover. He is too proud of his good looks already." Before he had been in office a week, Cleveland recalled the treaty of annexation from the Senate, much to the distress of Reed's young friend, Roosevelt, who felt "very strongly" about "hauling down the flag," as he called it.

The motive of the annexationists had been economic self-interest. It took Mahan to transform the issue into one of national and fateful importance. In the same March that Cleveland recalled the treaty, Mahan published an article in the *Forum* entitled "Hawaii and Our Future Sea Power," in which he declared that command of the seas was the chief element in the power and prosperity of nations and it was therefore "imperative to take possession, when it can righteously be done, of such maritime positions as contribute to secure command." Hawaii "fixes the attention of the strategist"; it occupies a position of "unique importance . . . powerfully influencing the commercial and military control of the Pacific." In another article published by the *Atlantic Monthly* in the same month, Mahan argued the imperative need, for the future of American sea power, of the proposed Isthmian Canal.

Captain Mahan's pronouncements were somehow couched in tones of such authority, as much a product of character as of style, as to make everything he wrote appear indisputable. He was already the author of *The Influence of Sea Power on History*, given originally as lectures at the Naval War College in 1887 and published as a book in 1890. Its effect on the naval profession abroad, if not at home, was immediate and tremendous, and even at home, although it had taken three years to find a publisher, it excited the attention of various thoughtful persons concerned with national policy. Theodore Roosevelt, who as the author at twenty-four of a book on *The Naval War of 1812* had been invited to speak at the Naval War College, heard and became a disciple of Mahan. When *The Influence of Sea Power on History* was published he read it "straight through" and wrote to Mahan that he was convinced it would become "a naval classic." Walter Hines Page of the *Forum* and Horace E. Scudder of the *Atlantic Monthly*, editors in the days when magazines were vital arenas of opinion, regularly gave Mahan space. Harvard and Yale conferred LL.D.'s. Nor were all his professional colleagues traditionalists opposed to things new. His predecessor at the Naval War College, Admiral Stephen Luce, who had selected Mahan to succeed him when Luce himself was named to command the North Atlantic Squadron, brought his squadron to Newport so that his officers could hear the lectures of this new man who, Luce predicted, would do for naval science what Jomini in the days of Napoleon had done for military science. After the first lecture, Luce stood up and proclaimed, "He is here and his name is Mahan!"

What Mahan had discovered was the controlling factor of sea power; that whoever is master of the seas is master of the situation. Like M. Jourdain who spoke prose all his life without knowing it, it was a truth that had been operative for a long time without any of its operators being consciously aware of it, and Mahan's formulation was stunning. His first book was followed and confirmed by a second, *The Influence of Sea Power on the French Revolution*, published in 1892. The original idea had come to him "from within" when, on reading Mommsen's *History of Rome*, "it struck me how different things might have been could Hannibal have invaded Italy by sea . . . or could he, after arrival, have been in free communication with Carthage by water." All at once Mahan realized that "control of the sea was an historic factor which had never been systematically appreciated and expounded." It was "one of those perceptions that turn inward darkness into light." For months, while on leave in 1885, before taking up his duties at the War College, he read at the Astor Place branch of the New York Public Library, following his clue through history in mounting excitement and with every faculty "alive and jumping."

In the United States the building of navies with more than coastal defence capacity was traditionally regarded as a sacrilege against the original idea of America as a nation which could live without aggression and demonstrate a new future to the world. In Europe the nations who had exercised power upon the seas for centuries were suddenly made aware by Mahan of what they had. A commentator signed "Nauticus" remarked that sea power, like oxygen, had influenced the world through the ages, but just as the nature and power of oxygen remained unrealized until Priestley, "so might sea power but for Mahan."

Ordered to command the flagship of the European Station in 1893 (much against his will, for he would have preferred to stay at home and continue writing), Mahan was received in England with unprecedented honors. He was invited by the Queen to a state dinner at Osborne, dined with the Prince of Wales and was the first foreigner ever to be entertained by the Royal Yacht Squadron, which gave a dinner in his honor with a hundred guests, all admirals and captains. In London, John Hay, who was visiting there, wrote to him that "all the people of intelligence are waiting to welcome you." Lord Rosebery, then Prime Minister, invited him to a private dinner with just himself and John Morley at which they talked until midnight. He met Balfour and Asquith, visited Lord Salisbury at Hatfield, and dined again with the Queen at Buckingham Palace. Wearing a red academic robe over his dress uniform and sword, he received a D.C.L. from Oxford and an LL.D. from Cambridge, said to be the only man ever to receive degrees from both universities in the same week.

After a temporary escape to the Continent, where, equipped with guidebook, umbrella and binoculars, he traced Hannibal's marches, he was seized upon by his most enthusiastic disciple, Wilhelm II, who invited him to dinner aboard his yacht, the *Hohenzollern*, during Cowes Week. With effect that was to be epochal on world history, *The Influence of Sea Power on History* had planted in the Kaiser the idea that Germany's future was on the sea. By his order, a copy of Mahan's book was placed on every ship in the German Navy and the Kaiser's personal copies in English and German were heavily underlined and bristling with marginal comments and exclamation marks. "I am just now not reading but devouring Captain Mahan's book and am trying to learn it by heart," he informed a friend by telegram in 1894, when Mahan was in Europe. "It is a first class book and classical in all points. It is on board all my ships and constantly quoted by my Captains and officers." The Japanese were no less interested. *The Influence of Sea Power on History* was adopted as a text in Japanese military and naval colleges and all Mahan's subsequent books were translated into Japanese.

The obvious corollary of Mahan's thesis was the peremptory need to develop the American Navy, at that time moribund from neglect. As Cleveland's Secretary of the Navy, William C. White, said in 1887, it did not have the strength to fight nor the speed to run away, and in Mahan's judgment it was not a match for Chile's Navy, much less Spain's. In 1880, when serious discussion began of an Isthmian Canal, which in the absence of adequate naval power would constitute more of a danger than an asset, he had written, "We must without delay begin to build a navy which will at least equal that of England when the Canal shall have become a fact. . . . That this will be done I don't for a moment hope but unless it is we may as well shut up about the Monroe Doctrine at once."

From then on he continually badgered friends, colleagues and correspondents on this theme. His passion was for naval power, not for ships, as such, for he did not enjoy sea duty and looked nothing at all like a sailor. Well over six feet tall, wiry, thin and erect, he had a long, narrow face with narrowly placed pale-blue eyes, a long, straight, knifelike nose, a sandy moustache blending into a closely trimmed beard over an insignificant chin. All the power of the face was in the upper part, in the eyes and domed skull and the intellectual bumps over the eyebrows. Born the year after

Reed, he was fifty in 1890, and though exceptionally reserved and retiring, he was capable, according to his wife, of sudden roars in "his quarter deck voice." His brother called him Alf. He had little sense of humor, a high moral tone and shared the respectable man's horror of Zola's novels, which he forbade his daughters to read. So precise were his scruples that when living on naval property at the War College he would not allow his children to use the government pencils.

His friends and acquaintances were few and his social life, except on the occasion of his tour of duty abroad, virtually nonexistent. External expression of his personality was limited; his life was inner. He was like a steam kettle in which the boiling goes on within an enclosed space and the steam comes out through a single spout. Like Reed he was intensely clear-thinking and definitive in his conclusions. Apropos of a trip ashore at Aden, where he visited a colony of Jews, he wrote, "I am without anti-Semitic feeling. That Jesus Christ was a Jew covers his race for me." In a total of sixteen words he settled to his own satisfaction a problem that had harassed mankind for nineteen centuries and had reopened in his own days full of new trouble and malignance. Samuel Ashe, his lifelong friend since they had been classmates at Annapolis, said, "He was the most intellectual man I have ever known."

In 1890 the Navy at last began to build. On the recommendation of the Policy Board appointed by Harrison's Secretary of the Navy, Benjamin Tracy, Congress reluctantly and not without strong objections from inside and out authorized three battleships, the *Oregon, Indiana* and *Massachusetts*, and a fourth, the *Iowa*, two years later. They were the first fruits of Mahan's long campaign. The policy which these ships expressed, though far from being generally accepted at once, represented a fundamental change in the direction in which Mahan was pointing: outward. They meant recognition that America must create a fleet capable of meeting successfully the best that a potential enemy could send against her. Canada was regarded as a hostage to restrain Britain, and the political balance in Europe was considered likely to prevent any potential European enemy from sending its full fleet into American waters. The object was therefore to be supreme in these waters and this meant a fleet capable of protecting the American coasts by taking offensive action against enemy bases anywhere from Newfoundland to the Caribbean. Such was to be the function of the new battleships. They were of the 10,000-ton class, with an average speed of fifteen knots, a coal capacity sufficient for a cruising radius of 5,000 miles at moderate speed, four 13-inch guns, and eight 8-inch guns. In combination of armor and firepower they represented the best in design and construction of the time. At their trials, the *Indiana* in 1895 followed by the *Iowa* in 1896 soberly impressed the British as a match for Britain's first-line ships, of which the latest of the "Majestic" class were 15,000 tons with four 12-inch and twelve 6-inch guns.

The ships lent heart to Mahan's disciples. Roosevelt, still on the Civil Service Commission, was not yet widely heard, but his friend and political mentor, Senator Henry Cabot Lodge of Massachusetts, was the principal political voice in Washington of Mahan's views. Son of a family whose fortune had been made in clipper ships and the China trade, author of various biographies and histories of the Colonial period, Lodge was led into political life through his deep interest in American history. His grandfather and namesake, Henry Cabot, could remember as a boy hiding under the sideboard to watch President George Washington at breakfast in his father's home. Elected to the House in 1886, Lodge made an immediate impression by his frequent and able speeches and proved himself an adroit master of political strategy and tactics. He was shrewd, worldly, forceful and possessed of both energy and intelligence. Along with Roosevelt he was a champion of civil service reform and an inner member of the select group which gathered around the two non-participants, John Hay and Henry Adams, who watched government half wistfully, half cynically from the ringside. Representing the party in opposition, Lodge and Roosevelt had no influence on Cleveland; but they believed and they preached with fervor.

"It is sea power which is essential to every splendid people," Lodge declaimed in the Senate on March 2, 1895. He had a map of the Pacific set up with Britain's bases marked by very visible red crosses and he used a pointer as he talked to make Mahan's point about the vital position of Hawaii. The effect was dramatic and reinforced by the speaker being, as he wrote to his mother, "in desperate earnest." Hawaii must be acquired and the Canal built. "We are a great people; we control this continent; we are dominant in this hemisphere; we have too great an inheritance to be trifled with or parted with. It is ours to guard and extend." As he spoke, Senators came in from the cloakrooms, members of the other House appeared, and also messengers and journalists, until soon the chamber was filled and men were standing around the walls. Lodge could feel he had their "absolute attention. . . . When I sat down everybody crowded around to shake my hand . . . which hardly ever happens in the Senate." In an accompanying article that month in the *Forum*, Lodge stated flatly that once the Canal was built, "the island of Cuba will become a necessity" to the United States. He did not say how the necessity was to be made good; whether the United States was to buy the island from Spain or simply take

it. He offered the opinion, however, that small states belonged to the past
and that expansion was a movement that made for "civilization and the
advancement of the race."

At this juncture History lent a hand. On February 24, 1895, the Cuban
people rose in insurrection against Spanish rule and on March 8 a Spanish
gunboat chased and fired on an American merchant vessel, the *Alliance,*
which it supposed to be bent on a filibustering errand. This "insult to our
flag," as it was called, evoked a burst of comments from prominent members of the Senate Foreign Relations Committee which showed that Lodge
had not been speaking only for himself. The American appetite for new
territory was making itself felt. Senator Morgan of Alabama, Democratic
chairman of the Committee, said the solution was clear: "Cuba should become an American colony." Reed's colleague but not his friend, Senator
Frye of Maine, agreed that "we certainly ought to have the island in order to
round out our possessions" and added with simple candor, "If we cannot
buy it, I for one, should like an opportunity to acquire it by conquest."
Another Republican, Senator Cullom of Illinois, expressed even more
plainly what was moving inside the American people. "It is time some
one woke up," he said, "and realized the necessity of annexing some
property—we want all this northern hemisphere." It was not, in 1895,
necessary to disguise aggressiveness as something else. As yet the Senators
were not talking in terms of support for Cubans rightly struggling to be
free, because the *insurrectos,* who were burning American property as
enthusiastically as Spanish, had not yet been presented in that light.

With President Cleveland standing robustly against expansion, the
exuberant greed of certain Senators had little effect on policy. It was an
act by Cleveland himself, at the end of the year, that brought into open
explosion the new American mood. His emphatic assertion of the Monroe
Doctrine over Venezuela, in defiance of Britain, marked the beginning of
a new period in American life as vividly as if a signal flag had been run up
to the top of the American flagpole. No question of gain, territorial or
otherwise, was involved in Venezuela; it was simply a question of asserting
an American right, as it seemed to Cleveland and especially to his exceed-
ingly assertive Secretary of State, Richard Olney. The burst of chauvinism,
jingoism and general bellicosity that it touched off startled everyone,
though it came less from the common man than from the rich and powerful
and vocal. The Union League Club had 1,600 members, proclaimed one
of them, and "we are 1,600 to a man behind Mr. Cleveland in this matter.
. . . There is absolutely not one dissenting voice." Congratulations from
other Republicans, stung to admiration, poured in upon the White House,

including one from Theodore Roosevelt. The New York *Times* exaggerated matters in headlines which had no relation to the reports beneath them. PREPARATIONS FOR WAR and COUNTRY IS AROUSED, they ran, or, WANT TO FIGHT ENGLAND: *Army and Navy Men Profess Great Eagerness to Go to War. Talk of Invasion of Canada.* The Army bureau chief who was quoted, far from talking about invading Canada, gave a careful and sober statement of American naval and military inadequacies and stated his belief that America would "make a sorry spectacle at war with England."

The surge of militancy evoked by the Venezuela Message shocked people who still thought of the United States in the terms of its founders, as a nation opposed to militarism, conquest, standing armies and all the other bad habits associated with the monarchies of the old world. This tradition was strongest in New England, and was stronger among the older generation—roughly those who were over fifty in 1890—than among the new. They were closer to Jefferson, who had said, "If there is one principle more deeply rooted in the mind of every American, it is that we should have nothing to do with conquest." They took seriously the Declaration of Independence and its principle of just power deriving from the consent of the governed. They regarded the extension of American rule over foreign soil and foreign peoples as a violation of this principle and a desecration of the American purpose. The original American democracy was to them a torch, an ideal, an example of a brave new world that had set its face against the old. They wanted nothing to do with titles of rank and nobility, knee breeches, orders or any of the other insidious trappings of monarchy, and when in the Navy the title of Admiral was first proposed, an officer fumed, "Call them Admirals? Never! They will be wanting to be Dukes next."

First-generation immigrants who had come to the United States beckoned by the American dream were as deeply devoted to the founding principles as those in whom they had been bred for generations. Some came out of the balked revolution of 1848, seeking Liberty, like Altgeld's father and like Carl Schurz, now sixty-six, who as journalist, editor, Cabinet minister and Senator had been a power and reformer ever since Lincoln's Administration. Some came to escape oppression or poverty and to seek opportunity, like the Scottish weaver who arrived in 1848 with his twelve-year-old son, Andrew Carnegie, or like the Dutch-Jewish cigarmaker who came from a London slum in 1863 with his thirteen-year-old son, Samuel Gompers. Some came, like E. L. Godkin, editor of the *Nation* and the New York *Evening Post,* not as a refugee from oppression, but as a voluntary exile from the old world, lured by America as a living demonstration of the democratic ideal. To them, as to men whose ancestors had come in the 1630's, America was a new principle, and they saw the new militancy as its betrayal.

Godkin, filled with "anxiety about the country," determined to oppose the Venezuela Message even if he should jeopardize his paper with the "half-crazed public." Son of an English family settled since the Twelfth Century in Ireland, where he had been born and brought up, he had served as correspondent for English papers during the Crimean War and the American Civil War. He became editor of the *Nation* when it was founded in 1865 by a group of forty stockholders who supplied $100,000 with the stated purpose of championing the labouring class, the Negro, the cause of popular education and "true democratic principles in society and government." In 1883, while remaining at the *Nation*, he succeeded Carl Schurz as editor of the *Evening Post* and through the medium of these two organs made himself, as William James said, "a towering influence on all thought concerning public affairs."

He was a handsome, bearded, hot-tempered Celt, delighting in combat, brooding in melancholy, vivacious, pugnacious and a muckraker before Roosevelt invented the name. So unrelenting was his pursuit of corrupt practices by Tammany politicians that on one occasion they had him arrested for criminal libel three times in one day. James Russell Lowell agreed with the opinion of an English journalist that Godkin had made the *Nation* "the best periodical in the world," and James Bryce, already famous as the author of *The American Commonwealth,* declared the *Evening Post* to be "the best paper printed in the English language." Closer to home, opinion was hotter. Governor Hill of New York said he did not care about "the handful of mugwumps" who read the *Evening Post* in New York City. "The trouble with the damned sheet is that every editor in New York State reads it." This was what accounted for Godkin's pervasive influence; that other makers of opinion took their opinions from him—though not, to be sure, all. "What fearful mental degeneracy results from reading it or the *Nation* as a steady thing," wrote Theodore Roosevelt to Captain Mahan in 1893.

In 1895 Godkin was sixty-four and feared the future. The United States, he wrote to a friend, "finds itself in possession of enormous power and is eager to use it in brutal fashion against anyone who comes along without knowing how to do so and is therefore constantly on the brink of some frightful catastrophe." Indeed, as the United States had at this moment exactly one battleship in commission, Godkin was not unwarranted in thinking the Jingoes "absolutely crazy." He believed the new spirit of "ferocious optimism," as he strikingly described it, would lead to eventual disaster.

William James, Professor of Philosophy at Harvard, was equally disquieted. "It is instructive to find," he wrote apropos of Venezuela, "how near the surface in all of us the old fighting spirit lies and how slight an appeal will wake it up. Once *really* waked, there is no retreat." His colleague at Harvard, Charles Eliot Norton, Professor of Fine Arts, who was regarded as the exponent and arbiter of culture in American life, protested the war spirit at a meeting in the Shepard Memorial Church in Cambridge. "The shout of brutal applause, which has gone up from every part of this nation," he said, makes every rational lover of his country feel the "greatest apprehension" for the future.

The white-haired, slender, stoop-shouldered figure, the husky yet musical voice speaking in its Boston Brahmin accent, the charm of that "supremely urbane and gentle presence" was never so at home as when against the herd. Born in 1827, only a year after Jefferson and John Adams died, Norton represented the puritan and militantly liberal conscience of an older generation. He was the son of Andrews Norton, "Unitarian Pope" of New England and Professor of Sacred Literature at Harvard, who had married Catherine Eliot, daughter of a wealthy Boston merchant, and was himself descended through a long line of ministers from John Norton, a Puritan divine who had emigrated to America in 1635.

Like Lord Salisbury, Norton believed in the dominance of an aristocratic class, which to him meant a class founded, not in landowning, but in a common background of culture, refinement, learning and manners. He saw it disappearing and protested regularly against encroaching vulgarity in his lectures. In parody of his manner a student said, "I propose this afternoon to make a few remarks on the hor-ri-ble vul-gar-ity of EVERYTHING." Another of his students at Radcliffe, in her diary for 1895, described him looking "so mildly happy and benignant . . . while he gently tells us it were better for us had we never been born in this degenerate and unhappy age." Norton became one of the first contributors to the *Atlantic Monthly* when it was founded by James Russell Lowell in 1857, later co-editor with Lowell of the *North American Review,* and was one of the forty stockholders who founded the *Nation.*

Writing to Godkin about the Venezuela Message, Norton thought it made "a miserable end for this century" and had done much to increase the "worst spirit in our democracy, . . . a barbaric spirit of arrogance and unreasonable self-assertion." What disturbed him more bitterly was the "deeper consideration" that the rise of democracy was not proving, after all, "a safeguard of peace and civilization," because it brought with it "the rise of the uncivilized whom no school education can suffice to provide with intelligence and reason." It might have been Lord Salisbury speaking. Norton felt the bitterness of a man who discovers his beloved to be not as beautiful—nor as pure—as he had believed. "I fear that America," he wrote to an English friend, "is beginning a long course of error and wrong and is likely to become more and more a power for disturbance and barbarism. . . . It looks as if the world were entering on a new stage of experience in which there must be a new discipline of suffering to fit men for the new conditions."

Yet his was not the desiccated and disappointed pessimism of Henry Adams, who drifted in and out of Washington and back and forth between Europe and America croaking his endless complaints like a wizened black crow; finding the century "rotten and bankrupt," society sunk in vulgarity, commonness, imbecility and moral atrophy, himself on the verge of "mental extinction" and "dying of ennui"; finding America unbearable and leaving for Europe, finding Europe insufferable and returning to America, finding "decline is everywhere" and everywhere "the dead water of the *fin de siècle* . . . where not a breath stirred the idle air of education or fretted the mental torpor of self-content." The Venezuelan crisis merely confirmed him in the belief that "society today is more rotten than at any time within my personal knowledge. The whole thing is one vast structure of debt and fraud." This was less a judgment on the current mood than a reflection of the rude shaking his nerves had suffered in the financial panic of 1893. Adams, like most people, saw society in his own image and ascribed his own impotence and paralysis to society at large. "Though rotten with decadence," he said of himself in 1895, "I have not enough vitality left to be sensual." The rotten old century, however, was bursting with vitality and he need only have looked at intimates of his own circle in the persons of Lodge and Roosevelt to have found the "ferocious optimism" that Godkin noted all around.

Although a decade older than Adams, Norton would allow himself occasional moments of optimism when he suspected that the loss of the values he loved might be the cost of a compensating gain in human welfare. "There are far more human beings materially well off today than ever before in the history of the world," he wrote in 1896, and he could not resist the thought, "How interesting our times have been and still are!"

The last few years had indeed been full of incident. Cleveland, for all his good will, was beset by hard times. Industrial unrest gripped the nation. Depression followed the panic of 1893. In 1894 Coxey's Army of the unemployed marched on Washington, and the bloody Pullman strike angered and frightened both sides in the deepening warfare of labour and capital. In the Congressional elections that November, the Republicans regained the House with a huge majority of 140 (244–104), and when in December, 1895, the new Fifty-fourth Congress assembled, the familiar great black figure with the great white face was again enthroned in the Speaker's Chair.

Reed was now at the zenith of his power. The dangerous battle of his first term was long past and the guerrilla warfare of two terms as minority leader over, leaving him with unlimited control. "He commands everything by the brutality of his intellect," said a member. His well-drilled ranks, though occasionally, and as time went on, increasingly, restive, could not break the habit of obedience. When the Speaker waved his hands upward members would stand as one man, and if by chance they rose to claim the floor when he wished them silent, a downward wave made them subside into their seats. "He had more perfect control over the House than any other Speaker," wrote Senator Cullom of Illinois.

Stern on dignity and decorum, he permitted no smoking or shirtsleeves and even challenged the cherished privilege of feet on desk. A member with particularly visible white socks who so far forgot himself as to resume that comfortable posture, received a message from the Chair, "The Czar commands you to haul down those flags of truce."

With no favorites and no near rivals, he ruled alone. Careful not to excite jealousy, he avoided even walking in public with a member. Solitary, the stupendous figure ambled each morning from the old Shoreham Hotel (then on Fifteenth and H Streets), where he lived, to the Hill, barely nodding to greetings and unconscious of strangers who turned to stare at him in the street.

He had a kind of "tranquil greatness," said a colleague, which evolved from a philosophy of his own and left him "undisturbed by the ordinary worries and anxieties of life." Reed gave a clue to it one night when a friend came to discuss politics and found him reading Sir Richard Burton's *Kasidah*, from which he read aloud the lines:

> Do what thy manhood bids thee do,
> from none but self expect applause,
> He noblest lives and noblest dies
> who makes and keeps his self-made laws.

Secure in his self-made laws, Reed could not be flustered. Once a Democratic member, overruled by Reed on a point of order, remembered that the Speaker had taken a different position in his manual, *Reed's Rules*. Hurriedly, he sent for the book, leafed through its pages, pounced on the relevant passage and marched to the rostrum in anticipatory triumph to lay it before the Speaker. Reed read it attentively, cast a glance down at the man from his glowing hazel eyes and said with finality, "Oh, the *book* is wrong."

During the Venezuela crisis he said little publicly, kept the Republicans in the House under firm control and trusted to Cleveland's basic antipathy for foreign adventure, which he shared, to withstand the Jingoes' eagerness to annex this and that. Reed was unalterably opposed to expansion and all it implied. He believed that American greatness lay at home and was to be achieved by improving living conditions and raising political intelligence among Americans rather than by extending American rule over half-civilized peoples difficult to assimilate. To him the Republican party was the guardian of this principle and expansion was "a policy no Republican ought to excuse much less adopt."

The year 1896 was a Presidential one and Reed wanted the nomination. With the Democrats torn by their discords, chances of a Republican victory looked favorable and the nomination was a prize worth fighting for. "He is in excellent health and spirits," reported Roosevelt, and "thinks the drift is his way." Appearing with his moustache shaved off, Reed seemed to one reporter to feel the "necessity of taking himself seriously," which tended to muffle his wit. As a contender for the nomination his position was complicated by the fact that the most vigorous campaigners on his behalf were Lodge and Roosevelt, whose views on expansion were fundamentally opposed to his own, although this had not yet become a touchstone. "My whole heart is in the Reed canvass," said Roosevelt.

Reed would not go out of his way to build up support for himself by the usual methods. When members demanded private appropriation bills for their districts without which they feared they would be unable to cultivate sentiment for his nomination, he was unmoved. "Your bill will not be allowed to come up even with that Reed button in your coat," he said to one member. When the railroad magnate, Collis P. Huntington, of the Southern Pacific, three times asked to see Reed's campaign manager, Representative F. J. Aldrich, Reed said yes, Aldrich might call on him, "But remember, not one dollar from Mr. Huntington for my campaign fund!" Aldrich, who went to see him anyway, confided that Reed would not permit any but a few donations from personal friends and had collected a total of $12,000. Disgusted, Huntington disclosed that Reed's rivals were not so particular about money. "The others have taken it," he said, revealing that he had placed his bets across the board.

Another man was spending money liberally on behalf of a rival candidate. Mark Hanna, the boss of Ohio, had cast a President-maker's eye on Reed in the previous campaign but had found him too sardonic, his oratory too Eastern and his personality hardly amenable. As Henry Adams said, Reed was "too clever, too strong-willed and too cynical" to suit the party chiefs. Since then Hanna had found his affinity in a man the antithesis of Reed—the amiable, smooth-speaking, solidly handsome McKinley, of whom it was said that his strongest conviction was to be liked. He was a man made to be managed. He had never made an enemy and his views on the crucial currency question, as a biographer tactfully put it, "had never been so pronounced as to make him unpopular" either with the silver wing or the gold-standard group. Reed now had cause to regret that in naming McKinley chairman of the Ways and Means Committee he had opened his path to prominence as sponsor of the Mc-Kinley Bill on the tariff. Since the Fifty-first Congress, when McKinley had ventured some objections to the Speaker's methods in the matter of the quorum, Reed had had little use for him. He considered him spineless, an opinion to which he gave immortal shape in the phrase, "McKinley has no more backbone than a chocolate eclair." *

Hanna saw in McKinley less an eclair than a kind of Lohengrin and felt sure he could secure his nomination as long as McKinley's rivals remained divided and did not unite behind any one of themselves, especially not behind Reed, the only one who had the stature for the Presidency. Hanna shrewdly judged Reed too inflexible, however, to be willing to bend for the sake of gaining the others' support. He was right. Eastern leaders, finding the Reed camp dry of inducements, pledged their votes elsewhere. Reed was not making it easy for would-be supporters. When a political chieftain from California asked for a promise of a place on the Supreme Court for a man from his state, Reed refused, saying the nomination was not worth considering unless it were free of any deals whatsoever. The California chieftain was soon to be seen basking in Hanna's entourage. When Governor Pingree of Michigan, who controlled the delegates from his state, came to Washington to see Reed, Aldrich had the greatest difficulty in persuading him to leave the Chair and come down to his office where the Governor was waiting. When at last he did, Pingree held forth on

* This has also been ascribed to Roosevelt. It is not certain to whom the credit belongs.

his views on free silver, which were obnoxious to Reed, who immediately said so. "Pingree wanted to be for Reed," reported Aldrich helplessly. "He went away and espoused the cause of McKinley."

Reed could see the trend but he could not have changed himself. "Some men like to stand erect," he once said, "and some men even after they are rich and high placed like to crawl."

When in a masterly speech he tore, trampled and demolished free silver, which was less a question of currency than of class struggle, Roosevelt, filled with enthusiasm, wrote him, "Oh Lord! What would I not give if you were our standard-bearer." At times, however, Roosevelt confessed to being "pretty impatient" with Reed, who would not satisfy his insistence on support of a big navy. "Upon my word," he complained to Lodge, "I do think that Reed ought to pay some heed to the wishes of you and myself." It was a vain hope to express of a man who was not given to "heeding" anyone's wishes. To Lodge's annoyance, Reed also refused "to promise offices from the Cabinet down or spend money to secure Southern delegates." Hanna, well supplied with funds, was busy in the South collecting white and Negro Republican delegates who were for sale. "They were for me until the buying started," Reed said.

He was not sanguine and already, in a letter to Roosevelt before the Convention met, talked of retiring to the private practice of law. "In a word, my dear boy, I am tired of this thing and want to be sure that my debts won't have to be paid by a syndicate [a reference to McKinley's]. . . . Moreover the receding grapes seem to ooze with acid and the whole thing is a farce."

At St. Louis in June, Lodge made his nominating speech. Reed received 84 votes on the first ballot in comparison to 661 for McKinley and the grapes receded beyond reach.

President Cleveland likewise was rejected by the Democratic Convention in favor of an ambitious thirty-six-year-old Congressman from Nebraska, known for his crowd-catching oratory, who treated the Convention to the most memorable rhetoric since Patrick Henry demanded liberty or death. "Clad in the armor of a righteous cause . . . a cause as holy as the cause of liberty. . . . You shall not press down upon the brow of labour this crown of thorns. You shall not crucify mankind upon a cross of gold!" When the hysteria was over, Governor Altgeld turned a "weary face and quizzical smile" to Clarence Darrow and said, "I have been thinking over Bryan's speech. What did he say, anyhow?"

The campaign roused the country to extremes of emotion and reciprocal hate. It was Silver against Gold, the People against the Interests, the farmer against the railroad operator who siphoned off his profits in high freight charges, the little man against the banker, the speculator and the mortgage holder. Among the Republicans there was real fear that a Democratic victory, coming after the violence of Homestead and Pullman, would mean overturn of the capitalist system. Factory owners told their men that if Bryan were elected "the whistle would not blow on Wednesday morning." Even the *Nation* supported McKinley. When he won, business settled back in its seat, reinforced in its rejection of social protest. "Mark Hanna's era," wrote a contemporary looking back, "marked a climax of this easy defiance by the strong. I well remember the charming bulldog manner in which Hanna took up defense of unlimited private monopoly. . . . It was a note that can never be sounded quite so fearlessly again."

The arena was now cleared for a different battle, in which Reed's fate and his country's were to be decided. Cleveland had refused to be budged when Congress passed a resolution which by recognizing the Cuban rebels as belligerents would have permitted the sale to them of arms. The resolution was "only an expression of opinion by the eminent gentlemen who voted for it," he said, and since the power to recognize rested exclusively with the Executive he would regard it "only as advice," which left "unaltered the attitude of this Government." Now he was replaced by McKinley, who, though personally opposed to war with Spain, was unpracticed in the art of living up to his convictions. In Spain Premier Canovas was dead, leaving weaker hands in control. In New York William Randolph Hearst, having bought the *Journal*, was adapting himself to the dictum of the editor of England's first halfpenny paper, the *Daily Mail*, who on being asked what sells a newspaper, replied, "War." Hearst was helping to manufacture a war by horrendous stories of Spanish cruelties, Cuban heroism, American destiny and duty, empurpled by the demands of a circulation battle with Joseph Pulitzer's New York *World*.

A new factor in the world was the victory of Japan over China in their local war of 1895, which caused a sudden recognition of Japan as a rising power in the East and startled Kaiser Wilhelm II into coining a phrase, *die Gelbe Gefahr*—"the Yellow Peril." The rise of Japan gave urgency and cogency to the demand for the Isthmian Canal and to Captain Mahan's contention that Cuba in the Caribbean as well as Hawaii in the Pacific were necessary for the Canal's strategic defence. In a number of articles appearing in 1897 Mahan showed that the Carribbean was a vital military crossroads which could be controlled either from Jamaica or Cuba, and he set about proving professionally and unanswerably that Cuba from the point of view of situation, strength and resources was "infinitely superior."

His voice echoed in the Senate through Lodge, who repeated the argument that the Canal would make a Cuba a "necessity." As extra inducement to Senators more materially than strategically minded, he expanded on how that "splendid island . . . still sparsely settled and of almost unbounded fertility" offered great opportunities for the investment of American capital and as a market for American goods. Roosevelt, although he had no such forum, was earnestly pleading the same cause wherever he had a hearing. The vociferous campaign he and Lodge were waging reached an august listener who was not pleased.

President Charles William Eliot of Harvard, the "topmost oak" of New England, speaking in Washington on the much-debated issue of international arbitration, denounced the doctrine of jingoism as "offensive." Associated with countries where there had always been a military class, it was, he said, "absolutely foreign to American society, . . . yet some of my friends endeavor to pass it off as patriotic Americanism." He then laid down firmly the principles which he believed made America different from the old nations. "The building of a navy and the presence of a large standing army mean . . . the abandonment of what is characteristically American. . . . The building of a navy and particularly of battleships is English and French policy. It should never be ours." The American policy was reliance upon strength in peace, whereas Jingoes were a creation "of the combativeness that is in man." He specifically identified Lodge and Roosevelt as Jingoes and privately, it was learned, called them "degenerated sons of Harvard."

Eliot spoke with unmatched authority. Descended from Eliots and Lymans who had been settled in New England since the Seventeenth Century, he belonged to a group who felt themselves the best. "Eliza," protested Mrs. Eliot when a friend joined the Episcopal church, "do you kneel down in church and call yourself a miserable sinner? Neither I nor any of my family will ever do that!" His father, a mayor of Boston and a Congressman, was also, as treasurer of Harvard, a member of the seven-man Corporation, Harvard's governing body, which an English observer called "government by seven cousins." His own quarter of a century as president of Harvard had been an unremitting battle against the traditionalists to transform the college from an Eighteenth Century backwater into a modern university. During that time he had, as President Hyde of Bowdoin said, been "misunderstood, maligned, misrepresented, hated," and Eliot himself confessed that in all his public appearances during those years, "I had a vivid sense that I was addressing a hostile audience." Being a fighter, this did not halt him. He was not naturally an ingratiating man. Over six feet tall, with "an oarsman's back, a grave and sculptured head," he was a "noble presence" born to command. A strawberry birthmark which covered one side of his face and pulled a corner of his lip into a seeming superciliousness had set him apart from boyhood and given him a quality of loneliness. With this to overcome and the additional handicap of being, as Professor of Chemistry, a scientist, he had nevertheless been named president of Harvard at thirty-five. His ideal of behavior, in his own words, was that of "a gentleman who is also a democrat." He was inflexible about what he thought was right. When a star baseball player was left off the Harvard team because of low marks, Eliot was heard to remark that this was no loss because he was a player who resorted to deception. "Why," he explained, "they boasted of his making a feint to throw a ball in one direction and then throwing it in ANOTHER!"

Against the strenuous lethargy of the diehards he succeeded in opening the curriculum to modern studies, introducing the elective system, assembling a faculty that gave Harvard its golden age, raising the Law School and Medical School to prestige and prominence and through his influence modernizing the whole American system of higher education. When in 1894 at the age of sixty he celebrated his twenty-fifth anniversary as president, opposition had given way to respect and admiration. He was suddenly recognized as Harvard's greatest president and the "first private citizen of the country." It was said that the Boston Symphony could not open without him and the sanguine birthmark appeared no longer as a blemish but as "an emblem of triumph over the handicaps of life."

To Roosevelt, then thirty-eight, Eliot himself seemed one of the diehards who refused to understand that America's manifest destiny lay outward. Having imbibed deeply from Mahan, Roosevelt felt urgently the need of his country to equip itself for the role of greatness which the times were shaping. The distaste for that role of many of the influential men of his time made his voice shrill with frustration. "If ever we come to nothing as a nation," he wrote Lodge after learning that they had been called "degenerated sons of Harvard," "it will be because the teaching of Carl Schurz, President Eliot, the *Evening Post* and futile sentimentalists of the international arbitration type" will produce "a flabby timid type of character which eats away the great fighting features of our race."

It was maddening to him that now, when war with Spain was in prospect, just such a flabby timid character was in the White House. Roosevelt was determined that there should be someone inside the Administration alert and capable of making ready for great events. He had set his heart on bringing together the man who understood the new destiny—

himself—with the instrument upon which all depended—the Navy. Mc-
Kinley's Secretary of the Navy was an easygoing and friendly gentleman
and former Governor of Massachusetts, John D. Long. Roosevelt believed
that if he himself were appointed Assistant Secretary he could, through
superior force of energy and ideas, take over the real command of that
office.

So did everyone else. Long somewhat apprehensively said, "Roosevelt has the character, standing, ability and reputation to entitle him
to be a Cabinet minister—is not this too small for him?" The only thing
against him, Lodge wrote to his friend after seeing McKinley on his behalf,
was "the fear that you will want to fight somebody at once." Nevertheless
McKinley, persuaded as usual by more forceful characters, appointed
Roosevelt on April 5, 1897, and he was confirmed on April 8. S. S. Mc-
Clure, the explosive and perceptive editor of *McClure's Magazine,* sensed
whence the appointment came and where it would lead. "Mahan must be
seen and talked to at once," he wrote to his co-editor. "He is the greatest
naval biographer and student of this century and his field is going to
become more and more popular." An identical twin of his time, McClure
knew what his twin would do. "Roosevelt seems big from here," he continued. "Write to him and try to get his naval stuff. Mahan and Roosevelt
are just our size." This was indeed so. McClure shared their feeling of
power and muscle and largeness of opportunity. When in the last year
of the century he wanted Walter Hines Page for an editor, he telegraphed
him, "Should see you immediately. Have biggest thing on earth." When
Page agreed to come, McClure was jubilant and replied that they would
make the strongest editorial combine in the world. "Oh my dear boy, *we*
are the people with the years in front of us!"

Now the long-thwarted annexation of Hawaii was revived. Roosevelt
in the effort to galvanize McKinley reported to him on April 22 that the
Japanese had sent a cruiser to Honolulu. He wrote to Mahan asking him
how to solve the political problem of acquiring the islands. "Do nothing
unrighteous," was the classic answer, "but take the islands first and solve
afterward." If he could have his way, Roosevelt replied, they would be
annexed "tomorrow," and Spain turned out of the West Indies and a dozen
new battleships built at once, half of them on the Pacific Coast. He reported a regrettable disposition on the part of Congress to stop naval
building until finances were firmer. "Tom Reed to my astonishment and
indignation takes this view."

Still firm in command of the Republican members, Reed could subdue
any unhealthy lust among them for annexation, but as Speaker he was

bound to pilot Administration policy through the House. The question was, what was Administration policy: the soft reluctance of McKinley or the "outward" drive of Lodge and Roosevelt powered by the ideas of Mahan and the persuasions of the sugar trust? The answer came in June, when a new treaty of annexation was concluded with the Hawaiian government, signed by McKinley and sent to the Senate for ratification. Although there was little likelihood of assembling two-thirds of the Senate in favor of it, the anti-expansionists were worried. Carl Schurz, whom McKinley, always anxious to please, had earlier assured of his disinterest in Hawaii, faced him with the issue after dinner in the White House, over cigars. Very uncomfortable, McKinley pleaded that he had sent the treaty to the Senate only to get an expression of opinion. Nevertheless, Schurz left with a heart "heavy with evil forebodings." In England the *Spectator* said somewhat nervously that the treaty marked "an end to the historic policy of the Republic since its foundation . . . and will mean its gradual evolution into a less peaceful and possibly militant power."

With regard to Cuba, the country was becoming increasingly excited. Reed regarded the Hearst-fabricated furor over Spain's oppression with contempt and Republican espousal of Cuba's cause as hypocrisy. He saw his party losing its moral integrity and becoming a party of political expediency in response to the ignorant clamor of the mob. Without compunction he suppressed the resolution recognizing the belligerence of the "Republic" of Cuba. He too took to the magazines to argue against expansion—in an article whose title, "Empire Can Wait," became a rallying cry for the opponents of Hawaii's annexation. It spoke the awful name; as yet the outright words "empire" and "imperialism," which connoted the scramble for Africa then at its peak among the European powers, had not been used in the United States. James Bryce, perhaps the only Englishman who could have been allowed to give advice, urged Americans to have nothing to do with a policy of annexation. America's remote position and immense power, he wrote in the *Forum*, freed her from the burden of armaments crushing the European powers. Her mission in the world was "to show the older peoples and states an example of abstention from the quarrels and wars and conquests that make up so large and lamentable a part of the annals of Europe." To yield to the "earth-hunger" now raging among the European states would be "a complete departure from the maxims of the illustrious founders of the republic." Behind his sober words could be sensed the love a man feels for the object of his life's work and a pleading to America not to contradict the promise that hung about her birth.

Mahan's mind, planning the strategy of a war with Spain, had already leapt beyond Hawaii to the far-off Spanish possession of the Philippines. What motivated him was not earth-hunger but sea power, the controlling idea which had drawn from him the grand orchestral words about the British Navy in the Napoleonic wars: "Those far distant, storm-beaten ships upon which the Grand Army never looked, stood between it and the dominion of the world." At the end of 1897 he entered the rising debate with a book, *The Interest of America in Sea Power*, in which were collected his major articles over the past seven years. He also advised Roosevelt on the appointment of a new commander of the Asiatic Squadron who could be trusted to act with vigor when the test should come. The chosen officer was Commodore George Dewey and his task was foreseen. "Our Asiatic Squadron should blockade and, if possible, take Manila," Roosevelt wrote to Lodge on September 21, 1897, and he took care to obtain the necessary coal to prepare the Asiatic Squadron for action.

On February 15, 1898, the United States armored cruiser *Maine* blew up and sank in the harbor of Havana with the loss of 260 lives. Although the cause of the explosion was never ascertained, it was impossible in the mood of the time to assume other than a dastardly Spanish plot. The proponents of war burst into hysteria; the peace-minded were outshouted. McKinley hung back, but fearful of a split in his party, soon gave way to the clamor. Speaker Reed did not. During the two months in which negotiations aimed at forcing Spain into war were being pursued, he did his best to hold back the wave, limiting time for debate and quashing resolutions recognizing Cuban independence. When Senator Proctor, who owned marble quarries in Vermont, made a strong speech for war Reed commented, "Proctor's position might have been expected. A war will make a large market for gravestones. " He was attacked by the pro-war press and his rulings aroused resentment in the House, which, on the whole—like the country—wanted war. "Ambition, interest, land-hunger, pride, the mere joy of fighting, whatever it may be" acknowledged the Washington *Post*, "we are animated by a new sensation. . . . The taste of Empire is in the mouth of the people even as the taste of blood in the jungle."

It was too strong for Reed to control. Asked by reporters one morning at breakfast at the Shoreham for comment on the stampede for war, he showed a letter he had just opened from Governor Morton of New York urging him to step down from the chair to the floor of the House and dissuade the members from intervention. "Dissuade them! The Governor might as well ask me to step out in the middle of a Kansas waste and dissuade a cyclone!" He could not keep the ultimatum to Spain from coming to the floor, and the vote for it in the House of 311 to 6 was a measure of the cyclone. To one of the six Reed said, "I envy you the luxury of your vote. I was where I could not do it."

War was declared on April 25, 1898. Mahan, then in Rome, asked by reporters how long he thought the war would last, replied with what proved dead reckoning, "About three months." Returning at once he was appointed one of the three members of the Naval War Board. Roosevelt sent him a plan of campaign for action in the Philippines and on receiving his comments wrote, "There is no question that you stand head and shoulder above the rest of us. You have given us just the suggestions we want."

On April 30 Commodore Dewey's squadron steamed into Manila Bay and with a day's bombardment, loosed by the classic order, "You may fire when ready, Gridley," destroyed or put out of action the Spanish squadron and shore batteries. Never had the country felt such a thrill of pride. GREATEST NAVAL ENGAGEMENT OF MODERN TIMES was one headline. It faced the country suddenly with a new problem which none but a few had thought of: What to do next? The American people on the whole, as Mr. Dooley said, did not know whether the Philippines were islands or canned goods, and even McKinley confessed "he could not have told where those darned islands were within 2,000 miles." The disciples of Mahan knew well enough where they were and what must become of them. Within four days of Dewey's victory Lodge wrote, "We must on no account let the islands go. . . . The American flag is up and it must stay." Since there had been a Filipino independence movement in existence for thirty years, for which many had fought and suffered prison, exile and death, Senator Lodge's simple solution took little account of the consent of the governed. Its leader was Emilio Aguinaldo, a young man of twenty-eight who had been in exile in Hong Kong. Upon Dewey's victory, he had returned at once to the Philippines.

In America the outbreak of a war to be carried to the enemy and posing no danger to the homeland did not silence its opponents but galvanized them. Suddenly they became an entity with a name: the Anti-Imperialists. Professor Norton, now over seventy, brought upon himself torrents of abuse and threats of violence to his house and person by urging his students not to enlist in a war in which "we jettison all that was most precious of our national cargo." Although a Boston Irish politician proposed to send a lynching party for him and the press called him a "traitor" and even Senator Hoar of Massachusetts denounced him, Norton's grief at his country's course was too great to be contained. At a meeting of the Congregational Church in Cambridge he spoke of how bitter it was that now, at the end of a century which had seen the greatest advance in knowledge and the hope of peace, America should be turning against her ideals and "plunging into an unrighteous war."

Others in Boston spoke out. Moorfield Storey, president of the Massachusetts Reform Club and Civil Service Reform League, and a former president of the American Bar Association, was one; Gamaliel Bradford, a rampant critic of government known for his one-man crusades through a flow of letters to newspapers, was another. The first Story (minus the *e*) had settled in Massachusetts in 1635 and Bradford was descended from the first Governor of the Plymouth Colony. Together they assembled a meeting of protest at Faneuil Hall, and here on June 15, 1898, three days after Aguinaldo in the Philippines issued a declaration of independence, the Anti-Imperialist League was founded. Its president was the eighty-year-old Republican George S. Boutwell, former Senator from Massachusetts and former Secretary of the Treasury under President Grant. Its stated purpose was not to oppose the war as such, but to insist that having been undertaken as a war of liberation, it must not be turned into one for empire. The quest for power, money and glory abroad, the League maintained, would distract from reform at home and bring in its train a strong central government destructive of traditional states' rights and local liberties. Americans had enough to do to solve the problems of municipal corruption, war between capital and labour, disordered currency, unjust taxation, the use of public office for spoils, the rights of the colored people in the South and of the Indians in the West, before taking alien peoples under their rule.

These were the problems that absorbed reformers—many of whom, together with independents and dissenters of various kinds and distinguished Democrats who had perforce become the anti-expansion party, now banded together under the banner of the League. Its forty-one vice-presidents soon included ex-President Cleveland; his former Secretary of War, William Endicott; former Secretary of the Treasury, Speaker Carlisle; Senator "Pitchfork Ben" Tillman; President David Starr Jordan, of Stanford; President James B. Angell, of the University of Michigan; Jane Addams; Andrew Carnegie; William James; Samuel Gompers, president of the American Federation of Labor, and numbers of other Congressmen, clergymen, professors, lawyers and writers. The novelist William Dean Howells thought the war "an abominable business." When his friend Mark Twain came home from an extended trip abroad, he too became a member of the League. Besides Godkin's *Evening Post,* its chief voices were the Boston *Herald*, the Baltimore *Sun* and the Springfield *Republican*, while two other Republican papers, the Boston *Evening Transcript* and the Philadelphia *Ledger*, also gave it support.

On the side of the Anti-Imperialists was a strong sentiment, growing out of the troubles with the Negroes after the Civil War, of reluctance to take on new colored populations. Nothing but more trouble would accrue, said Godkin harshly in the *Nation*, from "dependencies inhabited by ignorant and inferior races" with whom Americans had no union "other than would be necessary for purposes of carpet-baggery and corruption." Carl Schurz used the same argument against the Canal, saying that "once fairly started on a career of aggrandizement" the imperialists would insist that the Canal be bordered on both sides by American territory and would want to annex countries "with a population of 13,000,000 Spanish-Americans mixed with Indian blood" who would flood Congress with twenty Senators and fifty or sixty Representatives. Hawaii, where Orientals greatly outnumbered the whites, posed the same threat.

The Anti-Imperialists did not sweep up with them the Populists and followers of Bryan and those soon to be known as Progressives. While these groups opposed standing armies, big navies and foreign entanglements and were in theory anti-imperialist, anti-militarist and anti-European, they were simultaneously imbued with a fever to fight Spain as a cruel European tyrant stamping out liberty at America's doorstep. Bryan called for war as loudly as Theodore Roosevelt and in sincere flattery, if less promptly, had himself appointed Colonel of the Third Nebraska Volunteers, too late to see action in Cuba. Most vociferous of all was a young lawyer from Indianapolis, already famous at thirty-six as a political orator and soon to become a leader of the Progressives. The taste of empire, the rising blood of nationalism expressed in terms of wide-flung dominion, found in Albert Beveridge its most thrilling trumpet. Like Bryan, he possessed that dangerous talent for oratory which can simulate action and even thought. The war sent Beveridge into transports of excitement.

"We are a conquering race," he proclaimed in Boston in April, even before the victory of Manila Bay. "We must obey our blood and occupy new markets and if necessary new lands. . . . In the Almighty's infinite plan . . . debased civilizations and decaying races" were to disappear "before the higher civilization of the nobler and more virile types of man." Pan-Germans in Berlin and Joseph Chamberlain in England also talked of the mission of the superior race, variously Teutonic or Anglo-Saxon, but Beveridge had nothing to learn from them; it was all his own. He saw in present events "the progress of a mighty people and their free institutions" and the fulfillment of the dream "that God had put in the brain" of Jefferson, Hamilton, John Bright, Emerson, Ulysses S. Grant and other "imperial intellects"; the dream "of American expansion until all the seas shall bloom with that flower of liberty, the flag of the great Republic." It was not so much liberty as trade that Beveridge saw following the flag. American factories and American soil, he said, were producing more than the American people could consume. "Fate has written our policy for us; the trade of the world must and shall be ours. . . . We will cover the ocean with our merchant marine. We will build a navy to the measure of our greatness. . . . American law, American order, American civilization will plant themselves on those shores hitherto bloody and benighted but by those agencies of God henceforth to be made beautiful and bright."

Beveridge was so carried away by the opportunities for greatness that the sword he waved flashed almost too nakedly. He spoke of the Pacific as "the true field of our operations. There Spain has an island empire in the Philippines. . . . There the United States has a powerful Squadron. The Philippines are logically our first target."

During the summer while others volunteered and fought in Cuba and sickened of yellow fever and over five thousand died of disease, Beveridge's personal obedience to the call of blood remained rhetorical. He poured scorn on the Anti-Imperialist arguments. "Cuba not contiguous? Porto Rico not contiguous? The Philippines not contiguous? . . . Dewey and Sampson and Schley will make them contiguous and American speed, American guns, American heart and brain and nerve will keep them contiguous forever! . . . Who dares to halt it now, now when we are at last one people, strong enough for any task, great enough for any glory destiny can bestow?" In the following year Beveridge was elected Senator. "We're a gr-reat people," remarked Mr. Dooley. "An' the best iv it is, we know we ar-re."

Theodore Roosevelt in these months was at the front. Though he held a high and crucial office he had made up his mind in advance to give it up, if war came, for active service. Men like himself, as he wrote privately to a friend, having been taunted with being "armchair and parlor Jingoes, . . . my power for good whatever it may be, would be gone if I didn't try to live up to the doctrines that I have tried to preach." He resigned as Assistant Secretary of the Navy immediately after Manila, declined the command of a volunteer cavalry regiment which was offered him by Secretary of War Alger, but asked to serve as Lieutenant Colonel on condition that the command was given to his friend Colonel Leonard Wood of the regular army. This was done. By June 24, two months later, he was in action at San Juan Hill. By July 3 the land fighting was over, the ebullient Rough Rider was a hero and was triumphantly elected Governor of New York in November.

Meanwhile in a Congress flushed with war, advocates of the annexation of Hawaii saw renewed opportunity. Still unable to muster two-thirds of the Senate, they had decided to resort to annexation by a Joint Resolution, which required only a simple majority. The resolution had been introduced in the Senate on March 16 but Reed had been able to prevent its coming to the floor of the House all during the excitement in April. His ruthless command, commented the Washington *Post* on April 15, made him "the most dangerous antagonist in public life." He was in fact the only man whom the dauntless Beveridge did not care to take on. When urged to write to Reed to persuade him not to oppose expansion, Beveridge replied, "I feel that any effort of mine upon the Gibraltar-like mind and will of the Speaker would be absolutely ineffectual."

After the war reached the Pacific, however, even Reed was finding it hard to maintain his iron control. Exasperated, he told Champ Clark of Missouri he wished Dewey would "sail right away from that place. It will make us trouble for all time to come if he does not." The annexationists argued that if the United States did not take Hawaii, Great Britain would, or alternatively Japan, who was already plotting to gain control by encouraging the influx of Japanese subjects subsidized by their government. Besides, it now lay clearly in the American path. "We need Hawaii just as much and a good deal more than we did California," McKinley told his secretary, George Cortelyou, on May 4. "It is Manifest Destiny."

On May 4 the resolution was introduced in the House. Reed stifled it for three weeks against growing pressure. The excuse that control of Hawaii was necessary for the defeat of Spain in the Pacific he regarded as a pure pretext conceived by the sugar interests and imperialists. In this he was at odds with the President, almost all his party in Congress and with friends outside. "The opposition now comes exclusively from Reed, who is straining every nerve to beat Hawaii," Lodge wrote to Roosevelt. Reed even went to the length of enlisting help from the Democrats. When the future Speaker, Champ Clark, a good friend though a Democrat, asked Reed to put him on the Ways and Means Committee, Reed begged him to go on the Foreign Affairs Committee instead, where he needed Clark's help as "a man who believes as I do and who is a fighter."

"If you put it that way," Clark replied, much affected, "I'll stand by you." He agreed to sacrifice the place he had long coveted to help his party's most uncompromising opponent.

Restiveness in Reed's own party was increasing. On May 24 Republican members of the House took the unusual step of signing a petition for a caucus to consider the resolution. It presented Reed with a frontal challenge of all that he had fought for in his battle against the silent quorum. The fundamental premise of that battle and of Reed's Rules was that the will of the House as expressed by the majority must prevail. Reed knew that from his unassailable height above the floor and with his mastery of procedural techniques he could, with Clark's collaboration, fend off a vote on the Hawaii Resolution, but he could not change sentiment. He knew that his own, the majority, party wanted annexation and that the House on the whole was in favor of it. By summoning all his authority he might frustrate the resolution, but if he did, his success would nullify what he had earlier won: the reform which assured that the House really controlled itself, that no tricks of procedure, no arbitrary rules of a Speaker could obstruct the will of the majority. The purpose of the quorum battle had now come to a test, and with tragic irony, against himself. He would have to choose between his hatred of foreign conquest and his duty as Speaker; between, on the one hand, his own deepest beliefs, and on the other, Reed's Rules.

There was only one choice he could make. Knowing too well the value of what he had accomplished in the Fifty-first Congress, he bowed to the majority. Debate opened on June 11, and on June 15 the resolution passed by 209 to 91 with practically unanimous Republican support. Reed was not in the Chair. Representative Dalzell, substituting, announced before the vote, "The Speaker of the House is absent on account of illness. I am requested by him to say that were he present he would vote No." Reed had taken a stand, said the *Nation*, "absolutely alone" among his party. "Courage to oppose a popular mania, above all to go against party, is not so common a political virtue that we can afford not to pay our tribute to the man who exhibits it."

Annexation of Hawaii was formally ratified on July 7, four days after the war in Cuba was brought to an end by a naval battle off Santiago. There the Spanish fleet, attempting to run the American blockade, was destroyed by the superior fire of the five so-lately-built battleships, *Indiana, Oregon, Massachusetts, Iowa* and *Texas*. With the surrender of Santiago two weeks later, Spanish rule came to an end, defeated, not by the Cuban insurgents, but by the United States. When it came to negotiation of peace terms, all the passion lavished during the past three years on the cause of Cuban liberty, all the Congressional resolutions favoring recognition of an independent Cuban Republic and disclaiming intention to annex it proved a serious obstacle to Senator Lodge's "necessity." To take Cuba as the fruit of conquest was impossible, however alluring its strategic and mercantile advantages, but a smaller island, Porto Rico, at least was available. Required to renounce Cuba and cede the smaller neighbor, Spain was eliminated from the Western Hemisphere. The degree of Cuba's independence and nature of her relations with the United States was left to be worked out in the presence of an American occupation force. The result was the Platt Amendment of 1901, establishing a virtual American protectorate.

In the meantime preliminary peace terms were signed in Washington on August 12, leaving the even more troublesome question of the Philippines to be negotiated by peace commissioners who were to meet in Paris to conclude a final settlement. Drawing up a balance sheet of the war, Lodge could say with some satisfaction, "We have risen to be one of the great world powers and I think we have made an impression upon Europe which will be lasting." Mahan writing on the same subject to Mrs. Roosevelt was rather more pompous: "The jocund youth of our people now passes away never to return; the cares and anxieties of manhood's years henceforth are ours."

At home the Anti-Imperialists—through meetings, protests, speeches, articles, petitions, and public conferences—were attempting to hold their country back from plucking the archipelago in the Pacific which seemed to glow with the fatal evil of the apple in the Garden of Eden. Carl Schurz urged McKinley to turn the Philippines over as a mandate to a small power, such as Belgium or Holland, so that the United States could remain "the great neutral power of the world." In France it was the "Dreyfus summer," and Americans, too, in those months felt that their country had reached a moment critical for its character and future. In public and private the debate raged whether to keep the Philippines or turn them over to self-government by the Filipinos. Even the usually hard-headed Mahan caught the fever of righteousness and wrote to an English friend about America's duty to keep the Philippines, *"Deus Vult!* It was the cry of the Crusader and the Puritan and I doubt if man ever utters a nobler."

A three-day conference to consider "some of the most momentous problems in the history of the Republic" was convened at Saratoga in August by leaders in public life both for and against expansion. The favored theme of the expansionists, which called forth their most energetic arguments, was a vision of the vast untapped markets of the Orient with their limitless opportunities for American enterprise. Speaking for the Anti-Imperialists, Henry Wade Rogers, president of Northwestern University and chairman of the Conference on opening day, forcefully made the point that it was not necessary to annex territory in order to trade with it. But he could not summon passion equal to that of Judge Grosscup, notorious as the man who had issued the injunction in the Pullman strike, who delivered an exuberant paean to "the new career of commercial activity upon which I trust we are about to enter." With the Philippines and Hawaii in her hands, the United States would control the path to Asia, a whole continent with "doors swinging inward that will lead us to one half the desirable territory and one third the population of the earth."

Samuel Gompers spoke against conquest of foreign lands not only as a betrayal of American principles but as a danger to the standards of American wage-earners. Strange combinations were wrought in the cause of anti-imperialism. When, at a later meeting in Chicago, Gompers declared that retention of the Philippines would show that "our war was without just cause," Andrew Carnegie sent him a telegram of congratulations saying, "Let us stand together to save the Republic."

President McKinley, after soul-searching and prayer, had arrived at the decision desired by his advisers and popular with his party: the Philippines must be kept. In Paris, Spain's commissioners were given to understand that the time for dickering was over; possession talked. They would have to yield or face renewal of the war. A token payment of $20,000,000 was offered to grease acceptance of the inevitable. On December 10 the Treaty of Paris was signed, transferring sovereignty of the Philippines to the United States, with the $20,000,000 to follow upon ratification. "We have bought ten million Malays at $2.00 a head unpicked," remarked Reed acidly, and in the most prescient comment made by anyone at the time, he added, "and nobody knows what it will cost to pick them."

Although by now it was half expected, Aguinaldo and his forces learned of the settlement in bitterness and anguish, many of them hardly able to believe that their liberators and allies had turned into a new set of conquerors. Without an organized army or modern weapons, they prepared to fight again, while waiting for a still possible default. The strong anti-imperialist current in the United States was known to them and there was hope that the Senate would fail to ratify the treaty.

Reopening on December 5, 1898, the winter session of Congress was dominated by the fight over the treaty, more intense than that over Hawaii.

Every vote counted. To gather their two-thirds, the Republicans led by Lodge as chief Whip had to utilize every artifice, every argument, every avenue of pressure upon their own members and whatever Democrats might be amenable, while the anti-expansionists struggled to hold firm just enough Senators to make a third plus one. In the House at this time certain members proposed to Reed a coalition of Democrats and anti-imperialist Republicans in order to pass a House resolution against the treaty which would lead to its defeat in the Senate. Though it was no secret in Washington's inner circles by now that he "despised" the Administration, Reed refused. While he remained its pilot, he was not prepared to lead a revolt against it. His task as Speaker was filled with gall. "Reed is terribly bitter," wrote Lodge to Roosevelt, "saying all sorts of ugly things about the Administration and its policy in private talks so that I keep out of his way for I am fond of him and confess that his attitude is painful and disappointing to me beyond words."

The public was not happy about the Philippine adventure and confused as to its duty. Democrats and Populists especially had felt the war in Cuba to be in the cause of freedom. Now, through some sorcery of fate, the war had turned into a matter of imposing sovereignty over an unwilling people by right of conquest. America had become the new Spain. In this unhappy moment impressive advice was offered through the combined effort of two men with the same extraordinary sensitivity to history-in-the-making. On February 1, 1899, S. S. McClure published in a two-page spread in his magazine an exhortation in verse by Rudyard Kipling addressed to the Americans in their perplexity.

> Take up the White Man's burden
> Send forth the best ye breed,
> Go bind your sons to exile
> To serve your captives' need;
> To wait in heavy harness
> On fluttered folk and wild,
> Your new-caught sullen peoples,
> Half-devil and half-child. . . .
>
> Take up the White Man's burden
> The savage wars of peace,
> Fill full the mouth of Famine
> And bid the sickness cease. . . .
>
> Ye dare not stoop to less——

The note of righteousness was reinstated; Kipling had struck the perfect combination of noble destiny and unselfish mission. Widely reprinted and quoted, the poem spread across the country within a week, doing much to reconcile the hesitant to the imperial task.

In Washington it appeared as if opponents of the treaty might be successful, for the Republicans lacked one vote to make up the two-thirds for ratification. Suddenly, William Jennings Bryan arrived in Washington and to the amazement of his followers urged them to vote *for* the treaty. As leader of the Democratic party, he fully intended to be the standard-bearer himself in 1900, but he recognized the need of a new standard. Calculating that he could not win on a repetition of the silver issue, he was perfectly prepared to give it up in favor of imperialism, a new crown of thorns. He was sure that retention of the Philippines would be productive of so much trouble as to make a flaming campaign issue—but it must be consummated first. Consequently, he told his party, it would not do to defeat the treaty. This extraordinary reasoning astounded and even shocked those legislators who had thought a principle was involved. Senator Pettigrew, the "silver" Senator of South Dakota, was "so incensed that I finally told him he had no business in Washington on such an errand." In the delicate balance that prevailed, the most important issue since Secession depended on the votes of one or two vacillating Senators. Some were affected when Bryan argued that to ratify the treaty would end the war.

At this point, with the vote scheduled for February 6, with the outcome uncertain, with each side anxiously canvassing and counting every possible aye and nay, the Filipinos rose in their own war of independence. Their forces attacked the American lines outside Manila on the night of February 4. In Washington, although the news intensified the frenzied speculation, no one could be certain what effect it would have. A last-minute petition signed by ex-President Cleveland, President Eliot of Harvard and twenty-two other men of national prominence was addressed to the Senate, protesting against the treaty unless it included a provision against annexing the Philippines and Porto Rico. "In accordance with the principles upon which our Republic was founded we are in duty bound to recognize the rights of the inhabitants . . . to independence and self-government," it said, and pointed out that if, as McKinley had once declared, the forcible annexation of Cuba would be "criminal aggression by our code of morals," annexation of the Philippines would be no less so. Its text was unanswerable but it offered no judgeships, political futures or other coin that Lodge and Bryan were dealing in.

When the Senate voted on February 6, the treaty won by 57–27, with a one-vote margin. It was "the closest, hardest fight I have ever known," said Lodge. In the aftermath one thing on which all agreed was that Bryan had swung the deciding votes. By the time the vote was counted 59 Americans were dead and 278 wounded and some 500 Filipinos were casualties in the Philippines. The cost of picking Malays was just beginning to be paid.

"The way the country puked up its ancient principles at the first touch of temptation was sickening," wrote William James in a private letter. Publicly, to the Boston *Evening Transcript,* he wrote, "We are now openly engaged in crushing out the sacredest thing in this great human world—the attempt of a people long enslaved" to attain freedom and work out its own destiny. The saddest thing for men such as James was the parting with the American dream. America, Norton wrote, "has lost her unique position as a leader in the progress of civilization, and has taken up her place simply as one of the grasping and selfish nations of the present day."

To many others the knowledge of American guns firing on Filipinos was painful. The anger of the Anti-Imperialists deepened and their membership increased to half a million, with branches of the League in Boston and Springfield, in New York, Philadelphia, Baltimore, Washington, Cincinnati, Cleveland, Detroit, St. Louis, Los Angeles, and Portland, Oregon. "We are false to all we have believed in," wrote Moorfield Storey. "This great free land which for more than a century has offered a refuge to the oppressed of every land, has now turned to oppression." Still unwilling to give up, he hoped for leadership from Reed, whom Roosevelt had called "the most influential man in Congress." Writing to Senator Hoar, Storey begged him to "persuade Mr. Reed to come out as he should. He is very sluggish and lacks aggression in great matters. If he would come out I think he might really be the next President."

It was too late. Reed's sluggishness was that of a man for whom the fight has turned sour. Others whose main interest lay in non-political fields could feel as deeply without being shattered. Reed's whole life was in Congress, in politics, in the exercise of representative government, with the qualification that for him it had to be exercised toward an end that he believed in. His party and his country were now bent on a course for which he felt deep distrust and disgust. To mention expansion to him, said a journalist, was like "touching a match" and brought forth "sulphurous language." The tide had turned against him; he could not turn it back and would not go with it.

Like his country, he had come to a time of choice. He could go on to another term as Speaker, but already he could see signs of growing feeling in the House that he was too hostile to the Administration to continue as its principal lieutenant. Joe Cannon and others of his old associates were antagonized by his attitude and his remarks about the President but none dared attempt a contest to unseat him. The President lacked the nerve to come out openly in support of anyone else. Reed knew he could hold his command but it would be a term at bay against a pack snarling at his feet. He became "moody and ugly" in these days and curt to old colleagues whom he saw deserting him.

To retain office as Speaker would be to carry through a policy in the Philippines abominable to him. It would be to continue as spokesman of the party of Lincoln, which had been his home for so long and which had now chosen, in another way than Lincoln meant, to "meanly lose the last best hope of earth." To his longtime friend and secretary, Asher Hinds, he said, "I have tried, perhaps not always successfully, to make the acts of my public life accord with my conscience and I cannot now do this thing." For him the purpose and savor of life in the political arena had departed. He had discovered mankind's tragedy: that it can draw the blueprints of goodness but it cannot live up to them.

In February, 1899, after the vote on the treaty, he made his choice. Although he said nothing publicly at this time, rumors that he intended to withdraw from politics began to appear in the press. When reporters came to ask him about his hostility to the Philippines policy and the Nicaragua Canal bill, he brushed aside their questions with an expression of "fatigue and disgust." In April, after the close of the Fifty-fifth Congress, he authorized an announcement. The unbelievable proved true. Speaker Reed would retire from Congress and after a vacation in Europe would take up the private practice of law in New York as senior partner in the firm of Simpson, Thacher and Barnum.

"Congress without Tom Reed! Who can imagine it!" exclaimed an editorial in the New York *Tribune*. Everywhere was felt a half-frightened sense as of some great landmark being removed, leaving a gaping hole at the feet of observers. The *Times,* never one of his admirers, was moved to a full-column editorial on the "national loss." It felt "there must be something wrong in the political condition" that made such a man leave public life for the private practice of law. Its Washington correspondent called the event a "calamity" for Congress in the degree to which it would reduce the level of ability after the Speaker departed. Godkin in the *Evening Post* mourned the passing from political life of that rare phenomenon, "a mature, rational man."

Reed himself offered no public explanation of his going except to say, in a farewell letter to his constituents in Maine, "Office as a ribbon to stick in your coat is worth no-one's consideration." Cornered in the Manhattan Hotel in New York by reporters who urged that the public would want to hear from him, he replied, "The public! I have no interest in the public," and turned on his heel and walked away.

Military operations in the Philippines swelled in size and savagery. Against the stubborn guerrilla warfare of the Filipinos, the U.S. Army poured in regiments, brigades, divisions, until as many as 75,000—more than four times as many as saw action in Cuba—were engaged in the islands at one time. Filipinos burned, ambushed, raided, mutilated; on occasion they buried prisoners alive. Americans retaliated with atrocities of their own, burning down a whole village and killing every inhabitant if an American soldier was found with his throat cut, applying the "water cure" and other tortures to obtain information. They were three thousand miles from home, exasperated by heat, malaria, tropical rains, mud and mosquitoes. They sang, "Damn, damn, damn the Filipino, civilize him with a Krag . . ." and officers on occasion issued orders to take no more prisoners. They won all the skirmishes against an enemy who constantly renewed himself. A raiding party which missed Aguinaldo but captured his young son made headlines. Reed, coming into his office that morning, said in mock surprise to his law partner, "What, are you working today? I should think you would be celebrating. I see by the papers that the American Army has captured the infant son of Aguinaldo and at last accounts was in hot pursuit of the mother."

Aguinaldo fought for time in the hope that anti-imperialist sentiment in America would force withdrawal of the forces already sickening of their task. The longer the war continued, the louder and angrier grew the Anti-Imperialist protests. Their program adopted at Chicago in October, 1899, demanded "an immediate cessation of the war against liberty." They collected and reported all the worst cases of American conduct in the Philippines and all the most egregious speeches of imperialist greed and set them against the most unctuous expressions of the white man's mission. They distributed pamphlets paid for by Andrew Carnegie, and when the League's executive head, Edward Atkinson, applied to the War Department for permission to send the pamphlets to the Philippines and was refused, he sent them anyway.

Anxious to end the war and placate the "new-caught sullen peoples" and govern creditably, the Administration sent various committees to investigate the atrocities, to find out what the Filipinos really wanted—short of self-government, which they said they wanted—and to report on what form of civil government to give them. In April, 1900, the shy, kindly, three-hundred-pound Judge William Howard Taft was sent out to set up a civil government, armed with a charter drawn up by the new Secretary of War, Elihu Root, which granted the Filipinos a liberal degree of internal autonomy. Since neither they nor the Americans were ready to give up fighting, the attempt was premature, but Taft stayed on, determined to govern in the interest of "the little brown brother" as soon as he was given a chance. When friends at home, concerned for his welfare, sent anxious queries about his health, he cabled Elihu Root that he had been out horseback riding and was feeling fine. "How is the horse feeling?" Root cabled back.

Despite difficulties there was no re-thinking or hesitancy among the dominant Republicans about the new career upon which America was launched. The bill for constructing the Nicaragua Canal was in the Senate and so was Albert Beveridge, more closely allied with the Almighty than ever. "We will not renounce our part in the mission of our race, trustees under God, of the civilization of the world," he said on January 8, 1900. He informed Senators that God had been preparing "the English-speaking and Teutonic peoples" for this mission for a thousand years.

Some of Beveridge's generation found the new image of America repugnant. Hearing the sound of "ignoble battle" coming "sullenly over the Pacific seas," William Vaughn Moody wrote his "Ode in a Time of Hesitation," which appeared in the *Atlantic Monthly* in May, 1900. Are we still the "eagle nation" he asked, or:

> Shall some less lordly bird be set apart?
> Some gross-billed wader where the swamps are fat?
> Some gorger in the sun? Some prowler with the bat?

This was the conscience of the few, felt too by Godkin, who, in his disillusion, said a strange and clairvoyant thing at this time. "The military spirit," he wrote to Moorfield Storey in January, 1900, "has taken possession of the masses to whom power has passed."

As the war passed its first anniversary with the American forces deeply extended, there was one event ahead that might yet bring it to an end: the coming Presidential election. In this the Anti-Imperialists and Aguinaldo placed their hopes. Its earliest oddity was a boom for Admiral Dewey, partly inspired by the desperation of some Democrats to find any candidate other than Bryan. Having concluded after some study of the subject that "the office of President is not such a very difficult one to fill," the Admiral announced he was available but as his wording did not inspire confidence and he seemed vague as to party, his candidacy collapsed. Bryan loomed.

The Anti-Imperialists were caught in an agonizing dilemma. McKinley represented the party of imperialism; Bryan in Carl Schurz's words was "the evil genius of the anti-imperialist cause," loathed for his betrayal in the matter of the treaty and feared for his radicalism. Schurz met with Carnegie, Gamaliel Bradford and Senator Pettigrew at the Plaza Hotel in New York in January, 1900, in an effort to organize a third party so that the American people would not "be forced by the two rotten old party carcasses to choose between two evils." Carnegie subscribed $25,000 on the spot, while the others made up a matching sum. Shortly afterward, members of the steel trust with whom Carnegie was then negotiating the sale of his company told him that if he opposed McKinley the deal would not go through. Preferring United States Steel to a third party, Carnegie withdrew his support, received his shares and retired from business. Schurz and the others, however, held a Liberty Congress at Indianapolis, at which they called on Reed to be their candidate, but neither Reed nor anyone else wanted the vain task of leading a mugwump party. At Kansas City in July the inevitable happened: Bryan was chosen.

Campaigning on imperialism as he had planned, Bryan ranged the country as strenuously as before. He was tarnished, but his magnetism, his passion and his sincerity-of-the-moment still reached through to the people and even across the Pacific. In Bryan, but for whom the Treaty of Paris would have been defeated, the Filipinos placed their faith. "The great Democratic party of the United States will win the next fall election," Aguinaldo promised in a proclamation. "Imperialism will fail in its mad attempt to subjugate us by force of arms." His soldiers shouted the war cry, "Aguinaldo-Bryan!"

In their Chicago platform, anticipating the election, the Anti-Imperialists had said, "We propose to contribute to the defeat of any person or party that stands for the subjugation of any people." There was nothing to do, as a friend wrote to ex-President Cleveland, but "to hold your nose and vote" for Bryan. The modified rapture of such people for the Democratic candidate won them the name thereafter of the "hold-your-nose-and-vote" group. So distasteful to the *Nation* were both candidates that it refused to support either, preferring, as a dissatisfied reader complained, to "sit on a fence and scold at both."

The Republicans had no such difficulties. Although they preferred to be called expansionists rather than imperialists, they were proud of the condition whatever its name, and believed in its goals. Forthright as usual, Lodge said, "Manila with its magnificent bay is the prize and pearl of the East; . . . it will keep us open to the markets of China. . . . Shall we hesitate and make, in coward fashion, what Dante calls the 'great refusal'?" Secretary Hay having pronounced the policy of the Open Door, China's markets were much on men's minds. During the summer of the campaign, the siege of the legations at Peking by the Boxers and the American share in the relief expedition pointed up the far-flung role the country was now playing. Its most convinced and vocal champion was McKinley's new vice-presidential nominee, Theodore Roosevelt, who took the President's place as chief campaigner. Unsure of victory, for the "full dinner pail" was more a slogan than a fact, he campaigned so vigorously and indefatigably that to the public and cartoonists the Rough Rider with the teeth, pince-nez and unquenchable zest appeared to be the real candidate. He derided the specter of militarism as a "shadowy ghost," insisted that expansion "in no way affects our institutions or our traditional policies," and said the question was not "whether we shall expand—for we have already expanded—but whether we shall contract."

The country listened to thousands of speeches and read thousands of newspaper columns raking over every argument for and against imperialism and every aspect of the war in the Philippines. It learned, thanks to the efforts of the Anti-Imperialists, more about the conduct of its own troops than the public usually does in wartime. Dumdum bullets, so thoroughly disapproved (except by the British) at The Hague Peace Conference the year before, were found to have been issued to some American troops. In the end the American people, like the British in their Khaki election of the same year, approved the incumbents. What a people thinks at any given time can best be measured by what they do. McKinley and Roosevelt were elected by 53 per cent of the votes cast and with a greater margin over Bryan than had been received in 1896. Expansion and conquest were accepted and the break with the American past confirmed. Still at war in the Philippines, America moved into the Twentieth Century.

For Aguinaldo, after the election, there was nothing more to hope for. Retreating into the mountains, still fighting, he was captured by trickery in March, 1901, and in captivity in April signed an oath of allegiance to the United States together with a proclamation to his people calling for an end to resistance: "There has been enough blood, enough tears, enough desolation."

Professor Norton voiced the elegy of the Anti-Imperialists. "I reach one conclusion," he wrote to a friend in the month of Aguinaldo's capture, "that I have been too much of an idealist about America, had set my hopes too high, had formed too fair an image of what she might become. Never had a nation such an opportunity; she was the hope of the world. Never again will any nation have her chance to raise the standard of civilization."

Six months later came Czolgosz's shot and McKinley's place was taken by Roosevelt, "that damned cowboy," as Mark Hanna said when he heard the news. The remark was not astute. It was an architect of the new age who now became its President at forty-three.

Reed wrote him a letter of good wishes but the exchange was formal and the gulf remained. Living in New York, Reed formed a congenial companionship with Mark Twain, whose wit and turn of mind and sardonic outlook matched his own. They were guests together on board the yacht of the multi-trust capitalist Henry H. Rogers for a long cruise of which the epic legend survives that Reed won twenty-three poker hands in succession. He visited Washington now and then, once arguing a case before the Supreme Court and entertaining the justices by his rather remarkable style of delivery. He did not revisit the floor of the House but would hold court and see old friends in the office of the Ways and Means Committee. On doctor's orders he succeeded in losing forty pounds but his health was worrisome. In the summer of 1902 he was the central figure at Bowdoin's centennial celebration, where he enjoyed "a rare good time" such as, he said, "we may have again but cannot sanely look for." In December he was back in Washington and while in the Committee Room at the Capitol, was suddenly taken ill. He proved to be in the terminal stage of a chronic nephritis. Five days later, on December 6, 1902, he died, aged sixty-two. Joe Cannon, his successor as Speaker, said of him, "His was the strongest intellect crossed on the best courage of any man in public life that I have ever known." With those two qualities and his "self-made laws," Reed had stood his ground on the swampy soil of politics, uncompromising to the end, a lonely specimen of an uncommon kind, the Independent Man.

4

"Give Me Combat!"

FRANCE: 1894–99

4

"Give Me Combat!"

"THE PERMANENT glamour of France" was a phrase used by an Englishman of the nineties, Sir Almeric Fitzroy, secretary to the Duke of Devonshire. He felt that every child of Western civilization owed a debt to the country from which "came the impulse that dissolved the old world in agony and gave life and passion to the present." For two years, from the summer of 1897 to the summer of 1899, the agony of that old dissolution returned. Rent by a moral passion that reopened past wounds, broke apart society and consumed thought, energy and honor, France plunged into one of the great commotions of history.

During those "two interminable years" of struggle to secure the retrial of a single individual unjustly convicted, "life was as if suspended," wrote Léon Blum, a future premier, then in his twenties. It was as if, in those "years of tumult, of veritable civil war . . . everything converged upon a single question and in the most intimate feelings and personal relationships everything was interrupted, turned upside down, reclassified. . . . The Dreyfus Affair was a human crisis, less extended and less prolonged in time but no less violent than the French Revolution."

It "would have divided the angels themselves," wrote the Comte de Vogüé, on the opposite side from Blum. "Above the base motives and animal passions, the finest souls in France flung themselves at each other with an equal nobility of sentiments exasperated by their fearful conflict."

The protagonists felt a grandeur in the storm that battered them. Decadence was exorcised in the violence of their feelings and they felt conscious again of "high principles and inexhaustible energies." Hate, evil and fear encompassed them as well as courage and sacrifice. Their combat was epic and its issue was the life of the Republic. Each side fought for an idea, its idea of France: one the France of Counter-Revolution, the other the France of 1789; one for its last chance to arrest progressive social tendencies and restore the old values; the other to cleanse the honor of the Republic and preserve it from the clutches of reaction. The Revisionists, who fought for retrial, saw France as the fount of liberty, the country of light, the teacher of reason, the codifier of law, and to them the knowledge that she could have perpetrated a wrong and connived at a miscarriage of justice was insufferable. They fought for Justice. Those on the other side claimed to fight in the name of *Patrie* for the preservation of the Army as the shield and protector of the nation and of the Church as the guide and instructor of its soul. They assembled under the name of Nationalists and in their ranks sincere men were partners of demagogues and succumbed to methods that were reckless and brutal and terms that were foul, so that the world watched in wonder and scorn and the name of France suffered. Locked in mutual ferocity and final commitment the contenders could not disengage, although their struggle was splitting the country and fostering opportunity for the enemy at their frontiers, which every day the enemy measured.

"We were heroes," proclaimed Charles Péguy, who transmuted and exalted the political movements of his day in mystical terms inherited from Joan of Arc. In 1910 he wrote, "The Dreyfus Affair can only be explained by the need for heroism which periodically seizes this people, this race— seizes a whole generation of us. The same is true of those other great ordeals: wars. . . . When a great war or great revolution breaks out it is because a great people, a great race needs to break out, because it has had enough, particularly enough of peace. It always means that a great mass feels and experiences a violent need, a mysterious need for a great movement, . . . a sudden need for glory, for war, for history, which causes an explosion, an eruption . . ." If the values and forces Péguy saw in the Affair were large, it was because they were those of that time and that experience. The Affair made men feel larger than life.

The *casus belli* was condemnation of a Jewish army officer for treason in behalf of Germany; the object of the battle was on the one hand to prevent, on the other to obtain, a reopening of the case. Because it was weak, the Government employed all its weight on the side of its would-be destroyers to brace and support the original verdict. It was not the stable, respected, solidly embedded government enjoyed by the English, but insecure, thinly rooted in public confidence, flouted and on the defensive. Twice since 1789 the Republic had gone down under resurgent monarchy. Emerging as the Third Republic after 1871, France had revived, prospered, acquired an Empire. She nourished the arts, gloried in the most cultivated capital, and raised, on the hundredth anniversary of the Revolution, the tallest structure in the world, the daring, incredible Tower that soared above the Seine, a signal flag of her vitality and genius.

Always, however, in political life the nation was at odds with itself, galled from within by the unreconciled, unsubdued adherents of the *ancien régime* and Second Empire, oppressed from without by the superior strength of Germany and the sense of unfinished war between them, hankering for *revanche* without the means to achieve it. In 1889 discontent with the Republic came to a head in the attempted coup d'état of General Boulanger supported by all the elements of Counter-Revolution who made up the collective Right—the Church, the two hundred families of business and finance, the displaced aristocracy, the royalists and the followers and sympathizers of these groups. Boulanger's attempt ended in fiasco memorable for the remark of the Premier, Charles Floquet, "At your age, General, Napoleon was dead." Nevertheless his attempt shook the Republic and stirred up both the expectations and the frustrations of the Right.

The arrest, trial, conviction and sentencing of Captain Alfred Dreyfus, an artillery officer assigned to the General Staff, which took place in the months October to December, 1894, was not a deliberate plot to frame an innocent man. It was the outcome of a reasonable suspicion acted on by dislike, some circumstantial evidence and instinctive prejudice. Evidence indicated betrayal of military secrets to Germany by some artillery officer on the General Staff. Dreyfus, besides fitting the requirements, was a Jew, the eternal alien: a natural suspect to absorb the stain of treason. As a person he was not liked by his brother officers. Stiff, silent, cold and almost unnaturally correct, he was without friends, opinions or visible feelings, and his officiousness on duty had already attracted unfavorable attention. These characteristics appeared sinister as soon as he came under suspicion. His appearance, the reverse of flamboyant, seemed the perfect cover for a spy. Of medium height and weight, medium brown hair, and medium age, thirty-six, he had a toneless voice, and unremarkable features distinguished only by rimless pince-nez, the fashionable form of eyeglasses in his milieu. His guilt was immediately presumed. When motive and material proof could not be found, the officers who were charged with the inquiry, especially Major Henry and Colonel du Paty de Clam, made up for it by helpful construction and fabrication. Certain that they were dealing with a vile traitor who had sold secrets of military defence to the traditional enemy, they felt justified in supplying whatever was needed to convict him. The dossier they assembled, later to be known as the "Secret File," was persuasive enough to cause the General Staff chiefs sincerely to believe Dreyfus guilty, but it lacked legal proof. Knowing this, and dealing in a case particularly sensitive because of the involvement of Germany, and fearing the blackmail of the press, the then Minister of War, General Mercier, ordered, and the Government of which he was a member permitted, Captain Dreyfus' court-martial to be held *in camera*. When the questions of the five military judges indicated their doubts, the Secret File was submitted to them and withheld from the defence. Convinced by these documents, the judges reached a unanimous verdict of guilty. The death penalty for political crimes having been abolished in 1848, the sentence was life imprisonment. On the prisoner's refusal to confess and persistence in maintaining his innocence, he was ordered confined to Devil's Island, one of three prison islands off the coast of South America used for desperate criminals. A barren rock two miles long and five hundred yards wide, it was cleared of all but guards to accommodate Dreyfus alone, in a stone hut under perpetual surveillance. The unanimity of the military court seemed confirmed by a published rumor that Dreyfus had confessed, which, as it passed from journal to journal, acquired the force of an official statement and satisfied the public.

The next three years were marked by intense efforts both to uncover and to conceal the truth. The long, painful struggle for judicial review, or "Revision," as it was known, originated in the doubts of a few scattered individuals uneasy about the closed trial, who suspected a miscarriage of justice. They uncovered the illegality of the trial—on the basis of material not having been shown to the defence—and accumulated evidence pointing to the probable true culprit, a raffish and exotic officer, Major Ferdinand Walsin-Esterhazy. Their pressures and pryings caused the officers originally responsible for constructing the case against Dreyfus to try to strengthen its weaknesses. Major Henry of the Counter-Espionage Bureau, which by nature dealt in forgery and extra-legal procedures, forged a letter, supposedly from the Italian military attaché, Major Panizzardi, to his German colleague, incriminating Dreyfus after the event, and on this letter, thereafter, the Army's case hung. Each move in the campaign for Revision set off renewed efforts inside the General Staff to shore up the case and cover past fabrications in the Secret File by new ones. Officers succumbed to the mood of conspirators. There were secret meetings, warnings and blackmailings, clandestine relations between Paty de Clam and Esterhazy, dis-

Thomas B. Reed

Captain (later Admiral) Alfred Thayer Mahan

Charles William Eliot

Samuel Gompers

The mob during Zola's trial (drawing by Théophile Steinlen)

Le Pouvoir Civil

The "Syndicate" (drawing by Forain)

Allégorie

L'Affaire Dreyfus.

"Allegory" (drawing by Forain)

Coucou, le voilà!

La Vérité sort de son puits.

"Truth Rising from Its Well" (drawing by Caran d'Ache)

guises in false beards and dark glasses, and various melodramatic enterprises so deeply entangling the Army in acts it could never explain that
by now it could not afford to face a reopening of the case. Anyone agitating
for Revision or raising a question of Dreyfus' lawful conviction became
ipso facto the Army's enemy and by extension the enemy of France.

The Army was not political, not particularly clerical, not exclusively
aristocratic or royalist, not necessarily anti-Semitic. Although many of its
officers were all these things, the Army as a body was part of the Republic,
not, like the Church, its antagonist. Despite the anti-Republican sentiments
of individual officers, it accepted its role as an instrument of the state. The
Republic, needing the Army, was working to make it a more serious,
professionally trained body than the operatic corps of the Second Empire,
which from the Crimea to Sedan plunged into battle with more dash than
staff work. As a whole, the officer corps was still dominated by the
graduates of St-Cyr who came largely from county families still mentally
barricaded against the ideas of the Revolution. Its cult was that of a class
distinct from civilians, little concerned with or aware of what was going
on in the rest of the nation. It was a club loyal to its membership and
cultivating its distinctiveness of which the visible mark was the uniform.
Unlike British officers, who never wore uniform off duty, French officers
before 1900 never wore anything else. Poorly paid, slowly promoted,
drearily garrisoned for long stretches in some provincial town, their re-
compense was prestige: the honors, immunities and cachet of their caste;
in short, the esteem in which they were held.

The esteem was great. In the eyes of the people the Army was above
politics; it was the nation, it was France, it was the greatness of France.
It was the Army of Revolution as of Empire, the Army of Valmy in '92
when Goethe, watching, said, "From this day forth commences a new
era in the world's history." It was the Army of Marengo, Austerlitz and
Wagram, the *Grande Armée* that Lavisse proudly called "one of the most
perfect instruments of war history has ever seen"; the Army of the cuirasse
and saber, of the képi and *pantalons rouges,* of Sebastopol and the Malakoff,
of Magenta and Solferino, the Army that had made France the greatest
military power in Europe until the rise of Prussia, the Army of tragedy as
of glory, the Army of the Last Cartridges at Sedan, of the wild cavalry
charge that evoked the German Emperor's cry, *"Oh, les braves gens!"*
Twenty-five years later, under the never-absent shadow of Germany, the
Army was both defender of the nation and instrument of *revanche*. It was
the means of restoring, someday, the national glory. Men lifted their hats
when the colonel and the colors at the head of a regiment marched by.

In the words of a character whom Anatole France was satirizing—though not misrepresenting—the Army "is all that is left of our glorious past. It consoles us for the present and gives us hope of the future." The Army was *les braves gens*.

In the course of the Affair it became the prisoner of its friends—clericals, royalists, anti-Semites, Nationalists and all the anti-Republican groups who made its honor the rallying cry of their own causes, for their own purposes. Caught in the trap of its early commitment to Dreyfus' guilt, and of the forgeries and machinations by its officers to establish that guilt, the Army's honor became synonymous with maintenance of the original verdict. It was a fort to be defended against Revision.

Resistance to Revision was grounded in the belief that to reopen the trial was to discredit the Army and a discredited Army could not fight Germany. "Revision means War," proclaimed the royalist *Gazette de France* and a war fought with a disorganized Army is *"la Débâcle,"* the name given to the defeat of 1870. How could soldiers go into battle under officers they had been taught to despise? asked the royalist Comte d'Haussonville. Although he thought the idea of an innocent man in prison "intolerable" and the campaign against the Jews "revolting," nevertheless the Dreyfusard campaign against the Army was worse because it destroyed confidence in the officer corps. It was this fear of what would happen if the Army were weakened by distrust that intimidated the Chamber and turned the populace against Revision. The Army was their guarantee of peace. "France loves peace and prefers glory," it was said, and this sentiment too was mauled by Revision. By casting doubt on the infallibility of the General Staff Revision was equivalent to sacrilege against *la gloire militaire* and anyone favoring it was pro-German if not a traitor.

Mystified by the complexities of documents, facsimiles, trials and the Secret File, the people could not reconcile the idea of forgeries deliberately prepared to convict an innocent man with their idea of the Army which meant parades, uniforms, boots, epaulets, guns and flags. How could officers who rode proudly past on horseback, sword in hand, to the sound of music and drums, be imagined bent over tables in stuffy offices carefully forging handwriting and piecing letters together with scissors and glue? There was nothing brave or military about this, therefore it could only be calumny. The people were patriotic and Republican, believed what they read in the newspapers, loved the Army and hated and feared the "others"—*sans-patrie*, incendiaries, church-burners, Dreyfusards—who, they were told, were sworn to destroy it. They shouted *"Vive l'Armée!"* and *"Vive la République!"* "Down with Dreyfusards!" "Down with the Jews!" "Death to traitors!" *"Vive Mercier!"* and any other form of incantation that would serve to banish evil and reassure their faith.

The Army was personified in terms of the Affair by General Auguste Mercier, who as Minister of War in 1894 had originally ordered Dreyfus' arrest and through the consequence of that act became the idol of the Army's supporters and the symbol of its cause. At parties of the *haut monde,* ladies rose to their feet when General Mercier entered the room. Sixty-one, tall, thin, straight and well groomed, he had strongly carved features, a curved nose framed by the sharp upturned points of a "Kaiser" moustache, and expressionless eyes, usually half-closed except when they opened for a cold, direct glance. A veteran of the campaigns in Mexico and at Metz in 1870, he was welcomed by the Staff, on his appointment as War Minister in 1893, as a true soldier who was not a politician. When the Anarchist, Vaillant, had thrown his bomb in the Chamber, Mercier had sat through the smoke and uproar without moving a muscle except to catch a fragment which had bounced off the seat behind him and hand it to the deputy sitting there, saying without expression, "You can have it back." In character firm, decisive and thoughtful, in manner urbane and reserved, he was invariably polite and never abandoned, as the combat grew vicious, the usage *Monsieur* where others used *"sale bête"* or *"ce salaud"* as prefix to the name of a despised opponent.

In 1894 faced with the existence of treason on his Staff and realizing the legal weakness of the evidence collected against Dreyfus, he had ordered his arrest in the hope of extracting a confession. When this was not forthcoming and while the investigating officers were desperately seeking evidence to strengthen the case, the arrest was leaked to the anti-Semitic paper, *La Libre Parole,* which asserted that Dreyfus would not be tried because Mercier was in the pay of the Jews. Under the goading of this and other papers, Mercier had summoned the military editor of *Figaro* and told him what he sincerely believed: that he had had from the beginning "proofs that cried aloud the treason of Dreyfus" and that his "guilt was absolutely certain." He thereby, before the trial, tied the Army to Dreyfus' guilt and locked the terms of the Affair into a position that could never be broken. The issue was instantly recognized at the time. "Today one must be either for Mercier or for Dreyfus; I am for Mercier," said his parliamentary aide, General Riu, to reporters. "If Dreyfus is acquitted, Mercier goes," wrote the royalist editor, Cassagnac, in *l'Autorité,* adding, since Mercier was a member of the Government, "If Dreyfus is not guilty then the Government is." Thereafter every repetition of the choice only hardened the issue.

At the trial, it was General Mercier who authorized submission of the Secret File and its withholding from the defence—the act that made the trial illegal. Fully recognizing the decisive nature of what he had done, Mercier lived up to it during the next two years, through all the mounting evidence of forgeries and false conviction, with increasingly arrogant and positive assertions of Dreyfus' guilt. Once Dreyfus had been convicted on false evidence, any reopening of the case would reveal the Ministry of War, the General Staff and himself as dishonored; in short, as a colleague said, if in a retrial "Captain Dreyfus is acquitted, it is General Mercier who becomes the traitor." Through every reinvestigation and taking of testimony, the trial of Esterhazy, the trial of Zola, the inquiry of the Court of Appeals, the final trial at Rennes, he beat back the forces of Revision and held the citadel of the false verdict. Angular, haughty, icy-faced, never wavering in self-control even when the whole structure he had built was tottering, he reminded an observer of the character in Dante's Inferno who looked around him with disdain, "as if he held Hell in great contempt."

All the strength, except truth, was on his side. Each time the Dreyfusards brought forward new evidence which they were certain this time must force a retrial, it was quashed, suppressed, thrown out or matched with new fabrications by the Army, supported by the Government, by all the *bien-pensants* or right-thinking communicants of the Church, and by the screams and thunders of four-fifths of the press. It was the press which created the Affair and made truce impossible.

Variegated, virulent, turbulent, literary, inventive, personal, conscience-less and often vicious, the daily newspapers of Paris were the liveliest and most important element in public life. The dailies numbered between twenty-five and thirty-five at a given time. They represented every conceivable shade of opinion, calling themselves Republican, Conservative, Catholic, Socialist, Nationalist, Bonapartist, Legitimist, Independent, absolutely Independent, Conservative-Catholic, Conservative-Monarchist, Republican-Liberal, Republican-Socialist, Republican-Independent, Republican-Progressist, Republican-Radical-Socialist. Some were morning, some evening, some had illustrated supplements. Of four to six pages, they covered, besides the usual political and foreign affairs, news of the *haut monde,* of *le turf,* of fashions, of theatre and opera, concerts and art, the salons and the Academy. All the most admired writers, among them Anatole France, Jules Lemaître, Maurice Barrès, Marcel Prévost, contributed columns and critiques and their novels ran serially across the bottom of the front page. Editors on important issues contributed signed editorials of passionate invective. The press was daily wine, meat and bread to Paris. Major careers and a thousand minor ones were made in journalism. Everyone from Academicians to starving Anarchists made a supplementary living from it. Prominent politicians when out of office turned to journalism for a platform and an income.

Newspapers could be founded overnight by anyone with energy, financial support and a set of opinions to plead. Writing talent was hardly a special requirement, because everyone in the politico-literary world of Paris could write—and did, instantly, speedily, voluminously. Columns of opinion, criticism, controversy, poured out like water. *Le Temps,* Olympian and responsible, led all the rest. Its outsize pages were read by everyone in public life, its reviews decided the fate of a play, its editorials on foreign affairs written by André Tardieu were of such influence that the German Foreign Minister, Von Bülow, remarked, "There are three Great Powers in Europe—and M. Tardieu." Only *Le Temps* in its eminence remained above the battle, although inclining gradually toward Revision. *Figaro,* following it in importance, proved vulnerable. Its editor, Fernand de Rodays, after hearing Dreyfus cry out his innocence on the occasion of his military degradation, believed him. Three years later he published the first evidence against Esterhazy as well as Zola's first articles. Although he was a father and father-in-law of officers, his enraged colleagues of the Nationalist press denounced him as a traducer of the Army and organized a campaign to cancel subscriptions to *Figaro.* The management succumbed and De Rodays was ousted, an affair of such moment that Paris gossip said he had been paid 400,000 francs to support Dreyfus and the management 500,000 to get rid of him.

The blackmail of the Nationalist press, wrote Zola, who suffered its extremes, afflicted France like a "shameful disease which nobody has the courage to cure." The mischief-makers were the privately supported organs of special interests or of individual editors who were likely to be men either of rabid principles or none at all. There was Ernest Judet of *Le Petit Journal,* who led the campaign to smear Clemenceau with the mud of Panama and who, when Clemenceau became Premier in 1906, barricaded his villa at Neuilly as if to defend it against a siege. Devoured by a perpetual terror of Freemasons, Judet carried a loaded revolver and a leaded cane weighing twelve pounds. There was the old royalist, Paul de Cassagnac, who started the fashion in journalism for abuse and insult, and attacked everyone and everything from habit regardless of consistency. There was Arthur Meyer, a converted Jew, son of a tailor, grandson of a rabbi, an ardent Boulangist and royalist who was editor of *Le*

Gaulois, which specialized in the doings of the *haut monde.* It was the paper read by the world of the "Guermantes." Meyer's wholehearted adoption of that world's opinions and prejudices took a certain courage or a thick skin, for he was no Charles Swann who melted into his surroundings, but in appearance resembled the anti-Semitic caricatures of Jews. He nevertheless had married into the Faubourg—a dowerless daughter of the Comte de Turenne—was accepted into the circle of the Duchesse d'Uzès, became friend, adviser and confidant of the late Pretender, the Comte de Paris, and set masculine style by the cut of his morning coat and the fold of his cravats.

Henri, Comte de Rochefort, of *l'Intransigeant,* was the kind of journalist whose capacity for mischief is unfettered by doctrine: the more unsettled his convictions, the more brilliant and scathing his pen. A constitutional "anti" described by a friend as "a reactionary without knowing it," a bright-eyed cynic and "aristo" with a pointed white beard and an exuberant laugh, Rochefort combined in his person almost every tendency, no matter how opposite, of the Third Republic. His *Adventures of My Life* filled five volumes. He had been everything from an antagonist of Napoleon III to an associate of General Boulanger and his daily column was the delight of the most impressionable and excitable portion of the public.

Approached by the early Dreyfusards on the theory that he would relish a challenge to prove innocent a condemned man whom everyone believed guilty, Rochefort had been cordial, but was dissuaded from the adventure by his manager, Ernest Vaughan, on the ground that public opinion would not stand for disrespect of the Army. Rochefort found the other side just as exciting and when Vaughan meanwhile changed his mind, they quarreled, with the historic result that Vaughan departed to found his own paper, *l'Aurore,* and to provide an organ for the Dreyfusards which they had hitherto lacked. Rochefort retaliated with the most mischief-making story of the Affair. He informed his readers that a letter from the Kaiser to Dreyfus existed which the President of the Republic had been forced by threat of war to return to the German Ambassador, Count Münster, but not before it had previously been photographed. *L'Intransigeant* could say with "absolute certainty" on the authority of a high military personage that this was the "secret document" on which Dreyfus had been convicted.

So befuddled was the public mind by the fumes of mystification and intrigue rising from the Affair that the story was widely believed. It haunted efforts for Revision at every turn. It added fuel to the argument that Revision meant war. What acted on public opinion in the Affair was never what happened but what the Nationalist press and whispered rumor said happened. Intervention by Count Münster had indeed taken place for the purpose of officially denying any contact with Dreyfus but the view the public had of this incident was of a virtual ultimatum. The generals, whose thinking for good reason was dominated by the problem of Germany, used this as their excuse for not reopening the verdict and argued it so convincingly they convinced themselves. General Mercier testified he had sat up until midnight with the President and Premier after the interview with Count Münster waiting "to learn if war or peace would be the issue." General Boisdeffre, Chief of General Staff, angrily said to Princess Mathilde Bonaparte, when she argued the innocence of Dreyfus, "How can you say such a thing to me who has seen and held in his hands Dreyfus' own letters to the German Emperor?" Furious, the renowned hostess shouted, "If you have seen such letters they can only be apocryphal. You cannot make me believe in such a thing." Whereupon Boisdeffre strode out of the room in a rage and the Princess, letting out a sigh of relief, exclaimed, *"Quel animal, ce général!"*

What was truth and what people persuaded themselves was truth became hopelessly blurred. The German Government's several denials of any knowledge of Dreyfus were ignored on the ground that Berlin would not know the names of spies its agents dealt with. On the other hand, the Nationalist papers pictured Germany as affronted to the point of threatening war by France's condemnation of Dreyfus in the face of its denials. Any willingness to consider Revision was denounced as cowardly submission to German pressure—and proof of the power of the "Syndicate."

A creation of the anti-Semitic press, the "Syndicate" represented the Right's idea of evil. It was supposed to be a subterranean fellowship of the Jews, a black and sinister conspiracy whose forces were mobilized to reverse the conviction of Dreyfus and to substitute a Christian as the traitor in his place. Any development in the case unfavorable to the Nationalists could be ascribed to the "Syndicate." Any prominent or respected person who proclaimed himself in favor of Revision was in the pay of the "Syndicate." Evidence of the Army's forgeries was itself forged by the "Syndicate." The Nationalists said it had spent ten million francs since 1895 for corrupting judges and handwriting experts, suborning journalists and ministers. They said its funds supplied by the great Jewish bankers were deposited in the vault of an international bank in Berlin. They said its German adviser was Pastor Günther, the Kaiser's personal chaplain. Its aim was to break down the nation's faith in the Army, reveal its military secrets and, when defenceless, open its gates to the enemy. It was personified by the cartoonists as a fat Jewish-featured figure in rings and watch chains wearing an expression of triumphant malevolence, standing with one foot on the neck of a prostrate Marianne. As the animus of the Affair grew, the "Syndicate" swelled in Nationalist eyes into a monstrous league not only of Jews but of Freemasons, Socialists, foreigners and all other evilly disposed persons. It was said to be drawing on funds from all France's enemies, who were using Dreyfus as an excuse to discredit the Army and divide the nation. The humiliation suffered at Fashoda at the hands of England was seen as engineered by the "Syndicate." The "Syndicate" was everywhere; it embodied the hates and fears of the Right. It was the Enemy.

The sudden and malign bloom of anti-Semitism in France was part of a wider outbreak. As a social and political force anti-Semitism emerged in the late Nineteenth Century out of other expanding forces which were building tensions between classes and among nations. Industrialization, imperialism, the growth of cities, the decline of the countryside, the power of money and the power of machines, the clenched fist of the working class, the red flag of Socialism, the wane of the aristocracy, all these forces and factors were churning like the bowels of a volcano about to erupt. "Something very great—ancient, cosmopolitan, feudal, agrarian Europe," as a contemporary said, was dying and in the process creating conflicts, fears and newfound strengths that needed outlet.

A classic outlet was anti-Semitism. As scapegoat to draw off discontent from the governing class, it appeared in Germany under Bismarck in the seventies and in Russia in the eighties. The pogroms of 1881 and the subsequent disabling May Laws awoke in Jews a recognition of Mazzini's dictum, "Without a country you are the bastards of humanity." Anti-Semitism served equally as scapegoat for the propertied class, and its virulence at this time reflected a profound unease under a sense of impending breakup of the old order. Old values were giving way. Anarchist assaults, Socialist agitation, the growing self-consciousness of labour were threatening position and property, and nothing so generates hostility as a threat to possessions. In the West the new antipathy afflicted cultivated men like Balfour's secretary, George Wyndham, and Theodore Roosevelt's particular friend, the English diplomat Cecil Spring-Rice. Henry Adams expressed it rabidly and incessantly: he lived only in the wish to see the end of "infernal Jewry" and all "gold-bugs"; "we are in the hands of Jews who do what they please with our values"; "I read with interest *France juive, Libre Parole* and all"; "I pass the day reading Drumont's anti-Semitic ravings."

In men of this class the sentiment sprang from hatred of the new power of money (although nothing concerned Adams himself more than money), that is, of new "gold-bug" money deriving from stocks and shares and financial operations, in place of the acceptable form deriving from land and rents. The Jewish problem, explained the Duc d'Orléans during the Affair, was one of economic war. The day was approaching when all persons with attachment to the land and thus to their country would have to defend themselves against "the anonymous and vagabond" fortunes of the Jews, who had gorged themselves on the ruin of the Union Générale with the Government as their accomplice. The Union Générale was a Catholic bank founded with the blessing of Pope Leo XIII with the express purpose of attracting the investments of the faithful. On the advice of their priests, the aristocracy invested in it their capital, and modest Catholic families their savings. When, owing to the superior resources and shrewd maneuvers of its rivals, including the Rothschilds, the Union Générale collapsed in 1882, rich and poor Catholics alike lost their funds. The Jews were blamed. The Jewish "question" began to be discussed in the clerical and royalist papers. Secret plots and malignant powers were attributed to them. All the arguments which the Jew had inspired as the perennial stranger who persisted in retaining his own identity were revived. Jews were not Frenchmen; they were aliens within the French body, probably conspiring against France, certainly against the Church; they were promoters of the anti-clerical movement and enemies of Catholic *bien-pensants*.

French anti-Semitism, like its virulent appearances elsewhere in history, required the juncture of an instigator with circumstance. The instigator in this case was the previously unknown Edouard Drumont, who in the wake of the collapse of the Union Générale wrote a two-volume book, *La France Juive,* published in 1886 to instant success. It was a polemic compounded of Rothschilds and ritual murder, not a philosophical treatise like Gobineau's earlier *Essay in Racial Inequality,* which had its greatest appeal across the Rhine where the inhabitants were engaged in constructing a theory of a master race. Drumont's central theme was the evil power of Jewish finance. The book was widely read and reprinted and its author, a hearty, red-faced, thick-bodied man with a bushy black beard, thrived. In 1889 in association with the Marquis de Morès he founded the National Anti-Semitic League to fight "the clandestine and merciless conspiracy" of Jewish finance which "jeopardizes daily the welfare, honor and security of France." At its first big public meeting the Duc d'Uzès, the Duc de Luynes, Prince Poniatowski, the Comte de Breteuil and other members of the aristocracy felt gratified at finding themselves seated next to real workmen from the butcher shops and slaughterhouses who in turn were delighted to find themselves sharing their opinions with noblemen.

After the success of the book and the League, Drumont's next step was inevitably a newspaper. In 1892 he founded *La Libre Parole,* just at the time when the anger of bilked investors in the Panama loan fell upon its two leading promoters, Cornelius Herz and the Baron de Reinach, both Jews. Drumont's paper in foaming philippics and raging pursuit of the evildoers, became a power. It undertook at the same time a campaign to drive Jewish officers out of the Army as a result of which two of them fought duels with Drumont and the Marquis de Morès. The Marquis went to the unusual length of killing his opponent and was charged with foul play but acquitted in court.

When Dreyfus was condemned, *La Libre Parole* explained his motive to the public: revenge for slights received and the desire of his race for the ruin of France. *"A mort! A mort les juifs!"* the crowd howled outside the railings of the parade ground where the ceremony of his degradation took place.

The cry was heard by the Paris correspondent of the Vienna *Neue Freie Presse,* Theodor Herzl, who was standing amongst the crowd. "Where?" he wrote later. "In France. In republican, modern, civilised France, a hundred years after the Declaration of the Rights of Man." The shock clarified old problems in his mind. He went home and wrote *Der Judenstaat,* whose first sentence established its aim, "restoration of the Jewish state," and within eighteen months he organized, out of the most disorganized and fractional community in the world, the first Zionist Congress of two hundred delegates from fifteen countries. Dreyfus gave the impulse to a new factor in world affairs which had waited for eighteen hundred years.

The first Dreyfusard was Bernard Lazare, a left-wing intellectual and journalist who edited a little review called *Political and Literary Conversations* while he earned a living on the staff of the Catholic and Conservative *Echo de Paris*. An Anarchist in politics, a Symbolist in literature, and a Jew, he wore bifocals over shortsighted eyes whose gaze, said his friend Péguy, "was lit by a flame fifty centuries old." Suspecting the verdict from the start, he had learned from the commandant of the prison that Dreyfus, far from having confessed, had never ceased to declare his innocence. With the help of Mathieu Dreyfus, who was convinced of his brother's innocence, and after a prolonged search for evidence, hampered by silence, obfuscation and closed doors, Lazare finally brought out a pamphlet entitled, *A*

Judicial Error; the Truth About the Dreyfus Case. Although three thousand copies had been distributed to ministers, deputies, editors, journalists, and other opinion-makers, it had been ignored. Lazare's and Mathieu Dreyfus' visits to men of influence succeeded no better. "They bore us with their Jew," said Clemenceau. Comte Albert de Mun, the eminent Catholic social reformer, refused to see them and the Socialist leader, Jean Jaurès, was cold. The Socialist paper, *La Petite République,* reviewing Lazare's pamphlet, reached the required Marxist conclusion that "strikers are unjustly condemned every day without having committed treason and deserve our sympathies more than Dreyfus." Socialists could see no cause for concern in the Affair. Under the conditions of class war, the misfortunes of a bourgeois were a matter of indifference to them. Their traditions were anti-militarist, and Dreyfus, besides being a bourgeois, was an Army officer. Miscarriage of justice as applied to a member of the ruling class was a twist they were more likely to appreciate than deplore.

But the ripples of doubt started by Lazare spread and the Dreyfusard movement was launched. It caught up Lucien Herr, librarian of the Ecole Normale Supérieure, heart of the academic world. Here the keenest students in the country were prepared by the most learned professors for careers as the future teachers of France. Herr was a believer in Socialism, a friend and preceptor of the student world. During the summer vacation of 1897 he used to ride over every afternoon to discuss ideas with his young friend, Léon Blum. One day he said point-blank, "Do you know that Dreyfus is innocent?" It took Blum a moment to place the name; then he remembered the officer convicted of treason. He was startled, having like most of the public accepted the report of Dreyfus' confession as the official version. Herr's influence was pervasive. "He directed our conscience and our thought," wrote Blum. "He perceived truth so completely that he could communicate it without effort."

Elsewhere men who had been collaborators of Gambetta in the founding of the Third Republic, and to whom the principles for which it stood were sacred, stirred and felt uneasy. Two especially became active: Senator Ranc, a leading Radical and a member of the first Government of the Republic, and the younger Joseph Reinach, who in his twenties had been Gambetta's chief secretary. As the nephew and son-in-law of the venal Baron de Reinach of Panama ill-fame, he had cause for extra sensitivity, although it was less Jewish sympathies than concern for French justice that moved him. They found their champion in a man universally respected, Senator Scheurer-Kestner, Vice-President of the Senate, a founder of the Republic and onetime editor of Gambetta's paper *La République Française.*

As a native of Alsace who after 1871 had chosen to live in France, he had been appointed Senator for life and was regarded as the embodiment of the lost province. A dignified gentleman of substance, old family and quiet elegance, he represented the aristocracy of the Republic. When a reporter from *La Libre Parole* came to interview him and sat himself down in an armchair, "the Duc de Saint-Simon himself," it was said, "could not have been more scandalized" than Scheurer-Kestner, who was outraged at anyone from such a paper entering his house. When he learned that the Army had suppressed evidence showing the man on Devil's Island to be innocent and Esterhazy to be the real author of the document used to convict him, he was horrified.

This evidence had been discovered by an Army officer, Colonel Picquart, who had been appointed new chief of the Counter-Espionage Bureau some months after Dreyfus' conviction. When he presented his findings to the Chief and Assistant Chief of the General Staff, Generals Boisdeffre and Gonse, he met a wall of refusal either to prosecute Esterhazy or release Dreyfus. When Picquart insisted, Gonse asked him why he made such a point of bringing Dreyfus back from Devil's Island.

"But, General, he is innocent!" Picquart replied. He was told that this was "unimportant," the case could not be reopened, General Mercier was involved, and the evidence against Esterhazy was not definitive. When Picquart suggested that matters would be worse if the Dreyfus family, known to be investigating, turned up the truth, Gonse replied, "If you say nothing no one will know."

Picquart stared at him. "That is abominable, General. I will not carry this secret to my grave," he said, and left the room. Trained as a soldier, as loyal and obedient to the service as any other officer, with no ax to grind, no personal motive, nothing to gain in public notoriety as was to move later actors in the Affair, Picquart acted then and thereafter, at certain risk to his career, from purely abstract respect for justice. He was, if anything, anti-Semitic, and on one occasion, when asked to take Reinach, who was a reserve officer, on his staff during maneuvers, had objected, saying, "I can't stand the Jew." For Dreyfus he cared no more than for Reinach. It was the fact that the Army could knowingly condone punishment of an innocent man that he could not stomach. When he would not desist in his pressure he was transferred to an infantry regiment in Tunisia. Subject to Army discipline he could make no public disclosures, but he contrived a brief return to Paris on leave during which he disclosed the facts to a friend who was a lawyer, and left a sealed report to be given in the event of his death to the President of France. Subsequently, when his disclosure became known, he was recalled, arrested, tried and convicted of misconduct, discharged from the Army, later rearrested and imprisoned for a year.

Meanwhile his information had been given by his lawyer to Scheurer-Kestner, a personal friend, who instantly spoke out, asserting Dreyfus' innocence to fellow Senators and demanding a judicial review. He bore down upon the Government, harassed the Ministers of War and Justice, repeatedly interviewed the Premier and President. They stalled, put him off and promised "inquiries." National elections were due in May, 1898, only eight months off. A retrial would raise a howl by the mischief-making press and involve a public inquiry into Army affairs that, once started, could lead anywhere, with undesirable effects both on Russia, with whom France had recently concluded a military alliance, and on Germany. These matters of state, foreign and domestic, outweighed a question of justice for a solitary man on a distant rock; besides, to men who want to stay in office, the nature of justice is not so clear as to those outside. The ministers allowed themselves to be persuaded by the General Staff, on the strength of Major Henry's forged letter, which they had no reason to suspect, that Dreyfus must be guilty after all and Esterhazy probably an accomplice, or some other sort of unfortunate complication not justifying the terrible disturbance of a retrial.

Scheurer-Kestner hammered in vain. He thereupon published a letter in *Le Temps* informing the public that documents existed "which demonstrate that the culprit is not Captain Dreyfus," and demanding a formal inquiry by the Minister of War to "establish the guilt of another."

At the same time, *Figaro* published letters from Esterhazy to a cast-off mistress, one in facsimile, written during the Boulangist era, which expressed disgust for his own country in startling terms. "If I were told that I would die tomorrow as a Captain of Uhlans sabering Frenchmen, I should be perfectly happy," he had written, and added a wish to see Paris "under a red sun of battle taken by assault and handed over to be looted by 100,000 drunken soldiers." These extraordinary effusions of venom and hate for France in the handwriting of the *bordereau* * on which Dreyfus' guilt hung seemed to the Dreyfusards like a miracle. They thought their battle won. But they learned, as Reinach wrote, that "justice does not come down from heaven; it must be conquered." The journals of the Right immediately denounced the letters as forgeries fabricated by the "Syndicate." Esterhazy himself, a gambler in debt, a speculator on the Bourse, a fashionable and witty scoundrel, married to the daughter of a marquis, a

* The document recovered from the wastebasket of the German military attaché which was the original evidence of treason. It was a list of the information supplied.

man of sallow and cadaverous countenance with a crooked nose, a sweeping black Magyar moustache, the "hands of a brigand" and the air, wrote an observer, "of an elegant and treacherous gipsy or a great wild beast, alert and master of itself," was now transformed by the Nationalist press into a hero and his innocence made an article of faith.

To the same degree, Scheurer-Kestner was vilified and the public encouraged to demonstrate on the day he was to make a statement in the Senate. Tall, upright, pale, with high forehead, white beard and the austere air of a Huguenot of the Sixteenth Century, he walked to the tribune with measured step, as if he were mounting a scaffold. Outside in the foggy winter afternoon, crowds filled the Luxembourg Gardens howling against a man of whom they knew nothing. He read his appeal to reason in a slow heavy voice to antagonistic Senators who punctuated his speech with boos and insulting laughter. His reminder that he was the last deputy of French Alsace, which at any other time would have moved them, was met with cold silence, and, when he finished, hostile looks followed his return to the floor. A month later in the annual re-election for officers of the Senate he was defeated for the vice-presidency, the office he had held for nearly the life of the Republic.

His battle aroused the formidable support of Clemenceau, the government-breaker, *l'homme sinistre,* as the Conservatives called him, fearsome in debate, in opposition, in journalism, in conversation and in duels with pistol or épée. He fought a duel with Paul Déroulède over Panama and with Drumont over the Affair. He was a doctor by training, a drama critic who promoted Ibsen, an old and intimate friend of Claude Monet, whose work, he wrote in 1895, was guiding man's visual sense "toward a more subtle and penetrating vision of the world." He commissioned Toulouse-Lautrec to illustrate one of his books and Gabriel Fauré to write music for one of his plays. "Only the artists are on the right path," he said at the end of his life. "It may be they can give this world some beauty but to give it reason is impossible."

Out of office and Parliament since Panama, Clemenceau, when persuaded of the facts about Dreyfus by Scheurer-Kestner, saw the shape of a great cause and seized upon it, though not only as a vehicle of political ambition. To Clemenceau the menace of Germany was the dominant fact of political life. "Who"—he demanded, enraged by Esterhazy's vision of Prussian Uhlans sabering Frenchmen—"who among our leaders has been associated with this man? Who is protecting Esterhazy? . . . To whom have the lives of French soldiers and the defense of France been surrendered?" After Germany came anti-clericalism. "The French Army is in the hands of the Jesuits. . . . Here is the root of the entire Dreyfus case." Every day in *l'Aurore* he cut and thrust at the issues of the Affair, writing 102 articles on it in the next 109 days, and altogether nearly five hundred over the next three years, enough, when collected, to fill five volumes. Through all rang the bell of justice. "There can be no patriotism without justice. . . . As soon as the right of one individual is violated, the right of everyone is jeopardized. . . . The true patriots are we who fight to obtain justice and to liberate France from the yoke of gold-braided infallibility."

The Dreyfusard cause, too, had its opportunists. Urbain Gohier, an ex-monarchist who now professed to be a Socialist, lashed at the Army in *l'Aurore*. Its officers were "generals of debacle," "Kaiserlicks" who knew nothing but "flight and surrender" and brought no victories except over the French; they were "the cavalry of Sodom" with retinues of kept women. "One half of France is slinging invective at the other," worriedly wrote the French-born Princess Radziwill, née de Castellane, from Berlin. Married to Prince Anton Radziwill, the Prussian member of an international family of Polish origin who "loves to talk English while his brother, a Russian, talks French," she had dedicated herself to a goal of Franco-German rapprochement. "No one can see how it will finish," her letter continued, "but it cannot go on like this without real moral danger."

The danger was more than moral. Germany watched carefully the internal conflict that absorbed all France's attention. Her periodic denials of dealings with Dreyfus were designed less in the interest of justice than of aggravating French dissension. Happy in the consciousness of innocence, the Kaiser was not reluctant to inform visitors and royal relatives that France had convicted an innocent man. Through the family international of European royalty the word spread. In St. Petersburg in August, 1897, when the case had not yet become the Affair in France, Count Witte, the leading Russian minister, said to a member of a visiting French mission, "I can see only one thing that could cause great trouble in your country. It is this business of a captain condemned three years ago who is innocent"

The assumption so carelessly taken for granted in St. Petersburg was passionately rejected in the French Chamber in December by a sincere and honorable man of lofty ideals. To Comte Albert de Mun the innocence or guilt of Dreyfus was infused with another meaning; transformed, no less than the bread and wine of the sacrament, into another nature. Belief in Dreyfus' guilt was belief in God.

The fusion of these ideas lay in the condition of chronic war between the Church and the Republic. Since the Revolution, the Church had been on the defensive against the purpose of the Republic in the words of Jules

Ferry, "to organize mankind without God or King." The religious orders, furiously resisting the effort of the Republic to displace them from control of education, saw their hope of survival in restoration of the Catholic monarchy. This was what brought the Church in France into position in the Affair. It was the ally of the Army in its own mind as well as in Republican propaganda, which always linked "the Sword and the Censer." In the Jesuits the Republic saw the militant and aggressive general staff of clericalism who pulled the strings which moved the Dreyfus plot. The Jesuit leader was Father du Lac, confessor of both General Boisdeffre and the Comte de Mun, who were regarded as his mouthpieces.

To Pope Leo XIII, a realist looking on from outside, it seemed possible the Republic was here to stay. After the collapse of the Boulanger coup he could no longer believe that restoration of the monarchy was a serious possibility. Besides, he needed French support in his struggle with the Italian state. In the Encyclical of 1892 he urged French Catholics to reconcile themselves to the Republic, to support, infiltrate and ultimately capture it, in a policy called the *Ralliement*. Catholic progressives rallied, others did not and the Left did not trust the policy. "You accept the Republic," said Léon Bourgeois, leader of the Radicals to a meeting of Ralliés. "Very well. Do you accept the Revolution?" De Mun was one who never had.

When, in the midst of the Affair, de Mun arrived at the peak of a French career—election to the French Academy—he chose Counter-Revolution as the theme of his address. The Revolution, he proclaimed, was "the cause and origin of all the evils of the century"; it was "the revolt of man against God." He believed the ancient ideals and ideas were about to "reappear in our time with irresistible evolution" and revive "the social concepts of the Thirteenth Century." To heal the wounds of social injustice under which the working class suffered and re-Christianize the masses alienated by the Revolution had been the goal of his political career.

As a young cavalry officer out of St-Cyr, de Mun first became acquainted with the lives and problems of the poor through the charitable work of the Society of St-Vincent de Paul in his garrison town. During the Commune, as an aide to General Galliffet, who commanded the battalion that fired on the insurgent Communards, he saw a dying man brought in on a litter. The guard said he was an "insurgent," whereupon the man, raising himself up, cried with his last strength, "No, it is you who are the insurgents!" and died. In the force of that cry directed at himself, his uniform, his family, his Church, de Mun had recognized the reason for civil war and vowed himself to heal the cleavage. He blamed the Commune on "the apathy of the bourgeois class and the ferocious hatred for society of the working class." The responsible ones, he had been told by one of the St. Vincent brothers, were "you, the rich, the great, the happy ones of life who pass by the people without seeing them." To see and discover them de Mun had worked among the poor. "It is not enough to perceive the wrong and know its cause," he said. "We must admit ourselves responsible and confess that society has failed in its duty toward the working class." He determined to enter politics but his candidacy for the Chamber and his activities had been resented in the Army. Forced to choose, he had resigned his commission and broken his sword.

Yet in the Chamber his love for the Army remained and formed the theme of his most stirring speeches. Delivered with the adoration of a disciple and the fire of a champion, they made him known as *le cuirassier mystique*. He was the finest orator of his side, "the Jaurès of the Right," who brought to perfection the carefully taught art of the spoken word. A tall figure of dignified bearing, controlled gestures and exquisite manners, he was incomparable in authority when he rose to his feet. He spoke with force of conviction and conscious architecture of phrase, using his voice like a violin, sonorous and vibrant or muted and trembling, in long harmonious rhythms, sudden broken stops and eloquent perorations. His oratorical duels against two major opponents, Clemenceau and Jaurès, were spectacles of style and drama which audiences attended as they would Sarah Bernhardt playing *l'Aiglon*.

Although diehards accused him of being a Socialist and of encouraging subversive ideas and disturbing the established order, his essential loyalties were those of his class. He had been a supporter of Boulanger and until 1892 a royalist of sufficient stature to have the Comte de Chambord * as godparent for one of his children. When Leo XIII, however, called for the *Ralliement*, although most French royalists were stunned and rebellious, de Mun renounced royalist politics—if not sympathies—to become a leader of the Ralliés. Although his aim was social justice, he rejected Socialism as the "negation of the authority of God while we are its affirmation. . . . Socialism affirms the independence of man and we deny it. . . . Socialism is logical Revolution and we are Counter-Revolution. There is nothing in common between us and between us there is no place for liberalism."

His words defined the chasm, and his position on one side of it was inevitable. It led him in the Affair to embrace the brigands and fight on the terms established by Drumont. It was he who introduced the "Syndicate" into the first debate on the Affair in the Chamber. "What is this mysterious

* The last Bourbon Pretender, grandson of Charles X, who styled himself Henri V and died in 1883.

occult power," he demanded, looking directly at Reinach, "that is strong enough to disrupt the entire country as it has for the last two weeks and to throw doubt and suspicion on the leaders of our Army who"—here he stopped as if choked by his strength of feeling—"who may one day have to lead the country against the enemy. This is not a question of politics. Here we are neither friends nor opponents of the Government; here there are only Frenchmen anxious to preserve their most precious possession . . . the honor of the Army!"

His proud manner and thrilling voice brought the deputies to their feet in transports of applause. Reinach felt the entire Chamber swept by an overmastering emotion and incapable of individual reflection. "I felt on my head the hatred of three hundred hypnotized listeners. I crossed my arms; one word, one movement would have transformed this frenzy into fury. How struggle against a whirlwind?" Jaurès was silent and many of the Left were applauding from "the enthusiasm born of fear." Imperiously de Mun demanded from the Government an unequivocal statement confirming Dreyfus' guilt. The Minister of War, General Billot, obeyed, declaring "solemnly and sincerely, as a soldier and leader of the Army, I believe Dreyfus to be guilty." The Premier followed with an appeal to all good Frenchmen, in the interests of the country and the Army, to support the Government "struggling with such difficulties and harassed by such furious passions." The passions were at once expressed in a duel between Reinach and Alexandre Millerand, a Socialist, who in unprecedented support for the Government by one of his party, denounced the Dreyfusard accusations of the Army as "disloyal."

Other members of the nobility besides de Mun also served as deputies, but always as royalists in opposition. None took any share in the actual business of governing under the Republic. Among them was the Duc de la Rochefoucauld, representing the older nobility ante-dating the Empire, whose money came from Pommeroy champagne and Singer sewing machines and who, as president of the Jockey Club, was the acknowledged leader of the *gratin,* or "crust," of French Society. Others were the Marquis de Breteuil, representing a district in the Hautes-Pyrénées, and his friend the Comte de Greffulhe, whose yellow beard and air of combined rage and majesty caused him to resemble the king in a pack of cards. Possessor of one of the largest fortunes in France and a wife who was the most beautiful woman in Society, he and she served as Marcel Proust's models for the Duc and Duchesse de Guermantes. Another deputy was Count Boni de Castellane, the dandy and arbiter of taste of his circle. Tall and slim, with pink skin, blue eyes and small neat golden moustache, he had married the dour American heiress Anna Gould, and with her dowry built a marble mansion furnished with precious antiques to exhibit the perfection that taste endowed by money could reach. At the party to celebrate its opening a footman in a scarlet cloak was stationed at the curve of the staircase, and when the Grand Duke Vladimir asked, "Who is that Cardinal over there?" the host replied, "Oh, he is only there to make an agreeable effect of color against the marble." Count Boni's assessment of the Affair was that the Jews "in their insensate desire to save a co-religionist" were arrogantly interfering with judicial process and simultaneously, or alternatively, were making Dreyfus "the pretext for a campaign against the Army which doubtless originated in Berlin." In either case they were "insupportable to me." This on the whole represented the view of the *gratin,* who in the words of a notable apostate among them, the Marquis de Galliffet, "continue to understand nothing."

Some among them had literary or other distinctions. Comte Robert de Montesquiou, aesthete extraordinary, lavished on himself silks of lavender and gold, wrote elaborately symbolist poems and epitomized decadence to both Proust and Huysmans in their characters, the Baron de Charlus and des Esseintes. Montesquiou was what Oscar Wilde would have liked to have been if he had had more money, less talent and no humor. The Prince de Sagan, another notorious pederast who wore a perpetually fresh boutonniere and a perfectly waxed moustache, vied with his nephew, Count Boni, as the high priest of elegance and fought a duel with Abel Hermant, in whose satirical novels of the life of the rich and libertine he considered himself libelled. The Comtesse Anna de Noailles wrote poetry and glided through her lovely rooms in long white floating garments like "the ghost of something too beautiful to be real." At her parties everything was required to focus on her. She did not trouble much about her guests, "merely smiled upon them when they arrived and softly sighed when she saw them going away." The Comte de Vogüé, novelist and Academician, influenced the course of French literature by his studies of Turgenev, Tolstoy and Dostoevski which brought the great Russians to French attention.

These were the outstanding members. The bulk of the other one thousand or so who made up the *gratin* were chiefly distinguished, as one of them said, by "the certitude of a superiority that existed despite appearances to the contrary." Comte Aimery de La Rochefoucauld was noted for "the almost fossil rigidity of his aristocratic prejudices." Disgusted at improper protocol in a certain household, he said to a friend of his own level, "Let us walk home together and talk about rank." Of the Duc de Luynes he remarked that his family were "mere nobodies in the year 1000."

Of the same breed was the Duc d'Uzès, whose ancestor, when the King expressed surprise that none of his family had ever been Marshal of France, replied, "Sire, we were always killed in battle too soon."

The *gratin* were not hospitable; some families however wealthy "never offered so much as a glass of lemonade to their friends." The men considered themselves the only ones of their sex who knew how to dress or make love and exchanged tributes from the famous courtesans. They took their orders from the ranking members of their class and were ardently Anglophile in manners and customs. The Greffulhes and Breteuils were intimates of the Prince of Wales, *le betting* was the custom at Longchamps, *le Derby* was held at Chantilly, *le steeplechase* at Auteuil and an unwanted member was *black-boulé* at the Jockey Club. Charles Haas, the original of Swann, had "Mr" engraved on his calling cards.

At the château of the Duc de Luynes at Dampierre, an English visitor found a veneer of modernity in the automobiles, the billiard room, the London clothes of the men and the chatter of women, "but under this thin glaze a deadness of the Dead Sea. All the books are safe under lock and key in the library outside the house. In the house there is no book, no newspaper, no writing paper and only one pen." Two sisters—the Duchesses de Luynes and de Brissac—and their friend, the Comtesse de Vogüé, all on the point of becoming mothers, were "splendid creatures," very easy to get on with if one talked of nothing but sport. The host was Lord Chamberlain to the current Pretender. Their kind "are children, arrested in intelligence, who hate Jews, Americans, the present, the past two centuries, the Government, the future and the fine arts."

Under the law of the Republic all Pretenders to the throne lived in exile. Bonapartist hopes were lodged in Prince Victor Napoleon, grandson of Jerome Bonaparte, while legitimist allegiance went to a grandson of Louis-Philippe, the Comte de Paris, of whom Thiers said, "From a distance he looks like a Prussian, from close up like an imbecile." On his death in 1894 he was succeeded by his son, the Duc d'Orléans, a hare-brained young man who in 1890 had dashingly appeared in France with declared intent to "share the French soldier's *gamelle* [mess]," that is, to do his military service. Being equally celebrated for his romance with the prima donna, Nellie Melba, he was irreverently known thereafter as "Gamelba," a name coined by Rochefort. Before the Affair, his cause seemed moribund; but in the Affair the royalists found a new rallying point, new hope and excitement and in the anti-Semites, new partners and energy. Anti-Semitism became the fashion, although with certain unwanted effects on Society, for parvenus were able to force their way in by virtue of the degree of warmth with which they espoused the new cause. "All this Dreyfus business is destroying society," complained the Baron de Charlus, and the Duchesse de Guermantes found it "perfectly intolerable" that all the people one had spent one's life trying to avoid now had to be accepted just because they boycotted Jewish tradesmen and had "Down with Jews" printed on their parasols.

Important neither in government nor in culture, the *gratin* were important only in providing the background, motive, stimulus and financial backing to reaction. In the Affair the only serious leader to emerge from their class was de Mun. It was he who forced the Government to prosecute Zola for libel of the Army in his public letter, *J'Accuse,* and thus brought on the trial which made the case a national, no longer containable, issue. Had the Government had its way it would have taken no action, for discussion and testimony and above all cross-examination were to be avoided. But led by de Mun, the Right in its wrath demanded revenge and his authority exercised a spell. When no one from the Ministry of War was present in the Chamber to reply to Zola's attack, de Mun demanded that the session be suspended until the Minister of War could be summoned so that nothing should take precedence over defence of the Army's honor. A deputy suggested that the matter could wait while other business continued. "The Army cannot wait!" de Mun declared haughtily. Obediently the deputies filed out until the Minister arrived and afterward, swept up in a passionate oration by de Mun, voted to proceed against Zola.

"A colossus with dirty feet, nevertheless a colossus," Flaubert had called Zola. Although he was probably the most widely read and best-paid French author of the time, the brutal realism of his novels had aroused the disgust and resentment of many. He dug mercilessly into the base, sordid and corrupt elements of every class in society, from the slums to the Senate. Peasants, prostitutes, miners, bourgeois businessmen, alcoholics, doctors, officers, churchmen and politicians were exposed in gigantic detail. Worse, the supposedly beneficent Nineteenth Century itself was exposed in his picture of the terrible impoverishment brought upon the masses by industrialization. The doors of the Academy never opened to him. His account of 1870 in *La Débâcle* infuriated the Army and after *Germinal* he was classed as a champion of the workers against the established order. He was an agnostic who believed in science as the only instrument of social progress. Already, however, a literary reaction against realism and the "bankruptcy of science" was taking place.

In the year before Dreyfus' arrest, Zola's fame had reached its peak upon publication of the final novel in his immense twenty-volume panorama of French life. At a party given by his publisher to celebrate the occasion on the Grand Lac in the Bois de Boulogne, writers, statesmen, ambassadors, actresses and beauties, celebrities of every kind from Poincaré to Yvette Guilbert, were present. Where was he to go from here? The Dreyfus case opened a new road to greatness, but only to a man capable of taking it. It required courage to challenge the State, the training and genius of a great writer to compose *J'Accuse,* and sympathy with suffering to inspire him to act. Zola had known suffering: In his youth he had spent two unemployed years in the garret of a shabby boardinghouse, often so hungry that he set traps for sparrows on the roof and broiled them on the end of a curtain rod over a candle.

His first article on the Affair, after summarizing the evidence against Esterhazy—the handwriting, the *petit bleu,* the Uhlan letters—had asserted, "Truth is on the march and nothing will stop it." When a month later the Army ordered Esterhazy's court-martial, the Dreyfusards, believing this was a roundabout way of succumbing to Revision, were exuberant. In fact, it was a device for dealing with the Esterhazy problem through a trial whose verdict the Army could control. Esterhazy was acquitted and acclaimed by the mob as the "martyr of the Jews." The verdict "came upon us like the blow of a bludgeon," wrote Blum. It was as if Dreyfus had been condemned a second time. The march of truth had, after all, been stopped.

The only way to force the evidence onto the record was to provoke a civil trial. This was the purpose of Zola's open letter addressed to the President of France. He conceived it on the day of Esterhazy's acquittal with deliberate intent to bring himself to trial. He told no one but his wife and did not hesitate. Locking himself in his study, he worked without stopping for twenty-four hours, mastered the intricacies and mysteries of what by now had become one of the most complex puzzles in history and wrote his indictment in four thousand words. He took it over to *l'Aurore* on the evening of January 12, and it appeared next morning under the title suggested by Ernest Vaughan (or, according to another version, by Clemenceau): J'ACCUSE! Three hundred thousand copies were sold, many to Nationalists who burned them in the streets.

In separate paragraphs, each beginning "I accuse," Zola specifically named two Ministers of War, Generals Mercier and Billot, one "as accomplice in one of the greatest iniquities of the century," and the other of "possessing positive proofs of the innocence of Dreyfus and suppressing them." He accused the Chiefs of the General Staff, Generals Boisdeffre and Gonse, as accomplices in the same crime, and Colonel du Paty de Clam (he knew nothing about Major Henry) as its "diabolical author."

He accused the War Ministry of conducting an "abominable campaign" in the press to mislead the public and conceal its own misdeeds. He accused the first court-martial of conducting an illegal trial and the Esterhazy court-martial of covering that illegal verdict "on order" as well as of the judicial crime of knowingly acquitting a guilty person. The accusations were made in full awareness of the law of libel "to hasten the explosion of truth and justice. Let them bring me to court. Let the inquiry be in broad daylight. I wait."

The public was aghast; such charges flung at the military leaders of the nation seemed equivalent to an act of revolt. Many Revisionists felt Zola had gone too far. He had inflamed an already heated situation almost unbearably by frightening and angering the middle classes and increasing their support of the Army and their dislike of the Dreyfusards. Following de Mun's resolution next day, the Government announced that Zola would be prosecuted. Hatred, filth and insults were spewed on him by the press and in songs sold on the streets. He was viciously caricatured. "Pornographic pig" was polite among the names he was called. Packages of excrement were mailed to him. He was burnt in effigy. Placards were distributed reading, "The answer of all good Frenchmen to Emile Zola: *Merde!*" Evoking one of the major emotions of the Affair, the attacks denounced him as a "foreigner," in reference to his Italian father. In fact, Zola had been born in Paris of a French mother and brought up in the home of her parents in Aix-en-Provence.

The Government's suit, filed in the name of General Billot as Minister of War, ignored all the accusations relevant to Dreyfus and confined itself to the single charge that the court-martial of Esterhazy had acquitted him "on order." By this device the presiding judge could exclude any testimony not bearing precisely on that point. In a fiery protest against this procedure, Jaurès thundered in the Chamber at the Government, "You are delivering the Republic to the Jesuit Generals!" at which a Nationalist deputy, the Comte de Bernis, assaulted him physically, causing such an uproar that the military guard was required to restore order.

J'Accuse drew world attention to the Affair and gave it the proportions of heroic drama. That the French Army could be accused of such crimes and the French author best known to the foreign public be attacked in such terms were equally astounding. The world watched with "stupor and distress," wrote Björnstjerne Björnson from Norway. When the trial opened, the Dreyfusards were conscious of that audience. "The scene is France; the theatre is the world," they said. The trial transformed the Affair from the local to the universal.

The writer of his time who most truly touched the universal, Chekhov, was profoundly stirred by Zola's intervention. Staying in Nice at the time, he followed the trial in growing excitement, read all the verbatim testimony and wrote home, "We talk here of nothing but Zola and Dreyfus." He found the anti-Semitic and anti-Dreyfus tirades of the St. Petersburg *New Times*, the leading daily which had published most of his own stories, "simply repulsive" and quarreled with its editor, his old and intimate friend.

Foreign opinion, except as conditioned by feeling about the Jews, saw the issue chiefly as one of Justice and could not understand the obstinate refusal of the French to allow Revision. Foreign hostility itself became a factor in the refusal. "French papers ask why foreign countries take such an interest in the Affair," wrote Princess Radziwill, "as if a question of justice did not interest the whole world." It did, but in France the Affair was not only that. It was not a struggle of the Right against the Left, because men like Scheurer-Kestner and Reinach, Clemenceau and Anatole France, were not men of the Left. It was fought in terms of justice and patriotism, but fundamentally it was the struggle of the Right against Reason.

Zola's trial opened on February 7, 1898, and lasted sixteen days. The atmosphere at the Palais de Justice on the Ile de la Cité "smelled of suppressed slaughter," said a witness. "What passion on people's faces! What looks of hatred when certain eyes met!" The courtroom was crammed to the window sills with journalists, lawyers, officers in uniform, ladies in furs. Marcel Proust climbed every day to the public gallery, bringing coffee and sandwiches so as not to miss a moment. Outside the windows Drumont's claque, paid at forty sous a head, hooted and jeered. All the Army officers concerned in the trials and investigations of Dreyfus, Esterhazy and Picquart stood up and swore to the authenticity of the documents, including specifically the Panizzardi letter which was declared to be "positive proof" of Dreyfus' guilt. (The Foreign Minister, already advised by the Italians that it was a forgery, had wanted to call off the trial but the Government had not dared for fear of an Army revolt.) General Mercier, upright, haughty, unmoved, "entrenched in his own infallibility," affirmed on his honor as a soldier that Dreyfus had been rightfully and legally convicted. Attempts by the defence to cross-examine were met over and over again by the presiding judge with the sharp order, "The question will not be put." Statements by Zola or by his lawyer, Maître Labori, or by Clemenceau, who, though not a lawyer, was appearing for *l'Aurore,* were met by inarticulate roars from the packed audience. Zola, appearing nervous and sullen, kept his temper until, tormented beyond endurance, he spat out "Cannibals!"—the word used by Voltaire in the Calas affair. Esterhazy, called to testify, was greeted by the crowd with shouts of *"Gloire au victime du Syndicat!"* On the steps of the court, Prince Henri d'Orléans, cousin of the Pretender, shook the hand of the author of the Uhlan letters and saluted in him the "French uniform."

"Paris palpitated," wrote an English visitor, and he felt a lust for blood in the air. Mobs broke the windows of Zola's house and of the offices of *l'Aurore*. Shops closed, foreigners departed. A wave of anti-Semitic riots organized by Drumont's lieutenant, Jules Guérin, erupted in Le Havre, Orléans, Nancy, Lyon, Bordeaux, Toulouse, Marseilles and smaller towns, and reached a peak in Algiers where the looting and sack of the Jewish quarter lasted for four days, with many beaten and in some cases killed. In Paris an employment office opened where toughs were hired at five francs a day or two francs for an evening to shout, "Down with the Jews! Long live the Army! Spit on Zola!" When Zola left the court on one occasion, in company with Reinach, the crowd flew at them, yelling, "Drown the traitors! Death to the Jews!" and they had to be rescued by police. Thereafter, mounted police escorted Zola's carriage to and from the court every day, and were sometimes forced to charge the screaming mob threatening to assault it. Zola's friend Desmoulins, acting as bodyguard, carried a revolver.

In the Court, despite obstructions and jeers, truth was advancing. Neither Labori, young and vehement, of whom it was said, "He is not an intellect, he is a temperament," nor Clemenceau, hard, merciless, invincible in debate, could be bullied or silenced. The jury was rumored to be inclining toward acquittal. General Boisdeffre, taking the stand, warned, "If the nation does not have confidence in its Army chiefs . . . then they are ready to transfer to others their heavy task. You have only to say the word." It was a threat of collective resignation by the General Staff if the jury acquitted. Boisdeffre made it plain: Zola or us. This was the issue, not the guilt or innocence of Dreyfus, which the jury had to decide. Its members came mostly from the petty bourgeoisie: a tanner, a market gardener, a wine-dealer, a clerk, a landlord and two workmen. With implied threat *La Libre Parole* published their names and business addresses and letters from readers warning of vengeance if the "Italian" were acquitted.

In his closing speech, Zola, constantly interrupted by boos and hissing, swore by his forty years of labour and forty volumes of French literature that Dreyfus was innocent. He had acted to save his country from "the grip of lies and injustice" and though he were condemned, "France will one day thank me for having helped to save her honour." Clemenceau concluded, "Your task, gentlemen of the jury, is to pronounce a verdict less upon us than upon yourselves. We are appearing before you. You will appear before history."

Zola was condemned by a vote of 7–5 and the wonder was that five jurors had the courage to vote for acquittal. Outside, the Place Dauphine was black with people screaming in triumph. "Listen to them, listen to them!" said Zola as he was preparing to leave. "They sound as if they were waiting for someone to throw them meat." Clemenceau told a friend that in case of acquittal he was "quite certain not a single Dreyfusard in the court or corridors would have escaped with his life." Zola received the maximum penalty, a year's imprisonment and a fine of three thousand francs and on rejection of an appeal was persuaded by the insistence of his friends to escape to England. He should have been sent "to join his friend Dreyfus on Devil's Island" was Henry Adams' comment, "with as much more French rot as the island would hold, including most of the press, the greater part of the theatre, all the stockbrokers and a Rothschild or two for example." The sentiments were his own, not paid for like those of the Paris mob which they so accurately reflected.

The trial was a tornado that whirled all the vocal elements of society into its vortex. "Every conscience is troubled," wrote *Le Petit Parisien*. "No one reasons any more; no discussion is possible; everyone has taken up a fixed position." Families divided and even servants. In the most famous of the Caran d'Ache cartoons the father of a large family at dinner commands, "No one is to speak of it!" The next panel shows a wild melee of overturned table, knives and forks flying and chairs used as weapons, under the title, "They spoke of it!"

Organizing their efforts the Dreyfusards formed the League for the Rights of Man, which sponsored protest meetings and sent lecturers around the country. They drew up a petition for Revision which made the schism in society visible and inescapable. Called the "Protest of the Intellectuals," it began appearing day by day in *l'Aurore* with successive signatures. It cut jagged divisions between those who signed and those who refused. The organizers were Marcel Proust and his brother Robert (whose father refused to speak to them for a week in consequence), Elie Halévy and his brother Daniel and their cousin Jacques Bizet, son of the composer, all in their late twenties. Almost the first signature they obtained was their greatest coup: that of "the ultimate flower of Latin genius" and leader of Academicians, Anatole France. "He got out of bed to see us, in his slippers with a head cold," wrote Halévy. " 'Show it to me,' he said, 'I'll sign, I'll sign anything. I am revolted.' " He was a rationalist, revolted by unreason. A cynic and a satirist of human folly, he had sympathy neither for crusades nor for Dreyfus as an individual who, he perceptively suggested, was "the same type as the officers who condemned him; in their shoes he would have condemned himself." But he hated the crowd and out of contradictory spirit was usually to be found against the Government.

He wrote prose clear as a running brook. He had lived in the home and adorned the salon of his mistress, Mme Arman de Caillavet, since 1889, when, after a final quarrel with his wife, he walked out in dressing gown and slippers, carrying on a tray, quill pen, inkstand and current MS, and proceeded down the street to a hotel, sent for his clothes and never went home. Mme Arman exercised over him the tyranny of devotion and when he was lazy locked him up to make him write. His series of novels about the current day centering around M. Bergeret had been appearing serially in the violently right-wing *Echo de Paris* since 1895 and continued to appear there through the Affair, in ironic commentary on the print around them. France's signature enchanted the Revisionists and astonished both sides. He was "altogether one of us"; he should have never sided with "them," lamented Léon Daudet.

On its first appearance the Protest of the Intellectuals had 104 signers and within a month 3,000, among them André Gide, Charles Péguy, Elisée Reclus, Gabriel Monod, scholars, poets, philosophers, doctors, professors and one painter, Claude Monet, from sympathy with Clemenceau. The only political action of Monet's life, his signature caused a quarrel with Degas and they did not speak again for years. Now almost blind, Degas used to have *La Libre Parole* read to him each morning, and regarded with contempt the *arrivistes* of the Republican era. "In my time," he said disdainfully, "one did not arrive."

Artists and musicians, though on the whole politically indifferent, tended if anything toward the Nationalist camp. Debussy sat with Léon Daudet's circle at the Café Weber in the Rue Royale. Puvis de Chavannes was another Nationalist sympathizer.

Professors and teachers from the Sorbonne, the Ecole Normale, the Faculty of Medicine, the secondary schools and provincial universities, signed; many were opposed, many refrained for fear of reprisals. "If I sign," said a school principal to Clemenceau, "that ass Rambaud [the Minister of Education] will send me to rot in the depths of Brittany." The distinguished scientist Emile Duclaux, successor to Pasteur, signed immediately, saying that if they were afraid of revision in the laboratory, truth would never be reached except by accident. Following his lead, scientists entered the Affair and some suffered for it. Professor Grimaux of the Polytechnic, who both signed and testified at Zola's trial, was removed from the chair of chemistry. Heated arguments arose as to whether such great masters as Hugo, Renan, Taine or Pasteur would or would not have signed. Pupils and teachers were at odds, students divided, committees were formed for and against, especially in the provinces where the faculties were under Catholic influence.

Like an ice floe cracking, the intellectual world split over the Protest, and as the Affair progressed, the two halves spread wider and wider apart. Former friends passed each other in silence and any words they might have said "would never have carried across the worlds that lay between them." When Pierre Louÿs, author of *Aphrodite,* took the opposite side from his friend Léon Blum, without further communication they never saw each other again. When the Protest was being circulated, three journalist friends of Léon Daudet tried to persuade him, appealing for three hours over lunch to "my patriotism, my intelligence, my heart." Before the Affair he had dined at the home of the Laboris, where Madame sang the songs of Schumann and no evening could have been more delightful; "he robust and eloquent, she full of talent, charm and good will." He was welcome too in the charming house on the Pont-de-l'Arche of Octave Mirbeau, who owned Van Gogh's "Field of Iris" and where Madame welcomed one with "affectionate and sumptuous hospitality" and the cuisine was incomparable "from the butter to the wine, from the cooking oil to the soup." After the Affair the word "Nationalist" was to Mirbeau a synonym for "assassin," and Democracy was to Daudet "the poisoned terrain." Soon after Zola's trial Daudet was writing weekly diatribes of unexampled ferocity for *La Libre Parole* and *Le Gaulois.*

Maurice Barrès, the brilliant novelist who combined literature with a political career, was another whom his friends expected to be a Revisionist. Léon Blum asked for his signature feeling perfectly certain of him, but Barrès said he wanted to think it over and when he wrote it was to refuse. Though professing friendship and respect for Zola he said he felt doubtful and in his doubt chose "the instinct of patriotism." Within months he was to find the mystic answer in terms of blood and soil; to explain Zola as a "denaturalized Venetian" and the Jews on the same principle: that they "have no country as we understand it. For us our country is the earth of our ancestors, the land of our dead. For them it is the place of their best interest." Becoming the intellectual leader of the Nationalists, Barrès supplied them with words to pre-empt patriotism for the Right.

A new recruit, small but wickedly effective, in the form of a four-page weekly of caricatures called *Psst!*, was brought out by Forain and Caran d'Ache, who composed it sitting together at a table in the Café Weber. Caran d'Ache drew comic strips of inspired simplification. Forain was an artist whose sharp views of Parisian society were incisive and brilliant in black and white, although his oils evoked Degas' deadly comment, "He paints with his hands in my pockets." His cover design of a Prussian officer standing behind a dark and cynical figure representing the Syndicate and manipulating in front of its face the mask of Zola, compressed in one picture all the elements of the Affair as the Nationalists saw it. Reinach, the favored target of *Psst!*, was usually pictured as an orangutang in a top hat with heavily Jewish features going repeatedly to Berlin to confer with spike-helmeted Prussians. Scheurer-Kestner and other Revisionists appear as hook-nosed Jews in bankers' fur-collared coats, paying out German funds, using the Army képi for a football or picking weeds from the grave of Ravachol as a "bouquet for Zola." Throughout appears a stalwart wooden soldier, standing straight and brave, unwincing among the villains, forever valiant—the Army. The Intellectual is a lanky figure with oversized head, the star of David on his brow and carrying a pen bigger than his body, who registers his "disgust with everything French." The only variation in subject is the occasional appearance of "Oncle Sam" as the "New Gargantua" making a meal of Spain, Hawaii, Porto Rico and the Philippines.

The Affair pervaded life at all hours and places. Going to a new dentist, Léon Blum found a young man with the manner and bearing of a cavalry officer who suddenly said as his patient sat down, "All the same, they will not dare touch Picquart!" Gaston Paris, the scholarly medievalist and Academician, concluded an erudite article on Philip the Good with a stirring invocation to justice which at once categorized him. Paul Stapfer, doyen of the Faculty of Letters at Bordeaux, was suspended because in a funeral oration for a colleague he made a discreet allusion to the Revisionist opinions of the deceased. A tempest blew up in the Légion d'Honneur when it "suspended" Zola and succeeded in angering both the military members who had demanded his ouster and those members who were his partisans. Anatole France and others removed the red ribbon from their coats. At the cafés, Nationalists and Revisionists sat at different tables on opposite sides of the terraces. Whole villages took sides. A resident of Samois, fourteen miles from Paris, said everyone in his village was Dreyfusard while at Francoville, three or four miles away, everyone almost without exception was anti-Dreyfusard.

In February, 1898, at the Dîner Bixio, a dining club of the elect who met for the pleasure of each other's conversation, the Affair found everyone "troubled and grieved"; in March the Marquis de Galliffet said he would not go out or visit on account of it; in May conversation turned for a while to the question, "Did the Americans blow up the *Maine* themselves?" otherwise talk was only of the Affair; in November everyone was depressed: "I cannot remember a dinner so black," wrote one member in his diary.

The opening night of Romain Rolland's play *Les Loups* was a battlefield. He had written it in six days to show the world that France was torn by "one of the most redoubtable problems that can engage the human conscience, a dilemma worthy of Corneille: whether to sacrifice country or justice." The presence of Colonel Picquart in a box and of Colonel du Paty de Clam in the orchestra brought the audience to a peak of excitement. Picquart after his first arrest had just been discharged from the Army, and came to the theatre as the guest of Edmond Rostand, whose *Cyrano de Bergerac,* produced a few months earlier, had raised him to the height of celebrity. For a decade French theatregoers had languished under the skepticism, symbolism and Ibsenism of the Théâtre Libre. "We needed reassurance, ideals, panache," wrote a critic, "and then came Cyrano! Our thirst was assuaged." Cyrano's spirit was there that night.

When the character representing Picquart in the play confronted his opponent, the audience exploded before he could be heard. "The whole theatre shook from floor to roof." The usual *Vive!*'s and *A bas!*'s reached a fury in which someone was moved to cry, *"A bas la patrie!"* and a thirteen-year-old Anarchist in the balcony squealed, "Down with Christianity!" Rolland thought to himself, "My ideas are lost, but no matter, the play doesn't count. The real spectacle is there in the audience. This is history being acted!"

The carnage continued next day. *Echo de Paris* and *La Presse* dismissed their drama critics, the Collège Stanislas canceled a reception for Mme Rostand, and two papers opened a campaign to boycott *Cyrano,* whose popularity, however, proved stronger than its author's association with Picquart. In his diary Rolland wrote, "I would rather have this life of combat than the mortal calm and mournful stupor of these last years. God give me struggle, enemies, howling crowds, all the combat of which I am capable."

It was the same sentiment Péguy voiced: boredom with peace. Others shared it. That summer, Senator Ranc recalled, one was constantly expecting some surprise attack. "One day we would be warned not to sleep at home for fear of assault by anti-Semitic gangs, the next for fear of arrest by the police. It was exciting; one felt alive; nothing is so good as a time of action, and combat in the consciousness of a cause."

From the day early in the Affair when Joseph Reinach announced to the guests at Mme Emile Straus's salon that Dreyfus had been wrongfully convicted, the polarization of the salons began. Heretofore they had linked the worlds of fashion and intellect, bridged the sharp political divisions between classes and coteries. They were to France what the country-house party was to England. They were the market-place of ideas, the stock exchange of social and political favors united by one absorbing concern: who would obtain the next seat in the Academy, who would don the dark-green uniform and, watched by the elite of Paris, deliver his eulogy of the defunct Immortal whose place he was taking? Now they began to pull apart into separate units, frustrating the unifying and mixing process that had been their greatest contribution.

As a rule each salon had its *grand homme*. Mme Aubernon, doyenne of the hostesses, began with Dumas *fils* and finished with D'Annunzio. Mme Emile Straus, on the other hand, the beautiful Geneviève of the liquid black eyes and ardent glance, attracted too many to concentrate on one. Daughter of the composer Halévy and widow of Georges Bizet before she married Straus, leaving disconsolate a train of adorers, she had assembled at her salon the soul and salt of Paris before the ravages of the Affair. Henri Bergson the philosopher, Réjane the actress, Lord Lytton when he was British Ambassador, Professor Pozzi the surgeon, Henri Meilhac, the librettist of Offenbach's operas, Jules Lemaître, Marcel Prévost, Forain, Proust, and the Princesse Mathilde, who held her own salon on Wednesdays, all came to her Saturday afternoons on the Boulevard Haussmann, bringing still hot the happenings of the Chamber, the Quai d'Orsay, the theatres and the editorial offices. After Reinach's announcement, Lemaître left, allowing himself from then on to adorn only the right-wing salon of the Comtesse de Loynes. Other separations followed.

Mme Arman de Caillavet's Sunday salon on the Avenue Hoche where Anatole France was the permanent star was the Revisionist center. Clemenceau, Briand, Reinach, Jaurès and Lucien Herr were regulars. Mme Arman wanted only writers and politicians and snubbed the nobility except for Mme de Noailles, who was a Dreyfusard and would appear "like an Oriental princess descending from her palanquin . . .

to set ablaze the torrent of her words by the fire of her glance." Anatole France's books lay on all the tables and the Master himself stood in the midst of a crowd coming and going and gathering around him while he discoursed on a chosen theme, interrupting himself to greet arriving guests, bowing to left and right, introducing one to another, bending to kiss the hand of a pale feline figure wrapped in chinchilla, and keeping up the flow of his talk on the poetry of Racine, the paradox of Robespierre or the epigrams of Rabelais.

The Affair superseded Rabelais. At Mme Aubernon's, where guests of both camps were still invited, discussions that touched upon it immediately became impassioned. "This petition of the so-called 'Intellectuals' is preposterous and impertinent," declared Ferdinand Brunetière, editor of the magisterial *Revue des Deux Mondes*. "They have coined the name to exalt themselves above others as if writers, scientists and professors were better than anyone else. . . . What right have they to meddle in a matter of military justice?" Victor Brochard, Professor of Ancient Philosophy at the Sorbonne, replied heatedly, "Justice is based not on courts but on law. . . . To convict a man on evidence not shown to him is not only illegal; it is judicial murder. . . . Today it is not the Generals or Rochefort or the brawlers of *La Libre Parole* or Esterhazy or your Duc d'Orléans who represent the French conscience. It is we, the intellectuals."

Headquarters of the Right was the salon of Mme de Loynes on the Avenue des Champs Elysées, where Jules Lemaître reigned. After an initial career as a demi-mondaine she had married the elderly Comte de Loynes, become a recognized power in the making of Academicians and, in the course of time, governess, mother, sister and presumably mistress to Lemaître, although some unkind gossip said their friendship was platonic. Her guests met at dinner on Fridays in a room furnished in plush with a nude marble Minerva on the mantel and what Boni de Castellane described as a "shoddy" Meissonier on the wall. Lemaître, the celebrated drama critic of the *Journal des Débats,* was an immensely prolix writer who could turn his hand to plays, poetry, short stories, critical essays, biographies and assorted speeches, political pieces, opinion and polemics. His works, when ultimately collected, filled fifty volumes. Though essentially dilettante in spirit, he had saved the French theatre in a famous cry of alarm in the *Revue des Deux Mondes* from being inundated by the heavy waves rolling in from the north—Ibsen, Hauptmann, Sudermann and Strindberg—and had duly entered the portals of the Academy. The fruits of democracy and manhood suffrage he found disillusioning. "The Republic cured me of the Republic," he wrote; "life had already cured me of romanticism." Disenchanted as well with "literary games," he craved the role of a man of action, the restorative of a cause that not merely fluttered the pages of reviews but moved live men to passion. With ceremony and cheers in Mme de Loynes' dining room he was named president of the Ligue de la Patrie Française, organized by the Nationalists to unite the intellectuals of the Right against the "enemies of *la patrie*." Its Committee included among others de Vogüé, Barrès, Forain, Mistral the poet of the Provençal revival, Vincent d'Indy the composer and Carolus Duran the painter. The Ligue de la Patrie attracted 15,000 to its first meeting and gained 30,000 members in the first month. Lemaître was chosen president in order to have an Academician equal to Anatole France, but, given to mockery and grumbling, he lacked the spirit of a leader and after five minutes of argument, if he failed to impose his views, would drop out of the discussion.

As vice-president, the gentle poet François Coppée was no more effective. More or less bludgeoned by his friends into accepting the post, he was wrapped in nostalgia for the past and wrote verse romances about the humble of earlier times. When asked by an English friend, "*Que faites vous, Maître, dans cette galère?*" ("What are you doing in with that bunch?"), he replied, "To tell you the truth, I am not quite sure." He was able to explain, however, a vague feeling that the religion and patriotism which had made France great were vanishing and unless revived would disappear in the rising tide of materialism.

The real energy and leadership of the League was supplied by Barrès, Drumont, Rochefort and Déroulède, leader of the older Ligue des Patriotes. At policy sessions Drumont would laugh uproariously and say, "Those fellows will be the death of me." Rochefort, who listened only to himself, would say impatiently after a long discussion, "Yes, yes, it's sickening—what *canaille*!" and then tell some anecdote that enchanted Coppée. "Each one of us is serious individually," Lemaître confessed to Mme de Loynes, "but together we become frivolous."

Yet they felt the cause was deadly serious. Behind all the disputes over the *bordereau* and *petit bleu,* wrote Léon Daudet, "could be heard the tramp of the barbarian legions." Dreyfusism was the foreigner at the gates. It was revolution. It was Jews, Freemasons, freethinkers, Protestants, Anarchists, Internationalists. Everyone saw in it his own enemy. Barrès saw everything that was "un-French"; Arthur Meyer saw "an alliance of Anarchism and Dreyfusism" of which "twice monstrous cult" the two priests were Anatole France and Octave Mirbeau. Brunetière saw "individualism . . . the great malady of our time . . . the Superman of Nietzsche, the Anarchist, the *culte de moi*."

The strong man of the Radical Government which took office after the elections of May, 1898, was its Minister of War, Godefroy Cavaignac, a civilian. He was a man of rigid Republican righteousness, a "sea-green incorruptible," who regarded himself as the chastiser of parliamentary corruption. He had initiated the Panama inquiry and loathed Clemenceau. As Minister of War for a six months' tenure in 1895, he had accepted the honesty of the Secret File and firmly believed Dreyfus guilty. The outgoing Premier, Méline, had attempted to deal with the case by denying that any case existed after the rendering of a verdict, but Cavaignac decided to face the issue squarely. He reinvestigated the documents and convinced himself that although Esterhazy was involved, the Dreyfus verdict had been just. He thereupon ordered the arrest of both Esterhazy and Picquart and went to the Chamber determined to bury Revision for good. Grim and commanding, he told the members that Esterhazy had been wrongfully acquitted and would be dealt with as an accomplice but that "I am completely certain of Dreyfus' guilt." He went back over the entire history of the case, rebuilt the structure which the Dreyfusards had bit by bit proved false and in final proof cited Dreyfus' supposed confession and the Panizzardi letter which Méline, who had been Premier until two weeks ago and was sitting in the audience, knew from the Italians was a forgery. When Cavaignac finished the Chamber was on its feet cheering. He had lifted the terrible burden and they voted 545–0 (with nineteen abstentions including the silent Méline) for a national *affichage,* or "posting," of his speech outside every town hall in France. "Now the odious case is buried," said de Vogüé that night at his club. "Now Dreyfus is nailed to his rock until he dies!"

For the Dreyfusards it was an unbelievable blow, an "atrocious moment." A journalist came hot from the Chamber to bring the news to Lucien Herr, who was in his study with Léon Blum. They were struck mute; tears were close to the surface; they sat immobilized by consternation and despair. Suddenly the doorbell rang and Jaurès burst in, brushed aside the gesture of his friends inviting him to mourn and berated them in a tone of triumph. "What, you too? . . . Don't you understand that now, now for the first time we are certain of victory? Méline was invulnerable because he said nothing. Cavaignac talks, so he will be beaten. . . . Now Cavaignac has named the documents and I, yes I, tell you they are false, they feel false, they smell false. They are forgeries. . . . I am certain of it and will prove it. The forgers have come out of their holes; we'll have them by the throat. Forget your funeral faces. Do as I do; rejoice."

Jaurès went out and wrote *Les Preuves* (The Proofs), a series of articles beginning that week in the Socialist paper, *La Petite République,* which stunned its readers and marked the first collaboration of Socialism with a cause of the bourgeois world. Through the Affair the bridge of class enmity was crossed.

Jaurès himself had been a declared Dreyfusard since before Zola's trial. Short, stocky, strong, red-faced and jovial, he radiated the joy of battle. With his big head, rough beard and careless clothes finished off by drooping white socks, he looked like the accepted image of a labour leader. He was not, however, of working-class origin but came from the poorer branch of a respectable bourgeois family, and had been a student at the Ecole Normale, where he excelled in Greek and Latin and the humanities and was a friend and classmate of Henri Bergson and his rival for the highest honors. When waiting to testify at Zola's trial he had paced up and down the corridors with Anatole France reciting Seventeenth Century poetry. In the Chamber when he climbed with heavy, purposeful steps to the tribune and tossed off a glass of red wine before speaking, auditors tensed with expectancy, either worshipful or hostile. He spoke with a "splendid amplitude" in a voice almost too loud which he could easily have lowered and still have been heard in the last rows of any hall but which, as Rolland said, was a sensual pleasure to him when he let it out to the full. He could speak at this pitch for an hour and a half to two hours at a time. Using no notes, he could not be fazed by interruptions which served only to supply him with new inspirations. When heckled he played with his opponent "like a huge cat with a mouse, caressing him, making him jump this way and that, . . . and then with a sharp blow, flattened him with a final word."

He was never a sectarian who put a particular orthodoxy ahead of the ultimate goal, a habit which afflicted the Socialist movement. For Jaurès, who led the Carmaux strike in person, the ultimate aim of working-class power was not a theory but a realizable goal and Socialist unity a necessity for its achievement. Once persuaded of Dreyfus' innocence by Lucien Herr and others, he believed that Socialism, by abstaining from combat against injustice, would diminish itself. By making the cause of justice its own it would place its mark on the ultimate victory, open to itself a new path to power and cover itself with moral glory. The Affair, as he saw it, could become the catalyst of a united front of the Left which the Socialists should lead.

His colleagues in the Socialist party shared his enthusiasm not at all. Moderates like Millerand and Viviani did not want to be mixed up in this "obscure and dangerous" business; the extremists led by Jules Guesde, while personally Dreyfusard, opposed party action as an effort diverting working-class strength from a cause not its own. At a caucus of the party after *J'Accuse,* to decide what action to take if the Right demanded the prosecution of Zola, the moderates squirmed, preferring discretion to valor on the eve of the election. "Why risk our re-election for Zola?" they said. "He is not a Socialist; . . . he is after all nothing but a bourgeois." As the factions argued, Guesde in impatient disgust threw open the window with an ostentatious gesture for fresh air and cried, "Zola's letter is the greatest revolutionary act of the century!" But it was no more than a gesture and he signed the manifesto which declared, "Leave it to the bourgeoisie to tear themselves to bits over *patrie*, law, justice and other words that will remain empty of meaning as long as capitalist society endures." The iniquity of the Affair should be used as a weapon with which to beat the bourgeoisie, not as a cause to "mobilize and immobilize the proletariat behind one faction of the bourgeois world." The Dreyfus case was nothing but a power struggle between two bourgeois factions: on the one hand the clericals and on the other the Jewish capitalists and their friends. Socialists could not support one side against the other without violating the class struggle. "Between de Mun and Reinach," proclaimed Guesde, "keep your complete freedom."

But as de Mun had said, between the two sides there was no room for freedom. "You can hardly imagine how tormented I am!" Jaurès said to Péguy. "Our enemies are nothing—but our friends! They devour me because they are all afraid of not being elected. They pull at the back of my coat to keep me from going to the tribune." Shaking them off, Jaurès refused to remain silent and did indeed lose his seat in the election of May, 1898, although more because of industrialist opposition in his district than because of the Affair. Turning instead to *La Petite République* for a platform, as Clemenceau had to *l'Aurore*, he wrote a daily political column. When he began *Les Preuves* class hatred was so rooted in Socialist tradition that in order to rally the Left in the fight for justice it was necessary to de-class Dreyfus. "He is no longer an officer nor a bourgeois," Jaurès wrote. "In his misery he has been skinned of all class character. . . . He is simply a living witness to the crimes of Authority. . . . He is nothing less than mankind itself." He tore into the evidence, took up each one of Cavaignac's arguments and documents, separated rumor and blackmail, tracked down forgery. The impact of his logic and his strenuous seriousness revived the Dreyfusards. Cavaignac was enraged. At a dinner of the Cabinet he proposed to arrest all the leading Revisionists on a charge of conspiracy against the state and named Mathieu Dreyfus, Bernard Lazare, Ranc, Reinach, Scheurer-Kestner, Picquart, Clemenceau, Zola and others. When one of his colleagues asked sarcastically, Why not the lawyers too, Cavaignac replied, "Of course," and added Labori and Dreyfus' lawyer, Demange.

Nevertheless *Les Preuves* had shaken him. To answer certain of Jaurès' charges, he ordered yet another examination of the documents, this time by an officer not previously involved in the case. Working at night by the light of a lamp this officer noticed that the writing paper of the crucial Panizzardi letter was gummed together from two halves of the same brand of paper ruled in lines of faintly different colors. Colonel * Henry had used the blank parts of two real letters from Panizzardi to construct his document. The crucial letter was a forgery. Alerted by this find, the investigating officer looked further, was led down dark warrens of discrepancies and dutifully reporting his discoveries, laid ruin in the lap of the Minister of War.

Cavaignac, conqueror of the Affair, saw the whole of the case he had presented to the Chamber and the country shattered like glass. Its crux was a fraud; the statement on which he had won national acclaim was a fraud. For a man of his principles, to hush up the discovery was impossible; he had to face the tragedy of being wrong. Not being of the Army made it easier. He ordered the arrest of Colonel Henry, who was taken to Cherche Midi where Dreyfus had been lodged. That night, August 31, 1898, Colonel Henry committed suicide with the razor they had left for him.

Army officers, when they heard the news, were aghast; some wept. It was a stain on the Army's honor "worse than Sedan," said one. Léon Blum, vacationing in Zurich, opened the door of his hotel room at 10 P.M. to the porter who brought the news. "I don't think that ever in my whole life have I felt an equal excitement. . . . The immense, the infinite joy that rushed through me had its sources in the triumph of *reason*. The truth had actually won." This time, at last and for certain, it seemed to the Dreyfusards they had accomplished their task. In a sense they had, for the truth was now disclosed. To impose it was another matter.

Cavaignac resigned and within two weeks his successor, the sixth Minister of War since Dreyfus' arrest, also resigned. The Government, surrendering to what was now unavoidable, submitted the case to the Cour de Cassation (literally, "Court of Breaking"), whose task was to decide

* He had been promoted.

whether a given verdict should be upheld or broken. The action, taken as mistrust of the Generals, caused another War Minister to resign. Awaiting the Court's decision whether or not to accept the case, Paris boiled with excitement. If the Court took the case, the Secret File must come under civilian review, which the Army was committed to prevent. In England the sober *Spectator* thought the logic of the situation must lead to an Army coup d'état. In Paris the royalists and wild men of the Rightist leagues, hoping to provoke exactly that, spread rumors of a plot, called meetings, sent out their hired bands to shout in the streets. It was Déroulède's longed-for hour.

An irrepressible agitator, a poet and a deputy, long-legged and long-nosed like Don Quixote, Déroulède saw windmills to charge in every aspect of the Republic. A veteran of 1870, he had founded his Ligue des Patriotes in 1882 to keep alive the spirit of *revanche*. It bore the legend "1870–18——" with the second date left significantly blank and a motto of noble meaninglessness, *France Quand Même*. Déroulède wrote patriotic verse, loathed the royalists as much as the Republic and had "the political vision of a child." To foment a crisis he now joined forces with Jules Guérin, active head of the Anti-Semitic League, which was receiving a subsidy from the Duc d'Orléans, who hoped to ride in on the tail of the crisis. Tension grew when a strike of 20,000 construction workers on the site of the Exposition of 1900 caused the Government to bring in troops to occupy the railroad stations and patrol the boulevards. Word spread of a coup planned for the reopening of the Chamber on October 25. Déroulède and Guérin called for a huge protest meeting in front of the Palais Bourbon to demonstrate "confidence in the Army and abhorrence of traitors."

The Socialists, or a part of them, suddenly discovered the Republic was worth saving. However dedicated to overthrow of the existing system, they did not want it overthrown by the Right. Besides, they were discovering from their local committees that their neutrality in the Affair was compromising them with some of their constituents. "Because we seem to oppose all forms of bourgeois republicanism," wrote a party worker from the provinces, "many people take us for the allies of monarchist reactionaries."

The Socialist leaders, sending out notices by *pneumatique,* called an emergency meeting of their several groups to organize a united front in face of the peril, and such seemed the urgency of the moment that they succeeded in forming a joint, if temporary, Committee of Vigilance. Following proper revolutionary procedure, it decided to hold meetings every night and call upon the people for mass demonstrations. Clashes with the Rightist leagues, riots, even civil war loomed. In awful anxiety the Dreyfusard League for the Rights of Man called upon all Republicans to disdain fracas in the streets, but Jaurès saw Socialist opportunity: "Paris is trembling with resolve . . . the proletariat is organizing." Warned, however, by Guesde that to provoke an outbreak would be playing the game of the Generals, who were believed to be waiting for a riot to seize power, the Committee of Vigilance had second thoughts. Socialists would provoke nothing, it announced. "Revolutionary groups are ready to act or abstain, according to the circumstances."

So certain were the royalists of "the day" that André Buffet, *chef de cabinet* for the Duc d'Orléans, telegraphed the Pretender that his presence in nearby Brussels on October 24 was "indispensable." The Duke, who was hunting in Bohemia, replied, "Should I come at once or can I wait here? Urgent business." Adamant, Buffet wired back, "Approach frontier necessary," but the Duke, better advised, stayed away.

The day came, crowds surrounded the Chamber, filled the Place de la Concorde and nearby streets, slogans were shouted, red flags waved. "It seemed like the eve either of a new Commune or of a coup by a dictator." The atmosphere was threatening: troops and police were everywhere. The day passed, however, and the Republic still stood, for the Right lacked that necessary chemical of a coup—a leader. It had its small, if loud, fanatics; but to upset the established government in a democratic country requires either foreign help or the stuff of a dictator. As Clemenceau had harshly said when Boulanger shot himself on the grave of his mistress, inside the "Man on Horseback" was only "the soul of a second lieutenant."

Events rushed on. On October 29 the Cour de Cassation announced it would accept the case and begin its inquiry. VICTOIRE! proclaimed *l'Aurore* in the same type as J'ACCUSE! Revisionists hailed the decision as re-establishing civil power over the military. Then the Court demanded the Secret File. The Minister of War refused and resigned. The Government fell. For the next seven months the Court became the focus of the battle. From this point on, the Right was on the defensive and the Affair entered its period of greatest frenzy. The Court was excoriated by the Nationalist press as the "sanctuary of treason," a "branch of the synagogue," the "lair of Judas," a "combination of Bourse and brothel." The judges were variously "hirelings of Germany," "valets of the synagogue" and "rogues in ermine." Pressures of all kinds were exerted, both sides were accused of corrupting the judges, and the Nationalists succeeded in forcing the case out of the Criminal Chamber, which was considered too favorable, to the united Court of three chambers, which was considered more susceptible to pressure.

A Dreyfusard tempest raged at the same time over Picquart. To keep him from testifying before the Cour de Cassation the Army had transferred him to Cherche Midi preliminary to a court-martial. The League for the Rights of Man organized public protest meetings every night, in the provincial cities as well as in Paris. Jaurès' name and prestige drew 30,000 to a meeting in Marseilles. He, Duclaux the scientist, Anatole France, Octave Mirbeau and Sebastian Faure were the favorite speakers. Workers and bourgeois, students and professors, working women and Society women crowded the halls and overflowed onto the sidewalks, applauded the famous orators and marched together to shout *"Vive Picquart!"* under the prison walls of Cherche Midi. Signatures for a protest on Picquart came in this time not by hundreds but by thousands, including thirty-four members of the Institut de France, a measure, as Reinach said, of the distance covered by truth on the march. Among the new names were Sarah Bernhardt and Hervé de Kerohant, editor of *Soleil*, formerly against Revision, who signed the protest as "Patriot, Royalist, Christian." The historian and Academician Ernest Lavisse felt strongly enough to act, and as his gesture of personal protest, resigned his chair at St-Cyr.

Even the Anarchists, hitherto resolutely contemptuous and indifferent, were swept into the cause. Formerly they had denounced the Dreyfus "parade," in the words of their newspaper, *Le Père Peinard*, as a "bunch of dirty types" led by Clemenceau and by "the old exploiter Scheurer-Kestner, the toad Yves Guyot [editor of *Le Siècle*], the hideous Reinach, three malefactors who helped to concoct the *lois scélérates*." Now, however, when their bourgeois enemies cried out the sufferings of the two martyred prisoners of Devil's Island and Cherche Midi, the Anarchists did the same for their own martyrs sent to forced labour in French Guiana. With a new interest in these cases the League for the Rights of Man succeeded in obtaining pardons for five of them.

Some on the Right could no longer keep their heads turned from the truth. Mme de Greffulhe, goddess of the *gratin*, becoming secretly convinced of Dreyfus' innocence, wrote to the Kaiser asking to visit him to ascertain if the Germans really had employed Dreyfus as a spy. The only answer she received was a large basket of orchids. Proust chronicles the change in his character, the Prince de Guermantes, who confesses to Swann that after Colonel Henry's suicide he has begun to read *Le Siècle* and *l'Aurore* secretly every day. He and his wife, unknown to each other, have asked the Abbé to say a mass for Dreyfus and his family, and discovered to each other's astonishment that the Abbé too believes him innocent. Meeting the maid on the staircase carrying breakfast to the Princesse and concealing something under the napkin, the Prince discovers it to be *l'Aurore*.

Below the trapped obstinacy of the Generals, some in the Army were deeply troubled. "Just among ourselves with no outsiders present," an officer said to Galliffet while riding in a train, "we are not as anti-Revisionist as people think. On the contrary we too would like to see the light and see the culprits punished so that if wrongs have been committed the Army will not bear the responsibility." He felt that if Picquart were tried and convicted public opinion would turn against the Army.

The Army's cup of bitterness was filled when in the same week that the Cour de Cassation began its inquiry the order was given withdrawing Colonel Marchand from Fashoda. Jaurès lashed at the imperialist adventure as a crime of capitalism which had frivolously imperiled peace without preparing for the consequence of challenging England. As if his already strong intuitive perceptions had been sharpened by the Affair, he wrote with foreboding, "Peace has been left to the whim of chance. But if war breaks out it will be vast and terrible. For the first time it will be universal, sucking in all the continents. Capitalism has widened the field of battle and the entire planet will turn red with the blood of countless men. No more terrible accusation can be made against this social system." In his time it was still possible to suppose the fault lay in the system, not humanity.

The Affair continued in its frenzy. When Reinach wrote a series of articles in *Le Siècle* accusing Colonel Henry of having had a "personal interest" in ruining Dreyfus, Drumont persuaded Mme Henry to sue him for libel and opened a public subscription in her behalf which became the rallying point for Nationalists of every degree. A banner reading "For the Widow and Orphan of Colonel Henry against the Jew Reinach" was stretched across the windows of the offices of *La Libre Parole* on the Boulevard Montmartre and lit up at night. Within a month fifteen thousand persons had contributed 130,000 francs. Their names and comments provided a history of the Right—of that or any time. Five hundred francs, the top sum, was subscribed by the Countess Odon de Montesquiou, née Bibesco, and thirty sous by a lieutenant "poor in money but rich in hate." There were all varieties of hate, chiefly for Jews, expressed in suggestions for skinning, branding, boiling in oil, burning with vitriol, emasculation and other forms of foul or physical punishment. There was hate for foreigners and intellectuals and even a "500-year-old hate for England" but there were many who gave their francs out of love or pity for the widow and child. An abbé contributed for "defence of eternal law against Judaeo-

Christian deceit," a music professor for "Frenchmen against foreigners," a civil servant "who wants God in the schools," an anonymous donor "ruined by a Jew after six months of marriage," a workingman as "the victim of the anarchist capitalists Jaurès and Reinach." There were innumerable "true patriots" and one "Frenchman sick at heart." There were *Vive!*'s for Drumont, Rochefort, Déroulède, Guérin, Esterhazy, the Duc d'Orléans, *l'Empereur, le Roi*, the Heroes of Austerlitz and Jeanne d'Arc. Reinach was the chief target; Dreyfus received hardly a mention. General Mercier subscribed a hundred francs without comment; the poet Paul Valéry three francs "not without reflection."

Suddenly and strangely on top of all the excitement, the President of France, Félix Faure, died. The public sensed something unexplained and the truth in fact was too embarrassing to be told. Proud of his amatory prowess, President Faure died in the performance thereof in a ground-floor room of the Elysée. An aura of something hushed up was added to the atmosphere already charged with aggression and suspicion.

In the election of a new president, held in the midst of hysterical battle over jurisdiction of the Court, Emile Loubet, President of the Senate, a steady, simple Republican and product of peasant stock, won over the Conservative Méline. As Premier at the time of the Panama scandal, Loubet was despised by the Nationalists. They called his election an "insult to France," a "challenge to the Army," a "victory for Jewish treason." Their hired mobs sent to hoot his progress from the Gare St-Lazare to the Elysée raised such a clamor that even the band playing the "Marseillaise" could not be heard. "The Republic will not founder in my hands," said Loubet calmly. "They know it and it maddens them."

The Right in a state of ungovernable excitement was prepared to make it founder. "In a week we will have driven Loubet from the Presidency," boasted Jules Lemaître. The state funeral of Faure was fixed on as the occasion for a coup d'état. The Army must be persuaded to save the country. The "Leaguers" thought they could do it by a cry, a gesture, an occasion, and did not concern themselves with serious organization. Their plan was to intercept the military escort of the cortege while it was returning from the cemetery to its barracks in the Place de la Nation, and lead it to seize the Elysée. Déroulède joined by Guérin led a band of two hundred patriots into the streets, caught hold of the bridle of General Roget, commander of the escort, shouting, "To the Elysée, General! Follow us, General, follow us! To the Place Bastille! To the Hotel de Ville! To the Elysée! Friends await us. I beg you, General, save France, establish a Republic of the people, kick out the *parlementaires!*" The General kept his head and kept moving, the crowd, ignorant but willing, shouted, "Save France! *Vive l'Armée!*", the troops sweeping Déroulède and his followers with them, marched on to the barracks and entered. Déroulède, throwing open his coat to reveal his deputy's scarf, emblem of parliamentary immunity, was nevertheless carted off to the police station to be indicted for insurrection and provide at his trial one more cause for combative passions. The fiasco did nothing to daunt the expectations of the Right. In the following month the Anti-Semitic League received 56,000 francs from the Duc d'Orléans and 100,000 from Boni de Castellane.

Hardly had breath been drawn when the verdict that all France was awaiting was announced by the Cour de Cassation. Forty-six judges in scarlet and ermine declared for Revision. A cruiser was sent to bring Dreyfus back from Devil's Island for retrial. Zola returned from England with an article which *l'Aurore* headlined in the now familiar type, JUSTICE! He saw all factional and party lines now dissipated in one great division separating France into two camps: the forces of reaction and the past against the forces of justice and the future. This was the logical order of battle to complete the task of 1789. With the unquenchable optimism of their age the Dreyfusards hailed the Court's decision as the herald of social justice for the century about to be born. A great burden of shame seemed lifted and replaced by pride in France. "What other country," wrote a correspondent of *Le Temps* at The Hague where the Peace Conference was assembled, "has had the privilege of making the world's heart beat faster as we have for the last three years?" Revision meant not only the triumph of justice but of "the liberty of mankind." Others beside Frenchmen felt this universality. William James, traveling in Europe, wrote as he saw daylight breaking through the Affair, "It may be one of those moral crises that become starting points and high water marks and leave traditions and rallying cries and new faces behind them."

The Nationalists were flung into paroxysms of wrath. Caran d'Ache drew a cartoon showing Dreyfus with a smirk and Reinach with a whip ordering, "Come here, Marianne." On the facing page he drew Zola emerging from a toilet bowl holding a toy Dreyfus, with the caption, "Truth Rising from Its Well."

Fury at the Court's decision was vented the next day on the head of President Loubet when he attended the races at Auteuil. It was the Sunday of *le Grand Steeple,* the most fashionable event of the season. When the President's carriage drove up to the grandstand, groups of well-dressed gentlemen wearing in their buttonholes the white carnation of the royalists and the blue cornflower of the anti-Semites, and brandishing their canes, shouted in pounding rhythm, *"Dé-mis-sion!* [resign] *Pa-na-ma! Dé-mis-sion! Pa-na-ma!"* Through the howls and threats Loubet took his seat. Suddenly a tall man with a blond moustache, wearing a white carnation and white cravat, later identified as the Baron Fernand de Christiani, detached himself from the group, dashed up the steps two at a time and struck the President on the head with a heavy cane. Ladies screamed. A sudden silence of general stupor followed, then an uproar as the assailant's companions rushed to rescue him from the guards. As some were arrested others converged on the police in yelling groups, striking with their canes. The scene was *"un charivari infernal."* General Zurlinden, Governor of Paris, telephoned for reinforcements of three cavalry detachments. Loubet, though shaken, apologized for the disturbance to Countess Tornielli, the Italian Ambassadress, in the seat beside him. "It was a place of honor," she replied.

In Loubet's top hat the Republic itself had been assaulted and the public was startled and indignant. Telegrams from committees and municipal councils all over France poured in expressing a loyalty deeper than might have been supposed from the experience of the last years. Loubet announced that as an invited guest he intended to appear at next Sunday's races at Longchamps. Forewarned, the leagues and newspapers of both sides called for demonstrations and assembled their battalions. The Government took extraordinary precautions. Thirty squadrons of cavalry and a brigade of infantry in battle dress were lined up along the route from the Elysée to Longchamps, while at the racecourse itself dragoons of the *Garde Républicaine* armed with rifles were stationed at every ten yards around the course and at every betting window. Mounted police guarded the lawn. More than 100,000 people turned out along the route and at the racecourse, many wearing the red rose boutonniere of the Left. Again the threat of the Right brought out the workers, less, perhaps, to defend the bourgeois state than to defy the representatives of the ruling class. The presence of more than six thousand guardians of the law prevented a major outbreak, but throughout the day demonstrators clashed, private riots and melees erupted, cries and counter-cries resounded, hundreds were arrested, reporters and police as well as demonstrators were injured. As the crowds flowed back to Paris in the evening the turbulence swept through the cafés; *"Vive la République!"* met *"Vive l'Armée!"* Bottles and glasses, carafes and trays were hurled, tables and chairs became weapons, police charged; anger, broken heads and national animosities mounted. Even outside Paris, in a pension in Brest where officers and professors boarded, "these young men equally animated by love of France" could no longer talk to or understand each other without coming to the point of a duel. It was time, urged *Le Temps*, for a "truce of God."

But it was not to be had. When again the Government fell in the week after Longchamps, the fears and difficulties to be faced in office were now so great that for eight days no one could form a Government. In the vacuum the man who came forward with intent to "liquidate" the Affair was able to impose conditions that would otherwise have been unacceptable. He was René Waldeck-Rousseau, fifty-three, the leading lawyer of Paris and a polished orator, known as the "Pericles of the Republic." A Catholic from Britanny, wealthy and wellborn, he was impressive in manner and British in appearance, with cropped hair and moustache, a taste for hunting and fishing, a talent for watercolors and impeccable clothes. Rochefort called him *Waldeck le pommadé* because he was so well groomed. Admired by the Radicals and approved by the Center, he represented the *juste milieu*.

With the retrial of Dreyfus ahead, the Affair was moving toward climax. To retain office under the terrible buffeting he could expect, Waldeck deliberately chose to form a Government which, by being equally obnoxious to both sides, would cancel the blows of either. He selected a Socialist, Millerand, as Minister of Commerce and a military hero, the Marquis de Galliffet, "butcher" of the Commune, as Minister of War. The tumult in press and parliament that greeted this remarkable expedient was unequalled. "Pure madness . . . absolute lunacy . . . monstrous . . . infamous!" came from both sides. The appointment of Millerand not only infuriated the Right; his acceptance created a scandal and a schism in his own party and in the Socialist International of major proportions and historic significance. Acceptance of office in a capitalist Government was a betrayal comparable to that of Judas. Profoundly saddened, Jaurès begged Millerand to shun the offer, but Waldeck had knowingly selected a man to whom the lure of office was strong. The Socialists now had to face the choice whether or not to support the Waldeck Government when it came to the Chamber for a vote of confidence. If the Government lost, the prospect was chaos. Jaurès was persuaded by Lucien Herr's argument: "What a triumph for Socialism that the Republic cannot be saved without calling on the party of the proletariat!" The Guesde faction, however, clung to the class struggle. Socialists, stated Guesde, "enter Parliament as though we were in an enemy State only in order to fight the enemy class." Jaurès warned that if Socialism persisted in this attitude it would sink to the level of "sterile and intransigent anarchism," but he did not prevail. The Union Socialiste broke apart; twenty-five of the parliamentary members agreed to

support the Government; seventeen refused. Guesde enchanted his group
with the exciting suggestion that it should greet the new Government's
appearance in the Chamber with cries of *"Vive la Commune!"* but, so as
not to find themselves allied with the Right, abstain when it came to a vote.

For ten minutes next day they stood hurling *"Vive la Commune! A bas
les fusilleurs! A bas l'assassin!"* at the new ministers. The object of it all,
General the Marquis de Galliffet, Prince de Martigues, nearly seventy, with
red-bronze face and bright eyes, looked mockingly on the scene, half
gratified, half-disgusted. He had fought in the Crimea, Italy, Mexico,
Algeria and at Sedan, where he had led his regiment into the last cavalry
charge with the reply to his commanding officer, "As often as you like, Sir,
as long as one of us is left." Impressed by the great Gambetta's patriotism
and fighting spirit, Galliffet became and remained a loyal Republican and
openly despised Boulanger. The eyes in his highly colored face were sunk
on either side of a nose like the beak of a bird of prey, but his figure was
vigorous and young and he still wore "the same air that had made his fortune, as of a bandit chief who feared nothing or a *grand seigneur* who
cared for nothing." Despite a silver-plated stomach and a limp from old
wounds, he played tennis in the Tuileries Gardens and his love affairs,
recounted with sparkle and ribaldry, were the delight of the Bixio. He told
how Mme de Castiglione showed him her nude portrait by Baudry, and
when he asked if she was really as beautiful as that, she disrobed and posed
on the sofa. "The picture was better," Galliffet concluded. He was called
the *sabreur de la parole* because he told stories "as if he were charging at
the head of his squadron." Devoted to the fighting efficiency of the Army
and to Picquart who had served under his command, he had become a
Revisionist. For this sin he was cut at the Jockey, and after he became a
Minister, resigned from the Cercle de l'Union, less because of his own
opinions than because of "imbecile" members who got themselves arrested
at Auteuil; as he said, "It's not possible to belong to a club if one has to
arrest the members; it's not sociable." Caustic and eccentric, proud of
having nothing to live on but his pension after having once been rich, he
possessed "courage, effrontery, intelligence, contempt for death and thirst
for life."

He needed all these to become Minister of War at the peak of the
Affair. Confronting the taunts of the Guesde extremists in the Chamber
he suddenly stood up and barked, *"L'assassin, présent!"* The din became
general. Nationalists, Radicals, Center, were shouting insults and shaking
fists. Millerand, a lawyer like Waldeck, with gray hair *en brosse*, a lorgnon,
a neat black moustache and a precise, aggressive manner, was wilting. His

moustache trembled and he looked "like a huge cat caught in a downpour." Galliffet was observed taking down names and explained later, "I thought I'd better invite those chaps to dinner." Waldeck, trying to speak, stood at the tribune for an hour without being heard for more than ten minutes. He fought desperately and succeeded in establishing the Government by a majority of twenty-six.

Galliffet joined it "without illusions," he wrote to Princess Radziwill, because of its promise to pacify France, "if that is still possible. The Rightist papers beg me to do another Boulanger and those of the Left want me to cut off the heads of all the Generals who displease them. The public is an idiot. If I touch a guilty general I am accused of massacring the Army; if I abstain I am accused of treason. What a dilemma. Pity me." Actually, although he found Loubet "too bourgeois," he was pleased to be a Minister and was very "gay and amusing" at the next meeting of the Bixio. He told a lively story of a rather large but lovely lady of forty-five who visited him at his office to propose a little deal involving 20,000 horses to be bought for the Army. There would be a million in it for him. "A million," he said to her. "That's not much considering the twenty-five million I got from the Syndicate as everyone knows. Go to see Waldeck. He is jealous of me because he only got seventeen million."

Six weeks later, on August 8, 1899, the retrial of Dreyfus by a new court-martial was scheduled to open in the garrison town of Rennes, a Catholic and aristocratic corner of traditionally Counter-Revolutionary Brittany. France quivered in expectation; as each week passed bringing the moment closer, the tension grew. The world's eyes were turned on Rennes. All the important foreign newspapers sent their star correspondents. Lord Russell of Killowen, the Lord Chief Justice of England, came as an observer. All the leading figures in the Affair, hundreds of French journalists and important political, social and literary figures crammed the town. The Secret File was brought from Paris in an iron box on an artillery caisson. No one anywhere talked of anything but the coming verdict. Acquittal would mean for the Dreyfusards vindication at last; for the Nationalists it would be lethal; an unimaginable blow not to be permitted. As if on order they returned to the theme of the first blackmail: Dreyfus or the Army. "A choice is to be made," wrote Barrès in the *Journal*; Rennes, he said, was the Rubicon. "If Dreyfus is innocent then seven Ministers of War are guilty and the last more than the first," echoed Meyer in *Le Gaulois*. General Mercier, leaving for Rennes to appear as a witness, issued his Order of the Day: "Dreyfus will be condemned once more. For in this affair someone is certainly guilty and the guilty one is either him or me. As it is certainly not me, it is Dreyfus. . . . Dreyfus is a traitor and I shall prove it."

At six o'clock on the morning of August 8 the Court convened with an audience of six hundred persons in the hall of the *lycée*, the only room in Rennes large enough to accommodate them. In the front row, next to former President Casimir-Périer, sat Mercier, his yellow lined face as expressionless as ever, and nearby, the widow of Colonel Henry in her long black mourning veil. Dignitaries, officers in uniform, ladies in light summer dresses and more than four hundred journalists filled the rows behind. Colonel Jouaust, presiding officer of the seven military judges, called out in a voice hoarse under the pressure of the moment, "Bring in the accused."

At once every chattering voice was stilled, every mouth closed, people seemed to hold their breath as with one movement every head in the audience turned toward a small door in the wall on the right. Every gaze fastened on it with a kind of shrinking awe as if fearful to look upon a ghost. For the accused was a ghost, whom no one in the room had laid eyes on for almost five years, whom no one there beyond his family, lawyers and original accusers had ever seen at all. For five years he had been present in all their minds, not as a man but as an idea; now he was going to walk through the door and they would look on Lazarus. A minute passed, then another while the waiting people were gripped in silence, an agonized silence, "such a silence as never before could have overtaken a crowd."

The door opened, two guards were seen; between them came forward a thin, worn, desiccated figure, a strange shred of humanity, seeming neither young nor old, with a shrunken face and dried-out skin, and a body looking almost hollowed out but holding itself erect as if not to falter in the last few yards between the door and the witness box. Only the pince-nez familiar from the pictures had not suffered. A movement of "horror and pity" passed through the watchers, and the look bent on him by Picquart whose life he had changed beyond repair was so intense it could be felt by the people in between. Others present whose careers he had changed or broken—Clemenceau, Cavaignac—saw him for the first time.

For four and a half years Dreyfus had hardly spoken or heard a spoken word. Illness, fever, tropical sun, periods of chains and brutality when the frenzy in France was reflected by his gaolers, had enfeebled him. He could barely speak and only slowly understand what was spoken to him. Mounting the three steps to the tribune he staggered momentarily, straightened himself, saluted with impenetrable face, raised his gloved hand to take the oath, removed his hat, revealed the hair turned prematurely white. He remained a statue. He knew nothing of the Affair, the battle of the press, the duels and petitions, riots, street mobs, Leagues, trials, libel suits, appeals, coups d'état; nothing of Scheurer-Kestner, Reinach, the arrest of Picquart, the trial of Zola, the court-martial of Esterhazy, the suicide of Colonel Henry, the attack on the person of the President of France. During the trial, the impression he made on many was unfavorable. Rigidly determined to allow nothing to show that would appeal to pity, he antagonized many who came prepared to pity. G. A. Henty who came like most of the English, believing him to have been framed, left voicing doubts. "The man looked and spoke like a spy . . . and if he isn't a spy I'll be damned if he oughtn't to be one." Henty spoke for the last romantics who expected abstract concepts like Justice to be unequivocal and people who behaved oddly to be spies.

In the end it was not the impression Dreyfus made that determined the outcome any more than it was he who made the Affair: it was the dilemma Mercier had formulated long ago and it was General Mercier among the hundreds of witnesses who dominated the trial. Cold in authority, haughty in self-assurance, he took full responsibility for the original order withholding the Secret File from the defence, which he said was a "moral" decision. When on the witness stand he refused to answer questions he did not like; when not on the stand he intervened without being asked. When the Secret File was under examination he ordered the public excluded and the Court obeyed him. When questioned on the Army's suppression of evidence, the cynicism of his answers, Reinach confessed, "was almost admirable, . . . as if crime might be the source of a kind of beauty." Mercier "has become hallucinated," wrote Galliffet. "He thinks France is incarnated in his person . . . but all the same he is an honorable man."

As the weeks of examination and testimony dragged on with the succession of witnesses personally and passionately involved, the contention of lawyers, the disputes of journalists and observers, the heated feelings of the town, suspense as to the verdict became almost insupportable. In Paris rumors of another coup d'état planned for the day Mercier was to testify caused the Government to raid the homes of a hundred suspects and arrest sixty-five in their beds, including Déroulède but missing Guérin, who got away, barricaded himself in a house in the Rue Chabrol with a cache of munitions and fourteen companions, where he held out against a somewhat lackluster police siege for six weeks. "I don't budge from my office from 7 A.M. to 7 P.M. seven days a week, in order to be prepared for anything," wrote Galliffet.

On August 14 the too eloquent and aggressive Maître Labori, who "looked like Hercules and pleaded like a boxer," was shot outside the court, but not killed, by a young man with red hair who ran away shouting, "I've just killed the Dreyfus! I've just killed the Dreyfus!" The name again had become an abstraction. The attack raised the temperature to the level of madness. Since the assailant had run away with Labori's briefcase and had not been caught, it seemed to the Dreyfusards a deliberate plot and one more proof that the Nationalists would stop at nothing. They denounced their opponents as "murderers," a "General Staff of criminals" and swore that "for every one of ours we shall kill one of theirs—Mercier, Cavaignac, Boisdeffre, Barrès." Wrote Princess Radziwill to Galliffet, "My God, what an end to the century!"

The end of the trial came on September 9 and all the world gasped at the unbelievable verdict. By a vote of 5–2 Dreyfus was condemned again with "extenuating circumstances" which permitted a sentence of five years, already served, instead of a mandatory life sentence. Since there could obviously be nothing extenuating about treason, the rider was provocative to both sides. It had been devised by the prosecution, which realized that it would be easier to obtain a verdict of guilty if the judges did not have on their consciences the prospect of sending Dreyfus back to Devil's Island.

The effect of the verdict was as of some awful disaster. People were stunned. Queen Victoria telegraphed Lord Russell, "The Queen has learned with stupefaction the frightful verdict and hopes the poor martyr will appeal it to the highest judges." "Iniquitous, cynical, odious, barbarous," wrote *The Times* correspondent, bereft of sentence structure. Like an angry Isaiah, Clemenceau demanded, "What remains of the historic tradition that once made us champions of justice for the whole of the earth? A cry will ring out over the world: Where is France? What became of France?" World opinion suddenly became an issue, more acutely because of the coming International Exposition of 1900. At Evian on Lake Geneva, where many of the *gratin* spent their summer holidays, Proust found the Comtesse de Noailles weeping and crying, "How could they do it? What will the foreigners think of us now?" In the Nationalist camp the same thought was cause for rejoicing. "Since 1870 it is our first victory over the foreigner," exulted *Le Gaulois*.

Strength of feeling everywhere was made plain; the whole world cared. Excitement in Odessa was "simply extraordinary"; there was intense indignation in Berlin, "disgust and horror" in far-off Melbourne, protest meetings in Chicago and suggestions from all quarters for boycott of the Exposition. In Liverpool copies of *The Times* were bought out in minutes and soon sold at a premium. From Norway the composer Grieg wrote refusing an invitation to conduct his music at the Théâtre Chatelet because of his "indignation at the contempt for justice shown in your country." The English, riding at the time a wave of anti-French feeling because of Fashoda, were most indignant of all. Hyde Park rang with protest meetings, newspapers denounced the "insult to civilization," industrial firms and cultural societies urged boycott of the Exposition as a means of bringing pressure on the French Government, travelers were urged to cancel proposed visits, a hotel-keeper in the Lake District evicted a honeymooning French couple and one writer to the editor asserted that even the question of the Transvaal "pales into insignificance before the larger questions of truth and justice." *The Times,* however, reminded readers that many Frenchmen had risked "more than life itself" to prevent the defeat of justice and could not be expected to abandon the struggle to redress the wrong of Rennes.

The fight did in fact go on, but public opinion was worn out. The Affair was one of those situations for which there was no good solution. Waldeck-Rousseau offered Dreyfus a pardon which, despite the fierce objections of Clemenceau, was accepted on grounds of humanity—since Dreyfus could go through no more—and with the proviso that it would not terminate the effort to clear his name. Galliffet issued to the Army an Order of the Day: "The incident is closed. . . . Forget the past so that you may think only of the future." Waldeck introduced an Amnesty Bill annulling all pending legal actions connected with the case and angering both sides: the Right because Déroulède was excluded; the Dreyfusards because Picquart, Reinach and others who had suffered injustice or had been sued could not clear themselves. Waldeck was adamant. "The amnesty does not judge, it does not accuse, it does not acquit; it ignores." Debate nevertheless continued furious and lasted for a year before the bill became law. Animosities did not close over. Positions taken during the Affair hardened and crystallized. Lemaître, who had entered it more for sensation than from conviction, became a rabid royalist; Anatole France moved far to the left.

The battle shifted from the moral to the political; from Dreyfus to the Dreyfusian Revolution. It remained the same battle but the terms changed. The issue was no longer Justice and Revision but the effort of the Government under Waldeck and his successor, Combes, to curb clericalism and republicanize education and the Army. The fight was waged as fiercely as ever over Waldeck's Law of Associations directed against the Religious Orders and over the affair of General André and the *fiches* when it was disclosed that the overzealous Minister of War in 1904 was using reports from Masonic officers on Catholic brother-officers to guide him in matters of promotion. Persistent and unrelenting efforts by Mathieu Dreyfus, Reinach and Jaurès succeeded against all obstacles in achieving a final Revision and a "breaking" of the Rennes verdict by the Cour de Cassation. On July 13, 1906, the eve of Bastille Day, almost twelve years after Dreyfus' arrest and seven years after Rennes, a bill restoring Dreyfus and Picquart to the Army was carried in the Chamber by 442–32, with de Mun still among the negatives. Dreyfus, decorated with the Légion d'Honneur, was promoted to Major and Picquart to General, the ranks they would have reached by the normal course of events. In 1902 Drumont failed of re-election to the Chamber; *La Libre Parole* declined and in 1907 was offered for sale with no takers. Zola died in 1902 and at his funeral Anatole France spoke the just and noble epitaph of the man who "for a moment, . . . was the conscience of mankind." In 1908 Zola's ashes were transferred to the Panthéon. In the course of the ceremony a man named Gregori shot at Dreyfus, wounding him in the arm, and was subsequently acquitted in the Assize Court. In 1906 Clemenceau became Premier and named Picquart his Minister of War. Picquart in the seat of Mercier, "that's something to see!" said Galliffet. "There are some things to console one for not being able to decide to die."

Rennes was the climax. After Rennes neither the fight for Justice nor the struggle of the Right against the Republic was over, but the Affair was. While it lasted, France exhibited, as in the Revolution, political man at his most combative. It was a time of excess. Men plunged in up to the hilt of their capacities and beliefs. They held nothing back. On the eve of the new century the Affair revealed what energies and ferocity were at hand to greet it.

5

The Steady
Drummer

THE HAGUE:
1899 AND 1907

5

The Steady Drummer

JOY, HOPE, SUSPICION—above all, astonishment—were the world's prevailing emotions when it learned on August 29, 1898, that the young Czar of Russia, Nicholas II, had issued a call to the nations to join in a conference for the limitation of armaments. All the capitals were taken by surprise by what *Le Temps* called "this flash of lightning out of the North." That the call should come from the mighty and ever expanding power whom the other nations feared and who was still regarded, despite its two hundred years of European veneer, as semi-barbaric, was cause for dazed wonderment liberally laced with distrust. The pressure of Russian expansion had been felt from Alaska to India, from Turkey to Poland. "The Czar with an olive branch," it was said in Vienna, "that's something new in history." But his invitation touched a chord aching to respond.

Fear of the swelling armaments industry was widespread. Krupp, the colossus of Essen, was the largest single business in Europe. Skoda, Schneider-Creusot, Vickers-Maxim, the distended combines of many mergers, with harsh names that grated on the ear, had interests in every camp, sold their products to customers on every continent and to both sides of every quarrel, profited from every dispute. Each year one or another of them produced a new weapon more efficient in deadliness, which, when adopted by the armed forces of one power, immediately required a matching effort by its rival. Each year the cost mounted and the huge piles of weapons grew until it seemed they must burst in final, lethal explosion.

The Czar's manifesto called for a stop to this process. Addressed to all the governments represented at St. Petersburg, it stated that although the longing for peace had been especially pronounced in the last twenty years, "the intellectual and physical strength of nations, labour and capital alike, have been unproductively consumed in building terrible engines of destruction." Today these were the last word in science, tomorrow they were obsolete and had to be replaced. The system of "armaments à l'outrance is transforming the armed peace into a crushing burden that weighs on all nations and if prolonged will lead inevitably to the very cataclysm which it is desired to avert." To arrest this exorbitant competition was now incumbent upon all.

The summons from such a source surpassed the wildest dreams of the friends of peace. It "will sound like beautiful music over the whole earth," said a Viennese paper. Phrases like "a new epoch in civilization," "dawn of a new era," "omen for the new century," appeared in the press of every country. In Belgium the summons was called a "veritable deliverance," an act of "colossal importance" whose author would go down in history as "Nicholas the Pacific." In New York it seemed a possible beginning "of the most momentous and beneficent movement in modern history—indeed in all history." Rome lauded "one of the great documents that honors its century," and Berlin greeted "the new Evangelist on the banks of the Neva" whose goal was noble and beautiful in theory however unrealizable in practice. Humanitarian but utopian was the consensus in London—except for Kipling who uttered dire warning. Britain and Russia were then close to conflict across India's Northwest Frontier, and Kipling's poem "The Bear that Walks like a Man," composed in response to the Czar's manifesto, told a grim allegory of a man maimed and blinded when the bear he hunted stood up as if in supplication and the hunter "touched with pity and wonder" withheld his fire only to have his face ripped away by the "steel-shod paw":

> When he stands up as pleading, in wavering, man-
>   brute guise,
> When he veils the hate and cunning of his little
>   swinish eyes;
> When he shows as seeking quarter, with paws like
>   hands in prayer,
> *That* is the time of peril—the time of the Truce
>   of the Bear! . . .

Suspicion of Russia's motive and cynical speculations were ample. The leading question was, had France, Russia's ally, been consulted in advance? Since disarmament presupposed satisfaction with the status quo and since France was vociferously unreconciled to the loss of Alsace-Lorraine, the action of her ally posed, as *The Times* said, a "most surprising enigma." From the French reaction it was clear she had not been consulted. *"Et l'Alsace-Lorraine?"* was *l'Intransigeant*'s one-line summary. Nevertheless many felt that coming at a time when "the intolerable pretensions and immeasurable ambitions" of Anglo-Saxon imperialism were agitating everyone's nerves and when the maintenance of peace was becoming more and more a "miracle of equilibrium," the proposed conference was welcome.

Each group saw reflected in the Czar's manifesto, as if in a magic mirror, the face of its particular opponent. To Germany it was obvious that if England did not consent to naval disarmament the Czar's gesture would amount to "a sword stroke in water" and a few days later the Kaiser pronounced his decisive dictum, "Our future lies upon the ocean." The British saw the major problem in Germany's naval ambitions. Socialists everywhere were sure that whatever the Russian motive had been, considering the cruelties of Czarist oppression, it was not love of humanity. The German Socialist Wilhelm Liebknecht pronounced it a "fraud." Many peace advocates considered it a response to the Spanish-American War, which seemed to them a prelude to world disaster. Many Europeans were convinced by the taking of the Philippines of the necessity of curbing American expansion. Americans themselves were not averse to the thought that the Czar had been prompted by their victory over Spain. Speaking for the anti-imperialists, Godkin sadly noted that the "splendid summons" came at a time when the United States was more deeply committed to "the military spirit and idea of forcible conquest" than ever before in her history.

The puzzle of motive remained. One explanation widely favored was that Nicholas had acted less for humanity than from a human desire to forestall the Kaiser, who was believed to be planning a similar proclamation, *urbi et orbi*, on his forthcoming visit to Jerusalem.

Colonel Henry's suicide in the Dreyfus Affair soon absorbed public attention and ten days later the world gasped again when the Empress Elizabeth was assassinated by an Anarchist. Americans were preoccupied in welcoming home the regiments from Cuba, and the British with Kitchener's march to Khartoum. From September on, the air darkened with the prospect of war between England and France; Fashoda, as the German Ambassador happily remarked, seemed to have obliterated the memory of Alsace-Lorraine. Peace was crowded out as a sensation.

Not, however, to the dedicated disciples of the peace movement in Europe and America, whom the Czar's summons had electrified. Among the best known of these was Baroness Bertha von Suttner, author of the anti-war novel *Die Waffen Nieder* ("Put Down Your Arms"), which Tolstoy called the *Uncle Tom's Cabin* of its cause. When the Baroness' husband came home waving the newspaper, like Emma Goldman bringing the news of Homestead, she was transported with joy. Letters of congratulation soon poured in from fellow workers in the International Peace Bureau, the Interparliamentary Union, the Peace and Arbitration Association. "Whatever may come of it," wrote Björnstjerne Björnson, "from now on the air is throbbing with thoughts of peace." The fervor of the movement was personified by the Baroness, born Countess Kinsky in 1843 into an aristocratic Austrian family of dwindling fortunes. Too strong-minded and energetic to sink into genteel decay, she had taken a position at the age of thirty as tutor-companion to the daughters of the Von Suttner family and had kindled a glowing and reciprocated passion in the son and heir, seven years her junior. But she was dowerless and they parted in Germanic anguish. "He knelt before me and humbly kissed the hem of my gown: 'Matchless, royally generous-hearted woman, your love has taught me to know a happiness which shall consecrate my life. Farewell!' " At this moment a newspaper advertisement by a "very wealthy, cultured, elderly gentleman living in Paris" who was looking for a mature, educated lady as secretary and manager of his household offered a way out, and the Countess found herself in the employ of the discoverer of dynamite, Alfred Nobel.

A strange, satiric idealist and pessimist, shy, melancholy, almost a recluse, though hardly elderly at forty-three, Nobel had made millions in the manufacture of explosives and was profoundly disturbed by its implications. He seemed less in need of a secretary than of someone to listen to him. "I wish," he told his new employee, "I could produce a substance or a machine of such frightful efficacy for wholesale devastation that wars should thereby become altogether impossible." Despite an immediate sympathy and "the intense intellectual enjoyment" of his society and a tentative hint of something more, the lady succumbed to heartache, left after a week, flew back to the arms of her adorer and eloped with him. After twelve years of marriage and a career as a writer, she discovered—with a sense of revelation—the International Peace and Arbitration Association of London. Its statement of purposes declared that now at the close of the Nineteenth Century the time had come for all men to consult and agree on a means for the peaceful settlement of disputes and the abolition of war. Instantly and passionately a convert, Bertha von Suttner threw herself into the effort to organize branches of the society in Vienna and Berlin. In 1891 her efforts, publicized by the *Neue Freie Presse*, succeeded in Vienna and the manifesto issued on the occasion expressed the ideals of peace advocates everywhere. They believed a new war to be morally impossible because "men have lost some of their former savagery and disregard for life," and physically impossible because new weapons were too destructive. They believed the masses though still dumb yearned for peace. While all governments insisted war must be avoided, all were massing armaments to prepare for it and this "monstrous contradiction" must end.

The Interparliamentary Union, formed in Paris in 1888 to bring together members of the various national parliaments in the cause of peace, now held Congresses each year in different capitals. In the United States the Universal Peace Union named as its chief goals gradual disarmament and a Permanent Court of Arbitration. Stemming from the Geneva settlement of the *Alabama* dispute between the United States and Britain, the arbitration movement was especially strong in these two countries. Its goal was to substitute judicial settlement for war. Its advocates believed that if a workable process could be arranged, at first by treaty between individual nations, later by general treaty, while at the same time war was shown to be so destructive as to be "impossible," man would ultimately rather arbitrate than fight. It was a view based on the premise that man was reasonable and that wars came from quarrels susceptible of settlement by other means. The time was one of belief in moral as well as material progress and did not include the view of war as a clash of forces like the winds that blow.

Nobel was an ardent advocate of arbitration, though not of disarmament, which he thought a foolish demand for the present. He urged establishment of a tribunal and agreement among nations for a one-year period of compulsory truce in any dispute. He turned up in person, though incognito, at a Peace Congress in Berne in 1892 and told Bertha von Suttner that if she could "inform me, convince me, I will do something great for the cause." The spark of friendship between them had been kept alive in correspondence and an occasional visit over the years and he now wrote her that a new era of violence seemed to be working itself up; "one hears in the distance its hollow rumble already." Two months later he wrote again, "I should like to dispose of my fortune to found a prize to be awarded every five years," to the person who had contributed most effectively to the peace of Europe. He thought it should terminate after six awards, "for if in thirty years society cannot be reformed we shall inevitably lapse into barbarism." Nobel brooded over the plan, embodied it in a will drawn in 1895 which allowed man a little longer deadline, and died in the following year.

The cause of arbitration almost scored a triumph in January, 1897, when Britain and the United States signed a treaty, negotiated by Secretary Olney and the British Ambassador, Sir Julian Pauncefote, for the settlement of all except territorial disputes, the memory of Venezuela being still warm. Resenting invasion of its control of foreign affairs, the Senate refused to ratify it by three votes. The defeat seemed a calamity, in Olney's words, "not merely of national but of world wide proportions." It shook the general belief in man's moral progress.

In this belief, fostered in the last ten or fifteen years by signs on every hand of society's improvement, the peace movement had its origins. The marvelous strides of science had brought the human race to a stage of material welfare ready to prove the faith of the Nineteenth Century that the better off man became the less aggressive he would be. Society now had running water and lighted streets, sanitation, preserved and refrigerated food, sewing machines, washing machines, typewriters, lawn-mowers, the phonograph, telegraph and telephone and lately, beginning in the nineties, the extraordinary gift of individual powered mobility in the horseless carriage. It seemed impossible that so much physical benefit should not have worked a spiritual change, that the new century should not begin a new era in human behavior; that man, in short, had not become too civilized for war. Science made all phenomena seem subject to certitudes and laws, and if man's physical world could be understood and controlled, why not his social relations also? "Social conditions are destined to become *different*," Baroness von Suttner wrote with conviction. The younger generation agreed. "We were sincerely persuaded in 1898 that the era of wars was over," wrote Julien Benda, a French intellectual who was thirty-one in that year. "For fifteen years from 1890 to 1905 men of my generation really believed in world peace."

Fear as well as faith impelled the peace movement, fear of the unchained energy of the machine age. The great surge in mechanical energy, the amazing new techniques and tools and new inventions following one upon the other, the fantastic capabilities of electricity, created an uneasy sense that man had gathered into his hands more power than he could control; power that could escape, run wild and destroy him unless put under limits. In 1820 the world disposed of 778 metric tons of mechanical energy (expressed in the coal equivalent of mineral fuels and water power) compared to 15,000,000 metric tons in 1898. Productivity per man had increased in proportion. Countries were swelling in size and strength. The death rate declined markedly, owing to developments in sanitation and medicine, with the result that since 1870 the population of Europe had increased by 100,000,000, as much as its whole population in 1650. In the same period Great Britain had acquired 4,700,000 square miles of territory, France 3,600,000, Germany 1,000,000 and Belgium 900,000, or seventy-seven times her own size. In the United States during the same period the population had more than doubled and the per capita output of manufactures multiplied four times. The profits of Carnegie Steel rose from $6,000,000 in 1896 to $40,00C,000 in 1900. A new prime mover, the internal combustion engine, succeeded the steam engine and brought into existence the oil industry. The steam turbine and diesel engine added new motor power; hydro-electric power throbbed in thousands of dynamos. Steamships increased in tonnage, speed and cargo space. Steel, the key product of the age, mushroomed in products and uses through invention of the Bessemer converter. The relative invention rate reached the highest point in history in the nineties. Aluminum and other light metal alloys were developed. The chemical industry created new materials and processes. The method of mass production, using interchangeable parts, known as the "American system," came into use in all industrial countries. Dynamite as a blasting agent made possible massive excavations for quarries and mine shafts and mammoth constructions like the Simplon Railway Tunnel and the Panama Canal. The manufacture of dynamite increased from 11 tons in 1867, the year Nobel first put it on the market, to 66,500 tons in 1897. Big business which was necessary to finance heavy industry formed cartels and trusts with vast financial resources.

Nowhere were the added strengths greater than in weapons and other forces of war. The increase in population made manpower available for huge standing armies, and following the German example, conscription was adopted by all the Continental powers after 1871. To arm and equip mass armies required the efforts of mass industry and the munitions companies gathered under their control raw materials, mines, foundries and transportation. Markets and profits were almost limitless and they responded with fierce vigor to the incentive. In the ten years from the mid-eighties to mid-nineties land warfare was revolutionized by the introduction of the magazine-loading small-bore rifle, the improved Maxim machine gun, and smokeless powder. Together these multiplied the range, rapidity and accuracy of firepower five times or more and changed the nature of battle. Infantry who had fired three rounds a minute at Waterloo could now fire sixteen rounds a minute. The small bore added distance to the trajectory and accuracy to the aim. Development of automatic recoil for field guns equally increased the rate of artillery fire. Above all, smokeless powder, patented by Nobel between 1887 and 1891, opened up and extended the battlefield. It cleared the field of vision, permitted concealment of guns, speeded reloading and increased the range and accuracy of artillery from one thousand to five or six thousand yards. Battle would now spread over vast distances and an army be brought under fire before it could see the enemy. The conditions were laid, if barely yet suspected, for the supremacy of artillery over the rifle. The torpedo and the mine equally extended the range of naval warfare and experiments gave awful promise of the submarine.

Some gloried in the energy coursing through the world's veins; others feared it, and felt with Ibsen, "We are sailing with a corpse in the cargo." The desire for nations to come together in some sort of mutual effort to apply a brake grew increasingly vocal and was loud enough for Lord Salisbury as Prime Minister to give heed to it in 1897. In his Guildhall speech of that year he saw the piling up of arms and the yearly improvement in "instruments of death" culminating, unless prevented, in a "terrible effort of mutual destruction which will be fatal for Christian civilization." Without mentioning disarmament, he said the only hope of preventing the disaster lay in bringing the powers together to act on their differences in a friendly spirit and eventually to "be welded in some international constitution." Never an optimist, Lord Salisbury did not go so far as to suggest that this would abolish war, but limited his hopes to "a long spell of prosperous trade and continued peace."

The Czar was neither more pacific nor more idealistic than Lord Salisbury; he was thirty in 1898, a narrow, rather dull-witted young man of no vision and only one idea: to govern with no diminution of the autocratic power bequeathed by his ancestors. His petty view of things, said Pobiedonostsev, Chief Procurator of the Holy Synod, was the result "of the influence of the many chambermaids who surround his mother." The effort to keep a constitution at bay was the sum of his exertions and he had little political energy or interest left for anything else. Unlike the mettlesome Kaiser, who itched to play a hand every time he read a dispatch, the Czar found world affairs rather mentally taxing. "Indeed," as he wrote his mother during the excitement over Fashoda and the Kaiser's visit to Jerusalem, "many strange things happen in the world. One reads about them and shrugs one's shoulders."

The proposal for a peace conference was not his own idea. It originated for certain practical reasons with the ministers of three critical departments—War, Finance, and Foreign Affairs—and its genesis lay in the simple condition that Russia was behind in the arms race and could not afford to catch up. General Alexei Kuropatkin, the Minister of War, had learned that Austria, Russia's chief rival, was planning to adopt the improved rapid-fire field gun firing six rounds a minute, already possessed by Germany and France. The Russians, whose field gun fired one round a minute, could not hope to finance the rearming of their entire artillery, because they were already, at great financial strain, engaged in rearming their infantry. If the Austrians could be persuaded to agree to a ten-year moratorium on new guns, Kuropatkin thought, both countries would be spared the expense—and why not? For whether both rearmed or both agreed not to rearm, "the final result, if the two groups went to war, would be the same."

Kuropatkin took his simple but grand idea to the Czar, who could see no flaw, and then to the Foreign Minister, Count Muraviev, who took the precaution of consulting the Finance Minister, Count Witte. Capable, energetic and unusually endowed for a Czarist minister with common sense and a hard head, Witte was trying, against the forces of lethargy, autocracy and erosion, to fit Russia for the modern industrial world. He grudged every ruble spent on arms, detested the interference of war and believed the arms race might become "more irksome than war itself." However, as he pointed out, Kuropatkin's Chinese philosophy of agreeing with the enemy in advance depended on trusting the Austrians, which was impossible, and would be harmful besides, as it would "merely reveal our financial weakness to the whole world." Instead he proposed an international, rather than a bilateral, moratorium on new weapons. He expatiated to Muraviev on the incalculable harm that growing militarism was inflicting on the world and the boon which could be conferred upon humanity by limiting armaments. These "rather trite ideas," as he wrote later, were new to Muraviev and apparently produced on him a profound impression. Within a few days he called a council of ministers to consider an appeal to the powers for a conference. The Czar's approval was obtained. If only the awful pace of the world could be slowed down, he and his advisers felt, and something done "to keep people from inventing things," Russia would benefit.

Just at this moment an impressive six-volume work called *The Future of War* was published in Russia. Its author, Ivan Bloch, and his ideas, were known to Witte, whether or not they influenced him. Bloch was a self-educated man and converted Jew who, not satisfied with making a fortune in railroad contracting, had gone abroad to seek higher education in economics and political science in foreign universities. In Warsaw, on his return from Western Europe, he had become a power in banking and the railroad business, which brought him into contact with Witte, and had published a number of scholarly volumes on industrial and monetary problems before embarking on the major work that was to give him a niche in immortality. His studies and his experience in business filled him with growing apprehension that the limited war of the past was no longer possible. Because conscription could call on a pool of the entire nation, he saw wars of the future absorbing the total energies and resources of the combatant states, who, unable to achieve decisive victory on the battlefield, would fight to exhaustion until they had brought each other down in total ruin. The interdependence of nations in finance, foreign trade, raw materials and all business relations, Bloch believed, meant that the victor could not be separated from the vanquished. The destructive power of modern weapons would mean a vast increase in slaughter. The one-day battle had become a thing of the past. Whole armies would become entrenched for weeks and months at a time; battles would become sieges; noncombatant populations would be drawn in. No modern state could achieve victory without the destruction of its resources and the breakup of society. War had become "impossible except at the price of suicide."

Bloch's conclusions led him to the peace movement (or the process may have been the other way around). To convince society of the danger, he used a persuasion more frightening than war—social revolution. If present conditions continued, he argued, nations faced either exhaustion in the arms race or the catastrophe of war, and in either case "convulsion in the social order." The waste of national resources on a sterile product was accountable for the growing anti-militarism of the masses. Therefore in preparing for war the governments were really "preparing the triumph of the social revolution." If they could be convinced of this, Bloch believed, they would be more willing to find other means than war of settling their disputes. His six volumes were a massive piling-up of facts on firepower, blockade, freight and cargo capacities, casualty rates and every military and economic factor to prove the vulnerability of the modern state. Like Marx, Bloch drew from a given set of circumstances the dogma of an inevitable historical conclusion. He believed that armament expenditure necessarily "exhausted" a nation, as Marx believed that capitalism progressively impoverished the proletariat. Neither Bloch nor any of the peace propagandists considered the degree to which the armament and attendant industries created employment.

Fear of social revolution being an effective argument in Russia, Bloch gained an audience with the Czar and his argument found an echo in the manifesto which was written by Muraviev. The Foreign Minister evidently felt its persuasiveness. In conveying it to the British Ambassador he particularly asked him to emphasize in his report that Russia's initiative for peace would show "the discontented and disturbing classes" that powerful governments sympathized with their desire to see national wealth used productively rather than in "ruinous competition." The Ambassador replied suavely that "it would be difficult to remain insensible to the noble sentiments which had inspired this remarkable document."

"It is the greatest nonsense and rubbish I ever heard of," wrote the Prince of Wales less suavely to Lady Warwick. When indignant he took on something of the tone of his mother. "The thing is simply impossible. France could never consent to it—nor *We*." He decided it was "some new dodge of that sly dog" and "subtle intriguer" Muraviev, who had "put it into the Czar's head." On the whole this expressed the view of the governments. Regarding the proposal with cold distaste, they accepted the invitation—because none wished to be the one to reject it—while expecting nothing to come of it but trouble. As the Austrian Foreign Minister said, it would make it more difficult in future for governments to present new military demands to their parliaments.

Dampened but determined, Muraviev sent out a second circular letter in January, 1899, with an agenda of eight topics. The first proposed an agreement not to increase armed forces or military budgets for a fixed period. The last proposed agreement on the principle of arbitration and the working out of procedures. Topics 2, 3 and 4 dealt with prohibition or restriction of new types of weapons and of predicted means of warfare, such as submarines, asphyxiating gases and the "launching of projectiles from balloons" for which no specific verb existed. Topics 5, 6 and 7 concerned the laws and customs of land warfare and the extension of the Geneva rules of 1864 to naval warfare. Topics 2–7 were resented by the peace propagandists, who wished to abolish war, not alleviate it. They suspected that these topics had been included to stir the interest and require the participation of the governments and their military representatives, as was indeed the case.

Chanceries buzzed, diplomatic pouches bulged with dispatches, ambassadors called on foreign ministers and endeavored in the prescribed conversational minuet to discover the intentions of the government to which they were accredited. Lord Salisbury appeared in a German report as "very skeptical" and the Emperor Franz Joseph as taking an "unfavorable" view and considering any limit on military development "unacceptable." In Rome the Marquis Visconti-Venosta declined to be a delegate to a conference "which was not likely to be attended by any very useful results." Washington would send delegates but would do nothing toward limitation of arms. Belgium awaited the conference with "regret and anxiety," fearing that any alteration in the laws of war would confirm the powers of an invading army or restrict the rights of legitimate defence against invasion. Berlin's reaction seemed expressed in the addition of three army corps to her forces. From capital to capital, reaction varied little: arms limitation was "impractical"; restriction on new developments unwanted; arbitration on matters involving "national honor or vital interest" unacceptable, although perhaps feasible on minor matters. Conduct of war, however, offered room for discussion.

Fearing that all the excited talk of the peace advocates about disarmament had caused misunderstanding of his proposal, Muraviev visited the capitals to explain in personal interviews that what Russia really wanted was simply a ceiling on the status quo. It seemed so sensible. The powers might even agree, he suggested, on a fixed percentage of their population to be called to arms, which would enable them greatly to reduce their armies while "retaining the same chances as before." "Idiot," noted the Kaiser on the margin of this memorandum.

No one was more agitated by the Czar's proposal than Wilhelm II, in whose mind the military function was equivalent to the State as well as to himself, who personified the State. The white cloak and shining helmet he liked to pose in, the sparkle and color of uniforms, the gallop of cavalry, the panoply of regimental colors, the complicated rattle of ordnance, the whole paraphernalia of officer corps and Army, and lately, the brilliant vision of power upon the sea, were all facets of the same jewel—armed force. Everything else, Reichstag, political parties, budgets, votes, were more or less extraneous nuisances—except diplomacy, which was only properly understood by monarchs and invariably bungled at lower levels.

The Kaiser had come to the throne at twenty-nine, in 1888, after his father's sad small reign of ninety days when liberal rule had flickered for a moment in Germany and gone out. His first proclamation on his accession was addressed, not like his father's, "To My People," but, "To My Army." It announced, "We belong to each other, I and the Army; we were born for each other." The relationship he had in mind was explained in advice to a company of young recruits: "If your Emperor commands you to do so you must fire on your father and mother." His sense of personal responsibility for the affairs of Germany and of Europe was expressed in the frequent "I's" and "My's" that bedizened his talk. "There is only one master in the Reich and that is I; I shall tolerate no other." Or, some years later, "There is no balance of power in Europe but me— me and my twenty-five army corps." He was willing, however, to make room for the Almighty who figured as the "ancient Ally of my House." Remarks like these caused heads to shake and people to reflect like the Prince of Wales "how different everything would have been" if the Kaiser's father had lived. Still, the Prince explained, his nephew's speeches did not sound so absurd in German as when translated into English.

The Kaiserin remarked that she had not seen her husband so annoyed for a long time as over the sudden intrusion—into a domain he considered his own—of "Nicky," the Czar, whom he was accustomed to patronize and advise in voluble letters in English signed "Willy." Whether or not he had planned some similar statement from Jerusalem, the real bite was, as his friend Count Eulenburg said, that he "simply can't stand someone else coming to the front of the stage."

Assuming at a glance that the proposal was one for "general disarmament," and immediately seeing the results in personal terms, the Kaiser dashed off a telegram to Nicky. Imagine, he reproached, "a Monarch holding personal command of his Army, dissolving his regiments sacred with a hundred years of history . . . and handing over his towns to Anarchists and Democracy." Nevertheless he felt sure the Czar would be praised for his humanitarian proposal, "the most interesting and surprising of this century! Honor will henceforth be lavished upon you by the whole world; even should the practical part fail through difficulties of detail." He littered the margins of ensuing correspondence with *Aha!*'s and *!!*'s and observations varying from the astute to the vulgar, the earliest being the not unperceptive thought, "He has put a brilliant weapon into the hands of our Democrats and Opposition." At one point he compared the proposal to the Spartans' message demanding that the Athenians agree not to rebuild their walls; at another he suddenly scribbled the rather apt query, "What will Krupp pay his workers with?"

Germany did not have the motive and the cue for peace that Russia had: straitened circumstances. Under-developed industry was not a German problem. When Muraviev in Berlin told Count Eulenburg that the guiding idea behind the Russian proposal was that the yearly increases would finally bring the nations to the point of *non possumus*, he could not have chosen a worse argument. *Non possumus* was not in the German vocabulary. Germany was bursting with vigor and bulging with material success. After the unification of 1871, won by the sword in the previous decade of wars, prosperity had come with a rush, as it had in the United States after the Civil War. Energies were let loose on the development of physical resources. Germany in the nineties was enjoying the first half of a twenty-five-year period in which her national income doubled, population increased by 50 per cent, railroad-track mileage by 50 per cent, cities sprang up, colonies were acquired, giant industries took shape, wealth accumulated from their enterprises and the rise in employment kept pace.

Albert Ballin's steamship empire multiplied its tonnage sevenfold and its capital tenfold in this period. Emil Rathenau developed the electrical industry which quadrupled the number of its workers in ten years. I. G. Farben created aniline dyes; August Thyssen governed a kingdom of coal, iron and steel in the Ruhr. As a result of a new smelting process making possible the utilization of the phosphoric iron ore of Lorraine, Germany's production of coal and steel by 1898 had increased four times since 1871 and now surpassed Britain's. Germany's national income in that period had doubled, although it was still behind Britain's, and measured per capita, was but two-thirds of Britain's. German banking houses opened branches around the world, German salesmen sold German goods from Mexico to Baghdad.

German universities and technical schools were the most admired, German methods the most thorough, German philosophers dominant. The Kaiser Wilhelm Institute was the leading laboratory for chemical research in the world. German science boasted Koch, Ehrlich and Roentgen, whose discovery of the X ray in 1895 was, however, as much a product of his time as of his country, for in 1897–99 in England J. J. Thomson had discovered the electron, and in France the Curies the release of energy by radioactivity. German professors expounded German ideals and German culture, among them Kuno Francke at Harvard, who pictured Germany pulsing with "ardent life and intense activity in every field of national aspirations." He could barely contain his worship of the noble spectacle:

"Healthfulness, power, orderliness meet the eye on every square mile of German soil." No visitor could fail to be impressed by "these flourishing, well-kept farms and estates, these thriving villages, these carefully replenished forests, . . . these bursting cities teeming with a well-fed and well-behaved population, . . . with proud city halls and stately courthouses, with theatres and museums rising everywhere, admirable means of communication, model arrangements for healthy recreation and amusement, earnest universities and technical schools." The well-behaved population was characterized by its "orderly management of political meetings, its sober determination and effective organization of the laboring classes in their fight for social betterment" and its "respectful and attentive attitude toward all forms of art." Over all reigned "the magnificent Army with its manly discipline and high standards of professional conduct," and together all these components gave proof of "the wonderfully organized collective will toward the higher forms of national existence." The mood was clearly not one amenable to proposals of self-limitation.

The sword, as Germany's historians showed in their explanations of the marvelous national rise, was responsible for Germany's greatness. In his *History of Germany in the Nineteenth Century,* published in five volumes and several thousand pages over a period of fifteen years in the eighties and nineties, Treitschke preached the supremacy of the State whose instrument of policy is war and whose right to make war for honor or national interest cannot be infringed upon. The German Army was the visible embodiment of Treitschke's gospel. Its authority and prestige grew with every year, its officers were creatures of ineffable arrogance, above the law, who inspired an almost superstitious worship in the public. Any person accused of insult to an officer could be tried for the crime of indirect *lèse majesté.* German ladies stepped off the sidewalk to let an officer pass.

In 1891 the Alldeutsche Verband (Pan-German League) was founded, whose program was the union of all members of the German race, wherever they resided, in a Pan-German state. Its core was to be a Greater Germany incorporating Belgium, Luxemburg, Switzerland, Austria-Hungary, Poland, Rumania and Serbia which, after this first stage was accomplished, would extend its rule over the world. The League distributed posters for display in shop windows reading, *"Dem Deutschen gehört die Welt"* ("The world belongs to Germans"). In a simple statement of purpose Ernst Hasse, founder of the League, declared, "We want territory even if it belongs to foreigners, so that we may shape the future according to our needs." It was a task his countrymen felt equal to.

Any outbreak of fighting among the nations, as in the Sino-Japanese War of 1895 or the Spanish-American War, stirred in the Germans a powerful desire to mix in. Admiral von Diederichs, in command of the German Pacific Squadron at Manila Bay, was edging for a quick grab at the Philippines, and only Admiral Dewey's red-faced roar, "If your Admiral wants a fight he can have it now!"—silently if conspicuously supported by movements of the British squadron—made him draw back. "To the German mind," commented Secretary Hay, "there is something monstrous in the thought that a war should take place anywhere and they not profit by it." Dewey, understandably, thought they had "bad manners." "They are too pushing and ambitious," he said, "they'll overreach themselves someday."

At the top of the German state was a government essentially capricious. Ministers were independent of Parliament and held office at the will of a sovereign who referred to the members of the Reichstag as "sheepsheads." Since government office was confined to members of the aristocracy and the premise of a political career was unqualified acceptance of Conservative party principles, the doors were closed to new talent. "Not even the tamest Liberal," regretted the editor of the *Berliner Tageblatt*, "had any chance of reaching a post of the slightest distinction." After the Kaiser's dismissal of Bismarck in 1890, no one of active creative intelligence held an important post. The Chancellor, chosen because he was such a relief from Bismarck, was Prince Chlodwig zu Hohenlohe-Schillingsfürst, a gentle-mannered, fatherly Bavarian whose motto, it was said, was: "Always wear a good black coat and hold your tongue." The Foreign Minister was Count Bernhard von Bülow, an elegant gentleman of extreme suavity and self-importance and a manner so well oiled that in conversation and correspondence he seemed always to be rubbing his hands like a rug merchant. He used to scribble notes on his shirt cuffs for fear of forgetting the least of His Majesty's wishes. In an effort to catch the effortless parliamentary manner of Balfour he practiced holding onto his coat lapel before the bathroom mirror, coached by an attaché from the Foreign Office. "Watch," murmured a knowing observer in the Reichstag when Bülow rose to speak, "here comes the business with the lapels."

Behind Bülow in control of foreign policy was the invisible Holstein who in the manner of Byzantine courts exercised power without nominal office. He regarded all diplomacy as conspiracy, all overtures of foreign governments as containing a concealed trick, and conducted foreign relations on the premise of everyone's animosity for Germany. The interests of a Great Power, he explained to Bülow, were not necessarily identical with the maintenance of peace, "but rather with the subjugation of its enemies and rivals." Therefore "we must entertain the suspicion" that the Russian objective was "rather a means to power than to peace." Bülow agreed. His instructions to envoys abroad breathed of pitfalls and plots and treated Muraviev's agenda as if it were a basket of snakes. It would be desirable, he wrote to his Ambassador in London, "if this Peace and disarmament idea . . . were wrecked on England's objections without our having to appear in the foreground," and he trusted the Ambassador to guide the exchange of views with Mr. Balfour toward that end.

Mr. Balfour, the acting Foreign Secretary for Lord Salisbury, was not an entirely suitable victim for Bülow's manipulations. However skeptical of results, the British Government, unlike the German, did not feel threatened by an international conference and did not intend to bear the brunt of wrecking it. Moreover, public enthusiasm could not be flouted in England. In the four months following the Czar's manifesto, over 750 resolutions from public groups reached the Foreign Office welcoming the idea of an international conference and expressing the "earnest hope," in the words of one of them, that Her Majesty's Government would exert their influence to ensure its success "so that something practical may result." The resolutions came not only from established peace societies and religious congregations but from town and shire meetings, rural district committees, and county councils, were signed by the Mayor, stamped with the county seal, forwarded by the Lord Lieutenant. Some without benefit of official bodies came simply from the "People of Bedford," "Rotherhead Residents" or "Public Meeting at Bath." Many came from local committees of the Liberal party, although Conservative groups were conspicuously absent, as were Church of England congregations. All the Nonconformist sects were represented: Baptists, Methodists, Congregationalists, Christian Endeavor, Welsh Nonconformists, Irish Evangelicals. The Society of Friends collected petitions with a total of 16,000 signatures. Bible associations, adult schools, women's schools, the National British Women's Temperance Association, the Manchester Chamber of Commerce, the West of Scotland Peace and Arbitration Association, the Humanitarian League, the Oxford Women's Liberal Association, the General Board of Protestant Dissenters, the Mayor of Leicester, the Lord Mayor of Sheffield, the Town Clerk of Poole, were among the signatories.

Bound volumes of the resolutions signed with a shaky "S." indicated that Lord Salisbury was keeping track of public opinion. A deputation representing the International Crusade of Peace headed by the Earl of Aberdeen and the Bishop of London visited Mr. Balfour, who received them with a graceful speech taking "a sanguine view of the diminution, I will not say the extinction, but the diminution of war in the future" and looking forward to the coming conference as a "great landmark in the progress of mankind," whether or not, he added, it produced any practical results. This was not altogether what Bülow had hoped for.

The epitome of the peace movement was the most ebullient and prolific journalist of an age rich in his kind, William T. Stead, founder and editor of the *Review of Reviews.* Stead was a human torrent of enthusiasm for good causes. His energy was limitless, his optimism unending, his egotism gigantic. As the self-estimated pope of journalism his registered telegraph address was "Vatican, London." During the eighties he had edited the Liberal daily, the *Pall Mall Gazette,* in a series of explosions that made it required reading in public life. "You are too strenuous, too uniformly strenuous," pronounced the Prince of Wales who read it regularly. Stead waded recklessly into crusades ranging from protection of prostitutes to a "Sane Imperialism." They included campaigns against Bulgarian atrocities, Siberian convict life, the desertion of General Gordon at Khartoum, Congo slavery, the labour victims of "Bloody Sunday" in Trafalgar Square, and for baby adoption, village libraries, Esperanto, international scholars' correspondence, and housing for the poor. His most notorious effort, published under the title "The Maiden Tribute of Modern Babylon," described his personal purchase of a thirteen-year-old girl for £5 as a means of dramatizing the procurement of child virgins for prostitution. The articles made a world sensation, and besides causing Stead's trial and imprisonment on a charge of abduction, succeeded in forcing an amendment raising the age of consent from thirteen to sixteen.

Stead visited Russia in 1889, where he interviewed Alexander III and became a champion of Anglo-Russian alliance and thus of everything Russian. He campaigned for a big navy at the instance of his friend Admiral Fisher; collaborated with General Booth on a book, *In Darkest England*; joined Cecil Rhodes in the cause of Imperial Federation and union of the English-speaking world. Deciding to reform Chicago after a visit there in 1893, he exposed its evils and laid out a scheme of regeneration in a book called *If Christ Came to Chicago* and organized a Civic Federation which included labour leaders and Mrs. Potter Palmer to put the scheme into action. During the visit he talked with Governor Altgeld and invited Fielden, one of the pardoned Anarchists, to share a speaker's platform.

The connecting principle running through his causes was belief in man's duty to amend society and extend the British sway. He liked to use the phrase "God's Englishman" and conceived of this figure as a righter of wrongs; anything that added to his power was a benevolent influence. He turned up so often on opposite sides of the same question, as in the case of arms limitation and a big navy, that he was accused of insincerity, although in fact, as of any particular moment, his sincerity was genuine, if nimble.

In 1890 he founded his own journal, the monthly *Review of Reviews*, with the expressed object of making it read throughout the English-speaking world "as men used to read their Bibles . . . to discover the will of God and their duty to their fellow man." Finding a monthly less satisfactory as a political organ, he yearned for a millionaire to back him in a daily of his own and once in Paris told a friend, "I went in to Notre Dame to have a talk with God about it."

Detested by some, he was a friend of the great, including, besides Rhodes and Fisher, James Bryce, Cardinal Manning, Lord Esher, Lord Milner, Mrs. Annie Besant and Lady Warwick, who arranged a tête-à-tête lunch for him with the Prince of Wales. He interviewed sovereigns, cabinet ministers, archbishops and helped all "oppressed races, ill-treated animals, underpaid typists, misunderstood women, persecuted parsons, vilified public men, would-be suicides, hot-gospellers of every sort and childless parents." His talk was a river and as a lecturer he "leaped over the face of the globe as though on a pogo-stick." Besides writing, editing, traveling, interviewing and lecturing, he wrote or dictated some 80,000 letters in his twenty-two years on the *Review of Reviews*, an average of ten a day. He espoused spiritualism and considered himself a reincarnation of Charles II, who through him was making amends for his previous life on earth.

He was short in stature, with high color, bright blue eyes and a reddish beard, and in defiance of black broadcloth wore rough tweeds and a soft felt hat. Strong in good will, he was weak in judgment. If he had possessed that quality in proportion to his qualities of mind and character, said Lord Milner, he would have been "simply irresistible." Seeing in him, in exaggerated form, all the attributes of the English people of his generation, an American journalist summed him up as "the perfect type of Nineteenth Century man." Milner saw him as a cross between Don Quixote and P. T. Barnum, which may have been the same thing.

Naturally a passionate advocate of arbitration, Stead saw it leading to the establishment of an international court of justice and eventually to a United States of Europe. Anticipating the Czar, he had in 1894 suggested an international pledge by the powers not to increase their military budgets until the end of the century. When the Russian proposal burst upon the world, Stead saw the greatest opportunity of his career. He determined at once on a personal tour of the capitals as part of a great campaign to convince people everywhere that the Czar was sincere and to arouse a collective cry of support for the Conference. The tour was to culminate in an interview with the Czar from which he was not deterred by the Prince of Wales's opinion, conveyed through Lady Warwick, that the young ruler, his wife's nephew, was "weak as water, . . . has no character and would not be the slightest use to you." On the way, Stead planned to interview the Pope, the Kaiser and the President of France, as well as King Leopold of the Belgians whom he would persuade to become spokesman of a league of small powers. To ward off possible official interference he called on Mr. Balfour at the Foreign Office, whom he found at first "nonchalant and ironical" but who quickly hardened in response to Stead's rhapsodies. Balfour failed to understand, he said, how Stead could contemplate so lightheartedly "the increasing growth and power of Russia." For their own time it did not matter, "but what of our children? . . . What kind of world will it be when Russia exercises a dominating influence over the whole of south-east Europe?" He did not, however, offer to put any obstacles in Stead's path.

Within a month of the first news, Stead was on his way. In Paris he failed to see President Félix Faure, although he did see Clemenceau, who said "nothing would come of the Conference" and refused to alter his opinion. King Leopold, the Kaiser and Pope Leo XIII likewise avoided him, but Nicholas II, in compliance with a promise which his father had given to Stead ten years ago, granted him not only one audience but three. The Imperial graciousness dazzled Stead, who, being unused to courts, took it for the man's character and did not realize it was the monarch's trade. In any case he was determined to produce a hero. The Czar, he told his readers, was charming, sympathetic, alert, lucid, with a keen sense of humor, hearty frankness, admirable modesty, noble gravity, high resolve, remarkable memory, "exceptional rapidity of perception and wide grasp of an immense range of facts," and all these were at the service of the cause of peace. Stead's paeans to Russia's intentions so far outdistanced her real aims that the Russian ministers complained to the British Government of being "much embarrassed." His articles, however, were manna to the peace movement. Back in London he brought out a new weekly, *War Against War*, organized the International Peace Crusade and did his hyperactive best to strengthen public demand for a Conference that could not, must not fail.

Public opinion was not all of a piece. If the Liberals—and not all of them—shared Stead's enthusiasm, the Conservatives did not. In all peoples there was much of what William Ernest Henley hymned as "the battle spirit shouting in my blood." It was what made Romain Rolland, who was one day to become famous as a pacifist, cry joyously in 1898, "Give me combat!" The materialism of the time, the increasing ease, the power of money to substitute for muscle, produced in many a feeling of distaste or even a seeking for the strenuous, as when young Theodore Roosevelt headed for the Rockies. People felt a need for something nobler and saw it glimmer in the prospect of danger and physical combat, in sacrifice, even death, on the battlefield. The journalist Henry Nevinson felt a martial ardor when he drilled as an officer of the Volunteers and offended his Socialist friends by declaring that he "would not care to live in a world in which there was no war." In later years it seemed to him the ardor had derived partly from ignorance of war and partly from the influence of Kipling and Henley.

Within narrow limits Henley was the Conservatives' Stead, although lacking Stead's elemental force and social conscience. No Teutonic homage to the master race could outshout his celebration of "England, My England," whose "mailed hand" guides teeming destinies, whose "breed of mighty men" is unmatched, whose ships are "the fierce old sea's delight," who is:

> Chosen daughter of the Lord
> Spouse-in-Chief of the ancient Sword.

> There's the menace of the Word
> In the song on your bugles blown
> England!
> Out of Heaven on your bugles blown!

This was patriotism gone mad and represented a mood, not a people. In the same mood Americans listened to Albert Beveridge rant, "We are a conquering race . . . we must obey our blood."

Such sentiments were among the indirect results of the most fateful voyage since Columbus—Charles Darwin's aboard the *Beagle*. Darwin's findings in *The Origin of Species,* when applied to human society, supplied the philosophical basis for the theory that war was both inherent in nature and ennobling. War was a conflict in which the stronger and superior race survived, thus advancing civilization. Germany's thinkers, historians, political and military scientists, working upon the theory with the industry of moles and the tenacity of bulldogs, raised it to a level of national dogma. Houston Stewart Chamberlain, Wagner's son-in-law, supplied a racial justification in his *Foundations of the Nineteenth Century,* published in German, which showed that Aryans, being superior in body and soul to other men, had a right to be masters of the earth. Treitschke explained that war, by purifying and unifying a great people, was the source of patriotism. By invigorating them it was a source of strength. Peace was stagnant and decadent and the hope of perpetual peace was not only "impossible but immoral as well." War as ennobling became by extension, in the words of Generals von der Goltz and Bernhardi, a necessity. It was the right and duty of the nobler, stronger, superior race to extend its rule over inferior peoples, which, in the German view, meant over the world. To other nations it meant over colonies. Darwinism became the White Man's Burden. Imperialism acquired a moral imperative.

Darwin's indirect effects reached apotheosis in Captain Mahan. "Honest collision" between nations was "evidently a law of progress," he wrote in one of a series of articles in 1897–99 in which he tried to instruct Americans in their destiny. This one was called "The Moral Aspect of War." In another, "A Twentieth Century Outlook," he wrote that nothing

was "more ominous for the future of our race" than the current vociferous
tendency "which refuses to recognize in the profession of arms—in war"
the source of "heroic ideal." In a private letter he wrote, "No greater
misfortune could well happen than that civilized nations should abandon
their preparations for war and take to arbitration." His thesis was that
power, force, and ultimately war were the factors that decide great issues
in a nation's fate and that to depend on anything else, such as arbitration,
was an illusion. If arbitration were substituted for armies and navies,
European civilization "might not survive, having lost its fighting energy."
Yet Mahan believed the Twentieth Century would reveal that man's conscience was improving. He could not have preached power so positively
if he had not believed equally in progress. His moral rectitude shines in a
photograph taken with his wife and two adult daughters. Four pairs of
forthright eyes gaze straight at the camera. Four keel-straight noses, four
firm mouths, the ladies' high-necked blouses fastened with bar pin at the
throat, the hats perched stiffly on high-piled hair, all express the person
"assured of certain certainties," a species soon to be as extinct as
Ribblesdale.

The necessity of struggle was voiced by many spokesmen in many
guises: in Henri Bergson's *élan vital*, in Shaw's Life Force, in the strange
magic jumble of Nietzsche which was then spreading its fascination over
Europe. Nietzsche recognized the waning of religion as a primary force
in people's lives and flung his challenge in three words: "God is dead." He
would have substituted Superman, but ordinary people substituted patriotism. As faith in God retreated before the advance of science, love of
country began to fill the empty spaces in the heart. Nationalism absorbed
the strength once belonging to religion. Where people formerly fought for
religion now they would presumably do no less for its successor. A sense
of gathering conflict filled the air. Yeats, living in Paris in 1895, awoke
one morning from a vision of apocalypse:

> . . . Unknown spears
> Suddenly hurtle before my dream awakened eyes,
> And then the clash of fallen horsemen and the cries
> Of unknown perishing armies beat about my ears.

Quite unconnected, in the same year, the tap of distant drums sounded in
the seclusion of A. E. Housman's rooms:

> On the idle hill of summer
> Sleepy with the flow of streams,
> Far I hear the steady drummer
> Drumming like a noise in dreams.

Far and near and low and louder
  On the roads of earth go by,
Dear to friends and food for powder,
  Soldiers marching, all to die. . . .

Far the calling bugles hollo,
  High the screaming fife replies,
Gay the files of scarlet follow:
  Woman bore me, I will rise.

The Hague, as the capital of a small neutral country, was selected as site of the Conference and May 18, 1899, was fixed as the opening day. Advance arrangements stirred up a number of old animosities and current quarrels. China and Japan, Turkey and Greece, Spain and the United States had just finished wars; Britain and the Transvaal were warming up to one which threatened to break out at any moment. As host nation and ardent supporters of the Boers, the Dutch almost strangled the Conference before it could be born by demanding invitations for the Transvaal and Orange Free State. Turkey objected to the inclusion of Bulgaria, and Italy threatened to bolt if inclusion of the Vatican implied its recognition as a temporal power. Seeing "very sinister import" in this, Germany immediately suspected Italy of planning to secede from the Triple Alliance and herself threatened to withdraw from the Conference if any other major power did. These matters being surmounted, the nations proceeded to the naming of delegates.

The choices reflected the ambivalence of the agenda, concerned on the one hand with peace by arbitration and on the other with the conduct of war. Although arbitration had not been mentioned in the Czar's manifesto it had been included in Muraviev's agenda and since then, in the public mind, had become the major goal. The Boston Peace Crusade held meetings every week through March and April demanding that the United States commit itself to the goal of "a permanent tribunal for the Twentieth Century." With Congress in crisis over the vote on the Peace Treaty with Spain, McKinley was urged to appoint President Eliot of Harvard in the hope of soothing anti-imperialist sentiment. As Eliot was unlikely to prove a manageable delegate, McKinley preferred a safer selection in Andrew White, former president of Cornell, now Ambassador in Berlin. Rising from Professor of History to civic eminence, White was a hardworking, high-minded man who believed in all the right things. At The Hague he was soon on friendly terms with the Duke of Tetuan, delegate of the late enemy, Spain, who shared with him "a passion for cathedral architecture and organ music." Alongside White was appointed a delegate certain to act as watchdog of American interests and take a hard-headed view of the proceedings with which by no stretch of anyone's imagination could he be considered in sympathy—Captain Mahan. His name appearing on the list deepened Germany's suspicions of the Conference. "Our greatest and most dangerous foe," noted the Kaiser darkly.

American instructions to the delegates began by rejecting the original purpose of the Conference. Arms limitation "could not profitably be discussed" because American arms were below the level of the European powers anyway and the initiative in this matter could be left to them. As to restrictions on the development of new weapons, it was considered "doubtful if an international agreement to this end could prove effective." The delegates were to support efforts to make the laws of war more humane and they were themselves to propose a specific plan for an arbitration tribunal. They were also instructed to propose the immunity of private property from capture at sea, a seemingly bland suggestion which contained depths of unplumbed trouble.

France named as her chief delegate a former premier and friend of arbitration, Léon Bourgeois, whose term of office in 1895–96 had been taken up in a stubborn effort to enact the graduated income tax against the violent opposition of the Senate. It had only narrowly been defeated. With the Dreyfus Affair threatening a government crisis at any time which might bring Bourgeois back to office, The Hague offered a happy opportunity to remove him from the scene. "Amiable, elegant and eloquent," according to a political colleague if not friend, Bourgeois "cultivated a fine ebony beard and expressed commonplace thoughts in a mellow voice."

Already aroused by the Affair to a mood of super-patriotism, insulted by Russia's failure to consult her in advance, determined to accept no fixing of the status quo, France welcomed the Conference no more than any other nation. "To renounce war is in a sense to renounce one's country," was the comment of a French officer on the Czar's manifesto. Mme Adam, Gambetta's friend and priestess of *revanche*, when invited to hear a lecture by Bertha von Suttner, replied, "I? To a lecture on peace? Certainly not. I am for war." France nevertheless sent to The Hague, as second to Bourgeois, a dedicated apostle of peace, Baron d'Estournelles de Constant. A professional diplomat until the age of forty-three, he had become increasingly disturbed at the trend of international affairs until one day in 1895, shocked by a frivolous threat of war in a minor dispute, he resigned from diplomacy to enter politics and the Chamber in the cause of peace. A handsome man of polished manners he brought to the Conference as an official delegate the fervor and voice of the peace movement.

As initiators, the Russians provided the president of the Conference in the person of their Ambassador to London, Baron de Staal, a nice old gentleman with long white side whiskers and a square-crowned derby. He was described by the Prince of Wales as "one of the best men that ever lived, . . . who never said anything that was not true," which was useful if not adequate equipment for his task. The real head of the Russian delegation was Feodor de Martens, Professor Emeritus of International Law at the University of St. Petersburg, who allowed no one to forget that he enjoyed a reputation as Europe's leading jurist in his field. He was "a man of great knowledge," said Witte, "but by no means broad-minded." A future Chief of Staff, Colonel Jilinsky was the military delegate.

Count Münster, German Ambassador to Paris, in the wastebasket of whose Embassy the Dreyfus Affair began, looked forward with little pleasure to being his country's chief delegate. "Beating empty air is always a tiresome job," he wrote to a friend. Arms limitation was *ausgeschlossen* ("out of the question"), the favorite German word. Arbitration was important but agreement probably hopeless. To save Russia's face the Conference could not be allowed to end in fiasco and its work must be covered with a "cloak of peace." A courtly white-haired gentleman whom Andrew White regarded as a "splendid specimen" of an old-fashioned German nobleman, Münster had once been stationed in England, had married an English wife and was pleased by nothing so much as being taken for an English gentleman. Besides the military and naval delegates, he had two legal associates, Professor Zorn of the University of Königsberg and Professor Baron von Stengel of the University of Munich, whose chief qualification was a pamphlet he had just published entitled *Eternal Peace* which ridiculed the forthcoming Conference and extolled the virtues of war. Although Stengel said nothing abnormally different from what many in other countries believed, he said it after the German fashion rudely and loudly and the Kaiser's prompt gesture in naming him a delegate needed no thumb to his nose to make the point. Stead, then in Berlin, protested, Bülow oozed explanations and the German comic papers caricatured Stengel as a bull introduced into a bed of tulips.

A kind of magic in the Conference had brought it to reality despite general contempt, and drew from Britain the compliment of a strong delegation. Its chief, Sir Julian Pauncefote, Ambassador to Washington, was, as the negotiator of the world's first arbitration treaty, the outstanding champion of the idea in official life. A calm, heavy-set, unfussed dignitary who reminded people of a polar bear, he accomplished wonders of diplomacy by acting on the principle: "Never give way and never give offence." "I never hesitated to open my whole heart to him," said Secretary Hay, "for he was the soul of honor and of candor." Accompanying him was the recently retired Speaker of the House, Sir Arthur Peel, whose impressive presence in the Chair had quelled the most troublesome members. "When Peel lost his temper it was like a storm at sea," said one of them. "He could put up with a bore but he hated a cad, whether well or ill dressed."

As military and naval delegates Lord Salisbury's government selected two exceptional men from the upper ranks of their respective services. Major General Sir John Ardagh, after winning honors in Hebrew and mathematics at Trinity College, Dublin, had changed from a clerical to a military career. Subsequently he had been an observer in the Franco-Prussian and Russo-Turkish wars, seen active service in Egypt and the Sudan and was now Director of Military Intelligence.

His naval colleague was the most unsubdued individualist of his time, possessed of a vigor and impetus remarkable in any time. Admiral Sir John Fisher was a force of nature entirely directed to the renaissance of British sea power through modernization of the Navy. His only other mania was dancing, which he pursued from hornpipe to waltz at every opportunity, with other officers if necessary when there were no ladies present. Whatever he fought for was a struggle against the weight and lethargy of "the way it has always been" and his career was that of a fierce broom sweeping aside obsolescence in men as well as ships. He demanded oil instead of coal twenty years ahead of his time, substituted training in gunnery for cutlasses, training in engines and engineering for rigging and the handling of sails, introduced destroyers, pioneered in ordnance, armor and battleship design. During the bombardment of Alexandria when an armored train was needed to transport a landing force, he invented one. He had been Commandant of the Torpedo School, Director of Naval Ordnance, Superintendent of Dockyards, Third Sea Lord, Controller of the Navy and was currently Commander-in-Chief of the Atlantic Station.

Born in Malaya, Fisher had a strange flat smooth-shaven face which inspired his enemies, who were innumerable, to hint broadly at Oriental ancestry. On his flagship when he "prowled around with the steady rhythmical tread of a panther, the quarter deck shook and all hands shook with it. When the word was passed, 'Look out, here comes Jack!' every-

one stood terribly to attention while the great one passed on and away."
Upon the orthodox his flow of ideas had an effect either paralyzing or
maddening. When he talked of some new scheme or program he held his
companion fixed with a glittering eye and emphasized every sentence with
a blow of his fist on his palm. When he wrote letters his emphasis took
the form of two, three or four lines under a word and he closed, not "in
haste," but "in violent haste!" or with the warning: "Burn this!" He liked
to quote Napoleon's maxim, *J'ordonne ou je me tais* ("I command or
I keep quiet"), but he was incapable of practicing the second half.

At the moment, in case of war with France over Fashoda, he had
conceived a plan to execute a naval raid on Devil's Island and kidnap
Dreyfus in order to land him on the coast of France to embarrass the
Army and sow dissension. For the motto of one of his destroyers he
chose *Ut Veniant Omnes* (Let them all come). His pretended principles
of battle were "Give No Quarter, Take No Prisoners, Sink Everything,
No Time for Mercy, *Frappez vite et frappez fort, l'Audace, l'audace,
toujours l'audace*," but this was intended more for moral effect than as
serious tactics. When Lord Salisbury appointed him naval delegate to
The Hague he remarked that there was no doubt Jacky Fisher would
fight at the Peace Conference. "So I did," wrote Fisher afterwards,
"though it was not for peace."

The Hague proved an inspired choice. The charm of the Huis ten
Bosch (House in the Woods), summer palace of the House of Orange,
where the Conference met, the pleasant half-hour's drive from the seashore
at Scheveningen, where many of the delegates stayed, the hospitality of the
Netherlands Government and smiling welcome of its people, the summer
weather and flowered countryside, could not fail to refresh the most cynical
spirits. Black-and-white cows grazed peaceably along the roadside, canals
reflected the radiant sky, the docile wings of windmills turned and sailboats
moved seemingly over meadows, on waterways hidden by the tall grass.
The once quiet town, a "gracious anachronism" of brick houses and cob-
blestone streets, bustled with welcome. Flags of all the nations decorated
the staid hotels, windows were polished, doorsteps scrubbed, public buildings burnished and refurbished. Brought to animated life by its visitors,
The Hague seemed to wake like a Sleeping Beauty from its Seventeenth
Century slumbers.

The Huis ten Bosch was a royal château of red brick with white window frames set in a park on the outskirts of the town. Its windows opened
on lawns and rose gardens, fountains and marble nymphs. In the woods

which gave the place its name delegates could walk and talk between sessions along avenues of magnificent beeches where birds sang and the sun glinted through the leaves.

Plenary sessions were held in the central hall three stories high, hung with golden damask and frescoed with the triumphs of past Prince Stadtholders on throne and horseback. From the ceiling painted cupids, naked Venuses, and Death as a leering skeleton looked down upon the newly installed rows of green-baize desks seating 108 delegates from 26 countries. Black coats predominated, varied by military uniforms, by the Turks' red fezzes and the blue silk gown of the Chinese delegate. The real work of the Conference took place in the subcommittees which met in the many small salons rich in Delft and Meissen, Chinese wallpaper and pale Persian carpets. Every day the Dutch hosts served a bountiful luncheon with fine wine and cigars under the crystal chandeliers of the White Dining Room, where the delegates could meet and talk informally. The taste and dignity of all the arrangements, the choice liqueurs, the beauty of the surroundings, the evening balls and receptions gradually began to mellow the mood of disdain in which the Conference began.

No such body had ever assembled "in a spirit of more hopeless skepticism as to any good result," Andrew White believed when he arrived. The great Professor Mommsen of Germany, most admired historian of his time, predicted the Conference would be remembered as "a printer's error in the history of the world." Even some of Baroness von Suttner's friends were less than hopeful. Prince Scipio Borghese, whom she invited to be present as an observer, replied that nothing would be more charming than to spend time with "*un groupe du high-life pacifique*," but unfortunately in May he would have to attend his sister's wedding in the depths of Hungary. During De Staal's opening address, spoken in a voice alternately quavering and firm, the president dropped his wooden gavel, which was immediately, almost eagerly, seized upon as an ill omen. De Staal's "deplorable" Russian ignorance of parliamentary procedure and his happy-go-lucky way of adopting rules and motions seemed to White to presage "hopeless chaos."

The Conference divided itself into three Commissions: on Armaments, on the Laws of War, and on Arbitration, which in turn divided into subcommittees. The chairman of the First Commission was Auguste Beernaert, former premier and chief delegate of Belgium, who had once been called by King Leopold II "the greatest cynic in the kingdom." A worldly politician in his early career, he had been the King's right-hand man in the vast enterprise of the Congo as well as in Leopold's efforts to fortify the Belgian frontier against invasion. Late in life, however, Beernaert had suffered a personality change and become a pacifist and regular attender of peace congresses. As President of the Belgian Chamber he still exercised political power. Professor de Martens of Russia was chairman of the Second Commission and Léon Bourgeois of the Third.

Delegates were uncomfortably aware of the conscience of the world over their shoulder in the person of a large *"groupe du high-life pacifique"* who had descended upon The Hague as observers. Expecting nothing but failure, the Conference had decided upon closed sessions from which the press was rigidly excluded. It proved a hopeless maneuver, since the press was led by W. T. Stead in person, acting as correspondent for the *Manchester Guardian.* Through importunate interviews and his myriad personal connections he was able to publish a daily chronicle of the Conference on a special page made available to him by the *Dagblad,* leading newspaper of The Hague. The delegates devoured it, all the other correspondents depended on it and the peace propagandists spread its news abroad to their home societies. Succumbing to the inevitable the Conference opened its meetings to the press.

Leading the observers was Baroness von Suttner, acting as correspondent for the *Neue Freie Presse* of Vienna. Convinced that May 18 was an "epoch making date in the history of the world," she earnestly dispensed tea and talk to the delegates and conferred on strategy with D'Estournelles, Beernaert and her other friends. Ivan Bloch came from Russia with trunks full of copies of his book for distribution. He gave lectures with lantern slides for the public and receptions for the delegates combining excellent suppers with pictures and charts on the development of firearms. Dr. Benjamin Trueblood, Quaker secretary of the American Peace Society, came from Boston, and Charles Richet, editor of *La Revue Scientifique* and director of the French Peace Society, from Paris. The Queen of Rumania under her pen name, Carmen Sylva, sent a poem. Mme Selenka of Munich brought a pacifist petition signed by women of eighteen countries; a Belgian petition with 100,000 and a Dutch petition with 200,000 signatures were submitted. Andrew White found himself inundated by people with "plans, schemes, nostrums, notions and whimsies of all sorts" and by floods of pamphlets and books, letters, sermons and telegrams, petitions, resolutions, prayers and blessings. Yet behind the cranks he sensed evidence of a feeling "more earnest and widespread than anything I had dreamed."

Count Münster on the other hand was disgusted. "The Conference has brought here the political riffraff of the entire world," he wrote to Bülow, "journalists of the worst type such as Stead, baptized Jews like Bloch and female peace fanatics like Mme de Suttner. . . . All this rabble, actively supported by Young Turks, Armenians, and Socialists into the bargain, are working in the open under the aegis of Russia." He saw Stead as "a proved agent in the pay of Russia" and the proceedings on the whole as a Russian plot to nullify Germany's military advantage. Even in his native land, however, the "rabble" found an echo when a committee of Reichstag deputies, professors and writers urged support of the aims of the Conference. Although opposed to any arrangement that could "even to infinitesimal degree lower Germany's position among nations," it hoped for some result to relieve Europe of the burden of armament taxation and to prevent the outbreak of wars.

Feeling themselves the cynosure of the world's hope, the delegates began to feel the stirring of a desire not to disappoint it. After the first two weeks of work, reported Pauncefote, they "became interested in spite of themselves." Some, at least, began to want to succeed, from *"amour-propre"* as van Karnebeek, the Netherlands delegate, said, if from nothing else. Some, affected by the coming together of so many nations, began to look ahead to "a federation of the nations of Europe. . . . That is the dream that begins to rise at The Hague. Europe must choose either to pursue the dream—or anarchy."

For arbitration some hope sprouted but for arms limitation, whether of present forces, budgets or new weapons, there was none. Despite the desperate efforts of the Russians and the warm support of the small states and many civilian delegates, every proposal for restriction or moratorium was shown to be "impractical" by the military delegates of the major powers. The issue came to a head when Colonel Jilinsky of Russia urged a five-year moratorium in a peroration calling on the nations to rid themselves of the burden that was crushing the life out of Europe. Eloquently supporting him, General den Beer Portugael of the Netherlands pictured the governments "bound together like Alpine climbers by the rope of their military organizations" and tottering toward the edge of the abyss unless they could halt by a "supreme effort." Rising to his feet, the German military delegate, Colonel Gross von Schwartzkopf, cut through the eloquence as if by a stroke of cold steel. The German people, he said, were "not crushed beneath the weight of armament expenditures. . . . They are not hastening toward exhaustion and ruin." On the contrary their prosperity, welfare and standard of living were rising. Carried away by his subject, Colonel Schwartzkopf did not shrink from taking upon Germany the duty of opposing the moratorium, saving any of the other major powers that awkward task. When it became clear that Germany would be a party to no moratorium of any kind and consequently that there was not the least chance of its being approved, the other nations were happy to vote in favor of submitting it for further consideration to a subcommittee. In this way, wrote Sir John Fisher, explaining his vote to his government, Russian feelings would be spared and the public would not feel that England was blocking full *discussion* of the proposal.

In committee at The Hague, Fisher behaved himself with surprising circumspection; unofficially he remained normal. "The humanizing of war!" he exploded. "You might just as well talk of humanizing Hell!" His reply to a "silly ass" who talked about "the amenities of civilised warfare and putting your prisoners' feet in hot water and giving them gruel," was considered unfit for publication. In Stead's autograph book he wrote, "The supremacy of the British Navy is the best security for the peace of the world." He stayed at the Hotel Kurhaus in Scheveningen which from his description appeared to suit him admirably: "Such a rush always going on. Band plays at breakfast and at lunch and at dinner!!! Huge boxes arrive continuously and the *portier* rushes about like a wild animal. Railway, telegraph and post offices in the hotel!" Among the naval delegates Fisher was treated with worshipful respect, and his promotion in the midst of the Conference to Commander-in-Chief of the Mediterranean Station "fetched all the foreigners very much," including even Baroness von Suttner who regretted his absence from a ball given by De Staal since he was one of the "jolliest dancers." He was called the "Dancing Admiral," and as he was personally most gracious and put on no airs, "no man at The Hague," reported Stead, "was more popular." His contact with the German delegates convinced Fisher that Germany, not France, was going to be Britain's opponent. He learned from the German naval delegate that all British ships would be useless in war as the Germans expected to sink them by hordes of torpedo boats.

Britain was favorably disposed to naval limitation as it would have curbed the German naval program and preserved the status quo. Her support depended, however, on finding a formula for inspection and control which Fisher reported was "absolutely unrealisable." He did not think highly of a Russian suggestion that the good faith of governments might be relied on. Russia should have said straight out, remarked the French delegate rather pitilessly, that her real aim was simply the assurance of peace for three years. The Germans would again hear of no limitation and Japan, according to a British report, "will only listen when she has reached the standard of the great naval powers, that is to say, never."

The United States' position was made unequivocal by its hard realist, Captain Mahan, privately if not in the public meetings. His government, he told the British, would on no account even discuss naval limitation; on the contrary, the coming struggle for the markets of China would require a "very considerable" increase in the American squadron in the Pacific, which would affect the interests of at least five powers. In every commission and discussion Mahan made his presence felt like a voice of conscience saying "No"; it was, however, a conscience operating not in behalf of peace but in behalf of the unfettered exercise of belligerent power. He had "the deepest seriousness of all," wrote one observer.

It led him to oppose his own government's traditional position in favor of the immunity of private property at sea. What had been good for the United States as a weak neutral, Mahan believed, would no longer be good for her as a Great Power. The right of capture was the essence of sea power, especially of British sea power, with which he believed America's interests were now united. He looked ahead to the rights of the belligerent rather than back to the rights of the neutral.

When White, according to instructions, attempted to have the matter put on the agenda, Fisher carried the opposition for Mahan. Take the case of neutral coal, he suggested: "You tell me that I must not seize these colliers. I tell you that nothing that you, or any power on earth, can say will stop me from seizing them or sending them to the bottom, if I can in no other way keep their coal out of the enemy's hands." For the opposite reason Germany, of course, supported the American proposal of immunity from capture. For once in favor of something, Count Münster jumped at the chance to put "our powerful influence behind this principle" and Bülow was delighted to approve a measure so obviously "in the interests of humanity in general." Both were pulled up short by their own naval delegate, Captain Siegel, whose reasoning suggested the mind of a chess-player trained by a Jesuit. The purpose of a navy, he pointed out to his government, was to protect the seaborne commerce of its country. If the immunity of private property were accepted, the Navy's occupation would be gone. The public would demand reduction in warships and refuse to support naval appropriations in the Reichstag. In short, Captain Siegel made it clear that if the German Navy was to have a *raison d'être,* property must be left open to seizure, even in the interest of the enemy.

Discussions of this kind stimulated and absorbed the participants. The conduct of war was so much more interesting than its prevention. When the restriction of new weapons or prohibition of as yet undeveloped ones came up for discussion, the military and naval men, as alert as Captain Siegel, keenly defended their freedom of enterprise. The Russian proposal that the powers should agree "not to radically transform their guns or increase their calibres for a certain fixed period" was allowed to founder on the problem of inspection and control. Sir John Ardagh pointed out there would be nothing to prevent a state from constructing rifles of a new pattern and storing them in arsenals until needed. This caused a Russian delegate, M. Raffalovitch, to reply hotly that "public opinion and parliamentary institutions" should be adequate safeguard. Considering the source, this was not impressive. Mahan raised the same objection to proposals for limiting the calibre of naval guns, thickness of armor plate and velocity of projectiles. Any form of international control, he said, would be an invasion of sovereignty, to which all the delegates at once agreed.

In the debate on extending the rules of the Geneva Red Cross Convention of 1868 to naval warfare, the question was raised of rescuing sailors from the water after battle. This was the occasion that evoked Fisher's explosion about feeding prisoners gruel. When the debate was over his chief was able to report, "Thanks to the energetic attitude and persistent efforts of Sir John Fisher all provisions of the original articles which were likely in any way to fetter or embarrass the free action of the Belligerents have been carefully eliminated."

An ominous issue developed on the rights of defense of an unarmed population against armed invasion. Ardagh proposed an amendment changing the "liberty" of a population to oppose the invader to its "duty" to do so, adding, "by all legitimate means of the most energetic and patriotic resistance"—which won him the enthusiastic response of the small powers. Colonel Schwartzkopf "opposed it tooth and nail," supported for once by the Russians. "If anything was required to show the need for some article of the kind," Ardagh reported, it was the "bitter resistance" of the Germans and Russians which accomplished the amendment's defeat. This committee then turned its attention more successfully to such questions as the treatment of spies and prisoners of war; the prohibition of poison; treachery and ruses; the bombardment of undefended towns; and rules governing flags of truce, surrender, armistice and occupation of hostile territory.

In the committee on limiting new weapons the negative trend had become somewhat embarrassing. Everyone was therefore delighted to fall upon the question of dumdum, or expanding, bullets, which offered an opportunity both to outlaw something and to vent the general anti-

British feeling of the time. Developed by the British to stop the rush
of fanatical tribesmen, the bullets were vigorously defended by Sir John
Ardagh against the heated attack of all except the American military delegate, Captain Crozier, whose country was about to make use of them
in the Philippines. In warfare against savages, Ardagh explained to an
absorbed audience, "men penetrated through and through several times
by our latest pattern of small calibre projectiles, which make a small clean
hole," were nevertheless able to rush on and come to close quarters.
Some means had to be found to stop them. "The civilized soldier when
shot recognizes that he is wounded and knows that the sooner he is attended to the sooner he will recover. He lies down on his stretcher and
is taken off the field to his ambulance, where he is dressed or bandaged
by his doctor or his Red Cross Society according to the prescribed rules
of the game as laid down in the Geneva Convention.

"Your fanatical barbarian, similarly wounded, continues to rush on,
spear or sword in hand; and before you have had time to represent to
him that his conduct is in flagrant violation of the understanding relative
to the proper course for the wounded man to follow—he may have cut
off your head." Behind the flippant words Ardagh was making the point
that war was a bitter business and, more politely than Fisher, was ridi-
culing the notion that it could be civilized. Unimpressed, the delegates
voted 22–2, against the unyielding opposition of Britain supported by the
United States, to prohibit the use of the dumdum bullet.

Unanimity, elusive so far, was at last achieved on one topic: the
launching of projectiles or explosives from balloons. Here was something,
almost untried, that almost everyone was willing to ban, especially the
Russians, for whom the prospect of adding a new dimension to warfare
was altogether too much. As Colonel Jilinsky almost plaintively put it,
"In the opinion of the Russian Government the various means of injuring the enemy now in use are sufficient." As regards air warfare, most
of the delegates were willing to agree and a permanent prohibition was
voted. The committee congratulated itself. Then suddenly at the next
meeting Captain Crozier, having had serious second thoughts after consultation with Captain Mahan, raised an objection. They were proposing
to ban forever, he said, a weapon of which they had no experience. New
developments and inventions might soon make airships dirigible, enabling
them to be steered by motor power over the area of battle and to take
part at a critical moment with possibly decisive effect, thus in the long
run sparing lives and shortening the conflict. Would it be in the humanitarian interest to prevent such a development? Instead of permanent

prohibition, Captain Crozier proposed a five-year ban at the end of which period they would have a better idea of the capabilities of airships. This time impressed, the delegates agreed.

A proposed ban on the use of asphyxiating gas failed of unanimity by one vote—Captain Mahan's. He stubbornly refused to withdraw his negative on the ground that the United States was averse to restricting "the inventive genius of its citizens in providing weapons of war." Nothing had yet been done toward inventing it, and if it were, Mahan believed that gas would be less inhuman and cruel than submarine attack, which the Conference had not outlawed. Against his lone negative, nevertheless, the delegates adopted a ban on asphyxiating gas.

In the world outside The Hague, Chinese nationalists under the name "Righteous Fists," or Boxers, were attacking foreigners in Pekin, Boers and British had reached the edge of war in South Africa, Americans had launched war upon Filipinos, there were labour riots in Italy, police shot and killed demonstrators in Spain, a parliamentary crisis over manhood suffrage exploded in Belgium and everyone was talking about the assault on the French President at the races. "How bored Europe would be if it were not for France," patriotically reflected the correspondent of *Le Temps*. M. Bourgeois rushed home to try his hand in the crisis but decided after all not to undertake the burden of government, and, as Jaurès commented rather sourly, "the angel of arbitration flies back once more to The Hague, to return when the danger is over."

Amid the charms of the Huis ten Bosch, the prospect of a largely negative outcome, so lightly assumed at the start, began to cause anxiety about the public reaction, especially that of the Socialists, society's "awful conscience." If the Conference were to end in mere pious but empty ceremony, it was feared, the Socialists would triumphantly denounce the failure as further evidence of the impotence of governments and declare themselves the true representatives of humanity against its masters. Delegates quoted to each other Baron d'Estournelles' story that when he left Paris, Jaurès had said to him, "Go on, do all you can at The Hague, but you will labour in vain. You can accomplish nothing there, your schemes will fail and we shall triumph." Through the summer, as one delegate said, the Socialists prowled around The Hague like a cat around a bird cage. In Amsterdam they organized a mass meeting of three thousand which denounced the pretended efforts of the governments and declared peace could never be achieved except through the organization of the masses against the capitalists.

"Why does no one write over the door of the Conference, *Mene*,

Tekel, Upharsin?" asked the anonymous correspondent of *Le Temps* who left such a vivid record of that summer. Watching Dutch fishermen's children playing in the streets and pairs of smiling girls who strolled by coquettishly, he wrote, "If this great assembly does not achieve its purpose, the stupid rivalries of states may one day mow down these young people and lay their corpses by millions on the battlefields."

Hope for the Conference now lay in the Arbitration Commission. The chief delegates of the major powers, Pauncefote, White, Bourgeois, Münster, de Staal, all sat on this commission; its labours were the center of attention; its members, drawn forward by the pull of public opinion, really worked; discussions were animated and strong feelings generated. The British, Russians and Americans had each come with a draft proposal for a permanent tribunal; Pauncefote's plan, which did not require obligatory submission of disputes, was accepted as the basis for discussion. Count Münster, flanked by his two professors, declared from the start that Germany was utterly opposed to arbitration of any kind in any form. The whole idea was nothing but "humbug," he told White, and "injurious" to Germany because his country, as he was not shy in explaining, "is prepared for war as no other country is or can be" and could mobilize in ten days, faster than France or Russia or any other power. To submit to arbitration a dispute which might lead finally to war would simply give rival powers time to catch up and cancel Germany's advantage of rapid mobilization. "Exactly," noted the Kaiser in the margin of Münster's report, "that's the object of this whole hoax."

The Kaiser invariably became frenetic at the mere mention of arbitration, which he saw an incursion on his personal sovereignty and as a plot to deprive Germany of the gains achieved by her matchless military organization. Nevertheless, with Pauncefote, White and Bourgeois determined to achieve something, the Commission persisted in the effort to hammer out some form of tribunal. The civilian delegates laboured against the heavy resistance of their own governments and military colleagues, who were deeply disturbed at the least hint of the compulsory principle. No one wanted to give up an inch of sovereignty or an hour of military advantage and at times the outlook seemed hopeless. On a day when the wind blew from the sea, Baroness von Suttner wrote in her diary, "Cold, cold are all hearts—cold as the draft that penetrates the rattling windows. I feel chilled to the bone."

But the necessity of presenting some result to the public was overriding, and tentatively, bit by bit, a tribunal, though puny, began to take shape. Any suggestion of giving it authority over disputes involving "honor or vital interest" caused it to totter toward collapse. The Austrian delegate saw no objection to a tribunal which could decide on minor matters of dispute "such as for instance the interpretation of a Postal or Sanitary commission," but he resolutely rejected anything more. The Balkan delegates in a group—Rumania, Bulgaria, Serbia and Greece—created a crisis when they threatened to walk out if a provision for "investigating commissions" was retained. With utmost difficulty, one agreement at a time, the tribunal's powers and procedures were defined—but not unanimously.

Germany would agree to nothing. The other nations who equally disliked the idea without wishing to say so could rely on Münster's daily negative vote to do their work for them. A tribunal without Germany's adhesion, White wrote despairingly, would seem to the world "a failure and perhaps a farce." He argued earnestly and daily with the German delegates to convince them that their obstruction would only result in the Czar becoming the idol of the plain people of the world and the Kaiser the object of its hatred. They had no right to allow their "noble and gifted" sovereign to be put in this position. He repeated D'Estournelles' story of what Jaurès had said, and when this seemed to make an impression he repeated it in a letter to Bülow and sought out Stead and told him to use it "in every way." Stead complied with such zest that Professor Zorn complained of the "terrorism of the Stead-Suttner press" and warned his government that to abstain from all collaboration raised the danger of Germany being denounced as the "sole troubler of peace." From St. Petersburg the German Ambassador warned Bülow that if the Conference brought forth nothing the Czar would be personally insulted and the world would ascribe the "responsibility and odium of failure to us."

Pressure began to tell. Münster was wavering when a despatch arrived from Berlin stating that the Kaiser had declared himself "strongly and finally" against arbitration. In desperation White persuaded Münster to send Zorn to Berlin and he himself sent Frederick Holls, secretary of the American delegation, to present the issue in person to the Kaiser and his ministers. Friday's scheduled meeting of the Arbitration Commission was postponed until they could report back on Monday. Returning to his hotel White found a visitor, "of all men in the world," Thomas B. Reed, whose "bigness, heartiness, shrewdness" and fascinating conversation helped him to pass the anxious weekend.

In Berlin the Kaiser eluded the interviewers but not a report from Bülow which regretfully advised that the "very popular" idea of arbitration had taken hold of the Conference, won the support of the English, Italians, Americans and even the Russians, leaving Germany in isolated opposition.

The margin grew lurid with the Kaiser's disgust. "I consented to all this nonsense only in order that the Czar should not lose face before Europe," he scribbled. "In practice however I shall rely on God and my sharp sword! And I shit on all their decisions."

This evidently being recognized as His Majesty's gracious consent, word that Germany would sign the arbitration agreement was received at The Hague two days later. At last something would come of the Conference and the awful spectre of nullity and a Socialist triumph receded. Delegates worked mightily to draw up a convention of sixty-one articles, while applying "a zeal almost macabre" to removing any trace of compulsory character. They were ready for a final vote in the closing week of the Conference when it was suddenly frustrated by, of all people, the Americans. Delegates were stunned. Deeply embarrassed, White announced that his delegation could not sign Article 27, the particular contribution of the French, which required signatories to consider it their "duty" to remind parties to a dispute of the existence of the tribunal.

White's painful predicament was the work of Captain Mahan, who was in turn reacting indirectly to Stead. Under the influence of Stead's over-enthusiastic reports, the *Manchester Guardian* had hailed the draft of the Arbitration Convention as a great pacific instrument which if it had been operative in 1898 would have required the European powers to bring Spain and the United States to arbitration and would have prevented the war between them. Reading the article, Mahan was appalled. The "honest collision" might have been missed. For the future he saw a net of entanglements spreading before America's unwary feet. Summoning his fellow delegates he insisted that Article 27 would commit the United States to interfere in European affairs and vice versa, and if signed, would lead the Senate to refuse to ratify the tribunal. Mesmerized and convinced by his implacable logic, White and the others on the delegation submitted, although all their careful work was risked. If the Americans refused to sign a part of the agreement, other nations might back out and the whole delicately assembled structure fall apart. Urgently White tried to persuade the French to drop Article 27 or at least qualify the word "duty." Bourgeois and D'Estournelles refused to change so much as a comma. Fiasco loomed. Closing ceremonies were scheduled for the following day, July 29. In desperate maneuvers White sought a compromise. At the last minute the Americans arranged to sign under a qualifying phrase disclaiming any obligation to "intrude, mingle or entangle" themselves in European politics. By forceps and barely breathing, Arbitration was pulled into the world.

Total results of the Hague Conference were three Conventions: on Arbitration; Laws and Customs of War on Land; and Extension of the Geneva Rules to Maritime Warfare; three Declarations: on Projectiles from Balloons, Asphyxiating Gases, and Expanding Bullets; six "Wishes" for future accomplishment; and a Resolution. The last expressed the opinion of the Conference that limitation of military expenditures and of new types of weapons was "highly desirable for the moral and material benefit of humanity" and should be the subject of "further study" by the states. It was a pious dirge for all that was left of the original Russian purpose, yet the delegates did not seem ready to bury the Hague idea. However cynically they had come and however stunted their product, most of them could not but feel a sense of having participated in something important and a desire that the foundations they had laid should not be lost. They registered the feeling in a "Wish" for a Second Conference at some future date—although the idea did not please everyone. Count Münster crustily departed saying he had no desire to see international conferences perpetuate themselves like "bad weeds."

Three months after the Peace Conference, Britain went to war in South Africa. The Dreyfus Affair had distracted attention from the Conference, one ex-delegate commented sadly, and now the Boer War seemed to contradict it. Its unconscious epitaph was left to Andrew White in the form of a reluctant tribute paid to his difficult colleague, Captain Mahan: "When he speaks, the millennium fades."

By the time the Second Conference met in 1907, again at The Hague, war, revolution, new alliances, new governments, new leaders and most notably a new century had intervened. The Twentieth was already unmistakably modern, which is to say it was absorbed in pursuit of the material with maximum vigor and diminished self-assurance; it had forgotten decadence and acquired doubt. Mechanical energy and material goods were redoubling and dominant, but whether beneficent had somehow become a question. Progress, the great certainty of the Nineteenth, no longer appeared so sure.

People felt awe at the turn of the century, as if the hand of God were turning a page in human fate. Cannons were fired at midnight in Berlin to mark the moment and one listener heard the sound "with a kind of shiver: one knew all that the Nineteenth Century had carried away; one did not know what the Twentieth would bring."

To begin with, it brought violence. The new century was born brawling, in the Boxer Rebellion, in the Philippines, in South Africa, although the brawls were still on the periphery. In 1900 France was restless and so filled with frustrated rage that *Punch* predicted her first act on the day after the International Exposition closed would be to declare war on England, "for they have been held in for so long it will be necessary to do something desperate at once." In 1900 the Kaiser exhorted German troops embarking on the punitive expedition to Pekin to emulate Huns in ruthlessness. In the course of the Boxer Rebellion he experienced the inconvenience of too much zeal in the munitions business. Learning that a German gunboat had suffered seventeen hits in a duel with Chinese forts equipped with the latest Krupp cannon, he sent Fritz Krupp an angry telegram: "This is no time when I am sending my soldiers to battle against the yellow beasts to try to make money out of so serious a situation."

Money and bigness governed. Morgan in 1900 bought out Carnegie to form with Rockefeller and a hundred other firms the corporate colossus, U. S. Steel, the world's first billion-dollar holding company. King Leopold of Belgium, the Morgan of Europe, a builder too big for his country, created a moneymaking empire out of the Congo while British and Americans, busy killing Boers and Filipinos, loudly deplored his methods. Three hundred men, it was said, "all acquainted with each other, controlled the economic destiny of the Continent."

In 1900 Oscar Wilde, a bloated ruin at forty-four, died in Paris, and Nietzsche, aged fifty-five and mad, died at Weimar. "Then in 1900," wrote W. B. Yeats, "everybody got down off his stilts; henceforth no one went mad; nobody committed suicide; nobody joined the Catholic Church or if they did I have forgotten. Victorianism had been defeated." Some welcomed, some regretted the defeat but the fact was clear. As if to mark the event, the Queen herself incredibly was no more.

The year 1900 conveyed a sense of forces and energy running away with the world. Henry Adams felt moved to evolve a "Law of Acceleration" in history. He felt as if he could never drive down the Champs Elysées without expecting an accident or stand near an official without expecting a bomb. "So long as the rate of progress held good, these bombs would double in force and number every ten years. . . . Power leaped from every atom. . . . Man could no longer hold it off. Forces grasped his wrists and flung him about as though he had hold of a live wire or a runaway automobile."

Adams' choice of simile was apt, for the automobile was one of the century's two most potent factors of future social change; the other was man's unconscious. Although unrecognized in potential, it too was formulated in 1900, in a book, *The Interpretation of Dreams*, by a Viennese doctor, Sigmund Freud. Although the book attracted little attention and it took eight years to sell out the edition of six hundred copies, its appearance was the signal that Victorianism indeed was dead.

The International Exposition of 1900 covering 277 acres in the heart of Paris displayed the new century's energies to fifty million visitors from April to November. If they could not for this Exposition equal the Eiffel Tower of the last, the French built with the same *élan* a new miracle of engineering and beauty in the Pont Alexandre III, whose low graceful arch spanned the Seine in a single leap. It was considered "peerless in all the world" and the two new permanent exhibition buildings on the right bank, the Grand and Petit Palais, were unanimously acknowledged to be "suitable and grand." Not so the Porte Monumentale, or main gate, in the Place de la Concorde, built of what appeared to one observer to be lath, plaster, broken glass, putty, old lace curtains and glue. At its top, instead of a traditional goddess of Progress or Enlightenment, a plaster Parisienne in evening gown welcomed the world with open arms. Although considered gay and chic by some, the gate was generally deplored as the epitome of the new vulgarity of the new century. Multicolored electric lights played on towering electrically powered fountains at night; the new Metro was opened in time; a track for automobile testing and racing was built at the Expo annex at Vincennes. Of all the wonders the public's favorite was the *trottoir roulant,* a double moving sidewalk circling the grounds, one half of which moved twice as fast as the other. In the temporary buildings, the architects, striving for sensation, had achieved what seemed exciting originality to some and "a debauch of stucco" to others. Industrial exhibits in the Palaces of Machinery, Electricity, Civil Engineering and Transportation, Mining and Metallurgy, Chemical Industries and Textiles, displayed all the extraordinary advances of the past decade.

Of the national pavilions the most popular was the Russian, an exotic Byzantine palace with a Trans-Siberian Railway exhibit in which the visitor could sit in a sumptuous railway carriage and enjoy a moving panorama of the scenery. The Viennese was a fantasy of *Art Nouveau* with fretwork balconies in the form of curling vines and the sinuous lines of the new style curving through ceramics and furniture. The United States had the greatest number of exhibits but Germany's show was the most imposing, clearly superior in quality and arrangement. It affirmed an intense will to surpass every other exhibitor. Germany's dynamos were the largest, the spire of her pavilion the tallest, its searchlight the brightest, its restaurant the most expensive. The Kaiser himself, it was rumored, had commanded the finest china and silver, the most delicate glassware, the most luxurious service, so that one felt in the presence, as one visitor said, of a real style "William the Second."

In all the Exposition the two largest single exhibits were Schneider-Creusot's long-range cannon and Vickers-Maxim's collection of ferocious, quick-firing machine guns. Beholders gazed at them with solemn thoughts. An English correspondent in particular was moved to philosophize on the real meaning of the Exposition for the new era it introduced. Schneider's great gun seemed to him to hold the world collected in Paris under its threat and to mark the passage of war from a realm of sport to a realm of science in which the making of weapons absorbed the ingenuity of mankind. If a lull ever came, he wrote, the arts of peace might revive, "but meanwhile the Paris Exhibition has taught us that the triumph of the modern world is purely mechanical."

The triumphs continued. In 1900 Max Planck broke the chains of classical Newtonian physics to formulate the quantum theory of energy. In Switzerland in 1905 Albert Einstein, a professor at the University of Zurich, published a striking paper on a new theory of relativity. In 1901 wireless telegraphy spanned the Atlantic and Daimler supplanted the horseless carriage with a vehicle distinctly a motorcar. In 1903 a motorized dirigible flying machine flew at Kitty Hawk. But no epoch is all of a piece. To some the almost daily new miracles accomplished by science and mechanics still carried, not a threat as to Henry Adams, but a promise of progress in social justice. "It seemed merely a matter of decades," thought Stefan Zweig, a young intellectual of Vienna, "before the last vestiges of evil and violence would finally be conquered."

In 1900 the German Naval Law precipitated the abandonment of isolation by England. Providing for nineteen new battleships and twenty-three cruisers in the next twenty years, it made explicit Germany's challenge to British supremacy at sea, the fulcrum of Britain's existence. It convinced Britain that she needed friends. In 1901 the Hay-Pauncefote Treaty put a bottom under good relations with the United States. In 1902 the isolation of self-sufficient strength, once so splendid and confident, was ended forever by a formal alliance with Japan. In 1903 the new King of England, Edward VII, prepared the ground for reconciliation with France by a visit of ceremony to Paris carried out with tact and aplomb. In 1904 the new policy culminated in an Anglo-French Entente, disposing of old quarrels, establishing a new friendship and fundamentally defining the balance of Europe.

At the same time, England set about refitting her physical forces to meet a world full of new challenges. Her Army having been revealed in action as something less than in step with modern times, Balfour, now Prime Minister, set up a Committee of Imperial Defence to formulate strategy and reorganize and modernize the armed forces. He appointed Sir John Fisher as one of its three members and would have appointed Captain Mahan to succeed Lord Acton as Regius Professor of Modern History at Cambridge but that King Edward objected on the ground that English historians were available. For all his rarefied pose, Balfour's appreciation of the two hard-headed veterans of The Hague revealed a bent parallel to theirs. In 1904 he appointed Fisher First Sea Lord. The new head of the Navy had momentous plans in mind.

In the same year, Russia went to war with Japan, soon to become mired in a series of losing campaigns marked by the surrender of Port Arthur in January, 1905, and a humiliating, although not decisive, defeat at the Battle of Mukden in March. Three weeks later the alarm bell rang for Europe in Morocco.

To Germany's intense resentment, the Anglo-French Entente had recognized a French sphere of influence in Morocco. Now that Russia could not come to France's aid, Bülow and Holstein determined on a test of strength that would expose the weakness, as they believed, of the Entente. On March 31, 1905, the Kaiser stunningly, if nervously, descended upon Tangier in a challenge that every nation recognized. Europe shook under the impact and the gesture succeeded too well. It completed the work of the Kruger telegram, convincing Germany's neighbors of her ultimate belligerent intent and of the need for more specific preparations than a mere Entente. "Roll up the map of Europe," Pitt had said in despair ninety-nine years before when Napoleon won at Austerlitz. In a different spirit England unrolled it now. She entered into military conversations with France, underpinning their partnership with arms and envisioning, for the first time since Waterloo, an expeditionary force to the Continent in aid of a specific ally against a specific enemy.

In May, 1905, the Russian Baltic Fleet met its fatal rendezvous in the Straits of Tsushima in the world's first head-on clash of modern capital ships on the high seas. Though the Russian fleet was annihilated, its defeat did not end the war, thus proving Bloch's thesis, though few realized it, that against the total resources of a nation, victories on the battlefield were no longer decisive. Japan's victory startled the Old World and warned the New. Three months after Tsushima, in July, 1905, the President of the United States offered to mediate between Russia and Japan, less to save the Russians than to halt the Japanese, who seemed to him to have gone far enough. Accepting the offer, the parties came to Portsmouth, New

Hampshire, in August to negotiate a peace treaty under the aegis of the President of the United States. It was a significant moment in Western history. For McKinley or Cleveland or Harrison to have played such a role would have been unimaginable, but a new strength and a new man were now at work.

"Theodore! with all thy faults . . ." was the one-line editorial in which the New York *Sun* had expressed its Presidential preference in the election of the previous year. Its candidate, now President in his own right, was exuberantly in charge of a country booming with prosperity. With industry stimulated by the Spanish-American War, the depression, unemployment and savage labour troubles of the nineties had subsided and the bitter class feeling of the McKinley-Bryan campaign of 1896 was dulled by the full dinner pail. The Progressives, who were the new Left, were expansionist and believed America's direction was "onward and upward." President Roosevelt leading the march settled the coal strike, "took" Panama, began the building of the Canal, challenged the trusts, slapped the name "muckrakers" on crusading journalists, bullied the Kaiser out of Venezuela, and when a presumed American citizen was kidnaped by bandits in Morocco, sent the American Fleet to the rescue with the resounding demand (phrased by John Hay): "We want Perdicaris alive or Raisuli dead!"

"The President is in his best mood," said his friend Jules Jusserand, the French Ambassador, "he is always in his best mood." He had the mental energy of a geyser and the flaws of Everyman. His Attorney-General, Philander Knox, rather admired the way the President ignored his advice and once remarked, "Ah, Mr. President, why have such a beautiful action marred by any taint of legality." President Eliot still did not admire him, although when Roosevelt came to Cambridge in 1905 for his twenty-fifth reunion Eliot had felt obliged to invite him to stay at his house. On his arrival, perspiring and in need of a wash, Roosevelt pulled off his coat, rolled it up and flung it across the bedroom so violently it knocked a pillow to the floor, took a large pistol from his pocket and slammed it on the dresser. After washing up, "he came rushing downstairs as if his life depended on it," and when Eliot asked, "Now, are you taking breakfast with me?" replied, "Oh no, I promised Bishop Lawrence I would take breakfast with him—and good gracious!"—clapping his right hand to his side—"I've forgotten my gun!" Retrieving it, the President of the United States rushed off to see the Bishop while the president of Harvard, horrified by violation of a Massachusetts law against carrying pistols, muttered, "Very lawless; a very lawless mind."

The pistol represented, perhaps, less a lawless mind than the creed of the time that life was a fight. No one felt it more deeply than Roosevelt. He despised Tolstoy's "foolish theory that men should never make war," for he believed that "the country that loses its capacity to hold its own in actual warfare will ultimately show that it has lost everything." He was infuriated when the peace advocates equated progress in civilization with "a weakening of the fighting spirit"; such a weakening, as he saw it, invited the destruction of the more advanced by the less advanced. He confused the desire for peace with physical cowardice and harped curiously on this subject: "I abhor men like [Edward Everett] Hale and papers like the *Evening Post* and the *Nation* in all of whom there exists absolute physical dread of danger and hardship and who therefore tend to hysterical denunciation and fear of war." He deplored what seemed to him, as he looked around, a "general softening of fibre, a selfishness and luxury, a relaxation of standards" and especially "a spirit such as that of the anti-imperialists." "That's my man!" the Kaiser used to say whenever Roosevelt's name was mentioned.

No President had a more acute sense of his own public relations. When Baron d'Estournelles came in 1902 to beg him to do something to breathe life into the Arbitration Tribunal, Roosevelt listened. "You are a danger and a hope for the world depending on whether you support aggression or arbitration," d'Estournelles said. "The world believes you incline to the side of violence. Prove the contrary."

"How?" the President asked.

"By giving life to the Hague Court." Roosevelt promptly instructed Secretary Hay to find something to submit for arbitration and Hay obligingly uncovered an old quarrel between the United States and Mexico over church property, the first dispute to activate the Tribunal. Having been Secretary of State during the Hague Conference and sympathetic to arbitration, Hay wanted to build up the prestige of the Tribunal and now arranged to divert to it the dispute over Venezuela's debts. Fearing that the President might accept a German proposal to act as individual mediator in this affair, he strode up and down the room exclaiming, "I have it all arranged, I have it all arranged. If only Teddy will keep his mouth shut until tomorrow noon!" That objective being happily accomplished, the Tribunal received another important case.

Arbitration treaties between individual countries slowly made progress. England and France agreed on one when they joined in the Entente of 1904 and Norway and Sweden concluded another when Norway, without the firing of a shot, became an independent state in 1905—an event hailed in itself as evidence that man was making progress. Two other international disputes of the time, the Dogger Bank affair between Russia and England and the affair of Venezuela's debts, were referred to the Arbitration Tribunal, whose existence proved an invaluable means of saving face and satisfying public opinion. The Hague idea seemed to be putting on flesh.

In the summer of 1904 the Interparliamentary Union, meeting at the St. Louis Fair, adopted a resolution asking the President of the United States to convene a Second Peace Conference to take up the subjects postponed at The Hague and to carry arbitration forward toward the goal of a permanent court of international law. At the White House, Roosevelt accepted the resolution in person, as well as a visit from Baroness von Suttner, who had a private talk with him on "the subject so dear to my heart." She found him friendly, sincere and "thoroughly impressed with the seriousness of the matter discussed." According to her diary he said to her, "Universal peace is coming; it is certainly coming—step by step." As the most unlikely remark of the epoch, it illustrates the capacity of true believers to hear what they want to hear.

Roosevelt felt the glamour of a world role and as convener of the Peace Conference considered himself no less fitted than the Czar. Accordingly on October 21, 1904, Hay instructed American envoys to propose that the nations reconvene at The Hague. That the Second Conference, like the First, was called while a war was in progress need not, he suggested, be considered an ill omen.

The nations accepted on condition that the Conference should not be convened until the Russo-Japanese War was over. No sooner was it over, however, than the Moroccan crisis erupted. Again President Roosevelt played a decisive role and was able to exercise his influence, this time privately, to persuade the Kaiser to agree to an international conference on Morocco. Held at Algeciras in January, 1906, with the United States as a participant, it proved to be a discomfiture for Germany, leaving her more bellicose than before. International tensions were not eased.

Three months before Algeciras, in October, 1905, the keel of *H.M.S. Dreadnought*, first of her class, was laid. With guns and armor plate manufactured by separate ordnance firms, she was ready for trials in an unprecedented burst of speed and secrecy, a year and a day later, achieving the greatest of military advantages—surprise. Designed by Fisher, the *Dreadnought* was larger, swifter, more heavily gunned than any battleship the world had ever seen. Displacing 18,000 tons, carrying ten 12-inch guns, and powered by the new steam-turbine engines, it made all existing fleets, including Germany's, obsolete, besides demonstrating Britain's confidence and capacity to rebuild her own fleet. Germany would now not only have to match the ship but dredge her harbors and widen the Kiel Canal.

In Fisher's mind, as in Clemenceau's, there was but one adversary. Half jokingly in 1904 he shocked King Edward by suggesting that the growing German Fleet should be "Copenhagened," that is, wiped out by surprise bombardment, evoking the King's startled reply, "My God, Fisher, you must be mad!" At Kiel in the same year, the Kaiser upset Bülow by publicly ascribing the genesis of his Navy to his childhood admiration of the British Fleet, which he had visited in company with "kind aunts and friendly admirals." To give such sentimental reasons for a national development for which the people were being asked to pay millions, Bülow scolded, would not encourage the Reichstag to vote credits. "Ach, that damned Reichstag!" was the Kaiser's reply.

Invitations to The Hague meanwhile had been reissued not by Roosevelt but by the Czar, who felt the necessity of regaining face. The upstart American republic had intervened enough. In September, 1905, as soon as his war was over, the hint was conveyed to Washington that he wished the right to call the Conference himself. Roosevelt amiably relinquished it. The Treaty of Portsmouth, which in a few months was to bring him the Nobel Peace Prize, had, he felt, been enough of a good thing. "I particularly do *not* want to appear as a professional peace advocate . . . of the Godkin or Schurz variety," he wrote to his new Secretary of State, Elihu Root.* His withdrawal did not please the peace advocates. Russia, as one of them said, was "not in the van of civilization." This became strikingly apparent upon the outbreak of the Russian revolution of 1905. Forced by the crisis to grant a constitution and a parliament, the Czar repudiated the action as soon as his regime regained control, and dissolved the Duma to the horror of foreign liberal opinion.

The time seemed not on the whole propitious for a Peace Conference, but one encouraging development was a change of government in England which brought the Liberals, the traditional party of peace, to power. The new Prime Minister, Sir Henry Campbell-Bannerman, known to all as C.-B., was a solid round-headed Scot of a wealthy mercantile family who had made himself unpopular in Court and in Society by denouncing British concentration camps in the Boer War as "methods of barbarism." Nevertheless, King Edward, forced to become acquainted, discovered him to be indeed, as a mutual friend had promised, "so straight, so good-tempered, so clever and so full of humor" that it was impossible not to like him. C.-B.

---

* Hay had died in July, 1905.

had the wit, tact and worldly wisdom that the King appreciated and the two gentlemen, who had a number of tastes in common, soon found each other congenial. They both went annually to Marienbad for the cure, they both loved France and shared a special friendship with the Marquis de Galliffet. Though a Liberal, C.-B. was, to the royal surprise, "quite sound on foreign politics." He spoke the most fluent French of any Englishman, delighted to shop in Paris, to eat French food and read French literature, Anatole France being one of his favorites.

As an old-fashioned Liberal automatically disposed to disarmament,* C.-B. in his first public speech as Prime Minister somewhat rashly pledged his party to work for it at the coming Conference, although the Czar's invitation, as opposed to 1898, had conspicuously omitted to mention the subject. Nevertheless, C.-B. boldly took it on, as well as a pledge to work for a permanent court of arbitration. "What nobler role," he asked, "could this great country assume than to place itself at the head of a League of Peace?" This may have somewhat overstepped the view of a hard bloc within his own Cabinet composed of Asquith, Haldane and Grey, who as Liberal Imperialists were not altogether as peace-minded as himself. With unexpected toughness at seventy, C.-B. had withstood their attempt to elbow him into the House of Lords so as to obtain leadership of the Commons for Asquith. He detested them all and was enjoying his triumph.

Soon the relentless dilemma that attaches to office caught up with his Government. After years of excoriating the Tories as warmongers, the Liberals now suddenly found themselves responsible for the country's safety. Although committed by election pledges to reduction of military and naval expenditure, once the General Election confirmed them in office they were not anxious to repudiate the work of modernizing the armed forces which the Tories had begun. C.-B. referred to the members of the Committee of Imperial Defence, Fisher, Lord Esher, and Sir George Clark, presumably in that order, as Damnable, Domineering and Dictatorial; but he had inherited them, not to mention the dreadnought program. Haldane, as Secretary for War, undertook to cut £3,000,000 from the Army estimates while at the same time, through sweeping reforms, achieving a more efficient fighting arm, as Fisher had done in the Navy. He created a General Staff and a reserve force called the Territorials. Officers' Training Corps were formed in the public schools and universities and supplied with arms, ammunition and instructors by the government.

---

* Limitation of armaments rather than disarmament was the question at issue, but the single word, being less awkward, was generally used at the time and the usage has been followed here.

Young men responded with enthusiasm. The calling bugle and screaming fife worked their magic, though chiefly upon the officer class. Recruitment of private soldiers for the Territorials dwindled after the first few years.

H.M.S. Dreadnought was commissioned in 1906, a strange triumph for the Liberals, and Fisher was demanding construction of three more dreadnoughts for 1907. He threatened, if refused, to resign and take three other members of the Board of Admiralty with him. The Liberal dilemma was painful but not beyond solution. By insisting that the Navy was defensive (which, considering the nature of blockade, was arguable), the Government managed to give Fisher his dreadnoughts and absolve the Liberal conscience at the same time.

Once more the nations found themselves committed to go to The Hague and intensely disliking the prospect. All through 1906 and half of 1907 they put off the uncomfortable day while pursuing desultory discussions of agenda. The Russian program, circulated in April, 1906, proposed arbitration and laws of war as subjects for discussion while continuing to ignore disarmament. Emerging from foreign defeats and domestic revolution, Russia was concerned with replenishing, not reducing, armaments and had called the Conference only to retrieve the initiative from the United States. As far as Izvolsky, the current Russian Foreign Minister, was concerned, disarmament was "a craze of Jews, Socialists and hysterical women." Since the advent of the Liberals in England, however, the question of disarmament could not be escaped. To put it on the agenda after the burial of 1899 was like propping up a dead man; not to put it on was to admit hopelessness and invite public condemnation. At a meeting of the Interparliamentary Union in London in April, 1906, C.-B. urged the delegates to insist at home "in the name of humanity" on their governments going to The Hague with serious intent to decrease military and naval budgets. The meeting was hardly a happy one, for on opening day, as delegates crowded around to congratulate the proud members of the youngest parliament, word came that the Czar had dissolved the Duma. C.-B., who was to give the address of welcome, was so shocked that he challenged the Imperial decision with the words, "Under one form or another the Duma will revive. In all sincerity, we can say, 'The Duma is dead; long live the Duma!' " His outspokenness earned an official Russian protest.

As to disarmament the Kaiser let it be known that if it was brought up for discussion in any form, his delegates would leave the Conference which in any case he "devoutly hoped would not take place." He was already being blamed at home by the militant Pan-Germans and Crown Prince's party for yielding at Algeciras instead of fighting, and German diplomats hinted to other ambassadors that he might even be deposed if Germany were forced to agree to any form of arms limitation arising from the Conference. During one of the periodic visits of King Edward required by royal relations, with usually disastrous results, uncle and nephew discussed the forthcoming Conference while remaining for once reasonably amiable, perhaps because on this subject they were not far apart. The King "entirely disapproved" of the Conference, the Kaiser wrote to Roosevelt, "and himself took the initiative of telling me that he considered it a 'humbug.'" According to his report, King Edward said it was not only useless, since in case of need nobody would feel bound by its decisions, but even dangerous as likely to produce more friction than harmony.

To Roosevelt it was apparent that modern Germany, "alert, aggressive, military and industrial, . . . despises the Hague Conference and the whole Hague idea." His anxiety at the time was lest the British Liberal Government would "go to any maudlin extreme at the Hague Conference." He told the new British military attaché, Count Gleichen, a cousin of the King, that he hoped Haldane and Grey would not let themselves be "carried away by sentimental ideas." He was afraid they might be "swayed by their party in that direction . . . but don't let them do it." He talked fully to Gleichen of his current idea for a limitation on the size of battleships rather than on naval budgets. Unaware that his proposed top limit of 15,000 tons was already outdated by the monstrous hulk then lying in Portsmouth dockyard, Roosevelt explained that he wanted to see the British Navy remain in the same relative position vis-à-vis the navies of Europe and Japan as at present. Conveying the message to the King, Gleichen added that he had found lunch at Roosevelt's home in Oyster Bay "extremely meagre," and with only two Negro servants in attendance and no one to meet him at the station, arrangements rather primitive altogether.

Once the *Dreadnought* was commissioned, the United States Navy could not lag behind and two of the new class were authorized by Congress at Roosevelt's request in January, 1907. The Navy, he wrote to President Eliot, was an "infinitely more potent factor for peace than all the peace societies" and the Panama Canal far more important than The Hague. With regard to the Conference he added, "My chief trouble will come from the fantastic visionaries who are crazy to do the impossible."

One of these was Andrew Carnegie, whose company, when he sold it in 1900 to Morgan for $250,000,000 in bonds, was producing one-fourth of all the steel in the United States and as much as all of England. Less shy than Nobel, Carnegie was now devoting his profits, while he was still alive, to the welfare of humanity. Next to providing libraries which presumably might make men wiser, he hoped also to make them more pacific, and had agreed on the urging of Andrew White to donate a building for the Arbitration Tribunal at The Hague.

He was now busily engaged between the White House and Whitehall in an effort to promote the cause of the Conference, but Roosevelt had lost interest after the British refused to consider his proposal of a limit on the size of battleships. However, Roosevelt managed to avoid commitments by telling highly placed correspondents what they wanted to hear. He was in correspondence with the sovereigns of both Germany and England, whom he addressed easily as "My Dear Emperor William" and "My Dear King Edward."

By now scarcely any public official except C.-B. and Secretary Root wanted disarmament on the agenda. Root thought it should be discussed even if nothing were accomplished, because, he said, results are never achieved without a number of failures: "failures are necessary steps toward success." C.-B. too felt the world must keep on trying. Though a childless man whose wife, his closest companion, had just died and who himself was within a year of his death, he continued his own efforts. In March, 1907, he took the unusual course for a Prime Minister of publishing an article on a current question of policy. Under the title "The Hague Conference and the Limitation of Armaments," it appeared in the first issue of a new liberal weekly, the *Nation* (of London). Although armaments and engines of war had increased since the First Conference, he wrote, so had the peace movement, which was now "incomparably stronger and more constant." He thought disarmament should be given a chance to make the same progress as arbitration, which now had acquired a "moral authority undreamt of in 1898." Britain, he pointed out, had already reduced military and naval expenditures (which was true if the program for the new dreadnoughts was left out of account) and would be willing to go further if other nations would do likewise. Admittedly this would not affect Britain's naval supremacy, since it would freeze the status quo, but the Prime Minister insisted on the thesis that the British Navy was not a challenge to any state or group of states. The argument was narrow steering between the rocks of conscience and the shoals of political reality and it pleased nobody. The Germans took it as proof of a British plot in concert with France and Russia to force the issue at The Hague before Germany could make good *H.M.S. Dreadnought*'s lead. Bülow announced

publicly in the Reichstag that Germany would refuse to discuss disarmament at the Conference. King Edward was equally irritated by the Prime
Minister's espousal of disarmament, as bad as his support of women's suffrage. "I suppose he will support the Channel Tunnel Bill next week!"
he said in disgust, but from that particular horror C.-B. refrained.

As Foreign Secretary, Sir Edward Grey professed himself ready at all
times to talk budgetary limitation at The Hague. Haldane talked earnestly
to the American diplomat, Henry White, of the need for reducing armaments and had gone to Germany in 1906 to feel out possible ground for
an agreement. But the hard fact behind the talk was that neither the British
Government nor any other had any intention of limiting its freedom to arm
as it pleased. The only person to mention the role of the munitions manufacturers was the King of Italy, who suggested that disarmament would
cause "an outburst of opposition" among them and he was sure the Kaiser
would never consent to "clipping the wings of Krupp." When, on behalf
of Russia, Professor de Martens toured the capitals to gather opinions as
Muraviev, now dead, had done before, the American Ambassador in Berlin
summarized the matter flatly: "De Martens does not believe and nobody
believes . . . there is the slightest likelihood of any steps toward practical
reduction of armaments being taken at the next Hague Conference."

These were the private exchanges of diplomats, but peace could not
be so rudely handled before the public, at least not in England and the
United States. It was not a question of the great mute unknown passive
mass. Who knew what opinion lay there? Mass opinion when formed
would blow with the winds of circumstance and more likely with the loud
circumstance of war than with peace. The vocal opinion, however, of the
thinking public—especially of the peace movement—would be outraged
by exclusion of disarmament from the Hague agenda. Peace Congresses
meeting annually—at Glasgow in 1901, Monaco in 1902, Rouen and Le
Havre in 1903, Boston in 1904, Lucerne in 1905, Milan in 1906—passed
resolutions demanding that governments make some serious effort to reach
a truce on armaments. Baroness von Suttner, who had been awarded the
Nobel Peace Prize in 1905, and her colleagues in the peace societies and
at the annual Lake Mohonk conferences in America, agitated as energetically as ever. In 1907 Jane Addams published a book, *Newer Ideals of
Peace*, incurring Roosevelt's displeasure but adding a respected voice to
the chorus.

Carnegie, seizing on C.-B.'s idea of a League of Peace or League of
Nations, as he variously called it, decided the Kaiser was the man to estab-

lish it because "I think he is the man responsible for war on earth." Having several times been invited to visit by the Kaiser, who liked millionaires, he now set forth to convince him of his duty. By letter in advance he explained how the Kaiser could earn in history the title of the "Peacemaker" and added in a covering letter to the American Ambassador, "He and our President could make a team if they were only hitched up together in the cause of Peace." At Kiel, on his arrival in June, 1907, he dined twice with the Kaiser and was invited to a third audience with results eerily echoing the interviews of Stead with the Czar and Baroness von Suttner with Roosevelt. Carnegie found his monarch "a wonderful man, so bright, humorous, and with a sweet smile. I think he can be trusted and declares himself for peace. . . . Very engaging—very; can't help liking him." Once out of reach of the sweet smile, Carnegie remembered his mission and wrote back urging a great gesture by the Kaiser at The Hague to convince the world that he was in reality the "apostle of peace."

Words and gestures of this kind were a habitual weakness of the peace advocates, with effect on the public, if any, that could only be deceptive. At the same time, political leaders told the public only what sounded virtuous and benign, while reserving the hard realities for each other. Only one man tried to instruct the public to take an honest look at war. Mahan, now an Admiral, continued to publish articles on the necessity of the free exercise of fighting strength and especially, in anticipation of the Conference, on the danger of a renewed demand for immunity of private property at sea. The military function seemed to him to need protection from the uncomprehending view of the layman. "The prepossession of the public mind in most countries," he wrote worriedly to Roosevelt after a tour abroad, was such that the question of war was "in danger of being misjudged and 'rushed.' "

It was this prepossession that required both the British and American governments to support inclusion of disarmament on the agenda. Neither Grey nor Roosevelt believed discussion would lead to any practical result and in talks with foreign ambassadors both explained that they were obliged to insist on it for "the sake of public opinion." Germany, Austria and Russia were determined to exclude it for fear that discussion might somehow trap them into an unwanted position. After months of intricate diplomatic negotiation, the Conference was finally announced without disarmament on the agenda and with so many reservations included in the various acceptances that it seemed probable the Conference might break up as soon as it met. Great Britain, the United States and Spain reserved the right to bring disarmament up for discussion; Germany, Austria and Russia reserved the right to abstain or withdraw if it were mentioned, and other nations reserved a variety of rights in between.

So burdened, the nations assembled on June 15, 1907. The first decade of the new century, now three quarters old, was already marked by three characteristics: a bursting economy, a burst of creative vigor in the arts, and the sound of steady "drumming like a noise in dreams." For all who did not hear it there were many who did, not all with dread. In the German Navy it was the custom of officers to drink to "The Day." At a spa near Bayreuth a group of German students and young naval officers made friends with a visiting Englishman and "in the friendliest and most amiable fashion discussed with me the coming struggle between our two countries." They argued that every empire had its day. England's decline must come as had that of Spain, Holland and France. Who should fill the throne but the strong, wise, noble and gifted nation whose development had been the outstanding factor of the Nineteenth Century and who now stood "poised for heroic enterprise." Germany seemed not the only one so poised. The new aggressive powers exhibited by Japan and the United States convinced Europe that these nations were approaching a clash. Following the furor caused in Japan by the California Exclusion Act, both these nations believed it themselves. "The tendency is toward war," wrote Secretary Root, "not now but in a few years' time."

The prospect was viewed by many of the ruling class more matter-of-factly than tragically. Lord Lansdowne, opposing the Old Age Pensions Bill in the House of Lords, said it would cost as much as a great war and the expense of the South African War was a better investment. "A war, terrible as are its consequences, has at any rate the effect of raising the moral fibre of the country" whereas the measure under debate would weaken it. And if the prospect of war appalled the spokesmen of the working class, violence as such did not. Georges Sorel in his *Reflections on Violence* in 1908 claimed that proletarian violence exercised in the interest of class war was a "fine heroic thing," a civilizing agent that could save the world from barbarism.

The Second Conference was larger in size, longer in duration and more voluminous in results than the First, but otherwise not very different. It lasted through October—for four months instead of two—and produced thirteen conventions, as compared to the previous three. Because the United States had insisted on the presence of the Latin-American states, much to the distaste of the European powers, 44 nations and 256 delegates were present as compared to 26 and 108 at the First Conference. The larger number made it necessary to meet in the Ridderzaal, seat of the Netherlands Parliament in the center of The Hague, rather than in the Huis ten Bosch in its lovely park. Many of the delegates were the same as before; many of the notable ones of 1899 were missing. Bourgeois of France and Beernaert of Belgium again headed their respective delegations, but Münster, Pauncefote and De Staal were dead; Andrew White had not returned; Mahan and Fisher were absent in body if not in spirit. The new president was again a Russian, M. Nelidov, an elderly diplomat like his predecessor whose voice and manner revealed his lack of sympathy with the Conference and who, being in ill health most of the time, left command of the Russian delegation to the pompous Professor de Martens who himself suffered from gout and was often confined to his room. The Russian delegation seemed divided among itself with its members quartered in separate hotels.

Baron d'Estournelles, who was to share the Nobel Peace Prize with Beernaert two years later, was again present for France, and Professor Zorn, looking yellow and emaciated, from Germany. Among the newcomers were Count Tornielli, representing Italy, whose wife had been seated next to President Loubet on the terrible day at Auteuil, and the notorious Marquis de Soveral, who represented Portugal. An intimate friend of King Edward, he was known as the "Blue Monkey" in London Society where it was said, "he made love to all the most beautiful women and all the nicest men were his friends." A whole block of newcomers was provided by the "impeccable dandies" of Latin America.

Pauncefote's firm presence was missed. When he died in 1902 Roosevelt sent his body home to England in a cruiser, saying, "I did not do it because he was Ambassador but because he was a damned good fellow." His place was taken, if not filled, by a judge, Sir Edward Fry, a tiny, unworldly Quaker of eighty-two, yet not so unworldly as to want to yield control of the British delegation to his associate, Sir Ernest Satow, an experienced diplomat, formerly minister to Pekin, who spoke French fluently which Fry did not.

Dominating the Conference were the chief delegates of the United States and Germany: Mr. Joseph Hodges Choate, who at seventy-five with white chin whiskers seemed to personify the Nineteenth Century, and Baron Marschall von Bieberstein, suave and up to date, who though only ten years younger was clearly a man of the new age. Choate was genial and shrewd, famous as a raconteur, Ambassador to England from 1899 to 1905 and a lawyer by profession whose brilliant defence of the rights of property before the Supreme Court in 1895 held off the income tax for another eighteen years. He owned a summer home at Stockbridge designed by Stanford White. His white hair gleaming beneath a glossy silk hat became a landmark of the Conference.

Baron Marschall, Ambassador to Constantinople, a huge handsome man with two *alt-Heidelberg* dueling scars on his cheek, wore "a mask of haughty intelligence that seemed to despise the *ensemble* of human folly." He played chess and the piano, cultivated roses, and smoked tiny cigarettes endlessly, occasionally flicking the fallen ash from the silk lapel of his coat with a gesture that seemed to say he treated human issues with no more compunction. He despised public opinion which he said was whatever the newspapers chose to make it. A government that could not control the press was not worth its salt. The best way to control a newspaper, he advised, was by "banging the door in its face." Equally firm were his opinions on his fellow delegates: De Martens was a "charlatan . . . with an explosive lack of tact"; Barbarosa of Brazil was the "most boring"; Fry was "a good old man completely lacking in experience of modern life"; Tornielli was "gentle and pacific"; Tsudzuki of Japan was a "superior" person who had studied in Germany, spoke German and "felt the utmost veneration for His Majesty"; the Russian military delegate, Colonel Michelson, who made a speech saying that war was terrible and everything should be done by mediation to prevent it, was guilty of talk which might have been understandable coming from Baroness von Suttner but coming from a colonel was a "scandal"; Choate was "the most striking personality" among the delegates with "extraordinary intelligence, profound legal knowledge and great political ability."

Baron Marschall himself shook the Conference when in the course of discussion on a proposal to restrict mine-laying he warned against the folly of making laws for the conduct of war which might be rendered useless by "the law of facts." The implications to be drawn from this excited wide press comment, including a letter to *The Times* from the Poet Laureate. Too indignant for poetry, Alfred Austin wrote that Marschall's words were a plain warning of future German aggression of which all her neighbors—Holland, Belgium, France and Austria—should take note. Britain "duly forewarned" should adopt military conscription and the Laureate closed with a line borrowed from his predecessor, Lord Tennyson: "Form! Form! Riflemen, Form!"

As before, peace advocates converged from all quarters upon The Hague, including Bertha von Suttner and Stead, who had once again appointed himself independent *rapporteur*. Again he published a chronicle of the proceedings, personalities, disputes and private deals, this time in the form of a four-page daily newspaper, the *Courrier de la Conférence*. Bloch was dead but Andrew Carnegie took his place and laid the cornerstone for the new Peace Palace, to which he had donated $1,250,000. It was agreed that all member nations should contribute materials representing their finest products for the building that was to express "universal good will and hope." As before, Socialists, and this time Anarchists and Zionists as well, held their international Congresses in Amsterdam during the Conference to capture some of the world limelight for their causes. The Dutch pastor and pacifist Domela Nieuwenhuis, who managed to combine Anarchism with religion and remain sincere, denounced Carnegie impartially with the delegates as a merchant of death who built a Temple of Peace, while accepting orders for munitions "even from the Japanese," an accusation accurate in spirit if not in time. "Let all workers regardless of nationality strike on the declaration of war and there will be no war!" Nieuwenhuis cried out.

The work of the Conference was organized as before in Commissions—on Arbitration, Rules of War on Land, Rules of War at Sea—with an additional Fourth Commission—on Maritime Law. Bourgeois and Beernaert were chairmen as before of the First and Second Commissions, Tornielli of the Third and De Martens of the Fourth. At the opening session Nelidov's address of welcome aroused no enthusiasm; the first days were gloomy, arrangements and assignments confused and acoustics in plenary session so poor that on one occasion delegates disputed energetically whether the last speaker had addressed them in English or French.

Carrying out their insistence that disarmament must be discussed if only to prove to the public its impracticability and their own honest intentions, the British brought the question to the floor. None of the nations walked out, because Sir Edward Grey's explanations in advance, however foggy, had conveyed a sufficiently clear impression that the matter would not be uncomfortably pursued; nor was it. Sir Edward Fry made a grave and moving presentation of the case, describing the appalling increase in engines of death and moved a resolution calling for "further serious study" in the same phrase of postponement as had been used in 1899. Nelidov agreed that if arms limitation was not ripe in 1899 it was not more so in 1907, and the delegates adopted Fry's resolution without a vote. The matter was disposed of in a total of twenty-five minutes. Stead raged at the "miserable and scandalous debacle" and even Secretary Root concluded that Grey's support had been merely a gesture to "satisfy English public opinion."

Although the world grew bored after Fry's "funeral oration" as Marschall called it, and even the journalists lost interest, the Conference settled down to serious work on the laws and techniques of war. When busied in drafting and disputing the problems of their trade—the rights and duties of neutrals, the recovery of international debts by force, the rules for opening hostilities—all matters which took war for granted as a fact of human life, the delegates became absorbed. Indeed, they worked harder than at the First Conference, as if war was not only a fact of life but an imminent fact. Committee meetings were held twice a day, lengthy documents had to be read, expert opinions examined, new drafts prepared, and endless confidential talks held to work out compromises. "Never since my examination for the bar have I worked so hard as in the last six weeks," Marschall reported to Bülow.

The launching of projectiles or explosives from balloons was reconsidered, and again avoiding any extremes of self-denial, the delegates renewed the prohibition for another limited term of five years. Neutral territory, a matter on which the Belgians were particularly sensitive, was agreed to be inviolable and a convention of twenty-five articles was worked out establishing rules of procedures in case it were violated. As a result of Japan's treacherous opening of hostilities against Russia by surprise attack in 1904, new and interesting discussions were held on this subject. They culminated in a convention whose signatories agreed not to open hostilities without previous unequivocal warning in the form of a declaration of war or ultimatum accompanied by a conditional declaration of war. Another convention of fifty-six articles was adopted redefining the laws and customs of land warfare. As a result of the Venezuela affair in 1902 a convention against the use of force to collect international debts except if the debtor had refused arbitration was agreed on. This represented one definite advance in international law.

Naval warfare was the subject of the fiercest struggle, with the right of capture of seaborne commerce as the central issue. As the basic weapon of blockade, Britain was determined to preserve the right of capture free of any restrictions. Germany was equally determined to restrict it by international prize court and other interferences. The use of submarines and underwater contact mines as weapons against blockade Germany was determined to defend and Britain to restrict. On the immunity of private property, Grey, at least, had learned Mahan's lesson if the American delegation had not. He instructed his delegates that Britain could not assent to a principle which "if carried to its logical conclusion would entail the abolition of commercial blockade." He added a reason, in his tortured way, which would certainly not have occurred to Mahan. Britain could not agree to anything, he wrote, which might "so limit the prospective liability of war as to remove some of the considerations which now restrain the public from contemplating it." Translated into simpler language, this meant that Britain could not agree to anything which might, by limiting the damages of war, cause people to enter on it more lightly. With the British Liberals it was obligatory to find a moral reason to fortify a natural policy of self-interest, a practice no one carried to higher perfection or more obscure expression than Sir Edward Grey.

Eight conventions on naval warfare were ultimately reached establishing rules, rights and restrictions for every possible means of injuring the enemy. It took thirteen articles to prohibit the use of underwater contact mines unless harmless one hour after being laid; another thirteen articles to regulate naval bombardment of shore establishments; fifty-seven articles to govern an international prize court. Other conventions dealt with the right of capture, the nature of contraband, the rights and duties of neutrals at sea but so unsatisfactorily that all these questions were resumed at a conference of naval powers in London in the following year.

On arbitration, the motive power, now that Pauncefote was gone, was chiefly American, with Secretary Root, a lawyer by profession, supplying the energy behind Choate. Root's object was to transform the tribunal established in 1899 from an optional court for litigants who agreed to arbitration into a Permanent Court of International Justice with permanent judges deciding issues of international law by "judicial methods under a sense of judicial responsibility." President Roosevelt supported the aim without strong conviction, confessing to Root midway through the Conference that "I have not followed things at The Hague." To his friend Speck von Sternberg, the German Ambassador, he expressed himself more forcibly as, for some reason, he habitually did to Germans. He could not take a proper interest in the Hague proceedings, he told Speck, because he was so "utterly disgusted" with the nonsense chattered by professional peace advocates.

The American proposal for a Permanent Court ran into strong opposition, one obstacle being Brazil's insistence that all forty-four nations be represented on it. The idea of having decisions made for them "by decayed Oriental states like Turkey or Persia . . . or a half-breed lawyer from Central or South America," in the words of one commentator, disgusted the major European powers. The crux, however, was once more compulsory arbitration. On this, reported Marschall to Berlin, would depend the final answer, "Was it a Peace Conference or a War Conference that took place in 1907?" Since his own country utterly rejected the compulsory principle, presumably he faced the answer. He did, not, however, fall into the error made by his predecessors of strenuous isolation. Instead, as Choate said, he was devoted to the principle of arbitration while opposing every practical application of it. The Conference attempted to work out a list of innocuous subjects for compulsory submission on which everyone could agree, but it failed of adoption when eight nations voted against it. In the end a Convention on the Pacific Settlement of International Disputes was adopted containing ninety-six articles of which the compulsory principle was not one. Consequently, no Court of Justice could be established.

One last point of contention remained: a Third Conference. Believers in the Hague idea wished to see the principle of the interdependence of nations established in the form of a permanent organization and periodic meetings. The day of nations as separate sovereign units was past and before breaking up they wanted a commitment to meet again. Nonbelievers, chiefly the major European powers, wanted no further limitation of their freedom of action and no more invasions of sovereignty by insistence on compulsory peaceful settlement. They resisted commitment to a Third Conference, more particularly because pressure for it came from the Americans. Secretary Root, faithful to his precept that successive failures were necessary to success, and believing that each of the Conferences had accomplished something toward making possible the next, had instructed Choate to obtain a resolution for a Third Conference. By committing the nations now, he intended also to wrest initiative and control from Russia. Choate fought hard against the reluctance of the other delegates which remained unbending until he threatened Nelidov that if no agreement were reached he would move the resolution publicly in plenary session. Opposition gave way. The delegates adopted a resolution recommending that the next Conference be held "within a period analogous to that which had elapsed since the preceding Conference," namely, eight years.

To have achieved this much, Root wrote to Roosevelt, was at least progress "toward making the practice of nations conform to their professed desire for peace." The desire was real enough. Twice it had brought the nation to The Hague. Twice man's inherent desire to police himself had wrestled against opposite tendencies. The goal of a new international order in which nations would be willing to give up their freedom to fight in exchange for the security of law was still ahead. The advance toward it taken at The Hague, as Choate said later, was necessarily "gradual, tentative and delicate."

He hoped for further progress at the next Conference in 1915.

6

"Neroism Is in the Air"

GERMANY: 1890–1914

6

"Neroism Is in the Air"

T HE BOLD bad man of music at the turn of the century, innovator in form, modern and audacious in concept, brilliant in execution, not immune to vulgarity, and a barometer of his native weather, was Richard Strauss. His every new work, usually conducted at its premiere by himself, crammed the concert halls with a public eager to be excited and music critics eager to whip their rapiers through the hot air of their profession. In the ten years from 1889 to 1899, when he was between twenty-five and thirty-five, Strauss produced six works, *Don Juan, Tod und Verklärung, Till Eulenspiegel, Also Sprach Zarathustra, Don Quixote* and *Ein Heldenleben*, which created a new form—or, as the critics said, "formlessness." Called tone poems, the compositions were rather condensed operas without words. At the premiere of *Don Juan* the audience called the composer back five times in an effort to make him play the piece all over again. At the premiere of *Heldenleben*, the passage depicting battle enraged some listeners to the point of leaving the hall and caused others to "tremble as they listened while some stood up suddenly and made violent gestures quite unconsciously." If to some Strauss was a sensationalist and corrupter of the pure art of music and to others the prophet of a new musical age, even the "inventor of a new art," one thing was clear: he retained for Germany the supremacy of music which had culminated in Wagner. He was "Richard II."

In one sense this made him the most important man in German cultural life, for music was the only sphere in which foreigners willingly acknowledged the superiority that Germans believed was self-evident. German Kultur in German eyes was the heir of Greece and Rome and they themselves the best educated and most cultivated of modern peoples, yet foreigners in their appreciation of this fact fell curiously short of perfect understanding. Apart from German professors and philosophers, only Wagner excited their homage, only Bayreuth, seat of the Wagner Festspielhaus, attracted their visits. Paris remained Europe's center of the arts, pleasure and fashion, London of Society, Rome of antiquity and Italy the lure of travelers seeking sun and beauty. The new movements and impulses in literature—Naturalism, Symbolism, Social criticism; the towering figures—Tolstoy, Ibsen and Zola; the great novels from Dostoyevsky to Hardy: all originated outside Germany. England after its great Victorian age was again in the nineties pulsing with new talent—Stevenson, Wilde and Shaw, Conrad, Wells, Kipling and Yeats. Russia again produced in Chekhov a matchless interpreter of man. Painters bloomed in France. Germany in painting had little but Max Liebermann, leader of the Secessionists, whose secession, however, took him no further than the presidency of the Prussian Academy of Fine Arts. In literature her outstanding figures were the playwright Gerhart Hauptmann, an offshoot of Ibsen, and the poet Stefan George, an offshoot of Baudelaire and Mallarmé.

In music, however, Germany had produced the world's masters and seen the procession crowned by Wagner whose dogma of a fusion of the arts became a cult in which foreigners eagerly joined. Wagner Societies from St. Petersburg to Chicago contributed funds to provide the Master's music dramas with a fitting home, and the "Bayreuth Idea" created intellectual ferment beyond Germany's borders. Germans believed their sovereignty of music would continue forever without serious challenge from any other country. While many of them, like the Kaiser, detested Strauss's modernity, his pre-eminence appeared to them happy proof that German musical supremacy was maintained.

Not only the major cities but every German city or town of substantial size had its opera house, concert hall, music academy, orchestral society and musical *Verein* of one kind or another. Hardly a German did not belong to a choral society or instrumental ensemble and spend his evenings practicing Bach cantatas over several steins of beer. Frankfurt-am-Main, a town of under 200,000 in the nineties, about the size of The Hague, Nottingham or Minneapolis, boasted two colleges of music, with distinguished teaching staffs and pupils from many countries, a new opera house, "one of the handsomest in Europe," which gave performances six nights a week, a Museum Society Orchestra of 120 players which gave concerts of symphonic and chamber music, two large choral societies also prolific in concerts, and in addition was host to numerous recitals by visiting artists. Besides activity of comparable kind in Berlin, Munich,

Cologne, Dresden, Leipzig, Stuttgart and other cities, music festivals lasting as much as a week in honor of some composer or special occasion were held widely and often.

The season at Bayreuth since Wagner's death had acquired an oppressive atmosphere of obligatory reverence. The cab taking a visitor to the Festspielhaus displayed a card pinned over the seat labeled "Historical!" indicating that the Master had sat there. Performances opened with a blast of trumpets as if commanding the audience to prepare for devotions. At intermission sausages and beer were consumed, followed by another trumpet blast; after the second act more sausages and beer and more trumpets and the same procedure after the third act. The faithful absorbed the Master's works "as if they were receiving Holy Communion," reported the young Sibelius, who came in 1894 eager for a great experience and could not leave soon enough. By 1899 when Thomas Beecham, aged twenty, arrived, he found there was a rift in the cult. Malcontents were proclaiming the decadence of the Festival, criticizing the reign of the widow, Frau Cosima, and clamoring for the removal of the son, Siegfried, as director. They said his management was feeble and uninspired, singers were poor and performances shoddy, while the group loyal to "Wahnfried," the Wagners' house, countered with charges of intrigue and jealousy.

By now Strauss was the new Hero, so acknowledged in his self-portrait in music, *A Hero's Life*. Reared in and accustomed to comfort, clad in the correct clothes of a diplomat, slender and six foot three inches tall, with broad shoulders and well-cared-for hands, a soft unlined face, a mouth shaped like a child's under a flaxen moustache and a cap of curly flaxen hair already receding from a high forehead, Strauss looked neither Promethean like Beethoven, nor poetic like Schumann, but simply like what he was: a successful prosperous artist. His works had been performed since he was twelve; as a conductor he was engaged by all the leading orchestras. He was self-possessed, conscious of superiority and comfortably rather than offensively arrogant, a consequence of being Bavarian rather than Prussian.

Bavaria's last King, Ludwig II, who adored Wagner and died mad, had sided with Austria against Prussia in 1866, and Munich's culture was oriented more toward Vienna than Berlin. Munich fostered the arts and considered itself the modern Athens, as opposed to the Sparta of Prussia, whose Junkers, like their ancient prototypes, despised culture as well as comfort. Bavarians, as Germany's southerners—and largely Catholic— enjoyed the pleasures of life, physical as well as aesthetic. In Munich, Stefan George was high priest of a cult of *l'art pour l'art* and beginning in 1892 edited for his worshipful disciples the literary review *Blätter für die Kunst,* which sought the German answer to questions of art, soul and style. Humor found a corner in Munich, where the satiric journal *Simplicissimus,* founded in 1896, and the comic journal *Fliegende Blätter* were published. In Munich the *Überbrettl,* a form of satiric café entertainment, flourished and mocked Berlin.

As a native of Munich, Strauss belonged to a culture antipathetic to Prussia, but as a German aged seven in 1871, he grew up parallel with the new nationalism of the German Empire. Born in 1864, five years younger than the Kaiser, Dreyfus and Theodore Roosevelt, he came of a family which combined beer and music, his native city's leading occupations, in that order. His grandfather was a wealthy brewer whose musically inclined daughter married Franz Strauss, first horn of the Munich Court Orchestra and professor at the Royal Academy of Music. He was said to be the only man of whom Wagner was afraid. Although he played Wagner's music "lusciously," he hated it and his emphatic objections to its demands on his instrument accomplished on one occasion the unique feat of rendering the Master speechless. Before a rehearsal of *Die Meistersinger* Wagner begged the conductor, Hans Richter, to play over the horn solo himself for fear Franz Strauss would declare it unplayable. Although Franz Strauss never became reconciled to his son's dissonances and departures from classical form, Richard Strauss used no instrument to more marvelous capacity than the horn, as if in tribute to the man who, when asked how he could prove the boast that he was the best horn player in the world, replied, "I don't prove it, I admit it."

Strauss's parents began his musical education at the piano when he was four and he began composing at six. He could read and write musical notation before he knew the alphabet. While at school he studied violin, piano, harmony and counterpoint with the conductor of the Court Orchestra. With the "superfluous vitality" that was to remain one of his most notable characteristics, he produced at the same time a flow of songs, instrumental solos and sonatas. When he was twelve his *Festival March* (Op. 1) was performed by his school and later published. Performance of his compositions at public concerts began with three of his songs when he was sixteen, a *String Quartet in A* (Op. 2) when he was seventeen and a *Symphony in D minor* (Op. 3) played by the Munich Music Academy to an enthusiastic audience in the same year. At eighteen, he wrote a suite for winds which received the accolade of a commission for another work of the kind from Hans von Bülow, leader of the ducal Orchestra of Meiningen and the outstanding conductor of the day. Trained by Bülow, the

Meiningen was the jewel of German orchestras, whose members learned their parts by heart and played standing up like soloists. Strauss wrote a *Serenade for Thirteen Winds* which Bülow invited him to conduct at a matinee concert without a rehearsal. The twenty-year-old composer led the performance "in a state of slight coma," having never conducted in public before. Becoming Bülow's protégé, he appeared with him as solo pianist in a Mozart concerto and at the age of twenty-one was appointed music director of the Meiningen, where he studied conducting under its recognized master. In composition his adored model at the time was Mozart, and Strauss's early quartets and orchestral pieces composed before he was twenty-one were works of great charm and style in the classical tradition.

The musical world of the eighties was immersed in the party politics of classical versus romantic. New works were heard less for themselves than as upholders of the one or followers of the other. Composers, critics and public revolved in a perpetual war dance around the rival totem poles of Brahms and Wagner. To his partisans Brahms, who died in 1897, was the last of the great classicists, Wagner was anti-Christ and Liszt a secondary Satan. *Lisztisch* was their last word of contempt. Wagnerians on the other hand considered Brahms stuffy and tradition-ridden and their own man a combined prophet, Messiah and Napoleon of music. Strauss, as his father's son and a disciple of Mozart, was anti-Wagner, but under Bülow became converted. Even Wagner's seduction of his wife could not dim Bülow's admiration for the seducer's operas. Strauss was affected also by the preaching of Alexander Ritter, first violinist of the Meiningen, who enjoyed extra prestige as husband of Wagner's niece and convinced Strauss that *Zukunftsmusik* (Music of the Future) belonged to the successors of Berlioz, Liszt and Wagner. "We must study Brahms," he asserted, "long enough to discover that there is nothing in him."

Strauss felt Ritter's influence "like a storm wind." It combined with the experience of a trip to Italy, whose sun and warmth acted on him as it had on Ibsen and other northerners, to inspire *Aus Italien*, his first work in a new form. It was called a "Symphonic Fantasia" of four movements which bore descriptive titles: "In the Campagna"; "Among the Ruins of Rome"; "By Sorrento's Strand"; "Scenes of Popular Life in Naples." The second movement was subtitled "Fantastic pictures of vanished splendor; feelings of melancholy and splendor in the midst of the sunny present": and was marked *allegro molto con brio,* an odd way to express melancholy but *molto con brio* was to be characteristic of Strauss.

Aus Italien picked up where Liszt and Berlioz left off. They also had experimented in narrative and descriptive music, though within traditional patterns of theme and development. These requirements sometimes stretched program music into strange shapes, as in the case of the German composer J. J. Raff, in whose *Forest Symphony*, according to one critic, the shades of evening in the finale fell three times. Strauss avoided this problem by discarding traditional patterns. He described without developing, tantalizing the listener with a series of dazzling glimpses but no resolution. The result, at the first performance of *Aus Italien*, conducted by the composer in Munich, was hisses and catcalls, "general amazement and wrath."

Refusing to be diverted from the path he had chosen, Strauss next produced an orchestral work on the theme of Macbeth, as Berlioz had done on King Lear and Liszt on Hamlet. Not the drama's events but the conflict within Macbeth's soul was his subject, expressed in the rich polyphony and fertility of musical idea which were to create his renown. Meanwhile on Bülow's resignation he had succeeded as conductor of the Meiningen Orchestra and in 1889 moved to Weimar as conductor in the post Liszt had held thirty years before. Combining classics with "madly modern" works, including Liszt's as yet unappreciated tone poems, he presented fresh and exciting programs which drew large audiences. In a discussion with a friend who declared his preference for Schumann and Brahms, Strauss replied, "Oh, they are only imitators and will not survive. Apart from Wagner there is really only one great master and that is Liszt."

At Weimar on November 11, 1889, he conducted the premiere of his own *Don Juan*. Its theme, as stated by Nicholas Lenau, author of the poem on which it was based, was not that of a "hot-blooded man eternally pursuing women," but of a man's "longing to find a woman who is to him incarnate womanhood and to enjoy in one all the women on earth, whom he cannot, as individuals, possess. Because he does not find her, although he reels from one to another, disgust at last seizes hold of him and this disgust is the Devil that fetches him."

In adopting this theme Strauss committed himself fully to the business of making music perform a non-musical function: making it describe characters, emotions, events and philosophies, which is essentially the function of literature. He was forcing instrumental music by itself, without singers or words, to do the work of opera or what Wagner called "music drama." Given the task, no one was better equipped to accomplish it. With his knowledge, gained from conducting, of the capacities of every instrument, his bursting talent and overflow of ideas, his mastery of the techniques of composition, Strauss, like a circus trainer, could make music, like a trained seal, perform dazzling miracles against nature. *Don Juan* proved an enthralling seventeen minutes of music with its snatches of amorous melody, its headlong passion, its marvelous song of melancholy by the oboe, its frenzied climax and strange end on a dissonant trumpet note of disenchantment. Its undeveloped themes, however, were disconcerting and its episodic form sacrificed musical to narrative sequence. Bülow nevertheless pronounced it an "unheard of success." Eduard Hanslick, the grand panjandrum of musical criticism who wrote for the *Neue Freie Presse* and other papers of Vienna and detested everything that was not Brahms or Schumann, denounced it as "ugly" with only shreds of melody and no development of musical idea.

The feuds of music were personified by Hanslick, who had worn out the word "ugly" on Wagner through a thousand repetitions until Wagner conferred immortality on him as the unpleasant Beckmesser in *Die Meistersinger.* Hanslick pursued Bruckner, a symphonic follower of Wagner, with such virulence that when the Emperor Franz Joseph granted Bruckner an audience and asked if there was anything he could do for him, Bruckner could only mutter, "Stop Hanslick." Strauss now emerged as another of the new breed to be scotched, and as each new work of his appeared, Hanslick and his school warmed to new degrees of invective.

But Strauss was on his way. Bülow dubbed him "Richard II" and the next year he produced a more ambitious work, *Tod und Verklärung* (Death and Transfiguration). In this a dying man in his final fever relives his life from the innocence of childhood through the struggles and frustrations of maturity to the death agony. At the end comes "the sound of heavenly spaces opening to greet him with what he had yearningly sought on earth." Based on an idea rather than on a literary text (although his mentor, Alexander Ritter, wrote a poem to fit the music *ex post facto*), it escaped the traps of the too specific and soared on great sweeping melodies supported by orchestral splendors. Strauss was twenty-five and had already outdistanced Liszt.

He continued to conduct, to encourage and perform the works of contemporaries and to compose his first opera, *Guntram,* which was rejected as imitation Wagner by a public already saturated with the real thing. No rigid partisan, Strauss conducted *Hänsel und Gretel* with as much enthusiasm as *Tristan und Isolde.* When Humperdinck, then an obscure teacher at the Frankfurt Academy, sent him the score, Strauss was delighted with it and wrote the composer, "My dear friend, you are a great master who has bestowed on our dear Germans a work which they can hardly deserve." His introduction of the opera at Weimar made Humperdinck famous overnight and rich soon afterwards.

In 1894 Strauss moved on to Munich as conductor of the Court Opera and following the death of Bülow led the Berlin Philharmonic concerts for the winter season of 1894–95. In the same year he was guest conductor at Bayreuth. "So young, so modern, yet how well he conducts *Tannhaüser,*" sighed Cosima Wagner. The summers Strauss devoted to his own compositions, working best, as he said, when the sun shone. During the concert season he appeared as guest conductor in different German cities and toured with the Berlin Philharmonic throughout Europe. In the years 1895–99 he conducted in Madrid and Barcelona, Milan, Paris, Zurich, Budapest, Brussels and Liège, Amsterdam, London and Moscow. Limitless in energy, he once conducted thirty-one concerts in thirty-one days. On the podium, making no show of extravagant gesture or muscular contortions, he used a firm, decided simple beat, a few hard angular movements and signaled for crescendo with a hasty bend of the knee joints. "He conducts with his knees," said Grieg. Tyrannical in his demands on the players, he was generous in praise of a well-performed solo no matter how short, and would step down from the podium to shake hands with the player when the piece was over. He was no longer the "shy young man with a large head of hair" whom Sibelius, then a young music student in Berlin, had seen rise from a seat in the audience to acknowledge the applause at one of the early performances of *Don Juan.* His hair was already receding and it is doubtful if he had ever been shy. Now in his early thirties and with Bülow gone he was the most renowned conductor and exciting composer in Germany.

Between 1895 and 1898 he brought out three more new works which carried the symphonic poem to more daring feats of description and more boldly original subject matter than had so far been attempted in music. The marvels of polyphonic complexity were more stunning, the unresolved discords more disturbing and the uses of music in some places seemed deliberately provocative.

Nothing so clever, so comic, so flashing and surprising as *Till Eulenspiegel's Merry Pranks* had ever been heard. The brisk twinkling motif of the horn carries the medieval folk hero, Germany's Peer Gynt, on his picaresque progress, with every kind of instrumental device portraying his adventures as he gallops through the marketplace scattering pots and pans, disguises himself as a priest, makes love, and comes to a bad end in court with a long drum roll announcing the death sentence. An impudent twitter of the clarinet voices his final defiance on the gallows and a faint trill carries off his last breath as his feet swing in air. Strauss's program notes this time were more specific: "That was an awful hobgoblin," he noted over one passage, or, "Hop! on horseback in the midst of the market women," or, "*Liebegluhend*" (Burning with Love). The Till motif, becoming familiar as it came and went in different disguises, charmed the audience. It was music full of enchanting tricks, like the performance of a superlatively witty and nimble magician. It delighted if it did not move. It expressed a bubbling imagination and unsurpassed skill, though not of course to Hanslick, who, using the favorite censure of outraged orthodoxy, pronounced it "the product of decadence."

For his next subject Strauss moved to the core of his time. By 1896, the world had discovered Friedrich Nietzsche. Living in solitude, disillusionment and chronic drug-blurred battle against insomnia, this other German had produced a body of work around the central idea of the Superman, which was to reverberate down the corridors of his country's life. Responding early to its influence, Strauss determined to make *Also Sprach Zarathustra* the subject of a tone poem.

Nietzsche's alluring concept of "rule by the best," of a new aristocracy which would lead humanity to a higher plane, of man rising to superior fulfillment to become *Übermensch*, seduced the imagination of Europe. It stirred both the yearning hope of human progress as well as the beginning disillusionment with democracy. Nietzsche rejected the democratic idea of equal rights for all men as hampering natural leaders from realizing their full capacities. Where Lord Salisbury had feared democracy as leading to political, and Charles Eliot Norton to cultural, debasement, Nietzsche saw it as a ball and chain holding man back from his highest attainment. He saw the dominant weight of mass tastes, opinions and moral prejudices as a "slave morality." Mankind's leaders should live by a "master morality" above common concepts of good and evil. The goal of human evolution was the *Übermensch,* the higher man, the "artist-genius" who would be to ordinary man as ordinary man was to the monkey.

Through *Also Sprach Zarathustra* and its sequels, *Beyond Good and Evil, The Will to Power* and the final *Ecce Homo,* Nietzsche roamed wildly. His ideas rolled and billowed like storm clouds, beautifully and dangerously. He preached Yes to the promptings of energy as good *per se*, regardless of conflict with conventional morality. Law and religion which discouraged such promptings frustrated man's progress. Christianity was a sop for the weak, the meek and the poor. The Superman had no need of God but was a law unto himself; his task was self-fulfillment not self-denial; he shook off the chains of tradition and history as the intolerable burden of the past. Nietzsche stated his credo, not in logical declarative language, but in a kind of prose poetry like the Psalms, meandering and obscure, full of mountain tops and sunrises, the singing of birds and dancing of girls, perorations to Will, Joy and Eternity and a thousand colored metaphors and symbols carrying Zarathustra on his soul's quest toward the goals of humankind.

When he published in the eighties no one listened. Despising the Germans for their failure to appreciate his work, Nietzsche drifted to France, Italy and Switzerland, working himself up, as Georg Brandes said, "to a positive horror of his countrymen." It was a foreigner, Brandes, a Dane and a Jew, who discovered him and whose articles on him, translated and published in the *Deutsche Rundschau* in 1890 introduced him to Germany and began the spread of his fame. By this time Nietzsche was mad and Max Nordau, the author of *Degeneration*, discovering this, naturally seized on him as a prime example of his case and lavished on him some of his most excoriating pages. Since Nordau's book was translated and read all over Europe and in the United States, it helped to make Nietzsche known. He was lauded as a seer, denounced as an Anarchist, examined and discussed by the reviews, English and French as well as German. His aphorisms were quoted as verse titles and chapter headings, he became the subject of doctoral dissertations, the model of a train of imitators, the focus of a whole literature of adulation and attack. Because of his abuse of the Germans as vulgar, materialist and philistine, he was particularly welcomed in France, but this did not prevent his becoming a cult in his native land. The sap was rising in Germany and Germans responded eagerly to Nietzsche's theory of the rights of the strong over the weak. In his writings these were hedged about with a vast body of poetic suggestion and exploration, but taken crudely as positive precepts they became to his countrymen both directive and justification. By 1897 the "Nietzsche Cult" was an accepted phrase. In a bedroom in Weimar a man leaning against a pillow, staring at an alien world out of sad lost eyes, had bewitched his age.

To the "artist-geniuses" of real life *Zarathustra* was irresistible. In Paris when a friend read passages of it to the peasant-born sculptor Rodin, one of the great movers of art forms of his time, he became so interested that he returned every evening until the whole book had been read aloud. At the end, after a long silence, he said, "What a subject to put into bronze!" Under the same thrall Strauss saw the subject in music and in fact Nietzsche himself had written that the whole of *Zarathustra* "might be considered as music." It was not Strauss's intention to set Nietzsche's text to music but, modestly, "to convey musically an idea of the development of the human race from its origin through the various phases of evolution, religious as well as scientific, up to Nietzsche's idea of the *Übermensch*." The whole was to be his "homage to the genius of Nietzsche."

When it became known that Germany's most advanced composer was at work on a tone poem inspired by Germany's most advanced philosopher, admirers grew nervous and enemies sharpened their pens. The finished piece, composed over a period of seven months in 1896 and scored for thirty-one woodwinds and brasses, timpani, bass drum, cymbals, triangle, glockenspiel, two harps and organ beside the usual strings, took thirty-three minutes' playing time, almost twice as long as *Till*, and was performed under the composer's baton within three months of its completion. Trumpets sounded the opening, swelling into an immense orchestral paean by the whole ensemble which seemed to depict less the sunrise stated in the program notes than the creation of the world. Its magnificence was breathtaking. The end came with twelve strokes of a low bell gradually dying away to a pianissimo trembling of strings and winds and ending in the famous "enigma" of a B major chord in the treble register against a dark mysterious C in the bass. In between there was again the Strauss wizardry of polyphonic effect and enough musical ideas for a dozen pieces: "Science" was expressed by a fugue containing the twelve tones of the chromatic scale and the Dance theme of girls in a meadow, introduced by high flutes in a halting waltz rhythm, seemed to catch all the joy and freshness of a green world. It was, however, more Viennese than Bacchic and somehow cheapened by bells and triangles. Three days after the premiere *Zarathustra* was performed again in Berlin and within the year in all the major German cities as well as in Paris, Chicago and New York, evoking from critics new excesses of both savagery and eulogy. To Hanslick it was "tortured and repulsive," to the American James Huneker "dangerously sublime," to the eminent musicologist Richard Batka "a milestone in modern musical history" and Strauss "pre-eminently the composer of our time."

In Germany because of the plethora of performances, with a festival every week and continuing operas, concerts, choral societies and chamber music, success was almost too easy; orchestras were ready to grasp a composition the instant it was finished. *"There is too much music in Germany,"* wrote Romain Rolland in italics. As an observer deeply interested both in music and in Germany, he explained: "This is not a paradox. There is no worse misfortune for art than a superabundance of it." Germany, Rolland thought (not without French bias), "has let loose a flood of music and is drowning in it," a situation which did not leave Strauss unaffected. Early prominence and now pre-eminence in his field and confident mastery of his medium afflicted him with a desire to dazzle, and in his next composition, *Don Quixote*, he let his affinity for realism run unreined.

Realism was a German passion. Brünhilde at Bayreuth was always accompanied by a live horse which, affected by equine stage fright or the galloping music of the Valkyrie, invariably misbehaved in the middle of the stage to the relish of the German audience if not of visiting foreigners. The painter Philip Ernst, father of Max Ernst, when painting a picture of his garden omitted a tree which spoiled the composition and then, overcome with remorse at this offence against realism, cut down the tree. When Strauss used a wind machine in *Don Quixote* to represent the turning sails of the windmills, people could not be blamed for wondering if this were not carrying literalism to inartistic excess. His muted brasses representing the bleating of sheep aroused the critics' scorn, although it could not be denied that he conveyed with extraordinary skill not only the sound of bleating but a sense, almost a view, of the crowded mass of animals moving and shoving against each other.

The critics' blasts only added to Strauss's notoriety and drew greater crowds to his concerts. At thirty-four, admitted the English critic Ernest Newman, he was "the most talked of musician in the world." Although the Kaiser disapproved of his music, the German capital could not afford to do without him. Six months after the premiere of *Don Quixote* he was offered and accepted the conductorship of the Berlin Royal Opera.

Berlin meant Prussia, the natural enemy of Munich and Bavaria. The North German regarded the South German as easy-going and self-indulgent, a sentimentalist who tended to be deplorably democratic, even liberal. In his turn, the South German regarded the North German as an arrogant bully with bad manners and an insolent stare who was politically reactionary and aggressively preoccupied with business.

Architecturally, Berlin, Europe's third largest city, was new and not beautiful. It belonged in style to what in America was called the Gilded Age. Its main public buildings, streets and squares, built or rebuilt since 1870 to house suitably the new national grandeur, were heavily pretentious and florid with gilding. Unter den Linden, a mile long with a double avenue of trees, was laid out with obvious intent to be the biggest and most beautiful boulevard in Europe. It ended naturally in an Arch of Triumph at the Brandenburg Gate. The gate led in turn to the famous

Sieges Allee in the Tiergarten, with its glittering marble rows of helmeted Hohenzollerns in triumphant attitudes. When the statues were raised at the Kaiser's direction, Max Liebermann, who had a studio overlooking the Tiergarten, lamented, "All I can do is to wear blue goggles but it is a life sentence." The imposing Reichstag building was of maximum size to make up for its minimum powers. Along the Leipzigerstrasse and Friedrichstrasse, department stores and the head offices of banks and mercantile houses bulged with the rich excitement of business that was growing daily. The city was spotlessly clean and the population so orderly that a Berlin landlady's bill included three pfennings for sewing on a trouser button and twenty for removing an inkstain. Police were efficient, though an English visitor found them "extremely rough and even brutal." The lure of vice was aggressively flaunted, food was uninteresting, ladies unfashionable. Prussian thrift stifled elegance. Berlin women of the middle class wore homemade clothes with plaid blouses, muddy-brown skirts, sack coats like traveling rugs, square-toed boots and nondescript hats that went with everything and matched nothing. They had stout figures, raw complexions and wore their hair pulled back and pinned in a braided coil.

Society, owing to the lack of intercourse between its rigidly maintained categories, was stiff and dull. Unless ennobled by a *von,* businessmen, merchants, professional men, literary and artistic people were not *hoffähig,* that is, not received at court and did not mix socially with the nobility. Nor did they mix among each other. Every German belonged to a *Kreis*, or circle of his own kind whose edges were not allowed to overlap those of the next one. The wife of a Herr Geheimrat or Herr Doktor did not speak to the wife of a tradesman, nor she to the wife of an artisan. To congregate or entertain or marry outside of *Kreis* borders invited disorder, the thing Germans feared most. Perhaps to compensate for social monotony, some Germans, according to one report, ate seven meals a day.

Since the unification of Germany had been accomplished under the leadership of Prussia, the ruling caste was drawn from the landowning Junkers, or Prussian nobility, who were numerous, poor and backward. Looked down on by the Catholic nobility of Württemberg and Bavaria as coarse, tasteless and unfitted for social leadership, the Junkers made up in assertiveness what they lacked in education. They dominated the Army, which in Germany dominated the State, and in the wake of Bismarck, their greatest exponent, filled most of the government offices though not the business life of the capital, which was grasping and intense. Though an anti-commercial class, they were its willing agents and their Government was the most frankly commercial in Europe. The Kaiser, who admired money, included in his circle the wealthier and more cosmopolitan non-Prussian nobility. Court life was notable for minute rules of behavior and immense state dinners accompanied by very loud music. Jews, unless converted, were not received, with the occasional exception of a Court Jew, like the Kaiser's friend Albert Ballin. Although the Jews numbered about one per cent of the population, anti-Semitism was fashionable, stimulated by their rapid progress in science and the arts, business and the professions after legal emancipation was confirmed for the Empire in 1871. Despite the emancipation, however, professing Jews were excluded from political, military and academic posts and from the ranks of the *von*, an exclusion which, fortunately for Germany, did not make them feel any less devotedly German. Bleichroder, the banker who gave Bismarck the necessary credit for the Franco-Prussian War; Ballin, the developer of maritime trade; Emil Rathenau, founder of the Allgemeine Elektrizitäts-Gesellschaft, which electrified Germany; Fritz Haber, discoverer of the process for fixing nitrogen from the air, which made Germany independent of imported sources of nitrogen for explosives, were all born Jews and among them were responsible for a major proportion of Germany's booming energies. The German ruling class was likewise supported by an intensely industrious middle and lower class who applied themselves earnestly and worked incessantly, taking few holidays. They were better educated on the whole than those of other countries. Prussia had enforced full-time school attendance for children from seven to fourteen since the 1820's and by the nineties had two and a half times as many university students in proportion to the population as England.

The sovereign who ruled over this thriving people was busy and dynamic like them, but more restless than thorough. He was into everything and alert to everything, sometimes with useful results. When the Barnum and Bailey Circus played Germany in 1901, the Kaiser, hearing about the remarkable speed with which trains were loaded, sent officers to observe the method. They learned that instead of loading heavy equipment separately on each freight car from the side, the circus people laid connecting iron treads through the whole length of the train on which all equipment, loaded from one end, could be rolled straight through. By this means three trains, of twenty-two cars each, could be loaded in an hour. The circus technique promptly went to feed the insatiable appetite for speed of the German mobilization system. The Kaiser's observers also noted the advantages of the great circus cooking wagons over stationary field kitchens, and adopted them for the Army so that meals could be cooked on the move.

The Kaiser took immense care always to wear appropriate uniform for every occasion. When the Moscow Art Theatre played Berlin, he attended the performance in Russian uniform. He liked to arrange military pageants and festivals, especially the annual spring and autumn parades of the Berlin garrison on the huge Tempelhof Field, where formations of 50,000 troops, equivalent to several divisions, could maneuver. He felt himself no less an authority on the arts, on which he held decided if not advanced views. When Gerhart Hauptmann, author of *The Weavers*, a gloomy working-class drama, was designated by the judges to receive the Schiller Prize in 1896, the Kaiser awarded it instead to Ernst von Wildenbruch, a favorite of his own who produced historical dramas in the style of *William Tell*. When the Rhodes scholarships were established, the Kaiser nominated Germany's candidates, "vulgar rich people," according to a member of Balliol, "who don't have a good effect at all." One shot a deer in Magdalen College park and had to be recalled by the embarrassed monarch's order. The Kaiser liked to think of himself, as he explained in his speech dedicating the Sieges Allee in 1901, as an "art-loving prince . . . around whom artists could gather" and in whose reign the arts could flourish as in classical times "in the direct intercourse of the employer with the artist." As the employer in this case, he had given to the sculptors of the statues "clear and intelligible tasks" and "ordered and defined" their work but thereafter left them free to carry out his ideas. He could now take pride in the results, which were "untainted by so-called modern tendencies."

Art, he announced, should represent the Ideal. "To us Germans great ideals, lost to other peoples, have become permanent possessions" which "only the German people" can preserve. He cited the educational effect of art upon the lower classes, who after a hard working day could be lifted out of themselves by contemplation of beauty and the Ideal. But, he sternly warned, "when art descends into the gutter as so often nowadays, choosing to represent misery as even more unlovely than it is already," then art "sins against the German people." As the country's ruler he felt deeply hurt when the masters of art "do not with sufficient energy oppose such tendencies."

The theatre too, he explained in 1898, should contribute to culture of the soul, elevate morals and "inculcate respect for the highest traditions of our German Fatherland." So that the Royal Theatre, which he invariably referred to as "my theatre," should perform this function, he arranged a series of his favorite historical dramas for working-class attendance at suitable prices. He was a stickler for accuracy of detail in scenery and costumes and, for a ballet-pantomime on Sardanapalus, ransacked the museums of the world for information on Assyrian chariots.

He liked to attend and even personally direct rehearsals at the Royal Opera and Royal Theatre. Driving up in his Imperial black and yellow motorcar, he would establish himself at a big business-like table in the auditorium, furnished with a pile of paper and array of pencils. An aide in uniform stood alongside and held up his hand whenever the Kaiser signed to him, whereupon the performance halted, the Kaiser with gestures explained what improvements he wanted, and the actors tried again. He referred to the actors as "*meine Schauspieler*," and once when one of them, Max Pohl, was suddenly taken ill, he said to an acquaintance, "Fancy, my Pohl had a seizure yesterday." The acquaintance, thinking he meant a pet dog who had had a fit, commiserated, "Ach, the poor brute."

In music the Kaiser's tastes were naturally conservative. He liked Bach, the greatest of all, and Handel. As regards opera, to which he was devoted if it was German, he would say, "Gluck is the man for me; Wagner is too noisy." At performances he stayed to the end and frequently commanded concerts at the Palace, whose programs he arranged himself and whose rehearsals he attended, expecting them to have been rehearsed previously and everything to run smoothly. On a trip to Norway he summoned Grieg to an audience at the German Legation and having assembled an orchestra of forty players, placed two chairs in front for himself and the composer, who was requested to conduct the *Peer Gynt Suite*. During the music the Kaiser continually corrected the composer's tempi and expression and swayed his body in "oriental movements" in time to Anitra's dance which "quite electrified him." Next day the whole performance was repeated by a full orchestra on board the Imperial yacht, *Hohenzollern*.

Admiration for the Kaiser during the early part of his reign was a national cult. After the prolonged rule of his grandfather, Wilhelm I, followed by the painful three months' reign of a dying man, the advent of a young and vigorous monarch who obviously relished his role and played up to the glamour of a king was welcomed by the nation. His flashing eye and martial attitudes, his heroic poses enhanced by all that brilliant dress and stirring music could add, thrilled his subjects. Young men went to the court hairdresser to have their moustaches turned up in points by a special curling device; officers and bureaucrats practiced flashing their eyes; employers addressed their workers in the Kaiser's most dynamic style, as did Diederich, title character of Heinrich Mann's harsh satire of Wilhelmine Germany, *Der Unterthan* (The Loyal Subject): "I have taken the rudder into my own hands," he says on inheriting the family factory. "My course is set straight and I am guiding you to glorious times. Those who wish to help me are heartily welcome; whoever opposes me I will smash. There is only one master here and I am he. I am responsible only to God and my own conscience. You can always count on my fatherly benevolence but revolutionary sentiments will be shattered against my unbending will." The workers stare at him dumb with amazement and his assembled family with awe and respect.

The first half of the Kaiser's reign which began in 1888 coincided with the first flush of the Nietzschean cult. The monarch's ceaseless activity in every kind of endeavor made him seem to be the universal man, as if, rightfully in Germany, crowning the century of her greatest development, *Übermensch* had appeared, where else but at the head of the nation. Hero-worship was the natural consequence. Diederich in the novel sees the Kaiser for the first time at the head of a mounted squadron as he rides out with a face of "stony seriousness" to meet a workers' demonstration at the Brandenburger Tor. Transported by loyalty, the workers, who have been shouting "Bread! Work!" now wave their hats and cry, "Follow him! Follow the Emperor!" Running alongside, Diederich stumbles and sits down violently in a puddle with his legs in the air, splashed with muddy water. The Kaiser, catching sight of him, slaps his thigh and says to his aide with a laugh, "There's a royalist for you; there's a loyal subject!" Diederich stares after him "from the depths of his puddle, open-mouthed."

In Diederich, who is always brutalizing someone beneath him while sucking up to someone above him, Mann savagely portrayed one aspect of his countrymen—the servility which was the other side of the bully. The banker Edgar Speyer, returning to his birthplace in Frankfurt-am-Main in 1886 after twenty-seven years in England, found that three victorious wars and the establishment of Empire had created a changed atmosphere in Germany that was "intolerable" to him. German nationalism had replaced German liberalism. Great prosperity and self-satisfaction acted, it seemed to him, like a narcotic on the people, leaving them content to forego their liberty under a rampant militarism and a servility to Army and Kaiser that were "unbelievable." University professors who in his youth had been leaders of liberalism "now kowtowed to the authorities in the most servile manner." Oppressed, Speyer gave up after five years and returned to England.

What Speyer observed, Mommsen attempted to explain. "Bismarck has broken the nation's backbone," he wrote in 1886. "The injury done

by the Bismarck era is infinitely greater than its benefits. . . . The subjugation of the German personality, of the German mind, was a misfortune that cannot be undone." What Mommsen failed to say was that
Bismarck could not have succeeded against the German grain.

In the nineties, as a convinced believer in *Übermensch*, Strauss shared
the general admiration for the Kaiser. Personal experience as conductor
of the Berlin Royal Opera modified it. After conducting a performance
of Weber's tuneful *Der Freischütz*, one of the Kaiser's favorites, he was
summoned to the Imperial presence. "So, you are another of these modern
composers," stated the Kaiser. Strauss bowed. Mentioning a contemporary,
Schillings, whose work he had heard, the Kaiser said, "It was detestable;
there isn't an ounce of melody." Strauss bowed and suggested there was
melody but often hidden behind the polyphony. The Kaiser frowned and
pronounced, "You are one of the worst." Strauss this time merely bowed.
"All modern music is worthless," repeated the royal critic, "there isn't
an ounce of melody in it." Strauss bowed. "I prefer *Freischütz*," stated
the Kaiser firmly. Strauss deferred. "Your Majesty, I also prefer *Freischütz*," he replied.

If the Kaiser was not the hero he had supposed, Strauss was not long
in finding a better one—himself. This seemed a natural subject for his next
major work, unbashfully entitled *Ein Heldenleben* (A Hero's Life). Since
Aus Italien his subjects had never been moods or pictures, sunken cathedrals or pastoral scenes, but always Man: Man in struggle and search,
seeking the meaning of existence, contending against his enemies and
against his own passions, engaged in the three great adventures: battle,
love and death. Macbeth, Don Juan, the nameless hero of *Tod und Verklärung*. Till, Zarathustra, Don Quixote, were all voyagers on the soul's
journey. A portrait of the artist now joined their company.

Strauss's personal experience of the two first of the three great
adventures had been adequate if not epic. He had had battles with critics
which left wounds, and in 1894 he had married. Pauline de Ahna,
whom he met when he was twenty-three, was the daughter of a retired
General and amateur baritone who gave local recitals of Wagnerian excerpts. Following his lead, the daughter had studied singing at the Munich
Academy but had made little progress professionally until Strauss fell in
love with her and combined instruction with courtship so effectively that
in two years he introduced her to the Weimar Opera in leading soprano
roles. She sang Elsa in *Lohengrin,* Pamina in *The Magic Flute,* Beethoven's
Fidelio and the heroine of Strauss's own opera *Guntram*. Once, when re-

hearsing Elisabeth in *Tannhäuser,* she fell into an argument with him over tempo, and shrieking "frightful insults," threw the score at his head and rushed off to her dressing room. Strauss followed and members of the orchestra listened in awe to sounds of feminine rage audible through the closed door, followed by prolonged silence. Wondering which of the two, conductor or prima donna, might have killed the other, a delegation of trembling players knocked on the door and when Strauss opened it the spokesman stammered that he and his colleagues, shocked by the soprano's behavior, felt they owed it to the honored Herr Kapellmeister to refuse in future to play in any opera in which she had a role. "That distresses me," Strauss replied, smiling, "as I have just become engaged to Fräulein de Ahna."

The pattern of this occasion was retained in marriage. The wife shrieked, the husband smiled and evidently enjoyed being bullied. At parties Frau Strauss did not permit him to dance with other ladies. At home she practiced housewifery with "ruthless fanaticism," requiring her husband to wipe his feet on three different doormats before entering his own house. Every guest of no matter what age or rank was greeted by the order, "Wipe your feet." Floors were as clean as table tops and servants who failed to leave the contents of linen closets in mathematically perfect rows were pursued by the inevitable shrieks of wrath. Enthusiastically submitting to, as well as inflicting, punishment, Frau Strauss engaged the daily services of a masseuse of the violent school during whose visits Strauss was obliged to go for a walk to avoid hearing the tortured screams of his wife. She bore him one child, a son, Franz, born in 1897, who at once expressed the family tradition of *molto con brio* by "screaming like hell," according to a proud report to the child's grandparents.

When to her husband's accompaniment Frau Strauss sang his songs, which usually ended with a long coda on the piano, she flourished a large chiffon handkerchief which she would fling down with a gesture at the end to keep the audience's eyes on her instead of on the pianist. To guests she would explain in detail, while Strauss listened with an indulgent smile, how and why her marriage was a shocking *mésalliance*. She should have married that dashing young Hussar; now she was tied to a man whose music was not even comparable to Massenet's. During a visit to London when Strauss conducted *Heldenleben* and a toast was proposed in his honor at a dinner at the Speyers', his wife excitedly interrupted, "No, no!"—pointing to herself—"no, no! to Strauss *de Ahna*." Strauss merely laughed and seemed to an observer to enjoy his wife's claim of precedence.

She was responsible for his orderly habits. His worktable was a model of neatness, with sketches and notebooks arranged, filed and indexed as scrupulously as the records of a law firm. His handwriting was exquisitely clear and his scores "miracles of calligraphy," with hardly an erasure or correction. His songs might be dashed off at odd moments, sometimes during the intervals of concerts or operas when he was conducting, but his longer pieces were composed only at his summer home, first at Marquardstein in Upper Bavaria, later at his second home near Garmisch. Here in his studio he worked regularly from breakfast to lunch and often, or so he told an interviewer, through the afternoon and evening until one or two o'clock in the morning. He enjoyed writing his incredibly intricate scores, often so complicated in their excessive subdivision of groups and interweaving of melodies that the theme was beyond the reach of the listener's ear. Discernible to the eye of an expert score-reader who would marvel at the mathematical ingenuity of the scheme, such music was called *Augenmusik* (eye music) by the Germans. When complimented on his skill Strauss said it was nothing compared to that of a new young man in Vienna, Arnold Schönberg, who required sixty-five staves for his scores and had to have his music paper specially printed. Strauss's own facility was such that he said to a visitor, "Go right on and talk for I can write this score and talk at the same time." A symphonic poem took him three or four months, with scoring usually completed in Berlin between rehearsals and conducting engagements.

Visitors at the summer home were met by arrangements which exhibited a talent for organization on the part of Frau Strauss not inferior to that of the late Field Marshal von Moltke. A speaking tube was fixed to the gate under a sign telling the visitor to ring a bell and then put his ear to the tube. A voice over the tube demanded his name and if found acceptable, informed him the gate was now unlocked. Another sign instructed him how to open it and to be sure to close it behind him.

Frau Strauss did not permit dawdling. If her husband should be found on occasion wandering aimlessly around the house, she would command, *"Richard, jetzt gehst componieren!"* (Go ahead and compose!), and he would obey. If he worked too hard she would say, "Richard, put down that pencil!" and he would put it down. When he conducted the first performance in Vienna of his second opera, *Feuersnot*, Frau Strauss attended in the box of the Austrian conductor-composer Gustav Mahler and fumed throughout, as Frau Mahler recalled: "Nobody could like this trash; we were liars to pretend, knowing as well as she did that there wasn't an original note in it. Everything was stolen from Wagner and a dozen others better than her husband." The Mahlers sat in silent embarrassment not daring to agree, for "this shrew was quite capable of twisting the words in our mouths and suddenly screaming that we had made all those comments." After enthusiastic applause and many curtain calls, Strauss, beaming, came to the box and asked, "Well, *Pauksel*, what do you think of my success?"

"You thief!" she screamed. "You have the nerve to show yourself? I'm not going with you. You're rotten." Hurriedly pushed into Mahler's office, she continued her berating behind closed doors until Strauss stumbled out followed by his mate who announced in awful tones that she was returning to the hotel and "I sleep alone tonight."

"Can't I walk with you at least?" Strauss begged humbly.

"All right—ten steps behind me!" and she stalked off followed by the hero of the evening at a respectful distance. Later, looking subdued and exhausted, he rejoined the Mahlers for a late supper and spent the remainder of the evening with pencil and paper figuring out the royalties in the event of a major or minor success. Making money interested him as much as any aspect of his profession.

Strauss composed *Ein Heldenleben* in the summer of 1898, describing it as "a largish tone poem . . . with lots of horns, always expressive of the heroic." When finished it played for forty minutes, longer than any of his previous works. Artists had often portrayed themselves before, but Strauss, reflecting the national mood, was probably the first to name his self-portrait a Hero. He conducted the premiere himself on March 3, 1899, which, considering the provocative title, the nature of the music and the program notes, displayed considerable bravado. *Heldenleben* was divided into six sections, dealing with "The Hero," his "Adversaries," his "Consort," his "Battle," his "Works of Peace" and finally his "Escape from the World and Fulfillment of Life." In form it was an expanded sonata on a vast scale with recognizable statements of theme, development and recapitulation. After the Hero is proclaimed by the horns in a proud theme rising to fortissimo, the woodwinds introduce the Adversaries in busy, sniggering music that as plainly says "critics" as the bleating brasses in *Don Quixote* said "sheep." The Consort is played by solo violin in a series of cadenzas, alternately seductive and shrewish, with outspoken not to say painfully frank marks of expression on the score, among them, *"Heuchlerisch schmachtend"* (Hypocritically gushing), plus "frivolously," "haughtily," "affectionately," and at the last, in a passionate and moving love duet, "tenderly and lovingly." Meanwhile three trumpeters have tiptoed off stage and suddenly from a distance sound the call to arms. With fiercely scurrying strings, rattling kettledrums, fanfares of brasses and thunder of bass drums, the battle rages in a confused crescendo of noise that, not unlike real war, sounds as if all the generals had blundered. To the ears of 1899 it sounded "hideous." Through the turmoil the Hero's theme returns triumphantly. His Works of Peace, making the auto-biographical point unmistakable, are themes from the composer's earlier works. The Hero's final apotheosis is accomplished to muted solemn music which in later program notes Strauss designated as "funeral rites with flags and laurel wreaths lowered on a hero's grave."

Listening to the second performance at Cologne a few weeks later, Romain Rolland, fresh from his own exhilarating battle at the opening of *Les Loups*, was transported with excitement. Although some auditors hissed and some members of the orchestra even laughed at the music, "I clenched my teeth and trembled and my heart saluted the young Siegfried resurrected." In the "tremendous din and uproar" of the battle music, Rolland heard "the storming of towns, the terrible charge of cavalry which makes the earth tremble and our hearts beat." He thought it "the most splendid battle that has ever been painted in music." There were gulfs in which the musical idea disappeared for a time but emerged again, sometimes mediocre in melodic sentiment but grand in "harmonic and rhythmic invention and orchestral brilliance." Strauss seemed to Rolland to express a will "heroic, dominating, eager and powerful to a sublime degree." Touched too by the Nietzschean spirit, Rolland found this the reason why Strauss "is noble and at the present quite unique. One feels in him the force that has dominion over men." In the midst of admiration, however, Rolland also felt French and could not resist drawing political lessons. Now that Strauss, he decided, like Germany, had "proved his power by victory, his pride knows no limit." In him as a man "of vital energy, morbidly overexcited, unbalanced but controlled by an effort of will power," the Frenchman saw reflected the face of Germany. Neverthe-less Rolland became his friend and celebrator.

He had met Strauss for the first time eight years before in Bayreuth and again in January, 1899, when Strauss conducted *Zarathustra* in Paris. It was the Dionysus of Nietzsche let loose. "Aha!" Rolland wrote then, "Germany as the All-Powerful will not keep her balance for long. Nietzsche, Strauss, the Kaiser—giddiness blows through her brain. Neroism is in the air!" Rolland thought he could detect in the reiterated theme of Disgust in the tone poems and in the deaths that concluded them, a German "sickness hidden beneath the strength and military tautness." He heard it again in *Heldenleben*.

When on this occasion he called on Strauss at his apartment in Charlottenburg, Berlin's fashionable suburb, he found him more Bavarian than Nietzschean, with "a certain humorous buffoonery, paradoxical and satirical like that of Till Eulenspiegel." Like Till he delighted to scandalize the philistines. He alternated between energy and bouts of "laziness, softness and ironic indifference." Though cordial and well-behaved toward Rolland, he could be short with others, scarcely listening to what was said to him and occasionally muttering, *"Was? Ach, so so."* He behaved badly at table, sitting with his legs crossed at the side, holding his plate under his chin to eat and stuffing himself with sweets. In the drawing room he might lie down on a sofa, punching the cushions with his fists, and "insolently indifferent to those around him," fall asleep with his eyes open.

It was difficult to decide whether he was Till or Superman. In an article for the *Revue de Paris* Rolland presented him as "the artist-type of this new Germany, the reflection of a heroic pride close to delirium, of a Nietzschean egoism which preaches the cult of force and disdain for weakness." But he had to admit the picture was overdrawn. Rolland suffered from the same difficulty as Matthew Arnold's niece in Max Beerbohm's cartoon who was forced to ask, "Why, Uncle Matthew, oh why, will you not be always wholly serious?" Strauss would not live up to his image either and was quite prepared to admit it. "You're right," he wrote to Rolland. "I'm no hero; I haven't got the necessary strength; I'm not made for battle. . . . I don't want to make the effort. At the moment all I want is to make sweet and happy music. No more heroics." The fact was that in the surrounding Nietzschean ethos, *Heldenleben* had seemed like the thing to do; it reflected the national mood more than his own.

Strauss was a string plucked by the *Zeitgeist*. Although he had never known any but the most comfortable bourgeois circumstances, he sensed and expressed the revolutionary rumble of the working class in two of his finest songs so effectively that one, "Der Arbeitsmann" (The Workingman) became an anthem of the Socialist party. Another, "Das Lied des Steinklopfers" (Song of the Stonecutter), was his own favorite among his songs. When these were sung by Germany's leading concert baritone, Ludwig Wüllner, with the composer at the piano, they had such dramatic power that "hearing these grim defiant sounds," wrote a critic, "was like hearing the Marseillaise of tomorrow." Of another of his songs for the male voice, the "Nächtlicher Gesang" (Night Song), it was said that it could "make one shudder in broad daylight."

In *Heldenleben*, however, convinced admirers began to detect evidence of a deep-seated flaw in the composer. Ernest Newman believed Strauss had enriched music with more new ideas than anyone since Wagner and had "put into music a greater energy, a greater stress of feeling and a greater weight of thinking than any other composer of the day." Yet he did not seem able to restrain an unworthy desire to "stagger humanity." His technical facility and command over ideas was such that he could do anything he wanted and there was no limit to his inventiveness, but he could not keep it within bounds. Newman would willingly have left the hall during the "sniggering, snarling and grunting" of the Adversaries in *Heldenleben*, which he considered "freak" music like the sheep in *Don Quixote*. He felt a failure of taste, a streak of vulgarity in a man willing to spoil "two of the finest scores of the Nineteenth Century" with such "monstrosities" as these. Such reactions merely stimulated Strauss to further freaks as a sign of his contempt for what were claimed to be the "eternal" laws of beauty in music. The fact that he insisted on making the critics pay for their seats, causing "screams of agony" all over the Continent, did not help matters.

To the younger critics Strauss's discords and dissonances were not as distressing as his freaks. Lawrence Gilman, an American, thought the dissonance of the Battle music, like that depicting the mental confusion of Don Quixote, was "eloquent and meaningful" and quite different from that other kind achieved, as Whistler said, "by the simple expedient of sitting on the keyboard." Apart from the freaks there were enough marvels of music in Strauss's work to have put him above the sneers and carping; it was the non-musical aspect of his work—that is, the didactic realism of his program notes—which kept him in the center of critical furor. In the same spirit in which Philip Ernst, having omitted the tree from his picture, decided it must be cut down, Strauss insisted on painting the tree and then hanging a sign on it saying, "This is a tree." As a result critics leaped to take issue, as when Newman said of a trombone passage in *Zarathustra* labeled "Disgust," which followed "Delights and Passions," that "it no more suggests disgust than it does the toothache." It was no defence by his friends to insist that Strauss wanted his music to be listened to as music and that he added the program notes only under the urgent pressure of colleagues and publishers. An artist certain of his standards would not have made the concession and in any case the literary labels were in his mind and scribbled on his scores when he composed.

In France Claude Debussy, too, was writing descriptive music. Rather than literal and narrative, like that of Strauss, it was elusive and shimmering, after the manner of the Impressionists in painting and the Symbolists in poetry. The Symbolist credo was to suggest, not to name, an object. Where Strauss stated, Debussy suggested. "If people insist on wanting to understand what happens in a symphonic poem, we may as well give up writing them," he said. Literal meaning was a matter of equal unconcern to Sibelius. When asked by a friend after listening to a recording of his Fourth Symphony what it really meant, he said after a short pause, "Play the record again."

Debussy, however, admired Strauss, who was two years his junior, and acknowledged that the *Verklärung* (Transfiguration) in *Tod und Verklärung* "takes place before our very eyes." When he heard *Till Eulenspiegel* in 1903 he thought its flouting of musical laws amounted almost "to an hour of music in a lunatic asylum. . . . You do not know whether to roar with laughter or groan with pain and you are filled with wonder when you find anything in its customary place." Nevertheless he thought it a work of "genius" and was awed by its "amazing orchestral assurance" and the "mad rhythm that sweeps us along from beginning to end and forces us to share in the hero's pranks." What impressed him most about *Heldenleben*, which he also heard in 1903, was its "cyclonic energy." The listener is no longer master of his emotions: "I say again that it is impossible to withstand his irresistible domination." Debussy's own orchestral prelude, *L'Après-midi d'un Faune,* based on Mallarmé's poem, and his *Nocturnes* for orchestra, which appeared in the nineties, led Strauss to return the compliment. Debussy was "a remarkable and altogether unique genius," he said, "within his own limited domain."

Strauss was always rather surprised when someone else produced work of high quality. "I had no idea that anyone except myself was capable of writing such good music as this," he remarked "charmingly and characteristically" to Beecham on hearing a work of Delius. He never listened to Puccini and did not know *Manon* from *Tosca,* or *Butterfly* from *Bohème*, although Puccini's works were exactly contemporary with his own. Italian opera was not highly regarded in Germany. He was generous, however, in performing the works of other contemporaries. Unable to conduct modern music at the Berlin Royal Opera while the Kaiser's taste held sway, he founded an orchestra of his own, the Tonkünstler, to encourage "progressive principles" in music. Subsidized by private patrons, the Tonkünstler played all Liszt's tone poems in chronological order as well as Strauss's own works and introduced to Berlin performances of Tchaikovsky, Bruckner, Hugo Wolf, Elgar and, if not Debussy, at least his predecessors, Charpentier and d'Indy. Once in London on a visit to the National Gallery in company with Edgar Speyer and Edward Elgar, the group stopped in front of Tintoretto's "St. George and the Dragon" while Speyer remarked, "Here we have a revolutionary who broke ground at the very end of the glorious Venetian period. Shall we say that Tintoretto was to painting what our friend Richard Strauss is today to music?" Much struck by this remark, Strauss returned to the painting on their way back through the rooms, studied it again and exclaimed, "Speyer is right. I am the Tintoretto of music!"

From this height he could afford, and did not stint, encouragement of less renowned colleagues. On hearing a performance in Düsseldorf in 1902 of Elgar's *Dream of Gerontius,* based on a poem by Cardinal Newman, Strauss proposed a toast "to the welfare and success of the first English Progressive, Meister Edward Elgar, and of the young progressive school of English composers." Such tribute from Strauss startled the musical world and aroused the usual critics' uproar which it amused him to provoke. Though disliking the terms of the compliment all England was impressed and flattered. Strauss was no less appreciative of the ultramodern Schönberg, whose experiments in atonality so impressed him that he arranged for the young composer to be given the Liszt Fellowship and appointment as Professor of Composition in the Stern Academy in Berlin. On the occasion of the premiere of Mahler's *Third Symphony* in Cologne in 1902, Strauss decided its success by going up to the platform and applauding ostentatiously. From 1900 on, as president of the Allgemeiner Deutscher Musikverein, founded by Liszt, he invited foreign composers to conduct their new works at the Society's festivals. Sibelius, whom he invited to present his *Swan of Tuonela* in 1900, found him "extraordinarily amiable." When Strauss himself took the podium at these concerts he was greeted by the orchestra with a threefold fanfare and by the audience rising to its feet.

In England and the United States his renown was large and his appearances lionized. A Strauss Festival lasting three days was held in London in 1903 at which all his works from *Aus Italien* to *Heldenleben* were played. Strauss liked the English "very much," as he once told Rolland. For one thing they made traveling comfortable in places like Egypt, so that "you can always be sure of finding clean rooms and modern conveniences." For Strauss this proved they were a superior people and, according to the Nietzschean formula, they and not the Boers should have had Germany's sympathy during the South African War. "The Boers are a barbarian people, backward, still living in the Seventeenth Century. The English are very civilized and very strong. It's a thoroughly good thing that the strong should triumph."

In London he could enjoy the hospitality of Edgar Speyer, head of the syndicate which owned Queen's Hall and manager of its orchestra, who with his wife, a professional violinist before her marriage, made their home at Grosvenor Square a center of musical and artistic society. Here he could meet Henry James or Debussy, listen to Mme Grieg sing her husband's songs and enjoy a sumptuous dinner in company with John Sargent, to whom painting was a profession but music and food a matter of love. Noticing a gypsy band which had been wandering around London playing Spanish music, Strauss proposed that it be hidden in the garden to play during one of the Speyer parties, with results that tantalized Sargent, who was torn between his dinner and the need to run to the window to discover the source of the music.

In America, Strauss's compositions had been known and played ever since Theodore Thomas, conductor of the Chicago Symphony, had performed his *Symphony in F minor* in 1884 and the German-born Emil Paur of the Boston Symphony had played *Aus Italien* in 1888. Thomas and Paur, who later moved to the New York Philharmonic, continued to play Strauss's works as they came out, and in 1904 an American premiere was arranged for his newest work, *Sinfonia Domestica*, as the feature of a Strauss Festival to be held in New York. The composer was invited to conduct the new piece as well as a subsequent concert of his works in Chicago. Thomas, a fervent admirer over twenty years, considered him at this point in his career "the greatest musician now living and one of the greatest musical pioneers of all times."

With the new wealth of American business tycoons overflowing their coffers, the United States was developing a whole new audience and source of support for music and the arts. It was a time of exuberant expenditure and large ideas. When the rector of Trinity Church in New York wanted a new pulpit, he asked the senior partner of the leading architectural firm, McKim, Mead and White, to design him something "big, broad, ample and simple but rich in the right places." When the same McKim built the Boston Public Library a plaque was put up honoring the "splendid amplitude" of his genius. Splendid amplitude was in the air. Louis Tiffany designed for himself a house with a palatial flight of stairs leading up, between walls with complete Sudanese Negro huts built into them, to a hall so vast the ceiling was invisible in the dim light. In the center of the hall a black chimney soared to infinity, four immense fireplaces blazed, each with flames of a different color, mysterious light glowed through hanging Tiffany glass lamps and an invisible organist played the prelude from *Parsifal*.

The several major American orchestras subsidized by copper kings, railroad barons and their kind provided an important extra source of concert fees and royalties. Strauss was delighted to come and the concert-going American public breathlessly awaited the "most eminent of living composers," who, they were told by *Harper's Weekly*, uttered "imaginings of overpowering significance" and touched "the margin of the sublime."

Sinfonia Domestica, it was apparent on first performance, touched the ridiculous. Although it was performed by the composer's wish without program notes so that it could be listened to "purely as music," Strauss had already told an interviewer that it illustrated "a day in my family life" in the form of a triple figure representing "Papa, Mama and Baby." At the premiere it was presented only as Introduction and Scherzo, Adagio, Double Fugue and Finale, but, as usual, the composer soon obliged with an official analysis for subsequent performances which indicated the baby in its bath, the parents' happiness, the quarrels of aunts and uncles over family resemblances—"Just like his Papa!" "Just like his Mama!"— and similar stuff. Although there was tender melody of Strauss's finest in the cradle song and love duet, the dominant impression is of thumping and screaming and raucous confusion suggesting a maddened circus. If this is German home life, German history becomes understandable. Even longer than *Heldenleben*, the work astonished and offended most listeners. "If all the sacred elephants in India were driven into the Ganges at the same moment," said a renowned but unnamed conductor to Beecham when the piece was played in London some months later, "they could not have made half as much noise as that one little Bavarian baby in its bath." Gurgling bath water and ringing alarm clock were not what Wagner had meant by "the stuff of music." The vulgarity of the new century seemed suddenly confirmed by its most eminent composer. Strauss missed the point. "I do not see why I should not compose a Symphony about myself," he told Rolland. "I find myself quite as interesting as Napoleon or Alexander."

His choice of two world conquerors was indicative. In music the German assumption of superiority was by this time beginning to annoy other peoples. "German musicians always put a German arrival on a pedestal so that they can idolise it," wrote Grieg to Delius in 1903. "Wagner is dead but they must have something to satisfy their patriotism and they would rather have ersatz than nothing at all." In 1905 at a music festival in Strasbourg, capital of formerly French, now German, Alsace, the stated purpose was to bring French and Germans together through art. In a three-day program, however, only two French works were performed, while the first day of concerts began with Weber and ended with Wagner, the second day was devoted to Brahms, Mahler and Strauss and the last day entirely to Beethoven. The selection from Wagner of the last scene from *Die Meister-singer*, in which Hans Sachs denounces foreign insincerity and frivolity, suggested to one auditor a certain "lack of courtesy."

The world's increasing irritation with Germany appeared in the eagerness with which foreign critics seized upon evidence of a decline in Strauss's inspiration. Everyone jumped on *Sinfonia Domestica*. Newman was astonished that "a composer of genius should have fallen so low" and Gilman revealed the degree to which Germany was getting on the nerves of other nations. Quoting Matthew Arnold to the effect that Teutonism tends insistently toward the "ugly and ignoble," he wrote that "only a Teuton with a Teuton's failure of tact" could have contrived *Domestica*.

The *Zeitgeist* did not call for Papa, Mama and Baby. A restlessness fermenting under the superabundant materialism was producing in artists a desire to shock; to rip and slash the thick quilt of bourgeois comfort. Attuned as always, Strauss responded. *Sinfonia Domestica* had shocked by banality, but now he felt a need to unnerve and appall and went straight from Bavarian family life to a theme of depraved and lascivious passion—*Salome*, in Oscar Wilde's version.

A drama as lush and gruesome as Wilde trying hard could make it, *Salome* was a pursuit of sensation for its own sake, an effort to produce what Baudelaire called "the phosphorescence of putrescence." The original play, written in French in 1891, went into rehearsal in London a year later with Sarah Bernhardt in the title role, but performance was banned by the Lord Chamberlain on the ground that its presentation of St. John the Baptist was sacrilege. Upon publication (with copies for the author's friends bound in "Tyrian purple and tired silver"), the play was denounced by *The Times* as "an arrangement in blood and ferocity, morbid, bizarre, repulsive and very offensive." In 1894 an English translation by Lord Alfred Douglas appeared, illustrated with luscious evil by the truest decadent of them all, Aubrey Beardsley. Three of his drawings, considered indecent by the publishers, had to be withdrawn. In 1896, when Wilde was in Reading Gaol, *Salome* was produced in Paris by the actor-manager Lugné-Poë at his Théâtre de l'Oeuvre, with himself as Herod but without Bernhardt. The quintessence of decadence was overripe and it was not a success. In Germany, however, *Salome* matched a craving for the hor-

rendous and found its place. First produced in Breslau in 1901, its real
success came in 1902 with a production by Max Reinhardt at his Kleines
Theater in Berlin, where Strauss saw it.

More a poem than a play, Wilde's *Salome* was an exercise in purple,
an orgy in words, which succeeded on paper but embarrassed on the
stage. It offered the spectacle of Salome pouring out her hot erotic pleas
to the eyes, the hair, the limbs, the body and the love of Iokanaan, of
King Herod avid for his stepdaughter, of her voluptuous dance to excite
his lust and win her ghastly desire, of the black Executioner's huge arm
rising from the pit holding the bearded bloody head of the Prophet who had
scorned her, of her necrophilic raptures addressed to the head on the
platter and her final conquest of its dead lips, of Herod's climactic order
of horror and remorse, "Kill that woman!" and of her death crushed beneath the shields of his soldiers. Performed in flesh and blood it delighted
the Berlin audience. Wilde's moonlit fantasia, in Germany, came into its
own and enjoyed a phenomenal run of two hundred performances.

The undercurrent of morbidity in Germany, which Rolland had already
noticed, grew more apparent in the first decade of the new century. It
increased in proportion as Germany's wealth and strength and arrogance
increased, as if the pressure of so much industrial success and military
power were creating an inner reaction in the form of a need to negate,
to expose the worms and passions writhing within that masterful, prosperous, well-behaved, orderly people. It was as if Bismarck had perforce
produced Krafft-Ebing. Indeed Krafft-Ebing's *Psychopathia Sexualis* which
appeared in 1886 provided a well of lurid resource on which the German
drama, then the most vigorous form of national literature, could draw.

The theatre ranked with music and opera as a German pleasure and,
beginning in the nineties, broke out in a surge of problem plays stemming
from Ibsen and in new styles of acting and experiments in stagecraft.
Proclaiming the doctrine of Realism and Naturalism, the Freie Bühne
(Independent Theatre) of Berlin, copied after the Théâtre Libre of Paris,
opened in 1889 with Ibsen's *Ghosts* followed by Hauptmann's first play,
Before Dawn. Theatres sprouted and multiplied. Society's masks were torn
off and the "beast in man," Zola's objective, was enthusiastically exposed.
Besides Ibsen, Strindberg's cruel *Miss Julie,* Tolstoy's *Powers of Darkness*,
Zola's *Thérèse Raquin,* the symbolist and neo-romantic dramas of Maeterlinck, D'Annunzio and von Hofmannsthal, the social plays of Ibsen's disciple Shaw, the worldly satires of Arthur Schnitzler of Vienna and a
proliferation of German tragedies were performed. Student stage societies revived *Oedipus Rex* and Euripides, the Modern Touring Company

took the new drama to the provinces, and a people's theatre, the Freie Volksbühne, followed by the Neue Freie Volksbühne, allied it to Socialism. In Munich, the Intimes Theater was founded in 1895 by Ernst von Wolzogen, librettist of Strauss's opera *Feuersnot*. To achieve the same intimate atmosphere for experimental plays, Reinhardt founded the Kleines Theater in 1902, where, besides *Salome,* he produced Maxim Gorky's awful look at society's dregs, *The Lower Depths.*

Tragedy was the staple of the German theatre. Social comedies with happy endings were not a German genre. German fun was confined to buffoonery, either painful or coarse. Their tragedies were not so much curative, like Ibsen's, nor compassionate, like Chekhov's, but obsessively focused on mankind's cruelty to man, on his bent toward self-destruction and on death. Death by murder, suicide or some more esoteric form resolved nearly all German drama of the nineties and early 1900's. In Hauptmann's *Hannele* the child heroine dies of neglect and abuse in an almshouse, in his *Sunken Bell* Heinrich's wife drowns herself in a lake and he drinks a poisoned goblet, in *Rose Bernd* the title character, seduced and deserted, strangles her newborn child, in *Henschel* the title character hangs himself after betraying his dead wife by marrying a tart who lets his child die of neglect, in *Michael Kramer* a sensitive son is driven to suicide by an overbearing father, a popular theme in Germany rich in such fathers. In Sudermann's *Magda* only the father's fatal stroke prevents his shooting himself and his daughter, who needless to say is illegitimately pregnant, the invariable fate of the German heroine. An endless succession of them were driven in the grip of this circumstance to hysteria, insanity, crime, prison, infanticide and suicide. In Sudermann's *Sodoms Ende,* which varies the pattern if not the end, a dissolute young artist, corrupted by the wife of a banker, drives his foster sister to suicide and dies himself of a hemorrhage. In Wedekind's *Frühlings Erwachen* (Spring's Awakening), first effort of a playwright who was to exceed all the rest, the discovery of sex by adolescents conflicting with the prurience of adults produces total catastrophe: the fourteen-year-old heroine, being with child, dies, apparently of a mismanaged abortion; the boy is expelled from school and sent to a reformatory by his parents; his friend, unable to bear life, commits suicide and reappears in a graveyard with his head under his arm in a closing scene of opaque symbolism. In the course of the action a third boy, in a scene of explicit auto-eroticism, addresses a passionate love declaration to the picture of a naked Venus which he then drops down the toilet. First produced in 1891, the play was a sensational success and in book form went into twenty-six editions.

Born in the same year as Strauss, Wedekind was a writer of satanic talent who had been an actor, journalist, circus publicity agent, singer of grisly ballads for *Überbrettl* and while on the staff of *Simplicissimus* served a term in prison for *lèse majesté*. "I have the imagination of disaster—and see life as ferocious and sinister" exactly described him, though it was Henry James who said it of himself. *Frühlings Erwachen*, if taken as a plea for sex education, at least had a social message and a quality of pity, but thereafter Wedekind saw nothing but the ferocious and sinister. In the same years in which Freud was carefully arriving at his discovery of the subconscious, Wedekind saw an awful vision of it and stripped off every covering to show it as purely malignant. From 1895 on, his plays plunged into a debauch of the vicious and perverse which seemed to have no argument but that humanity was vile. *Erdgeist* (Earth Spirit) and its sequel, *Die Büchse der Pandora* (Pandora's Box), take place in a world of pimps, crooks, harlots, blackmailers, murderers and hangmen surrounding the heroine, Lulu, who represents sensuality incarnate both heterosexual and lesbian. Her adventures proceed through brothels and dives, seduction, abortion, sadism, necrophilia and nymphomania in what a contemporary critic called "a torrent of sex foaming over jagged rocks of insanity and crime." It was sex, not creative in its primal function, but destructive, producing not life but death. Lulu's first husband dies of a stroke, her second, bedeviled by her perfidy, cuts his own throat, her third on discovering her infidelity committed with his son is killed by her. After prison, degradation and prostitution, she ends, logically, slashed to death by a Jack the Ripper in a final lethal explosion of that erotic power which Shaw, a very different playwright, was celebrating at the same time as the Life Force.

The all-pervasive influence of Nietzsche was at work. Shaw's *Man and Superman* distilled from it a philosophic idea, but the Germans took Nietzsche literally. His rejection of conventional morality, which he meant as a steppingstone to a higher ground, they embraced as a command to roam the gutter. Sudermann quoted Nietzsche's words, "Only in the savage forest of vice can new domains of knowledge be conquered." As the domain of art if not knowledge, the same forest had lured the French decadents and the aesthetes of England in the movement that was abruptly terminated by Wilde's trial. In Germany the movement, carrying over into the new century, was pushed to new limits by Wedekind with a kind of frustrated ferocity. It was a form of rebellion against the overwhelming material success of the country, a sense of something wrong beneath the twelve-course dinners, the pomp of military parades, the boasts of "blood and iron." Wedekind and his kind were *Schwarzseher*, seers of black, of the black in man. They were a trend feeble in comparison with the dominant mood of self-confident power and pugnacity, yet who felt intimations of disaster, of a city ripe for burning, of Neroism in the air.

Strauss's antennae picked up whatever was in the air and he fixed unerringly on *Salome*—as the subject of an opera, not a tone poem. Using more instruments than ever, he composed a score of tremendous difficulty and exaggerated dissonance with the orchestra at times divided against itself, playing in two violently antagonistic keys as if to express the horror of the subject by horrifying the ear. Instruments were twisted to new demands, cellos made to reach the realm of violins, trombones to cavort like flutes, kettledrums given figures of unprecedented complexity. The musical fabric was dazzling. Strauss could write for the voice with no less virtuosity than for orchestra and the singers' parts seemed to grow more eloquent as the drama deepened in depravity. Salome's final song to the severed head thrilled listeners with a sinister beauty that did justice to Wilde's words:

"Ah! wherefore didst thou not look at me, Iokanaan! If thou hadst seen me thou hadst loved me. I am athirst for thy beauty; I am hungry for thy body and neither the floods nor the great waters can quench my passion. . . . Ah! I have kissed thy mouth, Iokanaan, I have kissed thy mouth."

When Berlin and Vienna refused performance, like London, on the ground of sacrilege, Strauss's great admirer, Ernst von Schuch, conductor of the Dresden Royal Opera, presented it there on December 9, 1905. The production, in a single act lasting an hour and forty minutes without interruption, spared the audience's sensibilities nothing. Iokanaan's head, made up in realistic pallor of death with appropriate gore, was held in full view; Salome's seven veils were ritually discarded one by one while Herod leered. Death under the soldiers' shields supplied a punishing catharsis. The audience responded with unbounded enthusiasm extending to thirty-eight curtain calls for cast and composer. In subsequent performances in other German cities *Salome* went on to huge success and, for Strauss, large financial reward not adversely affected by bans and censorship troubles. In Vienna owing to the objections of the Archbishop the ban held, but in Berlin over the strenuous objections of the Kaiserin a compromise was reached of the kind applied by the Church to the Song of Solomon. Performance was allowed on condition that the star of Bethlehem should appear in the sky as Salome died, presumably indicating the posthumous triumph of the Baptist over unnatural passion.

Kaiser Wilhelm nevertheless remained unhappy. Despite an affinity for coarse physical jokes practiced upon his courtiers to their intense embarrassment, his moral views were more Victorian than Edwardian and he was married to a model of German bourgeois respectability. The Kaiserin Augusta, known as Dona, was a plain, amiable woman who provided her husband with six sons and a daughter, had no interests outside her family and wore large feathered hats on every occasion, even when yachting. They were her husband's choice since his annual birthday present to her was invariably twelve hats selected by himself which she was obliged to wear. Her one mark on history was her insistence on a double bed in which she so often kept her husband awake with family discussions which made him irritable next day, that Chancellor Bülow suggested separate bedrooms for the good of the State. But against her conviction that a good German husband and wife should sleep together, his proposal was in vain. Already offended by Strauss's earlier opera *Feuersnot,* whose theme, bawdily expressed, was the necessity of a maiden yielding her virginity to restore fire to a village, the Kaiserin had caused its cancellation, at which the Intendant of the Royal Opera had resigned in protest. The Kaiser himself had removed the imperial coat of arms from the Deutsches Theater when it performed Hauptmann's *Die Weber* to a cheering Socialist demonstration in the mid-nineties. A decade had passed since then and to suppress on moral grounds an opera by Germany's leading composer would now have subjected the Kaiser to the sharp-tongued wit of *Kladderadatsch* and other irreverent journals. Accepting the compromise the Kaiser said, "I am sorry Strauss composed this *Salome*. It will do him a great deal of harm," upon which Strauss said that it had enabled him to build his new villa at Garmisch.

Outside Germany where taste was more prudish, *Salome* became "the storm center of the musical world." In New York a tense audience at the Metropolitan Opera on January 22, 1907, awaited the rise of the curtain with "foreboding," soon amply fulfilled. The music, when critics could tear their attention from portrayal of "a psychopathic condition literally unspeakable in its horror and abnormality," was acknowledged marvelous but perverted to means that "sicken the mind and wreck the nerves." The opera's theme, not humanly representative as the material of music should be, was considered variously "monstrous," "pestilential," "intolerable and abhorrent," "mephitic, poisonous, sinister and obsessing in the extreme." Its "erotic pathology" was unfit for "conversation between self-respecting men," and the Dance alone "ought to make it impossible for an Occidental woman to look at it." Rising in "righteous fury" the press agreed that popularity in Germany settled nothing for America and the Metropolitan bowing to the storm withdrew the production.

London did not even attempt it until three years later. A license was at first refused but this was overcome with the help of Mrs. Asquith, who invited Beecham, conductor at Covent Garden, for a visit in the country to enlist the help of the Prime Minister. By playing for him the march from *Tannhäuser* on the piano, the only piece of music Mr. Asquith knew, and assuring him that to like it was not a sign of philistinism, and by explaining that Strauss was "the most famous and in common opinion the greatest of living composers," Beecham won his support. In consultation with the Lord Chamberlain, changes in the text were worked out transforming all Salome's expressions of physical desire into pleas for spiritual guidance and, as extra precaution against sacrilege, requiring her final song to be sung to an empty platter.

In *Salome* Strauss had found his lode but where was there another Wilde? One appeared, and with a subject which promised to outdo *Salome*. Hugo von Hofmannsthal, a young poet and prodigy of Vienna, was already famous at twenty-six when he first met Strauss, ten years his senior, in 1900. The grandson of an Italian lady and a converted Jew ennobled as a baron, he embodied Vienna's cosmopolitan strains. When at sixteen and still a student in the gymnasium, he read his first verse play to Arthur Schnitzler, the listener felt he had "encountered a born genius for the first time in my life." Two years later, in 1892, under the pseudonym "Loris," he enraptured *Jung Wien,* the literary avant-garde of Vienna, with two verse plays, *Gestern* (Yesterday) and *Der Tod des Tizian* (Titian's Death), whose worldly knowledge and sophisticated weariness led Hermann Bahr, leader of the young literati, to suppose the author must be a titled diplomat of fifty. He was incredulous to find him a boy of eighteen, "a strange youth . . . fired by the slightest stimulus, but only with his intellect, for his heart remained cold." Self-indulgent, already a man of the world, "yet terribly sad in his precocious worldliness," Hofmannsthal was a combination of Edwardian Werther and Viennese Dorian Gray. Like Wilde an artist in language, he played on German as on a harp and in 1893, his next drama, *Tod und der Tor* (Death and the Fool), confirmed in him a poet who could raise his native language to the harmony of Italian. When words are used for their own sake the result may be musical but the thought murky. In 1905 Hofmannsthal concluded an essay on Wilde, in perfect if unconscious emulation of his subject, "He who knows the power of the dance of life fears not death. For he knows that love kills." To his contemporaries he seemed "absolute poetic perfection come into being." As an acolyte, for a time, of the circle which genuflected to Stefan George in Munich, von Hofmannsthal was absorbed in problems of symbol and paradoxes of "the truth of masks." As a Viennese he did not escape the pessimism that infused the capital of the oldest empire in Europe.

In Vienna, the *Kaiserstadt,* seat of the Congress that had pasted Europe together after Napoleon, the time was twilight. As the center of a centuries-old mixture of races and peoples and the unwilling allegiances of restless nationalities, the capital of Austria-Hungary had too many problems of political life too difficult to cope with—and so turned its attention to other matters: to culture and connoisseurship, dalliance if not love, refinement of manner above everything and seriousness in nothing but music. The tempo was easygoing, the temper flippant, the mood hedonism and a nonchalant fatalism. It was the land of the Lotus-Eaters, the "Capua of the Mind." Its Emperor was seventy-five in 1905 and had been holding together his difficult domains through a reign of fifty-seven years. Its sad wandering Empress was dead by an Anarchist's knife. Its court had retreated to the aristocratic purity of sixteen quarterings for every member. It was a place where something was visibly coming to an end; everyone knew it and no one spoke of it.

Vienna looked down on Berlin as parvenu and crude and expressed its feeling in a popular song:

> Es gibt nur eine Kaiserstadt
> Es gibt nur ein Wien,
> Es gibt nur ein Räubernest
> Und das heisst Berlin.*

In the city of Beethoven, music and opera were king and the man in the street discussed the rival merits of the bands who played in the Prater. Art and the artist were esteemed. In politics, in government, in morals, Vienna was "affably tolerant of all that was slovenly, . . . in artistic matters there was no pardon; here the honor of the city was at stake." That

---

* There's only one King's City,
  Vienna's its name;
  There's only one Robber's Nest,
  Berlin is the name.

honor was maintained by the bourgeoisie and the cultivated Jews, who were the new patrons of art. Franz Joseph had never read a book and nursed an antipathy to music. The nobility not only kept its distance from artistic and intellectual life but feared and contemned it. They had, however, the most accomplished social manners in Europe, and when Theodore Roosevelt was asked what type of person he had found most sympathetic on his European travels, he replied, "the Austrian gentleman."

In internal affairs the strongest political sentiment was anti-Semitism, which was outspoken but more routine than heated. Karl Luger, the handsome blond-bearded Mayor of Vienna and head of the Christian Socialist party, was the leading anti-Semite, though more officially than personally. "I myself decide who is a Jew," he used to say. Known as *der schöne Karl*, he was the most popular man in the city and his funeral in 1910 was a major event. Despite their handicap the Jews, who represented 10 per cent of Vienna's population, were fertilizers of its culture. They played a prominent part in press, theatre, music, literature, finance, medicine and the law. They supplied the conductor of the Vienna Court Opera and the country's leading composer in Gustav Mahler as well as Vienna's truest mirror in Arthur Schnitzler.

A doctor like Chekhov, Schnitzler was marked by the same melancholy underlying a tone of irony and mockery. Except in his tragedy of *Professor Bernhardi*, the Jewish doctor who was assimilated but never enough, Schnitzler's heroes were philanderers, seekers for meaning in love and art and life, but always, as became Vienna, a little listlessly. They were charming, good-natured, clever and sophisticated; voices of the wit, inconstancy, politeness and unscrupulousness of the Viennese soul—and of its lassitude. The hero of *Der Weg ins Freie* (The Road to the Open), six months after returning from a "melancholy and rather boring" tour of Sicily with his mistress before a final parting, reminds himself that since then he has done no real work, not even written down "the plaintive adagio which he had heard in the waves breaking on the beach on a windy morning in Palermo." He is obsessed by a feeling of the "dreamlike and purposeless character of existence." Discussing a heated debate in the Landtag he replies to a question, "Heated? Well, yes, what we call heated in Austria. People were outwardly offensive and inwardly indifferent."

Hofmannsthal after his first meeting with Strauss sent him a verse play for a ballet which he had written on discovering "Dionysian beauty" in the wordless gesture of the dance. Not so dedicated to pure art as not to value an association with Strauss, he hoped the Master would set his libretto to music. Strauss, however, was at the moment too busy with *Feuersnot* and other projects. Pursuing the Dionysian trail, Hofmannsthal began to make notes on Greek themes, on the relation of the supernatural to the bestial, on "phallic exuberance" and the "pathology and criminal psychology" of the tragedies then enjoying revival on the stage. Here he found, not the marble purity of the conventional classical Greece known to the Nineteenth Century, but Nietzsche's vision of a demonic Greece in whose sins and hates and forbidden bloodstained passions was the birth of tragedy, the earliest statement of man's compulsive drive toward ruin. The central tragedy, which Aeschylus, Sophocles and Euripides all had dramatized, was the chain of guilt in the house of Atreus from the sacrifice of Iphigenia to the murder of Agamemnon to the revenge of Electra and Orestes in their ultimate act of matricide. Hofmannsthal followed, but his *Elektra* turned out to be closer to Poe than Euripides, a nightmare of Gothic horror rather than a drama of man's fate.

His stage directions describe a palace courtyard at sunset where "patches of red light glimmering through the fig tree fall like bloodstains on the ground and walls." His characters surpass Salome in extravagant utterances of torment and desire, in ghastly longing for the double slaying of Clytemnestra and Aegisthus, in recollections of Agamemnon's gaping wounds, in sexual images of hatred appearing as a bridegroom, "hollow-eyed, breathing a viperous breath," whom Electra takes into her bed that it might teach her "all that is done between man and wife." Crazed with mutual hate, mother and daughter circle each other like mad dogs. Electra is a maniacal fury, feeding the vulture of revenge on her body, groveling in the dust of Agamemnon's grave at sundown, the hour when she "howls for her father" and sniffs among the dogs for the buried corpse. Clytemnestra is almost putrescent, with "a sallow bloated face" and heavy eyelids which she can only keep open by a "terrible effort." Dressed in purple, covered in jewels and talismans, she leans on an ivory cane, her train carried by "a yellow figure with the face of an Egyptian and the posture of a serpent." Sick with terror, evil dreams and an old lust, she is obsessed by the need to spill blood and drives herds of animals to the sacrifice in the hope that if the right blood flows she will be relieved of the nameless horror of her nightmares. It is no word, no pain that chokes her; it is nothing, yet so terrifying that her soul "hungers to hang itself and every nerve cries for death."

> Can one decay alive like a rotten corpse?
> Can one fall apart if one is not even ill?
> Fall apart wide awake like a dress eaten by moths?

She seems an allegory of Europe and the play a climax of the *Schwarzseher*, an apocalyptic vision of disaster. When, desperate for surcease from her dreams, Clytemnestra demands to know from Electra who must bleed and die that she may sleep at last, Electra cries in exaltation, "What must bleed? Your own throat! . . . and the shadows and torches shall envelop you in their black and scarlet net."

The play was produced by Max Reinhardt in Berlin in 1903, the year after *Salome*. Hofmannsthal was alert to its possibilities. To serve as a libretto for an opera by Strauss was then considered "to reach the summit of contemporary fame," and he repeatedly urged *Elektra* on Strauss as his next project. Though attracted, Strauss hesitated because of its similarity to *Salome* and cast about for some other theme of human nature driven to dreadful extremes. "Something like a really wild Cesare Borgia or Savonarola would be just what I am yearning for," he wrote to Hofmannsthal in March, 1906. Following a visit to The Hague, where he was haunted by Rembrandt's "Saul and David," he suggested a "raving Saul" as a possible subject. Ten days later he suddenly proposed, "How about a subject from the French Revolution for a change?" Hofmannsthal, with his drama already written, kept returning to *Elektra* and, although the marks of Wilde on it were obvious, he insisted that it was really very different. Eager for collaboration, he was persuasive and Strauss succumbed. Meanwhile, with one foot in the dominant camp, he composed five highly colored military marches for the Kaiser which won him the Order of the Crown, Third Class.

While Strauss was at work on *Elektra* a major scandal revealing rottenness in high places became public. The Eulenburg affair concerned homosexuals in the immediate circle of the Kaiser, but it was less their habits than the layers disclosed of malice, intrigue and private vendetta which shed a lurid glow on Germany. Three years earlier Fritz Krupp, head of the firm, on being accused by the Socialist paper *Vorwärts* of homosexual acts with waiters and valets, committed suicide. This time the central figure was Prince Philipp Eulenburg, former Ambassador to Vienna from 1894 to 1902, a suave and cultivated aristocrat who was the Kaiser's oldest and closest friend, sang songs to him beautifully at the piano, and gave him intelligent advice. As the only courtier to exercise on the whole a beneficent influence on the sovereign, he was naturally the object of the jealousy of Bülow and Holstein, who suspected the Kaiser of intention to make him Chancellor. Initiator of the scandal was Maximilian Harden, the feared and fearless editor of the weekly *Die Zukunft*, of which it was said that everything rotten and everything good in Germany appeared in its pages. Cause and motive had to do with Germany's diplomatic defeat at the Algeciras Conference which set off waves of recrimination among ministers, culminating in the removal of the spidery Holstein. He blamed Eulenburg, although in fact his removal had been secretly engineered by Bülow. Rabid for revenge, Holstein, who for years had kept secret police files on the private habits of his associates, now joined forces with Harden to ruin Eulenburg, whose influence on the Kaiser, Harden believed, was pacific and therefore malign. With Holstein's files at his disposal, Harden opened a campaign of innuendo naming three elderly Counts, all A.D.C.'s of the Kaiser, as homosexuals and gradually closing in on the friendship of Eulenburg with Count Kuno Moltke, nicknamed Tutu, "the most delicate of generals," commander of a cavalry brigade and City Commandant of Berlin. The Kaiser ditched his friends instantly and forced Moltke to sue Harden for libel, which was just what Harden wanted in order to ruin Eulenburg. Through four trials lasting over a period of two years, from October, 1907, to July, 1909, evidence of perversion, blackmail and personal venom was spread before a bewildered public. Witnesses including thieves, pimps and morons told of "disgusting orgies" in the Garde du Corps regiment and testified to abnormal acts of Eulenburg and Moltke twenty years in the past. A celebrated specialist in pathological conditions discoursed on medical details, Moltke's divorced and vindictive wife was called to testify, charges of subornation and perjury were added, Chancellor Bülow was himself accused of perversion by a half-crazed crusader for the legal rights of homosexuals and forced to sue, the verdict of the first trial in favor of Harden was reversed by a second trial and re-reversed in a third at which Eulenburg, now ill, disgraced and under arrest, was brought to court in a hospital bed. The public felt uneasily that justice was being tampered with, readers of *Die Zukunft* were given an impression of perversion everywhere and the prestige of Kaiser and court sank. At the same time in Vienna the Emperor's brother, Archduke Ludwig-Viktor, known as Luzi-Wuzi, became involved in a scandal with a masseur.

In England the three trials of Oscar Wilde had blazed and been put out within two months; the establishment turned its back on him and destroyed him. In Germany the establishment itself was on trial. In the midst of it, in October, 1908, came the tremendous gaffe of Kaiser Wilhelm's interview on foreign affairs in the *Daily Telegraph,* in which his more than usually indiscreet opinions, carelessly allowed to pass by Bülow, aroused the fury and hilarity of nations and questions as to his sanity at home. Some even demanded his abdication. Bülow, maneuvering neatly as he thought, virtually apologized in the Reichstag for his sovereign who never forgave him. Hurt and indignant, the Kaiser retired to the estate of his friend Prince Fürstenberg, where, in the course of an evening's festivities, Count Hülsen-Haeseler, chief of the Military Cabinet, appeared in a pink ballet skirt and rose wreath and "danced beautifully," affording everybody much entertainment. On finishing he dropped dead of heart failure. Rigor mortis having set in by the time the doctors came, the General's body could only with the greatest difficulty be divested of its ballet costume and restored to the propriety of military uniform. It had not been a happy year for the Kaiser, although six months later he at least had the satisfaction of forcing the resignation of Bülow.

Damage to the image of the ruling caste caused its members to swagger more than ever. As the Kaiser's prestige slipped, the trend of the extreme militants grew in favor of the Crown Prince, a strutting creature whose flatterers told him he resembled Frederick the Great, as indeed, facially, he did. In the eternal duel of reigning monarch and eldest son, Wilhelm II and "little Willy" felt required to outdo each other in bombast. "I stand in shining armor" and similar pronouncements of the Kaiser were of this period. The nation's mood of conscious power could absorb unlimited bombast. Germans knew themselves to be the strongest military power on earth, the most efficient merchants, the busiest bankers, penetrating every continent, financing the Turks, flinging out a railroad from Berlin to Baghdad, gaining the trade of Latin America, challenging the sea power of Great Britain, and in the realm of intellect systematically organizing, under the concept *Wissenschaft,* every branch of human knowledge. They were deserving and capable of mastery of the world. Rule by the best must be fulfilled. By this time Nietzsche, as Brandes wrote in 1909, held "undisputed sway" over the minds of his countrymen. What they lacked and hungered for was the world's acknowledgment of their mastery. So long as it was denied, frustration grew and with it the desire to compel acknowledgment by the sword. Talk of war became a commonplace. When the Kaiser's troublesome Rhodes scholars got drunk they threatened Oxford colleagues "with invasion and castigation at the hands of the German Army." In 1912 General Bernhardi, the leading military theorist of his day, proclaimed the coming necessity in a book of indisputable authority and conviction whose title was *Germany and the Next War.*

The other Germany, the Germany of intellect and sentiment, the liberal Germany which lost in 1848 and never tried again, had withdrawn from the arena, content to despise militarism and materialism and sulk in a tent of superior spiritual values. Its representatives were a caste of professors, clergy, doctors and lawyers who regarded themselves as the *Geist-aristokratie* (aristocracy of the mind) superior to the vulgar rich, the vulgar nobility and the vulgar masses. Unconcerned with social problems, unengaged in politics, they were satisfied with an indoor liberalism which fought no battles and expressed itself in abstract opposition to the regime, in contempt for the Kaiser and in the anti-militarist cartoons of *Simplicissimus*. They were personified by a professor of philosophy, Georg Simmel, whose lectures in a room overlooking Unter den Linden coincided with the hour of the changing of the guard. At the first sound of the military band Professor Simmel would abruptly stop talking and stand motionless in "an attitude of arrogant disgust and stoical suffering until the barbaric noise had faded away." Only then would he resume his lecture.

At the centenary celebration of the University of Berlin in 1910, the two Germanys met when the academic community found itself invaded by their fierce-moustachioed monarch in the golden cuirass and golden-eagled helmet of the Garde du Corps, with retinue in gorgeous uniform, heralded by the terrific blasts of a trombone choir. Satisfied that the Kaiser "looked even worse than his caricatures," the audience consoled itself with the thought that such an intrusion could not trouble their halls again for another hundred years.

Strauss completed the score of *Elektra* in September, 1908, with his publishers taking it from him page by page. Anticipating the prospect of another *succès de scandale*, they paid $27,000 for it, almost double the $15,000 paid for *Salome*, making Strauss's income from music in 1908 $60,000. The German public's appetite for sensation had become a habit and four cities competed for the honor of the premiere. Grateful to Schuch, Strauss gave it to Dresden, which in honor of the occasion scheduled a Strauss festival to include *Salome, Feuersnot, Sinfonia Domestica* and two performances of *Elektra*—five evenings of Strauss in succession.

Rehearsals of the new opera took place in an atmosphere of uproar; everything was larger, noisier, more violent than life. The score called for the biggest orchestra yet, sixty-two strings including eight bass cellos, forty-five winds including six bass trumpets and a contra-bass tuba, six to eight kettledrums as well as a bass drum, in all a total of about one hundred and twenty. The opera was performed in a single act lasting two hours without intermission with Electra on stage the entire time. Her part was longer than Brünhilde's in all of *The Ring* put together and her vocal intervals were considered "unsingable." The role of Clytemnestra was created by Mme Schumann-Heink, who, finding it "such a desperate one that it nearly killed me," never sang it again. In places where she was required to sing over the orchestra at fortissimo, Strauss, listening from the stalls, would scream over the din and crash, "Louder, louder, I say! I can still hear the Heink's voice!"

For a legendary drama set in 1500 B.C. he wanted everything to be "exact and realistic," insisting on real sheep and bulls for Clytemnestra's sacrifice. "*Gott in Himmel!* Strauss, are you mad?" howled the stage director in terror. "Imagine the cost! And the danger! What will they do when your violent music begins?" They would stampede, crash into the orchestra, kill the musicians, even wreck valuable instruments. Strauss was adamant. Von Schuch was called in to add his protest. Only after terrific arguments was Strauss persuaded to yield on the bulls and be content with sheep. Equally realistic in his music, he virtually took the role of words away from von Hofmannsthal. The tinkling of Clytemnestra's bracelets is heard in the percussion; when Chrysothemis speaks of a stormy night the storm rages in the orchestra; when the beasts are driven to sacrifice the noise of their hoofs makes the listener want to get out of the way; when the slippery pool of blood is described the orchestra gives a picture of it. The composer's mastery of his technical resources seemed superhuman and his breaking of musical laws more reckless than ever. As he put it, "I went to the uttermost limits of harmony and psychic polyphony and of the receptive capacity of present day ears."

When the evening came for the premiere on January 25, 1909, an international audience was assembled including opera directors from every country on the continent and, according to a possibly overwhelmed reporter, "200 distinguished critics." "All Europe is here," the hotel porter said proudly to Hermann Bahr, who came from Vienna.

Without overture or prelude the curtain rose as the orchestra thundered out Agamemnon's theme like the hammer of doom pounding on the great lion gate of Mycenae. No opera had ever opened so stunningly before. When the curtain fell after two hours of demonic intensity the audience sat for some seconds in stupefied silence until the "Straussianer" recovered and began to applaud. An opposition group hissed but most of the audience was too cowed to do anything until the claque won the upper hand and wrung curtain calls and ultimately cheers for the composer. The brutality of the libretto and the outrages upon musical form provoked the usual controversy. To some the music of *Elektra* seemed no longer music. "Indeed, many serious minded people consider Richard Strauss insane," wrote one benumbed listener. But on second hearing and at further performances which followed in Berlin, Munich and Frankfurt within four weeks of the premiere, the mastery of Strauss's score in conveying dread and impending horror leading up to the final murder was undeniable.

Listening to the music Hermann Bahr felt it expressed something sinister about the present time, a pride born of limitless power, a defiance of order "lured back toward chaos," and a yearning in Chrysothemis for some simple tranquil feeling. Though deeply disturbed he felt it had been a "marvelous evening" and returned to Vienna excited and uplifted. This was what Nietzsche had prescribed.

When it reached London a year later, in February, 1910, notoriety preceded it and musical warfare raged before a note had been heard. Strauss came himself to conduct two performances at a fee of £200 for each. The *Daily Mail* critic was struck by the sobriety of his gestures. "A tall pale man with smooth brow" whose steel-blue eyes flashed from time to time at singers or musicians, he conducted with head immobile and elbows as if riveted to his body. "He seemed a mathematician writing a formula on a blackboard neatly with supreme knowledge." After the performance *The Times* found the opera "unsurpassed for sheer hideousness in the whole of operatic literature," while the *Daily Telegraph* reported that "Covent Garden had never previously witnessed a scene of such unfettered enthusiasm." The rising controversy created a public demand that required Beecham to extend his season. From his point of view it was, excepting the death of King Edward VII some months later, "the most discussed event of the year." The truth was that by this time it could no longer be heard outside Germany without political overtones. George Bernard Shaw, believing that anti-German hysteria was responsible for the attacks on *Elektra*, leaned backward to the opposite extreme: In an article in the *Nation* he wrote that if once he could have said that "the case against the fools and the money changers who are trying to drive us into war with Germany consists in the single word, Beethoven, today I should say with equal confidence, Strauss." He called *Elektra* "the highest achievement of the highest art" and its performance "a historic moment in the history of art in England such as may not occur again in our lifetime."

Strauss recognized that in the style of *Salome* and *Elektra* he had gone as far as he could go. Suddenly, as after *Heldenleben*, having enough of the grand manner, he decided to give the public a comic opera for a change, in the style of Mozart's *Marriage of Figaro*, to prove that Strauss could do anything. As librettist Hofmannsthal approved and early in 1909 was at work drafting an "entirely original" scenario set in Eighteenth-Century Vienna, "full of burlesque situations and characters" with opportunity for lyrical melody and humor. On receiving the opening scene, Strauss found it delightful and replied, "It will set itself to music like oil and melted butter." Collaborating by correspondence through 1909 and the first half of 1910, librettist and composer constructed a new opera to be called *Der Rosenkavalier*.

The juvenile lead was to be sung by a woman dressed as a man. *Hosenrolle* (trouser parts) for women were a convention which Mozart himself had used for Cherubino but the Hofmannsthal-Strauss concept of Octavian was a rather different matter, not devoid of a desire to titillate. When Strauss's prelude to the opera describes with characteristic realism the pleasures of the sex act and the curtain rises on the Marschallin and her young lover still in bed, the discovery that both are women was likely to produce in the audience a peculiar sensation of which the authors were certainly aware. The idea was originally Hofmannsthal's. Strauss later claimed that the device was necessary because no man young enough to sing Octavian would have had the experience necessary to be an accomplished actor. "Besides," he added more frankly, "writing for three sopranos was a challenge." He met it, especially when the three sing together in the last act, with exquisite song. In *Elektra* the men's parts had been of small account and in *Rosenkavalier* the principle male part was that of a coarse lecher who appears either as unpleasant or ridiculous. Baron Ochs represented the German idea of the comic. As Strauss wrote to Hofmannsthal during the composition, he missed "a genuinely comic situation—everything is merely amusing but not comic." He wanted the audience to laugh; "Laugh! not just smile or grin."

The inevitable animals made their appearance in the form of a dog, a monkey and a parrot. When Strauss demanded from Hofmannsthal a love scene between Sophie and Octavian to which he could write a duet "much more passionate, . . . as it reads now it is too tame, too mannered and timid," Hofmannsthal replied pettishly that these two young creatures "have nothing of the Valkyrie or Tristan and Isolde about them" and he wished to avoid at all costs having them "burst into a kind of Wagnerian erotic screaming." This was hardly tactful and incompatibilities of temperament between composer and librettist were becoming evident. A touch of Tristan in fact appeared, not to mention some borrowing from Mozart and even from Johann Strauss. With bland anachronism a Viennese waltz, unknown in the Eighteenth Century, was a main theme.

By April, 1910, the full score of Act II was already at the printer before Strauss had received the libretto for Act III. Its situations contrived for the Baron's embarrassment turned out to have been adapted by von Hofmannsthal from *The Merry Wives of Windsor*, with the difference that, unlike Falstaff, Ochs remained unrelievedly unlikable. By the end of summer the opera was finished and on January 26, 1911, two years after *Elektra*, *Rosenkavalier* had its premier at Dresden. It was rarely to be off the opera stage thereafter. Composer and librettist endowed it with all the shimmer of super-civilized Vienna. It glistened like the silver rose that was its symbol. All Strauss's skill, resourcefulness and audacity—and his duality—were in the score. His highest gift of musical expressiveness could convey the bustle of an Eighteenth-Century levee, the delicious discovery of young love, the comic terror of the duel, the sweet sadness of the Marschallin's renunciation, and at the same time be used for coarse jokes and bottom-pinching humor. He gave the world a silver rose, beautiful, glittering and tarnished.

In 1911 Strauss was at the peak of the musical world, the most famous composer alive, "one of those," wrote a biographer of musicians, Richard Specht, "without whom we can no longer imagine our spiritual life." Although he and Hofmannsthal set to work at once on another opera, *Ariadne auf Naxos,* Strauss had reached his own peak and the palm was already passing.

In 1908 in Paris the Russian Ballet company of Sergei Diaghilev burst like a gorgeous tropical bird upon the Western world. Its season was a triumph of wild throbbing exotic splendor, another "flash of lightning out of the North." Instead of the tired routines of classical ballet it brought fresh excellence of music by contemporary Russian composers, new librettos, imaginative choreography and brilliant modern stage design, all assembled like a bed of jewels to set off a blaze of dancing that was virile and superb. The male dancer was the star, no longer a mere *porteur* to lift the ballerina, but a wind who brought vitality and zest sweeping onto the stage. Above all the rest was one, Vaslav Nijinsky. When he appeared with an astonishing leap into the air and seemed almost to pause there, people felt the excitement of perfection and knew they were seeing the greatest *ballon* dancer who ever lived. He was an angel, a genius, an Apollo of motion. He took possession of all hearts. The whole ensemble took Paris by storm. Devotees predicted the downfall of opera. "It was as if," wrote the Comtesse de Noailles, "something new had been added to the creation of the world on its seventh day."

New movements in the arts were erupting everywhere. At the Salon d'Automne in 1905 and 1906 the *Fauves* (Wild Beasts) led by Matisse exhibited in riotous color and distorted line their credo of painting independent of nature. In 1907–8 Picasso and Braque, discovering essential reality in geometrical forms, created Cubism. In its terms Léger celebrated the machine and a train of other artists followed. In Germany the new idea broke out in a school of Expressionists who searched for emotional impact through exaggeration or distortion of nature. Two Americans broke old molds: Frank Lloyd Wright at home and Isadora Duncan, who, touring Europe in the years 1904–8, introduced emotion into the dance. Rodin, speaking for his own métier but voicing a new goal for all the arts, had already said, "Classical sculpture sought the logic of the human body; I seek its psychology." Seeking it too, Marcel Proust in 1906 shut himself up in a cork-lined room to embark upon *Remembrance of Things Past*. Thomas Mann took up the search in *Death in Venice*. In Bloomsbury, Lytton Strachey prepared a new kind of biography. The Moscow Art Theatre demonstrated a new kind of acting. The Irish Renaissance flowered in Yeats and in J. M. Synge, who in *Riders to the Sea* and *The Playboy of the Western World* proved himself the only writer since Shakespeare to produce an equally fine tragedy and comedy. The time vibrated with a search for new forms and new realms. When on July 25, 1909, Blériot flew the Channel, confirming what the Wrights had begun, he seemed to mark a wiping out of frontiers, and everyone in Europe felt in his triumph "a soaring of feelings no less wonderful than that of the planes."

All the fever and fecundity of the hour seemed captured by the Russian Ballet. That it should come out of Imperial Russia, considered at once barbaric and decrepit, was as surprising as had been the summons to disarmament by the Czar. A great interest in things Russian aroused by the Franco-Russian Alliance and the Exposition of 1900 had inspired the enterprising Diaghilev to bring an exhibition of Russian art to Paris in 1906. Paintings and sculpture, ikons, priestly brocades and the jeweled marvels of Fabergé lent by the Imperial and private collections and by museums filled twelve rooms under the patronage of the Grand Duke Vladimir, Ambassador Izvolsky of Russia and Mme Greffulhe. The next year Diaghilev brought Russian music in a series of dazzling concerts with Rimsky-Korsakov conducting his own work, Rachmaninoff playing his own piano concerto, Josef Hofmann playing a concerto by Scriabine, and the magnificent basso Chaliapin singing excerpts from Borodin's *Prince Igor* and Moussorgsky's *Boris Godunov*. Building on the enthusiastic welcome, Diaghilev planned a greater triumph in a season of ballet and Russian opera. The Imperial Russian Ballet lent its leading artists,

Anna Pavlova, Nijinsky, Adolph Bolm and Tamara Karsavina, with Michel Fokine as choreographer. For stage design and costumes, Diaghilev obtained the gorgeous and barbaric talent of Léon Bakst, supplemented by outstanding painters, Soudeikine, Roerich, Alexandre Benois and others. The sensation of the first season was *Cleopatra,* whose music was a melange from at least five Russian composers. Russian themes mingled with Egyptian and Persian and even the original sorceress of the Nile could not have matched the ravishing beauty and figure of Ida Rubinstein borne on a palanquin surrounded by a whirling bacchanal of veils and rose leaves arranged to conceal the fact that as a dancer she was as yet barely trained. Paris found her almost "too beautiful, like strong perfume."

Every year for the next six years the Ballet returned with new and exuberant productions which revolutionized choreography and stage design. Music was dignified by a full orchestra, with Pierre Monteux engaged as conductor. Additional operas—Moussorgsky's *Khovantschina,* Rimsky's *Sadko* and *Ivan the Terrible*—besides *Prince Igor* and *Boris Godunov,* were added to the repertoire. Pavlova later left the company, but in 1909 in *Les Sylphides* she seemed to dancing "what Racine is to poetry," while Karsavina was "the exquisite union of classic tradition and revolutionary artistry." For the music of this ballet two of Chopin's piano compositions, *Nocturne* and *Valse Brillante,* were orchestrated by a pupil of Rimsky-Korsakov, Igor Stravinsky, then twenty-six, whom Diaghilev had commissioned after hearing his first performed orchestral work in St. Petersburg in 1908. In contrast to the classical delicacy of *Sylphides,* Fokine staged the savage Polovtsian dances from *Prince Igor* with Tartar-Mongol themes echoing in the music and a wild Asiatic horde of dancers against a scene in dull grays and reds, of low round-topped tents and rising columns of smoke stretching toward the infinite horizon of the steppe.

Emotion long absent from the ballet was infused by the voluptuous physical spectacles and intoxicating colors of Bakst. Houris of the Sultan's harem from the *Arabian Nights,* bacchantes from a Greek vase, Russian boyars in boots, harlequins and colombines of the Commedia dell'Arte, forest creatures in maroon, green and gold suggesting "the sparkling beauty of spotted pythons," tennis-players in modern dress took over the stage. Bakst inspired Paul Poiret and five years of women's fashions. When planning Rimsky-Korsakov's *Schéhérazade* with his associates, the red-haired Bakst in his elegant and scented clothes jumped on a chair and explained, in his guttural accent with explicit gestures, how the Sultan's bodyguard should cut everyone to pieces: "*everyone,* his wives and all their Negro lovers!" For *Schéhérazade* he designed a setting to suggest "dreadful deeds of lust and cruelty" which Fokine interpreted enthusiastically in a dance of Negro slaves whom the Sultan's wives persuade the eunuchs to liberate from their golden cages and who fling themselves upon the willing harem in an orgiastic dance of "spasms of desire." The sexual theme was a favorite of the Ballet. For *Thamar,* the Caucasian queen, a Cleopatra *à la russe,* Bakst designed a medieval castle above a river into whose waters rejected lovers fell to their doom. In her various roles as temptress the delicate and flower-like Karsavina conveyed vice, as the critics said, "with a great deal of verisimilitude."

When Rimsky died in 1908 Stravinsky composed a *Chant Funèbre* for a memorial concert in St. Petersburg. More than ever impressed, Diaghilev asked him to write the music for a ballet based on the Russian fairy tale of Prince Ivan and the Firebird. Set in a wood with a wicked wizard and twelve princesses under a spell, it evoked from the composer an imaginative score of mixed rhythms, graceful melody and a weird electric dance of demons. With Bolm as the Prince and Karsavina as the Firebird, it was performed in June, 1910, the first work of Stravinsky in his own right to be heard outside of Russia. Debussy rushed backstage to embrace him. The audience was delighted to appreciate music that was contemporary without being uncomfortable and Diaghilev was congratulated on every hand. He at once commissioned another ballet for the following season. When Stravinsky played for him a piece for piano and orchestra which he had already written on the adventures of Petrouchka, "the immortal and unhappy puppet, hero of every fair in every country," Diaghilev was enchanted. Together they worked out the scenes of the ballet, the carnival in the public square, the crowds and booths, the magician with his tricks, the gypsies and trained bear, the puppet show whose dolls come to life, the vain love of Petrouchka for the Dancer and his death at the hands of his rival, the Moor.

Petrouchka was music of power and vitality, close to the Russian people, with folk tunes and echoes of the hurdy-gurdy, humor and satire and poignant grief. Like Strauss, Stravinsky scorned development of themes but in a tradition he had inherited from the Russian "Five" rather than from Germany. Almost contrary to the nature of music, which traditionally depended on development and repetition, Stravinsky was terse and direct, aiming, as he said, "at straightforward expression in its simplest form. I have no use for 'working-out' in dramatic music. The one essential thing is to feel and convey one's feelings."

In this. *Petrouchka* succeeded and Paris acknowledged what Debussy's embrace had already recognized: the appearance of an original and major composer. Nijinsky as the puppet broke the audience's heart. Thrown by his master into a black box, rushing about waving his stiff arms in the air, pathetic in love and frantic in jealousy, his performance was a triumph just in time for the London season.

England greeted the Russian Ballet with a fervor equal to France. In the brilliant Coronation summer of 1911 "it was exciting to be alive." The heat broke records, festivities were at a peak, airplanes landed on country lawns, everybody was stimulated by the thrill of flight but the Russian Ballet "crowned all." It restored the dance to its "primal nobility," wrote Ellen Terry. It was a revelation in the harmony of the arts. Society, intellectuals, everyone with any pretensions to taste, flocked to Covent Garden "night after night, entranced." Nijinsky enraptured all who came: as the uncouth puppet, as the Negro slave in silver trousers of *Schéhérazade*, as Pierrot in a candle-lit garden chasing dancers dressed as butterflies to music by Schumann, as the Blue God rising from a lotus in a Chinese pool to music by Proust's friend Reynaldo Hahn, as the ghost of a rose in a costume of petals, flying out of a window in a famous leap that made people say his element was the air. Speaking no English and hardly any French, he became the darling of the dinner parties, speechless but smiling.

Impelled by triumph, like Strauss, to try for new sensation, Diaghilev in the season of 1912 succeeded in shocking Paris. He produced two new ballets by French composers. Maurice Ravel's *Daphnis et Chloé*, written for the occasion, was acknowledged by Stravinsky "one of the finest things by a French composer." Debussy's *L'Après-midi d'un Faune*, whose music was already known, was a scandal for non-musical reasons. Nijinsky was the Faun in skin-fitting tights painted in animal spots, with a tiny tail, a wig of tight curls made of gold cord, and two little curling horns. In a ballet lasting twelve minutes he chased nymphs in Greek gowns and, as the last escaped him, leaving behind her veil, fell upon it in a movement of sexual consummation. The choreography in this case was Nijinsky's own. The curtain fell upon hoots, whistles, and insults mixed with cries of *"épatant!"* and *"Bis, bis!"* Obliging, the company danced the ballet over again to "indescribable chaos." Next morning Gaston Calmette, the editor of *Figaro*, published a signed editorial on his front page under the title "Un Faux Pas" denouncing "the extraordinary exhibition of erotic bestiality and shameless gesture" and demanding its suppression in subsequent performances. Agreeing, if less excitedly, *Le Gaulois* found the final gesture *"de trop,"* while *Le Temps* with customary dignity expressed the "justified discontent" of the French people at this "regrettable adventure." A report quickly circulated that the Prefect of Police at Calmette's request had issued an injunction against further performance. In clubs, salons, cafés and lobbies of the Chamber no one talked of anything else; Paris momentarily was again in two camps. The excitable Russian Ambassador, M. Izvolsky, wanted to know if *Figaro* was attacking the Franco-Russian Alliance. Next day *Le Matin* published a letter from Rodin defending Nijinsky for restoring "freedom of instinct and human emotion" to the dance. The controversy transferred itself to Rodin, whose supporters issued a manifesto in which Jules Lemaître and Maurice Barrès were now on the same side as Anatole France and Octave Mirbeau along with ex-President Loubet, former premiers Clemenceau, Léon Bourgeois and Briand, Ambassador Izvolsky and Baron d'Estournelles. Forain, unreconstructed, published in *Figaro* an anti-Rodin cartoon. With every ticket for the second performance sold at a premium, the offending gesture was suppressed, leaving the Faun merely gazing on the veil with doleful regret.

In Vienna that season, where owing to a current Balkan War the mood was anti-Slav, a fiasco was barely averted. At rehearsals the orchestra of the Viennese Royal Opera, which could play anything put before it with accomplished ease, played the Russian music with ostentatious disapproval and deliberate mistakes. Monteux was helpless and when the enraged Diaghilev commented out loud on the behavior of these "pigs," the musicians downed their instruments and left the stage. Only by extracting an apology from Diaghilev next day was the crisis resolved. In Berlin the Kaiser attended a performance of *Cleopatra* and *Firebird*. Preferring the former, he summoned Diaghilev and told him he would send his Egyptologists to see it, apparently under the impression that Bakst's fantastic decor was authentic and the Russian potpourri a revelation of the real music of Ptolemaic Egypt.

Strauss too came to the performance and afterward complimented Stravinsky, adding a characteristic piece of advice. Referring to the muted mysterious opening of *Firebird*, where the Prince rides into the enchanted wood, he said, "You make a mistake in beginning your piece pianissimo; the public will not listen. You should astonish them by a sudden crash at the start. After that they will follow you and you can do what you like."

To capture Strauss for the Ballet was an obvious next task, and the Ballet's prestige in turn had already interested von Hofmannsthal, who opened negotiations. After obtaining Diaghilev's financial terms, he suggested to Strauss a ballet on Orestes and the Furies with Nijinsky portraying the hero's "terrible deed and terrible suffering" and the Furies "bursting forth horribly and triumphantly" in a dance of destruction at the end. It was hardly a fresh idea but Hofmannsthal wrote temptingly that it would provide the occasion for "wonderful, somber, grandiose music. . . . Think it over and please don't refuse." He enclosed a note of the terms which Diaghilev "takes the liberty of submitting to you." When Strauss promptly rejected the idea, Hofmannsthal hurriedly offered instead a libretto for a ballet based on Joseph and Potiphar's Wife which he had already written in collaboration with Count Harry Kessler, a German litterateur, amateur in politics and patron of the arts who like other Germans of liberal ideas had no place in official life. Applying pressure to Strauss, Hofmannsthal wrote that if he refused, Diaghilev—who liked the libretto—would commission a Russian or French composer. This worked. "Joseph is excellent," Strauss replied. "I'll bite. Have already started sketching it out."

Trouble soon developed. The libretto as conceived by its two sophisticated authors was a metaphysical version of the story of the Baptist and Salome, with Joseph as a God-seeker "whose secret is that of growth and transmutation, whose holiness is that of creating and begetting, whose perfection is that of things which have not yet been." He is confronted by a sensual woman who is ruined "by perception of the divine which she cannot conquer." These were not the most suitable ideas to express in music, much less the dance. Squirming, Strauss complained, "The chaste Joseph isn't at all up my street and if a thing bores me I find it difficult to set to music." He complained that Joseph in the ballet did nothing but resist the Queen's advances; "this God-seeker is going to be a hell of an effort." Hofmannsthal explained carefully that Joseph's resistance was "the struggle of man's intensified intellectuality" against woman's urge to drag him down, a clarification which did little to relieve Strauss's boredom with his task. His first sketches, which he played for Hofmannsthal in December, 1912, left his collaborator "disturbed" and conscious that "there is something wrong between the two of us which in the end will have to be brought into the open." For the time being he implored Strauss not to feel constrained by the demands of the dance but to write "unrestrained pure Strauss" expressing his own personality "with every conceivable freedom in polyphony and modernism in a manner as bold and bizarre as you may wish." Joseph remained chaste, however, and Strauss uninspired. In the meantime Diaghilev had another premiere ready for the season of 1913.

It was *Le Sacre du Printemps* (The Rite of Spring) by Stravinsky. Its theme was elemental, the rejuvenation of earth in spring. The form was a celebration of pagan rites in which a sacrificial maiden dances herself to death to renew the life of the soil. In contrast to the tired sophistry of *Joseph*, Stravinsky's scenario was simply a framework for dancers and

British delegation to The Hague, 1899. Front row, from left to right: Ardagh; Fisher; Pauncefote; Sir Henry Howard, Minister to The Hague. Arthur Peel is first on the left in the back row.

PARIS EXPOSITION, 1900

Porte Monumentale

Palace of Electricity

Alfred Nobel (portrait by E. Osterman)

Bertha von Suttner

The Krupp works at Essen, 1912

Richard Strauss, 1905

Friedrich Nietzsche, Weimar, 1900 (drawing by Hans Olde)

A beer garden in Berlin

Nijinsky as the Faun (design by Léon Bakst)

music. He opened not with a bang, as Strauss had advised, but with a slow trembling of woodwinds as if to suggest the physical mystery of budding. As the curtain rose on tribal games and dances, the music became vibrant and frenetic with primeval rhythms, the chant of trumpets, the driving beat of machinery, jazz metres and pitiless drums never before used with such power and abandon. It rose in intensity and excitement to a blazing climax and all the promise of a new age. It was the Twentieth Century incarnate. It reached at one stride a peak of modern music that was to dominate later generations. It was to the Twentieth Century what Beethoven's *Eroica* was to the Nineteenth, and like it, never surpassed.

The premiere conducted by Monteux on May 28, 1913, created almost a riot in the theatre. The abandonment of understood harmony, melody and structure seemed musical anarchy. People felt they were hearing a blasphemous attempt to destroy music as an art and responded with howls and catcalls and derisive laughter. Counter-demonstrators bellowed defiance. One young man became so excited he began to beat rhythmically with his fists on the head of an American in the audience whose own emotion was so great that "I did not feel the blows for some time." A beautifully gowned lady in a box stood up and slapped the face of a man hissing in an adjoining box. Saint-Saëns indignantly rose and left the hall; Ravel shouted, "Genius!" The dancers could not hear the music above the uproar and Nijinsky, who had choreographed the ballet, stood in the wings pounding out the rhythm with his fists and shouting in despair, *"Ras, Dwa, Tri!"* Monteux threw desperate glances to Diaghilev who signed to him to keep on playing and shouted to the audience to let the piece be heard. "Listen first, hiss afterwards!" screamed Gabriel Astruc, the French manager, in a rage. When it was over the audience streamed out to continue their battle in the cafés and the critics to carry it to the press, but as the music had hardly been heard, opinion was largely emotion. Not until a year later when the music was played again in Paris as a concert in April, 1914, was it recognized for what it was. With the performance of the *Sacre*, filling out a decade of innovation in the arts, all the major tendencies of the next half-century had been stated.

That summer Strauss completed *Joseph*. Meeting with Diaghilev and Bakst in Venice, Hofmannsthal planned a production that was to be "the most lavish and beautiful imaginable." It was to be set not in Egypt but in the Venice of Tintoretto and Veronese because as Count Kessler explained, "Too scrupulous an accuracy can but impede the freedom of imagination."

Already busy with several new works, Strauss was news. When in July he finished *Ein Deutsches Motette* for chorus and orchestra it was considered worth a cable dispatch to the New York *Times*. For the opening of a new concert hall in Vienna in November he composed a *Festival Prelude* scored for a bigger orchestra than ever: one hundred and fifty musicians including eight horns, eight drums, six extra trumpets and an organ. It was suitable to a year of national chest-thumping in celebration of the hundredth anniversary of the defeat of Napoleon at Leipzig and the simultaneous twenty-fifth anniversary of the Kaiser's reign.

For the Centenary a book called *Germany in Arms* was published with an introduction by the Crown Prince, who wrote: "It is the holy duty of Germany above all other peoples to maintain an army and a fleet ever at the highest point of readiness. Only then, supported by our own good sword, can we preserve the place in the sun which is our due but which is not willingly granted to us." Although the "gigantic conflagration" of nations, once started, would not be easily extinguished, this should not deter the German hand from the sword, "for the sword will remain the decisive factor till the end of the world."

More factually Karl Helfferich, director of the Deutsche Bank, published a survey of *Germany's Economic Progress and National Wealth, 1888–1913* which supplied overwhelming figures of the "impetuous and triumphant upward movement" of the last twenty-five years. Helfferich showed that the population had increased by more than a third, that Germany's excess of births over deaths was greater than any other country's except Russia, that economic opportunity and demand for labour had expanded faster than the population, that productivity of German workers and percentage of population gainfully employed had increased, that upward was the word for statistics on production, transportation, consumption, capital aggregation, investments, savings-bank deposits and every other factor of economic life. Helfferich's pages groaned under such phrases as "enormous development," "vast progress," "prodigious expansion," "gigantic increase."

That year an Englishman traveling in Alsace-Lorraine asked a waiter in Metz what nationality he considered himself. *"Muss-Preussen"* (Obligatory Prussian) the man replied, and for the rest of the journey the Englishman was heard by his traveling companion to mutter at intervals, *"Muss-Preussen*—we're all going to be *Muss-Preussen* before long."

Fear of the same ancient sin of pride that had prompted Kipling to write "Recessional" in the year of Britain's Jubilee now afflicted an occasional thoughtful German. Walther Rathenau, introspective and literary heir of the Allgemeine Elektrizitäts-Gesellschaft, published a long poem called "Festal Song" in *Die Zukunft* whose tone was a protest against the organized enthusiasm worked up for the Centenary. He too saw an apocalyptic vision and headed his poem with a text from Ezekiel, "Also thou son of man, thus saith the Lord God unto the land of Israel, 'An end, the end is come upon the four corners of the land. Now is the end come upon thee; it watcheth for thee; behold it is come.'" Rathenau quoted no more but readers who turned to Ezekiel would have found the judgment upon Tyre: "With thy wisdom and thy understanding thou hast gotten thee riches and hast gotten gold and silver into thy treasure and by thy traffick hast thou increased thy riches and thine heart is lifted up because of thy riches and thou hast said I am a God. . . . Therefore I will bring strangers upon thee, the terrible of nations and they shall draw their swords against the beauty of thy wisdom . . . and bring thee down into the pit and thou shalt die the deaths of them that are slain in the midst of the seas."

Voices like that of Rathenau, who did not have quite the courage to sign his own important name but used a pseudonym, were not heard. Such was German national sentiment that when Hauptmann's *Festspiel* in honor of the Centenary was produced by Max Reinhardt it was attacked by the Nationalists and closed on demand of the Crown Prince because it stressed liberation rather than the sword which had accomplished it. The mood culminated at Zabern, a small Alsatian town where ill-feeling between the German garrison and the natives provoked German officers to assault and arrest civilians. Becoming a *cause célèbre* the incident increased foreign hostility to Germany. When Colonel Reuter, the commanding officer of Zabern, was court-martialed and acquitted, the power of the Army over the rights of the citizen became a major political issue in Germany. If Army officers were put beyond the law, said a member of the Center party in the Reichstag, "then *finis Germaniae*." He was cheered by the majority, but Colonel Reuter received the Order of the Red Eagle, Third Class, and a congratulatory telegram from the Crown Prince saying, "Keep it up!"

The combination of Richard Strauss and Russian Ballet, awaited as a major event, was scheduled for May, 1914, with the composer conducting. Attempting to sum up his career so far, Lawrence Gilman in January found the same baffling duality in Strauss which had so often troubled historians of his country. His best work, Gilman wrote, as in the opening of *Zarathustra*, the finale of *Don Quixote*, the love passage in *Heldenleben*, the recognition of Orestes and Electra, was music of "terrifying cosmic sublimity" and *Elektra*, his masterpiece, would someday be recognized as "among the supreme things of music." Yet he could achieve "a degree of bad taste that passes credibility, be commonplace with a blatancy that sets teeth on edge" and irritate by his "staggeringly complacent habit" of writing music without point or coherence, reason or logic. He always stirred the waters, coming up now with something precious, now with mud, but the activity was indisputable. Gilman, who had not yet heard the *Sacre*, concluded that Strauss was "unequalled in music as an awakener, . . . the most dynamic, the most reckless, the most preposterous of all composers, . . . the most commanding music maker since Wagner."

Strauss arrived in Paris for rehearsals in April. Nijinsky, for whom the part had been created, was not to play it, having been banished from the company by Diaghilev in a jealous fury because of his marriage. A new young dancer from the Imperial Ballet, Léonide Massine, slim, barely seventeen, with great brown eyes, replaced him. Ida Rubinstein was the Queen and the Spanish painter José Maria Sert supplemented the designs of Bakst. In a Palladian hall with fountains, pillars of gold, marble floors, and ewers of crystal piled with fruit, Potiphar's wife in scarlet brocade was surrounded by slaves in pink and gold and a bodyguard of gigantic mulattoes in black plumes holding golden whips. Animal life was present in a brace of Russian wolfhounds. A variety of exotic dancers endeavor to relieve the Queen's "almost passionate weariness of life" in vain, until a shepherd boy, Joseph, is carried in asleep wrapped in yellow silk and who, on waking, dances his search for the divine, instantly arousing the Queen from passionate weariness to passionate desire. Her most strenuous efforts at seduction are repulsed, she denounces Joseph, guards prepare his torture and death and he is saved by an Archangel who carries him off to the sound of heavenly music while Potiphar's wife strangles herself with her rope of pearls.

Although the libretto was widely ridiculed and the music was considered second-rate Strauss, the production was so sumptuous and lascivious that everyone enjoyed it and the evening ended happily in a gala supper at Larue's given by the composer for his friends who had come from Germany, Austria and Italy for the premiere. After feasting on early strawberries and exquisite wines, each guest was presented by the waiter with his share of the bill.

The company went to London at the end of May for a two-month season of "extraordinary success." Chaliapin was declared "supreme" as Ivan the Terrible, Rimsky's last opera, *Coq d'Or*, and Stravinsky's new one, *The Nightingale,* were acclaimed and the "ultra-modern" *Joseph* to be given on June 23 with the composer again conducting, aroused eager expectations. At rehearsals with Karsavina, who had replaced Ida Rubin-stein, Strauss demonstrated how he wanted her to perform her dance of seduction. Starting from the far corner of her dressing room and singing the music "he would run, trampling heavily across the room, to the sofa representing the couch of Joseph."

On the night of the performance Drury Lane was crowded to the last seat by a bejewelled and brilliant audience "keyed up to concert pitch for a memorable event." To a young man among them, jostled by bare shoul-ders and gay laughter, everyone seemed to know one another as if at "an enormous but exclusive party." In the presence of the Prime Minister and Mrs. Asquith, the Russian company and the renowned composer, it seemed "an occasion of almost international importance." As applause filled the house the young man, leaning forward from his seat in the dress circle, could see the tall "world-weary" German composer take up his stand before the orchestra, "pink and imperturbable."

If the music won no new laurels, Strauss's visit was personally satisfy-ing. He conducted the Queen's Hall Orchestra in a program of his own and Mozart's music, which was considered one of the finest concerts of the season. On June 24 wearing the "most beautiful of all the Doctors' robes," the crimson silk and cream-colored brocade of a Doctor of Music, he received an honorary degree from Oxford.

A month later on July 25 the Russian Ballet closed its season with a joint performance of Strauss's *Joseph* and Stravinsky's *Petrouchka*. At the same hour that evening in Belgrade the Serbian reply to an Austrian ulti-matum was rejected by the Austrian Ambassador, who announced the severance of relations and left for home.

7

Transfer of Power

ENGLAND: 1902–11

7

Transfer of Power

L ORD SALISBURY, who had died in 1903, was not on hand to see the workings of democracy in the first major election of the new century, but he would not have been surprised. A new segment of society was rising, not yet to take the patricians' place, but by its pressure and through its surrogates to push them aside. The age of the people was under way.

It revealed itself in the cry "Pigtail!" which echoed through the constituencies in the General Election of 1906 with virulence equal to its irrelevance. No issue proved more exploitable than "Chinese Slavery" and the Liberals played it up as designedly as the Tories had used patriotic slogans in the Khaki Election of 1900. The slaves in question were indentured Chinese labour imported with the consent of the Unionist government to mine gold in South Africa. Billboards flamed with pictures of Chinese in chains, Chinese being kicked, Chinese being flogged. Sandwich men dressed as Chinese slaves paraded the streets. Cartoons showed the ghosts of British soldiers killed in the Boer War pointing to the fenced compounds where the Chinese were lodged and asking, "Did we die for this?" Working-class audiences were told the Tories would introduce Chinese labour into England if they won and pictures of a pigtailed coolie in a straw hat were labeled "Tory British Workingman." Thrown on a lantern screen at political meetings, the pictures, reported Graham Wallas, a Liberal sympathizer, aroused "an instantaneous howl of indignation against Mr. Balfour." The audience could not have told whether it howled from humanitarian indignation or fear of the competition of cheap labour. Underlying both these sentiments Wallas thought he detected a fear of the alien symbolized by the alien pigtail. The hideous yellow faces aroused "an immediate hatred of the Mongoloid racial type and this hatred was transferred to the Conservative party." In the howl of the audience he heard the force of the irrational in public affairs.

New men were appealing to a new electorate; were called forth, as was the yellow press, by the existence of a new electorate. People were more literate and to that extent more reachable and more gullible. The ha'penny *Daily Mail* had a circulation of over half a million, more than ten times that of *The Times*. Motorcars enabled candidates to reach a wider audience and the growth of cities made audiences larger. The force of the irrational was not necessarily wrong; it could just as well be right for the wrong reasons. It was not necessarily confined to what Matthew Arnold called the Populace, but the effect was greater because there were more of them.

When Arthur Balfour smoothly succeeded Lord Salisbury as Prime Minister after the end of the Boer War in 1902, the waves of change were already lapping at his feet. Business was good but competition from abroad was cutting into British supremacy in foreign commerce, moving into her markets, taking the lead in new industries. At home upper-class life was still delightful, but unemployment, hunger and want, all the ills, injustices and inequities collectively known as the Social Problem, were pressing against the ramparts of privilege in a tide of discontent impossible to ignore or repress. The demands of a new age were requiring from government more action, more imagination, more positive intention and measures than formerly. The Liberals, who now looked forward to their chance after ten years out of office, believed they could supply the need.

They were not a coherent group and never had been. Their dominant philosophy, as of liberalism anywhere, favored change and reform, but it was cut into by a thousand fissures of ideas and social background. In person the Liberals ranged from Whig aristocrats like Lord Rosebery to country gentlemen like Sir Edward Grey to men of business wealth like Campbell-Bannerman to landless intellectuals like Asquith and Morley to a unique and alien upstart from the Celtic fringe like Lloyd George. Some were Little Englanders who regarded Empire, in the words of John Bright, as "a gigantic system for providing outdoor relief for the aristocracy"; some were as fervent imperialists as the Tories. Some were Church of England, some Nonconformist, some Home Rulers, some unalterably opposed to Home Rule. Some were ardent Radicals dedicated to redistribution of wealth and political power, some were magnates of industry absorbed in making fortunes. Those who were Liberals from conviction rather than from family tradition or political expedient felt that between themselves and the Tories existed "a gulf as wide as any in previous time";

the gulf, as Herbert Samuel put it, between "the quietist and the reformer." Filled with the zeal of the reformer, Samuel believed that the principles of Liberalism "are nothing else than the application to public affairs of the religious spirit itself." Some Liberals were sincere, some were opportunists, some were demagogues, some like Lloyd George all three at once. They were the outs, eager for office, ready to answer the demands of a new time.

Their opponents were split among themselves, harassed by a series of domestic quarrels which had reopened since the Boer War with a peculiar vehemence. All the hatred and jealousy of Nonconformity for the Establishment blew up into a national tempest over the Education Act of 1902. Sponsored and largely drafted by Balfour himself, the Act added secondary to primary education as an obligation of the state with the object of making it available to all and of bringing all schools up to a uniform standard. Like the Compulsory Education Act of 1870 it had an economic motive: the recognition that unless the nation undertook to raise the level of schooling, it would continue to fall behind in the competition for markets. In effecting progress, the Act was perhaps the most important of the decade but its method was partisan. By favoring and, in fact, giving financial support to the schools of the Established Church—that is, the Church of England—while the Board Schools under local control were abolished, the Act infuriated the Nonconformists, who were traditionally Liberals. It supplied a cause to reunite the Imperialist and Radical wings of the Liberal party which had divided over the Boer War and Home Rule. Debate in the Commons took on the animus peculiar to the war of High Church against Low Church, Methodist clergymen wrote outraged letters to the papers, the Act was called "the greatest betrayal since the Crucifixion," protest meetings assembled in villages and leagues were formed pledged to non-payment of school taxes with all the fervor of Roundheads refusing ship money to King Charles. Lloyd George, already the champion of Welsh Disestablishment, encouraged the leagues with histrionic oratory. In throwing themselves into a revival of religious battle, people seemed to be on the hunt for excitement, as if the Boer War had created a taste for it while supplying its physical experience to less than two per cent of the population.

The cry "Votes for Women!" promised further trouble and those who raised it frankly called themselves "militants." They organized under the leadership of Mrs. Pankhurst in 1903 in opposition to the Suffrage group led by Mrs. Fawcett which believed in obtaining the vote by persuasion. Their first experiments in militancy, confined to heckling and unfurling banners at political meetings, while not yet serious, were one more evidence, as Lady Frances Balfour wrote, of "new winds blowing hard through society."

At the same time, mine-owners of the Rand were demanding license to import Chinese labour when African labour, finding enough work after the war to satisfy a low appetite, could not be obtained for the mines. Contract labour had horrid connotations from which the Government shrank, but the mine-owners were insistent, else they could not reopen, investments were tied up, Rand shares tumbled, and as the *Economist* frankly stated, it was a matter of £.*s.d.* "If the people of England and elsewhere who own Transvaal mining shares to the value of £200,000,000 want to get their money back with interest, then they will have to tackle this labour question in the right spirit."

The Government reluctantly consented, the Chinese were brought in and lodged in compounds; the Liberals, who had themselves introduced contract labour in British Guiana, now thundered in awful wrath. The Chinese compounds were no worse than England's dark satanic slums, where one water faucet and one privy often served twenty-five families, where beds were rented for three and the space under them for two. But humanitarian instincts grow fiercer in proportion to the distance by which their causes are removed and it is always easier to build Jerusalem in Africa than at home. Moreover the Chinese labour issue carried the smell of money which had hung about the Boer War from the start. It devalued the moral content which the imperialists liked to attach to the cause of Empire.

On top of these issues Joseph Chamberlain wrought havoc with Tariff Reform. When he launched his campaign for Protection he aroused against his party the fundamental British sentiment of laissez-faire, raised among the people old memories of hated Corn Laws and fears of a rise in food prices, handed the Liberals another issue in the cry "Free food!" and split his party between the old and the new Conservatives, between land and money. Manufacturers and businessmen, exponents of what H. G. Wells called "commercialized imperialism with all its push and energy," favored Protection. As an imperialist and businessman himself, Chamberlain saw it as a means of drawing together the mother country and all its dependencies in a vast Imperial tariff system which would stimulate trade within the Empire and prosperity at home, strengthen Imperial bonds, increase revenues for social legislation, and, not least, provide an issue of which he would be the hero. In the British Cabinet he was what Germany was among the nations: dynamic, ambitious, conscious of power and ability, fitted in his own mind for the top place and galled that it was held by another. Tariff Reform was his usurpation of the office he had missed. It wrecked the Cabinet. Chamberlain himself resigned, the better to carry his campaign to the country. Five Free Traders, including the Duke of Devonshire and the Chancellor of the Exchequer, also resigned. In the ranks a vigorous new M.P., Winston Churchill, waving the banner of Free Trade, crossed over to join the Liberals amid cries of "Rat!" from the Tories. Interminable debates raged over preferential duties, bounties, dumping, and other fiscal mysteries. The public, barely comprehending, took sides, Free Food leagues sprang up alongside the anti-school-tax leagues; the British people were rapidly becoming as contentious as the French.

As Prime Minister, Mr. Balfour, still suave, effortless, unaddicted to political dogma, refused to take a firm position, partly because he saw no firm ground on which to take one and partly because he believed a strategy of steering between extremes was the best way to hold his party together and his Government in office. He saw no virtue in a doctrinaire persistence in Free Trade and he could see advantages to British industry in some form of selective tariff, although he had no wish to swallow Chamberlain's program whole. The one thing he firmly believed was that continued direction of England's affairs by the Conservative party was more important than either Free Trade or Protection and this he was determined to maintain. Amid quarreling colleagues, resigning ministers, party apostasies, he eluded all pressures and coolly told the House that he would be ill performing his duty "if I were to profess a settled conviction where no settled conviction exists." He infused the issues with such philosophic doubt and infused his doubt with such authority as almost to mesmerize members on both sides. When called upon to explain his relations with Free Traders and Protectionists within his own party he "indulged the House with a brilliant display of disdainful banter." Exploiting all his parliamentary dexterity, he maneuvered the Government through session after session for more than two years, seeming almost to find amusement in the difficulty of his task. But the performance left his followers uneasy. They wanted the leader of their party to lead and instead, as Harry Cust said, "he nailed his colors to the fence."

Balfour's purpose, however, was serious. He wanted to retain office as long as he could in order to consolidate the Entente and the work of the Committee of Imperial Defence especially after the Tangier Crisis of 1905. He had given the order for rearming the artillery with a new quick-firing gun, the 18-pounder, and he was determined, as he explained later, "not to go out of office until we were so far committed to the expenditure that no Liberal Government could have withdrawn from that position."

Relentless, Chamberlain persisted in his campaign. Balfour's dancing on eggs grew increasing difficult as the exasperation of his own party and the impatience for office of the Opposition mounted.

Overshadowing all was the Social Problem. Investigations and reports appearing all at once after 1900 made harshly visible the fact and the consequences of extreme inequality in possession of material goods. In B. S. Rowntree's *Poverty: A Study of Town Life*, 1901, in the last volume of Charles Booth's *Life and Labour of the People of London*, 1903, in L. Chiozza Money's *Riches and Poverty*, 1905, in reports of the Royal Commission on Labour and in the Fabian Society's studies of the destitute, diseased and insane, evidence accumulated that the richest country in the world rested on a foundation of one-third of its population living "in chronic poverty, unable to satisfy the primal needs of animal life." Chiozza Money showed that economic inequality was particularly wide in England. In France, whose population was about the same, there were twice as many small estates between £500 and £10,000 as in England, but in the United Kingdom three times as many large estates over £50,000 and four times as many over £250,000 as in France.

The investigators produced the facts: sleep, diet, sanitation, privacy, even respiratory air, were inadequate for basic human needs. Professor Huxley had calculated that 800 cubic feet of air space per person was the ideal. Even the Poor House provided 300. In the slums people lived three to a bedroom of 700 cubic feet or, with children, eight and nine in a space of 1,200 cubic feet. Vermin lived with them, a piece of paper on the floor served as a toilet, fish on Sundays was the weekly protein for a family of eight, at two and a half ounces per portion. Children were stunted and pale, with rotting teeth, and if they went to school, sat dully at their desks or fell asleep. Ignorance and apathy as much as ill health were poverty's product; the slums were sloughs of wasted lives. Overcrowding in country villages was often as bad. In an Oxfordshire cottage a family of eight slept in two beds with a pair of thin blankets among them, in a Yorkshire cottage husband and wife and five daughters shared two beds and an attic floor, in Somerset a mother and three children slept in one room, five children of both sexes up to the age of nineteen in another.

For unskilled and unorganized labour, working conditions matched the slums. At the Shawfield Chemical Works in Glasgow in 1897, year of the Diamond Jubilee, workmen received 3*d*. or 4*d*. an hour for a twelve-hour day, seven days a week, spent amid poisonous vapors without a lunchhour rest. They ate lunch standing at the furnaces and if they took Sunday off were fined the next day's wages. Lord Overtoun, owner of the Works, a philanthropist who gave £10,000 a year to charity, was a leading member of the Sunday Observance and Sunday Rest Societies. In other industries workers could be arrested for taking a day off without permission. If they applied for it, the request could be refused; if they took it anyway they could be, and often were, hauled off to a day in gaol. Skilled workers organized in England's craft unions, the oldest in Europe, were better off. Numbering about one-fifth of all adult male workers, a larger proportion than in any other country, they had their own insurance and pension systems backed by large funds and they benefited from lower prices in their own cooperatives. Nevertheless, vis-à-vis capital, they were still on the defensive and the dark persistent presence of unemployment at their backs made them vulnerable.

England's economy since 1900 had recovered from the depression of the nineties and was on the whole prosperous, active and expanding. Shippers and shipbuilders, bankers and millowners were busy, coal mines were operating to capacity, and although in chemical, electrical and other new industries the British were not as enterprising as some foreign competitors, most businesses, despite ups and downs, were doing well. Yet the gap in distribution of profits was growing not less but greater. While the rich lived at an acme of luxury and leisure, the purchasing power of wages was falling and human material deteriorating. The minimum height for recruits for the British Army was lowered from five feet three inches in 1883 to five feet in 1900.

Something was wrong with the system. Somehow the great mechanical and material achievements of the recent past had twisted society out of shape. In the United States, where the process was accelerated, Thorstein Veblen was moved to make his inquiries into business enterprise and the Muckrakers to their searches in the slums and stockyards and the files of Standard Oil. In England, reformers, writers, crusading journalists, Fabians, Socialists, Radical Liberals were impatient for the remedy. The shrill cries of H. G. Wells warned that material progress without planning would lead to a future, as he depicted it in *When the Sleeper Wakes* in 1899, of higher buildings, bigger towns, wickeder capitalists, more downtrodden and desperate labour, a future where "everything was bigger, quicker, more crowded" . . . in short an "exaggeration of contemporary tendencies." Like a blue jay incessantly pecking and cawing at the ills of civilization, he demanded in *Anticipations* in 1900 and *A Modern Utopia* in 1905 the New Republic of a planned society and fervently expounded the possibilities for improvement which science had put in the hands of man.

Peace, Retrenchment and Reform which had satisfied as the Liberal creed for so long were no longer adequate. The optimistic Liberalism of the Nineteenth Century was past. An "indignant pessimism" inspired Charles Masterman's *From the Abyss* in 1902 and *In Peril of Change* in 1905. A young Liberal journalist, literary editor of the *Daily News*, devoutly High Church in religion, married to a Lyttelton whose uncle was a member of Balfour's cabinet, he was one of the new kind of Liberal, puzzled and disturbed by trends which betrayed the promise of the Nineteenth Century. Another was the lonely economist J. A. Hobson, author of *The Social Problem*, 1901. He saw the brilliant hopes of early Liberalism overcast by the doctrine of survival of the fittest and the energy for progress absorbed in material growth. Political Economy having failed to solve the Social Problem, he believed a new social science was needed to "furnish a satisfactory basis for the art of social progress." Hobson fixed on unemployment as the crux of the matter. He saw it as a waste of human resources and included in that waste the idle rich, of whom 250,000 males between the ages of twenty and sixty-five, according to a census of 1891, were without trade or profession. Under-consumption, the corollary of unemployment, was the chief source of trouble and he saw imperialism, not as the white man's burden nobly shouldered, but as the economy's drive to compensate for markets missing at home. Hobson's views, expressed in *The Psychology of Jingoism* in 1901 and *Imperialism* in 1902, were influential but offensive both to the imperialists and to the Fabians, who believed in imperialism. He was never offered a chair either by the major universities or by the London School of Economics, founded by the Fabians in 1894, to establish that new social science which was his goal.

What the Fabian Society wanted was Socialism without Marx or revolution, something like Macbeth without murder—an intellectual, respectable, gradual, factual, practical, "gas and water" English Socialism powered by the brains, hard work and infinite attention to detail of the Webbs and the brilliant common sense of Shaw. Founded in the eighties, expounding plans and arguments through the Fabian Tracts, it was an intellectual lobby bent on guiding existing political institutions toward the ultimate goals of Socialism. Fabians were the B's in Beatrice Webb's division of people into A's (aristocrats, artists and anarchists) and B's (benevolents, bourgeois and bureaucrats). They sought no working-class base but preferred to operate, as William Morris said, by "gradually permeating cultivated people with our own aspirations" and gradually influencing government toward their goals. They made splendid progress among those of their own kind but remained a scholastic regiment of seven or eight hundred, aloof from the people for whom they toiled. In England persons of the educated classes did not and could not penetrate the unions. Discrediting the Marxian dogma of mandatory class war, the Fabians believed that labourers and employees must gain their ends within the capitalist system because it was the employers' surplus capital which gave them work. In his lectures "disproving" Marx, Shaw, a tall, reedy, red-haired figure, emphatic, provocative and bold, held listeners spellbound as he poured out ideas in crisp, sharp sentences, unfaltering for an hour and a half. In *Major Barbara*, which opened in December, 1905, with Mr. Balfour in the audience, Shaw spoke through the mouth of the munitions magnate, Undershaft, on "the crime of poverty." "What you call crime is nothing: a murder here and a theft there. What do they matter? They are only the accidents and illnesses of life: there are not fifty genuine professional criminals in London. But there are millions of poor people, abject people, dirty people, ill-fed, ill-clothed people. They poison us morally and physically: they kill the happiness of society: they force us to do away with our own liberties and to organize unnatural cruelties for fear they should rise against us and drag us down into their abyss. Only fools fear crime: we all fear poverty."

The Webbs attacked the crime with mountainous reports and the English lubricant of social intercourse and conversation. Coldly bent on improving society, they were essentially authoritarians, impatient with the democratic process. They favored Protection, Joseph Chamberlain (with whom Beatrice had once contemplated marriage) and anything which strengthened the State and brought in revenue for more sewers, soup kitchens and unemployment insurance. They had no use for the Liberals, who understood neither the imperial nor Socialist demands of the new age, and had little faith in a Labour party of the untutored which would be incapable of imposing its will. What was needed was a strong party with no nonsense and a business-like understanding of national needs which would take hold of the future like a governess, slap it into clean clothes, wash its face, blow its nose, make it sit up straight at table and eat a proper diet. This could only be the Conservative party, regenerated by Chamberlain, advised by Mr. and Mrs. Webb, bestowing upon England the iron blessings of Tory Socialism.

Orthodox Socialism was represented by the Socialist Democratic Federation led by H. M. Hyndman, a wealthy product of Eton and Trinity College, Cambridge, which he had attended in the same year as the Prince of Wales. As devout in Marxism as it was detached from the working class, the SDF expressed all the fiercest revolutionary doctrines of continental Socialism, but, lacking followers, remained a voice without a body. "I could not carry on," said Hyndman, "unless I expected the revolution at ten o'clock next Monday morning." Presumably it was to drop from the sky, because in Hyndman's scheme the workers did not figure as initiators. "A slave class cannot be freed by the slaves themselves," he pronounced. "The leadership, the initiative, the teaching, the organization, must come from those who are born into a different position and are trained to use their faculties in early life." He complained of the peculiarly British technique by which the ruling class absorbed rising labour leaders who proved only too willing to sell out to the dominant minority (that is, the Liberals) after they had "obtained their education from well-to-do Socialists who have been sacrificing themselves for their sake." The tone suggests some justification for the friends who said that Hyndman, a cricketer, had adopted Socialism out of spite against the world because he was not included in the Cambridge eleven. Along with Robert Blatchford, editor of the *Clarion*, and other earnest spirits, Hyndman in meetings, articles, journalism and oratory, relentlessly pursued that Monday morning which he could not have survived and the British working class did not want.

In 1901 occurred a decisive moment in the shifting balance of political power. The Taff Vale judgment by the House of Lords, acting in its capacity as a court of appeal, held trade unions liable for the damage caused by strikes, thus putting in jeopardy their pension and benefit funds. It proved to be that act of the ruling class which convinced the English working class of the need for political representation. Until then English labour believed in fighting its battles against employers by direct action through trade unions rather than by political action through Parliament. Giving its political allegiance to the Liberals, English labour could not be drawn into support of a Socialist party and disapproved of class war. "The English working class," said Clemenceau, "is a bourgeois class." Continental comrades found the English Trade Union Congresses dull and uninspired because the members were not interested in debating ideas but only in immediate gains. To the French, said one visitor, such gains were the gathering of strength for the social revolution; to the British worker they were ends in themselves while "fundamental principles and eternal verities irritate him." He was not interested in a new social system, as Morley said, "but of having a fairer treatment in this one."

In 1892 the eternal verities found a voice in a Scottish miners' organizer with the zeal of a prophet. Keir Hardie, then thirty-six, was a short handsome man with smoldering brown eyes and hair brushed back from a domed forehead. Born in a one-room cottage on a Lanarkshire coal field and brought up with two adults and nine children in that room, where somehow his mother taught him to read, he went to work as a baker's errand boy at the age of seven. On one weekly payday, with his father out of work, his mother in bed with a newborn child and no food in the house, the family's small and only breadwinner walked the two miles to his place of employment in the rain, to arrive for the second day in a row fifteen minutes late. "You are wanted upstairs by the Master," said the girl behind the counter. Entering the room where the employer and his family sat around a mahogany breakfast table set with steaming coffee and hot rolls, he was told he was dismissed and, as a reminder against lateness, his week's wages were forfeit. On his empty way out the maid in silent pity gave him a roll.

Hardie believed in class war to the end. Liberals to him were no different from Tories but just another face of the employing class. When he stood for the first time as an independent labour candidate from mid-Lanark in 1888, the Liberal candidate—Sir George Trevelyan—explained to him how unfortunate it was that they should fight each other to the benefit of the Tories and proposed that if Hardie withdrew, the Liberals would assure him a safe seat and election expenses at the next general election and pay him as M.P. a yearly salary of £300. Hardie, who had never earned anything approaching that sum, refused. Although he lost on this occasion, receiving only 617 votes out of a total of 7,000, four years later he was elected as an independent from South West Ham. When he took his seat in the House wearing tweeds and a cloth cap, unlike others of his class who put on respectable black broad-cloth when they mixed in the world, it was as if the red flag had been raised at Westminster. He never succumbed to the capitalist embrace. During a debate on the unemployed he sat listening in growing rage while no word of sympathy for the starving was uttered and finally burst out, "You well-fed beasts!" On another occasion when a member was denouncing the unemployed as lazy vagabonds who did not want to work, Hardie suggested that an equal number of vagabonds could be seen "every day on Rotten Row in top hats and spats." When he addressed meetings, standing like a statue in hewn granite of the emancipated worker, with head thrown back and body erect, he seemed to express the "equality, freedom and triumphant self-reliance" which he wanted to infuse in the working class. With no salary or political funds to draw on, he supported himself, his wife and three children on what he could earn from journalism, the maximum he ever made being £210 a year.

In 1889 the desperate dockers' strike for 6*d*. an hour started the movement to organize the unskilled in industry-wide unions. It continued through the nineties with organizers moved by a sense of "religious necessity" and workers whom it was difficult to persuade that arbitration paid them better than "the fierce strikes in which their repressed emotions sought outlet."

The dockers' strike waged in the heart of London had thrust the realities of labour's battles under the eyes of capital and swept young men like Herbert Samuel into politics. Appalled by conditions among the strikers and by the sweatshops and squalid homes he saw in Whitechapel when canvassing there for his brother's candidacy for the LCC (London County Council), he decided "from that moment" that the House of Commons was "my objective and to take part in social legislation my aim." The strike also brought to prominence a rampant trade unionist, John Burns of the Amalgamated Engineers, union of the locomotive drivers, who was known as the "Man with the Red Flag" from his habit of carrying that item with him whenever he addressed meetings. Although the dockers were not his union, he took over management of the strike to help its leaders, Tom Mann and Ben Tillett. He kept on excellent terms with the police, organized food lines and procured the settlement which won the "dockers' tanner"—to the distress of Kropotkin, who thought a critical moment had been missed. "If Burns with 80,000 men behind him does not make a revolution," he wrote, "it is because he is afraid of having his head cut off." Burns, however, despite a period of vociferous Socialism, was too English to be revolutionary and never shared Hardie's refusal to compromise with capitalism. He preferred to fight labour's cause through whatever alliances suited the situation, and when elected to the LCC, collaborated with the Liberals. His hatred of Keir Hardie, according to Beatrice Webb, "reaches the dimensions of mania."

At the Trades Union Congress of 1893 Hardie generated enough support, against the opposition of Burns, to form an Independent Labour Party of which he was named chairman. Its declared Marxian purpose was to secure public ownership of "all means of production, distribution and exchange" and, lest there be any mistake, "to take charge of the revolution to which economic conditions are leading us." Not unnaturally financial support from the craft unions was shy. Two years later in the general election of 1895, which brought in Lord Salisbury's Government, the ILP failed to elect a single one of its twenty-eight candidates. It was "the most costly funeral since Napoleon's," commented Burns, not without satisfaction in which he was joined by Mrs. Webb. For Labour to act independently and insist on three-cornered contests, she declared, was "suicide." Yet the Conservative editor J. L. Garvin suspected that despite the fiasco the ILP might well prove to be "an increasingly powerful and disturbing factor in English politics."

At the same time, employers' associations—formed to resist the demands of labour—increased in number and joined in agreements to employ non-union labour. To create a "reserve" in case of strikes they organized Free Labour Registries, which were simply lists of strikebreakers under another name. In 1897 they were able to defeat the old and powerful Amalgamated Engineers in its strike for the eight-hour day which lasted thirty weeks. Taking the offensive by lockouts, they succeeded against other unions in re-establishing piecework and repudiating overtime pay. On occasion the Government lent troops in their support. Leaving nothing to chance, the associations in 1898 formed the Employers' Parliamentary Council to smother any nascent legislation unfavorable to their interests.

In 1900, reluctantly edging toward the political arena, a number of trade unions, representing about one quarter of the total membership, joined with the ILP and Hyndman's group to form a Labour Representation Committee for the election of political candidates. The Fabian Society lukewarmly and temporarily joined also. As Secretary, the Committee chose Ramsay MacDonald, a thirty-four-year-old Scot who emerged from obscure beginnings to be a founder of the ILP and was recognized for an astute political sense. On discovering that the intellectuals were not, after all, to control policy, Hyndman's group pulled out and the Fabians, finding the endeavor "not in our line," never played a role. Coal and Cotton and the older craft unions remained hostile. Of the committee's fourteen candidates put up for the general election of 1900, only two, Hardie and John Burns, were elected.

Then came the "staggering blow" of Taff Vale. On the strength of the decision other employers began to sue for damages, the unions lost case after case; with their funds held liable, the long-acknowledged right of strike was nullified and all the hard-won gains of collective bargaining suddenly vulnerable. Discouraged and disillusioned in the old principle of direct action, the unions faced into politics, determined to reverse Taff Vale in the only way possible: through Parliament. Union membership in the Labour Representation Committee more than doubled in two years and with union treasuries opening up, the Committee won three by-elections in 1902 and 1903, including one three-cornered contest at Durham. Will Crooks, a former cooper and borough councilman, born in a workhouse, Arthur Henderson of the Ironfounders, and David Shackleton, a weaver, took their places in the House called "the best club in London."

Here indeed were new winds blowing through society. Yet they did not as yet seriously ruffle the class represented by the Tories. Its prevailing mood remained on the whole complacent. Tory philosophy accepted a surplus labour force as the fulcrum of the profit system, an economic law of nature not to be disturbed by legislation. Upper-class life continued so comfortable and pleasant that it was difficult to feel any urgency about reforming what *The Times* imperturbably called "imperfections of the Social Order." When Keir Hardie in 1901 moved the first Socialist resolution ever presented to the House of Commons and spoke for twenty minutes on how the menace of the profit system, responsible for the Boer War, the Boxer Rebellion and the London slums, could be remedied by common ownership of land and capital, "Mr. Balfour, coming back from dinner, smiled pleasantly on the Speaker, doubtless calculating that things as they were would last his time."

By 1905 with a general election looming, concessions were necessary. Wooing the labour vote the Conservatives appointed a Royal Commission on Trades Disputes to report on the question of re-establishing the principle of non-liability. It even allowed a Trades Disputes Bill, which would have reversed Taff Vale, to go through committee and pass two readings in the House, though it did not go so far as to enact it. It faced unemployment sufficiently, if not very boldly, to enact an Unemployed Workmen's Act which established Labour Bureaus to register the unemployed and to help them find work and to pay compensation in certain cases. The Act applied, however, only to London and its spirit was one of limited patching. The Tories had no really remedial program to offer because they did not want one.

As a minority party the Liberals needed the support of labour to win, especially to win by a large enough margin to free them of the Irish incubus. For them the appearance of independent labour candidates in the field could mean disaster. Faced with the danger of three-cornered contests which could only take away their votes, the Liberals now needed not merely support but alliance. Labour in the person of Ramsay MacDonald was ready to listen. In 1903 he and Herbert Gladstone, Chief Liberal Whip, worked out a secret pact by which the Liberals agreed not to contest thirty-five seats in return for the voting alliance of those labour M.P.'s elected. Keir Hardie, who was not consulted, would have regarded the arrangement as not only betrayal but superfluous. The Liberals would eventually discover, in his opinion, that without the working-class vote they were helpless; at that point they would either come to Labour or "go the Tory way."

In mid-January, 1906, spread over a period of two weeks, as was then the custom, the General Election took place. Chinese slavery, Protection vs. Free Trade, the school tax, Taff Vale, all the issues aired over three years, resounded again. Chinese labour on the hills of Wales? roared Lloyd George rhetorically, "Heaven forbid!" The voice of the demagogue and the force of the irrational merely reinforced a general sense that the Tories had been in power too long and this time the demagogue and the irrational were right. People wanted a change and they got one.

The Liberals won in a gigantic landslide. They returned to Parliament with the unprecedented margin of 513–157. Not all of this was their own. Labour won a total of 53 seats, of whom 29 were elected by the Labour Representation Committee, and organized themselves in the House for the first time as a recognized party with their own Whips. The remaining 24 were trade-union representatives called Lib-Labs who accepted the Liberal Whip and did not affiliate with the Labour Party until 1909. All 53 voted with the 377 Liberals, as did 83 Irish, giving the victorious party an absolute, almost unwieldy majority of 356. Even without the Irish and Labour, their own majority of 220 made them free of ties to any group. For the first time they had what Gladstone always wanted, that "hideous abnormality," as one Tory called it, a Liberal majority independent of the Irish vote.

The Labour accomplishment was even more startling and its implication was not missed. A friend of Sir Almeric Fitzroy who lost his seat in Lancashire attributed his defeat to the uprising of Labour and did not believe that the tariff and other issues played much part in the outcome but rather "the conviction, for the first time born in the working classes, that their social salvation is in their own hands."

In recognition of the new arrival on the political scene, John Burns was named President of the Local Government Board, becoming the first workingman ever to hold Cabinet rank. "I congratulate you, Sir Henry," he replied when Campbell-Bannerman, the new Prime Minister, offered him the post, "it will be the most popular appointment that you have made," as in fact it proved. After a week's enjoyment of the ruling-class embrace, Burns told Beatrice Webb, "I am a different man from what I was a week ago." His enjoyment of Cabinet office was so patent that he reminded Sir Edward Grey of a sentence from the naturalist Gilbert White, "In June the tortoise grows elate and walks on the tips of his toes."

For the Tories the result was the most overwhelming electoral defeat of a party in living memory. In the debacle even Balfour lost his seat, as did his brother Gerald, two members of his Cabinet, Alfred Lyttelton and St. John Brodrick, his cousin Lord Hugh Cecil, and, "saddest fate of all," as *Punch* lamented, Henry Chaplin, Squire of England, after thirty-nine years as M.P. All subsequently found seats in by-elections but in the meantime the "new Demos" reigned in fat triumphant majority.

During the hectic days of canvassing in Manchester before the election, Balfour, with his extraordinary capacity for detachment, took time out to seek an answer to an older if less immediate question than whether or not he would return as Prime Minister. In 1903 Joseph Chamberlain had been asked by Theodor Herzl on behalf of the Zionists for support in obtaining a colonization charter for the Sinai peninsula. Unable to persuade the British authorities in Egypt, Chamberlain, who saw the Jews as enterprising agents of colonization, offered them Uganda in East Africa as a substitute for Palestine. In the time of agony of the Russian pogroms, when East European Jews were desperately seeking an escape from Europe, the Zionist Congress nevertheless refused the offer, and Balfour wanted to know why. Long concerned with the idea "that Christian religion and civilization owes to Judaism an immeasurable debt," he held the Uganda question in the back of his mind and in the heat of the election campaign questioned his political agent, a Mr. Dreyfus, about it. Dreyfus offered to bring along a friend and ardent Zionist, born in the Russian pale, Dr. Chaim Weizmann, then a thirty-two-year-old instructor of chemistry at Victoria University in Manchester. Balfour at his election headquarters in a Manchester hotel set aside fifteen minutes for his visitor and stayed to listen for over an hour. Weizmann was nervous at the prospect of explaining to the renowned statesman in his shaky English all the history and hopes, the divisions and crosscurrents of his people in fifteen minutes. "I plunged into a long harangue on the meaning of the Zionist movement . . . that nothing but a deep religious conviction expressed in modern political terms could keep the movement alive and that this conviction had to be based on Palestine and Palestine alone. Any deflection from Palestine was—well, a form of idolatry. . . . I was sweating blood and trying to find some less ponderous way of expressing myself. . . . Suddenly I said: 'Mr. Balfour, supposing I were to offer you Paris instead of London, would you take it?'

"He sat up, looked at me and answered: 'But Dr. Weizmann, we have London.'

" 'That is true,' I said, 'But we had Jerusalem when London was a marsh.' He leaned back and continued to stare at me. . . . I did not see him again until 1914." Of the future Declaration that was to bear his name, Balfour said at the end of his life that "on the whole [it] had been the thing he looked back upon as the most worth his doing."

On the morning after his electoral defeat, Balfour visited a friend who for the first time in his life saw him "seriously upset." However, he went to bed with a book, came down to lunch next day "quite rested and cheerful," played golf in the afternoon and again on the day following, appeared thoroughly to enjoy himself and showed no curiosity about the continuing election results, "not even looking at a newspaper." He ascribed the defeat to the rise of Labour and to the public's desire for a change. Real issues had played little part, he noticed, audiences having refused to listen to argument.

Behind his carefree golf Balfour had been thinking. "The election of 1906 inaugurates a new era," he wrote the next day to the King's secretary, Francis Knollys, and the sudden emergence of a Labour party was its salient fact. It was the bid for power of a new claimant. In letters to several friends on this and the following day, Balfour opened his mind: something more was going on than the "ordinary party change. . . . What has occurred here has nothing to do with any of the things we have been squabbling over for the last three years." Campbell-Bannerman "is a mere cork dancing on a torrent which he cannot control" and the full significance of the drama could not be understood unless it was seen in terms "of the same movement which has produced massacres in St. Petersburg, riots in Vienna and Socialist processions in Berlin." His mind traveling ahead to the implications of this new development, Balfour wrote, at that moment of swollen Liberal victory, "It will end, I think, in the break-up of the Liberal Party." More enlivened than depressed by the new terms of battle, he assured Knollys that he had no intention of withdrawing from politics, because "I am so profoundly interested in what is *now* going on."

More clearly than most he sensed the beginnings of a transfer of power, not a mere political transfer from the in-party to the outs but one more profound, to a new class which, though as yet far from the possession of power, by its pressure on the possessors was causing upheaval in the components of society.

Meanwhile he had no seat. "I am certainly not going to go about the country explaining that I am honest and industrious like a second footman

out of a place," he remarked. A seat in the City of London being found
for him, he returned to the House as Leader of the Opposition.

Others besides Balfour glimpsed in Liberalism's victory the portents
of its dissolution. To the Socialists this was the Marxian imperative. Robert
Blatchford predicted that the Liberal party would try to carry out "a half-
hearted policy in the hope of not estranging any of its moderate followers."
If they attempted really remedial social legislation they would lose the
support of their capitalist backers, who would defect to the Tories. If
they did nothing in social reform they would lose the support of the
Radicals who elected them. In either case this would be their last Government. "The most certain of all aids to our cause is the inevitable disinte-
gration of the Liberal Party."

The Parliament of 1906 convinced the Tories of the rise of Socialism
with its explicit threat to the existence of Privilege. Until now the landed
aristocracy and squirearchy had believed that they could speak for the
people, that their national interest was the same, that in that sense they
were one. They believed in the benevolent working of Tory Democracy
as long as it did not interfere with the existing order. They thought of the
populace in terms of the rural and servant class whom they knew. George
Wyndham, Chief Secretary for Ireland in Balfour's Cabinet, a dithyrambic
true-blue Tory who retained his seat in 1906, believed he had won, as he
wrote his mother, "because the working men love me. I won by their
hearts. . . . All my song has been the brotherhood of the Empire for us
all, fair terms for the Foreigner, and the glory of Empire for our children
with a little straight talk for Christianity in our schools. . . . I have opened
my heart to all their hearts and we just love each other. I won on Toryism,
Empire and Fiscal Reform. The Irish voted for me, the Fishermen voted
for me, the Soldiers voted for me, the Artisans voted for me! Simply because we liked each other and love the traditions of the past and the Glory
of the future."

Wyndham's charming Eighteenth Century picture, whatever the case in
his own constituency, was for England, as for the rest of the world in
1906, as dead as the Prince Regent. The agricultural class was disappearing, seeping into the cities, and between the industrial proletariat
which was replacing it and the patricians, there was no love or common
interest. Wyndham and his kind knew nothing of miners and millhands
and people who lived in long monotonous rows of urban houses. "Fancy,"
said Winston Churchill, born in Blenheim Palace, when canvassing with a
friend in Manchester they entered a particularly drab street, "living in one
of those streets, never seeing anything beautiful, never eating anything

savoury—*never saying anything clever!*" The partakers of that fate were the new voters.

Among the 377 Liberal M.P.'s, 154, or 40 per cent, were businessmen, 85 were barristers and solicitors, 69 were "Gentlemen," 25 were writers and journalists, 22 were officers and the remaining 22 included university professors, teachers, doctors and champions of causes. Among the defeated Tories the largest category was still Gentlemen, representing 30 per cent, followed by businessmen at 25 per cent and officers 20 per cent. Almost half the House, to the number of 310, were new men who had never sat in Parliament before. A noble lord on visiting the newly assembled body was relieved to find that few were in "unconventional dress," but *Punch*'s veteran correspondent Sir Henry Lucy found the tone, character and social behavior of the House "revolutionized." The Irish were a rough group notable for bad manners which they exercised deliberately, uncowed by the traditions of the House. Since it was English they hated it, and since the Liberal majority had no need of them, they had no bargaining value and could do little but take out their frustration in noise and nuisance value to impede any legislation that was not Home Rule. Their old, hard-fought, ever-foiled battle to unseat English rule and govern themselves was not helped but swamped by the size of the Liberal victory.

When Balfour returned, the hostile majority openly showed their dislike of him as leader and symbol of the defeated party. New members, according to Austen Chamberlain, were "intolerant and rude to him . . . jeered at him and constantly interrupted him." Unmoved, debonair as ever, he remained master of debate and was able within a year to re-establish his ascendancy and win the respect of his opponents who "felt he gave distinction to the House." Although many of the new Government were his personal friends, the man who sat in his old place, facing him across the Speaker's table, was not. Campbell-Bannerman was impervious, as a colleague said, to the "historic charm" of Balfour; "he simply could not see it." Early in the session he tried to puncture its spell. Required to state his party's position on a resolution against Tariff Reform, Balfour managed an evasion as ambiguous as of old, exasperating the Prime Minister. "Enough of this foolery!" C.-B. burst out. His predecessor was "like the old Bourbons—he has learnt nothing. He comes back with the same airy graces, the same subtle dialectics, the same light and frivolous way of dealing with a great question but he little knows the temper of the new House of Commons if he thinks these methods will prevail here. I say enough of this foolery!" It was a doughty effort, widely quoted, but it did not dispel the Balfour aura.

The real temper of the new House was represented by a different kind of man than either Balfour the patrician or C.-B. the old-fashioned Liberal. The two dominant figures of the new Government, each of whom was to serve in succession as Prime Minister, were both men for whom government was not an inherited function but a professional career. They were H. H. Asquith, son of a Nonconformist Yorkshire wool merchant, and David Lloyd George, son of a Welsh schoolteacher. In background and temperament totally dissimilar, they had both made their way to Parliament through the practice of law.

The most dynamic of the new ministers, Lloyd George had been named President of the Board of Trade, not one of the chief Cabinet posts but one that gave him Front Bench rank. In him A. G. Gardiner, editor of the *Daily News* and a particularly perceptive student of political character, saw "the portent of a new age—the man of the people in the seat of power." If not yet in ultimate power, Lloyd George was obviously on his way to it and his purpose was as clear as that of a fox in a hen coop. He was forty-two, eleven years younger than Asquith and eleven years older than Churchill. Sent to Parliament in 1890 by a borough in Wales in the cause of Welsh nationalism, he was a Nonconformist dedicated to Disestablishment and a Radical dedicated to social reform. His political bible as a young man was *Les Misérables,* which he carried with him in a shilling paper edition whenever he traveled. His stand against the Boer War at the risk of professional boycott and actual assault took moral as well as physical courage. He had strong political principles but no scruples. Small and handsome, fearless, ruthless, and honey-tongued, with bright blue eyes, brown moustache and intense vitality, he constantly pursued and attracted women and adroitly avoided the occasional legal consequences. As a public speaker he was the Bernhardt of the political platform who ravished audiences with Celtic lilt and strong emotion. In public no rhetoric for him was too theatrical, no rabble-rousing too extreme; in office, however, he was circumspect and shrewd, conscious, as he used to say, that "England is based on commerce," and that no party could live by appeal to Labour alone. His greatest gift was an acute, intuitive, unerring sense of what the moment demanded, coupled with the conviction that he was the man to supply it. He "swooped down on opportunity like a hawk," and with it in his grasp, was a man whom the party leaders could not choose but use, even if like Chamberlain among the Tories, he was a cuckoo who would use them.

Ahead of him as Chancellor of the Exchequer was Asquith and coming up fast from behind, Winston Churchill, who had been given a sub-Cabinet post as Under-Secretary for the Colonies in reward for coming over from the Tories. Asquith was a professional intellectual machine who worked by training and judgment of what was expedient rather than by any fundamental primal belief. He was implacable in logic, irrefutable in debate. "Go and bring the sledgehammer," ordered C.-B. on one occasion when Balfour was delicately slitting the Liberals to ribbons, and Asquith was duly sent for. A brilliant First at Oxford, to which he had won a scholarship, he was the finest product, wrote Gardiner, of the Balliol system, which avoids excessive zeal and "distrusts great thoughts even if it thinks them." He understood everything and originated nothing. Firm but passionless he might have been a judge and was a perfect chairman of the board. After a successful early career as a barrister, he no sooner became a Cabinet minister under Gladstone in 1892 than he was marked as the coming man even though he was so unaccustomed to Society that he used to give his arm to his own wife to take her in to dinner. That difficulty was rectified when she died and Margot Tennant, with an eye for coming men, decided to marry him. He fitted smoothly into the elite; he "has no egotism, no jealousy, no vanity," said a woman friend. He dominated by intellect but he did not excite or stir reaction. The public could never form a picture of or pin a label on him and he remains for history a man without a face.

The Government included a number of peers, none of them great landowners, among whom were the aged Marquess of Ripon, who later resigned, Lord Tweedmouth, who became mentally "unhinged" and also eventually resigned, and Lord Crewe, Rosebery's son-in-law, who "horrified" the current Prince of Wales (later King George V) by his habit of wearing a jacket instead of a morning coat in the House of Lords. The only representative of the great aristocracy was the renegade Tory, Winston Churchill. Not Free Trade alone had brought him over to the Liberals. By 1904 when he changed parties he knew the Tories were on their way out. Craving office, he did not want to wait and besides he could not afford to. Although the grandson of a duke, he had to make a living. Journalism and authorship would pay but not with the kind of opportunity he wanted. In America a man of his energy would have chosen business, but for an Englishman of his inheritance Government was the one career for the exercise of greatness.

Recognizing the challenge of the social problem, he believed the Liberals could meet it and he wanted to play a major share. Apart from ambition he was moved by his deep devotion and love for his old childhood nurse, Mrs. Everest. Through her he felt personally the fate of the old unemployed person, "so many of whom have no one to look after them and nothing to live on at the end of their lives." In 1904 he saw opportunity, seized it, made the right choice for the time and won his chance. From then on in all his speeches he preached Liberalism as the "cause of the left-out millions" to which the working class should attach themselves rather than to a destructive Socialism. Once in office he knew that unless the Liberals could win the trade-union vote away from the rising Labour party, they must eventually collapse. He set out to earn it, forming a team with Lloyd George to draft and enact legislation on wages and hours, pensions and social insurance. In a speech at Glasgow in October, 1906, he outlined a program virtually adopting the Fabian idea of a welfare state and far ahead of anything intended by the Government of which he was a minor member. "We want to draw a line below which we will not allow persons to live and labour," he announced boldly and went on to propose the state as a "reserve employer" of labour, the establishment of minimum standards and state ownership of railways. Beatrice Webb was very gratified: "Winston has mastered the Webb scheme," she noted in her diary, and having done that he could be classified as "brilliantly able."

The most outright opportunist called forth to match the new times appeared in Tory ranks. He was F. E. Smith, a new M.P. aged thirty-three, who was one day to become Lord Chancellor under the name Lord Birkenhead. His maiden speech in 1906 was the most sensational parliamentary debut of his time. Like Asquith a barrister and self-made, he too had won a scholarship to Oxford, where, as a star of the Union, he learned every trick, gambit and lunge of debate. An adventurer without connections among the great territorial interests, he was prepared to fight his way up by intelligence, audacity, driving ambition and sheer gall. When he stood up to speak for the first time in the House of Commons amid the dispirited remnants of the Tory debacle, members saw "a young man, elaborately dressed, slim and clean-shaven with a long hatchet face, scornful eye and hair oiled and smooth." Standing with his hands in his pockets and a look of contempt on his face, he began in a suave, self-assured voice a speech of "brilliant insolence and invective." It was so biting in tone and practiced in delivery that listeners hardly noticed the lack of subject matter. The speech was a series of sneers, sarcasm and personal allusion tossed into Liberal laps like firecrackers. The Tories sat up, startled and delighted. When the speaker quoted a slightly twisted version of Lloyd George's electioneering reference to Chinese slavery on the hills of Wales and Lloyd George interrupted from the Front Bench "I did not say that," Smith was undaunted. "Anticipating a temporary lapse of memory," he said smoothly, "I have in my hand the *Manchester Guardian* of January 16," and after reading the quoted remark, added with thrilling insolence, "I would rather accept the word of its reporter than that of the right honorable gentleman."

The whole performance was a triumph of calculated purpose. Smith saw that what was needed at that moment was attack to give heart to the defeated side. From then on he was a growing power. Lacking the keel of a considered philosophy of government, he traveled fast but without direction. His brains were as notable as Lansdowne's manners; they went to his head, said Margot Asquith. Ideas and principles did not interest him but only the play of material forces, and he was supremely confident of his ability to manipulate them. A legend later went the rounds that when he was at Oxford he and Sir John Simon had tossed to decide which party each should join since no party could contain them both. While probably untrue, the fact that it was told and considered apt was indicative. After one of Churchill's speeches addressed to the labour vote, Smith said publicly, "The Socialists had better not cheer the name of Mr. Churchill for he will most likely steal their clothes when they go bathing— if they do bathe, which I doubt." It was a sneer of an unforgivable kind and one which meant a new kind of man was on his way up. Churchill's retort, "Mr. Smith is invariably vulgar," did not prevent them from becoming the best of friends.

Change of government re-established the terms of an old conflict. When the Liberals held the Commons, the Conservatives, if they felt really threatened, could fall back on the veto power of the House of Lords, as they had done in 1893 to block Gladstone's Home Rule Bill. Between the proponents of Change and the proponents of Things-as-they-are, between the policy of Reform and the policy of Hold-fast, another clash was bound to come, as Lord Salisbury had foreseen. Stating its essence he had said, "We have so to conduct our legislation that we shall give some satisfaction to both Classes and Masses. This is especially difficult with the Classes because all legislation is rather unwelcome to them as tending to disturb a state of things with which they are satisfied." When the disturbance became too threatening the House of Lords would balk, not because they were lords but as the reserve defenders of Things-as-they-are. Repeated use of the veto to block the will of the Commons would precipitate a constitutional crisis. "As long as I am there," Lord Salisbury had said, "nothing will happen; I understand my lords thoroughly. But when I go, mistakes will be made: the House of Lords will come in conflict with the Commons."

Balfour made the first move even before Parliament met. In a speech at Nottingham on the night of his electoral defeat he said it was the duty of all Conservatives to ensure that their party "should still control, whether in power or in Opposition, the destinies of this great Empire." Asquith afterward saw in this a claim to reassert the power of the Conservatives through the House of Lords. Whether it was or not, the event soon followed. In April, 1906, the Liberal Government introduced a new Education Bill of their own to cancel the objectionable features of the Act of 1902. It abolished state support of denominational schools. At this the High Church party reacted as furiously as the Nonconformists had done in 1902. The issue was at once recognized as the opening of battle between the two Houses of Parliament. "Possibly the ministers feel," wrote Lord Esher, "that *all* their legislation will be nullified by the House of Lords and the sooner they have to stand up and fight the better."

Balfour, following his uncle's line of thought, feared that the Lords would let themselves be provoked into making mistakes. He at once suggested to Lord Lansdowne, Conservative leader of the upper House, that the Government's strategy would be to send up bills with more extreme provisions than needed, trusting to the Lords to amend or reject them until they had built up a case against themselves. Then the Liberals would appeal to the country for a mandate to limit the Veto. Never before, he warned, had the Lords been called on to play a role "at once so important, so delicate or so difficult."

The tone of debate in the Lords on the Education Bill showed no sign of caution and their temper was not improved when they received from the Commons a Plural Voting Bill designed to end the ancient usage whereby owners of land in more than one constituency had more than one vote. "Something will happen," said Lloyd George almost visibly rubbing his hands. "There will be a great game of football on that field before long, I can assure you." In December, fulfilling his anticipation and Lord Salisbury's foreboding, the Lords threw out both the Education and the Plural Voting Bills. Significantly, however, they did not interfere with the equally, if not more, unpalatable Trades Disputes Bill, although the Liberals would have been only too pleased if they had. This bill, reversing the Taff Vale judgment, had been introduced in the Commons and passed against the real wish of the Government and over the objections of several ministers because of the pressure of Labour joined by the Radical members. "We could not resist the numbers pledged to it," Haldane, the

Liberal Minister of War, admitted. Cautiously steered by Lansdowne, the Lords let the bill pass because they did not wish to antagonize the working class and cement its alliance with the Liberals.

Making the most of the rejection of the other two bills, Asquith denounced the situation as "intolerable" and warned that a way must be found "by which the will of the people expressed through their elected representatives will be made to prevail."

His challenge was explicit and the House of Lords was waking up. The home of England's 544 hereditary peers, including twenty-two dukes, and of the bishops and law lords who sat with them was a high, dark oak-paneled chamber ninety feet long filled by two banks of red leather benches. Stained-glass windows held portraits of royalty since the Conquest. Walls and ceiling were thick with elaborately carved gothic molding and heraldic emblems. Between the windows, statues of the barons of Magna Carta, inadvertent founders of the parliamentary system, looked down a little grimly on what they had wrought. At one end of the chamber under a golden canopy were twin thrones for the King and Queen flanked by tall candelabra standing like guardsmen at attention. Below the throne the Lord Chancellor presided on the Woolsack, a square cushioned bench. Crossbenches in the aisle accommodated princes of the royal family and peers not affiliated with party. Sovereigns and judges in scenes from English history lent their shadowy presence in murals on the upper walls. The light was subdued, the general tone one of dignified somnolence.

Now the prospect of assault began to fill the benches usually sparsely dotted with forty or fifty peers. Lansdowne encouraged his followers to speak, paid attention when they did and supported their efforts with the gracious manner of the grand seigneur which characterized him. Lord Curzon adorned debate with speech "so infinitely superior to that of the ordinary peer that it is quite difficult to believe that he is ever in the wrong." The Liberals' new Lord Chancellor, Lord Loreburn, lent an invigorating presence and paid the House the compliment of always being wide awake when he was on the Woolsack. He was the former Sir Robert Reid, known as "Fighting Bob," a Scot, a famous cricketer who had bowled for Oxford, a Radical strongly opposed to the Liberal Imperialists and a "fiery orator" in the Commons who now lectured the Opposition "in tones that almost made the sinner weep," and advanced "the most contentious proposition with the most entrancing plausibility." In the rhythm of Gibbon and the gallantry of Lord Tolloller bowing to Lord Mountararat in *Iolanthe,* Lord Curzon acknowledged Lord Loreburn as "courtesy personified, persuasiveness incarnate and dignity enthroned."

On the crossbenches sulked the Liberals' last Prime Minister, Lord Rosebery, who had resigned the leadership and as an Imperialist and opponent of Home Rule had announced, when C.-B. became party leader, that "emphatically and explicitly and once and for all I cannot serve under that banner." Acknowledged since Eton days for his brilliance, wit and charm, Rosebery, having won the Derby and married a Rothschild fortune, was too used to success to be an accommodator, and remained— in Morley's phrase—"a dark horse in a loose box." When he sulked he could turn "an eye like a fish" on his friends and wither them with biting sarcasm; when he charmed he encircled himself in adoration. His variability caused the public to lose trust in him and recalled to A. G. Gardiner the story of a rustic who, being asked if Wordsworth was not very fond of children, replied, "Happen he was but they wasna verra fond o' him."

During the years of crisis over Home Rule, Rosebery had been leader of the movement for reform of the House of Lords by some modification of the hereditary principle and had three times brought forward proposals toward that goal in the hope that self-reform would ward off attacks on the veto power. The reform movement was now revived with Lord Curzon as the leading spirit. Even Mr. Churchill, who liked to have a hand in everything, contributed his suggestion in an article for the *Nation* entitled "A Smooth Way With the Peers." He proposed a system by which peers should be appointed for each session to reflect the same majority as in the House of Commons at the time, not however to exceed 250. This would exclude the "frivolous, lethargic, uninstructed or disreputable elements." Most of the proposed reforms contemplated some system by which the peers would elect from among themselves those specially qualified by ability or services. But many preferred the simple principle which once had moved Lord Melbourne to say he liked the Garter "because there was no damn merit about it." Balfour sympathized. He advised Lansdowne to "avoid the fatal admission that the ancient ground of hereditary qualification is insufficient to qualify for the upper House. If it is not sufficient qualification it is no qualification at all. . . . I think it a fact that the accident of birth is more easily defended on what some people call its naked absurdity than birth plus services." The Government did nothing to encourage reform of the Lords because it did not want them reformed; it wanted an issue and an excuse to limit the Veto.

Faced with these exciting possibilities Lloyd George became quite impatient with his constituents' single-minded attention to Welsh nationalism and tactlessly told them, "I will say this to my fellow countrymen. If they find the Government moving its artillery into position for making an attack on the Lords, Welshmen who worry the Government into attending to anything else until the citadel has been stormed ought to be pushed into the guardroom." The military language was curious and the speech so much resented that its careless author had to hurry to Wales to declare with hand on heart, "Am I going to sell the land that I love? God knows how dear to me is my Wales!"

In June, 1907, Campbell-Bannerman told the Commons that the time had come to challenge the pretensions of the peers, supported as they were by Mr. Balfour, "at the winding of whose horn the portcullis of the House of Lords comes rapidly down." Lloyd George's choice of metaphor was equally picturesque. The House of Lords, he said, was not the watchdog of the Constitution but "Mr. Balfour's poodle." C.-B. moved a resolution stating that in order to give effect to the "will of the people, the power of the other House to alter or reject Bills passed by this House must be restricted by law" so that, within the lifetime of any one Parliament, the final decision of the Commons should prevail. The Labour party immediately offered an amendment proposing to abolish the House of Lords altogether. In introducing a resolution rather than a bill, the Government's purpose was clearly propaganda rather than action and after the resolution was adopted—without the Labour amendment—nothing further was done.

That summer the Second Hague Conference assembled. In April of the following year, 1908, C.-B., expecting death, resigned and died within a month. Succeeding to the premiership Asquith remodeled the Cabinet more nearly in his own image. Four of a very able group of under-secretaries were promoted to Cabinet rank, among them Walter Runciman, son of a wealthy shipowner, Herbert Samuel, son of a Jewish banking family and like Asquith a First at Balliol, and Reginald McKenna, son of a London civil servant who had taken a superior degree in mathematics at Cambridge. His appointment as First Lord of the Admiralty in place of Lord Tweedmouth prompted Morley to recall that when he had proposed a certain name to Gladstone for that post in 1892, Gladstone with great solemnity and a wave of his hand said, "Well, for the Admiralty I think we require what is called a *gentleman*!" And "Here we are," sighed Lord Esher, looking over the new Cabinet, "overwhelmed by the middle classes."

The most important change in the Cabinet was Lloyd George's promotion to fill Asquith's place as Chancellor of the Exchequer while his own vacated place as President of the Board of Trade was filled by Winston Churchill, fourth of the under-secretaries to be promoted. Churchill's career almost ended at this point when he had to fight a by-election at Manchester owing to a custom then in force which obliged an M.P. raised to Cabinet rank to have his seat confirmed by the electorate. In a hard contest, harassed by Suffragettes, Churchill lost, to the screaming delight of the Tory press. His defeat proved that the balance was already swinging back from the abnormal Liberal victory of 1906 and it made more urgent the Liberals' need of the labour vote. At Dundee, where Churchill was immediately offered another seat, he insisted that only with the workers' support could the Liberals have the strength to put their legislation through the House of Lords against the growing forces of Tory reaction. "With your support we shall overwhelm them. . . . Ah, but we must have that support."

As it proved, none of the social legislation carried through by the energetic team of Lloyd George and Churchill was blocked by the House of Lords. A Coal Mines Act establishing the eight-hour day for miners, a Trade Boards Act establishing minimum wages for piecework in the sweated trades, a Workman's Compensation Act establishing employers' liability for industrial accidents and the Old Age Pensions Act were passed and the team began work on the National Insurance Bill for unemployment and health insurance which was to be the crown of the Liberals' welfare legislation. None was obstructed by the House of Lords for the same reason that the Trade Disputes Act had not been. The oncoming conflict with the Commons, however, was not diverted.

All the challenges, resistances and emotions of the conflict were stuffed like gun-cotton into a new piece of legislation, the Licensing Bill. The darling object for twenty-five years of Liberal temperance reformers, mostly Nonconformists, who wished to reduce the drinking of the lower classes, the Bill was the Government's election debt to the Nonconformist voters. It was designed to reduce the number of public houses by thirty thousand over fourteen years by canceling their licenses according to a fixed ratio of the population. Since the public houses were owned by the brewing and distilling companies, the Bill was strenuously opposed by the vested interests, not to mention the drinking public. Every property owner allied himself with the distillers; the Bill took on an aspect as sinister as Home Rule, as threatening as Socialism. Balfour declared it to be a direct attack on the rights of property and Conservatives responded to it much as the working class had responded to Chinese slavery. A special meeting of Conservative peers was called at Lansdowne House in

Berkeley Square. The country peers, or "Backwoodsmen," as they were known, who were never consulted on anything outside the affairs of their own counties, were summoned. Some had never spoken in the House, some had never even been inside it, and, mistaking Lansdowne House for the House of Lords itself, thought the Bill was being decided then and there. "Some of us . . . met each other fresh from the hunting field and were able to compare notes about the past season and discuss possible winners of the spring handicaps." All agreed the Bill must be rejected, and "adjourned for a good lunch at the Carlton Club."

In this case they had the country with them, as was shown in a by-election at Peckham fought on the Licensing issue. It turned what had been a Liberal majority of two thousand into a Conservative majority of the same amount. For the moment it was not popularity but the principle of the thing that concerned the Liberals. The high-handed disposal of the bill by caucus in Lansdowne House enraged them. In November, 1908, when the bill was formally rejected by the House of Lords, Churchill, "perfectly furious," revealed in a private conversation that the Liberals' answer had already been decided. "We shall send them up such a Budget in June," he said, "as shall terrify them; they have started the class war and they had better be careful." In fact the Licensing Bill had nothing to do with the class war, nor was it the class war alone, but the accumulating pressures of a new age which were the cause of Liberal discomfiture.

By 1909, the year of the great Budget battle, Liberalism had run into the realities of a world grown too difficult for the building of Jerusalem. The Liberal program was not winning the working class. On the contrary Labour and Liberals were drawing apart. Labour, impressed by the extent of its own power as revealed in the election of 1906, was becoming more aggressive; strikes had begun again as soon as the unions recovered their freedom of action by the Trades Disputes Act. Liberals of the employing class responded like employers. No pact operated now, and in two three-cornered by-elections in 1907 Labour won. The victory of Victor Grayson, a raving Socialist, in the West Riding of Yorkshire raised frightening prospects. A former theological student with a gift for oratory and a fondness for drink, he preached Socialism as the deliverance of the poor with a fervor that swept through the mill towns like fire. His wild antics in the House twice caused his suspension and attracted attention all over Europe. The Kaiser was reported to have proposed invading England with an Army corps or two, proclaiming that he had come not as an enemy but as Victoria's grandson to deliver England "from the Socialist gang which is ruling the country." In cooperation with King Edward he would dissolve Parliament and re-establish autocratic monarchy as a feudatory of Germany.

Englishmen were increasingly conscious of the threat of Germany. "The danger now is," wrote Lord Esher to a friend in 1908, "that in Europe we have a competitor the most formidable in numbers, intellect and education with which we have ever been confronted." The necessity of facing that danger was one more blow to the Liberal creed. Traditional pacifist Liberalism was violated when Asquith and his fellow Imperialists in the Cabinet, who controlled foreign policy, agreed to give Sir John Fisher four new Dreadnoughts. Conservatives, dissatisfied, shouted the slogan, "We want eight and we won't wait." Haldane's Territorial Army was equally resented by the pacifists of his party, who claimed that it would cost too much and drain money from social reform. With the King's strong support it was enacted over their objections. "We are certainly living in hard times," mourned King Edward, "but yet I hope that peace may be maintained—but only because Europe is *afraid* to go to war."

The topic of invasion occupied both the official and the public mind. The Committee of Imperial Defence appointed an Invasion Inquiry in 1908 and summoned the ex-Prime Minister to give his views on the evidence it had collected. Balfour spoke for an hour in a closely reasoned and "luminous" exposition, "quite perfect in form and language," which according to Esher, a member of the committee, so "dumbfounded" Asquith, Grey, Haldane and Lloyd George that none of them could think of a single question to ask him. "The general opinion was that no finer exposition of this question has ever been made."

The Committee's conclusion that a successful invasion could not be mounted was not known to the public, which felt an awful fascination in the topic. Erskine Childers had raised it in an absorbing novel *The Riddle of the Sands*, in 1903 and William Le Queux more emphatically if less artistically in a novel called *The Invasion of 1910* which ran as a serial in the *Daily Mail* in 1906 and was advertised through London by sandwich-men dressed in Prussian blue uniforms and spiked helmets. In 1909 Guy du Maurier's play *An Englishman's Home*, which dramatized an invasion by the forces of "the Emperor of the North," opened at Wyndham's Theatre and played to packed houses for eighteen months. The idea of invasion became almost a psychosis. Living at Rye on England's south coast Henry James felt "exposed," as he nervously wrote a friend in 1909. He worried that "when [he did not say 'if'] the German

Emperor carries the next war into this country, my chimney pots, visible to a certain distance out at sea, may be his very first objective."

The prospect of war negated everything that orthodox Liberalism stood for, yet the Government had to adapt to it. Meanwhile the sex war raged at home. The Suffragette movement, which Charles Masterman believed to be an "outlet for suppressed energy," released a curious surge of sex hatred, a mutual "blaze of antagonism," as H. G. Wells called it, which fitted the other strangely violent quarrels afflicting England in the first decade of the Twentieth Century. Wells thought the main impulse of the Suffragettes—that swarm of "wildly exasperated human beings"—was "vindictive," an outburst against man's long arrogant assumption of superiority. Their open warfare followed almost immediately upon the advent of the Liberals, prompted by repeated postponements and refusal of the Government to introduce a bill of enfranchisement. Unable to obtain any satisfaction by legal means, the women resorted to tactics which were essentially "propaganda of the deed" and, like their prototype, anarchic in spirit. They turned up at every political meeting despite all doorkeepers' precautions and drowned out the speakers by ringing bells and shrieking for the vote. They besieged the Houses of Parliament and offices of Whitehall, attacked ministers on their doorsteps, in one case knocking down Mr. Birrell, the Minister of Education, and kicking him in the shins, broke department-store windows with hammers, set fires in mail boxes, penetrated the House and stopped proceedings by chaining themselves to the grill of the Ladies Gallery and keeping up the incessant shout, "Votes for Women!"

In 1909 under the Liberal Government occurred the first forcible feeding of imprisoned Suffragettes, a peculiarly revolting process in which both the victims, who invited it by hunger strikes, and the officials who performed it, writhed like animals. It was accomplished by means of rubber tubes passed through the mouth, or sometimes the nostrils, to the stomach. While the prisoner was strapped in a chair and held down by guards or matrons, liquid food was forced down the tubes by stomach pumps. Outside in the streets Suffragettes marched with placards proclaiming, "Stop Forcible Feeding!" and one threw herself at the King's feet in the midst of a court reception crying, "Your Majesty, won't you please stop torturing women!" Inside the prisons the Suffragettes persisted in the hunger strikes which provoked the treatment. The irrational was gaining ground.

Put off again and again by Asquith's promises to carry through Enfranchisement, which he made to secure quiet and never kept, the feminists in the years after 1909 slashed pictures in the National Gallery and set fires in cricket pavilions, race-course grandstands, resort hotels and even churches. They interrupted services in St. Paul's and Westminster, forced petitions on the King at court, engaged in "painful and distressing" struggles with police, forcing their own arrest and imprisonment. They endured starvation and pain with mad fortitude, invited humiliation, brutality and finally, when Emily Davidson threw herself under the hoofs of the horses in the Derby of 1913, even death. Although these extremes were not reached until the period 1910–14, the practice and the spirit were already strong by 1909.

Men, otherwise decent citizens, reacted in the ugly spirit of a Saturday night drunkard beating his wife. When a meeting addressed by Lloyd George in the Albert Hall in December, 1908, was broken up by militants who, shouting "Deeds not words!" tore off their coats to reveal themselves dressed in prisoner's gowns, the stewards, according to the *Manchester Guardian*, "went mad with fury and rushed upon the women, ejecting them with nauseating brutality, knocking them against seats, throwing them down steps, dragging them out by the hair." In other instances of the kind they were deliberately struck in the breast. Possibly the fury was provoked by woman's abandonment of feminine lures and her substitution of attack as a means of gaining her desires, which seemed to unsex her. It touched fundamentals. "These termagants, these unsexed viragoes, these *bipeds*!" thundered a Nonconformist minister, expressing more than all the editorials. The strange physical fury generated by the women's struggle for the vote was the most unsettling phenomenon of the Liberal era.

By 1909 a gathering pessimism converged upon the Liberals and those allied with them. "A thousand sad and baffling riddles" had somehow replaced the simple verities of politics, wrote Masterman, now a member of the Government as Under-Secretary of the Home Office. In 1909 he published *The Condition of England*, a book of profound discouragement. He saw the world divided vertically "between nation and nation armed to the teeth" and horizontally between rich and poor. "The future of progress is still doubtful and precarious. Humanity at best appears as a shipwrecked crew which has taken refuge on a narrow ledge of rock beaten by wind and wave; we cannot tell how many, if any at all, will survive when the long night gives place to morning."

Around him Masterman saw a complacent society reposing in an illusion of security but "of all the illusions of the opening of the Twentieth Century perhaps the most remarkable is that of security." Instead of security he saw "gigantic and novel forces of mechanical invention, upheavals of people, social discontents . . . vast implements of destruction placed in the hands of a civilization imperfectly self-controlled" in which "material advance has transcended moral progress."

James Bryce, another member of the Liberal Government as Chief Secretary for Ireland and since 1907 as Ambassador to Washington, found discouragement in the central theme of his life, the democratic process. In a series of lectures he delivered at Yale in 1909 on "Hindrances to Good Citizenship," he admitted that the practice of democracy had not lived up to the theory. The numbers who could read and vote had increased twenty times in the last seventy years but "the percentage of those who reflect before they vote has not kept pace either with popular education or with the extension of the suffrage." The "natural average man" was not exhibiting in public affairs the innate wisdom which democracy had presumed he possessed. He was more interested in betting at the races than in casting his vote. Old evils of class hatred, corruption, militarism, had recurred and new evils emerged. Although the world was undeniably better off than it had been, the faith of the Nineteenth Century in the ultimate wisdom of government of the people, by the people, had met "disappointment." For the man who once described himself as "almost a professional optimist," the Yale lectures were a painful confession.

The philosophers of Liberalism, looking around them, were making the equally painful discovery that laissez-faire, essence of the Liberal creed, had not worked. It had produced the evils of sweated labour, unemployment and destitution which Liberalism, unready for the wholehearted state intervention of the Fabian dream, could not cope with. In three years of office the Liberal Government, after coming to power in a new century with the greatest mandate in party history, had not been able to give shape to the great promise of 1906. By 1910 the number of men involved in strikes was the highest for any year since 1893. "We began slowly to lose what we had of the confidence" of working people, admitted Haldane, and "this gradually became apparent." J. A. Hobson and L. T. Hobhouse, the economic and moral philosophers of social planning, had come to the conclusion that neither man nor society was operating properly. In *The Crisis of Liberalism*, published in 1909, Hobson wrote that if Liberalism could not transform its role into a more positive one, then "it is doomed to the same sort of impotence as has already befallen Liberalism in most continental countries."

Hobhouse and a number of other investigators were concerned with man's curious refusal to behave rationally in what seemed his own best interest. The low level on which the populace reacted politically, the appeal of the sensationalist press and the new phenomenon of mass interest in spectator sports were disturbing. Henri Bergson's idea of man as moved by a force which he called *élan vital* had stimulated a new science of social psychology to probe the role of emotions and instinct as the basis of human conduct. One of the most influential of English studies of the mental processes at work in public affairs was Hobhouse's *Democracy and Reaction,* published in 1904. An Oxford don whose deep interest in the labour movement led him to leave the University for the staff of the *Manchester Guardian,* Hobhouse found that the average man "has not the time to think and will not take the trouble to do so if he has the time." His opinions faithfully reflect "the popular sheet and shouting newsboy. . . . To this new public of the streets and tramcars it is useless to appeal in terms of reason."

This was the public which had shouted "Pigtail!" and the phenomenon of herd behavior suddenly was recognized as an entity. The Columbus of this discovery was a surgeon, Wilfred Trotter, who named the phenomenon, gave it status as a subject for scientific study and quietly concluded his first voyage in sociology with a sentence as pessimistic as any ever written. "A quiet man," as a friend described him, with a wide variety of interests in philosophy, literature and science, Trotter, who was 36 in 1908, was to be judged thirty years later "the greatest surgeon of the present century in this country." He had "the head and face of a scholar redeemed from austerity by a smile of great charm and sincerity." In his two essays on "The Herd Instinct" in the *Sociological Review* in 1908 and 1909 he found man's social behavior springing from that same dark and sinister well of the subconscious whose uncovering marked the end of the Victorian age. He saw the subconscious as a force lacking "all individuality, will and self-control." It was "irrational, imitative, cowardly, cruel . . . and suggestible." Because of man's innate desire for group approval, he is at the mercy of this irrational force and vulnerable to the herd reaction. Unlike Kropotkin who in *Mutual Aid* assumed the herd instinct to be benevolent, Trotter considered it a factor for danger because its operation was unconscious and irrational. "It needs but little imagination to see," he concluded, "how great are the probabilities that after all man will prove but one more of nature's failures."

The herd instinct occupied two other investigators in 1908, William McDougall in *Social Psychology* and Graham Wallas in *Human Nature in Politics.* Wallas' life and thought were directed toward *The Great Society,* the title of a book he published in 1914. With Shaw and the

Webbs he was the fourth of the Fabian junta until he resigned in 1904 in protest against its support of Tariff Reform. A member of the LCC, chairman of the London School Board, a founder of, and professor of political science at, the London School of Economics, Wallas in his own words was "a working thinker." He was described by Wells as a "rather slovenly, slightly pedantic, noble-spirited man" in moustache and pince-nez whose lectures, though slow and fussy, were "penetrating and inspiring." To another student, G. D. H. Cole, he was "the most inspiring lecturer I have ever heard." In *Human Nature in Politics* he examined the evidence showing that man did not act according to rational assumptions. His hope was that the new methods of psychology and sociology would light the way toward more enlightened behavior in humanity's self-interest.

Wallas did not want to accept the implications of Darwinism which seemed to condone and accept as inevitable the native aggressiveness of human nature and to condemn mankind to ruthless struggle as a condition of progress. Yet he foresaw that, unless the irrational was controlled, nations would engage in a series of inter-empire wars until only England and Germany or America and China remained, and then finally, after a "naval Armageddon in the Pacific, only one Empire will exist" and the inhabitants of the globe, reduced by half, would have to begin all over again. Already the process seemed to be on the way with "Germany and ourselves marching towards the horrors of world war" merely because, having made entities of Nation and Empire, "our sympathies are shut up within them."

Lloyd George's Budget of 1909 was the fuse, deliberately lit, of one of the great quarrels which made the Liberal era, in the words of a participant, "so unprecedentedly cantankerous and uncomfortable." With Liberal prestige sinking, party leaders were aware that without a popular issue they might not win the next election. People were already beginning to calculate, Gardiner wrote, "when the election would come and by how much the Liberals would lose."

As Chancellor of the Exchequer Lloyd George had to provide £16,-000,000 of additional revenue for 1909, one-third toward the eight Dreadnoughts to which the Government had agreed, and two-thirds for implementing the Old Age Pensions Act. He chose to obtain it by a tax-the-rich program which, while neither unsound nor confiscatory, was framed as provocatively as possible with intent to goad the Lords to reject it so as to create an issue of Peers vs. People. The Budget raised the income tax on a graduated scale from 9*d*. to 1*s*. 2*d*. in the pound with

an extra supertax of 6*d*. on incomes over £5,000. (Already when the
Liberals' first budget had raised the income tax to 11*d*. in the pound, a
daughter of the Duke of Rutland recalled, "We all thought Papa would
die. He looked too ashen to recover.") The new Budget raised death
duties to a maximum of 10 per cent on estates of £200,000 or over, it
added a tax on motors and petrol which at this date affected only the
rich, and also on tobacco and alcohol of which the last was to prove
a political mistake.

It was none of these measures but a tax of one-fifth the value on "unearned increment" of land when it was sold or passed by death, plus
an annual tax of a halfpenny in the pound on undeveloped land and
mineral rights, which aroused the whole of the landowning class in furious
resentment, as it was intended to. The land clauses required registration
and valuation of property, which to the landowner was no less than the
bailiff's foot in the door, the State's trespass on a man's private property.
Lloyd George pressed it home in public mockery and appeals to the
populace as blatant as when Mark Antony wept over Caesar's wounds.
Personifying the enemy as "the Dukes," he told a working-class audience
of four thousand at Limehouse in London's East End, "A fully equipped
Duke costs as much to keep up as two Dreadnoughts . . . is just as great
a terror and lasts longer." When the Government wanted money to pay
for the Dreadnoughts, he went on, "we sent the hat around among the
workmen. They all brought in their coppers." Yet when "the P.M. and
I knock at the doors of Belgravia" and "ask the great landlords to give
something to keep the aging miners out of the workhouse, they say, 'Only
a ha'penny, just a copper' and they turn their dogs on us and every day
you can hear them bark. . . . It is rather hard that an old workman should
have to find his way to the gates of the tomb bleeding and footsore
through the brambles and thorns of poverty. We cut a new path for him,
an easier one, a pleasanter one, through fields of waving corn."

For a minister of the Crown it was a performance that no one but
Lloyd George could have given without blushing. If the Prime Minister
was embarrassed by it he gave no sign, a point which disturbed King
Edward, who let it be known that he "cannot understand how Asquith
can tacitly allow" speeches that would "not have been tolerated by any
Prime Minister until the last few years."

Furor exploded over the Budget exactly as its authors wished. Conservative leaders roared in protest. Lord Lansdowne called Lloyd George
a "robber gull." Mr. Chaplin denounced the Budget as the first step in
a Socialist war against property, the Law Society declared a land tax

unjust and unworkable, a meeting of City men headed by Lord Rothschild protested the valuation of property by "irresponsible tribunals" such as those which had "cost one Stuart his head and another his throne." The Duke of Norfolk announced he would have to sell a Holbein which he had lent to the National Gallery, the Earl of Onslow put up for sale parts of his Surrey estate, and Kipling in a hysterical poem, "The City of Brass," portrayed England riddled by hatemongers and crushed by tributes levied "on all who have toiled or striven or gathered possession," until without a defender "it passed from the roll of the Nations in headlong surrender!" No less a Cassandra, Lord Rosebery said the measure was "not a Budget but a revolution." Underlying it was the "deep, subtle, insidious danger of Socialism" and Socialism was the "end of everything . . . of faith, of family, of property, of monarchy, of Empire." His speech, addressed to a meeting of businessmen in Glasgow, was read next morning "with the greatest joy at every country house party in England, Scotland and Wales."

A new Labour M.P., Philip Snowden, himself one day to be Chancellor of the Exchequer, said it was necessary to make the rich poorer in order to make the poor richer and the Budget was the beginning of democratic government. Balfour retorted that "you cannot abolish poverty by abolishing riches" and "let them not associate democracy with robbery." The Duke of Rutland, close to apoplexy, proposed that all Labour M.P.'s should be gagged. As rage mounted, the King was forced to confess that the "foolish and *mean* speeches and sayings" of landowners and capitalists were causing immense harm.

Everyone including the common people was aware that the Veto, not the Budget, was the stake. When Minoru won the Derby that summer one man among the cheering crowd shouted, "Now King, you have won the Derby—go home and dissolve the bloody Parliament!" Churchill speaking at Leicester in September welcomed the struggle as likely to "smash" the Veto if the Lords rejected a Finance Bill. Balfour stripped the issue down to the land valuation clauses, which as "compulsory registration" were, he claimed, illegal in a finance bill; "How dare you describe it as a Finance Bill?" In fact, as Lord Salisbury had once pointed out over an earlier budget, there was no constitutional bar to the Lords throwing out a Finance Bill—only a practical one: they could not throw out the Government of the day along with it. To reject a budget and leave the Government in power would amount to deadlock. The Government's recourse, if driven, would be to advise the King to create enough peers to provide a Liberal majority in the House of Lords, as many as five hundred if necessary, a deluge that would drown the hereditary peerage. Nevertheless the mood of the Conservatives was against compromise. Act boldly, said Lord Milner, and "Damn the consequences." This, with Balfour's concurrence and under his guidance, was the decision.

"The whole political world is convulsed with excitement," wrote Beatrice Webb in her diary, as to whether or not the Lords would throw out the Budget. Debate opened in the House of Lords on November 22 and lasted for ten days. Peeresses and visitors, including the King of Portugal, packed the galleries, aged peers came down from the country who "could not even find their way to the Houses of Parliament"; altogether four hundred members took their seats, the largest number to assemble since the rejection of Home Rule. Noble members, from the ancient ex-Lord Chancellor, Lord Halsbury, to young Lord Willoughby de Broke, spokesman of the country group, proclaimed their duty to the country to reject the Bill. As a Liberal, Lord Ribblesdale admitted his distaste for Lloyd George as "half pantaloon, half highwayman," but he did not see anything really socialistic about the Budget, nor did he think the country would be seriously affected by "the sobs of the well-to-do." If it came to a division he would vote with the Government.

Lord Rosebery, after all his horrors, advised passing the Budget rather than risk "the very existence of a Second Chamber." The climax was Lord Curzon's speech, which one deeply moved peer said was the finest ever heard in the House in forty years. The Government, Curzon said, proposed to introduce any measure it liked and, provided it could be covered with the label of a Finance Bill, force the Lords to pass it— "a revolutionary and intolerable claim" amounting to Single Chamber government. Despite the consequences, he advised rejection in the hope of bringing about a reformed House of Lords acting as an "essential feature" of the Constitution and not "a mere phantom rendered equally impotent and ridiculous."

The division was called on December 1, 1909, the Lords filed solemnly into the lobbies, the vote to reject was 350–75. Next day amid loud enthusiasm in the Commons, the Prime Minister, declaring a breach of the Constitution had taken place, announced the Government would appeal to the country and called for a dissolution. Customarily recumbent on the Opposition Front Bench, Mr. Balfour, who had a cold, coughed, tapped his chest, took a pill and sniffed a restorative.

While preparing for the new election, Asquith's Government drew up a Parliament Bill for abolition of the Lords' Veto which they expected to introduce upon being returned to office. It provided that on bills certified by the Speaker as Finance Bills the Veto should be abolished and that other bills, if passed by three successive sessions of the Commons, should become law with or without the consent of the Lords. Talk flew around London about creation of peers; everyone from poets to tea merchants, "even Hilaire Belloc," as Wilfrid Blunt noted maliciously, saw visions of the coronet descending upon his own head. Asquith meanwhile dropped hints of guarantees already secured from the King which were without foundation.

In the period of campaigning before the election in January, 1910, it became clear that Lloyd George, for all his oratorical forays against the Dukes, had failed. The public could not get excited about the peers; Haldane confessed that 40 per cent of the electorate were doubtful and 20 per cent "highly detached," in short, returning to normal. To Alfred Austin, vacationing in the south of France, the election was deadly serious. Since his district was safely Conservative, he felt exonerated from the need to go home to cast his vote, "but I had the results telegraphed to me, every day, from the Carlton Club." At home, wrote Beatrice Webb, "we are all awaiting breathlessly the issue of the great battle." The issue proved unfortunate for all. The Liberals were returned but with a majority so reduced as to put them back in the grip of the Irish. Labour, crippled by the Osborne judgment of 1908 which declared the use of union funds for political purposes illegal, lost ten seats. The Conservatives gained 105 seats, enough to have been a victory but for the low point from which they started. Both sides were caught in a trap. To put the Budget through now, the Liberals needed the Irish votes and the Irish disliked the Budget because of the tax on whiskey. The price of their support was Asquith's promise to carry through abolition of the Lords' Veto in order to clear the way for Home Rule. During four years in office the Liberals had not once introduced a Home Rule Bill, but this now became, as Speaker Lowther said, "the crux which dominated the whole situation." No longer hopeless suppliants, the Irish appeared "sinister and powerful" and the connection between the two issues was made "direct, obvious and unmistakable." Whether they liked it or not the Government was now committed to carry the battle to its ultimate conclusion—a creation of peers or at least the King's promise to create them. Events from this point on rose to a pitch of bitterness unsurpassed since the Reform Bill.

Asquith formally introduced the Parliament Bill in February, 1910, with the announcement that if the Lords failed to pass it he would advise the Crown to take the necessary steps. Then ensued a turmoil of negotiations and intrigue, of pressures on and advices to the King, of inter- and intra-party bargaining behind the scenes, of visits and consultations in country houses, of conferences with the Archbishop of Canterbury. Almost unnoticed, the Budget, cause of it all, was passed, as Lansdowne had promised if the Liberals won the election. But the Budget by now was forgotten, replaced as an issue by the Parliament Bill dragging along behind it its ridiculous shadow of five hundred artificial peers. Though it absorbed for months the efforts, passions and utmost political skills of Crown, Ministers and Opposition, it was a spurious issue. No basic question of human rights and justice was involved as in the Dreyfus Affair. The Liberals insisted that the issue was the power of the Lords to frustrate the will of the Commons, yet, in fact, as Herbert Samuel admitted, "It is true they let through almost all our social legislation" except for the Education and Licensing Bills, one of which had been a composite of compromises satisfactory to no one and the other hardly a question on which to shatter the British constitution. What drove the Liberals forward in the full rage of attack was the need to vindicate themselves for their failing program and for selling their honor to the Irish. They felt justified because their view of the House of Lords, as expressed by Masterman, was that of an institution which would only "allow changes it profoundly dislikes when compelled by fear. . . . It can do little but modify, check or destroy other men's handiwork. It has no single constructive suggestion of its own to offer to a people confronting difficult problems."

What impelled the Conservatives in their equal rage of resistance was a determination to preserve the last rampart of privilege. To lose the Veto or to lose the Conservative majority in the House of Lords meant to lose their last check upon the advance of the besieging classes. They looked on the attainment of power by the Populace, wrote Masterman, who saw their point of view too, as the Deluge. "They see our civilization as a little patch of redeemed land in the wilderness; preserved as by a miracle from one decade to another" and the rise of the Populace as the rush of a crowd upon a tranquil garden, "tearing up the flowers by the roots . . . strewing the pleasant landscape with torn paper and broken bottles." Their resistance, however, was weakened by a split in their ranks. As leader of the party, Balfour held to a policy of warding off at all costs a creation of peers large enough to saddle the House of Lords with a permanent Liberal majority. This in his mind was "revolution." Loss of the Veto, that is, acceptance of the Parliament Bill, he considered a lesser evil. Opposed to this view a group of "Diehard" peers was beginning to form, taking its name from a famous regiment. Its symbol and champion was that "antique bantam of a fighting breed," Lord Halsbury, and its active organizer was Lord Willoughby de Broke, nineteenth baron of his line, one of the eighteen members of the House of Lords whose title was created before 1500. Before succeeding to it he had served in the House of Commons, and besides political flair, possessed "unbounded energy and a marked talent for forcible and humorous oratory." At forty-two he was a personality of ingenuous charm whose father's dying wish was that his son should do everything he could "to prevent motor cars being used for any purpose connected with hunting," and whose great-grandfather "had never tired of voting against the Reform Bill and died many a silent death in the last ditch, or in the last lobby, in defense of the existing order." Willoughby de Broke looked on industrialism and democracy as forces which had "reacted hideously on the nation at large," talked in hunting and racing metaphor and dashed about like a foxhound to rally the Backwoodsmen. In a circular letter addressed to them, Lord Halsbury urged each peer "to take your stand on your Constitutional hereditary right and stoutly resist any tampering with it."

In the midst of tense maneuvering around the throne, King Edward suddenly and unexpectedly died. Extreme Tories claimed the wickedness of the Government had caused his death and regarded the Liberals as regicides. There was a general sense as of an anchor slipping away and of a recognized order of things gone. People somehow felt that the familiar royal bulk had stood between England and change, between England and outside menaces. A song sung by the charwoman in *Pelissier's Follies* of 1909 was widely popular:

> There'll be no wo'ar
> As long as there's a King like good King Edward
> There'll be no wo'ar
> For 'e 'ates that sort of thing!
> Mothers needn't worry
> As long as we've a King like good King Edward.
> Peace with 'Onner
> Is his Motter
> So God Sive the King!

When he died people expected times would now get worse. "I always felt," said one Edwardian, "that he kept things together somehow."

In verse for the occasion the Poet Laureate urged Englishmen to cease their "fateful feuds" and "fractious clamors" and declare "a truce of God." In an effort to spare the new King a crisis at the moment of his ascending the throne, the parties agreed to try to reach a settlement in a Constitutional Conference attended by four leaders from each side including Asquith and Lloyd George, Balfour and Lansdowne. Through twenty-one meetings during the summer and fall of 1910 they discussed and bargained, tried out the idea of a popular referendum and came close to an agreement only to founder finally over Home Rule. The Conference at least demonstrated that the Parliament Bill itself was something less than a fundamental issue, but statesmen would not or could not disengage themselves from the combat. Lloyd George, who was nothing if not a realist, tried. Principles being now thoroughly muddied, he approached Balfour with a proposal for a Coalition which, being free of the pressures of party extremists on both sides, might solve both the Veto and the Irish questions. He did not really want creation of peers any more than Balfour, he admitted amiably, because "looking into the future, I know that our glorified grocers will be more hostile to social reform than your Backwoodsmen." Since it is believed that Lloyd George made his first overture to Balfour without informing Asquith, it is possible he also had in mind ditching the Prime Minister as he was ultimately to do six years later. When Asquith was informed of the proposal he neither joined nor enjoined it but remained in the background, faithful to his motto, "Wait and see."

Believing that the British system of government depended on the check and balance of two parties and that a Coalition was warranted only in case of national emergency, such as war, Balfour refused. He did not really believe the Liberals could force the King to give them the necessary promise and in any case he considered there was less "real public mischief" in the Parliament Bill than in the creation of peers. Further he believed that if sufficient Conservative peers abstained from voting, the number of new peers created could be kept to a minimum short of the "revolution" of a permanent Liberal majority.

When Conference and Coalition both had failed, a General Election once more was called, in December, 1910, the second within a year. With public apathy unshaken, the results, except for a Liberal loss of two seats, were identical with those of the previous election. The country, as Wilfrid Blunt wrote, "cares too little about abolishing the House of Lords to make a revolution for it."

By judicious bullying before the election, Asquith had succeeded in obtaining the fateful promise of creation of peers from King George, who was confused by the conflicting advice and devious maneuvers of his advisers. The horrid prospect of England's hereditary peerage submerged by a "battalion of emergency noblemen," all Liberals, pleased no one and the prospect of the world's laughter and ridicule even less. Nevertheless the Government went ahead partly because it was impossible to stop and partly because they believed that when it came to a test the Lords would prefer to lose their Veto than to be doubled by the middle class. At some undated stage in the proceedings Asquith drew up, or caused to be drawn up, a list of some 250 names for wholesale ennobling which, though it included Sir Thomas Lipton, did not altogether deserve Lloyd George's sneer about glorified grocers. On the list along with Lipton were Asquith's brother-in-law, H. J. Tennant, as well as his devoted admirer and future biographer, J. A. Spender; also Sir Edgar Speyer, Bertrand Russell, General Baden-Powell, General Sir Ian Hamilton, the jurist Sir Frederick Pollock, the historians Sir George Trevelyan and G. P. Gooch, the South African millionaire Sir Abe Bailey, Gilbert Murray, J. M. Barrie, Thomas Hardy, and Anthony Hope, author of *The Prisoner of Zenda.*

In February, 1911, the Parliament Bill was reintroduced in the Commons to the accompaniment of "a great roar of cheering which had in it not only a note of triumph but of resolution, determination." "We are in grim earnest," wrote Herbert Samuel, "and if the Lords reject the Bill, "nothing could suit us better." Passed by the Commons in May, the Bill was duly sent for consideration to "another place."

In June began the great transport strike which opened a new period of deep industrial warfare. It marked the change from individual "trades disputes" to action according to the Syndicalist pattern in which workers struck not against a particular employer but against a whole industry. Unskilled labour had become disgusted with the political methods which won them no wage increases and revolted against the leadership of the Labour party, which once inside Westminster had become absorbed in the parliamentary game, with MacDonald gradually displacing Keir Hardie. Mass labor wanted hard gains in more pay and recognition of its unions by employers. It was clamoring for direct action and growing increasingly aggressive. Assaults on mine-owners' property had marked the strike of thirty thousand coal-miners in the Rhondda Valley of Wales a few months previously. Ben Tillett and Tom Mann, leaders of the first great dockers' strike, in 1889, were now preaching the doctrine of Syndicalism derived from Sorel and the French CGT, which combined belief in revolution with trade unionism and rejected political action in favor of the final weapon of the general strike. Mann and Tillett succeeded in organizing thirty-six unions of seamen, firemen, cooks and stewards, dockers and teamsters into a National Transport Workers' Federation. When shipowners refused to negotiate with it, the strike was called in June. It was to last seventy-two days and involve 77,000 men. As it spread from London to Liverpool, Hull, Cardiff, Bristol and Southampton, all traffic stopped in nearly every port and riots, looting and arson followed in its wake. "It is revolution!" exclaimed an excited employer to a Board of Trade official. "The men have new leaders, unknown before; and we don't know how to deal with them."

At this juncture, on July 1, the German gunboat *Panther* arrived at Agadir in Morocco, precipitating an international crisis which teetered for several weeks on the imminent brink of war. In August, in the midst of the crisis, four railway unions joined the seamen's and dockers' strike, threatening a total stoppage of all transport. The Home Secretary, Winston Churchill, supplied military convoys to keep essential trains running and sent troops to strike centers. There were inevitable clashes; soldiers in Liverpool opened fire, killing two strikers and wounding two hundred. For appealing to the soldiers not to shoot at British workers even if ordered, Tom Mann was imprisoned on a charge of inciting the troops to mutiny. Although the strike was settled on emergency terms, owing to the foreign crisis, others of equal intensity followed during the next three years. After the gunfire at Liverpool, trade-union votes turned increasingly toward their own representatives, ending the alliance with Liberalism. In the clang of the realities of class war, Churchill's earnest plea to labour in 1908, "Ah, but we must have that support!" echoed now with the faint ironic note of a faraway horn. Dividing from labour, Liberalism's road to the political wilderness was open.

Against this background, Coronation Summer, the hottest in a generation, bloomed in the golden fullness of an open rose. There were dinner parties and extravagant receptions every night, garden parties every afternoon, country house parties every weekend, glitter and picnics and fancy dress balls. Even the heat was "splendid—such a summer as comes seldom in England." The Henley Regatta was held in ideal weather and clear days were on hand for every rite of the season, polo at Ranelagh, the Eton-Harrow cricket match at Lords, the Gold Cup at Ascot. Neither the prospect of war, a general transport strike nor even creation of peers could subdue the high spirits of the festivities. Newspapers used the language of crisis and indignant noblemen growled at "nothing short of revolution" but a guest came to a masquerade ball at Claridge's flippantly wearing a peer's mantle and coronet with "No. 499" pasted on it. Lady

Curzon was crowned Queen of Beauty at a Tournament of Knights organized by Mrs. Cornwallis-West, Churchill's mother, with tickets at £20 apiece. The Russian Ballet made its London debut at Covent Garden, Pavlova and Nijinsky danced at private parties, including one in a garden under a blue sky at Strawberry Hill, once the home and gothic extravaganza of Horace Walpole. Its new owner, Lady Michelham, owned nineteen yards of pearls and gave a dinner for sixty guests after the dance in the garden, at which the entrées were served in the form of lighthouses, lit up inside and surrounded by ortolans representing sea gulls with a surf of white sauce breaking over them. At a house party at Blenheim, the Duke, his cousin Winston, Neil Primrose, son of Lord Rosebery, and F. E. Smith played cards till dawn in a tent by candlelight on upturned barrels. "What shall we play for, F. E.?" asked Marlborough. "Your bloody palace, if you like," Smith answered, although what he staked himself is not recorded.

Yet it was not the same, not the England of Jubilee year. The strikes were a reminder of the rising pressure of the working class, as Agadir was a reminder of the pressure of Germany. The assurance of a time characterized in English memory long afterward in terms of "the golden sovereigns, the sense of honor, the huge red blocks on the map," was gone. The gaiety was "feverish," the fancy dress ball of the season was given by F. E. Smith, not by the Duchess of Devonshire (the Duke had died in 1908), and in London the last horse-drawn bus had disappeared from the streets; motor-taxis, of which there had been none at the turn of the century, now outnumbered horsecabs 6,300 to 5,000.

The upper class still found life and each other immensely agreeable. At a party given by Mrs. Hwfa Williams and entertained by the wit of the Marquis de Soveral, the conversation was so generally enjoyed that the guests who had come to lunch stayed until one o'clock in the morning. It may have been enjoyment or they may have stayed from boredom, the boredom of having nothing else to do. The laughter, the fun, the practical jokes, the undeniable high spirits of privileged life of the time were the other face of ennui. The endless talk "at luncheon, tea and dinner, at dances and gatherings far into the night," Masterman believed, was the talk "of a society desirous of being interested, more often finding itself bored, filled with a resolute conviction that it must 'play the game,' and that this is the game to be played." They were "an aggregation of clever, agreeable, often lovable people . . . trying with desperate seriousness to make something of a life spared the effort of wage-earning." Writing in 1909 he did not call it the boredom of peace, yet when he wrote of "the present Roman peace which has come upon the western races of Europe," it was almost with a reluctant sigh.

During the first week of July the House of Lords amended the Parliament Bill so as to cancel abolition of the Veto and to except Home Rule from legislation which could become law without their consent. On July 18 Asquith officially informed Balfour by letter that he was in possession of the King's promise to create peers, that the amendments were unacceptable and that he proposed to make a statement to the Commons that unless the Lords passed the bill in its original form he would ask the Crown to take appropriate measures. The Diehards flung themselves furiously into organizing resistance like settlers preparing a stockade against the Indians. "Let them make their peers," declared Lord Curzon at a Diehard meeting, "we will die in the last ditch before we will give in!" To those who did not sympathize they were known as "Ditchers" thereafter. Among them were the new Marquess of Salisbury, his brother-in-law the Earl of Selborne, and, in the Commons, his younger brother Lord Hugh Cecil, Austen Chamberlain, George Wyndham and the two adventurers, Sir Edward Carson and F. E. Smith. During that hot July, Lord Willoughby de Broke worked feverishly canvassing all the peers, arranging meetings and obtaining speakers. On July 12, fifty-three peers including five dukes signed a letter to Lord Lansdowne stating that unless the amendments were retained they would vote to reject the Parliament Bill at its final reading "even though the consequence be the creation of peers."

Balfour and Lansdowne, whom the King begged not to force him to the loathsome expedient, summoned a Shadow Cabinet of the Opposition of which a majority, though not all, were willing to follow their recommendation to surrender, that is, to let the Parliament Bill pass without a division, since to die in the last ditch, while upholding principle, would not prevent abolition of the Veto. Unless the Government were bluffing, the result would only be creation of peers *and* loss of the Veto. But the Ditchers were adamant. To call for a division, said Lord Halsbury, was his "solemn duty to God and country." Assuming that the "Hedgers," as the followers of Balfour and Lansdowne were now called, abstained, the Ditchers needed enough votes to outnumber the seventy-five Liberal peers. Willoughby de Broke believed he had sixty and hoped for eighty.

Once more a meeting was called at Lansdowne House in an effort to arrive at a concerted policy between Hedgers and Ditchers. Curzon had now come around to Balfour's view but old Lord Halsbury grimly maintained he "would divide, even if alone, rather than surrender." Balfour was urged to call another meeting of the Shadow Cabinet but he was becoming irritated and impatient with the "theatrical" attitude of the Diehards, especially of the commoners such as Smith and Chamberlain. The most he would do was to write a public letter to *The Times* addressed to a "perplexed peer" advising the necessity of passing the Bill. The Ditchers replied that the Bill would establish Single Chamber government and they could not absolve themselves from responsibility "for a contemplated revolution merely by abstention." As the climax of their campaign they organized a great banquet in honor of Lord Halsbury for which the demand for tickets exceeded the capacity of the hall. Amid gladiatorial speeches and toasts Lord Halsbury, appearing "very unwell, anxious and tired," expressed the determination of his group to fight to the end and received a tremendous ovation. Lord Milner, whose "Damn the consequences" might be said to have started the train of events, was a logical addition to the company. Among other speakers Austen Chamberlain denounced Asquith as having "tricked the Opposition, entrapped the Crown and deceived the people."

On July 24, the day when the Prime Minister was scheduled to make his announcement to the Commons, the Ditchers' supporters in that House, led by Lord Hugh Cecil and F. E. Smith, organized a protest which culminated in the "most violent scene in the Commons within living memory." All the anger and frustration of a class on the defensive exploded in a demonstration of hatred and hysteria. Smith entered it from love of attack, Lord Hugh from passionate sincerity. In him all the Cecils' hatred of change was concentrated without the cooling Cecil skepticism so notable in his cousin Arthur. All his convictions were white hot. He saw doom in modern materialist society, in the turning away from Church and land and in democracy's turning away from "natural" leaders. Tall and stooped like his father as a young man, with a somber, narrow face, he had his father's habit of twisting and turning his long hands and looked and behaved like Savonarola. Churchill, at whose wedding in 1908 he had been best man, wrote that in Cecil "I met for the first time a real Tory, a being out of the Seventeenth Century." In private conversation he was "so quick, witty and unexpected that it was a delight to hear him," and in the House he held members "riveted in pin-drop silence for more than an hour" with a discourse on the difference between Erastians and High Churchmen. Considered by Asquith "the best speaker in the House of Commons and indeed anywhere," he was in gift of speech as in opinions an English Albert de Mun.

Once when Gladstone visited Hatfield, Hugh, then a small boy, burst into his bedroom and hit him with his fists, crying, "You're a bad man!"

"How can I be a bad man when I am your father's friend?" asked Gladstone, who had not dominated a thousand debates for nothing. But this opponent was not to be sidetracked into debate; he dealt in finalities. "My father is going to cut off your head with a great big sword" was his answer.

The sword was now drawn against Mr. Asquith. At three in the afternoon, in a House already buzzing with excitement, with every seat taken and members standing in the gangway, clustered in dense groups like bees, and galleries packed with onlookers, the Prime Minister entered, looking flushed and a little nervous. Liberals rose to their feet waving their order papers and cheered for three minutes, drawing "fierce ejaculations" from the Opposition, who cheered in their turn when Balfour came in. As Asquith rose to speak he was interrupted before he could pronounce an audible sentence by shouts of "Traitor!" and "Redmond!" in reference to the Irish sword hanging over his head, followed by a low steady murmur of "Divide! . . . 'vide! . . . 'vide!" * which began, grew, died away, and each time Asquith opened his mouth, began again. Standing on the Opposition front bench below the gangway, his eyes blazing, his bony ungainly body swaying to the rhythm of his cries, his face ashen and contorted by "tremendous passion," Hugh Cecil faced him, possessed by a fanaticism which allowed him to believe that any tactic, however discreditable, was justified for the sake of the cause. Asquith looked at his screaming foes with scorn and wonder, his eyes coming to rest on Cecil with the fascinated gaze of someone held by the pacing of a caged tiger. In the galleries excited ladies stood on their chairs. Sir Edward Grey, with a grim face, moved over next to Asquith as if to protect him. Balfour, lounging opposite, watched his own followers with a look of amazed disgust. Several times Asquith tried to read his statement but nothing he said could be heard over the shouts of " 'vide! 'vide!" "Who killed the King?" and "Dictator!" What few words he managed to make heard only enraged his opponents and evoked more howls. Despite every effort of the Speaker the demonstrators refused to subside. For three-quarters of an hour Asquith stood his ground until finally "white with anger" he folded up his speech and sat down.

When Balfour rose to speak the Liberals did not retaliate, but when F. E. Smith, who was believed to be the instigator, stood up he was met

---

* The call for a vote, which is taken by division, that is, a physical separation of members into their respective lobbies.

by pandemonium. To have exaggerated the intensity of passion in the House that afternoon, wrote *The Times* correspondent, would have been impossible. Again the Speaker was helpless, and finally after the session had lasted two hours and amid continued shouts and an isolated cry from the Labour benches, "Three cheers for the Social Revolution!" he adjourned the House as a "disorderly assembly," for the first time in its history.

The brawling and abuse of the "Cecil scene," as it came to be known, astonished everyone. No Prime Minister had ever before been so disrespectfully treated. The press overflowed with indignant comment and letters pro and con. Many felt that the scene had been directed as much against Balfour's leadership as against Asquith. Blunt recorded that F. E. Smith, George Wyndham and Bendor (the Duke of Westminster) were "in the highest possible spirits at the commotion they have caused and consider they have forced Balfour's hand."

Publication next day of Asquith's unheard statement marked the point of no recall and the Conservative leaders had to face the possibility that the insurgents would actually bring about the "revolution" that Balfour most wished to avoid—creation of a permanent Liberal majority in the Lords. If the Diehards could muster more than seventy-five, creation of peers must follow—unless the Government was bluffing. Was it bluffing? Many still believed so; no one could be sure. Nor did anyone know how many peers would actually vote with the Diehards. In this crucial situation Lansdowne and the Hedgers had to undertake the terrible necessity of finding a number of Conservative peers who would sacrific principle if not honor to vote with the Government for the bill they detested. It was the only way to prevent a possible Diehard majority. How many would be needed for the sacrifice and how many would have the courage at the last moment to perform it was another of the painful uncertainties of the situation.

On August 10, the day for drinking the hemlock, the temperature reached a record of a hundred degrees and tension at Westminster was even higher, for, unlike previous political crises, the outcome was in suspense. By 4:00 P.M. the House of Lords had filled to the last seat with the greatest attendance ever known, with visitors' galleries jammed and peers standing in passages and doorways. They wore morning coats with wing collars, ascots, spats and light waistcoats and after the dinner recess many appeared in white tie and tails. The Diehards wore white sprigs of heather sent by the Duchess of Somerset, while many of the Hedgers wore red roses. As Halsbury marched to his seat with the air of a knight entering the lists he seemed to an observer to be accompanied by an almost audible sound of jingling spurs. In a shrill appeal to conscience he demanded defeat of the Bill. Lord Curzon spoke for the majority and afterward sat "pale and angry" while Lord Selborne sprang to the table and "in strident tones with dramatic gestures" fiercely renewed the intention to die in the last ditch. New suspense was injected by the speech of the Liberal leader, Lord Crewe, whose reference to the King's "natural reluctance" and whose own unhappy conclusion, "The whole business, I frankly admit, is odious to me," reinvigorated a belief that the Government was bluffing. Anxious counts and recounts took place. Of six peers who sat at the same table during the dinner recess, two of whom, Lord Cadogan and Lord Middleton, were former Conservative Cabinet members, not one had made up his mind how to vote. When, on reassembling, one of the "sacrificial" peers, Lord Camperdown, announced his intention to vote with the Government, the Duke of Norfolk, enraged, replied that if any Conservative peer voted for the Bill, he and his group would vote with the Diehards. Lord Morley, whose peerage was barely three years old, nevertheless felt "deeply moved" when obliged to make explicit the Government's intention to follow defeat of the Bill by "a large and prompt creation of peers." Upon request he repeated the statement. A pall settled on the chamber. The Archbishop of Canterbury urged members not to provoke an act that would make their House and indeed the country a "laughing stock." Lord Rosebery, whose vacillations had confused everyone but who had been expected to abstain, suddenly jumped up from the crossbenches and announced, in "this last, shortest and perhaps most painful speech of my life," that he would vote with the Government. Since, whatever the outcome, "the House of Lords, as we have known it, disappears," he said he intended never to enter its doors again, and he never did.

At 10:40 P.M. amid "intense excitement" the division was called. Abstaining peers who could find room squeezed onto the steps of the throne where they could remain without voting while the rest of the abstainers led by Lord Lansdowne left the chamber. The two groups, as they gathered to file out in two streams into the lobbies on either side of the chamber, appeared to the tense watchers in the galleries about equal in number. Counting was done by tellers with white wands who tapped the shoulder of each peer as he returned from the division lobby. Slowly the streams reappeared while from the open doors the tellers could be heard counting aloud, "one, two, three, four. . . ." For a quarter of an hour which seemed like a full hour the process continued. During an accidental pause in the Government stream, the undaunted Lord Halsbury was heard to whisper, "There! I knew we should beat them!" Lord Morley waited anxiously for the sight of the bishops' lawn sleeves, feeling certain that they would vote with the Government. The procession came to an end. The tellers brought their count to the Chief Whip, Lord Herschell, who handed the results on a piece of paper to the Lord Chancellor. Amid profound silence Lord Loreburn rose from the Woolsack, shook back the panels of his wig and in clear tones announced the result: for the Bill, 131; against, 114; majority, 17. Unable to contain her emotion Lady Halsbury hissed loudly from the Peeresses' Gallery. No cheers or enthusiasm came from the victors except for M.P.'s who dashed off with the news to their own House, where it was greeted with roars of triumph. The Lords left at once and in five minutes their hall was empty. Thirty-seven Conservative peers plus the two archbishops and eleven bishops had voted with the Government and those of them who appeared that night among a tumultuous gathering at the Carlton Club were greeted with cries of "Shame!" and "Judas!"

"The floodgates of revolution are opened," bawled Lord Northcliffe's *Daily Mail* next morning, but no waters poured through. With the Veto abolished the way was open for a Home Rule Bill which the Government introduced in the following session. In the event, the victory over the Lords proved irrelevant. Opposition to Home Rule merely shifted its ground and, in the fresh form of the Ulster rebellion, provoked a new and sterner crisis in which the existence of the Parliament Bill was immaterial. Ultimately it took a greater upheaval than abolition of the Veto to lift the Irish incubus off English politics.

Some weeks later Sir Edward Grey remarked to Winston Churchill, "What a remarkable year this has been: the heat, the strikes, and now the foreign situation."

"Why," said Winston, "you've forgotten the Parliament Bill," and a friend who recorded the conversation added, "and so he had and so had everybody."

On the morning after the vote in the House of Lords, the heat wave and the transport strike, which seemed about to become a general strike and to threaten a "real danger of social revolution," absorbed the country's attention. A chagrined peer could find "no evidence anywhere that the Constitutional crisis had agitated the country." On the same day a measure of perhaps greater significance passed the House of Commons: a Payment of Members Bill by which M.P.'s would henceforth receive an annual salary of £400. It had long been bitterly fought by the Conservatives and determinedly sought by Labour. Non-payment was regarded by the Labour party as depriving the working class of the right to be represented in Parliament by men from their own ranks. Especially was payment needed after the Osborne judgment cut off the use of union funds for members' salaries. To its opponents, Payment of Members marked the passing of politics as a gentleman's profession and as such was "more disastrous" even than the Parliament Bill. It would introduce a new and "intolerable type of professional politician," complained Austen Chamberlain. It would remove the "last check upon the inrush of mere adventurers," said *The Times*, then owned by that supreme adventurer Lord Northcliffe, and it would encourage the "invasion" of unpaid forms of public service "now efficiently carried on by men who can afford to be disinterested." For the patrician, free of pecuniary greed and partaking in government from a sense of civic duty, the point was valid but obsolete; society's needs had grown beyond him, nor had he ever been disinterested in defending the ramparts of his caste. Payment of Members measured another advance in the transfer of power.

The next act followed logically: Balfour resigned the leadership of the Conservative Party, which he had held in the House of Commons for twenty years. His announcement, made on November 8, 1911, after returning from a vacation in Bad Gastein, caused a political "sensation." Although a movement for his ouster under the slogan B.M.G. (Balfour Must Go) had taken shape, inspired by the insurgent wing under the influence of F. E. Smith and Austen Chamberlain, it had been expected that he would fight for control. But the final stages of the Veto crisis, the wildness of a meaningless battle, the preference of the Ditchers for gesture over thought, the rising influence of adventurers such as Smith, whom he detested, and the challenge to his own leadership displayed by the uncouth tactics of the Cecil scene, had accumulated in Balfour to the point of irritated indifference. Almost as a gesture of contempt he had not waited for the issue of the final vote in the House of Lords but left for Bad Gastein the day before. During his stay among "the cataracts, the pines and the precipices" he thought things over and reached a decision. He was sixty-three, his interest in philosophy was still strong and to face the necessity of returning to a fight for control, first of the party, then of the country, against the trends of a new age did not appeal to him. He belonged to a tradition in which government was the function of the patrician, whereas already, as he said in his speech of resignation, the demand upon administrators and legislators had become so heavy that the affairs of state must devolve upon those who were prepared "to be politicians and nothing but politicians, to work the political machine as professional politicians." The rush of the crowd upon the tranquil garden, as Masterman had depicted the rise of the Populace, was under way and Balfour was too much the philosopher to fight it.

His succession went to neither of the two chief contenders, Walter Long, representing the landed gentry, nor Austen Chamberlain, who canceled each other out, but to Bonar Law, a Glasgow steel manufacturer, born a Canadian, who read the newspapers regularly, ate meals of vegetables, milk and rice pudding and had the backing of another of the adventurers, his fellow Canadian Max Aitken, soon to be Lord Beaverbrook.

Balfour's departure inspired floods of press comment and political gossip and an impeccable tribute from Asquith to "the most distinguished member of the greatest deliberative body in the world." George Wyndham, rather more sour if more genuine, thought Balfour's refusal to fight was in character, arising from indifference which came from taking "too scientific a view of politics." "He knows," said Wyndham, "that there was once an ice age and that there will be an ice age again."

8

The Death of Jaurès

THE SOCIALISTS:
1890–1914

8

The Death of Jaurès

SOCIALISM was international. Its name as an organized movement, the Second International Workingmen's Association, said so. Its anthem, "The International," affirmed it and promised besides that "tomorrow the International will be the human race." Its founding Congress of 1889 had as joint presidents a Frenchman and a German, Edouard Vaillant and Wilhelm Liebknecht. Its membership at its height represented the Socialist parties of thirty-three nations and would-be nations, including Germany, France, England, Austria, Hungary and Bohemia, Russia, Finland, Holland, Belgium, Spain, Italy, Sweden, Norway, Denmark, Serbia, Bulgaria, India, Japan, Australia and the United States. Its flag was a solid red representing the blood of Everyman. Its essential thesis was that the class solidarity of workingmen transcended national frontiers in a horizontal division of society. Its holiday set aside the first of May to demonstrate proletarian brotherhood. Its slogan was "Workers of the World, Unite!"

Whether or not miners, factory hands, farm labourers, servants and other members of the working class, in whose interest Socialism existed, felt themselves to be international, their leaders believed it, practiced it, counted on it. At the Amsterdam Socialist Congress which took place in 1904 during the Russo-Japanese War, the Russian and Japanese delegates, Plekhanov and Katayama, were seated side by side. When the two men clasped hands, all 450 delegates rose to their feet in a tribute of thunderous applause. When Plekhanov and Katayama each made a speech declaring that the war had been forced upon his country by capitalism and was not a matter of the Japanese people fighting the Russian people, they were listened to in "almost religious silence" and sat down amid cheers.

Socialism was equally predicated on the concept of class war and on its eventual outcome, the destruction of capitalism. It regarded both the ruling class and the bourgeoisie as the enemy. The sentiment was reciprocated. The word "Socialist" had a ring of blood and terror, like "Jacobin" of the old days. During the quarter century following its founding in Paris in 1889 on the hundredth anniversary of the French Revolution, the Second International inspired growing apprehension in the ruling class. Vienna was "paralyzed with fright" when Viktor Adler, the Austrian Socialist leader, called for a one-day general strike and mass demonstrations throughout the Empire on the first May Day to demonstrate the workers' united strength. When Adler announced a workers' parade down the chestnut-bordered Prater where usually only the carriages of the wealthy appeared, the rich and their allies trembled, expecting the rabble would set houses on fire, plunder shops, and commit unimaginable atrocities on their march. Merchants let down their iron shutters, parents forbade children to go out of doors, police were posted at every street corner, troops were held in reserve. The bourgeoisie saw spreading before their feet what Henry George had called in *Progress and Poverty* "the open-mouthed, relentless hell which yawns beneath civilized society." They were made aware of the rising threat "of the House of Want upon the House of Have."

When the Second International was founded, the twelve-hour day and seven-day week were normal for unorganized labour. Sunday rest and the ten- or nine-hour day were the hard-won privileges of skilled labour in the craft unions, which represented barely one-fifth of the labour force. In 1899 Edwin Markham, struck by the bent brute figure of Millet's "Man with the Hoe," expressed both society's fear and responsibility in a poem named for the picture:

> Through this dread shape humanity betrayed,
> Plundered, profaned and disinherited,
> Cries protest to the Judges of the World,
> A protest that is also prophecy. . . .
>
> How will the Future reckon with this Man?
> How answer his brute question in that hour
> When whirlwinds and rebellion shake the world?
> How will it be with the kingdoms and the kings—
> With those who shaped him to the thing he is—
> When this dumb Terror shall reply to God
> After the silence of the centuries?

In 1899, when poetry still spoke to the public, Markham's poem caused a sensation. Newspapers throughout America reprinted it, editorials discussed it, clergymen used it as a text, school children studied it, debating societies debated it, and commentators called it "the cry of the *zeitgeist*" and, next to Kipling's "Recessional," the most "meaningful poem of the age."

The public conscience which responded to an artist's vision and a poet's words was frightened and angry when confronted with the real thing. When in 1891 the textile workers of Fourmies, a small industrial town in northern France, organized a May Day demonstration for the eight-hour day, police charged their parade and in the ensuing melee killed ten people, including several children. "Take care!" warned Clemenceau in the Chamber. "The dead are strong persuaders. One must pay attention to the dead. . . . I tell you that the primary fact of politics today is the inevitable revolution which is preparing. . . . The Fourth Estate is rising and reaching for the conquest of power. One must take sides. Either you meet the Fourth Estate with violence or you welcome it with open arms. The moment has come to choose."

There was little disposition toward open arms. When the Socialist leaders and unions of Belgium, after two previous bloody attempts, succeeded in 1893 in organizing a general strike for equal manhood suffrage, the essential precondition for the conquest of power, soldiers killed twelve before the strike ended. When the Pullman strike in the United States in 1894 stopped trains and the mail, Judge William Howard Taft of Cincinnati, far from a ferocious man, wrote to his wife, "It will be necessary for the military to kill some of the mob before the trouble can be stayed. They have only killed six . . . as yet. This is hardly enough to make an impression." Here was the class war in operation.

Socialism's ultimate aim was the abolition of private property and the redistribution of the world's goods to provide everybody with enough. The goal was the same as that of Anarchism; what caused the permanent conflict between the two groups was that the Socialists believed in organization and political action to achieve it.

Collective ownership was the answer of both to the terrible riddle posed by the Nineteenth Century: that the greater the material progress, the wider and deeper the resulting poverty. Marx drew from the riddle the central theme of his system: that this inherent contradiction within capitalism would bring about its breakdown. He proved it from the economic analysis of history. The effect of the Industrial Revolution had been to transform the worker from an independent producer who owned his own tools into a factory hand, a propertyless, destitute member of society, dependent for his livelihood on the capitalist who owned the means of production. Through the capitalist's accumulation of profits derived from the surplus value of the worker's product, the exploiters were becoming richer and the exploited poorer. The process could only end in the violent collapse of the existing order. Trained in class consciousness and prepared for this event, the working class would, at the moment of ripeness, rise in revolution to usher in the new order.

This Marxian doctrine of *Verelendung* (pauperization, or increasing misery) and *Zusammenbruch* (collapse) was the religious formula of Socialism, equivalent to "God is One" of another religion. It afflicted Socialism and the labour movement with a chronic schism between the necessity of collapse and revolution on the one hand and the possibility of gradual reform of the existing order on the other. As a schism between the future Absolute and the present Possible, it was present from birth, when the founders of 1889 split into two Congresses over the issue whether to permit cooperation with the bourgeois political parties. The true Marxists accused the French Possibilists of lying in wait at the Paris railroad stations to lead unsuspecting delegates from the provinces to the wrong Congress. Throughout the next twenty-five years the schism affected every act, decision and formulation of policy in the working-class movement, dividing negotiated gains from uncompromising class war, pragmatists from theorists, trade unions from parliamentary parties, the workers themselves, who wanted improvements in wages, hours and safety today, from the leaders, who agitated in their behalf for political power tomorrow.

The Marxian premise built into Socialism a chronic dilemma as well as a schism. As a movement on behalf of the working class it needed working-class support, which could only be obtained by showing practical results. Yet every practical result slowed or arrested the process of impoverishment. When walking with a friend who reached in his pocket to give money to a beggar, Johannes Miquel, in his youth an ardent Socialist, stopped him, saying, "Don't delay the Revolution!" This was the logical extreme of Marxism. Any reform inferred a common ground between the contesting classes; revolution assumed the absence of it. If there was no common ground, what then was the use of anything short of revolution? Orthodox Socialists skirted this gaping hole in the creed by contending that reforms should continue to be wrung from the possessing class in order to strengthen the workers for the final struggle. The several national parties always stated a minimum program of reforms to be obtained within the existing system and a maximum program for the destruction of capitalism and triumph of the class struggle. Increasingly the moderates, or "opportunists," as their opponents called them, concentrated on the minimum program and the acquisition of political power necessary to put it through, while the orthodox refused to concede that any interim successes interfered with the truth of "increasing misery."

On the final necessity of revolution the Socialist party programs were imprecise. They glossed over it both in order to appeal to the voters and because it remained a disputable point. Socialism was not a hard gemlike doctrine impervious to modification, but varied, depending on time, country, situation and faction. Whether or not a Socialist believed in revolution was largely a matter of temperament. For some it was "nothing if not revolution." For others what counted was the Socialist millennium, however achieved. For the orthodox Marxist, in any case, collapse was ineluctable and Capitalism not a system to be modified but an Enemy to be destroyed, a living tyrant armed with the weapons of its class: courts, army, judges, legislature, police, injunctions, lockouts.

Property had lasted too long, filling the world with wickedness, turning men against each other. The time for overturn had come. The social evils produced by capitalism—poverty, ignorance, racial prejudice and war, which was just another form of capitalist exploitation—would be wiped out and replaced by social harmony. Freed from false patriotism, workingmen linked by their underlying brotherhood would no longer fight each other. Freed from the greeds and frustrations imposed by capitalism, every individual could pursue "the unimpaired development of his personality," being guaranteed under the collective system sufficient means and liberty to achieve it.

As the chariot of a new and higher order of life, Socialism seemed to its advocates to carry a sacred trust and to impose upon them a moral duty to be worthy of the ideal. Because he believed drinking was disgracing and destroying the working classes, Viktor Adler adopted total abstinence to set a personal example. Socialism was the repository of the big words. When, as a student in Brussels, Angelica Balabanov, a young Russian revolutionary, listened to Socialist orators in the Belgian Parliament, "Parliament seemed to me then a sacred place where Science, Truth and Justice . . . were to conquer the forces of Tyranny and Oppression for the working class."

The goal gave an excitement, a meaning, a glow to Socialist lives which for many of them substituted for the usual drives of personal ambition and profit. Party militants and organizers in the early days worked for nothing. Since there was no money in the movement, there could be no corruption. Since it could offer no livelihood or gain, its leaders tended

to be idealists. It was a cause, not a career. It gave its disciples something
to work for and infused a passion which could be understood across the
barrier of language. At one Socialist Congress the Spanish leader Pablo
Iglesias spoke so eloquently in his native tongue that although the audience
did not understand a word, they burst into frequent applause. To the
workers who increasingly voted for it, in millions after the turn of the
century, Socialism gave self-respect and an identity. A workingman could
feel himself no longer an ignored anonymous member of a herd but a
citizen with a place in society and a political affiliation of his own. Unlike
Anarchism, Socialism gave him a party to belong to and, since the nettle
of revolution did not have to be grasped, an acceptable way to reach the
goal instead of by way of the lawless deed.

The cause drew men like the Italian Amilcare Cipriani, one of the
founders of the Congress of 1889. Type of the eternal rebel, he had fought
with Garibaldi's Red Shirts and as a volunteer in the Cretan insurrection
against Turkey and turned up in Brussels to join the comrades in the general strike of 1893. "Magnificent in cape and soft felt hat, with black beard
streaked with grey and eyes of flame," he carried a handbag in which
"there were doubtless more explosives than toilet articles . . . ready to
fight in any corner of the world for the cause of Revolution."

It drew men of troubled conscience from the upper class, like the
American Robert Hunter, married to a daughter of the banker and philanthropist Anson Phelps Stokes. Like others of his class, Hunter was startled
by the articles of the Muckrakers and moved to seek a remedy for social
injustice. He saw his first vision of the poor in settlement-house work,
discovered Socialism, and at the age of twenty-eight in 1904 wrote a small
classic, *Poverty*. With the undulled emotion of his time he described a
valley in Italy "so smiling and peaceful, with a thousand terraced gardens
on its exquisite slopes, under skies that enrapture the soul; and with men,
women and children whose faces with big eyes and sunken cheeks lacerate
the heart. . . . Great God, is not the Valley of the Tirano all the school
that Italy needs for Socialism? . . . The faces are with you when you eat
and your food sickens you. . . . Any man with a heart would become a
Socialist in Italy."

Valleys of the Tirano in every country made Socialists out of intellectuals who saw them and workers who were born in them. What both had
in common was faith that man had it in his power to make things better.
The obstacles were massive; the House of Have was old and strong and
entrenched. But the grievances of the working class were rising and were
concerned as much with social inequality as with pure want. The workers

resented disparity in suffrage, due to property qualifications. They resented the unequal working of compulsory military service, from which the privileged could be exempted; the bias of the law, which worked one way for the rich and another for the poor; the layers of hereditary privilege of all kinds, which the ruling class took for granted. Socialism was making the workers' wants conscious and articulate. The apathy of the masses which had disillusioned Bakunin and caused Lassalle to rail at "the damned wantlessness of the poor" was passing. They were beginning to know what they wanted, though on the whole it was not revolution. Socialism's inclusion of that goal was what gave it fervor and impetus, as in the case of Julius Braunthal, who joined the Austrian Socialist party at the age of fourteen "for the sake of the Revolution." But revolution appealed more to intellectuals who had no doubt of their capacity to manage society than it did to the working class.

Like a crack in a plank of wood which cannot be sealed, the difference between the worker and the intellectual was ineradicable in Socialism. Organized Socialism bore the name Workingmen's Association but in fact it was never any such thing. It was a movement not of, but on behalf of, the working class, and the distinction remained basic. Although it spoke for the worker and made his wants articulate, goals and doctrine were set, and thought, energy and leadership largely supplied by, intellectuals. The working class was both client and ultimately, in its mass strength, the necessary instrument of the overthrow of capitalism. As such it appeared as Hero; it was sentimentalized. In the illustrations for an English pamphlet commemorating the London Congress of 1896, the workingmen appeared as handsome strong-muscled Burne-Jones figures in smocks accompanied by indomitable women with long limbs and rippling hair. They were not the same race as Zola's soiled figures, harsh, hungry, consumptive and alcoholic. The reality was neither all one thing nor the other; neither all *lumpenproletariat* nor curly-bearded, clenched-fisted revolutionist. The working class was no more of a piece than any other class. Socialist doctrine, however, required it to be an entity with a working-class mind, working-class voice, working-class will, working-class purpose. In fact, these were not easily ascertainable. The Socialist idealized them and to be idealized is to be overestimated.

Owing to its internal quarrels, the founding Congress of 1889 did not lay down a body of doctrine to which the member parties were obliged to subscribe. Agreement went no farther than four resolutions which established four objectives as proper Socialist aims short of the maximum program: the eight-hour day; universal equal manhood suffrage; substitution of citizens' militias for standing armies; observance of May Day for a show of working-class strength.

While the first was the essential demand of the clientele, the second was fundamental to the whole Socialist purpose and program. The vote was the one means by which the masses could translate numbers into power; their only means to equalize the power of capital. For the same reason, the ruling class resisted it. Equal manhood suffrage at this date existed only in France and the United States, and only in national elections, not local government, in Germany. In most other countries the propertyless were disqualified or plural votes were given to taxpayers, university graduates and fathers of families. Socialists demanded the one-man-one-vote principle.

May Day, last of the four resolutions, was agreed on in response to a message from the American Federation of Labor, which planned to open its campaign for the eight-hour day on May 1, 1890. It was adopted at the suggestion of a French trade unionist, but the result was divisive because the Germans refused to commit themselves to a gesture likely to anger officialdom and evoke reprisals.

Nevertheless it was the Germans who spoke with most authority in the International. As the oldest and largest of the Socialist parties, the German party enjoyed the greatest prestige and, by virtue of the fact that Marx was a German, regarded itself as the Petrine rock, not to mention the Vatican, of Socialism. In 1890, released from the anti-Socialist law, it won 1,400,000 votes, nearly 20 per cent of the total, and thirty-five seats, in the elections for the Reichstag, a victory that dazed Socialists in the rest of the world. In practice, the German Social-Democratic party, as a result of its successes among the voters and its close ties with the trade unions, adapted itself to the possible. In theory it remained stoutly Marxist and at its Erfurt Congress in 1891 restated the Marxian view of history as official.

The Erfurt Program reaffirmed that the middle class, small businessmen and farmers, were being squeezed out, sinking along with the proletariat into increasing misery, and that the greater the masses grew in number, increasing the pool of labour, the sharper became the division between exploiters and exploited. Since the ultimate solution of public ownership could only be accomplished through the conquest of political power, the program of the party must be to gain political control, using trade unions as the source of votes but maintaining direction of policy in the party.

The Erfurt order for political action stamped its image upon the Second International, though not without the furious resistance of the Anarchists and their friends whose split with the Marxists on this issue had broken up the First International. Although not invited to the Congress of Zurich in 1893, the Anarchists arrived anyway, whereat August Bebel, the German chairman, a master of Marxian abuse, harangued them for having "neither program nor principles." In Zurich, "accustomed to German methods," he had no difficulty in having them expelled by force. In protest against such methods, Amilcare Cipriani resigned as a delegate. The Anarchists retired to conduct a diminutive counter-Congress in a café while the majority unanimously adopted a resolution recognizing the "necessity of organizing the workers for political action." Only those parties and groups accepting this principle could henceforth call themselves Socialists and take part in Congresses of the International. Not wishing to cut themselves off from their foundations, they made an exception for trade unions, which in future were to be admitted without being required to subscribe to the political principle. According to the Belgian delegate Emile Vandervelde, these difficult problems were solved in an atmosphere of "profound calm." It seemed anything but calm to a young British trade-union delegate, J. R. Clynes of the cotton workers, who had never been abroad before. He was astonished at the "verbal orgies" and violence of the Latin and Slav delegates and at the flareups of hostility in which one delegate flourished a knife and "everyone was yelling and struggling." Among Socialists, human bellicosity found its vent in factionalism whose vehemence Clynes tactlessly ascribed to "national rivalries and hatreds growing out of past wars."

Going for a swim in the Lake of Zurich Clynes saw "a ruddy beard on the surface of the water floating gently towards me" which proved to be attached to Bernard Shaw, also a delegate to the Congress, representing the Fabian Society. Having already discounted Marx and revolution, Shaw did not spare his contempt, in his reports of the Congress, for Wilhelm Liebknecht's duping of his followers with the "rhetoric of the barricade." The German leaders, he decided thereafter, were forty years out of date. At sixty-seven, Liebknecht, founder of the party in 1875, was now its elder statesman. Descended from a long line of university professors reaching back to the Eighteenth Century, he had been imprisoned for his role in the bourgeois revolution of 1848, and afterwards lived in exile in England for thirteen years, where he studied with Marx. When he died in 1900 a crowd of an estimated hundred thousand mourners and spectators lined the streets along the route of his four-hour funeral procession.

By all but Shaw the German party was considered the hope of Socialism, bearer of the torch in the country from which Marx expected revolution to come. Everyone was impressed by its size and strength, its wonderful organization, its twenty-eight secretaries and organizers, its training program for party workers, and its mounting membership. In the elections of 1893 the Social-Democrats increased their votes to 1,750,000, close to 25 per cent of the total, more than those of any other single party. Since it was against principle to join forces with any bourgeois party, the Social-Democrats in the Reichstag remained, despite their numbers, a relatively impotent group in what was in any case an impotent body. The fact of their existence, however, exerted a silent pressure which made the Government more reasonable toward concessions. The Kaiser, who in the first careless rapture of his dismissal of Bismarck had lifted the anti-Socialist law in 1890, recovered quickly. By 1895 he had decided that the Social-Democrats were a "gang of traitors" who "do not deserve the name of Germans" and by 1897 that the party "which does not stop attacking the person of the All-Highest Ruler must be rooted out to the last stump." In 1895 Liebknecht was arrested on a charge of *lèse-majesté* for a speech of which Shaw said that it could have been made "by Mr. Arthur Balfour to the Primrose League tomorrow with the approbation of England." But this was no special mark of repression, since it could happen to anyone in Germany.

National tended to outweigh class traits among the German Socialists: they were more obedient than bold. For all its size the party did not venture to play host to an International Socialist Congress on German soil until 1907. Despite fiery speeches its leaders were prudent in action; they restricted May Day demonstrations to the evening so as not to interfere with work. Work stoppage, said Liebknecht, was general strike and "a general strike is general nonsense." In Munich no May Day demonstration was permitted until 1901 and then only on condition that it took place outside city limits and did not form crowds in the streets on the way. Columns of Socialists, "their pockets bulging with radishes," accompanied by wives and children, marched briskly in dead silence through the city to a beer garden on the outskirts where they drank beer and munched their radishes and struck a Russian exile as "not at all resembling a May Day celebration of working-class triumph."

They were better off, however, than any Russian worker. Under the heavy throb of German industrial expansion, employment was increasing faster than the population. Unions, under these conditions, were successful in raising wages. Social legislation, originally bestowed from above by Bismarck to weld labour to his state, was the most advanced of any country. By 1903, 18,000,000 workers were insured against accident, 13,000,000 against old age and 11,000,000 against illness, with a total annual expenditure of $100,000,000 in social welfare benefits. Laws regulated wages, hours, time off, grievance procedures, safety measures, and the number of factory windows and toilets. With characteristic thoroughness Germany's rulers wanted to ensure physical efficiency, leaving as little as possible to chance and bringing everything possible under orderly rule. Professor Delbrück in 1897 publicly supported the right of collective bargaining on the ground that labour peace was necessary for national unity and national defense. To keep labour quiet by judicious concessions was considered the best method of smothering the Social-Democrats, whom the possessing class regarded with increasing enmity and fear.

August Bebel, the party's dictator, was believed by the bourgeoisie to be a kind of "shadow-Kaiser." A small-boned, narrow little man with white hair and goatee, he had been born in a barracks in 1840, the same year as Czar Reed. His father was an Army corporal and his mother a domestic servant. Taking up the carpenter's trade, he had joined the labour movement in the days of Lassalle; and on a charge of incitement to treason had been sentenced to four years in prison, a punishment fruitful in producing Socialists. In prison Bebel read much, received visits from Liebknecht and wrote a magisterial history of *Woman and Socialism*. His brains, Mommsen said, if divided among a dozen Junkers from east of the Elbe, were enough to make each of them shine among his peers. In the Reichstag, where he had debated Bismarck in "savage accents," Bebel was the spokesman of poverty and misery, loved and admired by the workers, who felt him to be a comrade. He would remain "the deadly enemy of this bourgeois society and this political order" until it was destroyed, he proclaimed at a party Congress in 1903. This was traditional verbiage. In fact, Bebel had no great illusions about the mass of his followers. "Look at those fellows," he said in 1892 to a correspondent of the London *Times* as they watched a march of a battalion of Prussian Guards; "80 per cent of them are Berliners and Social-Democrats but if there was trouble they would shoot me down at a word of command from above."

Of the outstanding figures of the Second International only he and Keir Hardie were of working-class origin. Karl Kautsky, fourteen years younger than Bebel, thinker and writer of the party and formulator of the Erfurt Program, whose commentaries on doctrine provided the text of endless discussion, was the son of intellectuals, a painter and a novelist. Viktor Adler of Austria was a doctor, Emile Vandervelde was the son of wealthy parents whom he described as "models of bourgeois virtue," and Jaurès of France came from the petty bourgeoisie.

As a doctor, Adler knew the human damage caused by undernourishment, overwork and squalor. He wanted to lead the workers to a new existence of "health, culture, liberty and dignity." Born of a wealthy Jewish family of Prague, he had studied medicine in order to treat the poor. Dressed in rags like a bricklayer, he investigated conditions in the Viennese brickyards where workers lived in company barracks guarded like prisons, five or six families to a dormitory room, and were paid in chits valid only in company stores. Before founding the Austrian party in 1889 he traveled in Germany, England and Switzerland to study workers' lives and social legislation which might be introduced in Austria. He was a short, scraggy, rather fragile figure with bushy hair and moustache, gold-rimmed spectacles, a pale face and one shoulder bent forward. Next to music he loved Ibsen and Shelley. Accepting revolution as the ultimate goal, he believed interim reforms were necessary in order to fit the worker physically and intellectually for his destiny. The struggle to secure these reforms against that "despotism mitigated by slovenliness," as he described the Hapsburg regime, was often discouraging and gradually wore down the edge of Adler's faith. Trotsky, who knew him in the early 1900's, found him a skeptic who had come to tolerate everything and adapt himself to everything.

In Belgium, whose population was the densest in Europe and where the process of industrialization had been fierce and rapid, the life of the working class was, in the words of one observer, an "inferno." Textile factories, steel mills, mines, quarries, docks and wharves used up labour as a mill grinds grain. Twenty-five per cent of all workers earned less than the equivalent of forty cents a day; another 25 per cent earned between forty and sixty cents. An investigation in Brussels showed 34 per cent of working-class families living in a single room. The Belgian illiteracy rate was the highest in northern Europe because child labour was used to such an extent that few had a chance to go to school. Concerned with "something more profound than doctrine," the labour movement had founded the Belgian Workers' Party in 1885 without the usual schisms because it could not afford them. The most solidified, disciplined and serious of the European Socialist parties, it was markedly proletarian though led by the ardent Vandervelde. A lawyer by training, an eloquent and admired speaker and prolific writer on labour problems, Vandervelde was "gushed" over by female Socialists who found him "charming and physically attractive." Together with the unions, the party organized a system of cooperatives where workers bought Socialist bread and Socialist shoes, drank Socialist beer, arranged for Socialist vacations, and obtained a Socialist education at the Université Nouvelle, where the French Anarchist and geographer Elisée Reclus lectured. Founded by Vandervelde and others in 1894, the same year the Fabians founded the London School of Economics, the Belgian school capped a Socialist world created inside a capitalist society.

By virtue of the extended suffrage won with workers' lives, the Belgian Workers' Party in 1894 elected twenty-eight deputies to the most bourgeois parliament in Europe. The advent of this solid bloc "firmly and recklessly prepared to take up arms against every institution of the existing regime" created a thrill of fear in the ruling class and a sudden vision among the faithful that Belgium might be the land where Socialism would first be realized. When a second attempt by general strike to win suffrage on the one-man-one-vote principle was called in 1902, many in the movement were reluctant to risk the gains that had been made, but the militants prevailed. Still aggressive and strong, the ruling class suppressed the strike by "murderous fusillade" in the streets of Louvain. Eight strikers were killed and it took the party many years to recover from the defeat.

If Germany had Marx, France had her Revolution and her Commune. Her Socialism was more spirited but, owing to its extreme factionalism, less solid and therefore less authoritative than Germany's. The Marxist matrix was the French Workers' Party, founded by Jules Guesde in consultation with Marx and Engels in 1879. Two years later Paul Brousse seceded to form the Possibilists on the principle that the emancipation of the workers was possible without revolution. Edouard Vaillant, heir of the old Communard Blanqui, headed a separate Socialist Revolutionary Party from which an extreme wing split off called the Allemanists for its leader, Jean Allemane. Guesde was the self-appointed keeper of the Marxian conscience, tirelessly preaching against backsliders and false idols. With thin black hair worn almost to his shoulders, the face of an emaciated Jesus and a pince-nez on his long didactic nose, he was a zealot who never for an instant relaxed total battle against the capitalist system. "Torquemada in eyeglasses" was a contemporary's epithet and Zola described him talking "with a whole range of passionate gesticulations and a perpetual cough." For Guesde nothing short of revolution was of any value; no touch of cooperation with the enemy classes permissible. He was an Impossibilist. He belonged to that category of Marxists rendered gloomy by their own prophecies of catastrophe. Mankind, absorbed by materialist districtions, was deteriorating. Postponed much longer, Socialism might not come in time to save it. "What will we Socialists do with a humanity so degraded?" he asked during the Dreyfus Affair. "We will come too late; the human material will be rotten when the time comes to build our house."

In 1893 Socialists in France, as in Belgium, won an impressive electoral victory: over half a million votes sending thirty-seven deputies to the Chamber. Dominant among them was the newly famous thirty-four-year-old Jean Jaurès, whose championship of the Carmaux strike in his home district of the Tarn had aroused sympathies all over France. The miners of Carmaux, an area of old and bitter labour disputes, succeeded in 1892 in electing as mayor the secretary of their union, a Socialist, who, upon being refused time off to perform his political duties, took it anyway and was thereupon dismissed from his job by the company. It was a blow at the intent of the vote, an insult to the suffrage understood by every heir of the Revolution. When the miners struck in protest, Jaurès, the former professor of philosophy, made himself their adviser, leader and spokesman. His opponent, the Marquis de Solages, master of Carmaux, owner of iron mines, glass works, timber forests, a title and a seat in parliament, was the epitome of capitalism with whom Jaurès fought an endless duel, through strikes and elections, that lasted most of his life. As a candidate of the French Workers' Party, elected from Carmaux, Jaurès entered the Chamber.

Short and heavy set, a "robust caryatid" with a "jubilant and humorous" face, Jaurès glowed with the warm vitality of the South. "Everything interested him, everything excited him," said Vandervelde. With his voice which had the volume and range of an organ, his command of debate, his formidable intelligence, inexhaustible energy and unquenchable enthusiasm, he drew leadership upon himself. When he spoke he was in constant motion with bearded head thrown back or body thrust aggressively forward and short arms flailing. "His shoulders trembled and his knees shook under the burden of his thought. All the force of his immense culture and conviction were poured into words to guide the multitude who believed in him toward a better future." He seemed to combine the solidity of earth with the mobility of fire. His phrasing was so admired that even political opponents would go to hear him as they would to hear Mounet-Sully speak Racine. Hearing him discuss astronomy at a dinner party, a guest wrote, "The walls of the room seemed to dissolve: we swam in the ether. The women forgot to re-powder their faces, the men to smoke, the servants to go in search of their own supper." Remy de Gourmont said, "Jaurès thinks with his beard," but the man who wrote *Les Preuves* and had been in youth the glory of the Ecole Normale thought more clearly than most. Although the French Socialist movement had no official chief, since it was constantly splitting and subdividing, uniting and splitting again, Jaurès, gradually replacing Guesde, came to be accepted as its leader.

He was the authentic Socialist, not in doctrine, but in the essence of the idea and the cause. He believed that man was good, that society could be made good and the struggle to make it so was to be fought daily, by available means and within present realities. He fought it wherever it appeared: in the Fourmies fusillade, at Carmaux, in the *lois scélérates*, over the bill for the income tax, in the Dreyfus Affair. His Socialism did not stem from Marx; it was, he declared simply, "the product of history, of endless and timeless sufferings." His Latin thesis for his doctorate was on the origins of German Socialism beginning with Luther, *De primis socialismi germanici lineamentis apud Lutherum, Kant, Fichte et Hegel*. Elected to the Chamber first as a Republican in 1885, when he was twenty-six and its youngest member, he had become discouraged with politics and had returned to the academic life as professor at the University of Toulouse, where his lectures were soon thronged by workmen and bourgeois townsmen as well as students and faculty. The labour struggles of Toulouse and the Tarn drew him back into public life and he announced himself a Socialist in 1890. Edouard Vaillant once said he never knew any kind of revolution Jaurès was not in favor of, but Jaurès' idea of revolution was rather of taking over than of overthrowing the State. His Marxism was fluid: he was a patriot as much as an internationalist and believed in individual freedom no less strongly than in collectivism. "We Socialists also have a free spirit; we also feel restive under external restraint," he said. If Socialist society of the future did not allow men to "walk and sing and meditate under the sky" whenever they chose, it would be unacceptable. He denied the Marxist concept of the bourgeois state as one in which the working class had no share. He saw the working class not as an outsider at the door waiting to take over but as part of the State now, needing to make itself felt now and needing to use the middle class as an ally in the struggle to reform society toward the realization of the Socialist ideal.

His faith had the strength of an engine. "Do you know how to spot an article by Juarès?" asked Clemenceau. "Very simple; all the verbs are in the future tense." Nevertheless, of all Socialists he was the most pragmatic, never a doctrinaire, always a man of action. He lived by doing, which meant advance and retreat, adaptation, give and take. A formal dogma that might have closed off some avenue of action was not possible for him. He was always the bridge, between men as between ideas. He was a working idealist.

Elected with him as Socialist deputies in 1893 were Alexandre Millerand, a hardheaded lawyer; René Viviani, renowned more for his moving oratory than for its content; and another lawyer, Aristide Briand, youngest of the group, the F. E. Smith of the Socialists, whose brains, ability and ambition were to prove stronger than his convictions. Briand "knows nothing and understands everything," said Clemenceau, adding that if he were ever accused of stealing the towers of Notre Dame, he would choose Briand to defend him. The Socialist deputies in the parliament of 1893–98 made their ideas and aims and immediate demands known to the country. Among themselves they had managed to agree in 1896 on a minimum definition known as the St-Mandé Program, formulated by Millerand, which stated that "a Socialist is one who believes in the collective ownership of property." It established as essential Socialist goals the nationalization of the means of production and exchange, one by one as each became ripe; the conquest of political control through universal suffrage; and international cohesion of the working class. In the Chamber they demanded as interim reforms the eight-hour day, the income and inheritance tax, old-age pensions, municipal reform, health and safety regulations in factories, mines and railroads. With Jaurès in the van, with Guesde in his piercing voice making the bourgeoisie tremble as he expounded the implacable march of Marxian history toward collapse, with the conservative defense led by de Mun, and with all the speeches reported in the papers, the debate developed into a great tournament of ideas which made Socialism from then on a main current of French life.

French trade unions, infused by the fierce Syndicalist rejection of political action, federated in the Confédération Générale du Travail in 1895 and kept aloof from Socialism. The antagonism reached a climax at the London Congress of the Second International in 1896, the most "tumultuous and chaotic" of all, when armed with mandates from the French unions the Anarchists (among them Jean Grave, representing the steelworkers of Amiens), made their last claim to membership in the Socialist family. The French factions split apart in frenzied antagonism over the issue, and when they caucused before the plenary session a "pandemonium of savage clamor" could be heard through the closed doors. After six days of strife during which the old quarrel between Marx and Bakunin was fought all over again, the Congress ended by excluding the Anarchists once and for all. A phase of Socialism had come to an end. Few doubted that new issues would not arise to divide the right and left wings of Socialism and keep open the schism between the Absolute and the Possible.

Before that expectation was fulfilled, Socialism in the United States took on a new dimension when the use of injunction in the Pullman strike made a Socialist out of Eugene Victor Debs. Named for Eugène Sue and Victor Hugo by his father, an émigré from Alsace, Debs was brought up on *Les Misérables*, the bible of father and son. He went to work as a railroad fireman at fourteen, founded the Brotherhood of Locomotive Firemen, and resigned from it in 1892 when he was thirty-seven to organize all railwaymen in an industrial union, the American Railway Union. When in 1893 and 1894 the Pullman Company cut wages by 25 to 33⅓ per cent without lowering rents in company houses and while continuing to pay dividends to investors, Debs called a sympathy strike on all trains carrying Pullman cars. More than a hundred thousand men came out in what developed into the greatest strike effort yet seen in the United States. Mobilizing all the powers of capital, the owners, representing twenty-four railroads with a combined capital of $818,000,-000, fought back with the courts and the armed forces of the Federal government behind them. Three thousand police in the Chicago area were mobilized against the strikers, five thousand professional strikebreakers were sworn in as Federal deputy marshals and given firearms; ultimately six thousand Federal and state troops were brought in, less for the protection of property and the public than to break the strike and crush the union. A regular Army colonel, drunk in a Chicago club, wished he could order every man in his regiment to take aim and fire at every "dirty white ribbon," the emblem of the strikers.

Although the union had agreed to furnish necessary men for the mail trains, delivery of the mail was made the pretext for an injunction, the most sweeping ever granted. As the arm of the State used in support of property, injunction was capitalism's most formidable weapon and the most resented. Attorney-General Olney, who had been a lawyer for railroads before entering the Cabinet and was still a director of several lines involved in the strike, persuaded President Cleveland of the necessity. The United States District Attorney in Chicago drew up the injunction with the advice of Judges Grosscup and William Wood of the Federal Circuit Court, who then mounted the bench to confirm their own handiwork. When Governor Altgeld refused to request Federal troops, the judges certified the need of them in order to justify the injunction. It was war, proclaimed Debs, between "the producing classes and the money power of the country." Refusing to obey the injunction, he was arrested along with several associates, imprisoned without bail, tried and sentenced in 1895 to a term of six months.

After his arrest the strikers, by then more or less starving, gave up. Thirty had been killed, sixty injured and over seven hundred arrested. In rehiring, Pullman imposed yellow-dog contracts, requiring every worker to relinquish his right to join a union. The American Railway Union was destroyed but the strike had made a hero of Debs and a villain of injunction. It showed that strikes could not be won when government sided with capital; therefore labour must attain political power.

Debs pondered the lesson in prison. He read *Progress and Poverty*, Bellamy's *Looking Backward, Fabian Essays,* Blatchford's *Merrie England* and Kautsky's commentary on the Erfurt Program. He received a visit from Keir Hardie. He became convinced that the cause of the working class was hopeless under capitalism, and when, in the election of 1896, the forces of Mark Hanna and McKinley defeated Bryan and Populism, his conviction was confirmed. Capitalism, too strong to be reformed, must be destroyed. In return, the ruling class felt no less strongly about "Debs the revolutionist." While campaigning for McKinley, Theodore Roosevelt said in a private conversation, "The sentiment now animating a large proportion of our people can only be suppressed as the Commune was suppressed, by taking ten or a dozen of their leaders out, standing them against a wall and shooting them dead. I believe it will come to that. These leaders are plotting a social revolution and the subversion of the American Republic."

Debs announced his conversion to Socialism in a manifesto in the *Railway Times* of January 1, 1897, saying, "The time has come to regenerate society—we are on the eve of a universal change." In association with other labour leaders and adopting the form of the name used in Germany, he founded the American Social Democracy, which became the party of native American Socialism. In its early years, with less than four thousand members, it was kept alive by the gold watch of Debs's brother Theodore, pawned periodically to keep the party newspaper going. Whenever Theodore Debs appeared in the doorway of a pawnshop in the Loop, its old German proprietor would call over his shoulder to the girl at the cash register, "Giff the Socialist chentleman forty dollars." The political period of American Socialism still lay ahead, when in the first twelve years of the new century, under changed conditions, Debs was to be four times his party's candidate for President and campaign across the country on board the railwaymen's Red Special.

For the moment, his rival was the Socialist Labor Party, drawn chiefly from the foreign born and existing largely on paper and in the mind of its fanatic dictator, Daniel De Leon. Born in Curaçao of Dutch-Jewish parents and educated in Germany, De Leon was convinced that only he was fitted to lead the class struggle. He had come to the United States at twenty-two, and having taken a law degree at Columbia and held a lectureship there in Latin-American history, he was scorned by union opponents as the "professor." Besides keeping up hot and incessant propagation of Socialist ideas in his weekly *The People,* De Leon ran for the New York State Assembly, for Congress and in 1891 for Governor without visible result. To draw organized labor into political action he launched the Socialist Trade and Labor Alliance, whose chief function was to excite the rage of the craft-union leader, Sam Gompers. Political action in Gompers' eyes was the devil's pitchfork and of De Leon he said that "no more sinister force" had ever appeared in Socialism. In 1901 a large faction of the Socialist Labor Party, opposing De Leon's "dictatorship," seceded, under Morris Hillquit and Victor Berger, to join Debs's group, which now renamed itself the Socialist Party of America.

Socialism's inveterate opponent, Gompers was the prototype of regular as opposed to revolutionary trade unionism. He was the outstanding exponent of the view that labour's fight must be carried on within, not against, the capitalist system. Dwarfish and stocky, "almost grotesque," with a huge head and heavy coarse features, he was, though ugly, an impressive personality who dominated any meeting in which he took part. When launched on one of his anti-Socialist tirades in the Federation, an old opponent in the Typographers' Union who enjoyed heckling him used to call from the floor, "Give 'em hell, Sam; give 'em hell." Sam never slackened in the effort. Having rejected the Old World, he deeply distrusted the Socialist tradition, though well grounded in it. As a young man in the cigarmaking trade, which, paying by the piece, allowed one worker to read aloud while the others made up his quota, he read Marx, Engels, and Lassalle to his fellow workers. "Learn from Socialism" but "don't join," advised his mentor, an exiled Swedish Marxist. "Study your union card, Sam," he would say, "and if the idea doesn't square with it, it ain't true."

With faith in the new society of America, Gompers rejected the pessimism of the Marxian premise. He believed unalterably that labour should keep out of politics, while using its power to bargain directly with employers. Regulation of wages, hours and working conditions should be achieved by union activity, not by legislative enactment. He founded the Federation in 1881, when he was thirty-one, in a room ten by eight with a kitchen table for a desk, a crate for a stool and tomato boxes supplied by a friendly grocer for files. By 1897 it had 265,000 members, by 1900 half a million, by 1904 a million and a half. When Bryan, angling for the union vote in 1896, promised that if elected he would appoint Gompers to his Cabinet, Gompers stood up to announce that under "no circumstances" would he ever accept any political office. He refused to allow the AF of L to come out in support of Bryan and Populism because, as he said, "these middle-class issues" diverted labour from its own interest, which was the union and nothing else.

As his power grew, he shaved off his walrus moustache, adopted pince-nez, a Prince Albert coat and a silk hat, and like John Burns, enjoyed hobnobbing with the great, negotiating with Mark Hanna or August Belmont. Yet he never made money for himself and was to die a poor man. While repudiating the class struggle he remained profoundly class conscious. "I am a working man. In every nerve, in every fibre, in every aspiration I am on the side which will advance the interests of my fellow working men." The task for union members was to "organize more generally, combine more closely, unite our forces, educate and prepare ourselves to protect our interests, that we may go to the ballot box and cast our votes as American freemen, united and determined to redeem this country from its present political and industrial misrule, to take it from the hands of the plutocratic wreckers and place it in the hands of the common people." This in effect was practical Socialism. So was his reaction fifteen years later when on a tour of Europe he saw visitors appalled at an exhibit of slum conditions in Amsterdam. He recorded their shock that any human being would stand this "gross insult" from civilization: "Why not revolt against it somehow?" Socialism was essentially the movement of those who felt impelled to "revolt against it somehow," and Gompers, as Morris Hillquit used to say, was a Socialist without knowing it.

In Europe in 1899 a new issue exploded in the ranks of Socialism when Waldeck-Rousseau, seeking a wide base for the Government that was to "liquidate" the Dreyfus Affair, offered Cabinet office to Millerand, who accepted. Never before had a Socialist stepped over the invisible barrier into the bourgeois camp to cooperate with any part of it. Although Jaurès had led, pushed and persuaded the Socialists, or a faction of them, to join the bourgeois Dreyfusard groups in the battle to save the Republic, to enter a bourgeois government was another matter. Millerand's case raised the fundamental issue of cooperation which from here on grew more pressing as with each year the Socialists played a greater role in national life. The dilemma presented itself: whether to remain condemned to an orthodox if sterile purity waiting for the final overthrow of capitalism, or to cooperate with the bourgeois parties left of center, supporting them against reaction and spurring them toward reforms. The question carried the further implication: whether Socialist goals might not, in the long run, be attained by way of reform?

While *le cas Millerand* threw French Socialists into a turmoil, the same issue rose up in Germany, not in the flesh, but, as befitted Germans, in theory. It came from the most impeccable origins, promulgated by a man of the inner circle, a protégé of Marx and Engels, a friend and associate of Liebknecht, Bebel and Kautsky and a member of the founding Congress of 1889. It was as shocking as if one of the apostles had disputed Jesus. The name of the man who presumed to revise Marx was Eduard Bernstein, and his new doctrine, as if not quite daring to give itself a name, came to be called simply Revision. A bank clerk as a young man, Bernstein, at the age of nineteen, had gone into exile in Switzerland in 1878, the year of Bismarck's anti-Socialist law. From here he edited the party paper, *Sozialdemokrat*, so effectively as to win the approval of Marx and the accolade of Engels, who called it "the best the party has had." In 1888 the German Government paid it the compliment of bringing pressure on the Swiss to expel the staff. Bernstein moved to London, where, like the Master, he spent his time in the reading room of the British Museum and made no attempt to return to Germany after the repeal of the anti-Socialist law in 1890. Though still under indictment for sedition, he could have appealed his case, but he was writing a book on the English Revolution according to the Marxian interpretation and besides he found the atmosphere of London sympathetic. This was symptomatic of his trouble. During these years he acted as correspondent for the new party paper, *Vorwärts*, and for Kautsky's

Neue Zeit. Headquarters of German Socialism in London was Engels' house in Regent's Park, where the exiles gathered for evenings of discussion around a table generously laden with thick sandwiches and beer and, at the proper season, Christmas pudding. On Engels' death in 1895 Bernstein and Bebel were named his literary executors.

The following year, as if restraint had been lifted by Engels' death, Bernstein's first heretical articles appeared. He was forty-six in 1896, an outwardly decent, respectable figure with rimless glasses and thinning hair who looked as if he might have been a bank teller all his life, rising perhaps to branch manager. His only noticeable feature was a long flaring independent nose. Acquainted with the Fabians—in fact, a good friend of Graham Wallas—he had for a long time felt a prejudice against them for their willingness to work within the capitalist order. At the same time the workings of democratic government in England impressed him and he could not resist the surrounding evidence that capitalism was somehow not approaching imminent collapse. Despite glaring inequalities of wealth and the "increasing misery" Marx had predicted, paradoxically the system was undeniably strong, even aggressive. The world seemed unfairly caught in a relentless spiral of prosperity, with results which seeped down to counteract the "increasing misery" in the form of increased employment. In London and in exile Bernstein suffered the disadvantages of independent thought and became increasingly prey to the suspicion that history was not following the path that Marx had charted. She had disobeyed the German *diktat*. Hegel had laid it down; Marx had hardened it; but history, with a Mona Lisa smile, had gone her own way, eluding the categorical imperative.

Like a man beginning to doubt the Biblical story of Creation, Bernstein was assailed by the agonies of failing faith. He became moody and irritable and at one point even applied for a job in a bank in the Transvaal. Eleanor Marx wrote to Kautsky that Bernstein was in bad spirits and making enemies. But intellectual courage won. From 1896 to 1898 he submitted a series of articles on "Problems of Socialism" to the *Neue Zeit* which instantly provoked outcries and tirades. The German Socialist world was thrown into an orgy of controversy, heightened when Bernstein embodied his ideas in an address which he sent to the German party's Congress at Stuttgart in October, 1898, and subsequently enlarged into a book, *Die Voraussetzungen des Sozialismus* (The Evolution of Socialism), published in March, 1899.

It set forth the facts contrary to Marx: the middle class was not disappearing; the number of propertied persons was increasing, not decreasing.

In Germany the working class was not sinking in progressive impoverishment but slowly making gains. Capital was not accumulating among a diminishing number of capitalists but was rather being diffused over a wider ownership through the medium of stocks and shares. Increased production was not all being consumed by capitalists but was spreading into increased consumption by the middle class and even, as they earned more, by the proletariat. In Germany the consumption of sugar, meat and beer was going up. The wider the spread of money, the less chance of any single economic crisis bringing about a final crash. If Socialists waited for that, Bernstein warned, they might wait indefinitely. In short, the grim twins, *Verelendung* and *Zusammenbruch,* were shadows.

In place of the Marxian dialectic, Bernstein suggested a capitalist economy capable of indefinite expansion and ability to adjust itself so as to rule out the supposedly inevitable breakdown. In that case the existing order was here to stay. If breakdown and revolution were not, after all, inescapable, then the Socialist goal might be an ethical democratic society based on the support of all classes, rather than on the proletariat alone. If revolutionary aims were abandoned, Bernstein declared, carried away on a wave of optimism, the working class could win the support of the bourgeoisie for reforms within the existing order.

The implication for "Millerandism" was clear. If capitalism and Socialism were not, after all, to be a stark choice of one or the other, if society was to continue with some of this and some of that, then there was no further point in Socialists excluding themselves from a role in government.

Revision meant in effect abandonment of the class struggle. It was a stake plunged into the heart of Socialism. Bernstein did not shrink. The workers, he brazenly suggested, were not, as Marx assumed, a coherent, homogeneous "class," conscious of themselves as "the proletariat" or likely to become so. They were divided between rural and urban, skilled and unskilled, factory and home, with different interests and different levels of earning power. Many were hostile or indifferent to Socialism and tended to share bourgeois morals and habits rather than sharing Socialist contempt for the bourgeois.

If class was not, after all the primary loyalty of the worker, then it followed that his interests like those of any citizen were bound up with the national interests of his country. Here was the terrible horizon of Revision. Bernstein even banished the cruel edict of the *Communist Manifesto*: "the worker has no Fatherland." When every workingman had the vote, he said, as in Germany, he acquired political rights and responsibilities and must therefore think in terms of the national interest.

Revision tore Socialism apart. Bernstein's open formulation of the case rallied adherents long troubled by their own doubts. Party leaders rushed to attack the heretic. He was accused of being "English." Kautsky refuted every argument in a book, *Bernstein and the Social-Democratic Program*, which was intended to dispose of him but somehow did not. Dispute swelled and penetrated every meeting, newspaper and policy committee. Charged with ignoring the final goal of Socialism, Bernstein made the shocking reply, "I confess openly I have little interest in what is generally called 'the final goal of Socialism.' This goal, whatever it may be, is nothing to me; the movement [for social progress] everything." He decided to come home to defend himself in person. Friends interceded for him with the Government, and Chancellor von Bülow, calculating that he would be a disruptive influence, allowed the indictment against him to lapse. Returning in 1901, Bernstein was elected to the Reichstag in a by-election in 1902. He became the editor of a Revisionist journal and the oracle of a Revisionist faction which sprang up within the party and continued to grow.

The appeal of Revision was that it offered an end to Socialist isolation, opened the door to participation and also to ambition. It allowed Socialists to feel themselves part of their country, however contrary the feeling was to the command of the prophet. It recognized another reality: that imperceptibly, in a way Marx had not foreseen, a transfer of power between classes was in fact taking place, like water seeping through a dam.

Revision had a fault which Viktor Adler noted. It was said of Adler that like Montaigne he should have adopted a pair of scales for his emblem and the motto *"Que sais-je?"* because he always looked for some evil in anything good and some good in anything evil. In a letter to Bernstein he wrote that he had brought into the open doubts which all Socialists felt at one time or another but that in the end Adler himself would side with the Revolutionaries because Revision carried the mortal danger that "Socialists would lose sight of Socialism."

In the French Socialist world, at the same time, the quarrels let loose by *le cas Millerand* were even more ferocious and divisive than those in Germany. Distressed though he had been at Millerand's acceptance of office, Jaurès, when forced to take a stand, supported collaboration as against no collaboration at all. At the French party's Congress in Paris in December, 1899, he denied that it would lead to personal corruption, as charged by the Marxists. Since, he argued, it was impossible to predict when the capitalist collapse would come, it was necessary to work for reforms while preparing the way. "We must not fight from a futile distance," he said, "but from the heart of the citadel." Enraged orations by his opponents filled the hall. "Tall, thin, desiccated, his eyes ablaze like black fire," Guesde preached the purity of Marxism and was citing Liebknecht when one excited Ministerialist, as the supporters of Millerand were called, shouted, "Down with Liebknecht!" The shock that passed over the faces of the Guesdists, a delegate said later, was as if someone had shouted "Down with God!" in Notre Dame. After three days of intense fracas the proposition was put, "Yes or no, does the class struggle permit a Socialist to enter a bourgeois government?" The vote was for No but was immediately followed by another vote permitting Ministerialism under exceptional circumstances. With Jaurès pleading for unity the Congress managed to close under a patched-up formula in which underlying antagonisms were unresolved. Two parties thereafter emerged: Guesde, Vaillant and Marx's son-in-law, Paul Lafargue, formed the Socialist Party of France committed to "no compromise with any fraction of the bourgeoisie" and to the destruction of capitalism. Jaurès, Millerand, Briand and Viviani formed the French Socialist Party committed to a reform program for "immediate realization."

Throughout the world in every Socialist party headquarters and meeting hall where the red flag stood dustily in a corner, Revision and *le cas Millerand* widened old schisms. While doctrinaire Socialists clung to original principles, the Revisionists were discovering that Socialism, like politics, was the art of the possible. More divided than ever, the Second International assembled for its fifth Congress in Paris in September, 1900, in the midst of the Exposition. With the city full of visitors and the center of world attention, Socialist leaders were anxious to prevent an open rupture. Kautsky contrived a resolution which, while refusing to approve Millerand's action, did not condemn it. Delegates called it the Kaoutchouc (india-rubber) Resolution because it was so elastic. Pounded in debate, slashed by the furious swordplay of De Leon, it occupied almost the entire time of the Congress. At one point a German delegate, Erhard Auer, let slip a regret that the opportunity for a *cas Millerand* was not likely to offer itself to German Socialists. Exposing a basic fact of life in his country, the remark caused an outburst of applause, hisses and outraged discussion in the corridors. Eventually, under the expert piloting of Jaurès, bent as ever on unity, the Kautsky Resolution was passed over the heads of an intransigent minority. Jaurès' theme, as at his own Congress, was: "We are all good revolutionaries; let us make that clear and let us unite!" But the fact was something less than the wish.

With the Boer War, the war in the Philippines and the Boxer Rebellion in progress, delegates found it easy to unite on a resolution put forward by Rosa Luxemburg stating that capitalism would collapse as a consequence, not of economic conditions, but of imperialist rivalries. Recommending Socialist parties to work against war by organizing and educating youth to carry on the class struggle, by voting against military and naval estimates and by anti-militarist protest meetings, the resolution was passed unanimously along with another denouncing the recent Hague Conference as a fraud.

The only concrete accomplishment of the Congress was a decision to establish a permanent organization in the form of a Bureau in Brussels of which Vandervelde was named chairman and Camille Huysmans, another Belgian, secretary. It was to pass interim resolutions, prepare agenda for Congresses and hold emergency meetings, if necessary, to which member nations would each send two delegates. As the budget allocated to it was minuscule, the Bureau, as time went on, did not acquire great prestige or executive power, and except as a mail drop, served chiefly to emphasize that the sinews of internationalism were slender.

Revision continued to cut deep inroads. Jaurès, while defending collaboration as a fact of political life, refused to accept Bernstein's revision of theory. In the controversy between Bernstein and Kautsky, he told a Socialist Student Conference in 1900, "I am, on the whole, with Kautsky." Bernstein was wrong, he said, about the proletarian and bourgeois classes merging at their edges. Between the class that possesses the means of production and the class that does not "there *is* a definite line of demarcation," although of course there were intermediate shadings; and from these, Jaurès, once more the professor, launched himself happily on the wings of philosophic discourse. "One goes from white to black, from purple to red, from night to day by these imperceptible transitions which allowed Heraclitus to say that in day there is always some night and in night some day. . . . In fact, it is a characteristic of extremes that they are approached by intermediary nuances. . . ." Jaurès sailed on, holding his audience entranced until with a snap he came back to the issue. However "radically antagonistic" the classes, that did not mean there could be no contact or cooperation, and he closed with a final appeal for Socialist unity "amid loud applause, prolonged acclamations and cries of *Vive Jaurès!*"

As one of the four vice-presidents of the Chamber after his re-election in 1902, Jaurès practiced cooperation daily, becoming virtual leader of the left bloc of the parties which supported the Government in its battles against the Army and the religious orders. Life was pushing him toward Revision. He attended garden parties at the British Embassy and a banquet in the Elysée Palace for the King and Queen of Italy in 1903. At the Bordeaux Congress of his party that year he argued that the State was not, as Guesde maintained, an impenetrable bloc to stand or be overthrown, but penetrable by reforms. As these were gained, one by one, the workers' state would one day be discovered to have replaced the bourgeois state and "we shall be aware of having entered the zone of Socialism as navigators cross into the zone of a new hemisphere, though there is no rope stretched across the ocean to mark it." But he acknowledged that the problem of reconciling collaboration with class struggle was "complicated." In their party Congress at Dresden that year the Germans were finding it painfully so.

The issue came to a head in the great "knee-breeches" debate. The Social-Democrats were fresh from an electoral victory in which they had polled over three million votes to win eighty-one seats in the Reichstag. To maintain rigid Marxian apartness under these circumstances, Bernstein argued, was senseless. He urged the party to assume the prerogatives of its strength, namely, to accept one of the vice-presidencies of the Reichstag which was its due. Since this required paying an official call upon the Kaiser in court costume, the problem provided matter for days of passionate dispute. Imagine Socialists dressed up in knee-breeches, stockings and buckled shoes! scolded Bebel. To make the Socialist party *hoffähig* (acceptable at court) was an insult to the entire working class. Bernstein suggested that the issue was less a question of what Socialists wore than of what they did in Parliament, but the debaters were too absorbed in the awful yet alluring prospect of knee-breeches to listen to him.

The debate on Revision continued for three days with fifty speakers participating. Bernstein's expulsion was demanded by a group led by Rosa Luxemburg, whose small, frail body contained an outsize passion for revolution. Born in Poland in 1870, the daughter of a Jewish timber merchant, she was not good-looking save for a pair of fine black eyes. She had a limp, a deformed shoulder, a powerful intellect and a strong, clear voice. Retaining always a slight Polish accent, she was a formidable orator whose eloquence so aroused an Inspector of Police, posted at one of her meetings, as to make him forget his official status and applaud loudly. Rosa sent him a note saying, "It is a pity that a man as sensible as you should be in the police but it would be a greater pity if the police should lose so human an example. Don't applaud any more."

With Karl Liebknecht, son of Wilhelm, she represented the militant revolutionary left wing, centered in Leipzig, whose organ was the *Leipziger Volkzeitung,* edited by Franz Mehring. As the party increased in size and influence and its writers and advocates inevitably mixed in bourgeois circles, she led the resistance to growing respectability. For Revision, or "parliamentary and trade-union cretinism" as she called it, with its "comfortable theory of a peaceful passage from one economic order to another," she had only burning contempt. She believed in the revolutionary instinct and creative revolutionary energy of the unorganized masses which were to erupt spontaneously when history required it. The task of the party, as she saw it, was to educate, guide and inspire the masses in anticipation of the historic crisis, not to soften the revolutionary impulse through reform.

Between the Radicals and the Revisionists, the General Council of the party arbitrated, maintaining its balance without too much difficulty. As one of the leaders, Georg Ledebour, said, the party was 20 per cent radical, 30 per cent revisionist and the rest "will follow wherever Bebel goes." Bebel arranged the usual compromise. Without expelling Bernstein, the Dresden Congress defeated his motion for cooperation and passed a resolution reaffirming the policy of class struggle "which we have triumphantly pursued hitherto," and "decisively" rejecting any policy or tactics of "accommodation to the existing order." Thus the largest Socialist bloc in Europe maintained fidelity to Marx on paper while the facts of Revision continued to flourish.

Revisionists were not blind to the implications of abandoning the primacy of the class struggle. Nationalism was in the air and they felt its invigorating force. As Socialists they wanted to participate in national life, not to stay shut out, waiting for the promised collapse which never came. In the *Socialist Monthly* Bernstein used the English experience of imperialism and its relation to employment to argue that the fate of the working class was "indissolubly tied up" with the nation's external affairs, that is, with its foreign markets. Labour's interest, he said forthrightly, lay in a "*Weltpolitik* without war."

While the Germans disputed at Dresden, Revision cut a historic schism among the Russian Social-Democrats, who held their own party Congress of sixty members that year in London. No *cas Millerand* or even knee-breeches appeared on their horizon, nevertheless they split between Bolsheviks and Mensheviks over the issue of collaboration in the future. The former insisted on revolution and dictatorship of the proletariat in one leap with no interim accommodation; the latter believed this could not be achieved until Russia had first passed through a bourgeois stage of parliamentary government during which Socialists would have to collaborate with the liberal parties.

As a member of the Second International, the Russian party was perennially represented at international Congresses by its founder, Georgi Plekhanov, who had lived so long in exile that he had lost touch with affairs inside his own country. Apart from him, the other Russians in exile had little or no contact with the Socialists in whose countries they lived. Absorbed in their own fierce factional quarrel they held their own Congresses with little role in the International. Moving through London, Paris, Geneva and Munich, Plekhanov's rival, Lenin, leader of the Bolshevik faction, relentlessly poured out his denunciations of "opportunism" and "social-chauvinism." Now and then he visited the Bureau at Brussels, but no one, wrote Vandervelde, paid much attention to this "little man with the narrow eyes, rusty beard and monotone voice, forever explaining with exact and glacial politeness the traditional Marxist formulas."

Elsewhere the facts of political life were making a necessity of Revision whether the Marxists liked it or not. Industry was expanding, bringing with it a rise in trade-union membership which increased the lever of pressure in the hands of the working class. While the battle of capital and labour continued as fiercely as ever, the working class through the Socialist parties was enlarging its representation in every European Parliament. In Italy, where the peasants' unions and agricultural cooperatives were strongly Socialist, the party increased from 26,000 votes and 6 seats in Parliament in 1892 to 175,000 votes and 32 seats in 1904. In France, Jaurès' party, followed by the imprecations of Guesde and his followers, was performing a role in national life; and Jaurès himself was emerging as the real if not nominal leader of the Government's majority in the Chamber. In the Socialist world he moved forward to challenge the domination of the great German monolith at the next Congress of the International, held in Amsterdam in August, 1904.

The duel of Jaurès and Bebel made the Amsterdam Congress remembered by everyone present as the most stimulating of all the meetings of the Second International. Five hundred delegates attended, of whom about two hundred at any one time understood the language of the speaker. The platform was draped in red stamped with a gold monogram of the initials I.S.C., which, with the *S* twining around the *I* bore a startling resemblance to a well-known symbol of capitalism. Overhead a banner bore in Dutch the device on which everyone could still agree, *Proletaariers van alle Landen, Vereinigt U!* (Workers of the World, Unite!)

Factions were multiple. Britain had four delegations: the ILP led by Keir Hardie, the Socialist-Democratic Federation by Hyndman, the Labour Representation Committee by Shackleton, and a Fabian group. France had three delegations and the United States two, with the inevitable De Leon casting his scorn on all. He disapproved of the "social and picnic" aspect of the Congress, of delegates rustling papers and conversing and walking about during speeches, visiting with foreign friends, introducing one to another, arriving and departing and slamming doors. He pronounced Jaurès an "unqualified nuisance in the Socialist movement," Bebel its "evil genius," Adler "absurd," Vandervelde a "comedian," Hyndman "too dull" to understand what was going on, the British trade unionists "disastrous," Shackleton a "capitalist placeman," and Jean Allemane a "flannel-mouthed blatherskite." The only party which did not betray the working class by "revisionist flapdoodlism" was his own, whose attitude at all times was "sword drawn, scabbard thrown away."

Cooperation was the question to be settled, placed on the agenda by demand of Guesde. Bebel's object was to impose the Dresden Resolution of the German party upon the International. It provided, he said, the correct guidance for Socialists at all times in all circumstances since it stated the fundamental antagonism between the proletarian and the capitalist state. He took occasion to cite the growing strength of the German party. Jaurès retorted that if Socialists were as strong as that in France, they would "make something happen." Between the appearance of German strength and the reality of their influence, he said, launching upon a major offensive, there was a startling contrast. Why? Because "there is no revolutionary tradition among your workers. They never conquered universal suffrage on the barricades. They received it from above." All the deputies in the Reichstag were powerless, for the Reichstag was itself powerless in any case. It was the very helplessness of the German Socialists which enabled them to take an uncompromising stand on doctrine. What weighed most heavily upon Europe now was not the bold attempt of French Socialists to play a part in their national life, "but the tragic impotence of German Social Democracy." Passionately he defended his main thesis: that Socialists without abandoning principle must be the "marching wing" of democratic progress, even if necessary in liaison with bourgeois parties.

"Certainly Germany is a reactionary, feudal, police state, the worst governed country in Europe" except for Turkey and Russia, Bebel replied, "but we scarcely need anyone from the outside to tell us how dismal our conditions are." Jaurès' policy, he said, would corrupt the proletariat. The Dresden Resolution was the only safe guide. Shrilly Rosa Luxemburg

denounced Jaurès as *"der grosse Verderber"* (the great corrupter). When
he stood up to reply, asking who would translate for him, she answered,
"I will, if you like, Citizen Jaurès." Looking around with a broad smile
Jaurès said, "You see, Citizens, even in battle there is collaboration."

Refusing to give up the principle of class war, the majority voted
for the Dresden Resolution against Jaurès, combining, as Vandervelde
said, doctrinal enmity with personal sympathy. "We remembered the
Dreyfus Affair" and the "magnificent ardor" of Jaurès' great battle against
the accumulated forces of reaction, but the majority could not nerve themselves to cut the umbilical cord to Marx. In a final effort to close the rifts
of Revision, the Congress adopted a last resolution stating it to be "indispensable" to have only one Socialist party in each country henceforth.
All who claimed the name of Socialist must work for unity in the interest
of the working classes of the world, to whom they would be responsible
for "the mortal consequences of a continuance of their divisions."

A problem that had not yet been their main concern made a tentative
appearance at Amsterdam. With the echo of the Russo-Japanese War in
their ears, delegates discussed working-class responsibility to society in
the event of another war and the feasibility of a general strike. German
Marxist ardor cooled at the very word. To talk general strike was one
thing; to get the unions to act on it quite another. So far as the German
trade unions were concerned, the "political mass strike," as they called
it, was anathema. If the Fatherland were attacked, said Bebel, old as he
was, he with every other Social-Democrat would shoulder a rifle and fight
to defend his country. Looking very grave, Jaurès said to Vandervelde
on their way out, "I think, my friend, I am going to apply myself to the
study of military questions."

On his return home, as a loyal Socialist in obedience to the Amsterdam
decision, he moved back toward a rapprochement with Guesde, reuniting
the two parties in the following year as the Socialist Party, French Section
of the Workers' International, commonly called, from its French initials,
the SFIO. It declared itself to be "not a party of reform but a party of
class struggle and revolution" and verbally repudiated collaboration.
Although this was a defeat for his position, Jaurès did not make a fetish
of words. He let doctrine follow action and could the more easily concede
formula to Guesde since he himself was the real leader of the union. Cooperation for him was not an end in itself but an avenue of action.

For some it proved indeed the corrupter in a political sense. In 1906,
the same year in which the ILP entered the House of Commons and
John Burns the Cabinet, French Socialists polled 880,000 votes and won

fifty-four seats in the Chamber. Briand, who had been active in the matter of disestablishing the religious schools, was offered the post of Minister of Education. He accepted and in the ensuing bitterness left the party. A few months later Viviani followed him into office as Minister of Labour. Together with Millerand, who now called himself an Independent Socialist, they held a succession of offices from now on, with Briand reaching the premiership within three years and Viviani five years later. Carrying cooperation to its logical extreme, they became, as Ambassador Izvolsky said, "reasonable through the exercise of power."

In 1905 the great Marxist event, Revolution, suddenly took place—in the wrong way in the wrong country. Russia had not reached the highly industralized stage which Marx had predicated as necessary for collapse. The rising was not the work of a self-conscious disciplined proletariat but simply of exasperated human beings. No one was surprised that it failed, but the most extraordinary aspect of its passage was that it left Socialism virtually untouched.

All over the world people were horrified by the Cossacks' shooting down of workers on their march to the Winter Palace with their petition to the Czar. When news of the "fiendish massacre" was heard at a Trade Union Congress in Liverpool, the immediate reaction was to raise a fund of £1,000 for the families of the murdered men. When the Russian workers' protest became a general strike in October, forcing the regime in its fright to grant a Constitution, the event created a profound impression as a triumph of the working class. Workers in Europe held mass meetings, cheered and waved red flags. "Long live the Russian Revolution! Long live Socialism!" shouted Italian peasants fifteen hundred miles from St. Petersburg. But no spark from the Russian fire ignited a general conflagration. The long-awaited spontaneous uprising had occurred, but no Western working class was prepared to overthrow capitalism. Only the Austrian Socialists alertly used the example to bring to a climax their campaign for universal suffrage.

Seizing the opportunity to work on the fright inspired in the rulers by Russian events, Viktor Adler in Vienna proclaimed a general strike for November 28. He worked on the preparations for a month in advance. One party member in a factory where the workers were not Socialists could not bring them to join; no one would talk about the Revolution or the proposed strike or "touch a political subject with a ten-foot pole." The demonstration, however, was a success. In Vienna, the Mariahilfer-strasse was black with thousands of marchers packed so tightly that it

Arthur James Balfour, about 1895

Coal strike, 1910

CAPITAL

eamen's strike, 1911

David Lloyd George, about 1908

August Bebel

Keir Hardie

"Strike" (oil painting by Théophile Steinlen)

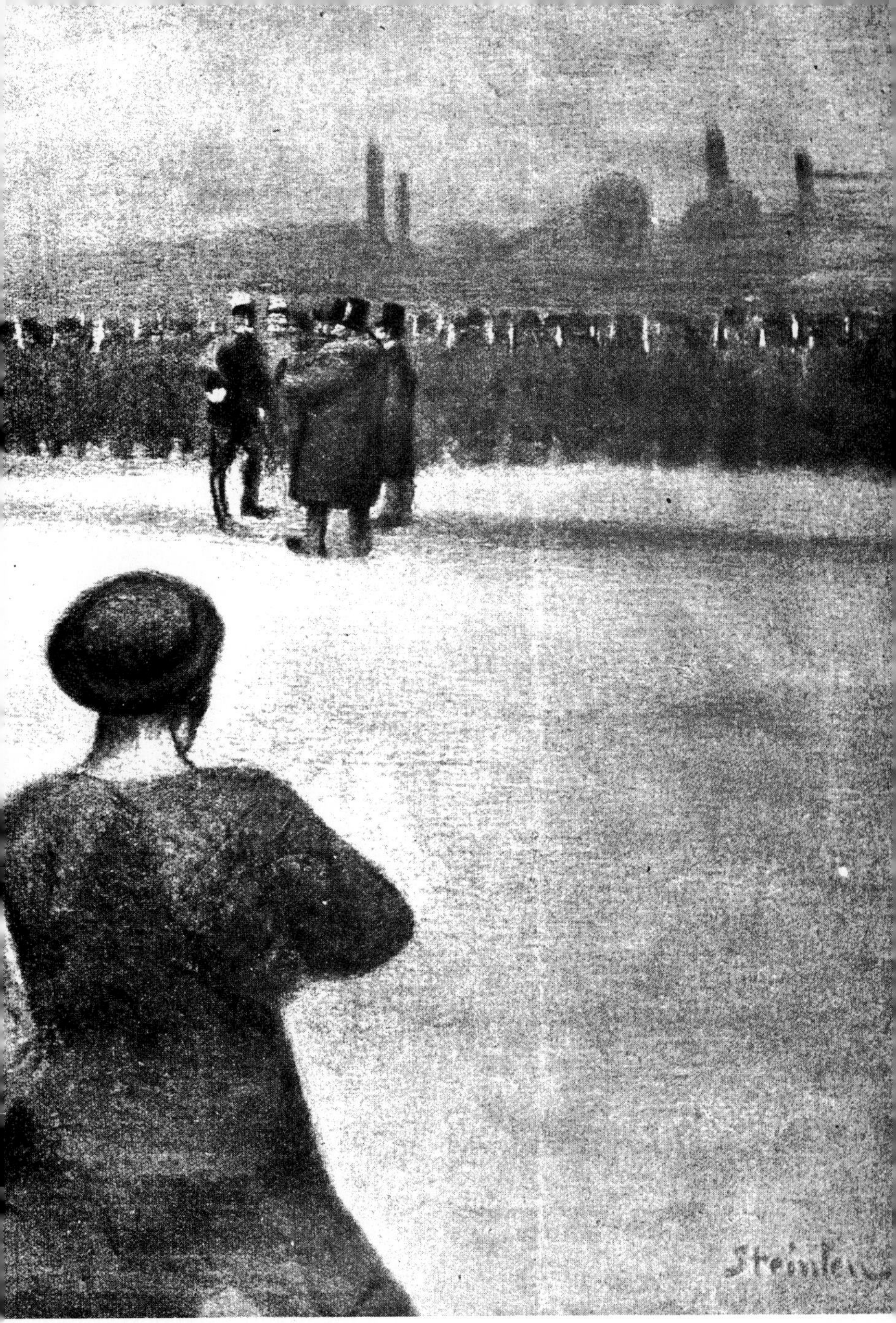
Steinlen

Jean Jaurès

took an hour to cover the half mile to the Ringstrasse, where the parade was joined by even greater crowds from other districts of the city. The tramp of the masses, the clenched fists, the red flags, raised again the terrible vision of Mme Hennebau in *Germinal*. The Austrian regime, frightened by the demonstrations, yielded the promise of manhood suffrage, which went into effect in 1907, virtually the only positive result of the Russian rising.

German Social-Democrats, too, arranged demonstrations for reform of the electoral system in Prussia, which was organized according to the tax roll. The great number of small taxpayers at the base who paid the same total amount as the fewer middle third and as the very few rich at the top were not permitted to elect more than one-third of the local representatives. The Socialists always elected their full third of the municipal councils, but even when they had the votes, could never win control. Nor, confirming Jaurès' taunt, could they win it on the barricades. Against the steel of the Prussian government, their demonstrations won no improvements.

One effect of the Russian revolution was to lose the Socialists votes. In the German election of 1907 middle-class voters represented by the Progressive party, which previously, when it came to a choice, had supported the Social-Democrats in preference to the reactionary parties, voted for the Conservative candidate. They were influenced too by heavy propaganda of the Navy and Pan-German Leagues, who wanted the election to register an overwhelming mandate for nationalism and imperialism. In the "Hottentot Election," as it was called from the current war in Germany's African colonies, the Socialists for the first time since 1890 lost seats.

Leon Trotsky, despairing at the repression under which the Russian revolution now seemed "hopelessly and permanently trampled," was struck by the lack of interest among the European Socialists. Meeting Kautsky in 1907, a small, delicate man with clear blue eyes and snow-white hair and beard who looked like "a very kind grandpapa" though only fifty-three, he found him "hostile to the transfer of revolutionary methods to German soil." On paper, revolution had a lovely glow; the reality in the streets was less welcome. The abortive experience in Russia revealed that the Western working class on the whole wanted no part of it. As a result, Revision was encouraged and Revision signified the further from class, the nearer to nationalism.

Industrial war did not slacken. Labour after 1905 listened increasingly to the Syndicalist teaching of direct action. Its source and influence was strongest in France, where Anarchists had long vigorously denounced the parliamentary method as a sham which diverted the labour movement from revolutionary aims to political issues and favored the leadership of intellectuals. In Syndicalist eyes the Socialist politicians, as members of a national parliament, became essentially part of the bourgeois world, taking on its codes and losing touch with the working class. Syndicalists insisted class war was economic, not political, and should be waged by strike, not debate. With the increasing infiltration of the Anarchists, the trade-union movement adopted revolutionary Syndicalism and direct action as its official doctrine at the CGT Congress of 1906. Direct action against employers consisted of the strike, the slowdown, boycott and sabotage; against the State it included propaganda, mass demonstration, resistance to militarism and to patriotism, a delusion fostered by the capitalists to perpetuate their power. Every gain by the workers was to be considered as strengthening them for the final battle and for the supreme last act of the class war—the general strike, the "revolution of folded arms" which, paralyzing the bourgeois world, would emancipate the working class and win control of the means of production.

In Italy where suppression of the labour movement by police and troops had long been brutal and the gulf of mutual hatred and fear between the classes was deep, the general strike was twice attempted under Syndicalist leadership, in 1904 and 1906, at a cost of savage strife and workers' lives. In France the defeat of one strike after another during the years of Clemenceau's Radical Government from 1906 to 1909 revealed the gap between Syndicalist preaching of the general strike and the actual power of the workers. Labour in France was still largely agricultural and a large share of industry was conducted in small non-union enterprises. CGT membership was not a major proportion of all industrial labour and, reflecting the old antagonism between Anarchists and Socialists, was more frequently at odds with the party than united in mutual support.

Employers fought back violently with dismissals and lockouts against CGT efforts to organize new trades and were frequently abetted by the use of troops, which Clemenceau claimed were necessary to prevent violence against non-strikers. In the strikes by miners of the Nord in 1906, by dockers at Nantes and by vineyard workers of the Midi in 1907, by construction workers in 1908, troops were dispatched by the Government in each case with a resulting total of 20 killed and 667 wounded. Strikes by postal workers and teachers were stamped out by threat of permanent dismissal on the ground that civil servants had no right to organize or strike against the government. CGT officials who had organized them were arrested on charge of incitement to rebellion. Against the stubborn resistance of employers a maximum limit of an eleven-hour day had been enacted in 1900, and a Sunday rest law and old-age pensions in 1906, but against the strike wave in the Clemenceau years, the hard hand of the Government behind the employer reflected Clemenceau's unsentimental dictum, "France is founded on property, property, property." The state's intervention nourished anger and disillusion. The Radical Government's recourse to violence, said Jaurès in 1909, and "its failure to reform society have produced a public lassitude, a muffled grumbling, an undercurrent of discontent. . . ." In the same year, a similar discontent with the Liberal Government in England was creating the same climate of restiveness.

In the United States the employers' counter-offensive also gathered force, backed by court decisions which used the Sherman Anti-Trust Act to outlaw picketing, boycott and strikes as restraint of trade. Like the hilltop signal fires of ancient times, Syndicalism sent its message across the Atlantic and it flared into existence in America with the founding of the Industrial Workers of the World in 1905. Created by Debs and "Big Bill" Haywood of the Western Federation of Miners in strange alliance with De Leon, the IWW was, by European standards, an impossible combination of Syndicalism and Socialism. It preached the doctrine of direct action, while Debs, its hero, campaigned as Socialist candidate for the Presidency of the United States.

American Socialism, like Russian, since it had no representatives in Congress and no role in government even at the municipal level, was protected from the temptations of collaboration. Debs by now had completely espoused the doctrine of class war to the end. Workers must be revolutionaries, not compromisers with the existing order. Their object was not merely to raise wages but to abolish the wage system. He saw Syndicalism as taking over the revolutionary spirit of original Socialism and as offering the means to achieve the promised goal through the trade-union methods in which he had grown up. In a letter to thirty trade-union leaders in December, 1904, he invited them to join in discussing "ways and means of uniting the working people of America on correct revolutionary principles." At its opening convention in Chicago on June 27, 1905, attended by miners, lumbermen, railwaymen, brewery workers and other industrial unions and Socialist factions, the IWW declared itself to be "the Continental Congress of the working class" which would unite skilled and unskilled in one great industrial union to overthrow capitalism and establish a Socialist society. Declaring for the ultimate weapon of Syndicalism, its slogan was "One big Union and one big Strike." According to Haywood—a one-eyed giant and "a bundle of primitive instincts"—the IWW would go down into the gutter to reach the "bums" and migratory workers and bring them up along with the whole mass of labour to a "decent plane of living." Scorning collective bargaining, agreements and political effort, it would work through propaganda, boycott, sabotage and the strike. Government, politics, elections were the bunk; the country should be run by the unions.

The IWW's rejection of political action set off a series of schisms and secessions which flew like woodchips from an ax. Debs was violently attacked by some Socialist colleagues for splitting the labour movement. De Leon broke away in 1908 and continued from his diminished outpost to fight for pristine principle. For Debs the goal was everything and any method which led to it, political as well as direct action, acceptable. Despite the Syndicalist principles of the IWW he ran again for President as the candidate of the Socialist party in 1908. In meetings across the country Haywood and others raised money in pennies and nickels to rent a locomotive and sleeping car to carry Debs on his campaign. Passing locomotive engineers tooted their whistles as the Red Special with red banners streaming from its roof and rear platform went by. Debs had a way of making people believe in the attainability of Socialism. Without brass bands or loud-speakers, his voice, smile and outstretched arms were enough. He "actually believes that there can be such a thing as the brotherhood of man," said a hard-bitten organizer who confessed himself pained when anyone else called him Comrade. "But when Debs says Comrade, it's all right. He means it." Families in wagons with red flags stuck in the whip sockets came for miles across the prairies to greet the Red Special at railroad stops. Torchlight parades in the towns, mass meetings, children with bouquets of red roses, created an illusion in which Debs himself began to believe. Socialists, he wrote to a friend, are "thick as grasshoppers out here" and the farmers "are revolutionary to the core and ripe and ready for action." The "plutes" would get a shock when the votes were counted. But the total vote proved disappointing: 400,000, no more than in 1904.

In 1910 on the wave of the general Reform movement in the United States, Victor Berger, the first Socialist to win a seat in Congress, was elected from Milwaukee together with a Socialist city attorney, Socialist comptroller, two Socialist judges and twenty-one Socialist aldermen out of thirty-five. In 1911 a Socialist mayor was elected in Schenectady and by 1912 the party had elected mayors in fifty-six municipalities. But these were victories of Revision and the successful candidates were intellectuals—lawyers, editors, ministers—not workingmen. The labour movement at both wings, IWW and AF of L, refused to enter politics. In 1912 when the major parties engaged in a three-cornered contest for the Presidency, Debs ran again. Again it seemed, as Victor Berger wrote in the Milwaukee *Leader*, that Socialism was the coming order and "we are speeding toward it with the accelerating velocity of a locomotive." Touring New York's Lower East Side, Debs stood on a truck which "slowly plowed its way through a roaring ocean of people as far as the eye could see all up and down dark tenement streets." The vote was 900,000, double that of the time before, though only 6 per cent of the total. The IWW won its greatest victory that year in Lawrence, Massachusetts, where it organized a strike of textile workers against a pay cut. It fed and maintained an entire town of workers and their dependents for two months and won a wage increase. But the bitter and brutal defeat of the Paterson strike shortly afterwards began the decline of American Syndicalism.

In Germany Syndicalist doctrine of the general strike took little hold. Like other German institutions the unions were too orderly to be attracted by a measure which was the negation of all order and duty. The working class, whom Kuno Francke in 1905 lauded as so "well-behaved," shared the attachment to authority and obedience which in Germany seemed overdeveloped, as if, without its protection, some old Teutonic savagery, some inner Hun, might break out. The German Socialists were realistic about the general strike. Bebel opposed its use for political purposes because, he said, it could only be organized under extraordinary conditions to the accompaniment of a revolutionary state of mind among the workers. Among his countrymen, as he was only too aware, this was missing. When the Radicals of the party at its Mannheim Congress in 1906 proposed a *Massenstreik* in case of war, Bebel rejected it as futile. In the event of war, he said, the military would take over law and order, resistance would be folly and chauvinist fever in any event would grip the masses. Bebel, at least, never fed on, or encouraged, illusions.

At Mannheim a crucial if quiet struggle for power took place with results decisive for German and, through it, for world Socialism. Kautsky offered a resolution intended to subordinate the trade unions to the party in matters of policy. Their task, as Kautsky defined it, was to defend and improve the lot of the worker until the final advent of Socialism. Since the task of the party was achievement of the long-term maximum goal, its decisions must predominate.

During the past decade membership in the German unions had increased from 250,000 to 2,500,000, with funds in proportion. Unlike the French, they were in close communion with the party and its chief source of votes. Sam Gompers on his tour of Europe in 1909 was impressed by the cash benefits the unions paid in strikes and lockouts, by their organization and discipline, and by the improved conditions and increased wages they had won. Day labourers earned three marks and skilled labour six marks a day, or about thirty-six shillings or eight or nine dollars a week. Mealtimes were regulated, fines and penalties posted on the bulletin board, the right to organize was recognized by the government except for servants and farm labour; child labour under thirteen was outlawed and between the ages of thirteen and fourteen was restricted to six hours a day. Gratified that such progress disproved the Marxist theory of "increasing misery," Gompers was inspired to a paean of optimism by the status of the German worker, who appeared to him to live in an age of "the greatest production, the most wealth, the highest general intelligence and the best reasons for hope for his class that the history of the world has recorded." Even if, in his anti-Marxist enthusiasm, Gompers overstated the case, the German worker was clearly acquiring a stake in the existing order. The effect was not conducive to revolutionary ardor in the unions. The fear that they were becoming too embedded in the existing order inspired Kautsky's resolution to subordinate them to the political control of the party.

His motion was firmly defeated by the majority at Mannheim for fear of offending the trade unions. It was all very well to let Kautsky formulate theory, but when it came to practical matters the General Council of the party was nothing if not realistic. Defeat of the resolution meant, in effect, a victory for the trade unions. Since Kautsky's analysis had been correct, it also meant, in the country of dominant Socialist influence, preference for the existing order over the final goal. Bernstein's onetime heresy "I care nothing for the final goal . . ." was now canonical. After Mannheim, day-to-day activity became increasingly practical and revisionist, even while party declarations at Congresses and ceremonial occasions continued to reiterate the Marxist formulas.

Nationalism came in with the rising Revisionist tide. In the Reichstag on April 25, 1907, shortly before the opening of the Hague Conference, a Socialist deputy, Gustav Noske, made the trend explicit in a speech which caused a sensation. It was a "bourgeois illusion," he announced, to suppose that all Socialists believed in disarmament. While they looked forward to peace in the future, international economic conflicts at present were too strong to permit disarming. Socialists would resist just as vigorously as the gentlemen on the right any attempt by another nation to press Germany to the wall. "We have always demanded an armed nation," he said to the astonished gasps of his colleagues and the equally astonished delight and applause of the Right. Indignantly repudiated by Kautsky, who with considerable courage said that in the event of war, German Social-Democrats would regard themselves as proletarians first and Germans second, Noske nevertheless found many followers.

In Germany as in England the topic of coming conflict between the two countries was fashionable, fomented by the Navy League's slogans, "The Coming War!" "England the Foe!" "England's Plan to Fall on Us in 1911!" and the Pan-German accompaniment, "To Germany belongs the world!" In every country as the air thickened with talk of war, the instinct of patriotism swelled. Older, deeper, more instinctive than any class solidarity, it was not something easily eradicated on the say-so of the *Communist Manifesto*. Unhappily for world brotherhood, the worker felt he had a fatherland like anybody else.

In strident dispute, a voice, expressing the opposite tendency from Noske in Germany, was raised in France. It came from the Socialist Gustave Hervé, a shrieking prophet of anti-patriotism and anti-militarism. Once a follower of Déroulède, he had swung to the opposite extreme and attained national notoriety by his declaration during the Dreyfus Affair that as long as military barracks existed he would hope to see the tricolor flag planted upon the dunghill in their courtyards. This led to his dismissal as a teacher and trial for incitement to mutiny in which he was successfully defended by Briand. Regarding the mystique of *patrie* as a Moloch sucking workers into its armored jaws where they shed each other's blood, Hervé continued his campaign against army and country, undaunted by further trials and a term in jail. "We shall reply to the mobilization order by revolt!" he screamed. "Civil war is the only war that is not stupid." At the French Socialist party Congress of 1906, in the midst of the first Moroccan crisis, and again at the Congress of 1907, he embodied these sentiments in a resolution. All the Syndicalist intellectuals, devotees of Sorel, Bergson and Nietzsche, rallied to his support. They were the cultists of the "myth" of the general strike, not the men who would be called upon to practice it, for these were not present. The CGT did not come to congresses of the SFIO, and in any case it designed the general strike for purposes of revolution, not prevention of war.

Representing the diehard Marxists, Guesde led the opposition to Hervé on the ground that since war was inherent in the capitalist system and the predecessor of its death-throes, it was futile, and for Socialists self-defeating, to prevent it.

Jaurès, as the party's leading figure, had to guide the Congress to a position. With his faith that a good society was within man's grasp, he saw war as the great wrecker; not the opportunity of the working class, but the enemy of the workingman. To prevent it was to become, in the years ahead, his primary aim. He had long maintained that the general strike, unless well organized both as to means and ends, was "revolutionary romanticism," yet at the same time it was the only way the working class could make its power felt to prevent a threatened war. He was also inclined to support it because, in maintaining the precarious unity of the SFIO, it was important to make concessions to the Syndicalist-minded wing. No less a man of this world than Bebel, Jaurès remained also an idealist and dealt with the problem of the general strike by persuading himself that if war loomed, somehow the masses would be stirred by the necessary fervor to rise in spontaneous and effective protest without previous planning or organization. In this one area, a crucial one, Jaurès came closest to thinking "with his beard." He agreed to a resolution less explicit than Hervé's, but committing French Socialism to all forms of agitation against war, including parliamentary action, public meetings, popular protests, "even the general strike and insurrection."

It was rhetoric, but Jaurès believed or persuaded himself that "ceaseless agitation" could make it come true. He did not content himself with hoping but practiced agitation at Socialist mass meetings and on speaking tours throughout France. From this time on, at Toulouse, Lille, Dijon, Nîmes, Bordeaux, Guise, Reims, Avignon, Toulon, Marseille, and of course Carmaux, "at every railroad station in France, it seemed, Jaurès descended from a train at one time or another, suitcase in hand, the great salesman of peace." Abroad too, in London, in Brussels and other foreign capitals, his voice poured forth as if trying physically to lift his listeners to a fervor that could be translated into action if need arose. On one trip to England in company with Vandervelde they visited Hatfield, home of the Cecils, which Jaurès said interested him more than Oxford.

The problem of war, the effort to reconcile the trends between the extremes of Hervé and Noske dominated Socialism from now on. It came to a head at once at the next Congress, convened for the first time on German soil, in August, 1907. Although the working class of Berlin was a stronghold of Socialism, the party's leaders did not venture to hold the Congress in the capital under the nose of the Kaiser. The site they chose was Stuttgart, capital of Württemberg in South Germany. Eight hundred and eighty-six delegates representing twenty-six nations or nationalities assembled in the largest auditorium of the city. Among them were Ramsay MacDonald from England, De Leon and Big Bill Haywood from the United States, Plekhanov, Lenin, Trotsky and Alexandra Kollontay for the various Russian factions, Mme Kama of India, the "Red virgins," Rosa Luxemburg and Clara Zetkin, and among the polyglot translators, Angelica Balabanov from Italy accompanied by a "violently protesting bullish young man with a dark face," Benito Mussolini. As a demonstration of Socialist strength an outdoor demonstration was held on the opening day, a Sunday, in a field outside the city. Workingmen and their families came from all around, filling the streets leading to the field where a dozen red-draped platforms had been set up for the speakers. Bands played and choral societies sang Socialist hymns while vigilant police watched over the proceedings from two captive balloons. By 2 P.M. a crowd of fifty thousand had gathered to listen to the Socialist celebrities amid "extraordinary enthusiasm but no disorder." In his speech Bebel congratulated the British proletariat on its recent brilliant success at the polls, remarking with perhaps a touch of envy that while the Government had cleverly made John Burns a member of the Cabinet, he was sure it had not succeeded in changing the party's fighting tactics. Loud cheers greeted Jaurès' speech, delivered in German. Though he could memorize a German translation of his speech after one reading or recite long passages of Goethe by heart, he could not command enough colloquial German to engage a hotel room.

Afterwards in the hall amid the admirable German arrangements everyone, understandably, had a sense of deliberating under the eyes of the police. When Harry Quelch, an English delegate, disrespectfully referred to the Hague Conference, then in session, as a "thieves' supper," Chancellor von Bülow, who was not notably respectful toward the Conference himself, brought pressure on the Württemberg government to have him expelled. Immediately ill at ease, Bebel did not even protest. Quelch's empty chair was kept filled with flowers during the remaining sessions.

While the Congress divided as usual into committees on suffrage, women, minorities, immigration, colonialism and other problems, the Committee on Anti-militarism was the focus of attention. The duty of the working class in the face of rising militarism and threat of war, placed on the agenda by the French, unleashed five days of debate. In an opening tirade, Hervé again proposed mass disobedience to mobilization, in effect insurrection. Since this could be transformed into revolution, it was supported by the German Radicals led by Rosa Luxemburg and Karl Liebknecht, but the official weight of the party, from old Marxists like Bebel and Kautsky to new nationalists of the Noske variety, shifted solidly to the right. Debating "within earshot, so to speak, of the Wilhelmstrasse," as Vandervelde put it, the Germans muted their customary verbal tornadoes, though not only from discretion; the shift was ideological. Some admittedly, some still pretending otherwise, they were aligning themselves with the national mood, accommodating to the facts of life in an era of national expansion from which the worker derived material benefits. "It is not true that workers have no Fatherland," declared Georg von Vollmar, a leading Revisionist; "the love of humanity does not prevent us from being good Germans." He and his group, he said, would not accept an internationalism that was anti-national.

Jaurès proposed the same resolution as had just been adopted by the French Congress, emphasizing "agitation" and including the general strike as a last resort.

To expect an effective general strike without planning or organization was equivalent to expecting an army to march without orders, billets, supply depots, transport, food or ammunition. Even if the Second International could have agreed on a general strike, it had no power to give orders to its national components, each of whom would have had to organize the strike of its own people separately. Unless the action were simultaneous and international, the workers who accomplished it most effectively would only be opening their own country to defeat. As Guesde was forever pointing out, a general strike could only be made effective by the best organized and disciplined labour force. If successful its only result would be to lay open the more modern countries to military defeat by the backward. The dilemma was awful and insoluble. Jaurès kept it at bay because he thought of the general strike more as an idea to kindle the masses than as a real possibility. Walking with Bernstein in one of Stuttgart's parks, he tried to convince him of the inspiriting value of a declaration in favor of the strike. "All my objections concerned its impracticality," Bernstein said later, "but he kept coming back to the *moral* effect of such a commitment." As Clemenceau was to say long afterwards, it was Jaurès' fate "to preach the brotherhood of nations with such unswerving faith . . . that he was not daunted by the brutal reality of facts."

Bebel opposed the general strike as totally impractical. Tied to the unions, as the French party was not, the German party looked at the strike from the union point of view. Though every member may have been a good Socialist, the unions had no wish to lose their funds in a reckless gesture against the power of the State. Financial reserves to maintain a general strike even in peacetime were not available. To oppose defence of the Fatherland in a nation seized by war fever, Bebel said, would put the Socialists in an impossible position. Even Kautsky agreed. A strike was impossible without consent of the unions, he pointed out. Privately he and like-minded friends comforted themselves, like Jaurès, with the belief that somehow, if war came, the "infuriated" workers would rise against it.

Where was the voice of the worker, the man directly concerned, in all this talk of strike? It was not heard. The worker was at home concerned with the job, the boss, the broken window, the ailing child, tonight's supper, tomorrow's holiday. If he thought about a strike it was for wages; if he thought about war it was as some vague grand happening with an aura of excitement and valor. He thought less of striking against it than of marching to it, to smite the foreigner and protect his country. Bebel knew him. "Do not fool yourselves," he said to an English delegate, and repeated his old assertion that the instant the Fatherland declared itself in danger, "every Social-Democrat will shoulder his rifle and march to the French frontier."

If Bebel was still the Pope of Socialism it was as a secular Pope; the moral torch had passed to Jaurès, "the greatest hope of the Second International," in the words of Vandervelde's opening speech. He was brimming with energy, plunged into a great campaign against war, delighted to be in Germany. Seizing a huge foam-crowned mug at a country beer garden, he said, "Beer! Vandervelde, German beer!" with a fresh enthusiasm that his companion found irresistible. One night, returning from an outing via medieval Tübingen, he insisted on getting out in the pouring rain and darkness, although nothing could be seen, to stand in front of the illustrious University.

Bebel threw the weight of the party against an explicit commitment to the general strike less because he was convinced it was impractical than because he feared reprisals by his Government, perhaps even renewal of the anti-Socialist law. Grown middle-aged and successful since Engels' warning, "Legality kills us," his party had no desire to go underground again. In addition to the conflicting French resolutions, he had also to contend against the Radicals of his own party assisted by a formidable partner. Pointing him out to a friend, Rosa Luxemburg said, "That's Lenin. Observe his obstinate self-willed skull." Together she and he were determined that any resolution taken by the Congress on militarism should remind the working class of its duty to transform war into revolution. In private sessions Lenin engaged in prolonged negotiations with Bebel, who insisted that there should be "nothing in the resolution that would enable the public prosecutor in Berlin to outlaw the party." After many rewordings and discussions which Lenin found overlong but rich in dialectic, a satisfactory formula was worked out and tacked on to the main resolution.

As drafted by a committee under Bebel's direction, the final result managed to accommodate all points of view, short of Hervé's insurrectionary strike, in a form calculated neither to alarm the public prosecutor in Berlin nor alienate any important section of the Congress. Bebel had prevailed. The resolution did not mention general strike. It reaffirmed the class struggle, the nature of war as inherent in capitalism and the demand for citizen armies to replace standing armies, but stated that "the International is not in a position to prescribe in a rigid form the action to be taken by the working class against militarism." It recommended the usual "ceaseless agitation" and declared in favor of arbitration and disarmament. The addition sponsored by Lenin and Rosa Luxemburg, pruned to respectability, pledged the working classes and their parliamentary representatives to exert their utmost efforts to prevent the outbreak of war "by using the means which seem most effective to them"; if war should nevertheless break out they were to work for its speedy termination and meanwhile "exploit the crisis with all their strength thereby to hasten the abolition of capitalism."

In 1909 a people suddenly rose in a strike against war with tragic results. It was not an organized movement but, as in the Russian rising of 1905, a spontaneous outbreak. Red Week in Barcelona, called by the Spaniards *la semana tragica*, was a mass protest against the conscription of soldiers for a campaign in Morocco which was considered by the workers a war in the interests of the Riff mine-owners. A strike initiated by the Labour Federation of Barcelona became overnight an outpouring of the people themselves, especially the women, against war, rulers, reaction, the Church and all the elements of an oppressive regime. Stamped out in gunfire and blood, the rising aroused Socialist wrath over the trial and execution of one man, Francisco Ferrer, but excited no concern for the problems or techniques of revolt.

In the same year, a general strike was called by the National Federation of Labour in Sweden in protest against the increasing use of lockouts by employers. Involving nearly 500,000 strikers and lasting a month, it was broken by the Government's threat of permanent dismissal and loss of pensions and by the success of the upper classes in organizing brigades to carry on essential services. Activity was easier to organize than the inactivity of folded arms.

In the same year, the shadow of war moved nearer when Austria-Hungary annexed Bosnia-Herzegovina in a challenge which Russia, not yet recovered from her troubles, had to swallow, the more so as the Kaiser proclaimed his stand in "shining armor" at his ally's side. Austrian

Socialists could not resist a thrill of national pride. The Socialist *Arbeiter-Zeitung* of Vienna published a series of chauvinist articles which caused the Serbian bourgeois press malicious joy in pointing out that international solidarity of the working class was not so solid as supposed.

In England the anti-German wave swept up Blatchford, who for all his Socialism had, as an old soldier, supported the Boer War. With Hyndman he now conducted a campaign for conscription in his paper, the *Clarion*. Branding them as betrayers of Socialism, Keir Hardie still believed "absolutely that organized labour would never take part in another orgy of workmen's blood." Nor was he alone. The mystique of the working class standing as one, in heroic consciousness of itself, was strong. Sam Gompers, born to the working class himself like Hardie, and concerned all his life with workingmen and their affairs, believed in it. When he came to Europe to attend an international Trade Union Congress in 1909, the primary impression he took away was "the fact of the solidarity today in the sentiment of the masses of Europe." Still the unconscious Socialist, he believed the struggle of the workers for their rights would take precedence "over wars between nations in which working men have no cause." He knew and stated in another context that a general strike was "impossible in the current stage of organized labour"; nevertheless he too felt sure of a "deep seated resolve" among his class to refuse to take military duty's last step of shooting down their fellow workers. The spirit of the international trade-union congresses where delegates talked and broke bread together would, he wrote, spread back through their reports to all organized workers, who would understand and refuse to kill each other. "Even the unorganized" would read the accounts and listen to the returning delegates and take up this spirit of refusal. Statesmen knew very well that their next order, "To the front!" would be followed by "mass demonstrations for peace"—Gompers did not venture to say mass disobedience. "It is the general consensus of opinion," he concluded, "that the final obstacle to a war of nations in Europe today is the determined adverse attitude of the workers in the different countries."

Gompers was as practical and toughminded as any man who ever lived, but the age he lived in was sentimental. That, like Jaurès, he could believe in a final Halt! accomplished by "mass demonstrations" showed the extent to which the idea of the working class as Hero had taken hold.

His purpose in coming to Europe was to affiliate the AF of L with the International Federation of Trade Unions. If any action by organized labour was to make itself felt against war, this was the only body which could supply it, supposing it possessed both the will and the means. It had neither. Founded in 1903 at the suggestion of English and French

unions but opposed by the Germans, it represented twenty-seven federa-
tions of trades or industries with a membership of over seven million in
nineteen countries. The figures were more imposing than its real functions,
which were chiefly secretarial. It kept member unions informed of trade
conditions and did its best to frustrate employers' efforts to recruit foreign
strikebreakers. To conciliate the large and well-financed German unions,
its headquarters were in Germany and Carl Legien, chief of the German
National Federation of Trade Unions, was its Secretary. At its biennial
Congresses, political and social questions, usually brought forward by
the French, were not welcomed. In 1909 the Federation raised a strike
aid fund of $643,000 for the Swedish general strike, most of it coming
from the German and Scandinavian unions and very little from the British,
French or American. Solidarity was less than total. With German influence strong and with a non-political orientation, it was not a body to
interest itself in ideas of an international general strike.

One of its strongest units was the International Transportworkers'
Federation of seamen, dockers and railwaymen. Founded in 1896, it
represented forty-two unions in sixteen countries with a membership of
468,000. It was on the ITF that Keir Hardie, who like Jaurès had become
primarily concerned with the problem of war, rested his hopes of an international strike in the event of war. If the transport workers alone, or
together with the miners' International, downed tools, he believed they
could stop a war. Here again the problem was simultaneous action in all
countries, but Hardie's fervor carried him over that and he brought his
proposal forward at the next Socialist Congress, held in Copenhagen in
August, 1910.

As host city to the International in 1910 Copenhagen was a symbol
of the importance Socialism had reached. The Danish Socialist Party,
one of the strongest of the small countries, controlled the municipal
government of the capital. The committee, determined to impress the
world by its organization and efficiency, gave magnificent receptions and
a Socialist mayor delivered the address of welcome. Replying in a voice
of "ripe sonority which makes hearts vibrate," Vandervelde expressed
the delegates' sense of a great occasion when "a free people, masters of
their City Hall, welcomes the Red International." Socialist voters in the
world now numbered eight million. French Socialists were fresh from
an electoral victory in May in which they had won over a million votes
and increased their deputies from 54 to 76. Although it was not a matter
for unmixed pride, Briand, still calling himself an Independent Socialist,
was actually Premier. Socialism seemed to have reached a stage to exercise
effectively the "awful conscience" of mankind.

At Copenhagen it spoke through Keir Hardie, who proposed a resolution jointly with Edouard Vaillant of France, recommending that "the affiliated Parties and Labour organizations consider the advisability and feasibility of the general strike, especially in industries that supply war material, as one of the methods of preventing war and that action be taken on the subject at the next Congress." When proposing it, Hardie acknowledged that the workers were not ready to strike against war but he clung to the hope that they would be ready when the time came. "We must give them a great lead," he said. His resolution was supported by Vandervelde and by Jaurès, who was the more disposed to be sympathetic because he was in the midst of an effective effort, which partly depended on acceptance of the general strike, to draw the CGT closer to the SFIO. Further, his concern over the bureaucratic trend of the German party led him increasingly to consider the need for mass tactics.

The Germans and Austrians were solidly opposed to Hardie's motion on the same ground as before: that to advocate a strike in the event of war might lead to prosecution for treason and confiscation of funds. Bebel, ill and growing old, was absent, but even without him, German pressure secured a negative vote. As a compromise the resolution was referred to the Bureau in Brussels for reconsideration at the next Congress. To go on record even to this extent worried the Germans. They were only reluctantly persuaded to agree by Vandervelde's argument that if they refused, the British and French might pursue the plan independently. A resolution on anti-militarism was passed, virtually the same as that of Stuttgart, with the addition that organized labour in member countries "shall consider whether a general strike should not be proclaimed if necessary in order to prevent the crime of war." As nervously if not quite as quickly as capitalists had disposed of Disarmament at The Hague, Socialists disposed of the general strike.

Within weeks hard proof was given of labour's inability to win a transport strike. In France in October Premier Briand broke a general strike of railwaymen against all private and state-operated lines by conscripting the workers into the army for a period of three weeks, making absence from work subject to a charge of military desertion. On the excuse of national defense, Briand defended his action as dictated by a patriotic conscience. Even to an old Socialist his conscience did not dictate pressure on the companies for the wage increase the railwaymen were demanding.

History had reached 1910. The transfer of power to a new class whose signals Balfour had seen in the British general election of 1906 was a process in the making, not a fact. In a test of strength, as in the French railway strike, labour could not command real power. International action was hallucination. While the Socialists kept on talking about it and believing in it, they were dealing more in a hope and a theory than in flesh and bones. One genuine attempt at international working-class action was made at this time. While the Socialists in Copenhagen were discussing a possible general strike in war industries, the very men who would be crucial to it, the International Transportworkers (ITF), by nature the most international of the unions, were also in session in Copenhagen. Once during the Boer War pro-Boer Dutch members had urged an international boycott of British shipping but the ITF leaders had flatly turned down the proposal on the ground that it was just not possible at that stage to interest workers in an international movement for political purposes. Direct trade union purposes were another matter. Now in 1910 they decided to call an international strike of their own in the following year for redress of grievances against the shipowners.

The active instigators were the British delegates, Ben Tillett and Havelock Wilson, while the German delegate, Paul Muller, was strongly opposed, just as his compatriots were simultaneously opposing Keir Hardie's proposal at the Socialist congress. A seamen's strike at the present moment, Muller said, would be "absolutely insane" and would certainly end disastrously. The masters would triumph, the union leaders would lose their influence, the men would become destitute and would ultimately have to sue for peace on their knees. Since a shipping strike, like a strike against war, would operate to the advantage of the shipping trade in the countries whose unions did not go out, and since the Germans and British were rivals in shipping, the international principle was vital. Heavy pressure brought Herr Muller around and the Congress voted unanimously for a seamen's strike against the "brutal and callous" refusal of the shipowners in all countries to discuss the unions' demands for a conciliation board. All agreed that the strike "must and would be international."

At subsequent meetings of the seamen's committee at Antwerp in November and the following March, the British stated they would definitely strike in 1911 and the Belgians, Dutch, Norwegians and Danes pledged their support. The Germans, now claiming that they had no reason to strike, backed out. The date was set for June 14. In the meantime the Danes and Norwegians retired, the former because they had succeeded in winning a favorable five-year agreement and the latter because, on their demands being turned down, they felt themselves too weak to enforce them. In what developed into the great Transport strike of Coronation summer, the British struck anyway, along with the Belgians and Dutch, whose action was overshadowed by the dramatic British effort. Sympathetic action in other Continental ports was organized by the ITF, which prevented recruitment of strikebreakers and helped the British seamen win their demands. As a whole, however, the strike solidarity originally contemplated was not reached. As if in preview, the ITF endeavor of 1911 showed what might be expected of the working class in international action.

Socialism with steadfast heart remained, nevertheless, predicated in the event of war on a "rising" of the workers of the world. In this it shared the tendency of the age to clothe reality in sentimental garments. The public of the time was not represented by those doctors, writers and social psychologists who were beginning to look at man without illusions. These were the advance guard, as were "seers of black" like Wedekind. The public preferred the rosy view: the perfect pearly nudes of Bouguereau, the impossibly handsome Gibson girls—creatures that never were on land or sea. So, in their own way, did the Socialists.

The rosy view predominated in Germany, where in the general election of 1912 the Social-Democrats won an astounding 35 per cent of the total vote, amounting to 4,250,000 votes and 110 seats. The party was growing so fast and seemed so powerful that to other Socialists it appeared "irresistible" and the moment near and certain when the Socialist movement in Germany would "include the majority of the people and burst the fetters of the feudal-capitalist state." The existence of so many Social-Democrats in the country meant a proportionate increase of their numbers in the armed forces, leading to a time, surely, when it would be impossible for the Army to be used against the workers.

But the discrepancy between size and actual influence which Jaurès had brought into the open at the Amsterdam Congress remained, indeed grew more noticeable as the size of the party swelled. The uses to which the German parliamentary Socialists put their electoral triumph of 1912 were not impressive. When the Government that year increased its forces by three Army corps, they opposed the enabling bill but did not venture so far as to oppose the tax which was to pay for it. When one of their number, Philipp Scheidemann, was elected First Vice-President of the Reichstag, his announcement that he would not join in the official call on the Kaiser touched off a new version of the knee-breeches debate. All the parties, not only the Socialists, took part. The vital question at issue was whether Scheidemann would make the call if the Second Vice-President were absent and whether Bebel had or had not agreed that the

Socialists could join in the customary cheers for their Sovereign. In the upshot, Scheidemann's principles caused his election to be cancelled, thus averting serious problems.

Within the body of Social-Democracy, Revision was keeping pace with the growing nationalism of the country. Socialism's very success turned its sights away from the maximum program, toward the minimum and the possible. The red dawn of revolution receded. Believers repeated the Marxist formulas with untamed ardor, but conviction had passed to those who were still "illegals"—the Russians. At a meeting of the Leipzig left-wingers, a visiting Austrian Socialist referred to his hosts as revolutionaries. "We revolutionaries?" interrupted Franz Mehring. "Bah! *Those* are the revolutionaries," he said, nodding at Trotsky, who was a guest.

For Jaurès the overriding task had become the need to forge and impose a policy for preventing war in terms compatible both with the defence of France and faith in Socialism. In his country too, nationalism, *revanche*, the belligerent spirit, was rising. The pressure of Germany was omnipresent, the shadow of Sedan lengthening. To logical extremists like Guesde, peace and the interests of the working class were not necessarily equivalent, but to Jaurès they were. He now believed that the only way consistent with Socialism to meet the threat of war was through a citizen army. When the whole nation was an army of reserves, with everyone having taken six months' basic training, and with officers drawn from the ranks, the nation could not be drawn into belligerency in the interest of capitalist warmongers. In a war of defence against invasion only such an army of the whole nation, he argued, could hope to repel the terrible "submersion" that German use of reserves in the front line was preparing.

Jaurès' campaign was not merely Socialist oratory. As in *Les Preuves* in the Dreyfus Affair, he set about demonstrating the practicability of his case, studying and working out, over a period of three years, the means of reorganizing the military establishment. He embodied the results in a bill submitted to the Chamber in November, 1910, and in a book of seven hundred pages, *l'Armée Nouvelle,* published in 1911. Preaching his cause tirelessly in the Chamber, in *l'Humanité*, the Socialist paper of which he was founder and director, in meetings and lectures, he was thunderously abused as a "traitor," pro-German and "pacifist" by the cohorts of the Right, particularly by the vituperative *Action Française*.

The Balkans, where the interests of Russia and Austria clashed, was, as everyone knew, the hot-box of Europe. When in October, 1912, the Balkan League of Serbia, Bulgaria, Greece and Montenegro, encouraged by Russia, declared war on Turkey, it seemed the awful moment had come. In Belgrade, Trotsky watched the 18th Serbian Infantry marching off to war in uniforms of the new khaki color. They wore bark sandals and a sprig of green in their caps, which gave them a look of "men doomed for sacrifice." Nothing so brought home to him the meaning of war as those sprigs of green and bark sandals. "A sense of the tragedy of history took possession of me, a feeling of impotence before fate, of compassion for the human locust."

To demonstrate the unity of the workers of the world against war, the Bureau in Brussels convened an emergency Congress to meet in Basle on the Swiss border between France and Germany on November 24 and 25. Five hundred and fifty-five delegates hastened to Basle from twenty-three countries. A manifesto drawn up in advance by the Bureau was voted unanimously, proclaiming "readiness for any sacrifice" against war, without specifying what. Addresses by Keir Hardie, Adler, Vandervelde and all Socialism's most inspiring orators culminated in a speech by Jaurès, tacitly acknowledged by now the most influential figure of the movement. Bebel, though present, was in decline and making what proved to be his last international appearance.

Jaurès spoke from the pulpit of the Cathedral, given over to the Congress by the ecclesiastical authorities despite bourgeois fears of "dangerous" consequences. The sound of the church bells, he said, reminded him of the motto of Schiller's "Song of the Bells"; *Vivos voco, mortuos plango, fulgura frango* (I summon the living, I mourn the dead, I break the thunderbolts). Leaning forward urgently, he spoke to the upturned faces: "I call on the living that they may defend themselves from the monster who appears on the horizon. I weep for the countless dead now rotting in the East. I will break the thunderbolts of war which menace from the skies."

As it happened, these particular thunderbolts were broken by capitalist statesmen who summoned a Conference in London in December, 1912, which limited and, when reconvened in the following May, settled the war before it could expand into conflict between Russia and Austria.

In March, 1913, in a measure directly contrary to Jaurès' campaign, France acted to enlarge her Army by restoring the period of military service from two years to three. Jaurès threw all his energies into battle against it and in favor of the nation-in-arms. For the next six months the Three-Year Law was the dominant fact of French life. Enactment became the rallying cry of nationalism and resistance to it the symbol of the Left. Jaurès denounced the measure in the Chamber as "a crime against the Republic" and drew a crowd of 150,000 to an open-air protest meeting. Leadership of the opposition marked him as the outstanding spokesman for peace. As such he was made the object of further attack as a pacifist and pro-German. After seven weeks of furious debate, the Law was enacted on August 7. Persisting, as he had done through six years of embittered struggle after Rennes until Dreyfus and Picquart were reinstated, Jaurès now led the movement for repeal.

Bebel died that year at seventy-three. In a procession lasting three days, workers and Socialists from many countries filed past the coffin surrounded by hundreds of wreaths and bunches of red flowers. Leadership of the party went to his chosen successor, Hugo Haase, a lawyer and deputy from Königsburg. In August, 1913, in the presence of Andrew Carnegie, and representatives of forty-two states affiliated with the Permanent Court of Arbitration, the Peace Palace was opened at The Hague in what *The Times* called "the happiest circumstances." A survey of French student life in 1913 remarked that the word "War" had a fascination which "the eternal warrior instinct in the heart of man keeps reviving."

Working-class strength continued to grow. Union membership in Germany and Great Britain each reached three million by 1914 and one million in France. The Socialists of Denmark were the largest single party; in Italy Socialists increased their seats in parliament from 32 to 52 in the election of 1913; in France from 76 to 103 in the election of April, 1914. Belgian Socialists, besides electing 30 deputies and seven senators, held 500 municipal council seats. Long frustrated by the stubborn resistance of the ruling class to equal suffrage, they felt themselves strong enough at last to enforce their demand by a general strike. Against impatient radicals who wanted immediate action, Vandervelde and his associates insisted on long and careful preparation; even so, although 400,000 workers joined the strike and stayed out for two weeks, they could not prevail and the strike failed.

The Tenth Congress of the Second International was scheduled for August, 1914, in Vienna, to mark the fiftieth anniversary of the founding of the First International and the twenty-fifth of the Second. Faith in its purpose and its goal were high. In May a Franco-German Committee of Socialist deputies, including Jaurès and Hugo Haase, met at Basle to discuss measures for rapprochement between their countries. Their intention was good but its limit was talk. In England Keir Hardie in the midst of a speech to a conference of the ILP in April turned suddenly to face rows of children from Socialist Sunday Schools, seated behind the platform. Speaking directly to them, he pictured the loveliness of the world of nature and of the world of man as it could become. He spoke of how unnecessary were war and poverty and how he had tried to pass on to them a better world and how, although he and his associates had failed, they, the children, could yet succeed. "If these were my last words I would say them to you: Live for that better day."

At the end of June, news that Serbian patriots had assassinated the Archduke Franz Ferdinand, heir to the Austrian throne, in an obscure town in the annexed territory of Bosnia, provided a sensation of the kind to which Europe was accustomed. It passed without causing undue public alarm. Then suddenly, a month later, on July 24, with terrible impact, came the announcement that Austria had delivered an ultimatum to Serbia of such "brutality," in the words of *Vorwärts*, the German Socialist paper, that "it can be interpreted only as a deliberate attempt to provoke war." Full-scale crisis opened beneath Europe's feet. Would it be another like Agadir and the Balkan War, hot with challenge and maneuver but finally fended off? People waited in desperate hope. "We relied on Jaurès," wrote Stefan Zweig long afterwards, to organize the Socialists to stop the war.

Socialist leaders consulted. To wait to make a demonstration at Vienna a month hence might be too late. A readiness, a sense of gathering belligerence, could be felt in the atmosphere. The Bureau of Brussels summoned an emergency meeting of leading members for July 29. Jaurès, Hugo Haase, Rosa Luxemburg, Adler, Vandervelde, Keir Hardie and representatives of the Italian, Swiss, Danish, Dutch, Czech and Hungarian parties and of the several Russian factions, about twenty in all, assembled with a "sense of hopelessness and frustration." What could they do? How could they make the will of the working class felt? What indeed was that will? No one asked that question for none doubted that it was for peace, but one answer had already been given two days earlier in Brussels at a congress of trade unions attended by Léon Jouhaux, head of the CGT, and Carl Legien, the German trade-union chief. Jouhaux tried anxiously to find out what the German unions would do. The French, said Jouhaux, would call a strike if the Germans would, but Legien remained silent. In any case no plans had been prepared.

All week the Socialist press of every country roared against militarism, urged the working class of all nations to "stand together," to "combine and conquer" the militarists, to engage in "ceaseless agitation" as planned by the International. *La Bataille Syndicaliste*, organ of the French unions, stated: "Workers must answer the declaration of war by a revolutionary general strike." Workers poured out to mass meetings, listened to exhortations, marched and shouted, but of desire to strike there was no sign as there had been no plan.

On a rainy day in Brussels the Socialist leaders met in a small hall of the Maison du Peuple, the proud new building of the Belgian labour movement with its theatre, offices, committee rooms, café and shops of the cooperatives. As they met they learned that Austria had declared war on Serbia but that other nations were not yet engaged. The hope that some-

how the workers would rise—the "somehow" to which they had clung for
so long—was all that remained. Each delegate hoped his neighbor would
bring news of some great spontaneous outbreak in his country expressing
the workers' No! Adler's speech brought no hope of a rising in Austria.
Haase, too restless to sit still, reported protests and mass meetings in Germany and assured his colleagues that "the Kaiser does not want war; not
from love of humanity but from cowardice. He is afraid of the consequences." Jaurès gave an impression of "one who, having lost all hope of
a normal solution, relies on a miracle." Hardie was certain that the British
transport workers would call a strike but his confidence was assumed. A
few weeks earlier he had written, "Only the binding together of the Trade
Union and the Socialist movements will ever put the workers into a position
of controlling Governments, thus bringing war to an end." The one country where such binding had taken place was Germany. The delegates
talked all day but the only decision reached was to advance the date and
change the place of the Vienna Congress to August 9 in Paris, there to
resume discussion.

That evening a mass meeting was held in the Cirque Royale crowded
by Belgian working people from all parts of the city and its suburbs. As
the leaders mounted the platform Jaurès stood with his arm around
Haase's shoulders in a gesture which denied the enmity of Germany and
France. When he spoke at the climax of the meeting his eloquence mounted
until the hall shook with the force of it. He was "quivering, so intense was
his emotion, his apprehension, his eagerness to avoid somehow the coming
conflict." When he had finished, the crowd, on waves of enthusiasm,
poured into the streets to form a parade. Carrying white cards inscribed
"Guerre à la guerre!" they alternately shouted the slogan and sang "The
International" as they marched.

Next day, as the delegates departed, Jaurès, taking leave of Vandervelde, reassured him. "It will be like Agadir—ups and downs—but it is
impossible that matters will not be settled. Come, I have a few hours
before my train. Let's go to the Museum and see the Flemish primitives."
But Vandervelde, who was leaving for London, could not go and never saw
Jaurès again. On the train returning to Paris, exhausted from the strain,
Jaurès fell asleep. A companion, Jean Longuet, looking at his "wonderful
face," was "suddenly overcome with a feeling . . . that he was dead. I froze
with fright." On arrival, however, Jaurès woke up and, still persisting,
went to the Chamber to talk among the deputies and to the office of
l'Humanité to write a column for the morning.

Angelica Balabanov and other delegates who left Brussels by another
train were breakfasting in the station restaurant at Basle next morning

when two comrades of the German Central Committee rushed by in obvious excitement. "There is no doubt about war now," said one of the delegates who had just talked with the Germans outside. "They came here to put the money of the German party in safe-keeping." In Berlin that day Chancellor Bethmann-Hollweg assured the Prussian Ministry of State that there was "nothing particular to fear from the Social-Democratic party" and "there would be no talk of a general strike or of sabotage."

In Paris on July 31, the day of Germany's ultimatum to Russia and declaration of *Kriegsgefahr,* or preliminary mobilization, the public was tense with the knowledge that France stood on the edge of war. The Cabinet was in continuous session, the German Ambassador arrived and departed ominously from the Foreign Office, the life of the country was in suspense. Jaurès led a Socialist deputation to the office of the Premier, his former comrade, Viviani, and returned to organize party pressure in the Chamber. At 9 P.M. he left the office of *l'Humanité,* worn out from anxiety, to have dinner with a group of colleagues at the Café Croissant around the corner in the Rue Montmartre. As he sat eating and talking with his back to the open window, a young man who had been following him since the previous evening appeared in the street outside. Filled, as was later ascertained, with the demented zeal of the superpatriot, he pointed a pistol at the "pacifist" and "traitor" and fired twice. Jaurès slumped to one side and fell forward across the table. Five minutes later he was dead.

The news licked through Paris like a flame. Crowds gathered so quickly in the street outside the restaurant that it took the police fifteen minutes to open a passage for the ambulance. When the body was carried out a great silence fell. As the ambulance clanged away, escorted by policemen on bicycles, a sudden clamor arose, as if to deny the fact of death, *"Jaurès! Jaurès! Vive Jaurès!"* Elsewhere people were stupefied, numb with sorrow. Many wept in the streets. "My heart is breaking," said Anatole France when he heard. Informed at its night session by a white-faced aide, the Cabinet was stunned and fearful. Visions rose of working-class riots and civil strife on the eve of war. The Premier issued a public appeal for unity and calm. Troops were alerted but next morning, in the national peril, there was only deep grief and deep quiet. At Carmaux the miners stopped work. "They have cut down a mighty oak," said one. In Leipzig a Spanish Socialist student at the University wandered blindly through the streets for hours; "everything took on the color of blood."

The news of Jaurès' death appeared in the papers on Saturday, August 1. That afternoon Germany and France mobilized. Before evening, groups of reservists, carrying bundles and bouquets of flowers, were marching off to the railway stations as civilians waved and cheered. Enthusiasm and excitement were equal in every country. In Germany on August 3, Socialist deputies held a caucus to decide whether to vote for war credits. Only a few days ago *Vorwärts* had scorned the pretence of a defensive war. But now the Government talked of the Russian peril and French aggression. Bernstein, the reviser of Marx, assured them that the Government planned to build a "golden bridge" for the Socialists and as proof cited the fact that the Foreign Ministry had extended official condolences in the great loss they had suffered by the death of Jaurès. Of the total of 111 Socialist deputies, only 14, including Haase, Rosa Luxemburg, Karl Liebknecht and Franz Mehring, were opposed, but they obeyed the strict discipline of the majority. Next day the Social-Democrats voted unanimously with the rest of the Reichstag for war credits.

The Kaiser announced, "Henceforth I know no parties, I know only Germans." In France M. Deschanel, President of the Chamber, delivering Jaurès' eulogy before a standing assembly, said, "There are no more adversaries here, there are only Frenchmen." No Socialist in either parliament disputed these statements of the primary loyalty. Léon Jouhaux, head of the CGT, declared, "In the name of the Syndicalist organizations, in the name of all the workers who have joined their regiments and those, including myself, who go tomorrow, I declare that we go to the field of battle willingly to repel the aggressor." Before the month was out Vandervelde joined a wartime coalition Government in Belgium and Guesde a Government of "sacred union" in France. Guesde a minister! The tribal pull of patriotism could have had no stronger testimony.

In England where there was less sense of national danger than on the Continent, Keir Hardie, Ramsay MacDonald and a few Liberals spoke out against the decision to fight. Elsewhere there was no dissent, no strike, no protest, no hesitation to shoulder a rifle against fellow workers of another land. When the call came, the worker, whom Marx declared to have no Fatherland identified himself with country, not class. He turned out to be a member of the national family like anyone else. The force of his antagonism which was supposed to topple capitalism found a better target in the foreigner. The working class went to war willingly, even eagerly, like the middle class, like the upper class, like the species.

Jaurès was buried on August 4, the day the war became general. Overhead the bells he had invoked at Basle tolled for him and all the world, "I summon the living, I mourn the dead."

Afterword

The four years that followed were, as Graham Wallas wrote, "four years of the most intense and heroic effort the human race has ever made." When the effort was over, illusions and enthusiasms possible up to 1914 slowly sank beneath a sea of massive disillusionment. For the price it had paid, humanity's major gain was a painful view of its own limitations.

The proud tower built up through the great age of European civilization was an edifice of grandeur and passion, of riches and beauty and dark cellars. Its inhabitants lived, as compared to a later time, with more self-reliance, more confidence, more hope; greater magnificence, extravagance and elegance; more careless ease, more gaiety, more pleasure in each other's company and conversation, more injustice and hypocrisy, more misery and want, more sentiment including false sentiment, less sufferance of mediocrity, more dignity in work, more delight in nature, more zest. The Old World had much that has since been lost, whatever may have been gained. Looking back on it from 1915, Emile Verhaeren, the Belgian Socialist poet, dedicated his pages, "With emotion, to the man I used to be."

References

BIBLIOGRAPHY AND NOTES

The Bibliography, arranged according to chapter, is confined (with one or two exceptions) to those sources cited in the Notes and is not intended to be either systematic or thorough. It is simply a list of what I used, often of what I stumbled on, weighted heavily toward primary personal accounts. It is noticeably light on secondary interpretative studies. When I needed their guidance I used those as nearly contemporary to their subjects as possible, not because they are better books than today's but because they are closer in spirit to the society and the time of which I was writing. Modern scholarship, nevertheless, has given me a firm underpinning in many places, notably Halévy's great and reliable encyclopedia of English affairs, Pinson's and Kohn's studies of Germany, Morison's edition of Roosevelt's letters and two superbly informative biographies of subjects who were at the heart and core of their age, Goldberg's *Jaurès* and Mendelssohn's *Churchill*. Each, while focusing on an individual, is a detailed history of his surrounding period, amply and carefully documented. In a narrower field Ginger's *Debs* and in a still more restricted one Painter's *Proust* achieve the same result.

Several remarkable investigations made at the time I could hardly have done without: Bateman's study of landed income in England, Jack London's and Jacob Riis's studies of the poor, and Quillard's study of the contributors to the Henry Subscription. Certain novelists, such as V. Sackville-West, Anatole France, and Proust, were invaluable as social historians, as were certain memoirists: Blum and Daudet on opposite sides, Lady Warwick, Sir Frederick Ponsonby, Lord Esher, Wilfrid Blunt, Baroness von Suttner, Stefan Zweig, and especially Vandervelde, who alone among the Socialists provided an intimate personal view of his milieu, of the kind in which the ruling class is so prolific. Even more valuable, perhaps, are those occasional individuals endowed both

465

with a peculiar extra insight into their time and a gift for expressing it; who illumine what is happening around them by a sudden flash of understanding Romain Rolland is one, Masterman another. Although less central to this book, Trotsky, as revealed in his matchless phrase about the Serbian infantry, has that same mysterious ability to perceive—almost to feel—the historical meaning of the moment and to convey it in words.

Of all the sources listed, the outstanding work is unquestionably Reinach's (of which more is said in the Notes to Chapter 4); the most consistently informative and brilliant writer is A. G. Gardiner; the most striking fact to emerge from the assembled bibliography is the absence (except for Henry Adams, whom I find disagreeable) of first-rate memoirs by an American.

In an effort to keep the Notes to manageable length, I have given a reference *only* for those statements whose source is not obvious. When no reference is given, the reader may assume that any act or quotation by, or statement made to, a person whose memoirs or other work appears in the Bibliography, was taken from that person's account. For example, in Chapter 4, should a reader wish to know what is my source for the statement that Léon Blum and his friend Pierre Louÿs took opposite sides in the Affair and thereafter never saw each again, he should check the Bibliography under the names of the participants in the episode and, in this case, on finding a book by Blum, assume that Blum was my authority. When Mme Melba's guests throw peaches out the window or Lord Ribblesdale is quoted on the status of a lord, it may be assumed that the work of each cited in the Bibliography is the authority. Often, as when Strauss visits Speyer or makes a passing remark to Beecham, the source is the memoirist, not the principal. In general, when no reference is given, the name of the person mentioned in a particular conversation, correspondence or incident is the key to the source. While this method requires anyone interested to find the page number in the original book for himself, it has the advantage of not perpetuating mistakes, and any other method would have stretched out the Notes to a length equal to the text.

In cases where a book has served in several places it is listed under the chapter of its primary concern. *DNB* refers to the *Dictionary of National Biography*, *DAB* to the American ditto, *The Times* to the London newspaper, *NYT* to the *New York Times*. An asterisk denotes a source of particular value or interest.

1. The Patricians

Bibliography

ADAMS, WILLIAM SCOVELL, *Edwardian Heritage, 1901–6*, London, Muller, 1949.

ASQUITH, EARL OF OXFORD AND, *Fifty Years of British Parliament*, 2 vols., Boston, Little, Brown, 1926.

ASQUITH, MARGOT (Countess of Oxford and Asquith), *Autobiography*, Vols. I and II, London, Butterworth, 1920.

AUSTIN, ALFRED, *Autobiography*, 2 vols., London, Macmillan, 1911.

BALFOUR, LADY FRANCES, *Ne Obliviscaris*, 2 vols., London, Hodder & Stoughton, n.d.

*BATEMAN, JOHN, *The Great Landowners of Great Britain and Ireland*, 4th ed., London, Harrison, 1883.

BATTERSEA, CONSTANCE, LADY, *Reminiscences*, London, 1922.

BENNETT, ARNOLD, *Journals*, 3 vols., New York, Viking, 1932.

BENSON, E. F., *As We Were*, New York, Longmans, 1930.

BIRKENHEAD, FIRST EARL OF, *Contemporary Personalities*, London, Cassell, 1924.

BLUNT, WILFRID SCAWEN, *My Diaries*, 2 vols., New York, Knopf, 1921.

BUCHAN, JOHN, *Pilgrim's Way* (English title: *Memory hold-the-door*), Boston, Houghton Mifflin, 1940.

CARPENTER, RT. REV. WILLIAM BOYD, *Some Pages of My Life*, New York, Scribner's 1911.

CECIL, LADY GWENDOLYN, *Life of Robert, Marquis of Salisbury*, 4 vols., London, Hodder & Stoughton, 1921–32.

CHAMBERLAIN, SIR AUSTEN, *Down the Years*, London, Cassell, 1935.

CHANDOS, VISCOUNT (OLIVER LYTTELTON), *Memoirs*, London, Bodley, 1962.

CHURCHILL, RANDOLPH SPENCER, *Fifteen Famous English Homes*, London, Verschoyle, 1954.

——————, *Lord Derby*, London, Heinemann, 1959.

CHURCHILL, WINSTON S., *A Roving Commission: My Early Life*, New York, Scribner's, 1930.

COOPER, LADY DIANA (MANNERS), *The Rainbow Comes and Goes*, Boston, Houghton Mifflin, 1958.

CREWE, MARQUESS OF, *Lord Rosebery*, New York, Harper, 1931.

CURZON, LORD, *Subjects of the Day*, New York, Macmillan, 1915.

DUGDALE, BLANCHE E. C., *Arthur James Balfour*, 2 vols., New York, Putnam's, 1937.

ESHER, VISCOUNT REGINALD, *Journals and Letters*, ed. Maurice V. Brett, 3 vols., London, Nicholson & Watson, 1934–48.

FITZROY, SIR ALMERIC, *Memoirs*, 2 vols., London, Hutchinson, n.d.

FORD, FORD MADOX, *Return to Yesterday*, New York, Liveright, 1932.

*GARDINER, A. G. (editor of the *Daily News*), *Pillars of Society*, New York, Dodd, Mead, 1914.

*——————, *Prophets, Priests and Kings*, London, Dent, 1914 (new edition, first published 1908).

*HALÉVY, ÉLIE, *A History of the English People in the 19th Century*, Vol. V, 1895–1905; Vol. VI, 1905–14, New York, Barnes & Noble, 1961.

HAMILTON, LORD ERNEST, *Forty Years On*, New York, Doran, 1922.

HAMILTON, LORD FREDERICK, *The Days Before Yesterday*, New York, Doran, 1920.

HARRIS, FRANK, *Oscar Wilde, His Life and Confessions,* New York, The Author, 1916.

HOLLAND, BERNARD (former private secretary to the Duke), *Life of the Duke of Devonshire,* London, Longmans, 1911.

JEBB, LADY, *With Dearest Love to All: The Life and Letters of Lady Jebb,* ed. Mary Reed Bobbitt, London, Faber, 1960.

KENNEDY, A. L., *Salisbury, 1830–1903: Portrait of a Statesman,* London, Murray, 1953.

KIPLING, RUDYARD, *Something of Myself,* London, Macmillan, 1951.

LAMBTON, HON. GEORGE, *Men and Horses I Have Known,* London, Butterworth, 1924.

LEE, SIR SIDNEY, *King Edward VII,* 2 vols., New York, Macmillan, 1927.

LESLIE, SHANE, *The End of a Chapter,* New York, Scribner's, 1916.

LONDONDERRY, MARCHIONESS OF, *Henry Chaplin: A Memoir,* London, Macmillan, 1926.

LOWELL, ABBOTT LAWRENCE, *The Government of England,* 2 vols., New York, Macmillan, 1908.

LUCY, SIR HENRY, *Diary of a Journalist,* New York, Dutton, 1920.

———, *Memories of Eight Parliaments, 1868–1906,* London, Heinemann, 1908.

LYTTELTON, EDITH, *Alfred Lyttelton,* London, Longmans, 1917.

MACKINTOSH, ALEXANDER (a parliamentary correspondent for the provincial press), *From Gladstone to Lloyd George,* London, Hodder & Stoughton, 1921.

MAGNUS, SIR PHILIP, *Edward VII,* New York, Dutton, 1964.

———, *Gladstone,* New York, Dutton, 1954.

MARSH, EDWARD, *A Number of People,* New York, Harper, 1939.

MELBA, NELLIE, *Melodies and Memories,* New York, Doran, 1926.

MIDLETON, EARL OF (ST. JOHN BRODRICK), *Records and Reactions,* London, Murray, 1939.

MONEY, SIR LEO GEORGE CHIOZZA, M.P., *Riches and Poverty,* 10th rev. ed., London, Methuen, 1911.

MORLEY, JOHN, VISCOUNT, *Recollections,* 2 vols., New York, Macmillan, 1917.

MOUNT, CHARLES MERRILL, *John Singer Sargent,* London, Cresset, 1957.

NEVILL, RALPH, *London Clubs,* London, Chatto and Windus, 1911.

NEVINS, ALLAN, *Henry White,* New York, Harper, 1930.

NEVINSON, HENRY W., *Changes and Chances,* New York, Harcourt, Brace, 1923.

———, *More Changes and Chances,* New York, Harcourt, Brace, 1925.

NEWTON, LORD, *Lord Lansdowne,* London, Macmillan, 1929.

———, *Retrospection,* London, Murray, 1941.

NICOLSON, HAROLD, *Helen's Tower,* London, Constable, 1937.

NORDAU, MAX, *Degeneration,* tr., New York, Appleton, 1895.

PLESS, DAISY, PRINCESS OF, *Better Left Unsaid,* New York, Dutton, 1931.

PONSONBY, ARTHUR, *The Camel and the Needle's Eye,* London, Fifield, 1910.

————, *The Decline of Aristocracy,* London, Unwin, 1912.

*PONSONBY, SIR FREDERICK (First Lord Syonsby), *Recollections of Three Reigns,* New York, Dutton, 1952.

PONSONBY, SIR HENRY, *His Life from His Letters,* ed. Arthur Ponsonby, New York, Macmillan, 1943.

RAVERAT, GWEN, *Period Piece,* New York, Norton, 1952.

RIBBLESDALE, THOMAS, LORD, *Impressions and Memories,* London, Cassell, 1927.

RONALDSHAY, EARL OF, *Life of Lord Curzon,* 3 vols., London, Benn, 1928.

RUSSELL, GEORGE W. E., *Prime Ministers and Some Others: A Book of Reminiscences,* New York, Scribner's, 1919.

*SACKVILLE-WEST, V., *The Edwardians,* London, Hogarth, 1930.

SITWELL, SIR OSBERT, *Left Hand, Right Hand,* Boston, Little, Brown, 1944.

————, *Great Morning,* London, Macmillan, 1948.

STRACHEY, JOHN ST. LOE (editor of the *Spectator*), *The Adventure of Living,* New York, Putnam's, 1922.

VICTORIA, QUEEN, *Letters,* ed. G. E. Buckle, Vol. III, 1896–1901, New York, Longmans, 1932.

*WARWICK, FRANCES, COUNTESS OF, *Life's Ebb and Flow,* New York, Morrow, 1929. (Notes refer to this book unless otherwise stated.)

————, *Discretions,* New York, Scribner's, 1931.

WHARTON, EDITH, *A Backward Glance,* New York, Appleton-Century, 1934.

WILDE, OSCAR, *Letters,* ed. Rupert Hart-Davis, New York, Harcourt, Brace, 1964.

WILLOUGHBY DE BROKE, RICHARD GREVILLE VERNEY, LORD, *The Passing Years,* Boston, Houghton Mifflin, n.d.

WILSON-FOX, ALICE, *The Earl of Halsbury, Lord High Chancellor,* London, Chapman & Hall, 1929.

*WYNDHAM, GEORGE, *Life and Letters,* ed. J. W. MacNeil and Guy Wyndham, 2 vols., London, Hutchinson, n.d.

YOUNG, KENNETH, *Arthur James Balfour,* London, Bell, 1963.

Notes

PAGE
4   "An almost embarrassing wealth": H. H. Asquith, I, 273, 275.
5   "Nerve storms": Kennedy, 353.
5   Family threw cushions: Frances Balfour, I, 311.
5   "Poor Buller": Young, 168; talking to Lord Roberts: Russell, 54–55.
6   Horse an "inconvenient adjunct": Cecil, I, 176.
6   He told Dumas *fils: The Times,* Aug. 24, 1903.
6   "Jump on behind": Kennedy, 241.
7   Pepys on Hatfield garden: q. R. Churchill, *Fifteen Homes,* 74.
7   "Jump, dammit . . . !": *ibid.,* 71.
7   "Quite exceptional stupidity": Cecil, I, 1.
7   Birkenhead on the Cecils: Birkenhead, 177.
7   Disraeli quoted: Mackintosh, 50–51.

PAGE
7   "That black man": *ibid.*
7   Morley, "blazing indiscretion": q. H. H. Asquith, II, 277.
8   "Every sentence," said a fellow member: Ribblesdale, 173.
8   "I thought he was dead": *National Review,* "Lord Salisbury: His Wit and Humor," Nov., 1931, 659–68.
8   "When will all this be over?": Carpenter, 237.
8   Colleagues complained: Cecil, III, 177.
8   "Just a little more off here": Ribblesdale, 174.
8   His charm "no small asset": Hicks-Beach, q. Cecil, III, 178.
9   "I think I have done them all": *National Review, op. cit.,* 665.
9   Gladstone quoted: Mackintosh, 50–51.
9   "Not excluding the House of Commons": Lucy, *Eight Parliaments,* 114.
9   Queen Victoria quoted: Carpenter, 236.
9   "Bad on his legs": F. Ponsonby, 67.
10   "Oh, I daresay": Benson, 164.
10   "Splitting it into a bundle": *Quarterly Review,* Oct., 1883, 575.
10   Articles in *Quarterly Review:* quotations in this and the following two paragraphs are from Cecil, I, 149, 157–60, 196.
11   Speech against Disraeli's policy: July 5, 1867, *Hansard,* 3rd Series, Vol. 188, 1097 ff.
12   "Grim acidity": Gardiner, *Prophets,* 150.
12   "Rank without power": Cecil, II, 5.
12   Curzon quoted: Ronaldshay, I, 282.
12   "Secure and comfortable": Buchan, 75.
12   Duke of Devonshire on Harcourt's Budget: *Annual Register,* 1894, 121.
12   "Germ planted": *The Times,* July 17, 1895, leader.
13   "Dominant influences": q. Magnus, *Gladstone,* 433.
13   Dufferin taught himself Persian: Nicolson, 246.
14   "Those damned dots": Leslie, 30–31.
15   Stanley "an upper class servant": T. P. O'Connor, q. R. Churchill, *Derby,* 45.
15   Eton's "scugs": Willoughby de Broke, 133.
15   Cecil Balfour forged a check: Young, 11.
15   Sargent asked Ribblesdale to sit: Mount, 418.
15   *"Ce grand diable":* Ribblesdale, xvii.
16   "A race of gods and goddesses": Clermont-Tonnerre (*see* Chap. 4), I, 175.
16   "Divinely tall": E. Hamilton, 7.
17   Gentlemen sighed and told each other: Sackville-West, 122.
18   "Bohemia in Tiaras": Benson, 157.
18   Prince of Wales to Churchill: W. Churchill, 155.
19   "I shall call you the Souls": q. Nevins, 81.
19   Two sets of eyebrows: Melba, 226.
19   "I don't like poets": Wyndham, I, 67.
20   Harry Cust's "fatal self-indulgence": Margot Asquith, q. Nevins, 81.
20   Lord Morley's detective: Fitzroy, II, 463.
20   "Brilliant and powerful body": W. Churchill, 89.
20   "Knew each other intimately": Willoughby de Broke, 180.
21   Jowett's choice of undergraduates: Newton, *Lansdowne,* 6.
21   "No end of good dinners": Willoughby de Broke, 30.
21   "Effortless superiority": Leslie, 43.
22   "Poor fellow, poor fellow": Marsh, 183.
22   "Born booted and spurred": Gardiner, *Prophets,* 214.
22   "When I looked at life from the saddle": Warwick, *Discretions,* 78.

PAGE

23   Chauncey Depew's telegram: Robert Rhodes James, *Rosebery*, London, 1963, 355.

23   "Even policemen were waving their helmets": Lee, II, 421.

23   Londesborough's "gloss, speed and style": Sitwell, *Left Hand*, 154.

23   "Because the carriage had to go home": Raverat, 178.

23   Blunt's sonnet: "On St. Valentine's Day."

24   Duke of Rutland's chaplain: Cooper, 20.

24   Squire Chaplin in the hunting field: Lambton, 133; Londonderry, 227, 240.

25   "Sure of themselves": Sitwell, *Great Morning*, 10, 121–22.

25   Colonel Brabazon described: W. Churchill, 67; testimony quoted: Esher, I, 362.

26–7 Figures on income and acreage: Bateman, *passim*.

27   The "poverty line": set by B. S. Rowntree at 21*s*. 8*d*. for a family of five. In *Poverty, A Study of Town Life,* 1901.

28   "Eau de Nil satin": Warwick, 230.

29   "Then bwing me another": W. Churchill, 68.

29   "Squalid throng of homeless outcasts": A. Ponsonby, *Camel*, 12.

30   Kipling on venting chauvinism: *American Notes (see* Chap. 3), 45.

30   "Knew his own mind and put down his foot": Whyte (*see* Chap. 5), II, 115.

31   "A series of microscopic advantages": q. *Monthly Review*, Oct., 1903, "Lord Salisbury," 8.

31   Morley Roberts: q. Peck (*see* Chap. 3), 428.

33   "All his bad qualities": Hyndman (*see* Chap. 7), 349.

33   "I was a problem": to More Adey, Nov. 27, 1897, *Letters*, 685.

33   Lord Arthur Somerset: Magnus, *Edward VII*, 214–15.

34   Swinburne "absolutely impossible": H. Ponsonby, 274.

34   "Join it": Hyndman (*see* Chap. 7), 349.

34   "I dare not alter these things": Marsh, 2.

35   Austin on Germans and Alfred the Great: q. Adams, 76, n. 3.

35   Salisbury on Austin's poem: Victoria, *Letters*, 24.

35   An American observer quoted: Lowell, II, 507.

35   Austin's Jubilee wish: Blunt, I, 280.

36   Lord Newton on the Lords: *Retrospection*, 101.

36   Rosebery complained: Crewe, 462.

37   Halsbury "invariably objected": Newton, *Lansdowne,* 361; "jolly cynicism": Gardiner, *Prophets*, 197; Carlton Club: Wilson-Fox, 122; Lord Coleridge: *ibid.*, 124.

37   "Rule by a sort of instinct": q. Halévy, V, 23, n. 2.

38   "Greatest gentleman of his day": Newton, *Lansdowne*, 506.

38   "A new sense of duty": Holland, II, 146. All quotations, anecdotes and other material about the Duke are from this source unless otherwise specified.

39   "Take things very easy": H. Ponsonby, 265.

39   "This is damned dull": Mackintosh, 113.

39   Duchess "one of the handsomest women": F. Hamilton, 201.

40   "No face was more suited": F. Ponsonby, 52.

41   "Certain hereditary governmental instincts" and "a debt to the State": Esher, I, 126.

41   "He was always losing them": H. Ponsonby, 265 n.

42   Duke at coronation rehearsal: Lucy, *Diary*, 193.

43   "Do you feel nervous, Winston?": R. Churchill, *Fifteen Homes*, 105.

43   "The best of company": F. Ponsonby, 294.

PAGE

44   *Spectator* and subsequent quotations in this paragraph: Strachey, 406 and 398; Holland, II, 211, n. 1; *The Times,* Mar. 25, 1908.

45   "Go and tell him he is a pig": Mackintosh, 91.

45   "A point of honor to stand for their county": Sir George Otto Trevelyan, q. A. Ponsonby, *Decline,* 101.

45   Long and Chaplin described: Gardiner, *Pillars,* 217; *Prophets,* 212.

45   "Calm, ineradicable conviction": Gardiner, *Prophets,* 213.

45   "How did I ao, Arthur?": Londonderry, 171.

46   "Sit on his shoulder blades": q. Young, 100.

46   "The finest brain": q. Chamberlain, 206.

46   William James: letter of Apr. 26, 1895, *The Letters of William James,* ed. H. James, Boston, 1920.

46   "Oh dear, what a gulf": Battersea, Diary for Sept. 6, 1895.

46   "Lovely bend of the head": Margot Asquith, I, 166.

46   "No, that is not so": Margot Asquith, I, 162.

47   Darwin on Frank Balfour: Young, 8.

48   Cambridge friends: Esher, I, 182; society friends: Russell, 63.

48   Balfour on Judaism: Dugdale, I, 324.

48   Harry Cust's dinner: Bennett, I, 287.

49   Daisy White congratulated: Nevins, 81.

49–50 "Quite a good fellow": Frances Balfour, II, 367; "A sympathetic outlook": *ibid.,* II, 93.

50   "A natural spring of youth": *ibid.;* "a freshness, serenity": Fitzroy, I, 28.

50   Lord Randolph: *Life of Lord Randolph Churchill,* by Winston Churchill, II, 459–60.

50   Balfour on Socialism: q. Halévy, V, 231.

51   "What exactly *is* a Trade Union?": Lucy Masterman (*see* Chap. 7), 61.

51   "My uncle is a Tory": Margot Asquith, I, 154.

51   Churchill used the word "wicked": Blunt, II, 278.

52   "Relentless as Cromwell": Young, 105.

52   Morley, "took his foes by surprise": q. Russell, 66.

52   "The most courageous man alive": Blunt, II, 278.

52   Debated with "dauntless ingenuity": Morley, I, 225–27.

52   "If he had a little more brains": q. Buchan, 156.

52   "A bullet on a bubble": Andrew White (*see* Chap. 5), II, 430.

52   "I never lose my temper": q. Morley, I, 227.

53   "This damned Scotch croquet": Lyttelton, 204.

53   Reply to Lady Rayleigh: Fitzroy, II, 491; charmed Frau Wagner: Esher, I, 312.

53   "Supreme energy of Arthur": *ibid.,* 340.

54   "He never reads the papers": Whyte (*see* Chap. 5), II, 120.

54   Prince felt Balfour condescended: Halévy, VI, 231.

54   The Queen admired him: F. Ponsonby, 69.

54   Queen "much struck": Journal, Sept. 11, 1896, Victoria, 74.

54   Proust's housekeeper: q. Havelock Ellis (*see* Chap. 4), 377.

55   Queen Victoria, "No one ever": q. Hector Bolitho, *Reign of Queen Victoria,* 366.

55   Kipling, "a certain optimism": Kipling, 147.

55   Sir Edward Clarke, "The greatest poem": q. Amy Cruse, *After the Victorians,* London, 1938, 123.

55   "Joe's War": Kennedy, 315.

56   Salisbury on Chamberlain: Dugdale, I, 67.

56   Balfour to Lady Elcho: Young, 129.

PAGE

56   Entertaining three duchesses: Frances Balfour, II, 211.

57   "The difference between Joe and Me": q. Julian Amery, *Life of Joseph Chamberlain,* IV, 464.

57   "Let us defy someone": q. Adams, 78.

57   Duke of Argyll: Frances Balfour, II, 318.

58   Salisbury to German Ambassador: Hatzfeld to Foreign Office, July 31, 1900, *Grosse Politik (see* Chap. 5), XVI, 76.

58   Lady Salisbury: Frances Balfour, II, 290.

59   *Le Temps,* "What closes today?": q. *The Times,* July 15, 1902.

59   "Go up at once, Sir James": Blunt, I, 366.

2. The Idea and the Deed

Bibliography

ARCHER, WILLIAM, *The Life, Trial and Death of Francisco Ferrer,* New York, Moffat, Yard, 1911.

BARNARD, HARRY, *Eagle Forgotten: The Life of John Peter Altgeld,* Indianapolis, Bobbs-Merrill, 1938.

BERKMAN, ALEXANDER, *Prison Memoirs of an Anarchist,* New York, Mother Earth Publishing Co., 1912.

BRENAN, GERALD, *The Spanish Labyrinth,* Cambridge, University Press, 1950.

CHANNING, WALTER, "The Mental Status of Czolgosz, the Assassin of President McKinley," *American Journal of Insanity,* October, 1902, 233–78.

CHARQUES, RICHARD D., *The Twilight of Imperial Russia,* London, Phoenix, 1958.

CORTI, COUNT EGON, *Elizabeth, Empress of Austria,* New Haven, Yale Univ. Press, 1936.

Crapouillot, Numéro Spécial, l'Anarchie, Paris, January, 1938.

CREUX, V. C., *Canovas del Castillo, sa carrière, ses œuvres, sa fin,* Paris, Leve, 1897.

DAVID, HENRY, *History of the Haymarket Affair,* New York, Farrar & Rhinehart, 1936.

*ELTZBACHER, PAUL, *Anarchism,* tr. S. T. Byington, New York, Benjamin Tucker, 1908.

GOLDMAN, EMMA, *Living My Life,* Vol. I, New York, Knopf, 1931.

HAMSUN, KNUT, *Hunger,* New York, Knopf, 1921.

HARVEY, GEORGE, *Henry Clay Frick,* New York, Scribner's, 1928.

HUNTER, ROBERT, *Poverty,* New York, Macmillan, 1904.

ISHILL, JOSEPH, *Peter Kropotkin,* New Jersey, Free Spirit Press, 1923.

———, ed., *Elisée and Elie Reclus, in Memoriam,* New Jersey, Oriole Press, 1927.

KERENSKY, ALEXANDER, *The Crucifixion of Liberty,* New York, John Day, 1934.

KROPOTKIN, PRINCE PETER, *The Conquest of Bread,* New York, Putnam's, 1907.

————, *Mutual Aid,* London, Heinemann, 1902.

*————, *Paroles d'un Révolté,* Paris, Flammarion, 1885.

————, "Anarchism," in *Encyclopedia Britannica,* 11th ed.

*LONDON, JACK, *People of the Abyss,* New York, Macmillan, 1903.

*MAITRON, JEAN, *Histoire du Mouvement Anarchiste en France, 1880–1914,* Paris, Société Universitaire, 1951.

MALATESTA, ENRICO, *A Talk Between Two Workers,* tr., 8th ed., London, Freedom Press, n.d.

MALATO, CHARLES, "Some Anarchist Portraits," *Fortnightly Review,* September, 1894.

MILIUKOV, PAUL, SEIGNOBOS, CHARLES, and EISENMANN, L., *Histoire de Russie,* Vol. III, Leroux, n.p., n.d.

MIRSKY, D. S., *Russia: A Social History,* London, Cresset, 1931.

NEVINSON, HENRY W., *The Dawn in Russia: Scenes in the Russian Revolution,* New York, Harper, 1906.

NICOLAEVSKY, BORIS, *Azev, the Spy,* tr. George Reavey, New York, Doubleday, Doran, 1934.

*NOMAD, MAX, *Apostles of Revolution,* Boston, Little, Brown, 1939.

————, *Rebels and Renegades,* New York, Macmillan, 1932.

PILAR, PRINCESS OF BAVARIA, and CHAPMAN-HUSTON, MAJOR D., *Alfonso XIII: A Study of Monarchy,* New York, Dutton, 1932.

REGIS, DR. EMMANUEL, *Les Régicides dans l'histoire et dans le présent,* Paris, Masson, 1890.

*RIIS, JACOB A., *How the Other Half Lives,* New York, Scribner's, 1890.

*SAVINKOV, BORIS V., *Memoirs of a Terrorist,* tr. Joseph Shaplen, New York, Boni, 1931.

SOREL, GEORGES, *Réflexions sur la violence,* Paris, Pages Libres, 1908.

VIZETELLY, ERNEST ALFRED, *The Anarchists,* London, John Lane, 1911.

WOODCOCK, GEORGE, and AVAKUMOVIC, IVAN, *The Anarchist Prince: A Biographical Study of Prince Kropotkin,* London, Boardman, 1950.

Three useful books have appeared since this chapter was written: *Anarchism,* by George Woodcock, *The Anarchists,* by James Joll, and *The Anarchists,* an anthology, edited by Irving L. Horowitz.

Notes

I have not thought it necessary, in this chapter, to give separate references for each incident and quotation since they group themselves, according to subject, into easily identifiable sets of sources, as follows:

For the conditions of the poor, Riis, London, Hunter and Chiozza Money (*see* Chap. 1) were my chief contemporary sources. For the ideas and theories of Anarchists of all countries and for excerpts from their writings, Eltzbacher was particularly useful. For French Anarchism all quotations, unless otherwise stated, are from Maitron or Malato (himself one of the French Anarchists of the time), supplemented by *Crapouillot* and Vizetelly. For Emma Goldman and Alexander Berkman their own memoirs are the sources for all quotations. For Johann Most the chapter on him in Nomad's *Apostles* was the chief source. In the sections on Spanish Anarchists the quotations are taken chiefly from contemporary reports in the American press, as noted. For Czolgosz the essential primary source is Channing. For the Russians, Savinkov, himself a member of the Terror Brigade, and Nicolaevsky are primary (and indeed so fascinating that my first version of the Russian incidents, having grown altogether out of proportion, had to be condensed to a fifth of its original length).

Facts and quotations not covered by the foregoing, and which seem to require a specific reference, are separately noted.

PAGE

63   "A daydream of desperate romantics": Nomad, *Rebels,* 13.

65   Proudhon, "Whoever lays his hand on me": from his *Confessions of a Revolutionary.* "To be governed is to be . . .": from his *Idée générale de la révolution au vingtième siècle,* Epilogue.

65   "Abstract idea of right": Bakunin said this was Proudhon's point of departure, q. Nomad, *Apostles,* 15.

65   "Their power will be irresistible": q. Eltzbacher, 138.

66   "We reckoned without the masses": q. Nomad, *Apostles,* 205.

67   "The gentry had murdered the Czar" and "Broken and demoralized": Kerensky, 44–45.

67   Henry James, "sinister anarchic underworld": from his Preface to *Princess Casamassima,* his novel with Anarchist characters first published in 1886. Johann Most is said to have inspired the conception of the unseen Anarchist leader Hoffendahl in the novel. Another literary exercise in the theme was Joseph Conrad's rather shallow story "An Anarchist," published in *Harper's Weekly* for Aug., 1906, of which the chief point seems to be that Anarchists are people of "warm hearts and weak heads." It was followed in 1907 by his novel *The Secret Agent,* dealing with plot and conspiracy. Neither James nor Conrad was concerned with the underlying social origins or social philosophy of Anarchism.

68   August Spies quoted: David, 332–39.

68   "I want the Day of Judgment!": a story told by Robert Blatchford, q. London, 298.

69   "What is Property?": the title of his second treatise, *Qu'est ce que la propriété?* 1840.

69   "All mankind's tormentors": from his *Dieu et l'Etat,* 2nd ed., 1892, 11.

69   Wcman who made match boxes and young man in the river: Riis, 47 and London, 205–07.

69   "Eight hours of work": q. Maitron, 186.

70   Nevinson on Kropotkin: *Changes and Chances (see* Chap. 1), 125.

71   Shaw on Kropotkin: q. Woodcock, 225.

71   "Galloping decay" of states: *Paroles,* 8–10.

71   "Inertia of those who have a vested interest": *Paroles,* 275–76.

71   Brousse, "The idea is on the march": q. *Crapouillot,* 15.

71   "By dagger, gun and dynamite": q. *ibid.,* 15.

71–2   "Men of courage . . . the deed of mutiny": *Paroles,* 285.

72   "A single deed . . .": *ibid.,* 285.

72   *La Révolte* of March, 1891; q. Maitron, 240.

PAGE

72   Argument with Ben Tillett and Tom Mann: Ford (*see* Chap. 1), 110.

72–3   Plans for Anarchist society: Kropotkin's *Revolutionary Studies, Conquest of Bread, l'Anarchie dans l'évolution social.* Malatesta's *Talk Between Two Workers.*

73   Shaw: Tract No. 45, read to the Society Oct. 16, 1891, published July, 1893.

74   Royal Geographic Society's dinner: Woodcock, 227.

74   Elisée Reclus, "irresistible magnetism": Vandervelde (*see* Chap. 8), 37.

75   Jean Grave, "simple, silent, indefatigable": Malato, 316.

75   Malatesta's adventures: Nomad, *Rebels,* 1–47.

76   "Just as we saw him last": Ishill, *Kropotkin,* 40.

76   "All are awaiting the birth": *ibid.,* 9.

76   "A shining moral grandeur": Victor Serge in *Crapouillot,* 5.

77   "Breathe hatred and revolt": Malato, 317.

79   Kropotkin and Malatesta repudiate Ravachol: in *La Révolte,* Nos. 17 and 18, Jan., 1892, and *l'En Dehors,* Aug. 28, 1892, q. Maitron, 204, 221.

79   "Miniature Borgias": Nomad, *Rebels,* 26.

83   The shooting of Frick: in addition to Berkman, Harvey's *Frick* and *Harper's Weekly,* Aug. 6, 1892.

84   Altgeld and the pardon: Barnard, 217, 246; *NYT,* June 28, 1893.

85   "Madrid is sad . . .": Pilar, 50.

85   Pallas' attempt on Martínez de Camos: Creux, 295–96; *Crapouillot; NYT,* Sept. 25, 30, 1893.

86   Barcelona Opera House bombing: *NYT,* Nov. 9, Dec. 20, 1893, Jan. 3, 1894.

86   Montjuich tortures: Brenan, 168, n. 1.

87   Asquith-Balfour exchange on the Anarchists: *Spectator,* Nov. 18, 1893, 706, Dec. 2, 791; *NYT,* Nov. 11, 1893.

88   Paris "absolutely paralyzed": Ford (*see* Chap. 1), 107.

89   Laurent Tailhade, "a blessed time": Nomad, *Apostles,* 11.

89   Octave Mirbeau: Daudet (*see* Chap. 4), 70.

89   "That there need be no misery": Suttner (*see* Chap. 5), I, 313.

89   President caricatured in soiled pajamas: in *Père Peinard,* July 4, 1897.

90   Sebastien Faure's "harmonious voice": Malato, 316.

91   "Qu'importe les victimes . . .": q. Maitron, 217. (This is frequently quoted as *Qu'importes les vagues humanités pourvu que le geste soit beau?* but this seems to have a ring of the morning after.)

91   Duchesse d'Uzès: Maitron, 215.

94   Clemenceau on Henry's execution: in *La Justice,* May 23, 1894, q. Maitron, 226.

95   Trial of the Thirty, Felix Fenéon: Roman (*see* Chap. 4), 59, 95.

96   "Every revolution ends . . .": q. Nomad, *Apostles,* 6.

97   Corpus Christi bomb: *NYT,* June 9, Nov. 25, Dec. 2, 22, 1896.

97   Canovas: Pilar, 40; Millis (*see* Chap. 3), 80–81; *Nation,* Aug. 12, 1897; *Review of Reviews,* Nov., 1897.

98   Letter from prisoner of Montjuich: q. *Crapouillot.*

99   Angiolillo: Creux, 301–15; Nomad, *Rebels,* 23.

100   Empress Elizabeth and Luigi Lucheni: Corti, 456–93.

102   Plot to assassinate the Kaiser: *Spectator,* Oct. 22, 1898; *NYT,* Oct. 15/16, 1898.

102   Bakunin, Germans not fit for Anarchism: Nomad, *Apostles,* 169, n. 5.

103   International Conference of Police in Rome: Maitron; Vizetelly, 238.

104–5   King Humbert and Gaetano Bresci: *Outlook,* Aug. 10, 1900; *Harper's*

PAGE

       Weekly, Aug. 4, 1900; *NYT,* Aug. 3, 1900; *Review of Reviews,* Sept., 1900, 316–22.

105–6   Czolgosz: Channing; Nomad, *Apostles,* 298–99; *NYT,* Sept. 9, 1901.

107   *Harper's* and *Century* quoted: *Harper's Weekly,* Dec. 23, 1893, Aug. 28, 1897. "The Assassination of Presidents," by J. M. Buckley, in *Century,* Nov., 1901.

107–8   Roosevelt on Anarchists: *NYT,* Dec. 5, 1901.

108   *Blackwood's:* July, 1906, 128, apropos of attempt on King Alfonso.

108   Lyman Abbott: *Outlook,* Feb. 22, 1902.

109   Assassination of Canalejas: *Literary Digest,* Nov. 23, 1912; *Living Age,* Dec. 12, 1912.

110   "Outraged beyond endurance": in his Preface to *Major Barbara,* dated June, 1906, apropos of the attempt on King Alfonso.

110–2   Russian Socialist-Revolutionaries: in addition to Savinkov and Nicolaevsky, general background from Charques, Miliukov and Kerensky.

111   Plehve, "We must drown the revolution": Miliukov, 1056.

112   Grand Duke Sergei "conspicuous for his cruelty": Nevinson.

112   "A formless mass 8 or 10 inches high": Savinkov, 106–7.

112   Czar and brother-in-law on the sofa: Bülow (*see* Chap. 5), II, 178.

3. End of a Dream

Bibliography

There are two full-length biographies of Reed, one by Samuel McCall, who served with him in Congress and was later Governor of Massachusetts, and one by Professor Robinson, both listed below. Among friends, reporters, Congressional colleagues and other contemporaries who wrote about him are the following:

BROWMAN, W. H., "Thomas Brackett Reed," *New England Magazine,* April, 1890.

DAY, HOLMAN F., "Tom Reed Among His Neighbors," *Saturday Evening Post,* January 3, 1903.

DE CASSERES, BENJAMIN, "Tom Reed," *American Mercury,* February, 1930.

FULLER, HERBERT B., *Speakers of the House,* Boston, Little, Brown, 1909.

HINDS, ASHER C., "The Speaker of the House of Representatives," *American Political Science Review,* May, 1909.

KNIGHT, ENOCH, "Thomas Brackett Reed: An Appreciation," *New England Magazine,* April, 1904.

LEUPP, FRANCIS E., "Personal Recollections of Thomas Brackett Reed," *Outlook,* September 3, 1910.

*LODGE, HENRY CABOT, "Thomas Brackett Reed," reprinted in *The Democracy of the Constitution and Other Essays,* New York, Scribner's, 1915.

*McCALL, SAMUEL, *The Life of Thomas Brackett Reed,* Boston, Houghton Mifflin, 1914.

McFARLAND, HENRY, "Thomas Brackett Reed," *American Review of Reviews,* January, 1903.

PORTER, ROBERT P., "Thomas Brackett Reed of Maine," *McClure's,* October, 1893.

*ROBINSON, WILLIAM A., *Thomas B. Reed, Parliamentarian,* New York, Dodd, Mead, 1930.

ROOSEVELT, THEODORE, "Thomas Brackett Reed and the 51st Congress," *Forum,* December, 1895.

Other Sources

ADAMS, HENRY, *The Education of Henry Adams,* Boston, Houghton Mifflin, 1918.

———, *Letters,* ed. Worthington Chauncey Ford, 2 vols., Boston, Houghton Mifflin, 1930–38.

ALEXANDER, DE ALVA STANWOOD, *History and Procedure of the House of Representatives,* Boston, Houghton Mifflin, 1916.

BARRY, DAVID S. (Washington Correspondent of New York *Sun* and Providence *Journal*), *40 Years in Washington,* Boston, Little, Brown, 1924.

BISHOP, JOSEPH BUCKLIN, *Theodore Roosevelt and His Times,* 2 vols., New York, Scribner's, 1920.

BOWERS, CLAUDE G., *Beveridge and the Progressive Era,* Boston, Houghton Mifflin, 1932.

BRYCE, JAMES, *The American Commonwealth,* 3 vols., London, Macmillan, 1888.

*CLARK, CHAMP, *My Quarter Century of American Politics,* 2 vols., New York, Harper, 1920.

CROLY, HERBERT, *Marcus Alonzo Hanna,* New York, Macmillan, 1912.

CULLOM, SENATOR SHELLY M., *Fifty Years of Public Service,* Chicago, McClurg, 1911.

DUNN, ARTHUR WALLACE, *From Harrison to Harding,* 2 vols., New York, Putnam's, 1922.

DUNNE, FINLEY PETER, *Mr. Dooley in Peace and War,* Boston, Small, Maynard, 1898.

FOULKE, WILLIAM DUDLEY, *A Hoosier Autobiography,* Oxford Univ. Press, 1922.

FUESS, CLAUDE MOORE, *Carl Schurz, Reformer, 1829–1906,* New York, Dodd, Mead, 1932.

GARRATY, JOHN A., *Henry Cabot Lodge: A Biography,* New York, Knopf, 1953.

GODKIN, EDWIN LAWRENCE, *Life and Letters,* ed. Rollo Ogden, 2 vols., New York, Macmillan, 1907.

GOMPERS, SAMUEL, *70 Years of Life and Labour,* 2 vols., London, Hurst & Blackett, 1925.

GRIFFIN, SOLOMON B., *People and Politics Observed by a Massachusetts Editor*, Boston, Little, Brown, 1923.

HARRINGTON, FREDERICK, "The Anti-Imperialist Movement in the United States," *Miss. Valley Hist. Rev.*, September, 1935.

HOAR, SENATOR GEORGE FRISBIE, *Autobiography of 70 Years*, 2 vols., New York, Scribner's, 1905.

HOWE, M. A. DEWOLFE, *Moorfield Storey: Portrait of an Independent*, Boston, Houghton Mifflin, 1932.

JAMES, HENRY, *Charles William Eliot*, 2 vols., Boston, Houghton Mifflin, 1930.

KIPLING, RUDYARD, *American Notes*, New York, Munro's, 1896.

KOHLSAAT, H. H., *From McKinley to Harding: Personal Recollections of Our Presidents*, New York, Scribner's, 1923.

LANZAR, MARIA C., "The Anti-Imperialist League," *Philippine Social Science Revue*, August and November, 1930.

LODGE, HENRY CABOT, ed., *Selections from the Correspondence of Theodore Roosevelt and H. C. Lodge*, 2 vols., New York, Scribner's, 1925.

LONG, JOHN D., *The New American Navy*, 2 vols., New York, Outlook, 1903.

LYON, PETER, *Success Story: The Life and Times of S. S. McClure*, New York, Scribner's, 1963.

MCELROY, ROBERT, *Grover Cleveland*, 2 vols., New York, Harper, 1925.

MAHAN, CAPTAIN ALFRED THAYER, *The Influence of Sea Power on History*, New York, Sagamore Press, 1957.

————, *From Sail to Steam* (autobiography), New York, Harper, 1907.

————, *The Interest of America in Sea Power*, Boston, Little, Brown, 1897. (Collected articles from *Atlantic Monthly, Harper's Monthly, Forum* and *North American Review*, 1890–97.)

MILLIS, WALTER, *The Martial Spirit*, New York, 1931.

MITCHELL, EDWARD P., *Memoirs of an Editor*, New York, Scribner's, 1924.

NORTON, CHARLES ELIOT, *Letters*, ed. Sara Norton and M. A. DeWolfe Howe, 2 vols., Boston, Houghton Mifflin, 1913.

PECK, HARRY THURSTON, *Twenty Years of the Republic*, New York, Dodd, Mead, 1906.

PERRY, R. B., *Thought and Character of William James*, Harvard Univ. Press, 1948.

PETTIGREW, SENATOR RICHARD F., *Imperial Washington, 1870–1920*, Chicago, Kerr, 1922.

PLATT, THOMAS COLLIER, *Autobiography*, New York, Dodge, 1910.

POWERS, SAMUEL LELAND, *Portraits of Half a Century*, Boston, Little, Brown, 1925.

PRINGLE, HENRY F., *Theodore Roosevelt*, New York, Harcourt, 1931.

PULESTON, CAPTAIN WILLIAM D., *Mahan*, Yale Univ. Press, 1939.

ROOSEVELT, THEODORE, *An Autobiography*, New York, Scribner's, 1920.

*————, *The Letters*, ed. Elting E. Morison, Vols. I and II, Harvard Univ. Press, 1951.

SCHURZ, CARL, *Reminiscences,* Vol. III (continued by Frederic Bancroft), New York, McClure, 1908.

SPRING-RICE, CECIL, *The Letters and Friendships,* ed. Stephen Gwynn, 2 vols., Boston, Houghton Mifflin, 1929.

STEALEY, ORLANDO O., *Twenty Years in the Press Gallery,* New York (author), 1906.

STOREY, MOORFIELD, *The Conquest of the Philippines by the United States,* New York, Putnam's, 1926.

SULLIVAN, MARK, *Our Times,* Vols. I and II, New York, Scribner's, 1926.

TAYLOR, CHARLES CARLISLE, *The Life of Admiral Mahan,* New York, Doran, 1920.

VANDERBILT, KERMIT, *Charles Eliot Norton,* Harvard Univ. Press, 1959.

VILLARD, OSWALD GARRISON, *Fighting Years,* New York, Harcourt, 1939.

WOLFF, LEON, *Little Brown Brother,* New York, Doubleday, 1961.

Notes

All biographical facts, anecdotes and quotations by or about Reed are from Lodge, McCall or Robinson except where otherwise stated. All quotations from Roosevelt are from the Morison edition of his *Letters,* for which I have given the dates and dispensed with volume and page references.

PAGE

117   "Out of whose collar": De Casseres. The following quotations in this paragraph, in order, are from Clark, I, 287; Leupp; McCall, 248; Dunn, I, 165; Foulke, 110; Porter. "The ablest running debater" was said by Rep. John Sharp Williams, Democratic Leader of the House; "the greatest parliamentary leader" by Lodge; "far and away the most brilliant" by Clark, II, 10.

118   Henry Adams on his brother John: Sept. 1, 1894, *Letters,* II, 55.

119   Bryce, "apathy . . .": III, 326–28.

119   Lewis Morris, "Damn the consequences": "Biographical Sketches of the Four Signers from New York," *Americana,* Aug., 1914, 627.

121   "A human frigate" and "How narrow": Day.

121   "Calculated . . . to obstruct legislation": Rep. Frye of Maine.

121   "All the wisdom": Clark, I, 286.

123   "Voting for him on the sly": Porter.

123   Palmerston's popularity: Peck, 276.

123   Choate anecdote: Barry, 142.

123   On Balzac: Porter.

123   "We asked the Tom Reeds": Lodge, *Corres.,* I, 77, 120.

124   "Theodore, if there is one thing more than another": q. George Stimpson, *A Book About American Politics,* New York, 1952, 342.

124   "Theodore will never be President": Leupp.

124   "Ambitious as Lucifer": Cullom, 243.

125   "It becomes a tyranny": Dunn, I, 35.

126   "The largest human face": Clark, I, 277–78.

126 ff.   "The Chair directs": All remarks by the Speaker and Representatives in the account of the Quorum fight are from the *Congressional Record,* 51st Congress, First Session.

PAGE

126 ff. "Pandemonium broke loose": Dunn, I, 27. Reporters and other eye-witnesses quoted on the Quorum fight are Dunn, I, 24–32; Peck, 200–202; Fuller, 219–21. The New York *Times* gave the story four columns on page 1 on both Jan. 30 and 31.

129 Reed's Rules: Fuller, 228.

129 Roosevelt on Reed's reform; *Forum,* Dec., 1895.

129 "Biting a green persimmon": Mount (*see* Chap. 1), 192. Sargent had difficulty with the portrait and destroyed his first version. "His exterior somehow does not correspond with his spirit. What is a painter to do? . . . I could have made a better picture with a less remarkable man. He has been delightful." Reed claimed that he liked it although "I am willing to admit that the picture is not so good-looking as the original." The portrait now hangs in the Speaker's Lobby in the Capitol. As it seems to the author to convey little of Reed's personality, it is not reproduced here.

129 "They might do worse": Brownson.

129 "White House Iceberg": Platt, 215.

129 "The House has more sense": Alexander, 27.

130 "Look outward": "The United States Looking Outward," Dec., 1890.

130 "A voice . . . of our external interests": Puleston, 133. All subsequent biographical facts, anecdotes and quotations by or about Mahan are from Puleston unless otherwise stated.

131 "Don't tell Grover": Clark, I, 281–82.

131 Roosevelt read it "straight through": May 12, 1890, *Letters,* I, 221.

132 Origin of "Sea Power": Mahan, *From Sail to Steam,* 276–77.

133 Kaiser on Mahan: q. Taylor, 131.

133 Secretary White: Fuller, 211.

134 Mahan on the Jews: *From Sail to Steam.*

135 Lodge in "desperate earnest": q. Garraty, 52.

136 Comments of Senators Morgan, Frye and Cullom: Millis, 29.

136 Union League Club, *NYT,* Dec. 18, 1895.

137 "Admirals? Never!": q. Taylor, 12.

138 "A towering influence": q. Godkin, I, 221.

138 Lowell on the *Nation:* Godkin, I, 251; Bryce on the *Evening Post: ibid.,* 232; Governor Hill: Villard, 123.

138 Godkin on the United States in 1895: *Life and Letters,* II, 187, 202.

139 William James on "fighting spirit": to Frederic Myers, Jan. 1, 1896, Perry, 244.

139 Norton, "shout of brutal applause": *NYT,* Dec. 30, 1895.

139 "Supremely urbane": Daniel Gregory Mason, "At Home in the Nineties," *New England Quarterly Review,* Mar., 1936, 64.

139 Students on Norton: William D. Orcutt, *Celebrities on Parade,* 41; Josephine Preston Peabody, *Diary and Letters,* 73.

139 Norton to Godkin and to English friend: q. Vanderbilt, 211; to Leslie Stephen, Jan. 8, 1896, *Letters,* II, 236.

140 Henry Adams: "dead water of the *fin de siècle*" is from *The Education,* 331. Other quotations in this paragraph are from the *Letters,* Vol. II, in order, as follows: Sept. 9, 1894, 55; Aug. 3, 1896, 114; Apr. 1, 1896, 103; Apr. 25, 1895, 68; July 31, 1896, 111; Feb. 17, 1896, 99; Sept. 25, 1895, 88.

140 Norton, "How interesting our times": to S. G. Ward, Apr. 26, 1896, *Letters,* II, 244.

141 "The Czar commands you": Fuller, 238.

141 "Tranquil greatness": Powers.

141 Reading Richard Burton: Stealey, 413.

PAGE

142   "A policy no Republican": Knight.

142   Roosevelt on Reed campaign: Oct. 18, 1895; Dec. 27, 1895; Jan. 26, 1896.

142–4 Reed's campaign: Robinson, 326–34; Griffin, 344; Platt, 313.

143   Henry Adams on Reed: to Brooks Adams, Feb. 7, 1896, *Letters,* II, 96.

143   "Chocolate eclair": Robinson, 362, calls it Reed's "alleged" statement.
       Kohlsaat, 77, gives it to Roosevelt and Peck says it was a "favorite saying"
       of Roosevelt although this does not exclude its having originated with
       Reed. To the present author it bears the stamp of Reed's picturesque turn
       of phrase.

144   Roosevelt to Reed: McCall, 228; to Lodge: Mar. 13, 1896.

144   "In a word, my dear boy": Pringle, 159.

144   Altgeld to Darrow: q. Ginger (*see* Chap. 8), 188.

145   "The whistle would not blow": *ibid.,* 191.

145   "Mark Hanna's era": Norman Hapgood, *The Advancing Hour,* 1920,
       76–77.

145   What sells a newspaper, "War": Kennedy Jones, q. Halévy (*see* Chap. 1),
       V, 9.

146   Eliot's speech in Washington: New York *Evening Post,* May 18, 1896.

146   "Degenerated sons of Harvard": Roosevelt to Lodge, Apr. 29, 1896.

146–7 Eliot characterized: In addition to James's biography, the sources used
       were:

    BROWN, ROLLO WALTER, *Harvard Yard in the Golden Age,* New York,
       1948.

    HOWE, M. A. DeWOLFE, *Classic Shades,* Boston, 1928.

    MORISON, SAMUEL ELIOT, *Three Centuries of Harvard,* Harvard Univ.
       Press, 1937.

    SEDGEWICK, ELLERY, *The Happy Profession,* Boston, 1946.

146–7 "Eliza, do you kneel . . .": James, I, 33–34; "Misunderstood": Morison,
       358; "I had a vivid sense": Brown, 27; "An oarsman's back": Sedgewick,
       371–72; "A noble presence": Howe, 185; "A gentlemen who is . . .": *ibid.;*
       "Throwing it in ANOTHER!": James, II, 69; "First private citizen":
       ibid., 92; "An emblem of triumph": Sedgewick, 371–72.

147   "If ever we come to nothing": Apr. 29, 1896.

148   Secretary Long on Roosevelt: Bishop, I, 71; Lodge to Roosevelt: Mar.
       8, 1897, q. *ibid.*

148   McClure to co-editor: Lyon, 148; to Page: *ibid.,* 167.

148   "Do nothing unrighteous": q. Puleston, 182; Roosevelt's reply: May 3,
       1897.

149   Schurz's visit to McKinley: Fuess, 350.

149   *Spectator* on the Treaty: June 19, 1897.

149   "Empire Can Wait": *Illustrated American,* Dec., 1897.

149   Bryce in the *Forum*: Dec., 1897, "The Policy of Annexation for America."

150   "Far distant, storm-beaten ships": from his *Influence of Sea Power on the
       French Revolution.*

150   Reed on Senator Proctor: Dunn, I, 234.

150   "The taste of Empire": q. Morison and Commager, *Growth of the Amer-
       can Republic,* II, 324.

150   "Dissuade a cyclone": *NYT,* Apr. 7, 1898.

151   Roosevelt to Mahan: Mar. 21, 1898.

151   Mr. Dooley on the Philippines: Dunne, 43. When Mr. Dooley asked
       Hinnissy if he could tell where the Philippines were, Hinnissy, representing
       public opinion, replied, "Mebbe I cudden't, but I'm f'r takin' thim in,
       annyhow." Mr. Dooley wasn't so sure. "Th' war is still goin' on; an' ivry

PAGE

night, whin I'm countin' up the cash, I'm askin' mesilf will I annex Cubia or lave it to the Cubians? Will I take Porther Ricky or put it by? An' what shud I do with the Ph'lippeens? Oh, what shud I do with thim?": *ibid., 46–47.*

151   McKinley on the Philippines: Kohlsaat, 68.

151   Lodge, must not "let the islands go": to Henry White, May 4, 1898, Nevins (*see* Chap. 1), 136.

151   Norton, "We jettison . . .": text of the speech in *Letters,* II, 261–69. The politician who proposed lynching was the Hon. Thomas J. Gargan.

152   The Anti-Imperialists: Lanzar, Harrington, Howe, Fuess.

152   "An abominable business": *Mark Twain–Howells Letters,* Harvard Univ. Press, 1960, II, 673, n. 4. See also Mark Twain's "To The Person Sitting in Darkness," *North American Review,* Feb., 1901.

153   Godkin on "inferior races": Mar. 24, 1898, 216.

153   Carl Schurz, same argument: Schurz, 441.

153–4   Beveridge's speeches: Bowers, 68–70, 76; Storey, 38; W. E. Leuchtenberg, "Progressivism and Imperialism, 1898–1916," *Miss. Valley Hist. Rev.,* Dec., 1952.

154   "We're a gr-reat people": Dunne, 9.

154   Roosevelt, "my power for good": Mar. 29, 1898.

155   Beveridge on Reed: to George W. Perkins, May 31, 1898, Bowers, 71.

155   "Opposition exclusively from Reed": May 31, 1898, Lodge, *Corres.,* I, 302.

155   Reed begged Clark: Dunn, I, 289.

157   Lodge, "one of the great world powers": to Henry White, Aug. 12, 1898, Nevins' *White,* 137.

157   Mahan, "the jocund youth" and *"Deus Vult!":* Puleston, 201.

157   Schurz, "the great neutral power": Fuess, 354.

157–8   Saratoga conference: *NYT,* Aug. 20, 1898.

158   Carnegie, "Let us stand together": Harvey, *Gompers* (*see* Chap. 8), 89–90.

159   Reed "terribly bitter": Dec. 20, 1898, Lodge, *Corres.,* I, 370.

160   Bryan and the Treaty: Dunn, I, 283; Hoar, I, 197; II, 110; Pettigrew, 206. The dealing in judgeships and other bribes by the Republicans is discussed in W. S. Holt, *Treaties Defeated by the Senate,* Johns Hopkins, 1933, 171, and in Garraty, *Lodge,* 201–2.

161   "Closest, hardest fight": *ibid.*

161   William James: *Letters,* II, 289; Per. y, 240.

161   Norton, "lost her unique position": Nov. 18, 1899, *Letters,* II, 290.

161   Moorfield Storey, "We are false": Howe, 221.

161   "Most influential man": Mar. 3, 1898, *Letters,* II, No. 976.

161   Storey to Hoar: Howe, 218–19.

161   "Touching a match": *NYT,* Apr. 23, 1899.

162   "Moody and ugly": Dunn, I, 298.

162   "Fatigue and disgust": *NYT,* Feb. 21, 1899.

162   *Tribune:* q. Robinson, 380; *Times,* Apr. 19 and 23, 1899.

162   Godkin on Reed: *Letters,* II, 239, 241.

163   "The public!": *NYT,* Apr. 20, 1899.

164   "How is the horse feeling?": Pringle, *Life and Times of William Howard Taft,* 1939, I, 236.

164   Beveridge, "We will not renounce": q. Wolff, 303.

164   Godkin, "the military spirit": *Life and Letters,* 243.

165   Admiral Dewey on the Presidency: Sullivan, I, 311.

165   "Evil genius": Fuess, 366.

PAGE

165   Third party and Plaza Hotel meeting: Pettigrew, 320–21; Fuess, 362–63.

165   Aguinaldo on the election: Wolff, 252.

165   "Hold your nose": Lanzar, 40.

165   *Nation*'s dissatisfied reader: Oct. 18, 1900, 307.

166   Lodge on Manila; q. Wolff, 304.

166   Roosevelt on expansion: *ibid.*, 332.

166   Dumdum bullets; *ibid.*, 305.

167   Norton's elegy: to S. G. Ward, Mar. 13, 1901, Vanderbilt, 217. An effort to heal the breach between the Anti-Imperialists and the Administration was made by Senator Hoar in the spring of 1901, with embarrassing results. As President of the Harvard Alumni Association, he offered an honorary LL.D. to McKinley without consulting the Harvard Corporation. Although President Eliot regarded McKinley as a "narrow-minded commonplace man" (James, II, 118), the Corporation gave its approval. But when the Board of Overseers, which contained a number of Anti-Imperialists, was asked for its concurrence a storm was raised, led by Moorfield Storey and Wendell Phillips Garrison. Bitter feeling developed, debate was "very sharp," and Theodore Roosevelt, thrown into a frenzy, and denouncing Storey as a "scoundrel," marshaled the votes of the waverers by mail. Leaked to Godkin, who published it in the *Nation*, Apr. 25, 1901, the opposition in the Overseers became known to McKinley. Although the Board finally voted for his degree, reportedly by 26 to 3, he did not appear at Commencement, with the result that the LL.D., which could not be conferred in absentia, was not conferred at all. Roosevelt, *Letters*, III, Nos. 2010, 2012; Howe, 177; *NYT*, May 3 and 9, 1901.

167   "That damned cowboy": Kohlsaat, 100.

167   Twenty-three poker hands: A. B. Paine, *Mark Twain*, III, 1163.

167   Joe Cannon said of him: q. McFarland.

4. "Give Me Combat"

Bibliography

BARCLAY, SIR THOMAS, *Thirty Years: Anglo-French Reminiscences, 1876–1906*, Boston, Houghton Mifflin, 1914.

*BARRÈS, MAURICE, *Scènes et doctrines du Nationalisme*, Paris, Plon, 1925.

BENDA, JULIEN, *La Jeunesse d'un clerc*, Paris, Gallimard, 1936.

BERTAUT, JULES, *Paris, 1870–1935*, New York, Appleton-Century, 1936.

*BLUM, LÉON, *Souvenirs de l'Affaire*, Paris, Gallimard, 1935.

BORDEAUX, HENRY, *Jules Lemaître*, Paris, Plon, 1920.

BOUSSEL, PATRICE, *L'Affaire Dreyfus et la Presse*, Paris, Colin, 1960.

BRUNETIÈRE, FERDINAND, *Après le Procès: Réponse à Quelques "Intellectuels,"* Paris, Perrin, 1898.

CAMBON, PAUL, *Correspondence, 1870–1924*, 3 vols., Paris, Grasset, 1940.

CASTELLANE, MARQUIS BONI DE, *How I Discovered America*, New York, Knopf, 1924.

*CHAPMAN, GUY, *The Dreyfus Case: A Reassessment*, New York, Reynal, 1955.

CLARETIE, JULES, "Souvenirs du Dîner Bixio," *La Revue de France*, June 15, July 1 and 15, August 1 and 15, 1923.

CLEMENCEAU, GEORGES, *Contre la Justice*, Paris, Stock, 1900.

CLERMONT-TONNERRE, ELIZABETH (DE GRAMONT), DUCHESSE DE, *Mémoires*, 3 vols., Paris, Grasset, 1928.

*DAUDET, LÉON, *Au Temps de Judas: Souvenirs de 1880 à 1908*, Paris, NLN, 1920.

DELHORBE, CECILE, *L'Affaire Dreyfus et les Ecrivains Français*, Paris, Attinger, 1932.

ELLIS, HAVELOCK, *From Rousseau to Proust*, Boston, Houghton Mifflin, 1935.

FRANCE, ANATOLE, *M. Bergeret à Paris*, Paris, Calmann-Lévy, 1902.

GARD, ROGER MARTIN DU, *Jean Barois*, Paris, Gallimard, 1921.

GARRIC, ROBERT, *Albert de Mun*, Paris, Flammarion, 1935.

GIRAUD, VICTOR, *Les Maîtres du l'Heure* (Jules Lemaître), Vol. II, Paris, Hachette, 1919.

GOLDBERG, HARVEY, *The Life of Jean Jaurès*, Univ. of Wisconsin Press, 1962.

GUILLEMINAULT, GILBERT, ed., *La Belle Epoque*, 3 vols., Paris, Denoël, 1957.

HERZOG, WILHELM, *From Dreyfus to Petain*, tr. Walter Sorell, New York, Creative Age Press, 1947.

HYNDMAN, H. M., *Clemenceau*, New York, Stokes, 1919.

IBELS, H. G., *Allons-y!: Histoire Contemporaine*, Paris, Stock, 1898.

JAURÈS, JEAN, *Les Preuves: Affaire Dreyfus*, Paris, *La Petite République*, 1898.

LETHEVE, JACQUES, *La Caricature et la presse sous la Troisième République*, Paris, Colin, 1961.

LONERGAN, W. F. (correspondent of the *Daily Telegraph*), *Forty Years of Paris*, New York, Brentano's, 1907.

MARTET, JEAN, *Le tigre* (Clemenceau), Paris, Albin Michel, 1930.

MASUR, GERHARD, *Prophets of Yesterday*, New York, Macmillan, 1961.

MEYER, ARTHUR, *Ce que mes yeux ont vu*, Paris, Plon, 1912.

————, *Ce que je peux dire*, Paris, Plon, 1912.

*PAINTER, GEORGE D., *Proust: The Early Years*, Boston, Little, Brown, 1959.

PALÉOLOGUE, MAURICE, *An Intimate Journal of the Dreyfus Case*, New York, Criterion, 1957.

PÉGUY, CHARLES, "Notre Jeunesse," *Cahiers de la Quinzaine*, 1910. (This was a reply to Daniel Halévy's essay on the Affair written at Péguy's invitation and published by him in the *Cahiers de la Quinzaine*. It is reprinted in English translation by Alexander Dru in *Temporal and Eternal*. New York, Harper, 1958.)

POUQUET, JEANNE SIMON, *Le Salon de Mme Arman de Caillavet*, Paris, Hachette, 1926.

PROUST, MARCEL, *A la recherche du temps perdu*, Paris, Gallimard, 1921–27.

*QUILLARD, PIERRE, *Le Monument Henry: Liste des Souscripteurs*, Paris, Stock, 1899.

RADZIWILL, PRINCESS CATHERINE, *France Behind the Veil,* New York, Funk & Wagnalls, 1914.

*RADZIWILL, PRINCESS MARIE, *Lettres au Général du Robilant,* Vol. II, 1896–1901 (the Appendix contains her correspondence with General de Galliffet), Bologna, Zanichelli, 1933.

**REINACH, JOSEPH, *Histoire de l'Affaire Dreyfus,* 7 vols., Paris, Charpentier, 1901–11.

ROLLAND, ROMAIN, *Mémoires,* Paris, Albin Michel, 1956.

ROMAN, JEAN, *Paris Fin de Siècle,* New York, Arts, Inc., 1960.

SOREL, GEORGES, *La Révolution Dreyfusienne,* Paris, Rivière, 1911.

VIZETELLY, ERNEST ALFRED, *Emile Zola,* London, John Lane, 1904.

———, *Paris and Her People,* New York, Stokes, n.d. (1918).

ZEVAÈS, ALEXANDRE, *L'Affaire Dreyfus: Quelques Souvenirs personnels, La Nouvelle Revue,* January, February, March, 1936, Vols. 141 and 142.

ZOLA, EMILE, *La Vérité en Marche* (collected ed.), Paris, Bernouard, 1928.

Notes

Since my purpose in this chapter was not to retell the story of the Dreyfus Affair but rather to show French society reacting to it, I have not thought it necessary to document the historical events of the case unless they are controversial or obscure. The basic and essential source is still Reinach's stupendous work overflowing with facts, texts, documentation, insights, comments, eyewitnessed scenes, character portraits of the leading figures he knew and his own direct experiences, such as the moment in the Chamber during de Mun's speech when "I felt on my head the hatred of three hundred hypnotized listeners." Everything that anyone said or did connected with the Affair he made it his business to collect and record, including, besides obvious matters, thousands of peripheral details such as Scheurer-Kestner's disgust with the reporter or Count Witte's flash of clairvoyance. As a major actor in, not merely an observer of, the events, Reinach was vilified, calumniated, and caricatured more than anyone excepting Zola. Under these circumstances to have put together a work of such historical value is a feat perhaps unequaled, certainly unsurpassed, in historiography. The reader may take it that any statement or quotation in this chapter not otherwise accounted for is to be found in Reinach, to be located through his Index, which occupies the entire seventh volume.

The most thoughtful expression of the Nationalist point of view is Barrès' while the most vivid and vicious is Daudet's. The best modern account—reliable, objective and of readable length—is Chapman's. For the riots at Auteuil and Longchamps I relied on the contemporary press.

PAGE

171 "Would have divided the angels themselves": in *Journal des Débats,* Mar. 8, 1903, on death of Gaston Paris, q. Barrès, 9.

173 "At your age, General": q. Lonergan, 76.

PAGE

175   Lavisse on the Grande Armée: *Histoire de France Contemporaine*, III, 379.

176   Anatole France, "all that is left": The character is M. Panneton de la Barge in *M. Bergeret à Paris*, 65–70.

176   Comte de Haussonville quoted: Paléologue, 147.

176   "France loves peace and prefers glory": said by Albert Vandal, member of the French Academy, q. *Figaro*, Sept. 25, 1898.

177   Ladies rose for General Mercier: Proust, *Guermantes*, II, 150. The Duchesse de Guermantes caused a sensation at the soirée of the Princesse de Lignes by remaining seated when other ladies rose. It was this action which helped to defeat the Duc for the Presidency of the Jockey Club.

177   "You can have it back": Reinach, I, 2.

177   "If Dreyfus is acquitted, Mercier goes": Paléologue, 44.

178   Observer reminded of Dante: *ibid.*, 198–99.

179   Bülow, "There are three Great Powers": C. Radziwill, 298.

179   Gossip on de Rodays bribed: Radziwill, *Letters,* 106.

179   Zola, a "shameful disease": *l'Aurore,* May 13, 1902, q. Boussel, 216.

179   Ernest Judet's fear of Clemenceau: Daudet, 43.

180   Arthur Meyer's career: C. Radziwill, 297–307.

180   Rochefort and Kaiser's supposed letter: Blum, 78–80; Boussel, 157–59. The story of the letter appeared in *l'Intransigeant*, Dec. 13, 1897.

180   Boisdeffre and Princess Mathilde: Radziwill, *Letters,* 133–35. Princess Radziwill told the story to the Kaiser who commented, "It's a good thing for me that such a man heads the French General Staff . . . and all I wish is that they leave him where he is."

181–2 The "Syndicate": The Right's conception of the Syndicate is expressed in all seriousness by Daudet, 11–17, and satirized by Anatole France in Chapter 9 of *M. Bergeret*. The *Dépêche de Toulouse* on Nov. 24, 1897, affirmed the existence of a *Syndicat D*. and its expenditure of 10,000,000 francs: q. Boussel, 138. Other charges from *Libre Parole l'Intransigeant, Jour, Patrie, Eclair, Echo de Paris* given with dates by Reinach, III, 20; also "Le Syndicat," *l'Aurore*, Dec. 1, 1897, in Zola, 13–19.

182   "Something very great": Count Harry Kessler, q. Masur, 297.

182   Henry Adams on reading Drumont: July 27 and Aug. 4, 1896, *Letters,* 110, 116.

183   "Clandestine and merciless conspiracy": q. Herzog, 30.

184   Duc d'Uzès felt gratified: *ibid.*, 31.

185   "They bore us with their Jew": q. Goldberg, 216.

185   Socialist review of Lazare's pamphlet: Zevaès, v. 141, 21.

186   "The Duc de Saint-Simon himself": Reinach, II, 618, n. 1.

188   Esterhazy, "hands of a brigand"; "elegant and treacherous": C. Radziwill, 326–27; Benda, 181.

188   Scheurer-Kestner like a 16th-century Huguenot: Rolland, 290.

188   Crowds in the Luxembourg gardens: described by Clemenceau in 1908 in a speech dedicating a statue to Scheurer-Kestner.

188   Clemenceau on Monet: q. J. Hampden Jackson, *Clemenceau and the Third Republic,* New York, 1962, 81.

188   "Only the artists": Martet, 286.

189   Clemenceau on Esterhazy, Jesuits, justice: q. Boussel, 143; Reinach, III, 265. The degree to which contemporary attention was focused on the Affair may be judged from Clemenceau's five volumes of collected articles: *L'Iniquité* (162 articles from *l'Aurore* and *La Justice* up to July, 1898);

PAGE

Vers la Réparation, 1899 (135 articles from *l'Aurore,* July–Dec., 1898); *Des Juges,* 1901 (40 articles from *l'Aurore,* Apr.–May, 1899); *Injustice Militaire,* 1902 (78 articles from *l'Aurore,* Aug.–Dec., 1899); *La Honte,* 1903 (65 articles from *La Dépêche de Toulouse,* Sept., 1899–Dec., 1900).

189   "Generals of debacle" *et seq.:* Reinach, III, 258.

189   Anton Radziwill "loves to talk English": Spring-Rice (*see* Chap. 3), I, 184.

189   Witte, "I can see only one thing": Reinach, II, 542, n. 1.

190   Jules Ferry, "to organize mankind": q. Goldberg, 39.

190   Léon Bourgeois to the Ralliés: q. Chapman, 23.

190   De Mun's speech to the Academy: Mar. 10, 1898. Reprinted in his *Discours politiques et Parlementaires.*

190–2   De Mun's career: Garric, *passim;* on Socialism, *ibid.,* 94.

193   Galliffet, "continue to understand nothing": to Princess Radziwill, Sept. 22, 1899, 342.

193   Comtesse de Noailles, "too beautiful to be real" and "merely smiled": C. Radziwill, 337–38.

193   "Certitude of superiority": Clermont-Tonnerre, 113.

193   Aimery de la Rochefoucauld: "fossil rigidity" was Proust's phrase for the Prince de Guermantes, for whom de Rochefoucauld served as a model. "Mere nobodies in the year 1000": q. Painter, 189.

194   Duc d'Uzès, "we were always killed": Painter, 200.

194   *Gratin* not hospitable: Clermont-Tonnerre, 113.

194   English visitor of Duc de Luynes: Wyndham (*see* Chap. 1), I, 346, 480.

194   Thiers on Comte de Paris: q. Spender, *Campbell-Bannerman* (*see* Chap. 5), II, 59.

194   Gamelba: Lonergan, 120–21.

195   "All this Dreyfus business" and "Perfectly intolerable": Proust, *Guermantes,* I.

195   "Colossus with dirty feet": Flaubert, *Correspondence,* Apr. 18, 1880.

197   "Pornographic pig," "Merde!" and other reactions: du Gard, 8.

197   Björnson, "stupor and distress": Reinach, III, 314.

197   "The scene is France": q. Herzog, 144.

198   Chekhov on Zola's trial: Ernest J. Simmons, *Chekhov: A Biography,* Boston, 1962, 412–13.

198   "Smelled of suppressed slaughter": Paléologue, 131.

199   "Paris palpitated": Hyndman (*see* Chap. 7), 301.

199–200   Zola's trial: Paléologue, 131–33; Hyndman, *Clemenceau,* 176–77; Vizetelly, 450–56; *et al.*

199   Labori "not an intellect": q. Chapman, 175.

200   Zola, "Listen to them!": Guilleminault, I, 189.

200   Clemenceau, "not a single Dreyfusard": Hyndman (*see* Chap. 7), 301.

200   Henry Adams on Zola verdict: Feb. 26, 1898, *Letters,* 151.

201   Anatole France got out of bed: from unpublished diary of Daniel Halévy, q. Delhorbe, 95–96.

201   "Altogether one of us": Daudet, 66.

201   Monet quarreled with Degas: Stephen Gwynn, *Claude Monet,* New York, Macmillan, 1934, 92.

201   Degas read *Libre Parole:* Chapman, 182; on *arrivistes:* q. George Slocombe, *Rebels of Art: Manet to Matisse,* New York, 1939, 158.

201   Debussy and Puvis de Chavannes: Painter, 356; Reinach, III, 248, n. 2.

201   "If I sign" said a school principal: Clemenceau in *l'Aurore,* Jan. 18, 1898.

202   Emile Duclaux, Revision in the laboratory: Reinach, III, 169.

PAGE

203   "He paints with his hands in my pockets": René Gimpel, *Carnets,* Paris, 1963.

203   Gaston Paris: Reinach, IV, 150, n. 5; Paul Stapfer: Zevaès, v. 141, 202.

203   Whole villages took sides: Barclay, 135.

204   Dîner Bixio: Claretie. All anecdotes of Dîner Bixio are from this source.

204   Opening of "Les Loups": Rolland, 291–95.

204   "We needed reassurance, ideals": Adolphe Brisson on "l'Aiglon," in *Figaro,* Mar. 13, 1900.

205   Ranc, "warned not to sleep at home": q. Reinach, IV, 151.

205–6   The salons: Bertaut, 163–73; Wharton (*see* Chap. 1), 261, 273; Painter, 130, 201, 281; for Mme Straus, see esp. Bertaut, Painter, 110–16, Paléologue; for Mme Arman, esp. Pouquet, *passim;* Clermont-Tonnerre, I, 4–5, 13; Blum, 98; for Mme Aubernon: Paléologue, 114; Suttner (*see* Chap. 5), I, 282–84; for Mme de Loynes: esp. Meyer, *Ce que je peux dire,* 250–53, 287; Castellane, 195.

207   Lemaître, "The Republic cured me": q. Giraud, 72.

207   "Que faite vous, Maître?": Barclay, 142.

207   Meetings of Ligue des Patriotes: Meyer, *Ce que je peux dire,* 253–63; Daudet, 89–90.

208   De Vogüé, "Now the odious case": Paléologue, 151.

209   Reciting 17th-century poetry: Goldberg, 226.

209   His "splendid amplitude": Rolland, 298; "Like a huge cat with a mouse": *ibid.*

210   Socialists on Zola's trial: Jaurès' *Œuvres,* VI, 197, q. Goldberg; Reinach, III, 255, IV, 148; Zevaès, v. 141, 97, 199.

210   Jaurès, "how tormented I am": q. Goldberg, 220.

212   "Because we seem to oppose": from a letter of Nov. 7, 1898, in the Guesde Archives, Amsterdam, q. Goldberg, 243.

212–3   Socialist Committee of Vigilance: Zevaès, v. 141, 203.

213   André Buffet telegraphed Pretender: Details of the right-wing conspiracy and its financing were obtained from evidence at the subsequent trial of Déroulède, Reinach, IV, 332–42.

213   "Eve of a new Commune": Radziwill, *Letters,* 155.

213   "Soul of a second lieutenant": André Maurois, *The Miracle of France,* New York, 1948, 404.

213   "Sanctuary of treason," *et seq.*: Paléologue, 187–90.

214   Anarchists on Dreyfus "parade": Boussel, 170–72: Maitron (*see* Chap. 2), 307–18.

214   Mme de Greffulhe wrote to the Kaiser: André Germain, *Les clés de Proust,* 1953, 43. (I am indebted for this source to Mr. George D. Painter, the biographer of Proust.)

214   Change in the Guermantes: recorded in *Sodome* and *La Prisonnière.*

215   An officer said to Galliffet: Claretie, 50.

215   Jaurès, "If war breaks out": q. Goldberg, 245.

215–6   Contributors to the Henry Subscription: Quillard, *passim.*

216   Loubet's election: Paléologue, 203; "The Republic will not founder": q. Chapman, 254.

216   Lemaître on driving Loubet out: q. Goldberg, 247.

217   Anti-Semitic League funds: Reinach, IV, 573, n. 4; V, 113, 254, n. 1, from evidence at Déroulède trial.

217   *Le Temps,* "What other country": June 6, 1899.

217   William James, "one of those moral crises": June 7, 1899, *Letters,* II, 89.

PAGE

217–8   The attack on Loubet at Auteuil: *Figaro*, June 5, 1899.

218   Next Sunday at Longchamps: *Le Temps*, June 12/13, 1899. Henri Léon, the Nationalist leader and cynic in *M. Bergeret à Paris*, describes how hooligans yelled *"Pa-na-ma! De-mis-sion!"* under his orders. "I beat time for them and they yell the separate syllables. It was really done with taste."

219   Lucien Herr's argument: from *Vie de Lucien Herr*, by Charles Andler, q. Goldberg, 254.

219–20 Socialists split on support for Government: Zevaès, v. 142, 47.

220   Marquis de Galliffet, silver-plated stomach: Castellane, 99; "air of a bandit chief": Reinach, V, 168–69; on arresting members of his club: Radziwill, *Letters*, 340; "courage and effrontery": Reinach, *loc. cit.*

221   Millerand, "cat in a downpour": Suarez (*see* Chap. 8), I, 259.

221   "Invite those chaps to dinner": from Louis Thomas, *Le Général de Galliffet*, 1910, 247 (supplied by Mr. Painter).

222–3   Rennes trial: eyewitness accounts by Marcel Prévost, New York *Herald*, Aug. 8/9; Severine and others, q. in Reinach, V; Barrès, 146; Zevaès, v. 142, 53; Benda, 211; London *Times*, New York *Tribune*, Aug. 8/9. Evidently it is a rule that discrepancies in observation increase with intensity of emotion: Dreyfus' hair was "white" according to *The Times*, "auburn-grey" according to the *Tribune;* his moustache "jet black" according to *The Times*, "frankly red" according to the *Tribune*.

223   G. A. Henty: Hyndman, 184.

223   Galliffet, "I don't budge from my office": Radziwill, *Letters*, 340.

224   Labori "looked like Hercules": Meyer, *Mes Yeux*, 152.

224   "I've just killed the Dreyfus": Paléologue, 241.

224   Queen Victoria's telegram: Reinach, V, 544.

224   Clemenceau: In *l'Aurore*, Sept. 10, 1899.

224   Comtesse de Noailles weeping: Painter, 299.

224–5   Foreign reaction to Rennes verdict: *The Times*, Sept. 12, 13, 14, 1899; Barclay, 162.

225   Grieg's "Indignation": Finck, *Grieg* (*see* Chap. 6), 104.

226   Galliffet, "That's something to see": Lonergan, 369.

5. The Steady Drummer

Bibliography

Official publications of the proceedings of the two Peace Conferences at The Hague are the following:

FRANCE, MINISTÈRE DES AFFAIRES ETRANGÈRES, Documents Diplomatiques, *Conférence Internationale de la Paix*, 1899, Paris, Imprimerie Nationale, 1900.

————, *Deuxième Conférence Internationale de la Paix*, 1907, Paris, Imprimerie Nationale, 1908.

*GERMANY, AUSWARTIGEN AMT, *Die Grosse Politik der Europäischen Kabinette*, Berlin, 1924–25. Band 15: *Rings um die Erste Haager Friedenskon-

ferenz. Band 23: *Die Zweite Haager Friedenskonferenz.* (Referred to in Notes as *GP.*)

GREAT BRITAIN, FOREIGN OFFICE, *Correspondence respecting the Proposal of HM the Emperor of Russia for a Conference on Armaments,* Russia, No. 1 (1899), Cd. 9090, London, HMSO.

————, *Correspondence respecting the Peace Conference held at The Hague in 1899,* Misc. No. 1 (1899), Cd. 9534, London, HMSO. (The material in these two volumes is referred to in the Notes as F.O. 83, 1695-6-7-8-9 and 1700. These are the reference numbers for the autograph originals in the Public Record Office which I consulted in preference to the published version.)

————, *Correspondence respecting the Second Peace Conference held at The Hague in 1907.* Misc. No. 1 (1908), Cd. 3857, London, HMSO.

————, *Further Correspondence,* Cd. 4174, Misc. No. 5 (1908).

HAGUE, THE, *The Proceedings of The Hague Peace Conference,* 4 vols. Translation of the official texts (originally published by the Netherlands Ministry of Foreign Affairs), prepared in the Division of International Law of the Carnegie Endowment for International Peace; ed. James Brown Scott, Oxford Univ. Press, 1920–21, Vol. I, 1899; Vol. II, III, IV, 1907.

UNITED STATES, *The Hague Peace Conferences of 1899 and 1907,* ed. James Brown Scott, 2 vols., Baltimore, Johns Hopkins Press, 1909. The second volume contains the instructions to and reports of the American delegates and the correspondence in 1904 and 1906 relating to the calling of the Second Conference.

Other Sources

ADAM, PAUL, "Physionomie de la Conférence de la Haye," *Revue de Paris,* August 1, 1907, 642-72.

BACON, ADMIRAL SIR REGINALD HUGH, *The Life of Lord Fisher of Kilverstone,* 2 vols., London, Hodder & Stoughton, 1929.

BERGENGREN, ENK, *Alfred Nobel,* tr., London, Nelson, 1962.

BLOCH, IVAN S., *The Future of War,* tr., with a "Conversation with the Author" by W. T. Stead, Boston, Ginn, 1902.

BÜLOW, BERNHARD, PRINCE VON, *Memoirs,* 4 vols., Boston, Little, Brown, 1931–32.

CHIROL, SIR VALENTINE, *Fifty Years in a Changing World,* New York, Harcourt, 1928.

CHOATE, JOSEPH HODGES, *The Two Hague Conferences,* Princeton Univ. Press, 1913.

CURTI, MERLE, *Peace or War: The American Struggle, 1636–1936,* New York, Norton, 1936.

DAVIS, CALVIN DE ARMOND, *The United States and the First Hague Peace Conference,* Cornell Univ. Press, 1962.

DILLON, E. J., *The Eclipse of Russia,* New York, Doran, 1918.

FISHER, JOHN ARBUTHNOT, LORD, *Records,* London, Hodder & Stoughton, 1919.

FISHER, JOHN ARBUTHNOT, LORD, *Fear God and Dread Nought: Correspondence of Lord Fisher,* ed. Arthur J. Marder, Vol. 1, 1854–1904, Harvard Univ. Press, 1952; Vol. 2, 1904–14, London, Cape, 1956.

FULLER, J. F. C., *Armament and History,* New York, Scribner's, 1945.

HENDRICK, BURTON J., *The Life of Andrew Carnegie,* 2 vols., Garden City, Doubleday, 1932.

HULL, WILLIAM I., *The Two Hague Conferences,* Boston, Ginn, 1908.

JESSUP, PHILIP G., *Elihu Root,* 2 vols., New York, Dodd, Mead, 1938.

LEMONON, ERNEST, *La Seconde Conférence de le Paix,* Paris, 1908.

MOWAT, ROBERT B., *Life of Lord Pauncefote,* Boston, Houghton Mifflin, 1929.

NEF, JOHN J., *War and Human Progress,* Harvard Univ. Press, 1950.

NOWAK, KARL FRIEDRICH, *Germany's Road to Ruin,* New York, Macmillan, 1932.

PALMER, FREDERICK, *With My Own Eyes,* Indianapolis, Bobbs Merrill, 1932.

PINSON, KOPPEL S., *Modern Germany,* New York, Macmillan, 1954.

SPENDER, J. A., *The Life of Sir Henry Campbell-Bannerman,* 2 vols., Boston, Houghton Mifflin, 1924.

STEAD, W. T., "Character Sketch: Lord Fisher," *Review of Reviews,* February, 1910.

*SUTTNER, BERTHA VON, *Memoirs,* 2 vols., Boston, Ginn, 1910.

TATE, MERZE, *The Disarmament Illusion,* New York, Macmillan, 1942.

Temps, Le, Reports of Special Correspondent at The Hague.

USHER, ROLAND, *Pan-Germanism,* Boston, Houghton Mifflin, 1913.

*WHITE, ANDREW D., *Autobiography,* 2 vols., New York, Century, 1905.

*WHYTE, FREDERIC, *Life of W. T. Stead,* London, Cape, 1925.

WITTE, COUNT SERGEI, *Memoirs,* New York, Doubleday, 1921.

WOLFF, THEODOR (editor of *Berliner Tageblatt*), *The Eve of 1914,* tr. E. W. Dickes, New York, Knopf, 1936.

Notes

As primary sources for what was said and what occurred at The Hague, I used the delegates' reports to their Governments contained in the Foreign Office Correspondence and *Grosse Politik;* the account in diary form by Andrew White in his *Autobiography,* and the reports of the Special Correspondent of *Le Temps.* Written while events were still hot, these make livelier reading than the tedious verbatim proceedings, collected and edited afterward. (*Le Temps'* correspondent signed himself X or sometimes XX, suggesting the possibility of two different people. Inquiries to *Le Monde,* successor of *Le Temps,* and to the Archivist of the Quai d'Orsay failed to penetrate his anonymity.) Unless otherwise stated all quotations by the delegates are from these sources; specific references are given only where it seems important. All material relating to Baroness von Suttner, including Nobel's letters, is from her *Memoirs.* All quotations from Roosevelt are from his *Letters* (*see* Chap. 3).

PAGE

229 "The Czar with an olive branch": *Neue Freie Presse,* q. *Figaro,* roundup of press comment, Aug. 30, 1898.

230 "It will sound like beautiful music" and other press quotations in this paragraph: *ibid.;* also *The Times* and *Le Temps,* roundup of foreign press comment, same date.

230 Kipling: The poem was first published in *Literature,* Oct. 1, 1898.

231 "A sword stroke in water": q. *Figaro,* Aug. 31, 1898. "Our future": Nowak, 237.

231 Liebknecht: Suttner, II, 198.

231 Godkin, "splendid summons": *Evening Post,* Aug. 29, 1898.

234 Olney on defeat of Arbitration Treaty: Mowat, 171.

234 Julien Benda: (*see* Chap. 4), 203.

234 Figures on world's mechanical energy: W. S. and E. S. Woytinsky, *World Population and Production,* New York, 1953, 930, Table 394.

236 "We are sailing with a corpse": q. Masur (*see* Chap. 4), 237.

236 Salisbury's Guildhall speech: *The Times,* Nov. 10, 1897.

236 Czar and his mother's chambermaids: q. David Shub, *Lenin,* 72.

236 Czar's letter to his mother: *Secret Letters of the Last Czar,* ed. E. J. Bing, New York, 1938, 131.

237 Kuropatkin and genesis of Peace Conference: Witte, 96–97; Report of German Ambassador Radolin to Chancellor Hohenlohe, July 13, 1899, *GP,* XV, No. 4350; Dillon, conversation with Kuropatkin, 275–77.

237 "Keep people from inventing things": q. White, II, 70.

238 "Except at the price of suicide," *et seq.:* Bloch, xxxi, lxii, 349, 355–56.

239 British Ambassador's report: Sir Charles Scott to Salisbury, Aug. 25, 1898, Cd. 9090.

239 "It is the greatest nonsense": Warwick, 138.

239–40 Diplomatic reactions: *GP,* XV, Nos. 4223, 4224, 4236, 4237, 4248, 4249; also Foreign Office, Plunkett from Brussels, Jan. 11, 1899; Rumbold from Vienna, Feb. 3, 1899.

240 Kaiser, "Idiot": *GP,* XV, No. 4233.

240 "To my People": Pinson, 279; "When your Emperor commands": *ibid.,* 278; "There is only one master": *ibid.;* "Me and my 25 army corps": q. Bernadotte Schmitt, *The Coming of the War, 1914,* New York, 1930, I, 29; "Ally of my House": q. Chirol, 275.

240–1 Prince of Wales, "how different" and not so absurd: q. White, II, 113–14.

241 Kaiserin on Kaiser's annoyance: Bülow, I, 275; Eulenberg quoted: *ibid.*

241 Kaiser's telegram to Czar and subsequent comments: *GP,* XV, Nos. 4222, 4216, 4228, 4231.

241 Muraviev told Eulenberg: *ibid.,* 4231.

242 Kuno Francke pictured Germany: "German Ideals of Today," *Atlantic Monthly,* Dec., 1905.

243 Pan-German program and "We want territory": *Encyc. Brit.,* "Pan-Germanism."

243 Admiral Dewey, on German bad manners: Palmer, 115.

243 Hay, "To the German mind": q. A. L. P. Dennis, in S. F. Bemis, ed., *American Secretaries of State,* IX, 124.

243 "Sheepsheads": Pinson, 278.

244 "Not even the tamest liberal": Wolff, 310.

244 "Always wear a good black coat": q. Pinson, 286.

244 Bülow and the lapels: Nowak, 226.

244 Holstein's explanation and Bülow's instructions: *GP,* XV, Nos. 4255, 4217, 4245-6-7.

PAGE

245   Public resolutions: F.O. 83, 1699.

245   Balfour, "A sanguine view": *ibid.*

245–8   Stead: All the material on Stead in these pages is from Whyte's biography with the exception of the story about Charles II, which is from Esher, I, 229; the Prince of Wales's opinion of the Czar as "weak as water," which is from Warwick, 136; and the Russian complaint of being "embarrassed," which was relayed by Ambassador Sir Charles Scott, Jan. 14, 1899, F.O. 83, 1699.

248   Henley, "the battle spirit": from "Rhymes and Rhythms," No. XVI, first published in *Poems,* 1898.

248   Nevinson: *Changes and Chances* (*see* Chap. 1), 130.

250   Mahan, "no greater misfortune": q. Puleston (*see* Chap. 3), 171.

250   "Assured of certain certainties": T. S. Eliot, "The Waste Land."

250   Yeats' poem: in his autobiography, *The Trembling of the Veil,* 415.

251   Boston Peace Crusade "permanent tribunal": Davis, 62.

251   McKinley urged to appoint Eliot: *ibid.,* 68.

252   Kaiser on Mahan, "Our greatest foe": *GP,* XV, n. to 4250.

252   Bourgeois, "amiable, elegant": Zevaès (*see* Chap. 4), v. 141, 202; "cultivated fine beard": Suarez (*see* Chap. 8), I, 420.

252   "To renounce war": General Barail, q. *Figaro,* Aug. 31, 1898.

252   Mme Adam, "I am for war": Suttner, II, 233.

253   "Beating empty air": q. Davis, 88.

253   Baron Stengel's pamphlet: Drummond to F.O., Apr. 6, 1899; Tate, 230, n. 44.

254   "Never give way": Mowat, 300; "soul of honor": *ibid.,* 295.

254   "When Peel lost his temper": Birrell (*see* Chap. 7), 126–27.

254–5   Fisher: the material in these three paragraphs is from Bacon's biography except for the last line, "So I did," which is from Fisher's *Records,* 55.

255–6   The Hague during the Conference: chiefly from reports by the correspondent of *Le Temps,* May 10, 20, 24, 25; *Figaro,* May 20; White, Mowat, Suttner. The Huis ten Bosch was visited by author in 1963.

256   "A printer's error": q. Davis, 86.

256   Beernaert "greatest cynic": Neal Ascherson, *The King Incorporated,* London, 1963, 142.

257   Münster, "political riff-raff": *GP,* XV, 4327.

258   Reichstag deputies: *The Times,* May 11, 1899.

259   Fisher, "humanizing war!" *et seq.*: Stead, *Review of Reviews,* Feb., 1910, 117.

259   Hotel Kurhaus: *Letters,* I, 142.

259   Stead on Fisher: q. Bacon, I, 121.

259   He learned from German naval delegate: *ibid.,* 128, 177.

260   "Deepest seriousness": q. Taylor (*see* Chap. 3), 99.

260   Fisher on neutral coal: Bacon, I, 128.

260   Captain Siegel's argument: *GP,* XV, 4274.

262   Ardagh's speech on dumdums: June 14, F.O. 83, 1695.

263   "The angel of arbitration": q. Reinach (*see* Chap. 4), V, 173, n. 2.

263   Society's "awful conscience": Hunter (*see* Chap. 8), 30.

263   D'Estournelles' story of Jaurès: White, 300.

264   Kaiser, "this whole hoax": *GP,* XV, 4276.

265   Efforts to persuade Germany on arbitration: White, II, 265–313. Pauncefote Memorandum, June 19, F.O. 83, 1695, and other reports in F.O. 83, 1700; *GP,* XV, 4276, 4280, 4284, 4317, 4320, 4349.

266   Kaiser's disgust, "I consented . . .": *GP,* XV, 4320.

PAGE

266   "Zeal almost macabre": *Le Temps,* editorial, July 27.

266   Mahan blocks arbitration: Puleston (*see* Chap. 3), 211; White, 338–41.

267   As if the hand of God: Clynes (*see* Chap. 7), 98; "With a kind of shiver": M. Radziwill, *Letters* (*see* Chap. 4), Jan. 2, 1900, 237.

268   Kaiser to Fritz Krupp: from the Krupp archives, q. William Manchester, "The House of Krupp," *Holiday,* Dec., 1964, 110.

268   Three hundred men "all acquainted": q. Kessler (*see* Chap. 8), 121.

268   "Then in 1900," wrote Yeats: Introduction to *Oxford Book of Modern Verse.*

268   Henry Adams expecting a bomb: *Education,* 494–95.

269–70   Exposition: *l'Illustration* and *Le Monde Illustré, passim* through the summer; *Outlook,* Sept. 8, Nov. 10, 1900, Jan. 5, 1901; *Harper's Monthly,* Sept., 1900; *Blackwood's,* July, 1900; *Nation,* June 28, 1900.

270   "It seemed merely a matter of decades": Zweig (*see* Chap. 6), 3.

271   Balfour wished to appoint Mahan Regius Professor: Magnus, *Edward VII,* 306.

272   Jusserand and Philander Knox on Roosevelt: Jules Jusserand, *What Me Befell,* Boston, 1934, 241; Sullivan (*see* Chap. 3), II, 438 n.

272   Roosevelt's visit to Eliot: James, *Eliot* (*see* Chap. 3), II, 159.

273   Roosevelt, "foolish theory": to Spring-Rice, Dec. 21, 1907, VI, 871; "weakening of fighting spirit": *ibid.;* "I abhor men like Hale: to Speck von Sternberg, July 16, 1907, V, 721; "General softening of fibre": to Whitelaw Reid, Sept. 11, 1905, V, 19.

273   Kaiser, "That's my man!": Bülow, I, 658.

273   D'Estournelles' visit to Roosevelt: Suttner, II, 390–91.

273   Hay, "I have it all arranged": Tyler Dennett, *John Hay,* New York, 1933, 346.

275   Fisher proposes to "Copenhagen" German fleet: Bacon, II, 74–75.

275   "Ach, that damned Reichstag!": Bülow, II, 36–37.

275   Czar's hint conveyed to Washington: Roosevelt to Carl Schurz, Sept. 15, 1905, V, 30–31. The letter to Root, Sept. 14, 1905, V, 26.

275   C.-B., "so straight, so good-tempered": Lee (*see* Chap. 1), II, 442.

276   C.-B., "What nobler role": at Albert Hall, Dec. 21, 1905, Spender, II, 208.

276   Damnable, Domineering and Dictatorial: Bacon, I, 207.

277   Izvolsky, "a craze of Jews": *GP,* XXIII, 7879.

277   C.-B., "Long live the Duma!": C.-B. delivered the speech in French, Spender, II, 264.

278   Kaiser hoped Conference "would not take place": *GP,* XXIII, 7815. On King Edward's visit: *ibid.;* also 7823, 7825-26.

278   "Alert, aggressive, military": to Oscar Straus, Feb. 27, 1906, V, 168.

278   "Maudlin extreme": to Reid, Aug. 7, 1906, V, 348; talk with Count Gleichen: Lee, II, 437. Another visitor who found American amenities less than satisfactory was Count Witte. During his mission to the Portsmouth Peace Conference he said the only decent meal he had had in America was on board Morgan's yacht (Witte, 169).

278   Navy "more potent for peace": Sept. 22, 1906, V, 421.

279   Carnegie agreed to donate Peace palace: Hendrick, II, 164.

279   Root, "failures necessary steps": Jessup, II, 70.

279   First issue of the *Nation*: Mar. 2, 1907.

280   "I suppose he will support": Lee, II, 467.

280   Sir Edward Grey and all other diplomatic exchanges: Nevins (*see* Chap. 1), 249, 252, 258–59; Hull, 49–50; U. S., Scott, Vol. II; *GP,* XXIII, 7750, 7869, 7927, 7986.

PAGE
281 Carnegie's visit to Kaiser: Hendrick, II, 299–318.
281 Mahan, "prepossession of the public mind": Puleston (*see* Chap. 3), 270, 280.
282 German officers drank to "The Day": Usher, 1.
282 Visiting Englishman at spa near Bayreuth: Buchan (*see* Chap. 1), 55.
282 Root, "tendency toward war": Jessup, II, 25.
282 Landsowne on Old Age Pensions: *The Times*, July 21, 1908.
283 Marquis de Soveral: Warwick, *Discretions*, 20; also F. Ponsonby, 216 (*both* Chap. 1).
283 "A damned good fellow": q. Mowat, 297.
284 Baron Marschall's appearance and habits: Gardiner, *Pillars* (*see* Chap. 1), 160–68; Barclay (*see* Chap. 4), 281. His opinions of delegates: to Bülow, July 28, 1907, *GP*, XXIII, 7961.
284 Austin's letter to *The Times:* Oct. 17, 1907.
285 Domela Nieuwenhuis: Adam, 655.
285 Fry's speech and comments: Hull, 72–74; White, II, 291.
286–8 Proceedings of the Conference: Scott, I, 110, *et seq*. Baron Marschall's report to Bülow, *GP*, XXIII, 7963; Grey's instructions on limiting "prospective liability" is No. 11 in F.O. correspondence, Cd. 3857.
287 Roosevelt, "I have not followed": July 2, 1907, V, 700; "Utterly disgusted": July 16, 1907, V, 720–21.
287 "Decayed Oriental states": M. W. Hazeltine, "The Second Peace Conference," *North American Review*, Nov., 1907.
287 "Was it a Peace Conference?": q. Choate, 40.
288 "Gradual, tentative, delicate": Choate, 22.

6. "Neroism Is in the Air"

Bibliography

ALDRICH, RICHARD (music critic of the New York *Times* for this period), *Concert Life in New York, 1902–23*, New York, Putnam's, 1941.

BAUMONT, MAURICE, *L'Affaire Eulenberg et les Origines de la guerre mondiale*, Paris, Payot, 1933.

BEECHAM, SIR THOMAS, *A Mingled Chime*, New York, Putnam's, 1943.

———, *Frederick Delius*, New York, Knopf, 1960.

BERTAUX, FELIX, *A Panorama of German Literature, 1871–1931*, tr., New York, Whittlesey, 1935.

BIGELOW, POULTNEY, *Prussian Memories, 1864–1914*, New York, Putnam's, 1915.

BRANDES, GEORG, *Friedrich Nietzsche*, New York, Macmillan, n.d.

CLADEL, JUDITH, *Rodin*, New York, Harcourt, 1937.

*DEL MAR, NORMAN, *Richard Strauss*, New York, Free Press of Glencoe, 1962.

DUKES, ASHLEY, *Modern Dramatists*, Chicago, Sergel, 1912.

EKMAN, KARL, *Jean Sibelius*, New York, Knopf, 1938.

FINCK, HENRY T., *Grieg and His Music*, London, John Lane, 1909.

*———, *Richard Strauss*, Boston, Little, Brown, 1917.

———, *Success in Music*, New York, Scribner's, 1909.

GILMAN, LAWRENCE, *Nature in Music and Other Studies*, London, John Lane, 1914.

GOOCH, G. P., *Germany*, New York, Scribner's, 1925.

GRIGORIEV, S. L. (stage manager for Diaghilev), *The Diaghilev Ballet, 1909–29*, London, Penguin Ed., 1960.

HAMBURGER, *see* Hofmannsthal.

HASKELL, ARNOLD L. (director of the Covent Garden Royal Ballet), *Diagileff*, New York, Simon & Schuster, 1935.

HELFFERICH, KARL, *Germany's Economic Progress and National Wealth, 1888–1913*, Berlin, Stilke, 1913.

HOFMANNSTHAL, HUGO VON, *Selected Plays and Libretti*, ed. Michael Hamburger, New York, Bollingen-Pantheon, 1963.

HUNEKER, JAMES, *Overtones*, New York, Scribner's, 1904.

JEFFERSON, ALAN, *The Operas of Richard Strauss in Britain*, London, Putnam's, 1963.

KARSAVINA, TAMARA, *Theatre Street*, London, Constable, 1948.

KESSLER, COUNT HARRY, *Walter Rathenau*, London, Howe, 1929.

KOHN, HANS, *The Mind of Germany*, New York, Scribner's, 1960.

LAWTON, MARY, *Schumann-Heink*, New York, Macmillan, 1928.

LEHMANN, LOTTE, *Five Operas and Richard Strauss*, New York, Macmillan, 1964.

LOWIE, ROBERT HARRY, *Toward Understanding Germany*, Univ. of Chicago Press, 1954.

MAY, ARTHUR J., *The Hapsburg Monarchy*, Harvard Univ. Press, 1951.

MILLER, ANNA IRENE, *The Independent Theatre in Europe, 1887 to the Present*, New York, Long & Smith, 1931.

NEMIROVITCH-DANTCHENKO, VLADIMIR, *My Life in the Russian Theatre*, Boston, Little, Brown, 1936.

NEWMAN, ERNEST, *Richard Strauss*, London, John Lane, 1908. (With a valuable Memoir by Alfred Kalisch.)

NIJINSKY, ROMOLA, *Nijinsky*, New York, Simon & Schuster, 1934.

POLLARD, PERCIVAL, *Masks and Minstrels of New Germany*, Boston, Luce, 1911.

*ROLLAND, ROMAIN, *Correspondance; Fragments de Journal* (No. 3 in *Cahiers Romain Rolland*), Paris, Albin Michel, 1951.

———, "Souvenirs sur Richard Strauss," in *Les Œuvres Libres*, Nouv. Serie, No. 27, Paris, 1948. (Much of this duplicates material in the *Correspondance* and *Journal* and parts of both appear in Rolland's *Musicians of Today*, New York, Holt, 1914.)

ROSENFELD, PAUL, *Musical Portraits*, New York, Harcourt, 1920.

———, *Discoveries of a Music Critic*, New York, Harcourt, 1936.

SCHOENBERNER, FRANZ, *Confessions of a European Intellectual*, New York, Macmillan, 1946.

SHAW, GEORGE BERNARD, *The Sanity of Art* (originally published 1895), New York, Borri, 1907.

SHAW, STANLEY, *William of Germany*, New York, Macmillan, 1913.

SOKOLOVA, LYDIA, *Dancing for Diaghilev*, New York, Macmillan, 1961.

SPEYER, EDWARD, *My Life and Friends*, London, Cobden-Sanderson, 1937.

*STRAUSS, RICHARD, and HOFMANNSTHAL, HUGO VON, tr., *Correspondence*, London, Collins, 1961.

STRAVINSKY, IGOR, *Autobiography*, New York, Simon & Schuster, 1936.

TERRY, ELLEN, *The Russian Ballet*, London, Sidgwick, 1913.

THOMAS, ROSE FAY, *Memoirs of Theodore Thomas*, New York, Moffat, Yard, 1911.

THOMPSON, OSCAR, *Debussy, Man and Artist*, New York, Dodd, Mead, 1937.

TOVEY, DONALD FRANCIS, *A Musician Talks*, 2 vols., Oxford Univ. Press, 1941.

VAN VECHTEN, CARL, "The Secret of the Russian Ballet" and "Igor Stravinsky: A New Composer," in *Music After the Great War and Other Studies*, New York, Schirmer, 1915.

WERFEL, ALMA MAHLER, *And the Bridge Is Love*, New York, Harcourt, 1958.

WOOD, SIR HENRY, *My Life of Music*, London, Gollancz, 1938.

WYLIE, I. A. R., *The Germans*, Indianapolis, Bobbs-Merrill, 1911.

*ZWEIG, STEFAN, *World of Yesterday*, New York, Viking, 1943.

Notes

All biographical facts about Strauss not otherwise identified and all quoted comments about him by German critics and musicologists are from Finck. Separate references for comments or anecdotes by Rolland, Beecham, Newman, Mme Mahler (Werfel), Speyer, Stravinsky and others whose works are listed above are given *only* when the source is not obvious. By good fortune the celebration by major orchestras of Strauss's centenary in 1964, the year in which this chapter was written, enabled me to hear all his major works within the space of several months. Many of the program notes for these concerts, though ephemeral and therefore not listed in the Bibliography, were useful.

PAGE

291   "Tremble as they listened": Rolland, *Journal*, 125.

292   Frankfurt's musical life: Speyer, 79.

293   Bayreuth: Stravinsky, 60; Beecham, 55; Ekman, 125.

296   Shades of evening fell three times: Grove's *Dictionary of Music*, "Program Music."

296   "Oh, they are only imitators": q. Speyer, 143.

297   "Stop Hanslick": Werner Wolff, *Anton Bruckner*, New York, 1942, 103.

298   "So young, so modern": q. *Current Biography*, 1944, "Strauss."

300   "Positive horror of his countrymen": Brandes, 113.

300   Rodin on Nietzsche: Anne Leslie, *Rodin*, New York, 1937, 200.

301   "Too much music in Germany": *Souvenirs*, 232–33.

302   Brunhilde's horse: Haskell, 156.

302   Philip Ernst: *Current Biography*, 1942, "Max Ernst."

302   North and South Germans: Wylie, 29–38.

303   Max Liebermann on statues: Frederic William Wile, *Men Around the Kaiser*, Philadelphia, 1913, 168.

PAGE

303   Berlin Landlady's bill: Zweig, 113.

303   "Extremely rough": Chirol (see Chap. 5), 266.

303   Berlin women: Wylie, 192–93.

303   Seven meals a day: However unlikely, this was the report of the American Ambassador, James W. Gerard, *My Four Years in Germany*, New York, 1917, 56.

304   Number of university students in Prussia: Charles Singer, *et al.*, *A History of Technology*, Oxford Univ. Press, 1958, V, 787–88.

304   Barnum and Bailey's circus: Dexter Fellows, *This Way to the Big Show*, New York, 1936, 22; H. L. Watkins, *Barnum and Bailey in the Old World, 1897–1901*, 45. (I am indebted for these references to Mrs. Janise Shea.)

305   Kaiser at the Moscow Art Theater: Nemirovitch-Dantchenko. Material in this and the following four paragraphs is chiefly from the chapter "The Kaiser and the Arts" in the book by Stanley Shaw. The prize to Wildenbruch is from Lowie, 41; the Rhodes scholars from the *Letters* of Cecil Spring-Rice, II, 119; the adventure with Peer Gynt from Finck's *Grieg*, 145–46.

307–8   "Bismarck has broken": q. Kohn, 187–88.

308   Strauss's interview with the Kaiser was told to Rolland, q. Del Mar, 280–81.

309   Strauss becomes engaged: *ibid.*, 121–22.

309   Frau Strauss, character and habits: Lehmann, chaps. 2 and 3.

309   "Screaming like hell": Del Mar, 182.

309   Toast at the Speyers': Wood, 216.

310   "*Jetzt gehst componieren*": q. William Leon Smyser, in *The New Book of Modern Composers*, ed. David Ewen, New York, 1961, 396. "Put down that pencil": q. F. Zweig, *Stefan Zweig*, New York, 1946, 103.

312   "Neroism is in the air": *Journal*, Jan. 22, 1898, 118.

313   "Arbeitsmann" as Socialist anthem: Pinson (see Chap. 5), 262.

314   Made critics pay for seats: Huneker, in *NYT*, Nov. 24, 1912.

315   Debussy, "If people insist": Thompson, 183.

315   Sibelius, "Play the record again": Told by William Golding, q. Maurice Dolbier, in New York *Herald Tribune*, Apr. 21, 1964.

315   Debussy on Strauss: Thompson, 182–83.

315   Strauss on Debussy: Caesar Searchinger, "Richard Strauss As I Knew Him," *Saturday Review of Literature*, Oct. 29, 1949.

317   Sargent and gypsy band: Mount (see Chap. 1), 217.

317   Thomas, "the greatest musician": Thomas, 502.

317   "Big, broad, ample and simple": Charles Moore, *The Life and Times of Charles Follen McKim*, Boston, 1929, 85.

317   Tiffany's house: Werfel, 47–48.

318   "A day in my family life": Gilman, *Harper's Weekly*, Mar. 9, 1907.

318   "All the sacred elephants in India": Beecham, *Delius*, 129.

318   Grieg to Delius: *ibid.*, 129.

319   "Lack of courtesy" at Strasbourg: Rolland, 213.

319   "Tyrian purple and tired silver": Wilde to Frances Forbes Robertson, Feb. 23, 1893, *Letters* (see Chap. 1), 333.

319   *Salome* denounced by *The Times*: q. *ibid.*, 335 n.

319   Beardsley's drawings: *ibid.*, 344, n. 3.

322   "See life as ferocious and sinister": to A. C. Benson, June 29, 1896, *Henry James: Letters to A. C. Benson*, London, 1930, 35.

322   "A torrent of sex": Horace B. Samuel, *Modernities*, London, 1914, 135.

324   Star of Bethlehem: Del Mar, 281.

PAGE

324   Kaiserin's hats: Mary Ethel McAuley, *Germany in War Time,* Chicago, 1917, 183; double bed: Palmer (*see* Chap. 5), 222; canceled *Feuersnot*: Del Mar, 236.

324   Kaiser on *Salome* and Strauss's reply: Del Mar, 281.

324–5   *Salome* in New York: *Outlook,* Feb. 9, 1907; Gilman, *Harper's Weekly,* Feb. 9, 1907; Aldrich, 172–79.

325   *Salome* in London: Beecham, 161, 168–73.

325–6   Von Hofmannsthal: Zweig, 46–48; Hamburger, xxvii; Bertaux, 95.

326   "Capua of the mind": Bertaux, 92.

326   *"Es gibt nur eine Kaiserstadt"*: May, 309.

326–7   "Affably tolerant" and Franz Joseph never read a book: Zweig, 19, 21.

327   Roosevelt on the "Austrian gentleman": q. Wharton (*see* Chap. 1), 277.

327   Karl Luger: Zweig, 105; May, 311.

328   Hofmannsthal's notes on Greek themes: Hamburger, xxxii. The common assumption that Hofmannsthal's *Elektra* was influenced by Freud is historical conclusion-jumping for which there is no evidence. Ernest Jones, Freud's biographer, points out (*Freud,* I, 360, and II, 8) that the publication of *The Interpretation of Dreams* in Nov., 1899, awakened no interest in Viennese intellectual circles. Although Hofmannsthal owned a copy, there is no evidence when he acquired it and his correspondence does not discuss it. Hamburger, xxxiii.

329   "Summit of contemporary fame": Dukes, 68.

329–30   Eulenberg affair: Baumont; Wolff (*see* Chap. 5).

331   Hulsen-Haeseler's death: Zedlitz-Trutzschler, Robert, Graf von, *Twelve Years at the Imperial German Court,* New York, 1924. The episode is discussed in every biography of the Kaiser.

331   Rhodes Scholars: Spring-Rice, II, 119.

332   Professor Simmel: Schoenberner, 55–56.

332   University of Berlin centenary: *ibid.,* 58.

332   Strauss's income in 1908: Finck, *Success in Music,* 14.

333   *Elektra* rehearsals: Schumann-Heink (Lawton, 322–25). According to this version, Strauss said, "I still can't hear the Heink's voice," meaning, presumably, that he was addressing his "Louder!" to her. Finck, on the other hand, who says he obtained the story directly from Schumann-Heink herself, gives it the other way around, and his version is the one generally repeated. To the present author, it is a puzzle why Strauss should have wanted to drown out the singer's voice in a part he himself had composed, but since I am not the first to find his actions occasionally baffling, I have given the accepted version of the incident.

333   Premiere of *Elektra*: Arthur Abell, in *Musical Courier,* Feb. 17, 1909; Hermann Bahr's article, q. Rosenfeld, *Discoveries,* 141–42.

334   *Elektra* in London: Finck, 252–53; Beecham, 147; Jefferson, 22; GBS in the *Nation,* Mar. 19, 1910.

335   Strauss's explanation for female Octavian: Lehmann, chap. 2.

336   Comtesse de Noailles, "something new": q. Haskell, 184.

337   Rodin, "classical sculpture": q. Albert E. Elsen, *Rodin,* New York, Museum of Modern Art, 1964.

337   "A soaring of feelings" on Blériot's triumph: Zweig, 196.

338   Quoted descriptions of Rubinstein, Pavlova, Karsavina: Haskell, 188.

338   Bakst jumped on a chair: Grigoriev, 39.

339   *Schéhérazade*: Terry, 41–44.

339   Karsavina, vice "with verisimilitude": Van Vechten, 81.

339　Premiere of *Firebird*: Unless otherwise stated, Stravinsky is the source for this and other performances of his works for the Ballet.

340　"It was exciting to be alive" and "night after night entranced": Leonard Woolf, *Beginning Again*, New York, 1963–64, 37.

340–1　Premiere of *Faun*: Nijinsky, 172–74; Cladel, 218–21; *Le Gaulois*, May 30; *Le Temps*, May 31; *Figaro*, May 29–31; *Current Lit.*, Aug., 1912, "The Faun That Has Startled Paris."

341　Incident in Vienna: Nijinsky, 194–95.

341　Kaiser on *Cleopatra*: Stravinsky, 67.

343　Premiere of *Sacre*: Stravinsky, 72; Nijinsky, 202; *Figaro*, May 31; *Le Temps*, June 3; *Le Gaulois*, June 1, 1913; Van Vechten (*q.v.*) was the American who was hit on the head.

343　Kessler, "too scrupulous an accuracy": q. *Lit. Digest*, June 20, 1914.

344　Crown Prince's book: q. *The Times*. May 1, 1913.

344　"*Muss-Preussen*": Ford (*see* Chap. 1), 402–3.

345　Rathenau's "Festal Song": *Zukunft*, Oct. 26, 1912, 128–36. The poem was signed "Herwart Raventhal."

345　Zabern, "*finis Germaniae*" and "Keep it up!" (*Immer feste darauf!*): Wolff (*see* Chap. 5), 341–44. Full accounts of the Zabern affair are given by J. Kaestlé, *l'Affaire de Saverne*, Strasbourg, n.d., and Charles D. Hazen, *Alsace-Lorraine Under German Rule*, New York, 1917.

345–6　Gilman in January: *North American Review*, Jan., 1914.

346　Ballet's London season of 1914: *Annual Register*, Part II, 73.

347　Night of the performance at Drury Lane: Siegfried Sassoon, *The Weald of Youth*, 245.

347　Strauss at Oxford: *The Times*, June 25, 1914.

7. Transfer of Power

Bibliography

(in addition to those listed for Chapter 1)

BIRKENHEAD, EARL OF, *Contemporary Personalities*, London, Cassell, 1924.

BIRKENHEAD, SECOND EARL OF, *F. E., Earl of Birkenhead*, by his son, London, Eyre & Spottiswoode, 1960.

BIRRELL, AUGUSTINE, *Things Past Redress*, London, Faber, 1937.

BROCKWAY, FENNER, *Inside the Left*, London, Allen & Unwin, 1942.

BRYCE, JAMES, VISCOUNT, *The Hindrances to Good Citizenship* (Yale Lectures), Yale Univ. Press, 1909.

CLYNES, JOHN ROBERT, *Memoirs*, Vol. I, London, Hutchinson, 1937.

FULFORD, ROGER, *Votes for Women*, London, Faber, 1957.

GARDINER, A. G., *Portraits and Portents*, New York, Harper, 1926.

HEARNSHAW, F. J. C., ed., *Edwardian England, 1901–10*, London, Benn, 1933.

HOBSON, JOHN ATKINSON, *The Social Problem*, London, Nisbet, 1901.

HUGHES, EMRYS, *Keir Hardie*, London, Allen & Unwin, 1956.

HYNDMAN, HENRY M., *The Record of an Adventurous Life,* New York, Macmillan, 1911.

JENKINS, ROY, *Mr. Balfour's Poodle,* London, Heinemann, 1954.

JONES, THOMAS, *Lloyd George,* Harvard Univ. Press, 1951.

*MASTERMAN, C. F. G., *The Condition of England,* London, Methuen, 1909.

MASTERMAN, LUCY, *C. F. G. Masterman: A Biography,* London, Nicholson, 1939.

*MENDELSSOHN, PETER DE, *The Age of Churchill, 1874–1911,* London, Thames & Hudson, 1961.

NICOLSON, HAROLD, *King George the Fifth,* London, Constable, 1952.

NOWELL-SMITH, SIMON, ed., *Edwardian England, 1901–14,* Oxford Univ. Press, 1964.

PANKHURST, E. SYLVIA, *The Suffragette,* New York, Sturgis, 1911.

———, *The Suffragette Movement* (re-issue), London, Longmans, 1932.

POPE-HENNESSY, JAMES, *Lord Crewe: The Likeness of a Liberal,* London, Constable, 1955.

SAMUEL, HERBERT, *Grooves of Change* (English title: *Memoirs*), Indianapolis, Bobbs-Merrill, 1946.

———, *Liberalism,* London, Richards, 1902.

SOMERVELL, D. C., *The Reign of George the Fifth,* New York, Harcourt, 1935.

SPENDER, J. A., *Life of H. H. Asquith,* 2 vols., London, Hutchinson, 1932.

TROTTER, WILFRED, *Instincts of the Herd in Peace and War,* London, Allen & Unwin, 1916 (also Oxford Univ. Press, 1953, with a Foreword by F. M. R. Walshe).

ULLSWATER, VISCOUNT (JAMES LOWTHER), *A Speaker's Commentaries,* 2 vols., London, Arnold, 1925.

WALLAS, GRAHAM, *Human Nature in Politics,* Boston, Houghton Mifflin, 1909 (also 3rd ed., New York, Knopf, 1921).

WEBB, BEATRICE, *Our Partnership,* London, Longmans, 1948.

WELLS, H. G., *Experiment in Autobiography,* New York, Macmillan, 1934.

WILLIAMS, MRS. HWFA (FLORENCE), *It Was Such Fun,* London, Hutchinson, 1935.

Notes

(For all sources not listed above, see Chap. 1)

PAGE

351–2   Chinese Slavery: Lyttelton, 320–21; Pope-Hennessy, 69; Wallas, 127; Hearnshaw, 94.

352   Yellow press: the phrase was in use in England at that time: Lucy Masterman, 216.

352   "Outdoor relief for the aristocracy": q. Cecil, I, 167.

353   Education Act, "greatest betrayal": q. Adams, 123.

354   *Economist,* a matter of £ .s.d.: q. Adams, 103.

354   One water faucet and one privy: This and subsequent facts about the living conditions of the poor are from the chapter "Domestic Life," by Marghanita Laski, in Nowell-Smith.

PAGE

354 Contract labour in British Guiana: Alfred Lyttelton speaking in the House of Commons, March 21, 1904, demonstrated that these contracts, negotiated under Gladstone and Rosebery, were for longer duration (five years as against three) and more severe conditions than the South African contracts. (Hansard, IV series, v. 132, 283 ff.).

355 Cries of "Rat!": Mackintosh, 222.

355 Balfour on Tariff issue: Fitzroy, I, 191, 220; Spender, C.-B., II, 102.

355 Cust quoted: Sir Ronald Storrs, Memoirs, 37.

355 "Not to go out of office": Young, 232.

356 "In chronic poverty": Hobson, 12.

356 Conditions at Shawfield Chemical Works: Hughes, 91.

357 Hauled off to a day in gaol: Gompers (see Chap. 8), 29–30.

357 Army lowered minimum height: Nowell-Smith, 181.

357 Wells depicted it: Autobiography, 550.

358 A's and B's: Lord Beveridge, Power and Influence, 66–67.

358 William Morris, "gradually permeating": Hunter (see Chap. 8), 97.

359 Beatrice Webb contemplated marrying Chamberlain: Margaret Cole, Beatrice Webb, New York, 1946, 21.

360 "I could not carry on": q. Hesketh Pearson, Shaw, 68; "A slave class": Hyndman, 397.

360 Hyndman, a Socialist from spite: White (see Chap. 5), I, 98.

360 Clemenceau, "a bourgeois class": q. Hyndman, 300.

360 "Eternal verities irritate him": Hunter, 120.

361 Keir Hardie: Hughes, passim; Brockway, 17–18.

361 "Well fed beasts" and "Every day in Rotten Row": Hunter, 230.

362 "Religious necessity" and strikes as "outlet": Clynes, 83, 85.

362 "If Burns with 80,000 men": q. Webb, 23.

362 ILP's declared aims: Hughes, 66–67.

362 "Most costly funeral" and Garvin quoted: Hughes, 76.

363 Fabians, "not in our line": Edward Pease, q. Halévy, V, 263, n. 2.

364 "Imperfections of the Social Order": Aug. 23, 1902.

364 "Mr. Balfour, coming back from dinner": Parliamentary correspondent of the Daily News, q. Hughes, 113.

364 MacDonald-Gladstone secret pact: Mendelssohn, 322.

365 "Go the Tory way": Hughes, 69.

365 "Hideous abnormality": Willoughby de Broke, 249.

365 Burns congratulates C.-B.: Webb, 325; reminds Grey: q. Lucy Masterman, 112.

366-7 Balfour and Weizmann: Dugdale, I, chap. 19; Chaim Weizmann, Trial and Error, New York, 1949, chap. 8.

367 Friend saw him "seriously upset": Newton, Retrospection, 146–47.

367 Balfour's letters on Election results: Letter to Knollys, q. in full in Lee, II, 449; others in Esher, II, 136; Young, 255.

367 "Like a second footman": Dugdale, II, 49.

368 Blatchford predicted: q. The Times, Jan. 19, 1906.

369 "Never saying anything clever!": Marsh, 150.

369 Categories of new M.P.'s: Jenkins, 7.

369 Few in "unconventional dress": Newton, Retrospection, 149; Irish members' bad manners: ibid., 99.

369 C.-B. impervious to Balfour's charm: Birrell, 243.

370 "England is based on commerce": q. Gardiner, Prophets, 136.

371 "Bring the sledgehammer": Gardiner, Prophets, 54.

371 Took his own wife into dinner: Blunt, II, 300.

PAGE

371   "No egotism, no vanity": q. Gardiner, *Pillars,* 122.

372   Churchill motivated by Mrs. Everest: *Roving Commission,* 73. All subsequent statements by Churchill, unless otherwise noted, are from Mendelssohn.

372–3 F. E. Smith: Gardiner, *Pillars,* 95–103; *Portraits,* 122–28.

373   Salisbury on coming clash of Lords and Commons: Margot Asquith, 157; H. H. Asquith, *Fifty Years,* I, 174.

374   Conservatives "should still control": *The Times,* Jan. 16, 1906.

374   Balfour warns Lansdowne: Newton, *Lansdowne,* 354.

374   "Something will happen": at Llanelly, Sept. 29, 1906, Lee, II, 456.

375   Curzon "so infinitely superior": Newton, *Retrospection,* 161.

375   Loreburn: Willoughby de Broke, 260; Curzon, *Subjects of the Day,* 228.

376   Rosebery, "eye like a fish": F. Ponsonby, 382.

376   Churchill, in the *Nation:* Mar. 9, 1907.

376   Balfour on "hereditary qualification": q. Young, 266.

377   "Portcullis" and "poodle": These phrases graced the debate on the Lords' rejection of the Licensing Bill, June 24, 1907.

377   Morley recalled Gladstone saying: q. Esher, II, 303.

379   "Backwoodsmen" meet at Lansdowne House: Willoughby de Broke, 246–47.

379   Churchill "perfectly furious": Lucy Masterman, 114.

379   Victor Grayson: Brockway, 24–25; Halévy, VI, 105.

380   Kaiser's proposal to save England: Blunt, II, 210.

380   King Edward on "hard times": q. Magnus, 417.

380   Invasion psychosis: I. F. Clark, "The Shape of Wars to Come," *History Today,* Feb., 1965.

381   Henry James, chimney pots: Jan. 8, 1909, *Letters,* ed. Percy Lubbock, New York, 1920, II, 121.

381–2 Suffragettes: In addition to Pankhurst and Fulford, the list of Suffragette assaults is most conveniently found in successive volumes of the *Annual Register.* The Albert Hall meeting is quoted from Nevinson, *More Changes,* 321–25, as is also "Those bipeds!": 306.

382–5 A gathering pessimism: Masterman, 84, 120, 289; Bryce, 15, 39, 228; Hobson and Hobhouse, q. C. H. Driver, "Political Ideas," in Hearnshaw; Trotter described: *DNB;* quoted: 47; Wallas described: Wells, 509, 511; Cole, 222; quoted: 284–85.

385   "Cantankerous and uncomfortable": *DNB,* Lowther.

386   "We all thought Papa would die": Cooper, 11.

386–7 The Limehouse speech: July 30, 1909. The King's displeasure was expressed in a letter to Lord Crewe, q. in full, Pope-Hennessy, 72–73. Other reactions and comments chiefly from the *Annual Register.* Rosebery's Glasgow speech in Crewe, 511–12; Kipling's poem appeared in the *Morning Post,* June 28, 1909, and only once since, in the *Definitive Edition* of his Verse, London, Hodder & Stoughton, 1940. "Foolish and mean speeches": q. Magnus, 431.

387   "Now King, you have won the Derby": Fitzroy, I, 379.

387   Balfour and Salisbury on Finance Bill: Dugdale, II, 56; *Annual Register,* 1909, 118.

388 ff. Lords debate the Budget, *et seq.*: As the English love nothing so much as a political crisis, the literature on the Budget–Parliament Bill crisis is so extensive that it cannot be missed, or even avoided. In the recent publication of *Churchill As I Knew Him,* by Lady Violet Bonham-Carter, Asquith's daughter, it is still going on. Every biography or autobiography of

PAGE

the principal figures involved and every political memoir of the period discuss it, the major sources being: Newton's *Lansdowne*, Young's *Balfour*, Spender's *Asquith*, Lee's *Edward VII*, Nicolson's *George V*, Wilson-Fox's *Halsbury*, Pope-Hennessy's *Crewe*, Ronaldshay's *Curzon*, Crewe's *Rosebery*, Willoughby de Broke's *Memoirs* and Roy Jenkins' book on the whole affair, *Mr. Balfour's Poodle*. The major parliamentary debates were quoted fully in *The Times* as well as verbatim in Hansard, and the big scenes were described at length and in detail in the daily and periodical press. For material in the following pages, therefore, references are given *only* for odd items whose source might be hard to locate.

389   Haldane on public apathy: q. *Annual Register*, 245.

389   Speaker Lowther on the Irish: Ullswater, II, 85; "sinister and powerful" and "direct, obvious": Morley, II, 349–50.

391   "Antique bantam": from a poem by an admirer which appeared in the *Morning Post*, q. Pope-Hennessy, 123.

391   Charwoman's song: Sitwell, *Great Morning*, 57.

391   "He kept things together somehow": Sackville-West, 307.

391   Laureate's poem: Austin, II, 292.

392   "Our glorified grocers": Lucy Masterman, 200, told to her by Lloyd George.

393   Asquith's list: Spender, *Asquith*, I, Appendix.

393   "We are in grim earnest": *Grooves of Change*, 39.

394   Transport strike, "it is revolution!" q. Halévy, VI, 456.

394   Tom Mann imprisoned: Clynes, 154.

394   Even the heat was "splendid": Sir Edward Grey, *Twenty-Five Years*, London, 1925, I, 238.

395   Lady Michelham's party: Williams, 192–93.

395   "Your bloody palace": Birkenhead, 175.

395   "The golden sovereigns": Cyril Connolly, reviewing Nowell-Smith, *The Sunday Times*, Oct. 18, 1964.

395   Last horse-drawn bus and preponderance of motor-taxis: Somervell, 28; Nowell-Smith, 122.

397–8   Hugh Cecil: Churchill, 201; also Churchill's *Amid These Storms*, New York, 1932, 55; also Gardiner, *Pillars*, 39.

398–9   The Cecil scene: besides accounts in the daily press there are illustrations of the scene in *Punch*, Aug. 2 and 16; and *Illus. London News*, July 29.

399   "Disorderly assembly," for the first time: *The Times*, parl. corres., July 25, 1911.

400   Of six peers at dinner, none had made up his mind: Midleton, 275.

401   "You've forgotten the Parliament Bill": Christopher Hassall, *Edward Marsh*, London, 1959, 173–74.

401   "A real danger" and chagrined peer: Newton, *Retrospection*, 187.

403   Balfour, "nothing but politicians": q. Young, 315.

403   Asquith's tribute: Guildhall speech, Nov. 9, *Fifty Years*, II, 129–31.

403   Wyndham, "ice age": Blunt, II, 339.

8. The Death of Jaurès

Bibliography

BALABANOFF, ANGELICA, *My Life as a Rebel,* New York, Harper, 1938.

BEER, MAX, *The General History of Socialism and Social Struggles,* Vol. II, New York, Russell & Russell, 1957.

BERNSTEIN, EDOUARD, *My Years of Exile,* New York, Harcourt, 1921.

BRAUNTHAL, JULIUS, *In Search of the Millennium,* London, Gollancz, 1945.

COLE, G. D. H., *A History of Socialist Thought,* Vol. III, *The Second International, 1889–1914,* Parts I and II, London, Macmillan, 1956.

COLEMAN, MCALISTER, *Eugene V. Debs,* New York, Greenberg, 1930.

DELEON, DANIEL, *Flashlights of the Amsterdam Congress,* New York, Labor News, 1929.

DESMOND, SHAW, *The Edwardian Story,* London, Rockliff, 1949.

DULLES, FOSTER RHEA, *Labor in America,* New York, Crowell, 1960.

(L'EGLANTINE), *Jean Jaurès; Feuilles Eparses,* Brussels, l'Eglantine, 1924.

FISCHER, LOUIS, *The Life of Lenin,* New York, Harper, 1964.

FYFE, HAMILTON, *Keir Hardie,* London, Duckworth, 1935.

GAY, PETER, *The Dilemma of Democratic Socialism: Bernstein's Challenge to Marx,* New York, Collier, 1962.

GINGER, RAY, *The Bending Cross: A Biography of Eugene Debs,* Rutgers Univ. Press, 1949.

*GOLDBERG, HARVEY, *The Life of Jean Jaurès,* Univ. of Wisconsin Press, 1962.

GOMPERS, SAMUEL, *Labour in Europe and America,* New York, Harper, 1910. (For autobiography, *see* Chap. 3.)

HARVEY, ROWLAND HILL, *Samuel Gompers,* Stanford Univ. Press, 1935.

HENDERSON, ARCHIBALD, *Bernard Shaw,* New York, Appleton, 1932.

HILLQUIT, MORRIS, *Loose Leaves from a Busy Life,* New York, Macmillan, 1934.

*HUNTER, ROBERT, *Socialists at Work,* New York, Macmillan, 1908.

INTERNATIONAL SOCIALIST CONGRESS, *Proceedings;* published variously. Nos. 1, 1889, Paris, and 3, 1893, Zurich, are in German, entitled *Protokoll.* No. 4, 1896, London, is in English; Nos. 2 and 5–8 are in French, entitled *Compte rendu analytique.* No. 5 was published by the *Cahiers de la Quinzaine,* Paris, 1901.

JAURÈS, JEAN, *Bernstein et l'Evolution de la Méthode socialiste* (text of lecture delivered to Socialist Student Conference, February 10, 1900. Erroneously dated 1910). Paris, Socialist Party pamphlet, 1926.

JOLL, JAMES, *The Second International, 1889–1914,* London, Weidenfeld, 1955.

KLEENE, G. A., "Bernstein vs. 'Old-School' Marxism," *Annals of Am. Academy,* November, 1901, 1–29.

KRUPSKAYA, NADEZHDA K., *Memories of Lenin*, 2 vols., tr., New York, International, 1930.

LORWIN, LEWIS, L., *Labor and Internationalism*, New York, Brookings, 1929.
————, *The International Labor Movement*, revised ed. of the above, New York, Harper, 1953.

MANN, TOM, *Memoirs*, London, Labour Publishing Co., 1923.

ORTH, SAMUEL P., *Socialism and Democracy in Europe*, New York, Holt, 1913.

ROSENBERG, ARTHUR, *The Birth of the German Republic, 1871–1918*, New York, Russell & Russell, 1962.

SCHORSKE, CARL E., *German Social Democracy, 1905–17*, Harvard Univ. Press, 1955.

STEWART, WILLIAM, *J. Keir Hardie*, London, ILP, 1921.

SUAREZ, GEORGES, *Briand, sa vie, son œuvre*, Vols. I and II, Paris, Plon, 1938.

TROTSKY, LEON, *My Life*, New York, Scribner's, 1930.

*VANDERVELDE, EMILE, *Souvenirs d'un Militant Socialiste*, Paris, Denoël, 1939.

VAYO, JULIO ALVAREZ DEL, *The Last Optimist*, New York, Viking, 1950.

Notes

Unless otherwise stated all quotations by Jaurès are from Goldberg, by Debs from Ginger, by Bernstein from Gay, by Gompers, in the case of biographical facts, from his autobiography, and in the case of comments on European labour, from his *Labour in Europe and America;* by Vandervelde, DeLeon and others, following the principle already established, from their own works.

PAGE
407 In "almost religious silence": Hunter, 319.
408 Vienna "paralyzed with fright": Zweig (*see* Chap. 6), 61; Braunthal, 56.
409 Comments on Markham's poem: Sullivan (*see* Chap. 3), II, 236–47.
409 Clemenceau on Fourmies: Alexandre Zevaès, *Histoire de la 3me République*, Paris, 1926, 342.
409 Taft on the Pullman strike: *DAB*, Taft.
410 Marxists accused the French Possibilists: Joll, 33.
410 "Don't delay the revolution!": Bülow (*see* Chap. 5), I, 672. Miquel in later life became a Conservative and Minister of Finance, 1890–1900.
411 "Nothing if not revolution": DeLeon, 192.
412 Applause for Pablo Iglesias: Hyndman, 396.
412 Cipriani described: Vandervelde, 44.
412 Hunter on the Valley of the Tirano: in *Socialists at Work*, 55.
413 "Damned wantlessness of the poor": The phrase was circulating at the time without a clear claim as to authorship. Minus the adjective it appeared anonymously in a Fabian Tract of 1884, *Why Are the Many Poor*, and has been ascribed by Professor Gay in his book on Bernstein to William Morris. As *Verdammte Bedürfnislosigkeit* it was quoted by Shaw in his Preface to *Major Barbara*, without attribution but suggesting a German origin. Although some German scholars are reluctant to specify

PAGE

an origin, the attribution to Lassalle is made on the authority of George Lichtheim in a letter to the author.

413   English pamphlet on Congress of 1896: Walter Crane, *Cartoons for the Cause, 1886–96,* London, 1896.

415   Zurich Congress: Vandervelde, 144.

415   Shaw on Liebknecht: Henderson, 220.

416   Kaiser on the Socialists: Michael Balfour, *The Kaiser and His Times,* London, 1964, 159.

416   "By Balfour to the Primrose League": Joll, 76.

416   "General Strike is general nonsense": *ibid.,* 53, n. 2.

416–7 May Day in Munich: Krupskaya, I, 67.

417   Bebel a "shadow-Kaiser": Rosenberg, 44.

417   Mommsen on Bebel: Hunter, 227; "savage accents": *ibid.,* 226; "deadly enemy": q. Pinson, 212; "Look at those fellows": Chirol (*see* Chap. 5), 274.

418   Adler characteristics: Braunthal, Trotsky, Balabanoff, Joll, 38; "Despotism mitigated by slovenliness": Braunthal, 52.

419   "More profound than doctrine": Hunter, 134.

419   Vandervelde "gushed" over: Balabanoff, 15.

419   "Firmly and recklessly": Vandervelde, 46.

420   "Torquemada in eyeglasses": Nomad, *Rebels* (*see* Chap. 2), 65.

420   "What will we Socialists do . . . ?": Goldberg, 226.

420–1 Jaurès, "Jubilant and humorous": Hyndman, 398; "His shoulders shook" and discussed astronomy at dinner party: Severine, in *l'Eglantine,* 7–8; "Thinks with his beard": Clermont-Tonnerre (*see* Chap. 4), II, 251.

421   Vaillant on Jaurès: Hunter, 79.

422   Clemenceau, "all the verbs": Roman (*see* Chap. 4), 91.

423   The London Congress: Vandervelde, 145.

423   Army Colonel in a Chicago club: Ginger, 139.

424   Injunction advised by Grosscup and Wood: Allan Nevins, *Grover Cleveland,* New York, 1932, 618.

424   Roosevelt on "shooting": Pringle (*see* Chap. 3), 164.

425   Theodore Debs's gold watch: Coleman, 201.

425   "Almost grotesque": Hillquit, 93.

425   "Give 'em hell, Sam": Harvey.

426   "These middle class issues": q. Dulles, 181.

426   "I am a working man": Hillquit, 95.

430   "I confess openly . . .": Braunthal, 91; Gay, 74.

430   It was said of Adler: DeLeon, 37; his letter to Bernstein: Braunthal, 100.

431   "Tall, thin, desiccated" and "Down with Liebknecht!": Goldberg, 262.

431   Erhard Auer's regret: DeLeon, 66–67.

433   Knee-breeches debate at Dresden: Gay, 232, n. 39.

433   Rosa Luxemburg: Balabanoff, 22; Vayo, 61.

434   Georg Ledebour's estimate: Trotsky, 215.

434   Dresden Resolution: Pinson, 215–16.

434   *"Weltpolitik* without war": *ibid.,* 214.

435–7 Amsterdam Congress: Vandervelde, 152–62; DeLeon, *passim.*

437   Bebel would shoulder a rifle: Vandervelde, 161.

438   Isvolsky on Briand and Viviani: Goldberg, 455.

438   "Fiendish massacre": Clynes, 103.

438   Italians hail Russian Revolution: Balabanoff, 54.

438–9 Austrian suffrage strike: Braunthal, 64–68.

PAGE

441   "Property, property, property": q. Goldberg, 363.
441   Debs's letter of December, 1904: Coleman, 227–28.
441   "Bundle of primitive instincts": q. Dulles, 211.
443   "Slowly plowed its way": Ernest Poole, q. Ginger, 281.
443   Mannheim Congress: Schorske, 56.
444–5   Noske's speech in Reichstag: Pinson, 215.
445   Hervé; "We shall reply . . .": D. W. Brogan, *France Under the Republic*, 429.
446   "At every railroad station": M. Auclair, *La Vie de Jean Jaurès,* q. Goldberg, 381.
446   Hatfield visit: Vandervelde, in *l'Eglantine*, 38–40.
447   Mussolini described: Desmond, 207.
447   Police in balloons over Stuttgart: *The Times,* Aug. 19 and 20, 1907.
447   Quelch incident: Balabanoff, 82; Trotsky, 205.
448   Georg von Vollmar quoted: Pinson, 215–16.
448   Clemenceau on Jaurès' fate: in *l'Homme Libre,* Aug. 2, 1914.
449   "Infuriated" workers would rise: Braunthal, 106.
449   "Do not fool yourselves": Desmond, 206.
449   Jaurès at Tubingen: Vandervelde, 167.
449   "That's Lenin": q. Fischer, 58.
449   Lenin's parleys with Bebel: Supplied to the author by Louis Fischer from Lenin's "The International Socialist Congress at Stuttgart," *Works,* 5th ed., Moscow, 1961, XVI, 67–74, 514–15.
450   Stuttgart Resolution: Beer, II, 156.
451   *Arbeiter-Zeitung* of Vienna: q. Trotsky, 211.
451   Blatchford and Hyndman for conscription: Halévy (*see* Chap. 1), VI, 395.
451   Hardie believed "absolutely": Clynes, 25.
452   "Ripe sonority": report in *Le Peuple,* q. Vandervelde, 170.
452   8,000,000 Socialist voters: *The Times,* Aug. 31, 1910.
453   Hardie at Copenhagen: Cole, 83–84; Hughes, 197–98; Stewart, 302.
454   ITF and Boer War: Information supplied by K. A. Golding, Research Secretary, ITF, London.
454–5   ITF strike of 1911: Prior discussion of the strike at Copenhagen in 1910 from *The Times,* Aug. 25–29. Subsequent developments from Mr. Golding.
455   German Socialism appeared "irresistible": Braunthal, 46.
455   Scheidemann debate: *The Times,* Feb. 19, Mar. 9, 1912.
456   "We revolutionaries?": Trotsky, 213.
457   Basle Cathedral, "dangerous" consequences: *Annual Register,* 1912, 367.
457   Jaurès' speech: Joll, 155.
458   A survey of French student life: *Les Jeunes Gens d'Aujourd'hui,* q. Wolff (*see* Chap. 5), 275.
458   "If these were my last words": Brockway, 39.
459   *Vorwärts* on Austrian ultimatum: Vayo, 78.
459   "We relied on Jaurès": Zweig (*see* Chap. 6), 199.
459   Jouhaux's proposal to Legien: Joll, 162.
459   *La Bataille Syndicaliste: ibid.,* 161.
59–60   Brussels Conference: Balabanoff, 4, 114–18; Vandervelde, 171; Stewart, 340; Joll, 164.
460   Hardie, "Only the binding together": Fyfe, 136.
460   Jean Longuet quoted: Goldberg, 467.
461   Bethmann-Hollweg: Joll, 167.
461   Jaurès' death: *Humanité, Figaro, Echo de Paris,* Aug. 1/2.

PAGE

461 Spanish Socialist in Leipzig: Vayo, 81.

462 Bernstein, "golden bridge": Hans Peter Hanssen, *Diary of a Dying Empire*
Indiana Univ. Press, 1955, 15.

462 Kaiser, Deschanel, Jouhaux: *The Times, Echo de Paris*, Aug. 5.

Afterword

463 Graham Wallas: Preface to 3rd ed. of *Human Nature in Politics*, 1921.

463 Emile Verhaeren: *La Belgique sanglante*, Paris, 1915, *Dédicace*, unpaged

Index

amended by Lords, 396; accepted by Lords, 399-401

Paty de Clam, Colonel du (1853-1916), 173, 174, 196, 204

Pauncefote, Sir Julian (1st Baron), (1828-1902), 233; at First Hague Conference, 253-254, 258, 264; death of, 283

Paur, Emil (1855-1932), 317

Pauwels, Jean, 92

Pavlova, Anna (1885-1931), 338, 395

Payment of Members Act, 401-402

Payson (Representative, Ill.), 127

Peace Congresses, 233, 280

Pearl Harbor, U.S. acquisition of, 130

Peel, Sir Arthur (1st Viscount Peel) (1829-1912), 48, 254

Péguy, Charles (1873-1914), on Dreyfus Affair, 172; signs Protest, 201; and Jaurès, 210

People, The, 425

Père Peinard, Le, 78, 89; closes down, 91; on Dreyfus, 214

Petit Journal, Le, 179

Petit Parisien, Le, 200

Petite Republique, La, 185, 210

Pettigrew (Senator, S. Dak.), 160, 165

Philippine annexation: support for, 157-158; Senate ratification of, 158-161; Filipino revolt against, 158, 161-166

Picasso, Pablo (1881-   ), 337

Picquart, Colonel Georges (1854-1914), 220, 222, 225; discovers Dreyfus' innocence, 186; arrested and imprisoned, 187, 208; attends Les Loups, 204; public protest, 213-214; Minister of War, 226

Pissarro, Camille (1830-1903), 80, 89

Planck, Max (1858-1947), 270

Platt Amendment, 157

Plehve, Wenzel von (1846-1904), 111-112

Plekhanov, Georgy (1857-1918), 407, 435, 446

Pless, Daisy, Princess of, 29, 42

Plume, La, 91

Plural Voting Bill (1906), 374

Pohl, Max, 306

Poiret, Paul, 338

Pollock, Sir Frederick (1845-1937), 393

Poniatowski, Stanislas, Prince, 183

Ponsonby, Arthur (1871-1946), 29

Ponsonby, Sir Frederick (b. 1867), 42

Ponsonby, Sir Henry (1825-1895), 6, 54

Popolo, Il. 98

Populists, 153, 159

Portland, 6th Duke of (1857-1943), 28

Portsmouth, Treaty of, 271-272, 275

Possibilists (France), 419

Pozzi, Professor, 205

Presidential elections (U.S.): 1876, 121; 1888, 124-125; 1892, 130; 1896, 144-145, 272, 424, 426; 1900, 164-166; 1908, 442; 1912, 442-443

Presse, La, 204

Prévost, Marcel (1862-1941), 178, 205

Primrose, Neil, 395

Privy Council (Great Britain), 14

Proctor, Redfield (1831-1908), 150

Protection (Great Britain), 354-356; Fabians and, 359

"Protest of the Intellectuals," 200-202

Proudhon, Pierre (1809-1865), 64-65, 69, 73

Proust, Marcel (1871-1922): 337; at Zola's trial, 198; organizes Protest, 200; "Baron de Charlus," 193, 195; "Guermantes," 192, 195, 214-215; at Evian, 224

Proust, Robert, 200

Psst!, 203

Puccini, Giacomo (1858-1924), 315

Pulitzer, Joseph (1847-1911), 145

Pullman strike, 141, 145, 409; Debs in, 423-424

Punch, 15, 46, 53, 369

Puvis de Chavannes, Pierre, 201

Quarterly Review, 10

Queensberry, 9th Marquess of, 33

Quelch, Harry, 447

Rachmaninoff, Sergey, 337

Radziwill, Prince Anton, 189

Radziwill, Princess Marie (b. 1840), 221; and Dreyfus Affair, 189, 198, 224

Raff, Joseph Joachim, 296

Raffalovitch, 261

Railway Times, 424

Ralliement, 190, 191

Ranc, Arthur (1831-1908), 185, 205

Rathenau, Emil (1838-1915), 242, 304

Rathenau, Walther (1867-1922), 344-345

Ravachol (Anarchist) (d. 1892), 77-80, 93, 94, 96

Ravel, Maurice (1875-1937), 340, 343

Rayleigh, 3rd Baron (1842-1919), 48

Rayleigh, Lady (d. 1934), 53

Reclus, Elisée (1830-1905), 70, 76, 93, 95, 96, 201, 419; character of, 74

Reclus, Paul, trial of, 95

Reed, Thomas B. (1839-1902), described, 117-118, 141; early career of, 119-121; as Congressman, 121-124; as Speaker, 124-125; 141-142; quorum fight, 124-129; as Minority Leader, 129-130; and Cleveland, 131; in Venezuela crisis, 142; seeks Presidency, 142-144; and Hawaii, 149, 155-156; and Cuba, 148-151; on war in Philippines, 158; bitterness of, 159, 161; resigns, 162-163; refuses to join third party, 165; death of, 167

Reed's Rules, 129, 142, 156

Regis, Dr. Emanuel, 106-107

Reichstag elections: 1890, 414; 1893, 416; 1903, 433; 1907, 439; 1912, 455

Reinach, Baron de, 184, 185

Reinach, Joseph (1856-1921), 186; becomes Dreyfusard, 185; on justice, 187; focus of hatred in Chamber, 192; accompanies Zola, 199; caricatured in Psst!, 203; and salons, 205; and de Mun, 210; on Picquart Protest, 214; sued by Mme Henry, 215; and Amnesty Bill, 225; unrelenting efforts, 226